HAMPSTEAD

Building a Borough, 1650-1964

HAMPSTEAD
Building a Borough, 1650-1964

F. M. L. THOMPSON

Professor of Modern History, University of London

Routledge & Kegan Paul

London and Boston

First published in 1974
by Routledge & Kegan Paul Ltd
Broadway House, 68–74 Carter Lane
London EC4V 5EL and
9 Park Street
Boston, Mass. 02108, U.S.A.
Printed in Great Britain by
W & J Mackay Limited, Chatham

ISBN 0 7100 7747 5
Library of Congress Catalog Card No. 73–87319

Contents

Illustrations

MAPS

ACKNOWLEDGMENTS

Illustrations are reproduced by courtesy of the Local History Collections
of the Camden Public Libraries. Map 5 is by courtesy of the House of
Lords Record Office; Map 7 is reproduced by permission of the Church
Commissioners.

Preface

Hampstead vanished as a separate municipality in 1965, when the borough merged with those of St Pancras and Holborn to form the present London Borough of Camden. Such administrative changes could not, of course, abolish Hampstead as a place, and not a mere place either but one whose name is known round the world. The sturdy survival of the place, and the people who live in it or visit it, is indeed the chief reason for trusting that this history may retain some interest even though it appears several years after the demise of the borough. In a parting gesture of characteristic enlightenment the Hampstead Borough Council decided to commission a history, and I was privileged to receive that commission and the subsequent support of the London Borough of Camden, without which this book could not have been written. Apart from an injunction not to write an 'official' history or a narrow municipal history, and an encouragement to produce a work of 'a general historical nature' I was left entirely free, with a mark of confidence indispensable to the professional historian, to devise my own brief.

Writing with the monumental and fascinating volumes of T. J. Barratt, *The Annals of Hampstead* (1912), very much in mind it seemed to me that the important thing to do was not to attempt the impossible task of emulating them or attempting to bring their kind of treatment up to date; rather the first thing to do was to approach the development of Hampstead as a piece of urban history. Hence this book is an attempt to understand and explain the forces which have gone into the moulding and shaping of all those districts which lie within the ancient parish and more modern municipal boundaries of Hampstead, the places in which people live, work to a small extent, and play and enjoy themselves to a great extent. To a historian of landownership and agriculture, dusting off the hayseeds as he enters the unfamiliar world of city streets, the fundamental role of property rights, tenures and interests in determining the character of urban development has naturally been of great interest. Property was no doubt the major factor in deciding when houses were built in a particular place, why a road went this way rather than that, and how a neighbourhood came to have one social character rather than another. But in unravelling the apparently chaotic and mindless jumble of a nineteenth-century suburb superimposed on an eighteenth-century village, and pursuing its underlying rationality, contributory streams from religion, class, transport, employment, sickness and fever, and the open air lobby are all seen to have played a part. The Heath, indeed, especially the enlarged Heath of today, is Hampstead's main title to metropolitan significance, and a considerable part of the book is devoted to a re-interpretation of the reasons for its survival.

The emphasis of the book, in other words, is on the process of the creation of the urban environment of Hampstead; so that detailed treatment of what went on within that environment, socially, intellectually, artistically, politically, and civically must await separate inquiry. Another subject of great interest, the history of Hampstead Garden Suburb, finds itself excluded for the different reason that it lies outside the boundaries of Hampstead parish and borough.

Several of the collections of manuscripts used in this study are in public depositories, whose archivists and librarians have been most helpful: Camden Public Libraries, Greater London Record Office, Church Commissioners, and Dean and Chapter of Westminster. Other collections are in private hands, and I am most grateful to the following for access to their papers and for permission to quote from them: The Provost and Fellows of Eton College; Robin Bagot, Esq., of Levens Hall, Westmorland, for permission to consult the estate papers kept at Messrs Eland, Hore & Paterson, Lincoln's Inn Fields.

F. M. L. THOMPSON

Abbreviations

The following abbreviations are used in the footnotes:

CC Church Commissioners
DNB Dictionary of National Biography
DCW Dean and Chapter of Westminster [Muniments, Westminster Abbey]
Eccles. Comm. Ecclesiastical Commissioners
E/MW Maryon Wilson Papers [deposited in Greater London Council Record Office]
Eton Eton College Papers, Windsor
HBC Hampstead Borough Council
HJR Hampstead Junction Railway
HLRO House of Lords Record Office
HPL Hampstead Public Library
GLCRO Greater London Council Record Office
LGOC London General Omnibus Company
MBW Min. Metropolitan Board of Works, Minutes
RCO Recent Chapter Office [a class of records in DCW]
SC Select Committee

One

THE PREHISTORY OF
URBAN HAMPSTEAD

The growth of London since 1800 has been prodigious. So obvious a
fact would not be worth stating, but for the circumstance that this
growth has not so much filled up previously empty spaces on the map as
occupied particular districts which already had existences of their own.
This book is about one of these particular districts, Hampstead. Many
nineteenth-century observers of London, living through the time of
headlong numerical expansion, felt that the process had got out of hand
and was accelerating into an uncontrollable, mindless, urban sprawl.
The most vivid fear was of a continuous, undifferentiated mass of buildings stretching from the Thames to Brighton. Many twentieth-century
observers, living through the time of greatest spatial expansion in the
built-up area, have echoed these fears, seeing in their mind's eye stretch
upon stretch of identical suburban streets, endlessly repeated semi-
detacheds. Little is so overwhelming as the impression of sameness,
anonymity, and oddly regular disorder and repetition, produced by
looking down on London from the air. The intellectual traveller, bound
for some similar view of some other international city, generalises his
observations, and in the congested contemporary idiom talks portent-
ously of the transformation of metropolis into megalopolis. His expectations of the future, projections of an interpretation of present trends,
are less eloquent and vivid but of the same breed as Cobbett's.[1] The
common element is a vision which fuses the whole seething mass of the
city into one single entity. If this was the whole truth there would be
little point in writing this book, for there would be nothing worthy of
serious study between the conurbation as a whole, and the separate
individuals, families or social groups forming the elements from which
it is composed; no one particular place could have any special claims to
attention.

Other writers, more receptive to the visual impact of the detail of the

[1] A view whose adherents stretch from W. Cobbett, *Rural Rides*, January 1822
  (ed. G. D. H. and Margaret Cole, 1930) to Peter Self, *Cities in Flood* (1957).

[1]

urban environment, are impressed by the idiosyncrasies of the separate parts of the great Wen rather than by its overall unity, and conclude that London is nothing much more than a haphazard conglomeration of villages and small towns, more or less articulated by a transport system, and more or less held together by blocks and wedges of routine housing—standard for its particular period—interspersed between the old centres.[1] Greater London as such, on this view, amounts to little more than an inanimate infrastructure of the services essential to render the whole thing vertebrate and viable; true urban life resides in the urbanised village nuclei. London local historians, by and large, have implicitly adopted this standpoint, and vie with one another in the filial devotion with which they extol the uniqueness of their parish and its worthies, leaving the rest of London to form a dimly-perceived backcloth to the local play. If this was the whole truth, again there would be little point in the present work, for the reasons that local historians of Hampstead already abound, and a study which mainly emphasised the isolated individuality of Hampstead could not hope either to increase awareness and understanding of that uniqueness or to contribute to understanding the development of London as a whole.

Fortunately neither view is valid in its extreme form. Certainly the different London districts each possess their own distinctive character-istics, whether these are thought of in terms of topography, architec-tural appearance, social composition, or patterns of employment; and individuality of the thing studied is a fit ground for the exercise of historical curiosity. It is equally certain that the separate parts are interdependent, and together form a whole. A modern sociologist, hav-ing shown that this whole is a good deal less tightly-knit than many planners and others had supposed, still concludes that 'it is the Central Area which provides the common link without which Greater London would be rather like a conglomeration of independent towns and vil-lages'.[2] Admittedly in this 1964 overview Hampstead itself had almost been made part of the central area which held the rest of London to-gether; though simply casting it for this role did not ensure that it gave a convincing performance as one of the providers of employment and services for the outer areas of the conurbation. Taken historically, how-ever, the point is that in relation to an earlier much smaller central area Hampstead may be supposed to have been in the position of a modern

[1] Most commonly expressed by architectural historians, for example S. E. Rasmussen, *London the Unique City* (1934, Penguin ed. 1960), pp. 28–9; N. Pevsner, *The Buildings of England: London*, II (1952).

[2] J. H. Westergaard, 'The structure of Greater London', in *London, Aspects of Change* (Centre for Urban Studies Report No. 3, 1964), p. 109.

Finchley, Wimbledon, Richmond or Orpington. This supposition at once gives a more than local interest to a local study, for it must involve investigation of the character and development of this local-central relationship. If the history of its dealings with London should show that Hampstead's position has undergone a complete transformation, so much the better as a bonus for a specially interesting performance.

But it is not only the concept of Greater London as a kind of solar system, and the chance of uncovering earlier forms of life on one of the planets, which may give a history of the parish and borough of Hampstead another dimension besides that of the parish pump, however elegant. It is also the prospect that scrutiny of any one of the satellites may yield clues about the development of the whole system. However differentiated the London districts may have become—or always have been—and however much pre-metropolitan individuality they may have retained, all of them have by definition experienced in some form the impact of the general forces which created the expanding conurbation. Analysis of those general forces, which were an immense complex of demographic, economic, technological, social, and administrative factors, lies somewhat beyond the scope of a study of a particular small area which contributed barely four of the hundreds of square miles covered by modern Greater London. Analysis of their effects on the particular square miles called Hampstead, however, is part of the real meat of urban history. It is at this level that we may see the general forces made incarnate in real buildings and real inhabitants, and may escape from the abstractions and models of urban sociology to the awkward real world in which urban morphology, urban environment, and urban ecology were actually shaped. How was urbanisation, as a physical process, carried out; what determined the timing of the development; and why did the social segregation or class zoning so widely noted as a feature of nineteenth-century urban growth, emerge where and when it did: these are some of the questions which a local study may hope to illumine. They have indeed already been brilliantly illuminated by the history of Camberwell, the study in London history which pioneered this blend of the particular and the general.[1] The exercise is worth repeating, not because Hampstead is a more typical London suburb than Camberwell—far from it; but because Hampstead is very different, and has become almost the archetype of a high-class residential district.

The broad lines of the portrait of Hampstead can be indicated very

[1] H. J. Dyos, *Victorian Suburb: a Study of the Growth of Camberwell* (Leicester, 1961).

simply. Until the late seventeenth century it was simply high, rather than high-class or residential, and there is little to suggest that its history was substantially different from that of any other place within three to five miles of the City and Westminster. From then until the early nineteenth century the distinctive character of old Hampstead was formed, as a small satellite town of the metropolis, separated from it by open and generally steeply-sloping fields. By the 1820s the metropolitan building tide reached the southern shores of the parish, and from then until the early 1900s washed over it. Before 1914 the tide had passed on, lapping in this north-westerly direction at Golders Green, Willesden, Hendon and Finchley, and leaving behind it Hampstead fully developed apart from its great prize, Hampstead Heath. From 1907, when the Tube reached Golders Green and the actual building of Hampstead Garden Suburb began (lying in the area of the borough of Hendon), there was only a little fresh building in Hampstead until 1945, as stray pockets were filled up, having for one reason and another escaped all the nineteenth-century building waves; but in the main the district had the posture of a physically settled, though socially mobile, area. Since 1945, and especially since the middle 1950s, the builders have returned to Hampstead in force, and it has entered the stage of urban renewal and redevelopment, mainly in its most southerly and more low-lying parts, but also through the subdivision and cannibalisation of some of its surviving mansions on higher ground. This study is chiefly concerned with the two periods when the builders have been most active in Hampstead, either in covering open ground with houses or in demolishing and replacing existing houses; and principally it is concerned with the long period in the nineteenth century when Hampstead formed part of London's frontier beyond which lay open country. But so much of the future physiology and social temperament of Hampstead had already been determined before the brand new streets began to be laid out, that it would be a nonsense to start simply at the point in the late 1820s when the first unromantic pioneers straggled over the parish boundary from Camden Town in the south and hesitantly laid claim to Hampstead as metropolitan territory.

The romantic element had entered Hampstead considerably before this, local loyalists would say with the Romans, others would say with the neo-Romans of the late seventeenth century and their appetite for spas, the waters, and revelry. Visions of a Roman Hampstead rest upon little more than fertile antiquarian imaginations working on a large urn, unearthed near the Hampstead Wells in 1774, coupled to a somewhat vague supposition that the original Roman route from London to St Albans ran up and over the Heath until Watling Street was constructed.[1] It is indeed conceivable that the superior merits of the more direct route of Watling Street (Edgware Road), with its much easier gradients, were for a while outweighed by the problems of denser forest on the lower ground, and that temporarily the Romans might have found that it suited them to go up and down the Hampstead hill to gain a passage that was easily cleared. Nevertheless since the Romans did build Watling Street, and that fairly early in their occupation, Hampstead can at the most have lain on an imperial arterial road for only a brief time. Indeed the major influence of the imperial road-makers, and of their medieval successors who sensibly chose the way over the lesser heights and shallower gradients of Highgate for the line of the North Road to Barnet, was to leave Hampstead on the road to nowhere, wedged between what were the two principal land routes to the north and north-west for the entire period until the railways came. The fact that it was not on one of London's main lines of communication throughout this time simply confirmed Hampstead's topography in command of London's northern heights which it was folly to attempt to cross when they could be more cheaply outflanked; it also meant that Hampstead did not experience the appearance of such transit facilities as posting houses and hostelries, nor the incipient and widely-spaced ribbon development, which characterised many other places equidistant from the centre of London that were astride main roads and occurred in them during the eighteenth-century expansion of stage coach and waggon transport, if not indeed during the preceding century or more.

This natural isolation from main thoroughfares was to be important once London did begin to bring to bear its first faint, and wealthy, residential influence. Meanwhile Hampstead was like much of the rest of the near environs of medieval London. That is to say it was monastic land, in its case one of the manors of the Abbey of Westminster by grant of Ethelred confirmed in 986; and it was agricultural. It was no accident that medieval London was to a great extent encircled by royal and ecclesiastical lands, since it was clearly a great convenience to control a source of food close at hand, and those closest to the hand which controlled the disposition of land naturally received the lion's share of this convenience. This situation proved to be of benefit to historians and of little disadvantage to London. For at the very time when London began to grow rapidly, in the sixteenth century, it chanced that the ring of

---

[1] *Gentleman's Magazine*, XLVI (1774), p. 169; J. J. Park, *The Topography and Natural History of Hampstead* (1818), pp. 6–11.

corporate estates was effectively broken by the dissolution of the mona-
steries and by the necessities which forced the sale of crown estates, thus
removing any possible constrictions on expansion which might have
been imposed in succeeding centuries by corporate landowners who
conceivably could have remained legally or economically immune from
the lures of development.

The charm of the corporate landowner for the historian is that the
record-survival rate is much higher than in the case of private landowners with all the risks to which their records are subject, either because none were ever kept anyway, or because ownership changes or
mere periodic fits of office-tidying fever have led to their loss or destruction. Moreover even where land has not permanently retained its
corporate character there was a fair chance that when it passed into
private ownership it would do so in sizeable blocks, and would in this
way come to form part of those larger private estates which again have
greater record-survival chances than small or petty properties. In
Hampstead several estates had been detached from, or carved out of, the
Abbey of Westminster's manor before the Dissolution. Some land
clearly found its way into lay tenure, but the principal parcelling out
was for the foundation, in the twelfth century, of Kilburn Priory in
the west, and the endowment of the Hospital of St James with lands in
the south-east; and in the next century the Knights Templar received
lands to the north of Kilburn, probably the later Shoot-Up Hill estate.
On the dissolution of the Knights Templar in 1312 this was granted to
the Hospital of St John of Jerusalem, while Henry VI granted the
lands of the leper Hospital of St James to his new foundation of Eton
College.[1] Eton survived the Dissolution, and Westminster Abbey was
reincarnated, in the shape of the Dean and Chapter, in possession of the
Belsize part of the former Hampstead holding. The rest of the monastic
and charitable estates quickly passed into lay ownership; but while
some of the property, notably the Hospitallers' Shoot-Up Hill estate,
thereupon passed out of the realm of archives, much of it came to
owners who in varying degree, and at least for parts of the time since
1540, have fallen into the record-keeping class. Thus the largest Hampstead estate since the Dissolution has been the private one, of the lords
of the manor; and later owners of what had been Kilburn Priory lands
were in the property business in the nineteenth century in a sufficiently big way to have left record evidence behind them. These,
together with the still surviving corporate estates of Eton and of the

[1] Accounts of the descent of properties are to be found in Park, op. cit., and
T. J. Barratt, *The Annals of Hampstead* (3 vols, 1912).

Dean and Chapter, cover about 60 per cent of Hampstead's 2,247 acres.[1]

The direct influence of Hampstead's monastic past is not only that the historian of the nineteenth century is served by wide record coverage, admittedly also of widely varying quality and exceedingly thin in places; it is also that ownership of the land was largely concentrated into a few hands, and this was one of the crucial factors in the shaping of urban Hampstead. Against this, however, must be set the disappointing yield of evidence on Hampstead's pre-Dissolution economy. It would be exceedingly interesting to learn something of the economic functions and social conditions of a village and manor on the near outskirts of medieval London, but unfortunately there is little here to learn. The cultivated parts of Domesday Hampstead, not surprisingly, were largely in tillage, and there was also enough waste and woodland to support 100 swine.[2] Most of the manor, it seems, was run as one of the Abbey's home farms, though whether all the produce of the arable was carted to Westminster, or whether some may have been consumed on the spot at a small grange, possibly on the site of the later Belsize House, is not clear. Direct farming was given up in the fourteenth century, one of the metropolitan manors having been kept in hand for over a century after the Abbey had begun leasing out its more distant demesnes.[3] What kind of men the new lessees were we cannot be certain, but from the 60 or so holdings which appear in a roll of 1372 it seems likely that they were mainly peasant subsistence farmers, and that Hampstead was not yet within the normal circle of London's commercial food supply.[4] This is consistent with the valuation of Hampstead in the *Valor Ecclesiasticus* of 1535, which made it worth £53. 3s. 1d. net in rents; for although these customary rents may not indicate the real value of the land at all accurately, an average rent of under $6\frac{1}{2}d$. an acre for all the land excluding the Heath does not suggest anything but a very weak London influence on agricultural land values.[5] The statement in a valuation of 1549, made on the winding up

[1] See below, pp. 75–83, for a full discussion of the pattern of landownership. The reported, and reputed, acreage of the parish of Hampstead fluctuated somewhat; the figure taken here is the one most frequently given in the nineteenth-century census tables.

[2] Domesday entry quoted Park, op. cit., p. 88.

[3] Barratt, op. cit., I, 44; and Barbara Harvey, 'The leasing of the Abbot of Westminster's demesnes in the later Middle Ages', *Economic History Review*, 2nd ser. XXII (1969).

[4] Cited by J. Kennedy, *The Manor and Parish Church of Hampstead* (1906), p. 24.

[5] *Valor Ecclesiasticus, Temp. Henry VIII* (1810), pp. 403, 415, 422. On the

of the short-lived bishopric of Westminster, that there was 'of howse-ling people [communicants] within the said parish the number of 147', points in the same direction; if allowance is made for the children not included in this tally the total population cannot greatly have exceeded one person to ten acres, a density which could be matched by many well-settled, purely rural, parishes anywhere in the country.[1]

Although these scraps of evidence suggest that the proximity of the London market had not begun to have much effect on the type of farming carried on in Hampstead by the early sixteenth century, other straws in the wind hint at a less detached ruralism. In 1496 the Abbey made a contract for the production of 400,000 bricks at Belsize, and these were no doubt made in the field which was still known as Brick Field in the eighteenth century.[2] It is possible that in pursuit of some policy of estate autarky these bricks were for building operations in Westminster, though their costly cartage across miles of intervening land containing equally suitable brick earth ought to have made plain the unnecessary sacrifice involved in such behaviour. It is more plausible to suppose that the bricks were for local use, and that their making marks the building of the first large mansion on the Belsize site. At any rate a considerable country house was in existence there by 1550, which does not appear to have been then newly built, when 'the capital messuage of Belsis' was demised to Sir Richard Goodrich; it would need to have been a sizeable mansion to absorb so many bricks.[3] Affluent residents, however, were to hand. The house seems to have been occupied for a short time by a wealthy City mercer, Philip Oakham, and then from 1557 until his death there in 1568 by Armigil Wade (or Waad), an important royal official in the reigns of Henry VIII, Edward VI and Elizabeth, and a confidant of William Cecil.[4] Belsize had thus become a convenient country house for those with frequent business to do in London, and a commuter, possibly the first and certainly stately, had settled in Hampstead; it could be nearer the truth to say that the long weekend had arrived. The arrival of Belsize, which

---

general point see *The Agrarian History of England and Wales*, ed. Joan Thirsk (Cambridge, 1967), IV, 324–5.

[1] Kennedy, op. cit., pp. 61, 112. In the sixteenth century first communion might be administered at the age of ten, so that it is possible that the 147 'houseling people' were the whole population aged ten and upwards; the under-tens might have been about a quarter of the total population.

[2] Dean and Chapter of Westminster Muniments, Westminster Abbey [DCW], 16470, contract of 1496.

[3] DCW 16475, lease of 9 August 4 and 5 Philip and Mary with recitals.

[4] Ibid.; and see Barratt, op. cit., I, 75–82.

figured so prominently on the later local maps with its strikingly severe pentagonal grounds, was the large-scale and for a while *avant-garde* start to the colonisation of select parts of Hampstead by the villas of the wealthy, a long-drawn-out process occurring mainly from the late seventeenth to the mid-nineteenth centuries. The villas in their turn, by reason of the precise locations of their grounds and the precise terms of their tenures, were to be of great consequence in influencing the chronology and topography of true urbanisation.

While Hampstead of the villas made leisurely progress the influence of London was more directly apparent on farming Hampstead. The soils, which outside the sands and gravels of the heath were clays and heavy loams, combined with the techniques and requirements of subsistence farming, had placed Hampstead under the normal arable régime of the Middle Ages. Wheat and beans were presumably the usual crops, the ploughs and oxen went over most of the land, and the livestock of both peasants and lord lived largely by grazing the Heath. But if it became profitable to do so the soils could equally well support grassland farming, and the breadstuffs needed by the inhabitants could be purchased from elsewhere. It may be that the conversion to grass was started not by the pull of the London market, but by the push of labour shortage after the Black Death when lack of sufficient men to maintain former levels of arable cultivation forced a very general adoption of less labour-intensive practices. The first direct evidence of conversion, however, comes from the mid-sixteenth century, and suggests that the pull of London was the reason. In 1555, under one of the periodic Tudor Acts for preserving tillage and preventing the decay of houses of husbandry, commissioners held an inquest in Middlesex and were informed that in Hampstead a large gentleman grazier, John Slannyng, had not only felled a considerable area of wood in Ken Wood, Wyldes Wood and Chalcots, contrary to custom, in order to graze his horses, mares and cattle there, but was also 'keeping 140 acres in Hampstead, and the farm of Chalcots containing 120 acres more, in pasture instead of tillage', and that he let this land 'to butchers and inn-holders of London.[1] The object of the copyholders who made this presentment was to force the reinstatement of the plough. But clearly the economic advantages and the highest income lay with increasing specialisation on grass to satisfy the London demand, so that it is unlikely that pressure for traditional backwardness ever had much success.

It is possible that there was an intermediate stage in the progress

[1] Quoted in Barratt, op. cit., I, 60.

towards an all-grass Hampstead, at some time between about 1550 and 1700. At least one of the early eighteenth-century field names, Summer leys, implies that convertible farming had been practised in Hampstead, the system in which parts of the arable land were in turn laid down to temporary grass leys, where they could lie for several years before being ploughed once more.[1] This style of farming, which was well adapted to dairying, would have been very sensible for some farms in Hampstead during a period when the London-based demand for pure grazing pastures and hay meadows was not large enough to dominate all the farms in the parish. Farms entirely given over to permanent grass could scarcely have competed with similar provincial farms forming the breeding or fattening areas for London's meat supply, since the comparatively low stocking ratios which were within the capacities of that kind of farming could not have supported the rents of £1 an acre which Hampstead lands were yielding by 1700.[2] This level of rent, compared with Gregory King's average value of 8s. 8d. an acre for pasture and meadow for the whole kingdom in 1688, could have been produced from permanent grass only if it was entirely devoted to special uses, such as providing accommodation land for the droving trade and hay for London's stables and cowhouses. Undoubtedly some Hampstead farmers were taking part in these specialised forms of London agriculture, but there were limits to their adoption. On the demand side, the requirements of drovers and grazing-butchers were not unlimited, and in catering for this demand Hampstead had to face the competition of other places which were nearer to the main sheep and cattle routes. On the supply side, the monoculture of pure hay farming needed large supplies of manure, and as long as manure had to come by cart for several miles transport costs probably priced it out of the reach of most farmers, certainly of those who were any distance up the hill.

We may picture the Hampstead farmers of the early eighteenth century, therefore, as engaged in a range of enterprises with the emphasis on dairying, hay farming, and short-stay stock-keeping, and with the trend all the time towards laying more land down to grass. By the middle of the century all the estate evidence suggests that nearly

[1] Greater London Council Record Office [GLCRO], Maryon Wilson Papers [E/MW], E/MW/H/I/2310 A, 'A particular of the Manor of Hampstead belonging to Baptist Noel, Earl of Gainsborough, 1703/4'. For the introduction of convertible farming from 1560 onwards see E. Kerridge, *The Agricultural Revolution* (1967), especially pp. 194–221.

[2] GLCRO, E/MW/H/I/2310 A; every one of the ten farms on the manor had a rent of £1 an acre or slightly more in this rental of 1703/4.

all the land was under grass.[1] The cartographical evidence to the contrary of Rocque's 1744 *Survey of London* is highly suspect. His field markings indicate that about half the land in the parish was under the plough; but as comparison with a contemporary estate map shows that the field boundaries on Rocque's map were extremely inaccurate, it must be concluded that his portrayal of land use was also the result of guesswork and hazy memory rather than accurate observation.[2] The consolidation of holdings and the movement of rents on the manor lands is scarcely consistent with anything but a movement to grass: the ten separate farms of 1703 were reduced to four holdings at some time before 1766, and the total rents, which were about £450 in 1703, had become £753 in 1766 and £1,307 by 1787. Moreover the steward clinched matters by noting that in 1772 'Samuel Carr, the coachmaster in Oxford Road, offered me £3 an acre for any quantity of land in Hampstead:—462 acres at £3 is £1386 p.a.'.[3] The coachmaster's level had almost been reached by 1787, though it was not being paid by the coachmaster himself, whose application had simply been used as a yardstick of values; he had clearly wanted the land to use in his business, for grazing and for hay. Not surprisingly, when a public house was opened half-way up Haverstock Hill at about this time, it was named The Load of Hay.

By about 1800 only the odd plough or two was left in Hampstead. Eton's farm of Chalcots had only 18 of its 227 acres under the plough in 1796, and with a valuation of £4 an acre set upon it was reaching its peak as a grass farm.[4] The complete disappearance of the plough was registered by the Tithe Commutation Award of 1839, which shows that every single acre of agricultural land in the parish was meadow or pasture, save only for 6 acres of nursery ground.[5] Chalcots, which was the farm nearest to London (Chalk Farm), actually reached its all-time

---

[1] Ibid. and DCW 12450, field references to Survey of Lands belonging to the Dean and Chapter of Westminster in the Parish of Hampstead, 1734.

[2] J. Rocque, *Survey of London in 1744* (1746), compared with estate map DCW 12450 of 1734.

[3] GLCRO, E/MW/H/I/2310 A for 1703; E/MW/H/I/2280, an Account of the improvement of the Estate since Michaelmas 1766, for 1766 and 1787 and annotation referring to 23 November 1772. There was no market garden ground on this property, which might otherwise have explained the high average rents.

[4] Eton College Papers, Windsor [Eton], MS. College Records, XLIX, 19, Survey and Valuation of several farms in Hampstead, Hendon and Finchley, by Abraham and William Driver, 1796.

[5] GLCRO, Tithe Map and Apportionment, Hampstead, 1839. This map was surveyed in 1838.

peak in money rent in 1811, when it was valued at £6 an acre.[1] The Regent's Canal was opened shortly thereafter, in 1820, and although the Camden wharf was within a few hundred yards of the farm, the greater convenience and cheapness of water carriage of manure inwards and hay outwards was apparently outweighed by the strength of the competition from more distant grass farms which the canal brought into the market. The strength of the monopoly position, both as a hay farm and as a feeding farm, had been described by the surveyor in 1796:[2]

> The farm is in general very good land and in a high state of cultivation, which is occasioned in a great measure from its contiguity to London, from whence manure is so easily obtained. The crops of hay it produces annually are very great . . . The fences are in general very bad, which is partly occasioned by the great stock of cows fed upon the farm, and being so near the Metropolis, the wood is daily stolen and carried away.

By 1832 the lessee, from whom the actual farmer held as a sub-tenant, was arguing that ruinous competition caused by the canal had undermined the monopoly and the rent:

> The Middlesex farmers, it is well known, are not the race they used to be when they could get from six to seven guineas a load for their hay. The canals have ruined them . . . With respect to Chalcots the rent of £5.10 [an acre] is not to be got from a responsible tenant . . . little cowkeepers or others may be found to give that rent for a few acres, but what trouble to get the rent of such persons.

The actual rent which he then received from his tenant had fallen to £4. 8s. 0d. an acre.[3]

There was some special pleading here, for the opening of the canal had benefited rather than harmed the chief farm on the manorial estate, which was half-a-mile to a mile further from the canal and from London than Chalcots. The rent of this farm, variously known as Hall Oak or Manor Farm, which had still been £2. 11s. 0d. an acre in 1787, went to £3 an acre in 1798, and reached £5 an acre in 1819, where it remained until the 1840s; the decline then was not due to competition,

---

1 Eton, College Records, XLIX, 21, Valuation by John Trumper, 14 May 1811.
2 Ibid., XLIX, 19.
3 Ibid., XLIX, 42, Thomas Clarke to Rev. George Bethell [Provost of Eton], 7 March 1832.

whether canal- or rail-borne, so much as to the depredations of constant invasion by the London populace.[1] In agricultural terms, therefore, Hampstead reached its peak of prosperity in the early nineteenth century as the provider of fodder and standing room for part of London's meat and milk supply, and for some of London's horses. Market gardening, the even more highly specialised and profitable form of suburban agriculture, never established much of a hold in Hampstead. Presumably neither proximity nor improved transport could overcome the natural disadvantages of the less suitable soils and steeper hills of Hampstead in comparison with the riverside and valley areas which produced London's vegetables. There were, by the 1820s, one or two market gardens on the lower reaches of Haverstock Hill, and many small gardens were engaged in supplying the purely local market of Hampstead town. But by and large when the ground landlords and their advisers came to weigh the opportunity costs of building development in the nineteenth century, the element of alternative agricultural use was furnished by grass rents of the order of £4 to £6 an acre.

In the pre-nineteenth-century building development of Hampstead town the ground landlord had no opportunity costs; for it seems that virtually the entire town was built on encroachments and enclosures from the manorial waste, that is the Heath, so that no income at all was sacrificed by abandoning previous or alternative uses. It is true that some part of the town as it existed in 1703 had been built on copyhold lands, no less than 112 separate copyhold holdings with a house or houses on them being recorded in that year. Many of these holdings were no doubt of ancient and honestly agricultural origin, though many other copyholds had either been created out of the Heath or enlarged by encroachments, with building definitely in view. In 1703 it was possible to trace 27 acres which had recently been taken from the Heath for building copyholds; and although we may suppose that more heathland had gone the same way without getting into this surveyor's book, even a conservative estimate shows that the Heath lost 100 acres from the 340 acres which it was known to the 1703 surveyor to have covered at one time, before its area was stabilised early in the nineteenth century.[2] All this land was used for building or for furnishing

[1] GLCRO, E/MW/H/I/2280, for 1787 and 1798; E/MW/H/III/38/15, Case on the part of Sir Thomas Maryon Wilson as to the value of the lands required for the New Road [Finchley Road], November 1828.
[2] GLCRO, E/MW/H/I/2310 A, Survey of 1703, noting copyholds lately taken from the Heath. The map in Barratt, op. cit., II, 196 probably underestimates the extent of the Heath in 1680.

the houses with gardens, and contributed about one half of the built-up area of Hampstead in 1801. In the light of what happened later when it was thought that parts of the Heath might be used for building, it is curious to note that none of the seventeenth- or eighteenth-century nibbling at the Heath produced any protests from the inhabitants or the copyholders. The reason is plain: the encroachments were certainly profitable for the lord of the manor, who was able to charge increased entry fines on every change of copyholder, but they were equally profitable for the copyholders, who obtained valuable building plots. Where the lord of the manor and the copyholders were able to scratch each other's backs, they were quite content to remain silent about the shrinkage of the Heath.[1]

Much later, preservationists might bemoan the fact that the Heath had ever been touched, and might wish that the 312 acres of the 'remains of the Heath unimproved' recorded in 1703 had forever remained that way. Other preservationists, interested in Georgian buildings and in conserving the charm of eighteenth-century urban-village street views, have equally strong reasons—without perhaps being aware of them—for being grateful that the Heath-despoilers had been at work. For if there was to be any building at all in Hampstead from the late seventeenth century onwards, both law and economics indicated that it should take place on the Heath. Legally, no doubt, there were no obstacles to building on the freehold lands of the parish except such as might have been self-imposed. But we are entitled to assume that in the crucial cases self-imposed impediments were indeed formidable. Thus it is entirely likely that the freehold lands of the Earl of Gainsborough, the lord of the manor, were held under a family settlement which prevented both sales and the granting of any except farm leases. The ancient village was surrounded by these lands on the west and the Heath on the north and east. Even where there was a property gap, to the south, it was filled by the Chapter lands. These were not completely immobilised or frozen in their existing use by their tenure, it is true; but by slipping into the habit of leaving them on leases for lives which were perpetually renewed the Chapter had surrendered effective control to the lessee, and he in his turn did not have sufficient security to make plots easily available for building because there was always some risk that possession might revert to the Chapter. In terms of law the difficulties, imperfections and restrictions on ownership and leasing could have been overcome, at a price; for the devices for getting round such snags, whether sur-

[1] See below, chs 4–5, for the history of the Heath.

renders, fines and recoveries, or private estate bills, all had costs that would necessarily be reflected in one way or another in the price of houses. Patently there was no call to pay this price, when land from other sources was easily available for building, at no legal cost beyond the fees of the steward of the manor.

For there were no legal difficulties in taking in pieces of ground from the waste, and either expanding the holdings of existing copyholders or creating new ones. The process was simple; the resulting tenure was reasonably secure, and title to the properties was easily transferred, thus providing favourable proprietary conditions for building. To put it briefly, the lord of the manor had the power, with the consent of the homage (nominally all the holders of ancient copyholds in the manor) given in a general court baron of the manor, to 'approve' or enclose pieces of the Heath and grant them to applicants, who thereupon became copyhold tenants. Fees had to be paid, usually of three shillings to the lord and a guinea to the steward. Thereafter the new copyhold could be transferred like any other, by entry on the court roll, on payment of a fine equivalent to two years' full annual value every time the holding changed hands by death or sale. The only legal limit on these piecemeal enclosures was that the residue of the Heath which remained should always be sufficient to meet the established rights of the copyholders to pasture, turf, and the like. The petty scale of operations in the eighteenth century meant that this was never more than a hypothetical limit, since there was always plenty of common left for the tenants' stock to graze. In practice these powers began to be used for building purposes in the late seventeenth century, and continued to be used throughout the eighteenth century. The manor had 146 copyhold tenants in 1703, and by the early nineteenth century there were about 300. In these hundred years some holdings were no doubt subdivided, and such multiplication of individual tenants would not imply any expansion of the total land held by the group; on the other hand, in the course of time many copyholds no doubt managed to evade the grasp of the manorial administration, and pass themselves off as freeholds, thus escaping the later count. On balance, then, these figures probably give a fair impression of the size of the operation.[1]

[1] Copyholders were counted in the 1703 Survey, and again in 1829, GLCRO, E/MW/H/III/38/14, Brief for Mr Bollard to appear at House of Lords Committee hearing on behalf of Sir Thomas Maryon Wilson. The court rolls for the eighteenth century do not appear to have survived, and have not been deposited at the GLCRO with the other manorial records. Copious extracts from the court rolls were made, however, in the Brief for Mr Bollard, and in Hampstead Public Library [HPL], Documents in the case of Hoare v

What could be done within the law could also be done outside it altogether. Unless the manorial administration was extraordinarily vigilant it was impossible to prevent straightforward appropriation of bits of the common and waste, whether by resident tenants or by squatters, and whether done stealthily or boldly in full light of day. In general, existing villagers with legitimate established rights of their own might be expected to be jealous of and hostile to complete strangers and outsiders who tried to plant themselves on the common land, and their own self-interest would make them into reliable informers against such invaders. But self-interest would equally mean that villagers might from time to time enlarge their own holdings by taking in small pieces from the common, moving their fences forward inch by inch; and when it was a matter of a relative or a friend wanting to carve out a completely new holding by squatting, a villager would assist and connive. Certainly in Hampstead the administration found it difficult to detect or prevent their nibbling encroachment. The lords of the manor were never personally resident, and therefore were not themselves on the spot to watch everything that was going on; and their stewards were also non-resident, usually London attorneys or solicitors from the late seventeenth century onwards, who visited Hampstead perhaps two or three times a year at most. There was, it is true, also a bailiff for the manor, who did usually live on the spot. But as he was usually drawn from the ranks of the local copyholders and tenants, unswerving loyalty to the lord's interests was less than complete; and in any case the bailiff was often the tenant of one of the chief farms, whose business would occupy much of his attention. Hence it was only where the immediate interests of the inhabitants, and the bailiffs, were touched that vigilance was exerted; and immediate interests were apt to be agricultural, so that strangers with no rights of common were liable to find their cattle and donkeys hustled off the Heath into the manorial pound, which remained in use until well into the nineteenth century.[1] In other matters a blind eye was turned when plots were taken in from the Heath which did little harm to what was left—so much so that by the late nineteenth century the official line was that 'by tradition it is believed that the Town of Hampstead was built on the Waste by

---

Wilson, Chancery, 1866 H. No. 273, especially item 3 'Extracts from Court Rolls shewing Grants of Waste since 1783', and item 12 'List of Inclosures from the Heath, 1608–1866'; these extracts show the process of 'approvement' continuously in action.

[1] GLCRO, E/MW/H/III/38/14, Brief for Bollard, extracts court roll for 28 May 1759 instituting new methods for impounding strange cattle.

squatters.'[1] An exaggeration, no doubt, but a pardonable one to use when suggesting the role of squatting in the early growth of urban Hampstead.

In spite of the tradition, however, it is likely that this role was largely confined to the earliest period of urban growth, perhaps to the time of the Civil War and Protectorate when the royalist lord of the manor, Lord Campden, was either away fighting or found his estate sequestrated and in the hands of parliamentary commissioners, and when it is likely that the manorial administration was thrown into utter confusion. For although the prospect of free plots for the taking must always be irresistible for any developer, those with property rights can also be relied upon to take some care to ward off squatters once it is clear that their particular patch has become a popular district for building. This had certainly happened to Hampstead by the last decade or so of the seventeenth century, and from that time onwards we may doubt whether barefaced squatters managed to get away with anything more than perhaps the occasional small site for a single cottage. The sites for any substantial buildings, let alone groups or rows of houses, would come only through legitimate acquisitions. These plots in turn continued to come out of the Heath, not because they were free to the acquirer, but because they were virtually free to the supplier. The cost of such Heath-plots to the builder or house-owner, in terms of annual rents and entry fines, may well have been little different from what he would have had to pay if any alternative sites had been taken from ancient copyholds or from the demesne freehold. But from the point of view of the supplier, the lord of the manor, all income from new Heath-plots was an addition to gross income, while for plots taken from anywhere else there would be some deduction for the loss of income from previous use which he would have to set against new rents.

Local topography clearly did not inhibit this direction of expansion from the original village centre of the High Street–Heath Street– Church area, but neither did it dictate such lines of advance. To the east of this nucleus more or less level, or only gently sloping, ground was taken in from the Heath for housing. But the physically equally inviting level ground to the south and south-west quickly encountered the property boundaries, either of the lord of the manor's freehold or of the Dean and Chapter's estate, and for that reason it was not

[1] GLCRO, E/MW/H/III/38/16, Proceedings on the purchase of Hampstead Heath by the Metropolitan Board of Works, 1871, statement by F. J. Clark, Surveyor to the Manor.

the scene of early development, while, by way of contrast, the awkwardly sloping ground to the north and north-west of the old centre,
which on purely topographical grounds one might have expected
houses to shun, was in fact built over in the early stages, precisely because it was Heath-land. Admittedly the sloping ground had the great
attraction of offering simple and free drainage, and easily tapped water
supplies. Nevertheless, the inconvenience of some of the very steep
streets and alleys developed in seventeenth- and eighteenth-century
Hampstead was accepted primarily because of the property structure.
Moreover the compactness and congestion of much of this development, the close-packed tightness and narrowness of the surviving
examples such as Flask Walk or Perrin's Court which furnish one
element of Hampstead's charms, indicate that land was scarce and
precious, not to be squandered in over-spacious development. The
physical evidence confirms, in other words, that even the Heath-land
was not too easily come by for building purposes.

Why was any land wanted for building purposes at all at this time,
and what forces settled the character of the old town of Hampstead, as
it emerged by 1800? The traditional interpretation focuses entirely on
the discovery and exploitation of the Hampstead mineral waters at the
very end of the seventeenth century, and it is perfectly true that from
that time Hampstead developed in the next half-century as one of
London's fashionable spas. Before accepting this as the sole spur to
growth, however, it should be noted that the Wells began their commercial life only in 1698, when Susannah Noel, mother of the infant
lord of the manor the Earl of Gainsborough, granted six acres of the
Heath containing springs and wells to a syndicate, which was to apply
the profits of its enterprise to the easing of Hampstead's poor rate.[1]
There is some evidence that Hampstead was already developing in a
modest way as an upper-class residential satellite well before 1698. If
one starts with the notabilities, then the most renowned of the seventeenth-century residents was the parliamentarian and leading republi-
can, Sir Henry Vane. With his main seat at Raby Castle in Co. Durham,
Vane found it convenient to provide himself with another house near
to London, and settled on Hampstead. What he built for himself, at
some time in the 1640s, the surviving drawing shows to have been a
very considerable mansion. But though it was every inch a gentleman's
mansion, set in large grounds, the interesting thing about Vane House
was that it was set right on the edge of the village—on the site at the
top of Rosslyn Hill now largely occupied by the Soldiers' Daughters'

[1] Park, op. cit., pp. 51–2.

Home, whose buildings incorporate part of the seventeenth-century house. It was at Vane House that he was arrested at the Restoration, so that apart from his period of political retreat at Raby, following quarrels with Cromwell, Vane would seem to have been quite normally resident at Hampstead.[1] His household, by its demand for services and supplies, would therefore contribute to the growth of gentry-dependent trades in the village. On the opposite side of the road was a more modest gentleman's house, known in the eighteenth and nineteenth centuries as the Chicken House, which was visited by James I in 1619.[2] And somewhere near at hand was the house built by Sir Isaac Wake, a courtier who died in 1632, of whom John Aubrey remarked: 'He had a fine seate at Hampstead in Middlesex, which lookes over London and Surrey, where he made those delicate walkes of pines and firres, also corme-trese, etc. The Lord Chiefe Baron Wyld had it afterwards. His study was mighty pleasant.'[3] The employment created by these resident gentry, and a few more of their kind, was likely to have stimulated some town growth at Hampstead well before 1698.

Just how far this growth had gone can be gauged from the parliamentary survey of 1646 which itemised 146 separate dwellings in Hampstead, distinguishing with some care between 68 'houses' whose rental values ranged between £5. 5s. 0d. and £17. 10s. 0d. a year, and 78 'cottages' with rentals of £1. 10s. 0d. to £3. 15s. 0d. a year; in one case a 'cottage' was carefully noted as having been 'late a house'.[4] These 146 households might be taken to imply a population in the region of 600 to 650, well over twice the size of the probable population in 1549; but the great uncertainties as to the appropriate value of the hearth-multiplier to apply make such demographic calculations at the level of the individual parish highly approximate.[5] Of greater importance than such guesses at the total population is the social structure implicit in the balance between houses and cottages, for the gentry and comfortable classes in their houses were about as numerous as the villagers, labourers, and small tradesmen in their cottages, the structure of an urban rather than of an agricultural community. The hearth tax assessment of 1664 confirms the presence, and continued steady growth, of the merchant-gentry element, showing 104 houses being assessed to the tax; the return is unfortunately damaged and does not give a

[1] Barratt, op. cit., I, 140–6.
[2] Ibid., I, 105–10.
[3] John Aubrey, *Brief Lives* (ed. Anthony Powell, 1949), p. 318.
[4] Bodleian Library, Rawlinson D 715, f.76, 'Survey and Valuation of Hampstead, 28 April 1646', printed in Barratt, op. cit., III, 359–61, App. III.
[5] T. H. Hollingsworth, *Historical Demography* (1969), pp. 117–21.

complete list of the meaner dwellings which were exempt from hearth tax, so that it is impossible to deduce the full tally of dwellings of all sorts in 1664.[1] Nevertheless the return does show that Hampstead had a goodly number of sizeable houses: no less than 29 of the taxpayers were assessed for five or more hearths apiece, and three-quarters of the families lived in houses which had two or more hearths. This is a picture of a place which had definitely outgrown its rural village days, and was well on the way to becoming an urban village with a large wealthy upper-class element.

It was thus on this foundation that health-resort Hampstead was developed with the opening up of the mineral springs. It is perhaps unduly exact to date this precisely to 1698 and the grant to the Wells' Trustees. The waters were certainly not of any fashionable or medicinal note in 1665 or 1668 when Pepys made visits to Hampstead, or that garrulous diarist would have found space to mention the fact among his notes of his amorous and business activities there.[2] But they were definitely being drunk, and talked about, before 1697, for on stopping at Barnet in that year Celia Fiennes complained of the dirtiness of its waters, and commented that the well was:[3]

> full of leaves and dirt, and every time they dip it troubles the water, not but what they take up and let stand looks clear but I could not taste it; its being very deep and not done at the bottom with a bason as Tunbridg, so that it appears not to be a quick spring as Tunbridg or the Spaw or Hamsted waters, which have all fine stone basons in which you see the springs bubble up as fast, and by a pipe runs off as clear and fast; it more resembles Epsom for which reason I dislike that . . .

So by 1697 the spa at Hampstead had been in business long enough for various bits of plumbing to have been done. Celia Fiennes, with her keen eye for all that was latest in the plumbing line, is unlikely to have been mistaken in this sort of detail. It could well be that the basic engineering had been completed before the 1698 grant, for this speaks of medicinal waters which were already known as 'the Wells'.[4]

The first benefits of the waters may have been monopolised by the

[1] The 1664 Hearth Tax roll for Hampstead is printed in Barratt, op. cit., III, 366–7, App. VII.
[2] *Diary of Samuel Pepys* (ed. H. B. Wheatley, 1905), v, 11 (11 July 1665), VIII, 77 (17 August 1668).
[3] *The Journeys of Celia Fiennes* (ed. C. Morris, 1949), p. 121.
[4] Quoted in Park, op. cit., p. 51.

wealthy, the fashionable, and the hypochondriacs, for it was not until 1700 that the manor court ordered that a second spring,[1]

> lying by the Purging wells, be forthwith brought to the town of Hampstead, at the parish charge, and that the money and profits arising thereout be applied towards easing the poor's rate hereafter to be made.

The townsfolk were thus assured of their share of the chalybeate waters, which were thought to be the basis of the town's reputation for healthiness; though maybe this truly derived simply from the fresh air which had been the only quality worth extolling in Pepys's day. In truth, however, the townsfolk did not need their own private tap in order to benefit from the waters, for the people who came for a cure brought custom and trade, and openings for lodging-house keepers and speculative builders or property developers; while a separate trade in bottled waters sprang up which supported a small-scale health industry. The rapidity of these developments is startling, and Hampstead in the early eighteenth century had the bustle, and the stridency, of a mushroom town. Flask Walk was set up, dealing in the flasks of the bottled trade, and quite distinct from Well Walk, which led visitors direct to the cure. By 1700 supplies of the waters were being taken to London and a retail outlet had been established in Fleet Street, where flasks were sold for threepence each, with a home delivery service at a penny extra also available.[2] In 1701 the Wells' Trustees found a speculator, John Duffield, who took a lease of their property and rapidly built a large hall on the south side of Well Walk, part of which was a pump-room but most of which was fitted out as a ballroom and assembly room. The Assembly Room was in use by the autumn of 1701, and development of the rest of the estate followed swiftly on the appearance of a fashionable crowd in search of water or company. Perhaps both were found together, in the dancing and the music—a 'consort' being a happy rendering of the latter in a handbill of 1701—which were provided. For the less healthy, gambling dens and souvenir shops were soon opened; and it was at this time that the whole surrounding district, which became known as New End, was developed with residences and lodging houses, many of which still survive.

There can be no doubt of the appeal of Hampstead to the smart set at this time, aided, as we shall see shortly, by the rather different attractions of Belsize. It was this fashionable tone which gave the

[1] Loc. cit.
[2] *The Postman*, 20 April 1700; cited Park, op. cit., p. 52.

initial impetus to the growth of the resort. But at the same time Hampstead's very nearness to London meant that its popularity quickly spread to more disreputable elements, and to the lower orders, so that its exclusiveness was extremely short-lived. Already by 1709 it could be said that 'its nearness to London brings so many loose women in vampt-up old clothes to catch the City apprentices, that modest company are ashamed to appear here . . . it seems to me', the observer continued in an early example of prejudice, 'to be overstok'd with Jews and sharpers.'[1] By about 1715, it seems, Hampstead's career as a high-ranking London spa was finished. The occasion was appropriately marked by the Hanoverian succession, such a conclusive triumph for Whig principles that it led the top Whig group, the Kit-Kat Club, to discontinue its summer meetings at the Upper Flask near the Assembly Room.[2] The Assembly Room itself became a chapel in 1725. And in 1724 Defoe was writing of Hampstead's resort days as a thing of the past:[3]

> Hampstead indeed is risen from a little Country Village, to a City, not upon the Credit only of the Waters, Though 'tis apparent, its growing Greatness began there; but Company increasing gradually and the People liking both the Place and the Diversions together; it grew suddenly Populous, and the Concourse of People was Incredible. This consequently raised the Rate of Lodgings, and that increased Buildings, till the Town grew up from a little Village, to a Magnitude equal to some Cities; nor could the uneven Surface, inconvenient for Building, uncompact, and unpleasant, check the humour of the Town, for even on the very steep of the Hill, where there's no walking Twenty Yards together, without Tugging up a Hill, or Straddling down a Hill, yet 'tis all one, the Buildings encreased to that degree, that the Town almost spreads the whole side of the Hill.
>
> On the Top of the Hill, indeed, there is a very pleasant Plain, called the Heath, which on the very Summit is a Plain of about a Mile every way; and in good Weather 'tis pleasant Airing upon it, and some of the Streets are extended so far, as that they begin

---

[1] John Macky, *A Journey through England in Familiar Letters from a Gentleman Here to His Friend Abroad* (1714, but written in 1709: 5th ed. 1732) I, 88–9.

[2] Barratt, op. cit., I, 197ff. The Kit-Kat Club associated with Hampstead such well-known names as Marlborough, Kneller, Addison, Congreve, Steele, and Walpole.

[3] Daniel Defoe, *Tour through the Whole Island of Great Britain* (1724: 1927 ed.) I, 383–5.

to build even on the highest part of the Hill. But it must be confest, 'tis so near to Heaven, that I dare not say it can be a proper Situation for any but a race of mountaineers, whose lungs had been used to a rarify'd air . . .

But as there is (especially at the Wells) a Conflux of all Sorts of Company, even Hampstead itself has suffered in its good name; and you see sometimes more Gallantry than Modesty; so that the ladies who value their Reputation, have of late more avoided the Wells and Walks at Hampstead, than they formerly had done.

A resort does not of course cease to be a resort simply because it is no longer frequented by the cream of society. The replacement of the quality by more disorderly and dissolute elements, and the eclipse of the waters as the main draw, in fact probably meant that Hampstead had more visitors, not fewer. But the change in the character of the customers, now largely in the day-trip class, also meant that the physical development of Hampstead was halted. The visitors were, no doubt, good for trade, and the shopkeepers and others who provided them with drink, refreshment, and trinkets continued to flourish. The demand for lodgings and summer residences, however, tailed off. As Defoe had noted, 'this Place may be said to be prepared for a Summer Dwelling, for in Winter nothing that I know can recommend it'; and this kind of demand had sustained something of a building boom up to about 1720.[1] Then for the next twenty years or so there was little fresh house building, the changed character of Hampstead's attractions providing a local reinforcement for more general financial factors which damped down building activity at the time.[2]

It is difficult to say just how many houses were added to Hampstead in this early phase which transformed it into a true town. Already in 1704 a manorial survey recorded at least 200 houses which could still be made to acknowledge the manorial jurisdiction, and of which 50 were marked as having been taken from the Heath. The entry recording 'houses standing on the Heath, and orchards and gardens taken from the Heath', which occupied 27 acres in all, was in addition to the houses separately counted, so that this survey may witness the existence of something like 250 houses all told.[3] This growth, a virtual doubling

[1] Ibid., i, 384.
[2] The aftermath of the South Sea Bubble put a damper on building, by disturbing the capital market, but did not in itself account for the prolongation of inactivity until the 1740s. On the general rhythm of building in London, see J. Summerson, *Georgian London* (1945), pp. 5, 81.
[3] GLCRO, E/MW/H/I/2310A, 1703/4.

since 1646, was undoubtedly continued after 1704, but no evidence exists from which the size of Hampstead can be estimated at the time of the pause in the early 1720s. But if we make the conservative assumption that a further 50 houses were added between 1704 and 1720, then a place with at least 300 houses and between 1,200 and 1,400 inhabitants would justify Defoe's description of its rise from a country village to 'a magnitude equal to some cities'. Comparison with Hampstead at the time of the first census, in 1801, brings out the explosive nature of the urban growth induced by the mineral waters. In 1801 Hampstead had 691 inhabited houses and a population of 4,343, so that in the eighty years after 1720 the rate of growth was no greater than in the eighty years before.[1]

These years after 1720 saw at least one attempt to restore Hampstead to favour as a respectable health resort, in the 1730s; but although Hampstead did remain, and still remains, a pleasure resort, it never regained the front rank as a London spa, and its attractions for leisure and pleasure, though by no means negligible, played no more than a subsidiary role in its further development. The attempt once more to cry up the medicinal values of its waters was made by a local physician and patriot, Soames, in 1734.[2] But even if the Wells had truly possessed any curative powers, which later analyses make extremely doubtful, Hampstead was simply too close to London to be able to compete with Tunbridge or Bath, or even Epsom, for which the sheer cost of travelling provided the basic foundations of exclusiveness. The Soames promotion was followed a few years later by the conversion of a Queen Anne house in Well Walk, later known as Burgh House, into a new assembly room to replace the one which had become a chapel. This, the Long Room, certainly provided a social centre which was much used in the second half of the eighteenth century, both by the quality and by social aspirants, and both for indoor entertainments and for lavish private parties with dancing in marquees in the grounds.[3] But these Hampstead commemoration balls, though no doubt frequented by Londoners having a night out, were not the reason for Hampstead's further expansion; they were rather a sign of the kind of social life generated by that expansion, an expansion which was essentially bringing the upper classes and the wealthy to live in Hampstead as permanent residents, not as health- or pleasure-seekers.

[1] See Appendix for census details.
[2] Barratt, op. cit., I, 240.
[3] See the illustration [Barratt, op. cit., I, 263] of Thomas Osborne's guests dancing in a marquee at the Long Room in 1754. Osborne was a bookseller with aspirations to enter Hampstead society.

The sign that expansion had been renewed, and the evidence of its prosperous respectability, was the rebuilding of the parish church in 1744–7, when the old church, which had become very cramped especially when the congregation was afforced by all the summer residents, was replaced, on the same site, by a large, plain, nicely-proportioned brick structure designed by John Sanderson. The wealth which could build the new church, as well as its restrained elegance, was matched by Church Row, which was built at about the same time, or perhaps a little earlier. Church Row, now 'the best street in Hampstead' from an architectural point of view, was also the best street in Hampstead socially as soon as it was built.[1] Its comfortable family houses, with three principal storeys plus basement and attic floors, are very similar to many town houses of the same period, and some were probably occupied as such by gentlemen's families with a fair complement of servants; others were probably used as summer residences by families who also kept a London house, the wife, children and servants being established for the season while the master of the household, if still active in business, remained in town during the week and came up the hill for weekends. Such was a common pattern of life among the Hampstead gentry in the late eighteenth and early nineteenth centuries. And since Church Row houses were not provided with stables and had no private mews attached, the street was clearly not intended exclusively for carriage-folk who might have commuted daily to London in their own private transport; though stabling could be arranged in the nearby courts and alleys. If they were retired or persons of private means, the householders could well have been year-round Hampstead residents; but if they were business or professional men, they would have found little employment in Hampstead itself, and a public transport service so sketchy that they could not have relied on it to get them to an office in London daily. There were just two coaches a day running between Hampstead and Holborn or Covent Garden, in 1740.[2]

The regular, though not completely uniform, terrace arrangement of Church Row, which was paralleled in a smaller way in such developments as Hampstead Square and Elm Row, clearly indicates that as the middle of the eighteenth century approached Hampstead had moved away from any idiosyncratic, water-borne, urban growth. For there are

[1] Pevsner, op. cit., p. 195. Pevsner dates Church Row as *c.* 1720, and it certainly seems to have been built by the time of Rocque's map, 1746.

[2] *Complete Guide to London* (1740), ed. J. Osborn, p. 78.

counterparts of this type of eighteenth-century development in almost every village at a similar distance from London—Camberwell, Clapham, Dulwich, Twickenham, or Wandsworth, to select but a few—all of which were thus developing as residential or semi-residential town villages. Hampstead, by virtue of its special start, was simply one of the largest of these. It was, for example, to judge from the visual evidence of Rocque's map of 1746, at that time four or five times larger than Paddington which was still a tiny detached village, twenty times larger than Kilburn, a little halt four miles out from London on the St Albans road, and thirty or forty times as big as St Pancras, a mere resting place on the way to Hampstead or Highgate; while modern Camden Town, a little to the west of St Pancras, was then represented by no more than Old Mother Red Caps where one might take a drink before attempting the ascent of Haverstock Hill. Such was the measure of the advantage which height gave to Hampstead.[1]

In the second half of the eighteenth century Hampstead consolidated its position as a select residential town and summer station for some of London's wealthier professional and mercantile classes. Its peers in these functions were such places as Clapham, Chelsea, Hammersmith, Fulham, Putney, Greenwich, Stoke Newington, and of course its neighbour, Highgate. While all of these enjoyed a broadly similar kind of development there were many differences, some simple and some subtle, which gave to each a distinctive character and reputation whose strength or weakness broadly determined the social characteristics of full urbanisation in the nineteenth century. Thus those lying on level ground, at modest elevations, and with easy approaches from the centre were most vulnerable to mass invasion, and though they might preserve some of the physical appearance of their eighteenth-century hearts were poorly placed to maintain their eighteenth-century social status. The same topographical factors had, however, tended to make these places less exclusive and less sought after in the eighteenth century than the more elevated spots, since the easier and cheaper access had tended to lay them open to the slightly more vulgar new-rich in the first place. Hampstead clearly came in the top class in height and in social elevation; and its height and steepness of approaches were to contribute powerfully to the continuation of this state of affairs right through the nineteenth century. As between places at a similar remove from London and equally expensive to reach, however, the choice was not determined merely by relative heights above sea level. Differing views of the merits of local topography may certainly have entered into it; not

[1] See the northern section of Rocque's map, 1746.

everyone of the same level of social ambition and of means necessarily admired the exertions or the breezes which Hampstead's views entailed, and some may have preferred the gentler demands of Blackheath or the riverside at Putney. But as between Hampstead and Highgate, which acquired quite distinct ambiences at this time, the differences were clearly neither geographically nor aesthetically determined. It was at this level that economic and social factors were decisive. The property structure of Hampstead, as has been seen, led to a compact town development, with a few stately mansions outside; it did not permit the straggling development along the main road which at once made Highgate more bustling and more attractive to commercial men.

The very compactness of Hampstead's early development meant that its eighteenth-century housing was fairly well within a ring fence, so that short of redevelopment, which within the old town and within the nineteenth century was largely confined by financial rewards to the shops, Georgian Hampstead formed a fortress with built-in defences and a high survival rating. Other places, where the property structure and the sites permitted more spacious first development, were vulnerable later on because the gaps for further development and infilling were so large, and hence their eighteenth-century pieces might either be left as tiny isolated islands or altogether drowned by nineteenth-century building. Admirers of eighteenth- and early-nineteenth-century domestic architecture, therefore, have reason to be grateful to the particular distribution of landownership in Hampstead which caused such building to be hemmed in.

The social character of Hampstead, formed in the eighteenth century and projected forward to cast its glow over much of its nineteenth-century urbanisation, perhaps owed more to the forging of associations with particular occupations and individuals than to any of the features so far discussed. That is to say, when men of broadly similar wealth and tastes came to choose which district to live in, those who chose Hampstead rather than some close alternative did so because of the specific associations which Hampstead had acquired, and the local communities or social circles which went with them. In the popular mind Hampstead is pictured as an artists' colony, its associations literary and artistic with a radical flavour, spiced with progressive intellectuals and politicians. Such were not the associations which Hampstead earned in the eighteenth century, nor those which predominated in the following hundred years. Its reputation, once the gaiety verging on *risqué* depravity of the early 1700s subsided, rested on more solid,

[27]

earnest, and prosperous stuff than canvases, odes, or broadsheets. The first painter of any note to live in Hampstead, after all, was George Romney, and he did not come until 1796, and then only to indulge some building fancies at the top of Holly Bush Hill and not to continue with his career as a fashionable portrait painter.[1] It was only in 1821 that a painter, John Constable, settled in Hampstead in order to practise his art, of landscape painting, to be followed in the next year by a lesser light, John Linnell. There was indeed a literary association from much earlier, when Richard Steele lived in the parish for a year in 1712; but this was merely a year of temporary exile from London society enforced by loss of political favour, and can scarcely rank as a voluntary bestowal of literary grace. Authors and poets are certainly known to have visited Hampstead in plenty, but that signifies nothing more than that they visited such places as commonly were visited, as it might be Richmond, or Chiswick, or Greenwich, just as well as Hampstead. The first literary circle firmly based in Hampstead was that kept by Joanna Baillie in the opening decades of the nineteenth century; a minor dramatist herself, praised at the time and rapidly forgotten, she made her house on Holly Hill into something of a salon, frequently visited by her countryman Sir Walter Scott, by Wordsworth, and by Maria Edgeworth.[2] But it was not until Leigh Hunt came to live in Hampstead, first in a cottage at West End in 1812 and then in the Vale of Health from 1816, that any considerable literature was actually written in Hampstead. Hunt's poets' circle included John Keats, who lodged in Well Walk and then in Lawn Bank (in John Street, later renamed Keats Grove), and wrote his best poetry there between 1817 and 1820.[3] Undoubtedly Hampstead's most famous resident; but he did not reside there until after the general character of the area had already been settled.

There are, therefore, no grounds for supposing that the families which came to settle in Hampstead and caused its population to grow to 4,343 by the end of the eighteenth century were attracted there by its artistic and literary atmosphere, since it had none at the relevant date. They came, rather, simply because it was a desirable area for the prosperous and successful; and they were in the main families whose wealth rested on finance and trade, or the professions. Hampstead's business community in the late eighteenth century has not been much noticed

---

[1] E. Bell, 'George Romney in Hampstead', *Middlesex and Herts: Notes and Queries*, 1895.
[2] Barratt, op. cit., II, 112–21.
[3] Ibid., II, 135–40, 147–63.

by the local chroniclers, since eminence in this line did not strike them as eminence at all; but something of its nature can be judged from the memorials in the church and tombstones in the churchyard. These record the life and death in Hampstead in the later eighteenth century of East and West India merchants, publishers, booksellers, drapers, bankers, and inventors (John Harrison of the chronometer, Henry Cort of the puddling process). The chief benefactor of the parish in this period was John Stock, a resident who left £1,000 in 1781 for a charity to clothe, educate, and apprentice ten parish orphans. He was a wealthy draper and painter to the royal dockyards, who left most of his fortune of over £14,000 to charities, mainly to be administered by his own City company of the Painter-Stainers.[1] The impression from this source, however, is that the businessmen were surpassed in numbers, though not necessarily in wealth, by the professions.

Medical gentlemen had been drawn to Hampstead in the days when the curative powers of the chalybeate waters were in vogue, and some stayed on to advocate more simply the virtues of fresh air. A few of the doctors no doubt lived by local practice among the inhabitants and summer residents, but there would appear to have been more doctors than local patients could support, and some of the big names clearly conducted fashionable London practices from their Hampstead base. Such was William Pierce, the surgeon who endowed in 1771 a Friday evening lecturette to be given in the parish church by the curate. Sir William Duncan, physician to George III from 1760 until his death in 1775, was plainly in the same class, though Mark Akenside, an indifferent physician, is better known as a slightly less indifferent poet.[2] The doctors in their turn were overshadowed in eminence by the legal profession, and if Hampstead's image at the opening of the nineteenth century can be summed up in a single phrase it is as a lawyers' nest that it is best pictured.

The eagles in this nest were the Lord Chancellors. Eight lawyers reached the political head of their profession between 1760 and 1830, and of these two lived in Hampstead and one was an honorary Hampstead man. The most successful of the genuine residents is amply recorded in the street names of the area where his house stood, once as Wedderburn for his patronym and once as Rosslyn for his earldom, though Loughborough, the name under which most of his public career was conducted, is not similarly enshrined. The later developer, however, allowed him Eldon, Lyndhurst and Thurlow for company

[1] Park, op. cit., pp. 281–3, 334–59 ('Biographical notices').
[2] Ibid., pp. 280, 330–1, 340–1.

[29]

among his streets, fellow-Chancellors linked to Loughborough by profession if not to Hampstead by residence. The 'opposition' Chancellor of 1806, Erskine, has no street to his name, but he has his House, opposite Ken Wood. Both of them were no doubt following the lead of the most famous and successful lawyer of the century, Mansfield, who had bought Ken Wood in 1753 from Bute, and engaged the Adam brothers to rebuild the mansion. The house itself and its grounds lie over the parish boundary into St Pancras (Highgate), but the Ken Wood estate included farmland in Hampstead parish whose position on the eastern flank of the Heath was later to be of strategic importance, and the Mansfield family always retained an interest in Hampstead affairs.

The legal colony was not, of course, entirely composed of great names. Indeed the fashion may be said to have been set by one of the second eleven, the Master of the Rolls Sir Thomas Clarke who bought Branch Hill Lodge in 1745, and rebuilt it to Flitcroft's designs. Ownership passed to the son of Clarke's patron the Chancellor Macclesfield; and later occupants included a Master in Chancery, Thomas Walker, and Loughborough for a few years, so that Branch Hill acted as a considerable legal nursery. Alvanley lived in Frognal when he was Master of the Rolls at the end of the century; and tablets in the church speak of many Masters in Chancery, barristers, and judges. Whether Hampstead was good for the law, or the law good for Hampstead, is not entirely clear. For although it may seem obvious that it was simply a case of successful lawyers wanting to live in Hampstead, it could also be true that just one or two eminent and influential lawyers for neighbours might bring success to young men trying to build practices, so that it might not be ridiculous to have come to Hampstead in order to succeed in the law.

The root cause of the swarming of the lawyers, the presence of the queen bee, may have been pure chance. But it may be significant that Hampstead had no resident nobility or gentry of the established landed variety. Several lesser members of the traditional aristocracy were indeed buried in Hampstead, but mainly rather earlier: for example, the Irish Lord and Lady Ikerrin, in 1687 and 1688; in 1696 'Lord Wharton died at Hampstead, where he had been some time for the air'; the widow of Sir Charles Gerrard of Harrow, who was sister to the fifth Duke of Somerset, died at Hampstead in 1731; and much later, in 1810, an only daughter of the Earl of Lennox died there. A few aristocratic baptisms were also registered, such as Mary, daughter of the fifth Viscount Fitzwilliam, in September 1707, or Anne, daughter of

Sir Winwood Mowet, in July 1715.[1] The births clearly took place
during summer sojourns; the burials were of persons who had perhaps
come to Hampstead for health and had the misfortune to die instead,
for they were not permanent residents. The only genuinely resident
member of the old nobility who comes to light was Nathaniel Booth,
who lived in Hampstead certainly from 1748, when one of his infant
sons was buried there, until his own death in 1770; but he chanced to
become Lord Delamere only upon failure of heirs male in the direct
line, and was for most of his life a gentlemanly but minor civil servant.[2]
The absence of any established resident aristocracy meant that there
was no established family interest in Hampstead, no influential family
in control of Hampstead society. It was this social setting, perhaps, which
made Hampstead particularly attractive to the reigning lawyers, for
where no one was in possession empires could be carved out by the
freshly risen. A man of Wedderburn's ambition, for one, liked to rule
the roost, and would have fitted awkwardly into any local society in
which someone else was hereditary and undisputed head.

The lesser lawyers—along with the lesser civil servants, the merchants and bankers, and the men with private means—lived for the
most part in the town itself. The great lawyers required great houses,
and they lived in mansions set in private grounds, which made a major
contribution to the third element of eighteenth-century Hampstead,
the Hampstead of the villas, an element which needs to be set alongside
agricultural Hampstead and town-Hampstead in picturing the threshold of urbanisation. There was nothing very unusual about the
development of these large houses, each with its few acres of gardens
and mini-parks, in Hampstead; most places on the fringes of London
saw the appearance of similar comfortable villas during the eighteenth
century. What is perhaps unusual about Hampstead is that there were
not a great many of them before 1800, a reflection of the cautious, or
even restrictive, attitude of the landowners. Nevertheless this was a
form of development which the owners were ready to permit; or rather
one should perhaps say that it was a form of development which select
residents were willing to undertake on the terms which the owners
would concede. For these villas seem to have been built on rather short
leases of less than fifty years, or, what would generally be considered
much more discouraging from a building point of view, tenures of
quite uncertain duration that were sub-leases from a lessee who was
himself a lifehold tenant. The point was that a builder building for sale
would not take the risk of putting up houses on short or indefinite

[1] Ibid., pp. 334–59. [2] Ibid., pp. 332–3.

terms with no certainty of renewal, or of the future rents should renewal be granted. But select individuals, having decided on a promising site for a single large house, were quite willing to build on the tenurial sands, confident that they could cultivate a personal relationship with their landlord which would provide them with permanent occupation on reasonable terms.

The greatest lawyer had the largest house, Ken Wood, and this was in fact Mansfield's freehold estate; Branch Hill was also a freehold property, having been carved out of the Heath at some time after 1680. But two large lawyers' houses in Frognal, the Hall occupied by Alvanley in the late eighteenth century, and the Grove occupied by Edward Montagu, a Master in Chancery, at the same period, were both held of the lord of the manor on short terms, being part of his freehold demesne. One or two of the other well-known mansions were also freehold property, or, what amounted to the same thing from a building point of view, copyhold of inheritance: such were North End House, or Pitt House, owned by Lord North when Chatham retired there to brood in lonely melancholy in 1766 and 1767; and Heath House, opposite Jack Straw's Castle, which began a long connection with banking and philanthropy when Samuel Hoare the Quaker banker bought it in 1790. But Wedderburn, when as Lord Loughborough he moved from Branch Hill Lodge, moved to a leasehold house, then known as Shelford Lodge; he enlarged and improved it, and renamed it Rosslyn House to commemorate his own earldom.

Shelford Lodge stood on the Belsize estate, on its northern boundary; and it was held on a sub-lease from Lord Chesterfield, whose family had been the lessees of the entire estate from the Dean and Chapter of Westminster since Philip Stanhope had inherited the lease from his half-brother Lord Wotton in 1683. The Waad or Wade family, latterly of Battle Hall, Maunden, in Essex, had held the lease from the sixteenth century until about 1645; and after the disturbances of the Civil War the lease was granted to Lord Wotton's stepfather, one of Charles II's courtiers during the exile.[1] It is not known when Shelford Lodge was built, but it was certainly already there in 1734 when the Belsize estate was surveyed, the tenant being a Mrs Mules and the 'improved rent' or full annual value of the house being reckoned at £80, which meant that it was a sizeable residence.[2] It stood at the end of a

[1] Ibid., pp. 153–5; D. Lysons, *The Environs of London* (1795), II, 533; DCW 16476, lease for 21 years at £19. 2s. 10d. rent to Anne Wade, of Battle Hall, Maunden, widow. And see above, p. 8.

[2] DCW 12450, Survey and May of the Belsize Estate by John Grove of

private drive running parallel to Belsize Lane and roughly on the line of the present Lyndhurst Road. A little to the south were two other gentlemen's mansions of comparable size and seclusion: the White House, later known as Belsize House, on the north side of Belsize Lane, which was untenanted and therefore not valued in 1734; and Lord Paget's house, then lately built and lying between Belsize Lane and the drive to Shelford Lodge, and also valued at £80 a year.[1] Paget, a younger son of the Earl of Uxbridge (a descendant, after Waterloo, became Marquess of Anglesey), left no mark in the Hampstead histories, just as his house seems to have faded away before 1813.[2] Apart from Belsize itself, a considerable exception, the Belsize Estate had no other mansions of the first rank, but there were in 1734 nine other more modest gentlemen's houses, each valued at about £20 a year, detached houses with half an acre or so apiece, clustered round the top of Haverstock Hill on Belsize Lane and on the northern boundary of the estate. This was the limit of Belsize development in 1734, and it was still very nearly the limit in 1813, only one or two further houses, of the villa type, having been added in the interval. A small rash of houses shown in the 1813 map on the opposite or east side of Haverstock Hill running between Pond Street and a point opposite Belsize Avenue shows that the demand for ribbon development was present, but the property conditions to satisfy it were not: this little strip of developed land was ancient copyhold and outside the Belsize estate.[3]

The country villa or mansion demand, and the ribbon development demand, might have been more systematically exploited if the eighteenth-century lessees of Belsize had been profit-minded. The ground landlords of the estate, the Dean and Chapter of Westminster, washed their hands of its management and exploitation, contenting themselves with granting automatic renewals to the Earls of Chesterfield every time a life dropped in the lease. The reserved rent received by the Dean and Chapter remained fixed for ever at £19. 2s. 10d., plus ten cartloads of hay and five quarters of oats for the capitular stables; their renewal fine for the insertion of a new life had become stabilised, by the early eighteenth century, at $1\frac{1}{4}$ times the full rack rent value of the

Greenwich, July 1734. The 'improved rent' estimated at £80 can be compared with other houses put at £14 p.a. in the same document.

[1] Ibid. The White House was also later known as Belsize Court.

[2] Rocque's map, 1746, shows the same formal garden layout as the 1734 survey, but only a small house. Park's map, 1813 (in Park, op. cit.) shows no house on the site.

[3] Park's map, 1813.

estate, which they claimed was £775 in 1715, though Lord Chesterfield denied this and strove to prove that his 'clear yearly profit' after meeting taxes and estate expenses came to only £178. 18s. 7d.[1] How this particular dispute was settled the records do not tell, but it is plain that, as in the case of all beneficial leases, the lessors had surrendered the main part—perhaps 90 per cent—of the profits of ownership, and hence also the opportunities and risks of ownership, to the lessee. Even on the most extreme assumptions the rate of return to Lord Chesterfield was comfortably over 10 per cent on his outlay, so that unless he had been a fanatical profit-seeker he had every reason to be extremely happy to leave things as they were and not bother about any further development of his property. For if we assume that in his lease for three lives one dropped every 21 years, which is an unrealistically short interval; that he was forced to accept the Chapter's high valuation of 1715, and pay a renewal fine of £969; and that in the event he himself received in clear profit over the next 21 years no more than his own low estimate of £179 a year: then in return for an expenditure over the 21 years of £1,389 in fine and annual reserved rents to the Chapter, he would have received a clear £3,759, giving him a net profit of £2,376.

In reality, quite apart from this local financial disincentive, the Chesterfields were inclined to leave the Belsize estate alone and not trouble to realise its opportunities because they were absentees to whom the Belsize income was utterly insignificant beside the riches of their Nottinghamshire and Derbyshire estates, and because the one experience of thrusting enterprise at Belsize in the early eighteenth century was peculiarly shattering. It seems that after the original Armigail Wade the great house at Belsize was used as a residence by his son Sir William, also a royal servant, until he lost office in 1613, but was then abandoned. When it was acquired by Lord Wotton in the Restoration period it was put into service again, and used as his principal residence, apparently being extensively altered by him.[2] From the time of Wotton's death in 1683, however, the house was always in the occupation of under-tenants holding from the Chesterfields, and from time to time appears even to have been left unoccupied. Thus one Povey was the sub-tenant in the early eighteenth

1 DCW 16490, Belsize Renewal Fines, 26 July 1715: 'The rule of the Church of Westminster for some time has been according to the practice of many other churches and the Reason of the Thing, to take a year and one quarter's value for adding one life in a lease of three.' Ibid., 16481, Earl of Chesterfield's rental, 1707–14.

2 Lysons, op. cit., II, 533 speaks of an old print showing Belsize as a house of the time of Charles II. Park, op. cit., pp. 151–6 for the history of the house.

century, a not very successful but extremely prolix coal merchant, who
claimed that the books and treatises 'I have writ exceed 600 in number',
ranging from 'A discovery of indirect practices in the Coal Trade' in
1700 to a broadsheet in 1718 showing how he had done his bit to keep
Papist practices at bay by spurning a tempting offer to re-sublet
Belsize to the French ambassador, the Marquis de St André.[1] But he
was in trouble in 1714 as a sub-tenant when allegations were made to
Lord Chesterfield that he had been committing waste at Belsize, allegations which he refuted in typical style:[2]

> Committing damages and waste upon an Estate, which I have re-
> trieved from utter ruin? [he asked with a rhetorical flourish] The
> Mansion House and the outhouses were little more than a Heap
> of Rubbish: the land was overrun with Briers and Weeds: the
> Walls tottering and ready to fall down; but now it is manifest to
> every eye, that all things are in good repair and order. One com-
> plaint against me to his Lordship is, that I have taken away the
> Leaden Pipes, a pretty Story indeed: Have I wronged his Lord-
> ship in exchanging old Lead for new, and adding three times the
> weight of new lead to it over and above, which is to be seen on the
> Flats, and in the new Gutters I have laid? . . . Several Judges
> as well as Bishops who have done me the Honour of a visit, told
> me no Nobleman's Estate was ever more beautify'd by a Tenant,
> than my Lord of Chesterfield at Belsize is at this time, and other
> Improvements will likewise be made against next summer. [He
> added that he had laid out £2,200 in all in repairing] his Lord-
> ship's ruin'd Estate.

Before long, however, Povey tired of being visited by bishops and
judges and decided to recoup himself in more tangible manner for his
expenses in rescuing Belsize from dilapidation. So in 1720 he in turn
sublet Belsize to a Welshman, Howell, who proceeded to turn the place
into one of the most notorious pleasure gardens of the day. The opportunity, perhaps, was presented by the waning of the fashionable popularity of the Wells at Hampstead, and the astute Howell seized the
chance to entice and titillate the smart demi-reps with lavish amuse-
ments nearer to London and nearer to the foot of the hill. By Defoe's
time in 1724 Belsize had already run its giddy course of abandon:[3]

1 Park, op. cit., pp. 157–8.
2 DCW 16483, Charles Povey to Dean and Chapter, 9 June 1714.
3 Defoe, op. cit., I, 384.

At the foot of this Hill, is an old seat of the Earls of Chesterfield, called Bellsize; which for many years had been neglected and as it were forgotten. But being taken lately by a certain Projector to get a Penny, and who knew by what Handle to take the gay part of the World, he has made it a true House of Pleasure; Here, in the Gardens, he entertained the Company with all kinds of Sport, and in the House with all kinds of Game, to say no more of it: This brought a wonderful Concourse of People to the Place, for they were so effectually gratified in all sorts of diversions, that the Wicked part at length broke in, till it alarm'd the Magistrates, and I am told it has been now in a manner suppress'd by the hand of Justice. Here was a great room fitted up with abundance of Dexterity for their Balls, and had it gone on to a degree of Masquerading as I hear was actually begun, it would have bid fair to have had half the Town run to it: one saw Pictures and Furniture there beyond what was to have been expected in a meer Publick House; and tis hardly credible how it drew Company to it; But it could not be, no British Government could be supposed to bear long with the Liberties taken on such Publick Occasions: So as I have said, they are reduc'd, at least restrained from Liberties which they could not preserve by their Prudence.

In its first giddy flush Howell's advertising gave a decorous glimpse of the pleasures to be found.[1] He announced in 1723:

'Bellsize House is open every day; the public days are Mondays, Thursdays and Saturdays, with a good Concert of Musick in the Long Gallery during the whole season. The Proprietor is now provided with a Pack of good staunch Hounds, and a Huntsman, ready to show the Diversion of Hunting whenever the Company pleases; The Walks in the Garden and Parks are made very pleasant, where Gentlemen and Ladies have frequent Egress and Regress to Walk without any Expence. Any company that stays late,' [he prudently concluded] 'there are Servants with Fire-Arms to see them safe to London.'

An anonymous satirist of 1722 did not mince so many words:[2]

The scandalous lewd house that's call'd Belsize,
Where sharpers lurk, yet Vice in publick lies,
Is publicly become a Rendezvous,
Of Strumpets, common as in common Stews,

[1] *Daily Post*, 17 June 1723.
[2] Anon., *Belsize-House. A Satyr* (1722). In the Swiss Cottage Public Library.

. . . Convenient this defiled House is made,
To bring the Welsh Ambassador a trade.

For a short time Belsize, perhaps appropriately renamed The Wilderness at this time, was all the rage and outclassed London's other pleasure gardens of Vauxhall and Ranelagh in its raciness and daring. Sex, racing, and gambling were an irresistible mixture, and at the height of business between 300 and 400 carriages of the nobility and gentry were observed jostling into the park for a single race meeting and stag chase. The law moved in, as Defoe noted, in 1722, though it was to suppress unlawful gambling rather than to control the prostitution and promiscuity.[1] That was enough, however, to damage the attractiveness of the diversions, and the upper classes, for whom in any event novelty tends to wear off very quickly, moved away from the gardens soon after this. Povey was still the chief sub-tenant in 1734, and Howell was still presumably carrying on, offering entertainment to a lower class of clients; but the enterprise was faltering, and is last heard of in 1745 when a foot-race was advertised to be held there.[2] After this the mansion seems to have been left to decay, unoccupied; certainly the old house had been pulled down and replaced by a large, square, late-eighteenth-century red-brick mansion by the time Lysons was there in 1795.[3]

For Lord Chesterfield the experiment of running Belsize as a business had yielded no profits, since these had all gone to his sub-tenant and sub-sub-tenant; it had possibly brought him some opprobrium from the censorious. At any rate the rebuilding shows that he was convinced that the proper use of Belsize was as a large private residence, and he had presumably succeeded in finding a wealthy sub-tenant who was willing to rebuild. It was into this new house that the last of Hampstead's great politician-lawyers of the eighteenth century, Spencer Perceval, moved in 1798. A barrister by training, who prosecuted Tom Paine in 1792 and Horne Tooke in 1794, he rose to be Prime Minister in 1809 by way of the law offices of the government. He may have come to Hampstead because he married one of the daughters of the lord of the manor, Sir Thomas Wilson; although Belsize must have been handy for his *ménage* of thirteen children, he left in 1807 when he became Chancellor of the Exchequer. Meanwhile his habit of riding direct across the fields from Belsize to Westminster had been noted and stored away as a prestigious argument for future road development.[4]

[1] Park, op. cit., p. 248.
[2] Ibid., p. 249, DCW 12450, July 1734.   [3] Lysons, op. cit., II, 533.
[4] GLCRO, E/MW/H/III/38/15, Walpole Eyre to Sir Thomas Maryon Wilson, 6 December 1819.

The Belsize estate thus entered the nineteenth century largely as farmland, farmed from the house and steadings on the estate's southern edge at the junction of Englands Lane and Haverstock Hill, centrally placed for the two sections of the farm, that on the east and that on the west of the main road. But it was also equipped with two or three ample mansions, and a handful of more modest villas. It was ripe for the development of many more of these, and awaited only a change in the effective ownership; even so, the layout and boundaries of the few private suburban grounds and parks which did exist had already unknowingly determined much of the shape, timing, and even social character of the vast nineteenth-century building development itself, since it was these things which settled the form of the parcels in which dealings in the land could take place.

If the only faintly non-rural prehistory of the Belsize estate determined its nineteenth-century urban character, just as the small-scale urban prehistory of Hampstead town settled its later form, then the almost entirely agricultural prehistory of the Chalcots estate left it a blank sheet for the urban pen to draw on as it pleased. Chalcots enjoyed this fate because it was more low-lying than Belsize, and therefore not in such demand for elegant residences; and because its easier access to London made its hay farming that much more profitable and alternative uses for parts of the farm that much less attractive. In ownership and management terms it was very similar to Belsize, Eton College abdicating effective control to a beneficial lessee paying a nominal rent. The College could, however, always resume control relatively painlessly, since its habit was to let the estate on a series of twenty-year leases renewable every seven years on payment of a fine calculated at $1\frac{5}{8}$ times the current full annual value until 1818, when the rate of the fine was raised to $1\frac{7}{8}$ times the rack rental.[1] In practice, nevertheless, the College went on renewing the lease throughout the eighteenth century to the Earle family, as a matter of course, so that that family regarded themselves as hereditary lessees. The Earles in turn always put in a tenant to do the actual farming, and the Rhodes family became the equally hereditary tenant farmers of Chalcots. The sheer weight of tradition and inertia, therefore, even more than the technical nature of the tenurial arrangement in itself, accounts for the prolongation of pure haymaking at Chalcots. There were promptings, at the end of the eighteenth century, in the direction of change and enterprise, for

[1] Eton, College Records, XLIX, No. 53, Thos. Clarke to Geo. Bethell (the Provost), 18 May 1832.

when they valued the property for the renewal fine in 1796 the College's surveyors, Abraham and William Driver, made a point of stressing its ripeness for building. 'A considerable part of this Estate is very eligibly situate for building', ran their survey, 'being within 3 miles of London, and adjoining the Turnpike Road for a considerable extent.'[1] But no heed was taken of this advice, and apart from the farmhouse itself at the end of Englands Lane, there were only three very modest houses and a poor cottage on the estate at the beginning of the nineteenth century. One of these was Steele's Cottage, also on Englands Lane, which Richard Steele had used for his country exile in 1712; by 1832, and probably earlier, it was occupied as 'two Distinct Houses'.[2]

This was all that Chalcots had to offer. Some local histories suppose that the Chalk Farm Tavern was in Hampstead parish. If so, it would have been on the Chalcots estate; but in fact it lay just outside the southern boundary of the parish, and though much frequented by revellers and travellers to Hampstead it did not impinge on its property, only its propriety.[3] So Eton, which was to be the first beneficiary of the fruits of full urbanisation, missed out on the villa stage altogether, and had to rest content in the eighteenth century with its ancient annual rent of 410 gallons of wheat, 864 gallons of malt, 16 sheep of 44 lb each, 'entertainment' of £1. 0s. 6d., and £9. 15s. 6d. in cash. All of which was, of course, commuted into money, and produced £92 a year in the early nineteenth century. And every seven years the Provost and Fellows divided among themselves the renewal fine, which amounted to £1,395 in 1796, and reached £2,665 in 1811.[4] They were no doubt well content to make such hay while the sun shone.

---

1 Ibid., No. 19, Survey and Valuation by Abraham and William Driver, 1796.
2 Ibid., No. 50, Thos. Clarke to Geo. Bethell, 3 May 1832.
3 See, for example, Barratt, op. cit., II, 52–5, 282–7, III, 255–9, for the inclusion of Chalk Farm in Hampstead. Park's map, 1813, and the Tithe Map, 1838, however, both make it clear that it lay in St Pancras parish.
4 Eton, College Records, XLIX, No. 110, John Shaw to Geo. Bethell, 8 Sept. 1842, detailing the customary annual rent; fines calculated from No. 19, 1796, and No. 21, valuation by John Trumper, 14 May 1811.

Two

CHARACTER FORMATION
General influences

There are as many different ways of defining London as there are ways of looking at urban life. It can, for example, be seen as the business and financial headquarters of the economy, which is a small area, the traditional City; as the shopping, entertainment and highest-class residential district, which is a larger but still central area, the West End; as an administrative area, which has ballooned in the last century and a half, with landmarks in 1855, 1888, and 1964; as a policeman's beat, which from the formation of the Metropolitan Police District in 1829 covered a vast tract of country in order to embrace the rural hideouts of the criminal classes, an area which eventually filled up with people and became coterminous with Greater London; or as a string of dormitories held together by transport knots, which is an even larger area, with elastic boundaries that alter with the prevailing sociological and geographical winds. For the greater part of the nineteenth century, however, men had no great difficulty in understanding what they meant by the larger London, which they usually called 'the metropolis', even if it had no well-marked boundary lines: it was known to the census officials from 1831 as the Registration Division of London, and although the boundaries were subsequently altered in detail, this was substantially the same area as that administered by the Metropolitan Board of Works from 1856 and by the London County Council from 1888 to 1964.[1] It was only after the LCC began to function that the ordinary inhabitant was likely to be sure whether he definitely

[1] In the 1841 Census, for example, the census metropolis of 1831 was enlarged by the inclusion of the parishes of Stratford, Bromley, Camberwell, Fulham, Hammersmith and Stoke Newington; the townships of Deptford, Greenwich and Woolwich; and the manor of Hatcham: Parl. Papers, 1843, xxII, 468–9. Hampstead was not included in the census metropolis until 1861, shortly after it had been included in the statutory London of the Metropolitan Board of Works. The area and boundaries of Hampstead as an ancient parish, civil parish, registration district and metropolitan borough (under the 1899 London Government Act) were all identical for all practical purposes.

[40]

lived in London or not, so little known were the earlier administrative or registration divisions, so little direct part before then did even the ratepaying voters take in the government of London, and so little impact did any actions taken in the name of London as a whole have on the ordinary citizen. Nevertheless it was this area of the future LCC which was already thought of as constituting 'London' at the beginning of the century even if the major part of it was still empty; it was this area which was virtually entirely built-up by 1901; and it was this area which attained its maximum population, of $4\frac{1}{2}$ million, in 1921, and has subsequently gradually declined. It forms the proper context within which Hampstead's growth should be judged.

The London of 1801 with its population approaching 900,000 had reached the line of the New Road, the Marylebone Road of today, as a continuous built-up area, with fingers of sustained ribbon development pointing northward at Maida Vale, Camden Town and Kentish Town, and Islington. The New Road itself had been built between 1756 and 1760 as the first urban bypass in the world, and had naturally been routed through what was then open country in order to keep down the costs of land acquisition. For similar reasons of cheapness and avoidance of housing demolition the great encircling loop of the Regent's Canal was sent through open country, and its line thus marked the limits of the spearheads of development in 1811 when the route was laid out. Thus conveniently do great transport undertakings preserve for posterity the outlines of the cities they were promoted to serve. The outlines of the many satellites which served the London of 1801 are less well preserved, as they lacked any comparably striking physical arte-facts which might delineate them for ever to the casual passer-by. The discerning eye may still gauge their limits at succeeding dates from the styles of surviving buildings. But since architectural styles tended to be rather long-lived, and since different styles might have very long periods of overlap according to the whims of individual developers and builders and to the rate at which architectural fashions percolated downwards from the largest operators to the smallest one-house jobbing builder, this method of dating phases of expansion is very rough and ready. Maps, with which London was liberally supplied because the ceaselesss physical changes meant an unending demand from inhabi-tants and visitors alike for means of knowing where they were, and the census returns, provide much firmer ground. For the satellites of 1801 the census supplies the readiest means of comparison. Hampstead with its 4,343 inhabitants was already overshadowed by such places as Chelsea, Kensington, Deptford, Greenwich, Hackney, Wandsworth

THE GROWTH OF
HAMPSTEAD

CHILDS
HILL

West Heath

Paddington
Cemetery

0   ¼   ½   ¾   1mile

MAP 1 The growth of Hampstead

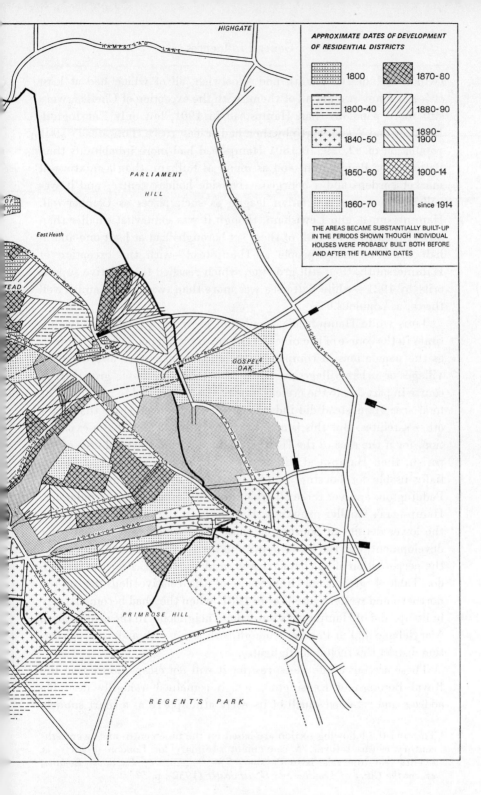

APPROXIMATE DATES OF DEVELOPMENT
OF RESIDENTIAL DISTRICTS

	1800		1870-80
	1800-40		1880-90
	1840-50		1890-1900
	1850-60		1900-14
	1860-70		since 1914

THE AREAS BECAME SUBSTANTIALLY BUILT-UP
IN THE PERIODS SHOWN THOUGH INDIVIDUAL
HOUSES WERE PROBABLY BUILT BOTH BEFORE
AND AFTER THE FLANKING DATES

PARLIAMENT
HILL

East Heath

GOSPEL
OAK

PRIMROSE HILL

REGENT'S PARK

(which includes Clapham), and Woolwich, all of which had at least twice as many people; all of them, with the exception of Chelsea, were still more populous than Hampstead in 1901, but only Kensington, Hackney and Wandsworth by then had at least twice Hampstead's 1901 population of 82,329. In 1801 Hampstead had more inhabitants than Battersea or Paddington, and as many as Fulham, then a mixture of market gardens and a bourgeois riverside holiday centre; and it was still in the same population league as such places as Camberwell, Hammersmith, and Lewisham, though it was somewhat smaller than any of them. By 1901 all of these six boroughs had at least one-and-a-half times as many people as Hampstead—with the exception of Hammersmith, then still growing, which reached this relative superiority by 1921—while Battersea was more than twice, and Camberwell thrice, as populous.[1]

Thus while Hampstead's population grew by a prodigious twenty times in the course of the nineteenth century it did not grow by so much as the populations of comparable satellites which were also detached villages or urban-villages in 1801. This relatively lesser growth is of course in part due to the preservation of the Heath, and in relation to its total area Hampstead did indeed conserve more open space than most other satellites. But this is a comparatively small part of the explanation, for if the area of the Heath is deducted from the total area of the parish, then Hampstead still possessed at least as many acres potentially usable for housing as, for example, Fulham, Kensington, and Paddington, and yet these all ended up with much larger populations. Hampstead's smaller growth is, therefore, in the main a reflection of the lower density of housing on those parts which were available for development, and the lower density in turn is the outward evidence of the perpetuation of its character as a residential district for the well-to-do. Table 1 gives some impression of the relative densities of the northern and western satellites in 1901, when they had become largely built-up, and of Hampstead's immediate neighbours in the central area, Marylebone and St Pancras (though both as a parish and as a registration district this included Highgate).

These are but crude measures, for it will not escape notice that the Royal Borough of Kensington, which remained a highly desirable address and retained much of its early atmosphere as a court suburb,

[1] This and the following section are based on the nineteenth- and twentieth-century census returns. A convenient summary for London districts, at twenty-year intervals, is in Pevsner, *The Buildings of England: London, except the Cities of London and Westminster* (1952), p. 37.

Table 1   Population and housing densities in 1901
(*Persons, and houses, per acre; no deductions from gross areas for open space, waste, water, unoccupied or agricultural land, roads, railways*)

	Persons	Houses
Hampstead	36·7	5·4
Camberwell	57·9	8·1
Chelsea	118·6	15·6
Fulham	80·7	10·0
Hammersmith	49·0	7·0
Kensington	79·3	10·8
Marylebone	88·2	9·9
Paddington	101·8	12·7
St Pancras	88·0	9·4

Source: *1901 Census of Great Britain*, B.P.P. 1902, CXX.

had nevertheless achieved double Hampstead's densities. In part this effect was due to differing styles of development, to the contrast between the tall and close-packed houses of Kensington's squares and terraces, which were no less fashionable and upper-class on that account, and the smaller villas, spaced out in their pairs, of Belsize Park. But in the main the effect was due to the fact that the borough and registration district of Kensington included districts of lower-middle-class and working-class housing of much higher density, in the Notting Hill district, as well as such fashionable quarters as Knightsbridge. Comparisons are not entirely invalidated by this feature, however, merely rendered difficult. For none of the census districts was homogeneous either in style of housing or in social character. St Pancras, for example, contained at least four quite distinct areas: a part of the old central area south of the New Road, which was the northern section of Bloomsbury; the eastern part of the Regent's Park development, a mixture of wealthy terraces and service and trading premises; the Camden Town core of dense nineteenth-century building; and the south-western section of Highgate. Paddington had wealthy districts in Bayswater and Warwick Avenue, separated by a wedge of crowded working-class housing alongside the Great Western Railway and immediately north of the Harrow Road. Marylebone encompassed the old aristocratic district of the squares between Oxford Street and the New Road, the greater part of the Regent's Park development, and most of St John's

Wood, the pioneer of suburban development in pairs of semi-detached villas; but it also included a sizeable cramped and lower-class district, between Lisson Grove and the Edgware Road. Camberwell could boast the fashionable Dulwich Village, as well as the unfashionable and seedy quarters of its northerly parts. Hampstead itself was by no means exempt from this heterogeneity; its affluent image was set by the old Town itself, by Belsize Park, and by the Fitzjohn's Avenue district; but very nearly half its population lived in less than one-third of its area, in the high-density housing of West Hampstead between West End Lane and Kilburn, and of the south-eastern corner of Hampstead, the Fleet Road district. Whether the swings gained what was lost on all these varied roundabouts it would be impossible to say without a highly detailed ward-by-ward and precinct-by-precinct analysis of each borough. But for general purposes the impression given by the comparison of the raw and unprocessed densities of Table 1 is a fair enough indication of the relative sparseness of settlement in Hampstead.

The contrast within administrative Hampstead can be illustrated from its constituent wards in 1901. The three western wards of West End, Kilburn, and Priory then contained 37,638 people in 5,506 houses; allowing for the small but densely developed Fleet Road area, which had no sort of separate administrative existence, there were something like 40,000 people and 5,800 houses in those districts which had turned into lower-middle-class and working-class Hampstead, at about 53 persons and 8 houses to the acre. In upper-class and upper-middle-class Hampstead, on the other hand, in Town, Belsize, Adelaide, and Central Wards, the remaining 42,000 people and 5,300 houses lived spaciously at 28 persons and $3\frac{1}{2}$ houses to the acre.[1] This was not, indeed, such gracious living as may have gone on in Dulwich, where on an acreage equal to that of the affluent part of Hampstead there were only 7 persons to the acre in 1901; and it was practically overcrowding in comparison with the stateliest of provincial suburbs, Edgbaston for example still keeping the rest of Birmingham at bay with only $1\frac{1}{2}$ houses per acre as late as 1955.[2] This may not show anything except the pitfalls in equating spacious with gracious living. Indeed it may be argued that below some ceiling which marked the

[1] *1901 Census of Great Britain*, Parl. Papers, 1902, cxx, Table 9.
[2] H. J. Dyos, *Victorian Suburb: a study of the Growth of Camberwell* (1961), p. 57; the Dulwich registration district contained 1,453 acres, which was within a few acres of the area of the four wards of Hampstead assigned to its 'spacious quarter'. For Edgbaston see D. A. Reader, 'The making of a garden suburb: Edgbaston in the nineteenth century', unpublished conference paper,

Urban History Group conference, Birmingham, 1970.

limit of what was acceptable for genteel suburban existence, that may perhaps have been of the order of 5–7 houses per acre, it was the higher rather than the lower densities of initial development which secured long-run stability for the residential character of a district. This was because an initial development which hit just the right degree of crowding, whether fortuitously or by cunning, could present a solidly prosperous front with no gaps or chinks for subsequent more intensive development that might introduce a discordant note into the neighbourhood.[1]

There was little that was discordant or unharmonious about the Hampstead prospect at the end of the nineteenth century. To Charles Booth, the most acute and thorough social investigator of the time, Hampstead appeared in 1889 as 'one of the largest and most prosperous of the well-to-do residential suburbs of London'; and when confirming in 1898 that this was a district for the wealthy, where 'building is entirely for the rich', he made it clear that its inhabitants were 'middle and upper class business and professional men, merchants, authors, journalists, musicians and others'.[2] Booth's statistics partly spelled out and partly obscured the meaning of these descriptions, showing that the larger Hampstead, considered as a registration district, came at the top of the league table for comfort and lack of poverty; though the smaller Hampstead, as used by the London School Board for the designation of one of its districts, was outclassed by several other high-class residential districts; the smallest Hampstead of all, however, the School Board subdivision of eastern Belsize Park and Chalcots—bounded by Haverstock Hill, Thurlow Road, Belsize Park Gardens, and King Henry's Road—could hardly be outshone, since 100 per cent of its residents lived 'in comfort' on Booth's definitions.[3] Some of the comparisons shown by this scheme of social ranking are reproduced in Table 2.

The implications, and explanations, of Hampstead's varied showings in the Booth ratings will be discussed in a later chapter. For the present

[1] The point is developed below, pp. 340–1.
[2] Charles Booth, *Life and Labour in London*, 1st ser. II (1902), pp. 424–5; 3rd ser. *Religious Influences*, I (1902), pp. 213–15.
[3] Ibid., 1st ser. II Table I. The School Board division of Hampstead contained 1,000 acres, and Belsize Park 643 acres, so that 604 acres of the full parish (later borough) were omitted from this part of Booth's survey. On the other hand the Hampstead Registration District (shown in Table 2 (i)) was identical with the full parish. Deducting the population of School Board Hampstead and Belsize Park from the population of Registration District Hampstead, suggests that in 1889 there were 2,305 persons in the 'missing' or at that time undeveloped 604 acres, which were mainly in west and north-west Hampstead.

Table 2   Social ranking of selected districts in 1889

(i)   *Census registration districts, in order of affluence*

	1	2	3
	% of population in classes E & F	% of population in classes G & H	% of population in comfort (cols 1 + 2)
Hampstead	52·5	34·0	86·5
Lewisham & Penge	44·5	37·4	81·9
Paddington	51·8	26·5	78·3
Chelsea	57·1	18·4	75·5
Kensington	42·1	33·2	75·3
Fulham	39·0	36·3	75·3
Marylebone	49·0	23·6	72·6
Camberwell	49·2	22·2	71·4
St Pancras	54·4	15·2	69·6
Holborn	45·8	5·3	51·1

(ii)   *School Board divisions, in order of affluence*

	1	2	3
	Total population	Persons per acre	% of population in comfort
Dulwich	32,336	18	98·7
Mayfair	31,316	96	97·3
Belgravia	23,262	82	95·0
Kensington	28,396	50	94·1
Peckham	30,124	66	94·1
Cromwell Road	36,049	97	94·0
Eltham	32,746	7	93·5
Kennington	32,407	94	89·4
Clapham	33,638	80	89·0
Belsize Park	33,437	52	88·3
Tyburnia (Bayswater)	27,194	88	87·6
West Brompton	34,641	103	87·4
De Beauvoir Town	29,179	85	87·3

St Peter's Park			
(Maida Vale)	36,285	100	87·1
Highbury	30,954	69	87·0
Streatham	28,662	22	87·0
Lavender Hill	29,623	64	84·7
Hackney Downs	30,029	79	84·5
Balham	35,223	31	84·2
Hampstead	31,151	31	83·8
Westbourne Grove	28,647	82	83·1
Shepherd's Bush	35,911	73	83·0
Camden Town East	31,799	81	82·2
Chalk Farm	29,282	130	82·0
Woolwich Common	33,762	21	81·2
Chelsea	32,746	99	79·9

Booth's classes E & F are the 'comfortably off' working classes; his classes G & H are the lower and upper middle classes, and the upper class.
Sources: Charles Booth, *Life and Labour in London*, 1st ser. II (1902); (i) from Booth's Table III, (ii) from Booth's Table I; in each case only a selection has been reproduced.

it should be noted that both the Hampstead and the Belsize Park of Table 2 (ii) were districts established chiefly for the administrative convenience of the School Board in levying school rates and in locating Board schools in divisions of roughly equal population, and did not correspond at all closely either with the current popular usage of the names as descriptive labels or with such precise tools of definition as property boundaries and house-type frontiers. In most respects these nuances meant that the well-being of the truly 'comfortable' neighbourhoods in the parish was understated. It should also be noted that there was, over London as a whole, no correlation between affluence and population density, partly because the 'comfortable classes', on Booth's definition, included all the better-off members of the working classes, and were simply being distinguished from 'the poor'. Moreover, the Hampstead of Table 2 (ii) included the entire Heath; if the 300 acres of the Heath, as it had by then become, are deducted from the 1,000 acres of this division, then its density is raised to 44 persons per acre of net potential building land. Even so, although the poorest group of School Board divisions invariably had very high population densities, of the order of 200 persons per acre, if the entire Table 2 (ii) is taken as constituting London's top group of poverty-free areas it is

[49]

apparent that both very high and very low densities were compatible with membership.[1]

Where any close pursuit of population densities tends to lead into the statistical thickets, recourse to the simplest and least ambiguous social indicator of all may help to pinpoint Hampstead's standing at the end of the nineteenth century. The ability to employ domestic servants, though it went pretty far down the social scale to the level of small shopkeepers, cashiers, and chief clerks, was nevertheless a sign of middle-class status. There was indeed a wide gulf between the family of a clerk, like Pooter, which could just manage to keep a single maid, and the true upper-middle-class family which retained a minimum of three servants.[2] These social differences are crucial in any attempt to delineate Hampstead's portrait; but for a more distant glimpse it does not particularly matter that such details fail to show when making a simple relation of total numbers of servants to total numbers of families; the snapshot of Table 3 is sufficiently revealing without them.

Table 3   Servant ratios in selected boroughs, 1901

	Number of domestic servants per 100 families or separate occupiers
Hampstead	81·4
Kensington	80·0
Westminster	65·8
Chelsea	55·2
Marylebone	51·4
Paddington	50·2
Holborn	22·3
Hammersmith	19·3
Fulham	18·6
St Pancras	16·9
Camberwell	15·3
Bethnal Green	5·8
LCC as a whole	24·5

Source: *1901 Census of Great Britain*, B.P.P. 1902, CXX, LCC Table 35A. Spaces in the list indicate omissions. The districts used are metropolitan boroughs.

[1] The mean density of this group is 69, and the median 80, persons per acre; but neither figure has any particular meaning.
[2] George and Weedon Grossmith, *The Diary of a Nobody* (1892).

[50]

Hampstead was the best-servanted borough in London, but when it came to butlers it slipped to seventh place in the league—or to sixth, if we exclude the City itself as being too peculiar a place to stand comparison with anywhere else. To employ indoor male servants, as butlers and footmen, was the mark of aristocratic style, and in this department the winners in 1901 were those boroughs which contained prominent aristocratic quarters: Westminster, Chelsea, Marylebone, Kensington, and Paddington, in that order; even modest Holborn, because it held part of Bloomsbury, had proportionately as many butlers as Hampstead.[1] In fact if one went calling in Hampstead at the turn of the century the chances were very high that the door would be opened by a domestic of some sort, but very low that it would be a footman holding out the salver for one's card. This more than anything else captures the Hampstead image: it was a comfortable, prosperous, desirable, attractive residential district with quite a few wealthy residents, but it was bourgeois through and through, with only a slender aristocratic or plutocratic top layer. The great question is, how had it managed to become like that? and more particularly, how had it contrived to emerge at the far end of the nineteenth century in such an unchallengeably solid middle-class position, far more securely so than all those other suburbs which had started the century with equal standing?

The question is indeed so great that this book is in large part an attempt to suggest an answer. Any explanation is necessarily complex, involving as it does so many different strands of topography, amenity, fashion, religion, demography, employment, transport, finance, and property. All of these must be unravelled and inspected before the threads can be woven together into an answer. The finished cloth, however, was not an exclusively home-produced article made in Hampstead; the design was subject to external influences, neither generated within nor operating within Hampstead. The chief of them were people, places, and timing. In their absence Hampstead either would not have grown at all, or might well have become a very different place.

It is of course obvious that the suburbs, all the suburbs, were developed only because the total population of London was continually growing. The general explanation of this growth is beyond the range of this study. It must suffice to note that the expansion of London's and especially the City's commercial and financial activities was perhaps of

[1] *1901 Census of Great Britain*, LCC Table 35A. Where Westminster had 12·5 indoor male servants per 100 families, Hampstead had 1·6.

[51]

greatest importance to Hampstead, though the effects of the capital city's functions in government, culture, entertainment, and shopping were only barely in second place. It can, however, be asserted that supplying the metropolis with food, drink, dresses and suits, gas, water, scavenging, luxury articles, and prostitutes, which furnished the employment that supported expansion in many districts, were of minor importance to Hampstead. With certain exceptions in shipbuilding and engineering, London as an industrial town manufactured chiefly for itself in the nineteenth century: Hampstead took no part in this.[1] The whole large fraction of London's expansion which is explicable in terms of London feeding on itself in providing for the production of commodities and basic services for its own use thus had no local significance, with some exceptions in the building industry itself, and in the provision of transport services.[2] Nevertheless, inasmuch as the portion of London's growth which was self-generated could not have occurred unless there had been a growing consuming classs requiring victuals and services, it was the growth of this consuming class which was of primary importance to the whole operation. In this sense it was the Hampstead-type expansion which epitomised the primary forces of London's growth; the expansion of non-producers, or at least of those who were not mainly concerned with producing for the local London economy, provided the market which dragged the rest of London into existence. To the extent that the motive power of this engine of London's growth was supplied by the spending of incomes created by the provision of the services in which the capital city specialised—banking, insurance, stock-jobbing, overseas and wholesale merchanting, shipbroking, West End retailing, Whitehall administration, dispensing justice and legal advice, and providing both fashionable and progressive culture—Hampstead was perhaps as representative as any other single suburb of the nature of the power-house. But to the extent that a proportion of the fuel came from rentiers spending incomes which originated quite outside London—from landed estates, ownership of home or overseas businesses, stocks and shares, or armed services' pay or pensions—then, although Hampstead was not destitute of men of

[1] Hampstead played some part in supplying central London with water, abortively in the sixteenth century, successfully from the early seventeenth century, but this created little if any local employment.
[2] In common with most suburbs, a large part of the work force which built Hampstead and kept its houses in repair actually lived in the district. Also, urban transport generated some local employment, while parts of Hampstead developed as dormitory areas for workers in the national transport system: see below, pp. 361–5.

property by any means, the previous discussion suggests that it was very
much less typical of this aspect of London's dynamic forces than were
the true aristocratic quarters.

The primary sector of Hampstead's growth is therefore to be explained in terms of its success in securing a goodly share—and, in relation to its area, what can be called a lion's share—of the pool of top
professional, mercantile, and artistic talent which created London. In
addition, the professional, financial, and mercantile activities which
made London also required multitudes to man (and, later on, to
woman) their offices. These second- and third-level occupations, the
great tribe of commercial clerks and secretaries, may be regarded as
essential elements in London's growth in a more fundamental way
than those occupations in the clothing, furniture, and luxury trades
which are properly viewed as deriving from a growth already under
way for other reasons. Hampstead, though it never became a clerk's
paradise on the scale of Islington or Camberwell, was not unrepresentative of this element either. The primary growth-generating sector,
however, possessed so powerful employment-generating capacities, via
its expenditure and consumption patterns, that it did not need to be
numerically very large in order to initiate a total expansion on the scale
of London's millions. Just as in London as a whole the secondary sector
of derivative trades and services greatly outnumbered the primary
sector, so it did in Hampstead: to take but a single example, there were
more than twice as many domestic servants in 1901 as members of the
controlling élite.[1] Moreover, while some of the derivative occupations
were organised for the London market as a whole, and were specialised
both in function and in location—as, for example, was most of the
production of luxury articles, and most of the furniture industry—
others necessarily existed to support purely local economies, and had to
be resident within them. Hampstead's own sub-economy, the market
primarily created by her quota of the controlling élite, required, besides the building workers already mentioned, local transport, retailing, clothing, and repair services. This category also outnumbered the
members of the controlling élite by almost two to one in 1901, and
roughly represents the members of the working classes who both lived
and worked in Hampstead.[2]

[1] *1901 Census of Great Britain*, LCC Table 35. The controlling élite has been
broadly defined to include all males in the Occupation Classification Groups I
(national and local government), II (armed services), and III (professions), plus
merchants and bankers from Group V, and rentiers and retired businessmen
from Group XXIII.

[2] Ibid. Locally-employed males only (apart from domestic service, females in

Such, in very broad terms, were the factors which caused Greater London to grow. Its spatial expansion clearly could not have occurred without some means of transport to link outlying districts with the centre: they could not live without receiving supplies from outside their own borders, and people had to be able to get to and fro before they could become viable. Though improved transport could not in itself create an accumulation of people of the London size, it has long been popularly supposed that it could and did substantially create the actual sprawling London of the nineteenth century. The idea that the metropolis was the child of the railways, particularly of the suburban commuting railways, is pleasantly easy to grasp but almost wholly mistaken. It has been seriously undermined by recent work on transport history;[1] but any endeavour to substitute for the railways some more humble and more flexible transport improvement as a prime agent of development—for example, horse-drawn omnibuses, or horse-drawn trams—is doomed to the same fate. For public transport of all and every variety and shape, whether stage coach, short-stage coach which was embryo-omnibus, full-blown omnibus, or tram, as well as railway whether above or below ground, almost always followed after a considerable amount of population growth and urban development had

Hampstead were only largely employed in the clothing trades, which quite probably served a purely local custom). The following Occupation Groups have been excluded, as likely to have been employed outside Hampstead: VI (railwaymen), VII (nurserymen), XI (jewellers, watchmakers, makers of electrical goods), XIV (brick, cement, pottery, and glass workers), XVI (workers in leather and skins), XVII (paper, printing, and book trades), and XVIII (makers of textile fabrics). Some from these groups, however—e.g. saddlery and harness makers, brickmakers, workers in printing and bookselling, jewellers and watchmakers—were undoubtedly locally employed. Unfortunately the census did not attempt to record places of work, and an estimate of those locally employed must therefore be attempted solely on the basis of occupational descriptions; the one used here, which includes those employed in horse transport, vehicle trades, building, furniture trades, druggists, dress trades, food, drink and tobacco, gas, water and electricity, and unspecified shopkeepers, is believed to be an under-statement. It has also been assumed that the entire controlling élite, as defined in the previous footnote, worked outside Hampstead, though this was obviously not the case for a number of the doctors, clergy, solicitors, teachers, and artists, let alone the retired officers, the rentiers, and the retired businessmen, and the local government workers. In order to argue the case for the minor role of regular travel to work, the figure for those working outside Hampstead has been purposely inflated to an upper limit.

[1] Notably by T. C. Barker [and Michael Robbins], *A History of London Transport*, I, *The Nineteenth Century* (1963), which puts bus and tram in the foreground; and by J. R. Kellett, *The Impact of Railways on Victorian Cities* (1969), which demolishes the view of railways as suburb-creators.

been achieved, and only preceded these in rare instances. Public transport, though extremely important, was important only in the later stages of urban development, when its nature could be decisive in either consolidating or transforming the character inherited from the initial phases. As far as transport was important at all in these early phases, it was private transport which mattered; and this, according to income and class, was a matter of shanks' pony or a horse and carriage. Before the motor car many people were indeed ready to walk vast distances to work, as much as three or four miles each way daily; nevertheless legging it home up hill at the end of a day's work cannot have been widely popular, and to this extent Hampstead's elevation was a built-in determinant of its social status in the 'carriage trade'. However, the importance of any form of regular daily transport can easily be exaggerated. On the same assumptions as were used for 1901 about the relationship between different occupations and place of work, less than 7 per cent of Hampstead's total population of nearly 12,000 in 1851 were likely to have been employed outside the district, and the actual numbers involved were puny: about 750 men and a mere 30 or so women. Hampstead's commuting logistics were plainly unlikely, at this stage, to have presented any formidable problems. To be sure, in relation to the male population alone Hampstead's commuting class of 1851 was of greater significance: it constituted about 27 per cent of all adult males, and when allowance has been made for the unoccupied adult males (chiefly rentiers, but including a few paupers, vagrants, and 'others in barns') it was nearly one-third of all employed males.[1] But the fact that the group was a significant proportion of Hampstead's breadwinners did not make the problems of its daily travel any greater.

Hampstead was, indeed, tolerably though not lavishly provided with public road transport. The growth in the services is shown in Table 4. In relation to the volume of public transport on the streets of London at any of these dates the Hampstead services were minute. There were, for example, reckoned to be about 1,800 daily journeys by short-stage coaches to the City and West End in 1825; and when the London General Omnibus Company was being launched in the early 1850s it was estimated that there were nearly 810 omnibuses in service, run by a

[1] Parl. Papers *1851 Census of Great Britain*, 1852/3, LXXXVIII, Pt 1, pp. 16–26. The Classes used in the 1851 Occupation Tables are differently numbered and arranged from the 1901 Census Groups, but the individual occupational designations used permit approximate, though not absolutely reliable, comparisons to be made.

[55]

*Table 4   Road transport services to and from Hampstead
Terminating in the City (Bank, Mansion House, Royal Exchange,
Holborn Bars) and in the West End (Tottenham Court Road)*

	Short stages		Omnibuses	
	No. of coaches	No. of daily journeys (return)	No. of buses	No. of daily journeys (return)
1740	—	1	—	—
1763	—	5	—	—
1770	—	14	—	—
1793	—	18	—	—
1799	—	43	—	—
1815	—	43	—	—
1825 (City only)	10	17	—	—
1834 (City only)	12	25	8	20
1838–9	13	—	7[a]	—
1856	—	—	{ 8 [b] 10	—

[a] Includes 1 serving Kilburn.
[b] Serving Swiss Cottage.

Sources: 1740 to 1815 inclusive: *Kent's London Directories*, 1825, 1838–9, and 1856: Appendices 1, 2, and 3 in T. C. Barker, *A History of London Transport*, I; the 1856 list refers to omnibuses handed over to the London General Omnibus Co. in 1856, which acquired the great majority, but not quite all, of the buses then running. 1834: B.P.P. *Accounts & Papers*, 1834, LI, no. 45, Statement of the no. of short-stage coaches, omnibuses, and flys passing through the City.

crowd of medium and small operators.[1] Allowing for the West End services, Hampstead may have had 40 short-stage daily journeys in 1825; and it may have enjoyed the services of as many as 24 omnibuses in all in 1856: in other words, Hampstead had only between 2 and 3 per cent of London's public transport, though this was at least four times the share which it could have expected on mere population grounds.[2]

[1] Barker, op. cit., pp. 4, 77, 81. The LGOC actually acquired 600 of the 810 existing omnibuses. If the Hampstead routes were served by their relative share of the non-acquired buses, there might therefore have been a maximum of 24 buses serving different parts of Hampstead in 1856.
[2] In the first half of the nineteenth century Hampstead's population was between 0·4 and 0·7 per cent of the population of the metropolis as a whole.

Until the last quarter of the eighteenth century the services were obviously much too infrequent to be used for daily travel to business, and the early short-stage operators were catering for a more casual traffic of day-trippers, holiday-makers, shoppers and the like. By the early nineteenth century some small part of the more plentiful services may have been provided at the morning and evening hours which business and professional men found convenient for regular daily travel. The Directories suggest that there were half-a-dozen trips inwards, and again outwards, at suitable hours; though the regular hourly services throughout the middle of the day equally suggest that the non-commuting traffic was more voluminous than the office-bound gentry.[1] If the six short-stage coaches were all loaded to capacity, which is unlikely, they could have carried about 75 Hampstead businessmen to their London desks. By 1856 the extreme capacity of the assumed 24 omnibuses would have been 480 passengers; presumably not more than half of them would have departed from the Hampstead end of a morning, and since these would all expect to pick up some passengers en route none of them would have begun their journeys full of Hampstead men. Their contribution to Hampstead commuting is thus likely to have been of the order of 200 regular passengers at most; in addition, not more than 100 could have been relying on the surviving short-stage coaches. On the most generous assumptions, therefore, less than half Hampstead's daily exodus was carried by public road transport, and the probability is that the true proportion was much less than this.[2]

By the early 1850s some Hampstead folk were travelling daily by train, but not very many. Hampstead lay across the main route to the north-west, and by the time all the trunk lines had been built three of them—the London and Birmingham (subsequently the London and North Western), the Midland, and the Great Central—ran through its territory. These, however, were built for long-distance through traffic and remained largely indifferent to their suburban potential, at least in their early years. The LNWR, for example, found that suburban traffic congested its lines and frustrated its profitable through traffic, and therefore dispensed with the local trains: it had 'tried a station at Kilburn', it was reported in 1853, 'but the length of the through traffic rendered it very difficult to carry out'.[3] The London and Birmingham's pursuit of a profitable goods traffic, which eluded it while freight had

[1] *Kent's London Directory* (83rd ed., 1815), p. 60.
[2] Carrying capacities of short-stage coaches and omnibuses from Barker, op. cit., p. 21. Estimate of total number of commuters in 1851, above, p. 55.
[3] H[ouse] of L[ords] R[ecord] O[ffice], Min. H. C. 1853, 8 June, Hampstead Junction Railway Bill, f.29 (George Berkeley, Engineer of LNWR).

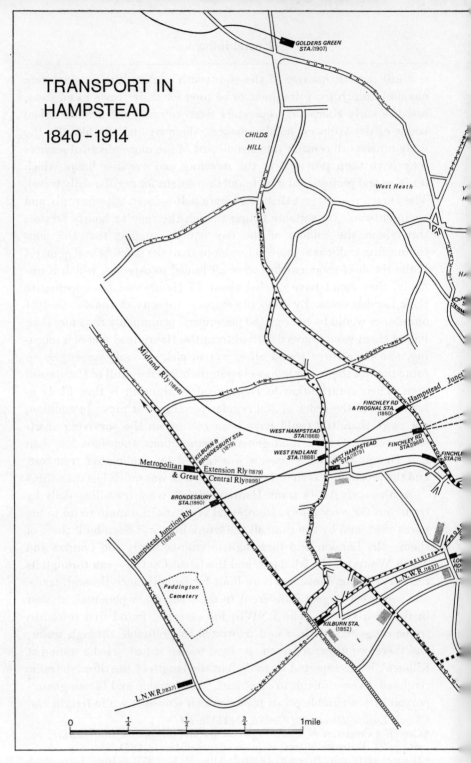

MAP 2 Transport in Hampstead, 1840–1914

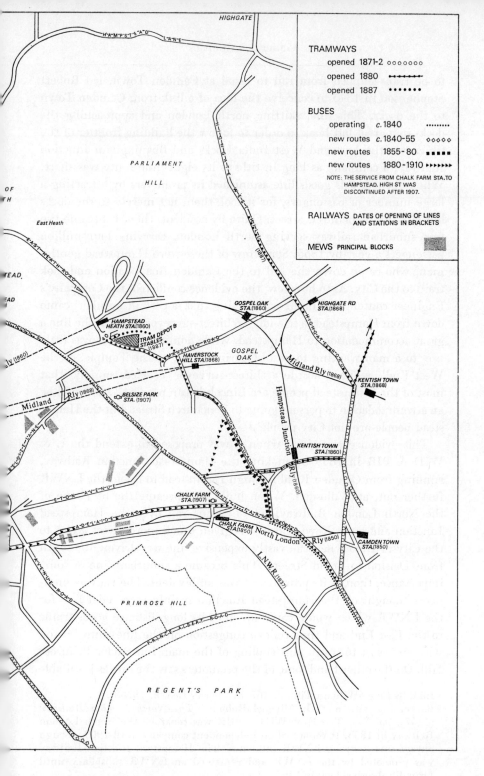

HIGHGATE

H·A·M·P·S·T·E·A·D LANE

PARLIAMENT
HILL

East Heath

EAST·HEATH·ROAD

E·A·S·T·H·E·A·T·H·R·O·A·D

GOSPEL OAK
STA.(1860)

HIGHGATE RD
STA.(1868)

HAMPSTEAD
HEATH STA.(1860)

TRAM DEPOT &
STABLES
(1887)

MANSFIELD·ROAD

HAVERSTOCK
HILL STA.(1868)

GOSPEL
OAK

Midland Rly (1868)

KENTISH TOWN
STA.(1868)

Rly (1860)

Midland Rly (1868)

BELSIZE PARK
STA.(1907)

F·L·E·E·T·L·A·N·E

Hampstead Junction

KENTISH TOWN
STA.(1860)

North London Rly (1860)

E·T·O·N A·V·E·N·U·E

CHALK FARM
STA.(1907)

CHALK FARM
STA.(1850) North London Rly (1850)

A·D·E·L·A·I·D·E·R·O·A·D

CAMDEN TOWN
STA.(1850)

A·V·E·N·U·E·R·O·A·D

PRIMROSE HILL

PRINCE·ALBERT·ROAD

L·N·W·R (1837)

REGENT'S PARK

to be trans-shipped from rail to canal at Camden Town, led Robert
Stephenson in 1845 to conceive the idea of a link from Camden Town
to the docks. This line, skirting north London and approaching the
docks in a great left hook in order to follow the building frontier of the
time, was the East and West India Docks and Birmingham Junction
Railway, a company as long in title as its eight-mile route was short.
When opened, this goods line astonished its promoters by attracting a
large number of passengers, for it took them not merely to the docks
but also into Fenchurch Street. Quite by accident, then, it became the
first suburban railway serving north London, carrying four million
passengers a year by 1853. Some few of these were Hampstead gentlemen, who came down the hill to the Camden Road station and took
train to the City. As to how few, the evidence conflicted: the Company's
Engineer contented himself with saying that 'a certain number' came
down from Hampstead; a friendly architect-surveyor thought the line a
great accommodation to Hampstead, while admitting that it was little
use 'to a man wanting to go to Charing Cross, or the Temple, or the
West End'; while a hostile architect-surveyor asserted roundly 'that
most of the Hampstead people are Lincoln's Inn people . . . it will be
an accommodation to persons going to Fenchurch Street, but the Hampstead people are not City people'.[1]

This evidence was given when it was proposed to extend the E &
WID & BJR in 1853 by making the Hampstead Junction Railway,
running from Camden Road through Hampstead to rejoin the LNWR
further out, at Willesden. When built, this became the backbone of
the North London Railway, whose trains ran over the Hampstead
Junction and on to Kew; and it was given much more direct access to
the City in 1865 when the vastly expensive line was driven due south
from Dalston to Broad Street.[2] This became a suburban line of some
importance, though its provenance was ambivalent. The railway engineers thought of the Hampstead Junction mainly as a relief line for
the LNWR which would carry much of its long-distance goods traffic
to the East End and thus relieve congestion on the lines into Euston
without resort to costly quadrupling of the main line under Primrose
Hill. On the other hand some of the promoters saw the line as justifiable

[1] Ibid., 8 June (William Tite, ff. 167–8; Charles Lee, ff. 187–8).
[2] Barker, op. cit., p. 163; Michael Robbins, *The North London Railway*
(1937), pp. 3–5. The E & WID & BJR was renamed the North London
Railway in 1853. It remained an independent company until 1909, though
always under strong LNWR influence. The Hampstead Junction Railway
was promoted by the LNWR and remained an LNWR subsidiary until
formally absorbed by it in 1867.

in itself for the short-distance suburban traffic which it would generate: 'there will be an increase in passengers,' it was forecast, 'the largest increase would be from Hampstead no doubt . . . I believe that buildings will be extended all along the line in a few years.'[1] In the event, when it was opened in 1860 this line, with its stations at Hampstead Heath, Finchley Road, and Edgware Road (with a fourth subsequently constructed at West End Lane), was very successful as a purely suburban line, and drew a large proportion of its traffic from Hampstead. Nevertheless, in arriving on the scene as late as 1860 it served to sustain and accelerate Hampstead's suburban career, rather than to initiate it, for the population had passed 19,000 before a train began to run, and the commuting class had grown to over 1,300.[2]

The London extension of the Midland, from Bedford, was opened to St Pancras in 1868, and although this was primarily designed as a main line its utility to the districts through which it passed was not ignored; stations were initially provided at West End Lane and Finchley Road, though since both of these then stood in open country it is unlikely that they had much custom for several years. In any case the Midland's suburban services, though they were not totally neglected on the pattern of the LNWR, were still at the end of the century infrequent and lethargic in comparison with those of the Great Northern, the Great Eastern, the North London, or almost any of the south London lines.[3] It was indeed not until Hampstead had become an old-settled area and the frontier had moved beyond it that it excited the provision of a truly custom-built suburban railway. This was the underground, authorised in 1893 as the Charing Cross, Euston, and Hampstead Railway, but not opened until 1907.[4] Popularly known as the Hampstead Tube until it became the Northern Line of the LPTB, it clearly acted as an enormous stimulus to, possibly as the essential precondition of, the growth of Golders Green; for Hampstead, however, it provided a service for a population which was already there; and, in the longer run, provided new inhabitants for houses which had been built long before.

Well in advance of the tube, a railway had crept just below the

---

[1] HLRO Min. (HJR), 8 June (Robert Stephenson, ff. 6–8, 10; George Berkeley, ff. 23–4, 32–3, 66).
[2] Parl. Papers, *1861 Census of Great Britain*, 1863, LII, 21–9; using the same occupational definitions as for 1851 and 1901.
[3] Kellett, op. cit., pp. 372–82 discusses the suburban practices and policies of the major railway companies.
[4] HLRO Book of Reference and Plan, 1892 (Charing Cross, Euston, and Hampstead Railway); the Act was 56 and 57 Vict. cap. ccxiv.

surface to the southern fringe of the parish. This was the Metropolitan
and St John's Wood Railway, promoted in 1864 and opened to Swiss
Cottage in 1868, which used the 'cut-and-cover' method of construction
for its single-track line from Baker Street under Wellington Road and
Finchley Road.[1] For almost a dozen years it served as a rather unpromising feeder for the Metropolitan line, until railway glory was
thrust upon it and it became the unique and priceless escape route for
the Metropolitan's dash to the open country and ultimately to Metro-
land itself. An undeniably suburban line, the M & StJWR was an extremely modest one, which reached Swiss Cottage nearly thirty years
after the immediate neighbourhood had been developed, and which did
very little to excite any further development in the near hinterland
during its years of independent operation between 1868 and 1879.
When double-tracked and taken over by the Metropolitan, this route
became what can only be called a suburban trunk line; but even so,
whatever its galvanising impact may have been on points further out
such as Willesden, Neasden, Kingsbury, Harrow—and later still on
Pinner, Northwood, Rickmansworth, Chorleywood, Amersham and all
stations to Aylesbury—its stimulating effects on home ground in
Hampstead were distinctly secondary.

Railways are a non-starter as a prime cause of Hampstead's growth,
though once they came they were undoubtedly a great convenience to
a fair number of Hampstead residents, who had come to live there for
quite other reasons in the first place. They were also of profound
importance in shaping and distorting urban development, which had to
accommodate itself to their presence and seized upon them as a means
of separating the sheep from the goats by using the device of the wrong
and the right side of the tracks. Urban communities adjusted to railways, and were not created by them. They were obliged to incorporate
railways into their fabric, whose texture was sometimes improved and
sometimes impoverished by such threads. Hampstead was on the whole
fortunate in the railway experience which was thrust upon it, and
gained more in ultimate convenience than it suffered from the diseases
of railway blight.[2]

Hampstead owed its nineteenth-century form infinitely more to the
fact that it abutted on St John's Wood than to the fact that St John's
Wood had its own rather smelly and ramshackle train service from
1868 onwards. Its proximity to Regent's Park likewise meant a great
deal more than the circumstance that the London and Birmingham

[1] 27 and 28 Vict. cap. ccciii.
[2] See below, pp. 371–2.

Railway gained access to Camden Town and Euston under a bit of
Primrose Hill, in 1837. Modern urban sociologists analyse the pheno-
menon of the social segregation or social zoning of residential areas in a
vast conurbation such as Greater London in terms of the concept of segments or wedges of predominantly a single type of housing and class of
residents, each succeeding outer arc in each separate wedge deriving
its character from its contact with its earlier-developed inside neighbour. Thus an original inner-core working-class district can be seen on a
map fanning outwards from this as an apex to colonise the outer parts of
a wedge for the working classes; and similarly for other central districts
originally occupied by the other classes. The model has obvious advantages over the earlier interpretations of social segregation in large cities,
which derived from Engels' analysis of Manchester in 1844 as a town
of concentric rings starting from a non-residential commercial centre
surrounded by an inner ring of working-class streets, and going on to a
middle ring for the middling bourgeoisie and ending with an outer ring
for the upper bourgeoisie and captains of industry.[1]

Actual examples do indeed suggest the real existence of partially
formed though never wholly complete social rings, but the chief
trouble with this pattern is not so much its failure to conform to reality
as its inability to cope satisfactorily with the mechanics of change. For if
the concentric ring pattern were to be completely maintained through a
period of rapid growth in the total size of the city, it would require that
the working classes should invariably move into the cast-off homes of the
middle classes as they took over what had previously been a middle-
class ring, and that while the middle classes would always be tending to
live in new houses during an expansion period, the working classes
would very seldom have any new housing built with them in mind.
Now it is quite true that a great deal of housing in the inner suburbs
which was built for a higher social class did in the course of time slip
down the scale and end up as working-class tenements, and this process
tends to confirm the ring theory. But this is only part of the story. The
rings were broken by the fact that several of London's nineteenth-
century inner suburbs were not only developed as middle- and upper-
class areas, but succeeded in staying that way despite the fact that
working-class areas had been subsequently developed much further out
than them, in other directions of advance into the country. Many of
these 'middle and outer zones of relatively low social status', as they
are circumspectly called, had in any case been developed as such directly

[1] F. Engels, *The Condition of the Working Class in England in 1844* (1950
ed.), pp. 45–6.

from open fields, with no intermediate stage of middle-class occupation.

The theory of wedge-like sectors is superior to the ring theory, when confronted with this kind of evidence about actual developments, because although it was initially framed as a means of formalising the description of an urban social structure observed at a point of time when development had been completed, it is capable of being adapted into a dynamic theory which can accommodate and help to explain the social characteristics of urban growth as a process of change. The dynamic force in the wedges is the factor of sympathy or contagion, by which each new outer edge or frontier zone of a given segment adopts, or is infected by, the style and reputation of the inner part with which it is in immediate physical contact. This concept is, inevitably, of no more universal applicability to the observed facts of London's growth than is the ring theory, since the westward spreading wedge that takes its root from high-class Bayswater and Kensington, for example, is classified as of 'relatively low social status' when it reaches industrial West London and parts beyond to Southall and Uxbridge. Nevertheless it is perhaps more useful for the historian of urban growth to look upon London as a dartboard with different coloured segments radiating from the bullseye, rather than as a target with different coloured rings.[1]

One explanation of Hampstead's character may therefore be sought in St John's Wood and Regent's Park, and the explanation of the upper- or middle-class character of these two districts may in turn be sought in their inner contact with the better-class streets and squares of Marylebone. There are of course some minor local difficulties about such explanations, since although the Midas-touch of the Portland estate (Cavendish Square, Portland Place, Harley Street, Devonshire Place, for example) plainly succeeded in imparting an aristocratic quality to the Regent's Park development immediately to its north, the equally upper-class Portman estate (Manchester, Portman, Bryanston, and Montagu Squares, for example) was apparently much less successful in affecting its northern neighbour, the Eyre estate. It was here that St John's Wood was developed in the decades immediately after Waterloo, and although it was affluent it was decidedly not aristocratic—definitely not even Forsyte country in the 1880s—and although it was middle-class it was often thought to be hardly respectable; providing house-room for officers' mistresses from the Barracks on the estate was

[1] The concepts and their application to Greater London, and the literature of the subject, are discussed by J. H. Westergaard, 'The structure of Greater London', in his report London, *Aspects of Change* (Centre for Urban Studies Report No. 3, 1964) and the social zones are mapped on p. 101.

one of its early reputations, and if this was undeserved, there was still a Bohemian feel about the place which gave some basis to these disapproving remarks. The distinction between aristocratic and middle-class is perhaps too fine for present purposes; and in truth Regent's Park and St John's Wood could not both have become upper-class since there simply were not enough aristocrats to live everywhere at once. From the Hampstead point of view, however, the difference between the Regent's Park terraces and villas, which were variants of aristocratic town houses, and the St John's Wood semi-detached and detached villas in their avenues and places, which were the prototypes of universal suburbia, was a critical one. John Nash certainly conceived of the Regent's Park development mainly in terms of its relationship with the West End and Westminster to which it was to be linked by the new thoroughfare of Regent Street which would ensure its acceptability as a fashionable town quarter enjoying the illusion of being in the country. But this was to be its social and material line of communication, and, as part of the staging of the illusion, the estate was not to be south-facing and inward-looking, but rather the master plan was for the estate to be facing outward, with its arms (the terraces to east and west of the Park) open to greet the country. That country was Hampstead. Not only did Nash think of the Hampstead and Highgate heights as the essential rural backcloth to his scheme, but also because they were heights he saw them, from the vantage point of 1812, as destined for good-class development in the future for which it was only meet that he should provide a fitting approach in the present. Twenty to fifty years on from Regent's Park, when estate owners and developers were laying out that hillside they may not have paused to reflect that they were destroying Nash's backcloth, but they were certainly conscious of the help which proximity to Regent's Park provided in making their building ventures 'go' as good-class speculations. Association by area was in this way a real factor in development policies, an element of the wedge theory which can be documented.[1]

What was true of Regent's Park was much more true of St John's Wood, for the influence in this case was not simply one of proximity but of direct imitation of layout and housing as well. Moreover this influence was directly transmitted by the property network. On the one hand, the Eyre estate reached up into Hampstead, its boundaries being

[1] For a guide to the large literature on the Regent's Park estate see Summerson, *Georgian London* (1945), ch. xiii, and Ann Saunders, *Regent's Park: a Study of the Development of the Area from 1086 to the Present Day* (1969). And see below, pp. 237–8, for the documentation of the Regent's Park and St John's Wood influences.

marked by what became Avenue Road, Swiss Cottage, Fairfax Road, and Belsize Road, so that eventually about a quarter of the St John's Wood development was part of Hampstead, a quarter which included a swathe of the largest type of paired villas on the entire estate, on both sides of Avenue Road and Finchley Road, and in St John's Wood Park. On the other hand, H. S. Eyre's architect and surveyor, who was responsible for the strategy of building operations from 1802 onwards, was John Shaw; and his son, the second John Shaw, was the surveyor who advised Eton College on the development of Chalcots as a building estate in the 1830s and supervised the builders. The link could hardly be closer. It may not be possible to determine individual responsibility for the revolutionary idea, in architectural and planning terms, of developing the Eyre estate with pairs of semi-detached houses set in irregularly aligned roads instead of with the traditional terraced houses arranged in grid-iron street plans. John Shaw apparently administered, but did not conceive, the scheme; and the idea owed much to Nash's little escapade in variegated village gothic in Park Villages East and West. Socially and economically, however, the idea clearly succeeded in tapping a new market of purchasers and occupiers who wanted their houses to be different from next door's, and wanted to have their own little gardens. This new demand may have been simply a matter of a shift in taste and fashion, a product of the romantic mood with its premium on individuality and nature, and a manifestation of the wish of everyman to have his own Strawberry Hill. It may, however, be susceptible of social and economic explanation, as the demand of new generations of the moderately well-to-do who were sentenced by their limited means to be permanent town-dwellers, and who therefore yearned for a way of deluding themselves that their homes were nevertheless still in the country. By contrast, the more wealthy who had set the previous tone were but seasonal town-dwellers, who wanted their town houses to be close-packed in terraces, formal and symmetrically uniform, because this made their season in town suitably distinct from the life in the country houses to which they could always retreat. Whatever the explanation of its origins it was the revolution on the Eyre estate which first made the state of semi-detachment incarnate and produced the first of innumerable Acacia Roads which through many derivations, many copies, and many debasements, gave suburbia to an insatiable middle-class world.[1]

[1] Summerson, op. cit., pp. 158–9 on the importance of the Eyre estate. See also A. M. Eyre, *St John's Wood: its History, its Houses, its Haunts and its Celebrities* (1913).

Before concluding, however, that the wedge theory works as perfectly as an explanation of the process of development as it does as a description of a static urban structure, it must be observed that Regent's Park and St John's Wood do not exhaust the list of areas of earlier settlement with which Hampstead was in direct contact. Indeed if social character had been invariably caught by physical contact like some contagious disease, then Hampstead ought to have suffered from a bad case of shingles, if not from schizophrenia. For to the south-east and east lay areas of very mixed character in Camden Town, Chalk Farm, Kentish Town, and Gospel Oak; and although these districts were still experiencing some fresh building at the same time as Hampstead, in the second and third quarters of the century, and were thus not completely formed in their characters before Hampstead reached the impressionable stage, nevertheless, with the partial exception of Gospel Oak, all of these neighbours had already acquired their general reputations before Hampstead was fairly born as a suburb. This is not to say that this group of neighbours was wholly innocent of good-class development. All of them, indeed, contained, and even managed to retain more or less permanently, pockets of spacious, modestly elegant, and highly respectable housing. But the important fact was that these were simply pockets, surrounded from the very first by great masses of indifferent or low-grade housing which stamped the prevailing character of these areas from a very early date. Some attempts at high-class development even contributed actively to social deterioration, for by unfortunate mistiming and optimistic miscalculation they launched large houses on to a sated market, and failing to find affluent tenants these at once became lodging houses or tenements.

By the time Nash drew up his Regent's Park scheme, in 1811, the character of the district to the east was sufficiently plain for him to be determined to keep it at bay with the barrier of Albany Street, to serve as the outer defence of his terraces and preserve 'that best-built part of the town from the annoyance and disgrace which threaten it on either side'.[1] Immediately to the east of the crown property was Lord Southampton's estate, and here inferior houses were going up on the land adjoining the Hampstead Road, fostered by short building leases, lax estate management, and over-eagerness to develop an outlying area ahead of any better-class demand. Nash might lament the wasted opportunity and complain that 'houses of such a mean sort as have been built at Somers Town, and are now building on Lord Southampton's

[1] Hugh C. Prince, 'North-west London, 1814–1863', in J. T. Coppock and H. C. Prince (eds), *Greater London* (1964), p. 100.

ground, should disgrace this apex of the Metropolis, particularly as there is sufficient space on the lower grounds for any increase of buildings required for the lower classes'.[1] Nevertheless the lower classes appropriated much of Lord Camden's estate as well, where active development began in 1812; while on Lord Somers's grounds the inhabitants were as unregulated and disorderly as the buildings, so that by 1826 the Bedford estate found it advisable to erect gates across the streets 'so as to shut out the low population of Somers Town'.[2] It was indeed only in Somers Town, and in Agar Town which was developed in gimcrack fashion astride the canal banks to the north, that the dregs of society came to rest, lodged in the crannies of uncontrolled and unsupervised building at its most unsavoury. These districts were from the first occupied as slums. Agar Town, dubbed by Dickens an 'English Suburban Connemara', supplied him with the material for a description of disorderliness which reeks of shanty-town filth:[3]

Along the canal side the huts of the settlers, of many shapes and sizes, were closely ranged, every tenant having his own lease of the ground. There were the dog-kennel, the cow shed, the shanty, and the elongated match-box styles of architecture. To another, the ingenious residence of Robinson Crusoe seemed to have given his idea. Through an opening was to be seen another layer of dwellings at the back: one looking like a dismantled windmill, and another perched upon a wall, like a guard's lookout on the top of a railway carriage. Every garden had its nuisance—so far the inhabitants were agreed—but every nuisance was of a distinct and peculiar character. In the one was a dung-heap, in the next a cinder-heap, in a third which belonged to the cottage of a costermonger, was a pile of whelk and periwinkle shells, some rotten cabbages, and a donkey; and the garden of another exhibiting a board inscribed with the words 'Ladies' School', had become a pond of thick green water.

This was the worst. Elsewhere Camden Town attained respectability, though it was respectability in generally cramped layouts and undistinguished terrace housing, and the respectability of industrious artisans and commercial clerks rather than that of the higher ranks. Moreover it was far from being an exclusively residential area. Even

[1] Ibid., pp. 96–7.
[2] Donald J. Olsen, *Town Planning in London* (1964), p. 148.
[3] Charles Dickens, *Household Words* (1851), quoted in H. C. Prince, op. cit., pp. 111–12.

before the railway arrived after 1835 there was considerable commercial and industrial activity in the district, in such businesses as stabling and laundering. The railway presence added to these activities through the direct employment created, the deterioration of residential property values, and to some small extent because of the improved transport facilities. By the 1840s a whole range of workshop industries flourished in the streets north of the Euston Road, in printing, engraving, musical instrument making, small-scale metal working, the clothing and furniture trades, and the like; while the newer industries had contributed the gasworks on the canal bank with Greek Revival cast-iron columns to support the gasholders.[1]

The picture should not be overdrawn. Hampstead's south-eastern neighbour was no social pariah, and was far from being a desolate and noisome wasteland. In particular the north-western part of the Southampton estate abutting Hampstead, and Eton College land, developed in a way which partly redeemed the start so much deplored by Nash. This little area, south of the Chalk Farm Tavern, had been only sketchily laid out with the rough lines of intended streets when the London and Birmingham Railway was projected, and little building had been completed; hence the choice of the route for the Euston extension in 1835, taking ground which was still open and keeping costly house acquisition and demolition to a minimum. After this, the area filled up rapidly, with the large Italianate terraces and pairs of villas of Gloucester Crescent, Oval Road, Gloucester Avenue, Chalcot Square, and Fitzroy Road—this last name commemorating the Southampton family origins.[2] This housing, if not of the aristocratic first-class, was decidedly above the fourth-rate, and did not bring disgrace on its neighbours in the Park. Nevertheless the Southampton estate never succeeded in getting more than this toehold in better-class development. Nearer to the High Street the streets which became Arlington, James-

[1] Parl. Papers *1841 Census of Great Britain*, 1844, xxvii, Occupation Tables, pp. 109–25, are not subdivided below the level of the Holborn Division, of which the St Pancras population constituted about one-third; 1851 Census, 1852/3, lxxxviii, Pt 1, Occupation Tables gike the St Pancras District separately.

[2] Gloucester Avenue was originally called Southampton Road; and the present Regent's Park Road began life as Gloucester Road. Chalcot Square and Chalcot Crescent commemorate the old Lower Chalcot Farm, while the half-circus formed by the junction of Chalcot Road and Regent's Park Road, on which the Baptist church stands, was the Chalk Farm Tavern tea garden. *P.O. London Directory*, 1850, endpaper map, shows the street layout in outline still, with a few houses built on Gloucester Avenue and Regent's Park Road, and Chalk Farm Tavern still in business.

town and Inverness were stocked with inferior terraces whose individual frontages were a bare fifteen feet. And although the Southampton area to the north of Prince of Wales Road, with the projected Malden Road as its spine and Queens Crescent as its chief arm, was laid out in 1841 for spacious development in pairs of semi-detached villas at a proposed density of less than four dwellings to the acre, the entire forty acres was in fact closely built up over the next couple of decades with orderly but extremely modest terraces. It was a district on Hampstead's doorstep, running up to the boundary marked by Maitland Park, and using the name and attraction of Haverstock Hill as its selling line.[1]

This part of Hampstead's eastern flank was backed by the Buck–Hawley estate, and topped by Gospel Oak. The first was a forty-acre site straddling the canal which was actively developed in the 1840s, when such streets as Buck Street, Hawley Crescent, Street, and Road were formed presumably to their ground landlords' present satisfaction even if not to their future glory. The estate was much troubled by railway interference, first by the E & WID & BJR in 1846, and then by the Hampstead Junction Railway in 1853. It is true that the building of these lines introduced the district to the assorted activities and squalor of life in the railway arches, and to the disturbing experience of trains rattling past a few feet from bedroom windows, the coal and cattle trains being particularly clanky and nocturnal in their habits. Nevertheless the railway inquiries established that the area did not suffer from the extremes of railway blight, simply because it had never started from any very elevated position. The architect William Tite gave the most emphatic evidence on this point, all his answers being calculated to convey with as much precision as politeness allowed the exact grade of social inferiority attained by the district. 'The houses on Buck's estate', he stated, 'are not small residences and semi-detached, they are streets of ordinary houses, and there are some villas but I think you could scarcely call them villas.' His view was that 'the line will do no more damage, to Buck's class of property, than the actual injury to houses taken, and overlooked by the line. It will not blight the whole estate.' The full meaning of the qualification, that little damage was to be expected on such a class of property, was brought out when he was asked about the effect on property amenities and values of the noise of cattle trains in the middle of the night, and disclosed that 'I should not

[1] Plan and particulars of sale of Lord Southampton's building ground on Haverstock Hill, and of freehold ground rents, 4 May 1841: in the MS. of George Head & Sons, surveyors, Baker Street.

like it myself, but there is a great difference between abuse in Lowndes Square, and this class of houses.'[1] The implied brutishness and insensitivity of the residents was no doubt as unwarranted as the assessment of their social status was just. Even the head of the syndicate of ground landlords, Louis William Buck, M.P., and his expert witness, Charles Lee, could put no better face on the matter than to claim that although the estate was covered with third- and fourth-rate houses they were still 'very respectable houses of their class, and very respectably inhabited.'[2] After all, there was little scope for appeal from the cold verdict of rentals of £25 to £40 a year for Buck's houses.

The same inquiry dealt with the character of Gospel Oak, through which the line approached South End and the southern edge of Hampstead Heath. Gospel Oak in 1853 consisted of a mere handful of houses actually achieved—'some 12 or 13 houses with a beershop at the corner' —but although the larger landowners in this part, Lord Mansfield and Lord Lismore, had no plans for development, the smaller properties were buzzing with schemes. Indeed the presence of a number of small properties, with their owners anxious for quick profits, seems to have been at the root of Gospel Oak's troubles. Tite said of the dozen houses already built 'I do not mean to say they are to be disregarded because they are humble, but they are very humble . . . some of them are very inferior, very ill-built and wretched.' The houses were mainly owner-occupied, and he sensed that 'they look a little like Land Society [similar to building society] houses, that is houses belonging to people in humble life, perfectly respectable in their way; and they look very like houses that have been built by persons for themselves.' When asked whether they were semi-detached cottages, he replied 'I should say that semi-detached suggests something better. They are houses in pairs.'[3] On top of this consignment of Gospel Oak to oblivion it emerged that the chief objector to the route from hereabouts, Dale, had merely put together some paper scheme for developing his property as soon as he got wind of the projected line, in the hope of getting some compensation. He was told that the line, with a station at Gospel Oak, would make his scheme go, and was easily bought off. His subsequent achievements in Dale Road and Vicars Road did nothing to earn redemption for Gospel Oak, apart from the supreme service of providing a site for the most

[1] HLRO Min. H.C. 1853, 8 June, Hampstead Junction Railway Bill, ff. 142, 147–8 (W. Tite, architect).
[2] Ibid., ff. 173, 218–19 (Charles Lee, surveyor; Louis William Buck).
[3] Ibid., ff. 32, 100–8, 160 (Whateley, counsel for J. L. Dale; Berkeley, railway engineer; W. Tite); and 10 June, ff. 1–2 (Merewether, counsel for the promoters).

bizarre and 'craziest of London's Victorian churches', St Martin, built in 1866.[1]

The post-railway growth of Gospel Oak was clearly most powerfully influenced by the railway itself. The Hampstead Junction line produced an offshoot from Gospel Oak in 1868, the Tottenham and Hampstead Junction, which provided a link with the Great Eastern's Lea Valley line; and also in 1868 the Midland extension to St Pancras was opened, running through Lord Lismore's part of Gospel Oak, which was laid out as intended building ground but not yet developed. The result of all this railway construction was to turn the whole area between Kentish Town Road and Gospel Oak station into railway-land, spread with sidings, engine sheds, and workshops, and liberally laced with interchange lines. With the jobs created by this activity, and with the proximity of the whole Kentish Town–St Pancras railway complex, the surrounding residential district became a natural railwaymen's quarter. Gospel Oak's function was to be one of the more salubrious parts of this quarter, respectable but emphatically working-class. Even before the railway imprint was so heavily laid upon the area, however, there were clear indications that it was destined for a somewhat modest and humble class of development, and that neither its ownership structure nor the character of its earliest settlers could ever have supported an expectation of attracting a wealthy middle-class community.

That being so, it is obvious that the influences gathering on Hampstead's south-eastern border in the 1840s and 1850s were of a vastly different type from those which could be expected from the direction of Regent's Park and St John's Wood. From the point of view of Hampstead's development into a comfortable, prosperous, and fashionable suburb the first set of influences had to be resisted as strongly as the second set were to be welcomed. It is clear in the hindsight of the completed urbanisation that one of the frontiers between superior and inferior sectors was established hereabouts. But it would be pure historicism to assert that it was inevitable that the frontier should be established in this particular place, and especially so since the area of doubtful desirability lay astride the main means of access to old Hampstead, which ran through Camden Town to Haverstock Hill. It would be

[1] Pevsner, op. cit., pp. 360–1. Confidence in Dale's intentions is hardly increased by the fact that the same Joseph Langham Dale appears to have been a considerable leaseholder and developer of 'instant slums' in the notorious Potteries district of North Kensington in the 1840s and 1850s: Patricia E. Malcolmson, 'The Potteries of Kensington: a study of slum development in Victorian London' (unpublished M.Phil. thesis, Leicester University, 1970), p. 34.

reasonable to suppose that in the absence of obstacles the natural line of advance for builders and inhabitants alike would have been the axis of the old road to Hampstead village. One great natural obstacle to permeation in this direction was of course the hill itself, and in a general sense it is true that the Northern Heights were destined by topography for upper-class occupation. The slopes gave advantages of drainage, water supply, and fresh air which the wealthier sort were prepared to pay for, thus driving property values beyond the reach of the lower ranks; while in any case the terrain discouraged industry and therefore the chance of work on the spot for the poorer sort, for whom daily journeys to work from a purely residential encampment on the hill would have been punishing either to the feet or to the pocket. It is therefore inconceivable that the Heights could in any circumstances have been occupied by a working-class suburb, and in a broad sense the contour lines provided Hampstead's defences against any such encroachment. Nevertheless along most of the south-eastern and eastern front the mixed-character force from Camden Town and Gospel Oak was halted and contained before its advance reached the hill proper, and before the gradient sharpened enough to slow its momentum. In other words it looks as though something more than a simple natural frontier was involved. At the same time, because the steeper slopes with their desirable potential lay behind and promised a future of attractive development which was worth conserving, the outlying defences in this direction did not need to be as blatant as the physical barriers erected to protect the Bedford estate or Regent's Park from contamination. Given the reinforcement of the hill in their rear, the property boundaries were sufficient in themselves to form an effective border, and to keep the sinister influences at bay.

In the Hampstead case the property boundaries were decisive in marking the line between residential sectors of sharply contrasting characters. But by itself the property structure probably would have been unable to produce the end-result of the wealthy suburb. Landowners, developers, and builders might propose, but their customers disposed. In Victorian London it was almost an everyday occurrence for the comfortable middle-class clients to fail to show up to take the houses designed to attract them; it was a standard routine for speculations to go sour for this reason, and through multi-occupation, tenementing, or other means houses built for single-family occupation by well-servanted middle-class households in fact passed straight into the tenancy of people lower down the scale. Which is but to say that housing suppliers had a persistent weakness for aiming at the upper end of the market, and collectively had a strong bias for exaggerating its size. So that within a century when total housing supply is generally held always to have fallen short of total need, if not of actual demand, there was generally a comfortable housing surplus for the middle-class house-hunter. When applied to the particular locality, this general situation meant that the mere fact that Hampstead's south-eastern border was protected by large blocks of property with owners resolved not to spoil their assets by permitting any haphazard, uncontrolled, or inferior development, was not by itself sufficient to ensure the success of schemes for creating a desirable residential district. The ownership pattern was capable of supplying the defensive resolves and the initial aspirations. Fulfilment of the aspirations depended on other and more on-going factors, capable of sustaining the character of the district over the whole span of the seventy or eighty years during which active development was in progress. On the one hand this was a matter of the creation and maintenance of a particular and distinctive image for the residential qualities of the neighbourhood, a reputation which could induce a sufficient stream of purchasers and tenants from the right income groups; the chief support of adequate demand was the attraction of living near or on the Heights and within reach of the Heath, a magnet whose force contemporaries believed to be more reliable than its permanence. On the other hand it was a question of the supply of building land being released only in such quantities and at such times as ensured that Hampstead largely avoided the debilitating effects of an overstocked market. This in turn depended on the timing and speed with which building tracts and plots were made available by owners, and although this was a subject of conscious control to some extent through deliberate estate policies, to a much greater extent this absolutely crucial matter of timing was determined fortuitously and in ways not only not intended but also sometimes vehemently resented by the owners. The accidents of family history, the intricacies of the land law, and the lucky chances of earlier tenurial arrangements, had a great deal to do with the emergence of Hampstead as Charles Booth found it.

Three

CHARACTER FORMATION
Hampstead of the
country villas

Pre-Victorian times bequeathed to Hampstead a structure of land-ownership which was remarkably favourable, not so much because of the concentration of ownership into a few hands, which was indeed striking but probably not unusual, but because of the strategic control which the distribution on the ground placed in the hands of the larger properties. The survey made in 1838 for tithe commutation gives a clear picture of the distribution of the land at a time when, outside the old town, it was still almost wholly agricultural; the outlines of this picture are displayed in Table 5.

Table 5   The structure of landownership in Hampstead, 1838 (to the nearest acre)

Size of estates (acres)	Landowners		Area occupied	
	Nos	%	Acres	%
Under 1	3	6·1	3	0·2
1 and under 5	14	28·5	40	2·4
5 and under 10	10	20·4	75	4·5
10 and under 25	12	24·6	189	11·3
25 and under 100	5	10·2	190	11·4
Over 100	5	10·2	1,169	70·2
Totals	49	100·0	1,666	100·0

Source: Tithe Apportionment, Hampstead, GLCRO.

This table covers about three-quarters of the land area of the parish. The remaining 533 acres were described in the Apportionment as 'common lands, private gardens, and waste'; the Heath, and small areas of manorial waste at West End, Fortune Green, and South End, perhaps covered 250–270 acres at this date, so that the built-up area of the old town, which was tithe-free and therefore not noticed in the survey, formed rather more than one-tenth of the total area.[1]

With five estates sharing 70 per cent of the land between them, there was indeed a high concentration of ownership into a few hands, but it was no higher than in contemporary Camberwell where seven land-owners held two-thirds of the land.[2] The convenience of Hampstead's big five in the days when they were farmland, and their strength when it came to building, was immensely assisted by their compactness. Eton's 200-odd acres, the Dean and Chapter of Westminster's 240 acres, and Henry Samuel Eyre's 140 acres, all lay within their own ring fences completely untroubled by any small properties in their midst, and Eyre's Hampstead property ran straight on from his larger Mary-lebone estate without any interruption. Only John Powell Powell's 170-acre estate was seriously split, lying in two almost equal halves divided by a half-mile strip containing many small properties. It is true that the largest estate of all, the 416 acres owned by Sir Thomas Maryon Wilson, the lord of the manor, was also in two blocks: there were 60 acres in a dozen fields along the east side of the Heath, but the remain-ing 356 acres lay in one continuous stretch to the west and south-west of the old town. Compactness, and the possibilities which this afforded for estate policies to follow an even course unmoved by the chance that intrusive small properties could be used for ill-considered and wounding antics, was by no means all. The entire eastern and southern borders of the parish were in the hands of the Wilson, Westminster, Eton, and Eyre estates, with the exception of a short stretch at the Kilburn end which was in the hands of Fulk Greville Howard. As a Hampstead land-owner Howard was certainly only of modest dimensions, with the 40-acre Abbey Farm that had once been Kilburn Priory, just spilling over into Marylebone. Howard, however, had married a great heiress, Mary Howard (and thereupon had changed his name from Upton) who in 1818

[1] The estates of the Dean and Chapter of Westminster, Henry Samuel Eyre, Fulk Greville Howard, and John Wrightson were also tithe-free by virtue of their descents from the former ecclesiastical lands of the Abbey of West-minster, the Hospital of St John of Jerusalem, Kilburn Priory, and the Hospitallers again, respectively. But these properties are included in Table 5, from data given in the Tithe Apportionment and from the separate estate records.

[2] H. J. Dyos, *Victorian Suburb? a Study of the Growth of Camberwell* (1961), pp. 40–1; identical-sized groups have been adopted in the present table to facilitate comparison.

succeeded to all the estates of the Earls of Suffolk and Berkshire except those, at Charlton Park, Malmesbury, which were settled to go with the title. Her inheritance gave her large estates in four counties, with a great house to go with each: Elford Hall in Staffordshire, Castle Rising in Norfolk, Ashstead Park in Surrey, and Levens Hall in Westmorland. Fulk Greville Howard, therefore, was a very large landowner indeed by marriage, his wife's 18,000 acres making him easily the largest private landowner connected with Hampstead.

Both the Dean and Chapter of Westminster and Eton College were considerable landowners elsewhere, both of them quite incidentally happening to own estates in neighbouring Hendon, which formed a major part of the site of the future Golders Green, while as corporate owners both institutions had a tendency to manage their properties with an endless future in view. Sir Thomas Maryon Wilson lived at Charlton House, Blackheath, where he had an estate as large and as potentially valuable as his Hampstead property; and he also owned agreeable country estates in Essex and Sussex, so that with more than 4,000 acres at his command all told there was a fair presumption that he would not be forced or tempted to do anything rash with his Hampstead land. Of the Hampstead border estate owners only Eyre does not seem to have been a substantial landowner on the national scale, in terms of acres; but his St John's Wood estate obviously made him into a landowner of very considerable wealth. All in all, therefore, these Hampstead owners were most amply backed by outside resources which gave them the financial security and outlook of large landowners who could afford to look on their Hampstead properties with fair detachment and reasonable immunity from catchpenny schemes and the temptations of quick profits.

Furthermore, behind this border screen of large properties the interior of the parish yielded only some 95 acres altogether, in fifteen small holdings of assorted sizes, up to the line of West End Lane; most of them were 'escaped' copyholds on the fringes of the old town, where infilling operations were likely to add to the established character of the older urban landscape, while two or three of them—the Carlile, Rhodes, and Key estates—were in the 10–15 acre range, large enough to be laid out as building estates with individualities of their own. The corollary was that the major portion of the land which was owned in units of less than 100 acres apiece lay in the north-west corner of the parish, beyond West End Lane. Indeed 60 per cent of the individual landowners were concentrated in the north-west, which contained only one quarter of the area; and they were scattered in a patchwork pattern

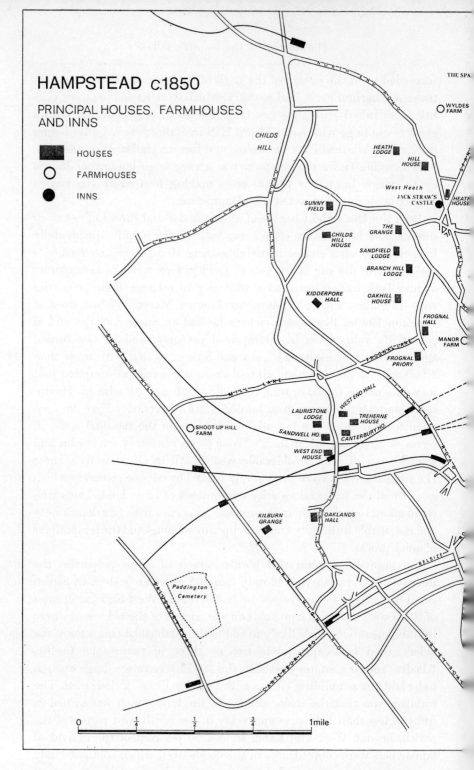

HAMPSTEAD c.1850

PRINCIPAL HOUSES, FARMHOUSES
AND INNS

⬛ HOUSES

◯ FARMHOUSES

⬤ INNS

THE SPA

◯ WYLDES FARM

CHILDS HILL

HEATH LODGE

HILL HOUSE

West Heath

JACK STRAW'S CASTLE

HEATH HOUSE

SUNNY FIELD

THE GRANGE

CHILDS HILL HOUSE

SANDFIELD LODGE

BRANCH HILL LODGE

KIDDERPORE HALL

OAKHILL HOUSE

FROGNAL HALL

MANOR FARM

FROGNAL PRIORY

WEST END HALL

LAURISTONE LODGE

TREHERNE HOUSE

◯ SHOOT-UP HILL FARM

SANDWELL HO.

CANTERBURY HO.

WEST END HOUSE

KILBURN GRANGE

OAKLANDS HALL

Paddington Cemetery

BELSIZE

0   ¼   ½   ¾   1mile

MAP 3 Hampstead c. 1850: principal houses, farmhouses and inns

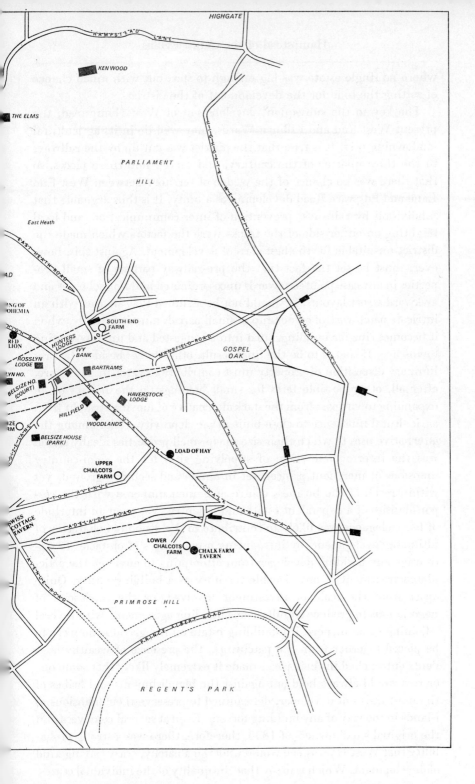

where no single estate was big enough to start out with much chance of setting the tone for the development of the district.

The key to the subsequent development of West Hampstead, the present West End and Kilburn Wards, may well lie in its agricultural landowning past. It is true that the district was cut up by the railways in the third quarter of the century, and carved into three pieces, so that there was no chance of the wedge of territory between West End Lane and Edgware Road developing as a unity. It is thus arguable that subdivision by railways, prevention of inter-communication, and local blighting on either side of the tracks were the factors which made the district unsuitable for the best class of development. Against this, however, must be set the fact that the pre-railway pattern of small properties in any case pointed towards unco-ordinated building schemes and awkward street layouts. It should not be assumed that an area with an intricate patchwork of ownership in small parcels must inevitably, when it becomes ripe for building, turn into a congested and unprepossessing townscape. If that is to be the final result, other forces besides the preliminary disposition of property must contribute towards it. There are, after all, other possible fates for small holdings on the fringes of an expanding town apart from the stark alternative of moving straight from agricultural innocence to close-built urban depravity. Chief among the alternative uses to which their size made small properties ideally suited was the intermediate stage of supplying sites for the semi-country mansions of merchant princes, set in ample and secluded grounds yet within reach of the business centre and unencumbered with the responsibilities of a dependent estate and tenantry. Yet even an interlude of leafy elegance was likely to contribute to the disjointed character of ultimate development, by introducing a new series of obstacles to discourage any building developer from attempting to envisage the articulated treatment of any sizeable territory as a building entity. Quite apart from the scale of investment involved, or the intricacies of negotiations to produce simultaneous building agreements with several adjoining small owners, if a building estate on the grand scale were to be pieced together from the patchwork, the presence of wealthy residents entrenched in their parks made it extremely likely that some one or two would always hold out against the blandishments and bribes of the most insistent developer, determined to preserve their mansions as islands in the way of any building torrent. Even at several removes from the original small owners of 1838, therefore, there was a strong probability that West Hampstead would undergo a patchy, crazy-paving kind of development. Which is to say that the quality of the individual crazes, the style of housing erected and the type of community actually attracted to them, could not be of the top class; but below that, did not need to be, and was not, of the poorest.

One consequence of the concentration of the smaller properties in the north-west corner of the parish was that most of the activity in the Hampstead land market concerned that district. There was of course nothing in principle to stop the freehold landowners elsewhere creating interests in their estates in the shape of long leases which could themselves become the subject of dealing and speculation, and in a building environment transactions in such interests were frequently of greater importance than the buying and selling of freehold land. Thus speculation in building values was by no means banished from the major part of Hampstead. But dealings in the ground itself were largely circumscribed geographically, and in so far as the land market effects observed in Camberwell were part of a general London experience—that 'the whole trend in the distribution of the ownership of the land during the nineteenth century was . . . towards a further multiplication of owners and a still more minute division of their holdings'—then the gap between West Hampstead and the rest of the parish could only widen as time passed.[1]

Owners of the larger estates might in some places contribute to the multiplication of small owners by disposing of bits of their estates piecemeal for building development; but in practice they did not do so in Hampstead. As a start, their institutional nature made the collegiate and capitular estates practically inviolable. At the beginning of the period it was legally impossible even to grant long leases for a definite term of years, as distinct from leases for lives or shorter leases with habitual renewals. Special legislation, the Eton College Act of 1826 and the Ecclesiastical Estates Leases Act of 1842, was necessary before it became possible to grant building leases. The sale of any corporate land was an even more difficult operation, and once it had become technically possible under such provisions as the Episcopal and Capitular Estates Management Act of 1851, or the belated but more liberal Universities and College Estates Act of 1898, the administrators of such estates continued to regard any sale as needing quite exceptional justification. This attitude persisted until the middle of the twentieth century, so that ownership of the soil of the Eton and Westminster estates remained virtually intact and untouched right through the period of building.

Similarly, the key estates which were in private ownership did not succumb to any temptation to indulge in selling off either whole

[1] Loc. cit.

[81]

portions or individual plots. For most of the nineteenth century the Howard and Wilson estates were not in a legal position to do so; the Eyre estate may, for all that is known, have had the legal power to sell, but certainly did not have the will. Both the Howard and Wilson estates were held under family arrangements, established either by wills or by marriage settlements, which meant that the powers of the owner for the time being over his land were limited, and did not extend to selling any part of it. Because of the terms of his father's will the powers of Sir Thomas Maryon Wilson were so extremely limited that he could scarcely deal at all with his Hampstead property during his lifetime (1821–69). Since all the Eyre estate records have vanished it is impossible to say whether Henry Samuel Eyre and his successors also held their estate as tenants-for-life under a family settlement.[1] But even if they did not, and were full owners of the fee simple, they had good reason for not wishing to exercise any legal powers to sell off land; for from the first days of the St John's Wood venture it was apparent that if he was to implement a scheme which would take very many years to complete, without incurring the additional risks of avoidable pitfalls caused by deviant developments arising in the path of the grand advance, it was vital for Eyre to retain the supreme control conferred by the ground landlord's position. Family interests and reasons of estate policy therefore combined to ensure that all three private estates held together as units of ownership throughout the century of active building. With few exceptions the territories of the five vital estates were the same in 1914 as they had been in 1838 apart from lands taken from them by compulsory purchase for railways and other public purposes.

The stability at this level of ownership was slightly unusual in terms of Hampstead's own previous experience, since the three private estates had all changed hands in the course of the preceding century. The same Earl of Chesterfield who was the eighteenth-century lessee of the Belsize estate had at one time been the owner of St John's Wood, which he sold to Henry Samuel Eyre the first in 1732. The manor of Hampstead and the freehold estate which went with it had been sold twice since the Dissolution took it from the Abbey of Westminster and placed it, after a spell in the possession of the short-lived bishopric of Westminster, in the hands of the crown in 1550. It was granted to Sir Thomas Wroth, a courtier who acquired considerable estates in the home counties, in 1551; after the death of his grandson it was sold, in 1620, to Baptist

[1] It seems that Sir John Summerson may have seen some Eyre MS. before 1939, but the present Eyre Estate Office believes that all the records were destroyed during the Second World War.

Hicks, a highly successful silk merchant and money-lender who propelled himself into the peerage as Viscount Campden.[1] Hicks's descendants became Earls of Gainsborough, and it was the third Earl who sold the Hampstead property to Sir William Langhorne in 1707. From then on the estate travelled by the ordinary, if involved, processes of inheritance and marriage through Margaret Maryon, a distant Langhorne cousin, to reach General Sir Thomas Spencer Wilson in 1777 through his marriage to Jane Weller, a Maryon great-niece and heiress. The Sir Thomas Maryon Wilson who inherited the estate in 1821 was the third Wilson to hold it.[2] Finally, the Kilburn Priory or Abbey Farm estate had a more involved, and a more commercial, history in its transit from the Knights Hospitallers of St John to the hands of Fulk Greville Howard.

The Hospital had held Abbey Farm along with Shoot-Up Hill Farm (the estate owned by John Powell Powell in 1838), and after the two had been separated by royal grants in 1546 they were reunited in 1595 in the possession of Sir Arthur Atye, the Earl of Leicester's secretary. Atye's heirs seem to have sold the estate in 1663 to an Edward Kelyng, who sold it in turn in 1673 to a pair of speculators, John King of the Inner Temple and Edward Jenkinson, a Westminster brewer, who quickly re-sold to Edward Nelthorpe, a London merchant. Nelthorpe's only child, Mary, married another merchant, Robert Liddell, who belonged to a younger branch of the Liddells of Ravensworth Castle, Durham. On the death of their son Henry Liddell without issue in 1768 the estate was inherited by a nephew, Richard Middleton of Chirk Castle, Denbighshire; this Middleton sold off the estate in two pieces in 1773, John Powell of Fulham buying the Shoot-Up Hill Farm, and Richard Marsh of Kilburn Bridge, Paddington, and Simondshyde Farm, near Hatfield, taking the Abbey Farm. It was from this Richard Marsh that Fulk Greville Howard bought Abbey Farm in 1819.[3]

[1] L. Stone, *The Crisis of the Aristocracy, 1558–1641* (Oxford, 1965), pp. 534–5.

[2] Manorial descent in HPL Documents in the case of Hoare *v.* Wilson, 1866, Plaintiff's Observations; and in T. J. Barratt, *The Annals of Hampstead* (1912), III, 64–6.

[3] The descent is outlined in Bagot MS., Lease No. 85, 30 November 1824, F. G. Howard to W. Carter; the account differs slightly from that given in Park, *The Topography and Natural History of Hampstead* (1818), pp. 199–202, and as it is in the form of an abstract of title is to be preferred. Park insists that Richard Marsh was still the owner at the time he was writing (1813), and as Park had possibly verified this by personal inquiry it must be accepted, although the recital of deeds made in 1824 indicates that Richard Marsh transferred the title in the estate, at least, to Daniel Chapman of Hitchin and his only child Ann, in 1794. Conceivably this was a preliminary to a marriage between Richard and Ann; but it was the Chapmans who

Howard clearly fastened on the Abbey Farm as a plain piece of speculation in real estate showing encouraging signs of ripeness for development, for he had no previous connections with the district and can have had neither the need nor any wish to turn Kilburn into a site for his own residence. The encouraging signs were that by 1819 building had begun on the Eyre estate, and though the action was still taking place far away to the south-east in streets like Alpha Road and Beta Place which have long since been obliterated by the Great Central Railway, still the St John's Wood Chapel had just been built, Lord's Cricket Ground had settled down on its new site, a house or two had gone up on Grove End Road, and most appetising of all a prolongation of the line of Grove End Road had been roughed out on the ground, the future Abbey Road leading right up to the boundary of the Eyre property by the West End Brook beside the Abbey Farm land.[1] Moreover, while a keen business eye could picture the early arrival of the builders at the back of Abbey Farm coming along Abbey Road, even a sober investor might well think in the hustling atmosphere of this quarter of London around 1819 that it would take them no time at all to reach the front of the Farm up the Edgware Road. A group of substantial villas had just gone up in Maida Vale, where a prolongation of Hall Road was later to cross the main road, and this smart line of gentlemen's residences under the name of Pine Apple Place looked like a very temporary halt in the unfolding of a ribbon of promising class which ought to reach Kilburn very quickly.[2]

So Fulk Greville Howard took possession of his new property in July 1819 and entered into his first building agreements before the end of the following September. Thus the most recent of the Hampstead estates to change hands became the first to launch into the venture of opening up fresh territory. As so often happened in real estate speculations, the glittering prospects were more dazzling than the experience at close quarters. The difficulty was partly that the Abbey Farm had some physical handicaps for building layout, the land beside the Brook being not too easily drained and forming an ample pond upstream from Kilburn Bridge; but it was mainly that the estate was a comparatively long way in fact from the building frontier, and that the eagerness of

---

conveyed to Howard in 1819, and Marsh was not a party to the conveyance, so that no such marriage ever materialised.

[1] Eyre MS., Book of Leases in force in 1903, showing building leases in Grove End Road running from September 1817. John Luffman's Map of London (1820), and Greenwood's Map of London (1827).

[2] Luffman's and Greenwood's maps; and T. C. Barker [and Michael Robbins], *A History of London Transport*, I, *The Nineteenth Century* (1963), p. 3.

PLATE 1 Belsize House in the mid-eighteenth century; after the fair (see p. 37)

PLATE 2 Thompson's folly: Frognal Priory about 1832 (see p. 120)

PLATE 3 Development on the Maryon Wilson estate: Downshire Hill and St John's Chapel in 1842 (see p. 126)

anticipation had foreshortened the interval between the perception of a building future and the actual arrival of the builders' workmen. It was not that the venture went completely sour on Howard, but there may well have been a long period when he felt he had burnt his fingers on the investment, and when it was only the ample outside family resources which prevented him from pulling out in disappointment and perhaps leaving Kilburn to a wholly inglorious fate. It turned out that Howard had come in on the tail-end of the Regency building boom, and when this finally petered out in the aftermath of the 1825 general financial crisis all that had actually been built on the Abbey Farm was one group of half a dozen fairly large villas and a second pocket containing eight cottages and some stabling. There the estate rested for over twenty years, and it did not really begin to go, and to fill up rapidly, until the 1850s. One can readily imagine that a less well-heeled speculator could only too easily have been caught short by this long stagnation and been forced to realise his assets for what they would fetch in a dull market, and that a slightly nibbled building estate such as this would almost inevitably have fallen apart into small morsels.

In his eagerness to get his new estate covered with houses and see a return on his purchase Howard played two distinct development lines. In one spot he dealt directly with some small jobbing builders, and in the second he dealt with a developer as an intermediary, who himself made sub-agreements with the actual builders. In both cases the arrangements were rather unfavourable to the ground landlord, but luckily for him the agreements were not so loosely drawn as to prejudice the future of the rest of the estate. In the first case, Howard made use of an existing farm lane leading from West End Lane to his Abbey Field to serve as an inexpensive residential road. Plots were taken in September 1819 by John Gelsthorp, a Marylebone carpenter, and by Henry Jay, a Kilburn carpenter who came to live on the site in Abbey Cottages, at remarkably high ground rents which were at the rate of about £67 per acre or between 3s. and 3s. 6d. per foot of frontage. Howard was sufficiently well advised by his agent, Thomas Hill Mortimer, of Albany, only to make agreements to grant 99-year leases once houses had been erected, and not to grant the leases themselves forthwith, for this provided an incentive to the lessees to get on with the building and a safeguard for the ground landlord that he could resume the land without trouble if no buildings appeared. But the agreements omitted to stipulate with any precision what kind of houses were to be erected, and the result was that rather small and cheap cottages, worth about £240 apiece, were placed on plots which had frontages ranging up to 80 feet

[85]

and which were of ample size to carry imposing residences. Moreover one smaller plot was used by Gelsthorp as the site for stabling and chaise-houses, not intended for the personal use of the relatively humble occupants of the cottages, but for letting to affluent residents from further afield. These two features, the stables and the unimpressive cottages, went a long way towards settling the future not merely of what became Abbey Lane and Kilburn Vale which were the immediate scene of activities, but also of the larger surrounding district of Kilburn, as a place of lower-middle-class and working-class occupation, mingled with the commercial and semi-industrial activities appropriate to the backstreets behind a shopping high street.[1]

The quality of the buildings put up by Gelsthorp and Jay was not helped by the small scale of their businesses, the obviously hand-to-mouth credit existence leading to early bankruptcy, which is revealed in the deeds. Gelsthorp operated on credit and loans from people in the same trade or same social level as himself, and when he went bankrupt in November 1821 his two chief creditors, John Scagell a bricklayer from Beckenham and Edward Kelly a scavenger from Paddington, became his assignees and sold his cottages and stabling by auction at the Yorkshire Stingo public house in the New Road. The purchasers were professional men in the City, one solicitor and one auctioneer; although the head leases were thereupon granted to them, the actual occupants were sub-tenants, probably weekly tenants. Jay lasted a little longer, borrowing among others from John Campbell a St Pancras slater and Richard Underwood a Brixton plumber, and failing only in January 1825, when these two became his assignees. His cottages were likewise auctioned off and acquired by investors, among them Howard's own agent, who left them in the occupation of the existing undertenants. Howard thus emerged unscathed by the failures of the two builders, and indeed the three-quarters of an acre they had covered yielded him a handsome £50. 13s. 0d. in ground rents. But they had covered it in a far from handsome way, and Howard found that for no very good reason he had created a little pocket of workers' cottages surrounded by open country, which remained to discourage better-class offers or indeed any offers at all for more development, for many years to come.

In the second case, Howard found a developer who was prepared to take the whole of Eight Acre Field, lying on the parish boundary with

[1] This and the following paragraphs are based on Bagot MS., Lease Nos 4 (24 December 1822), 6 (24 August 1824), 7 (24 June 1825), 8 (24 June 1825), and 9 (10 December 1822), which are the 99-year leases running from 29 September 1819 granted in fulfilment of the agreements with Gelsthorp and Jay.

Marylebone, and attempt to develop it as a secluded residential neighbourhood for the gentry. The developer was a surveyor, George Pocock who lived further down the Edgware Road at Kilburn Priory; and instead of imitating Pine Apple Place as a piece of ribbon development, he decided to lay out an accommodation road running down the middle of the field from the Edgware Road to nowhere. This road became Greville Place, and on either side Pocock laid out substantial building plots intended for comfortable villas or 'two having the appearance of one' as the agreements phrased it, for a class of occupiers who would have need of their own stables and chaise-house. For a few years after making his agreement with Howard in October 1819 Pocock was successful in finding takers for his plots, but there seems to have been no fresh building after 1825, and Greville Place was then left in suspense, six or seven large suburban houses pointed at the country behind, until the late 1840s.[1]

The takers were a mixture of building tradesmen who built on speculation and wealthy shopkeepers building for their own occupation. The Carew brothers of Edgware Road, one a stonemason and the other a sculptor, built a pair of substantial semi-detached villas with fashionable Grecian columns and porches in 1824, one of which the sculptor lived in himself and the other of which was sold for £1,400 to Samuel Chappell, a music seller in New Bond Street. William Jefferys, a plumber from Regent Street, and John Langdon, a surveyor from St Pancras, each built half of a similar pair; one half was retained by Langdon as his own house, and the other was sold to Thomas Dickins, the successful Oxford Street shopkeeper, for £1,664. James Banting, a carpenter from Cumberland Street, took two plots, on each of which he built a sizeable villa with its own two-stall stable, one of which was bought by a naval captain and the other, after Banting's bankruptcy in 1822, by Jonathan Robinson, a victualler in Crawford Street, Marylebone. Finally a wine merchant from Newgate Street bought a 75-foot frontage on which to build himself a house which he covenanted should be at least of the value of £700 in best quality materials, faced in composition, and to designs approved by Howard's agent.

Up to a point everyone involved in this little development had reason to be satisfied except for poor Banting who went bankrupt, and his creditors who had to be content with a payment of 12s. in the pound

[1] This and the following paragraphs are based on Bagot MS., Lease Nos 85 (30 November 1824), 86 (26 March 1828), 87 (25 December 1827), 122 (25 October 1823), 123 (6 May 1823), 124 (30 November 1824), and 125 (6 December 1822), which are in fact not leases but conveyances of the fee at perpetual rent charges.

on his debts. He was one more illustration of the fragility of the more substantial, or more venturesome, masters from the building trades who were so freely lured into building speculations on their own account in this boom. The almost insignificant activities on Howard's estate on Greville Place and Abbey Lane had between them drawn in at least eleven such carpenters, plumbers, slaters and masons either as principals or as creditors in order to produce fourteen assorted dwellings; and three of them, perhaps entering on the enterprise rather late in the boom, had been rapidly bankrupted. Pocock the developer did well out of the Greville Place operations, taking his reward for managerial and middleman's services of a not very onerous kind (he was at little expense in making the road, which was left to be properly made up and surfaced at the charge of the resident lessees) in outright sales of his rights over each building plot, for which the builders paid him sums ranging from £170 to £342 per plot. The builders who survived presumably did rather nicely, for the houses they sold for £1,400 and more when the market was firm probably cost them little more than £800 or so to build (they all contracted to expend not less than £700 per house and were unlikely to exceed the minimum by any great amount unless exceptionally certain in advance that they could sell the finished house), and were little different in size or style from the house for which the bankrupt Banting had to accept £893. The house-purchasers were no doubt well satisfied with their neat and pleasing villas, if not always with the bargains they had struck. Only the ground landlord's gratification at seeing a corner of his property well launched as an eligible close of prosperous retailers just making the grade as carriage-folk may have been tinged with regrets. At the end of it Howard had ground rents of £52. 10s. 0d. from Greville Place, far more amply secured by wealthy owner-occupiers than the ground rents from Abbey Lane, but he had still made a poor bargain. These ground rents were only at a rate of some £17 or £18 an acre, and much of the short-term profit had gone to the developer. Moreover he had signed away the long-term profits as well, for the original agreement with Pocock had provided that when any house was completed Howard would convey the freehold of the site to Pocock's nominee (the purchaser) at a perpetual rent charge.

This kind of tenure, which was akin to the system of feu-rents usual in Scottish town holdings and to the rent charges which were a common alternative to freehold tenures in many Lancashire towns, was never at all widespread in London. The long building lease, settling down in the early nineteenth century to 99 years as the most usual term, was understandably the most popular building tenure with London landlords, since at the expiry of the lease there was the lure of a juicy capital gain when the house itself as well as the site reverted to the ground landlord. As a set-off to the ultimate reversion one might expect the annual ground rent under a terminating lease to be proportionately lower than the annual payment under a perpetual rent charge; alternatively, the incomes from both methods might be equalised by an outright sale of the perpetual rent charge, so that at least notionally the interest from the purchase money assuming it to be invested, plus the rent charge, would be approximately the same as the ground rent under a building lease plus the discounted value of the reversionary interest.

Over Greville Place, however, Howard had slipped. His annual income was low, even if it had been ordinary ground rental from building leases. And he had made no sale to Pocock, received no lump sum from him. He had, on the contrary, agreed to grant Pocock or his assigns 99-year leases from 29 September 1819 as soon as tenements had been erected and slated, with an option that Pocock could also obtain the freehold of the ground at any time within ten years of the completion of the buildings on payment of a perpetual rent charge of 6d. per foot on the frontage.[1]

The financial arrangements certainly appear to have given fat pickings to the developer and a lean reward for the landowner. It may be that this was the kind of sacrifice which Howard had to make to get a rather remote piece of development off the ground as early as 1819; though the very much fatter ground rents which he obtained at the same date for the lower-class development even further out, at Abbey Lane, where on an acreage basis his income was at least three times the size, cast doubt on such a simple explanation. Either Howard was bamboozled over the terms agreed with Pocock; or, perhaps more likely, since Howard's adviser Mortimer seemed to know his way about the property market, highly favourable terms were given for this pioneer piece of classy development on the estate in the hope that Greville

[1] The terms of the original agreement with Pocock are most fully detailed in Bagot MS., Lease No. 86, F. G. Howard to John Edward Carew, sculptor, with the consent of George Pocock, and Joseph Carew, house mason. It is possible that some further houses were built under the 1819 Pocock agreement, besides those for which the conveyances at perpetual rent charges have survived. This is unlikely, since any such houses would be those remaining on 99-year leases where the option to acquire the freehold had not been exercised, and the estate office would therefore have had a strong incentive to keep track of them. Some doubt remains, however, because not more than half Pocock's take of eight acres seems to have been covered by 1825, yet neither Pocock nor his heirs ever re-emerge in the estate records to complete the covering of vacant land to which he must have retained a sound leasehold title under the 1819 agreement.

Place would be a loss-leader which would found a reputation for the vicinity and attract imitative proposals on more profitable terms. The point goes to the heart of the building policy of urban landowners, and hence to the centre of the problem of explaining the growth of districts of contrasting housing, since if the income of a ground landlord was actually lower per acre, though higher per house, the better the quality of houses erected, then it becomes difficult to see why a landowner should take any pains to encourage good quality housing, or indeed why he should not maximise his income by pushing for development of the lowest-quality housing at the highest densities consistent with respectable security for his rents, unless he entertained social or aesthetic objections to mean and congested little houses. The handling of the Abbey Farm estate in 1819 throws up the riddle in miniature, but offers no solution since all development was halted after 1825 and there was no follow-through from which one could tell whether rents per acre for good-quality suburban villa plots rebounded at least to the levels obtainable for indifferent cheap cottage sites.[1]

Apart from being rather discouraging financially at the building estate level, and inconclusive in establishing a proven cachet for the district, this first foray into exploiting the Abbey Farm may well have left Howard out of pocket on his investment. Unfortunately we do not know how much he paid for the farm in 1819, and can only guess that the lowest agricultural price would have been about £6,000 and the top building land price about double that.[2] Assuming that Howard gave something over the minimum, say £8,000, his income from the estate by 1825 was £103 from ground rents and perhaps £150 from the remaining thirty acres still run as meadow and pasture, so that he may have been enjoying a yield of 3 per cent on his investment; satisfactory if it had been a country property, but distinctly meagre for a speculation. The attempt to push forward on the Kilburn side in advance of the really massive metropolitan thrust must be judged a failure, though not a disaster.

While the owner took a hand in steering the formative processes on the Abbey Farm, albeit without instant success, the pre-development stage on the Belsize estate in the first half of the nineteenth century was shaped quite casually, without any general oversight or direction from the Dean and Chapter of Westminster. The fact that the owners

[1] See below, pp. 366–70.
[2] The values are conjectural, based on an assumed agricultural rental value of £5 an acre which is below that of neighbouring farms at the same date: see above, pp. 11–12.

simply sat back and let events take their course might in some places
have caused utter confusion. But on Haverstock Hill events were firmly
propelled by the attractions of the situation, the quiet, the clean air,
and the view out over London; these produced a ground-plan of interests
in the estate which set the stage for a more varied and probably more
successful development into building estates in the second half of the
century than could ever have been achieved by positive planning. The
event which set matters moving in Belsize after years of stability was
the decision in 1807 of the fifth Earl of Chesterfield to obtain a private
estate Act with powers to sell some of his inheritance to clear off accumulated debts.[1] Under these powers he sold his interest in the lease
for lives of Belsize, and in the same year it was bought by a syndicate
of four Hampstead men of property: Germain Lavie, James Abel,
Thomas Roberts, and Thomas Forsyth.[2] These four divided the estate
into eight lots, took their pick of what they wanted to keep and resold
the rest. The Dean and Chapter then granted eight separate leases in
1808; three to James Abel, two to Thomas Roberts, one to Thomas
Forsyth, and to the second purchasers one to Edward Bliss, a newly-
established country gentleman with his seat at Brandon Park in Suffolk,
and one to George Todd, a Baltic merchant who had made his fortune
and acquired his wife in Riga.[3] Lavie, who had a large house at West
End, apparently was interested only in the profits to be made from the
rapid resale, since he did not take one of the new leases, and survived
on the Belsize estate only as the father of a son aged four who was chosen
by Abel as one of the three lives named in his lease. The Belsize manor
was thus effectively split into eight leasehold estates. Each was held on
a lease for three lives, the lives being chosen by the lessee, so that each
lease thereafter came up for renewal at a different time; and each of the
five individual owners could deal with his estate as he pleased, within
the limits set by the duration of his lease. Hence these sub-estates had
different histories after 1808, and constituted internal barriers which
prevented the Dean and Chapter ever again treating the entire estate
as an entity.

The prime object of this exercise was to create a series of residential

[1] Private Acts, 47 Geo. III cap. lviii, Earl of Chesterfield. And see above,
pp. 37–8.

[2] Park, op. cit., p. 155; DCW RCO 32, Abstract of Title of B. G. Woodd to the
Hillfield estate, 1857, reciting James Abel's will of 1816.

[3] C[hurch] C[ommissioners], Lease 142561, 26 December 1808, Dean and Chapter of Westminster to Thomas Roberts, reciting the disposal of the manor and
estate of Belsize in eight leases. DCW RCO 32, Abstract of Title (1864) of
Devisees in Trust named in the will of Edward Bliss made in 1839; and RCO 32,
certificates showing that merchant George Todd married in 1797 in Riga.

estates, each house set in its few acres of park-like grounds and surrounded by its own paddocks and meadows to give a perfect impression of a country estate in miniature; a rural illusion which was yet, in the early years of the nineteenth century, more than a half-truth, and one which was within reach of the successful business or professional man whose affairs did not demand an excessively punctilious attendance at the office. To either side of Haverstock Hill sizeable houses appeared, grand enough for the lawyers to refer to them in deeds with respect as 'capital mansion houses' rather than as plain 'messuages', and the road up to Hampstead became even better punctuated with private drives than it already was with taverns. The shake-up in the leasehold ownership thus opened the way to meet the 'country seat' type of demand which had been frustrated by the indifference of the Chesterfields, and the first new building on Belsize land since 1734 seems to have begun soon after 1808.[1] Most of it, including all the large imposing seats, has long since been swept away to make room for some of the present roads and houses, and only one or two of the much smaller trifles, Hunters Lodge in Belsize Lane and a stuccoed terrace in Belsize Grove, remain from this period, surviving because they were smaller and therefore could be fitted into new building layouts and new ways of living. But though entirely vanished from view the mansions of Haverstock Hill represent more than simply one layer of Hampstead's past, fascinating and illuminating as it is to visualise the merchants and the bankers daily passing the sites of dozens of later Victorian houses lying concealed in their lawns and rose beds, as they took carriage down their drives. For like some glacial action which leaves its marks permanently on the landscape when the glacier has melted, the mansions and their grounds have left their imprint on the townscape in the line of a road maybe, in the angle of a garden fence, or in the frontier between one period and style of house and another.

This form of development embellished the Belsize estate and made a satisfactory addition to the Dean and Chapter's income in the haphazard manner to which they were accustomed: that is, the annual rents of the eight new leases were purely nominal and archaic, with their stipulations for delivering trusses of hay and pecks of oats, and were indeed precise subdivisions of the Chesterfield obligations thus stretching back unaltered to before the Dissolution; but the renewal fines taken by the Dean and Chapter for the insertion of a fresh life whenever one of the three dropped automatically rose with the annual value of the property, being calculated as twice the full current rack rental. Thus

[1] See above, p. 33.

they received tidy windfalls ranging from £700 to £900 each time a new life was up for insertion in one of the head leases of these mansions. Though they profited from the development, their connection with the estate was virtually confined to this unpredictable and intermittent financial link. For any building was done entirely at the discretion, and risk, of the lessees, over whom the Dean and Chapter had no control whatever. The risk of committing resources to building on the strength of such life leases of nominally unpredictable duration was theoretically immense, but in practice was assumed to be negligible. Tradition and custom indicated that the Dean and Chapter would always agree to insert a new life every time one died, at an agreed tariff; and it was confidently assumed that they would always continue to do so, since a refusal on their part would mean a resolve to sit it out until all the existing lives should run out, and during this time, which could well turn out to be seventy years or more, they would have to forego all their usual income from fines and subsist merely on the meagre trusses of hay. In the early 1800s it seemed manifestly absurd to imagine the comfortable and easy-going canons and their dean tolerating such short rations for a moment; and so the prospect of the occasional but succulent carrot of a fat renewal fine was enough to convince everyone concerned that an apparently wobbly tenure under a lease for lives, which might be ended at any minute by some chance accident, was for all practical purposes as sound as a foolproof tenure on a freehold estate. It was only events which were unforeseen and largely unpredictable in the 1800s— the reform of ecclesiastical estate management in the 1840s which placed the Ecclesiastical Commissioners in supreme control of the disposition of all church property, and the ripening of Belsize for intensive building exploitation—that rendered the absurdity a great deal less farcical. By this time, however, the deeds had been done, the investments had been made, the stately houses and their fringe of lesser gentlemen's residences already existed; and they were swept away not because their tenurial foundations turned out to be unsafe, but because the new alternative uses for their sites were more profitable to the house-owners and ground-owners alike.

Unfortunately it is not possible to unravel all the details of the tangled operations after the 1808 leases. The Dean and Chapter were not too methodical in keeping records, and in any case had only a remote interest in keeping track of what was going on; while those who were directly touched, the beneficial lessees, have left no archives. The detachment and carelessness of the Dean and Chapter is well illustrated by the fact that it took them nearly four years to discover, and then only rather by chance, that the unthinkable had happened and the South End Farm property had fallen into their full possession simply through the death in June 1868 of the last surviving life named in the 1808 lease. This opportune discovery in 1872 implied even more casual behaviour by the lessee, Thomas Roberts, or his executors and solicitors, who had apparently neglected to apply for the insertion of new lives when either of the other two original lives had dropped; for such negligence allowed the value of the Roberts property to dwindle gradually away to nothing.[1] It establishes, however, that one of the subdivisions of Belsize manor was of no residential interest. Thomas Roberts had kept one of his two pieces as farmland since 1808, and his association with the 50-acre South End Farm was simply that of a small agricultural landowner who left matters entirely to his tenant farmer, Joseph Pickett, who paid a rather low agricultural rent of about £2 an acre for the holding.[2] The only buildings on the farm were still in 1872 the farmhouse and outbuildings, which were roughly on the site of the present Hampstead Heath railway station and South End Green flats. The farm, being low-lying and astride the unsavoury Fleet brook which at any rate by mid-century was becoming an open sewer, had no attractions for parcelling out into seats for the town-gentry.

This was far and away the least attractive of the Belsize properties. Roberts's apparent indifference to the management of South End Farm may be explained by the fact that his other share in 1808 was Rosslyn House and some 21 acres of grounds in which it stood. Rosslyn House was one of the few mansions which were already on the Belsize estate, and which although altered and extended in the late eighteenth century, had been there, in the guise of Shelford Lodge, since before 1734.[3] It is not clear whether Roberts wanted it for his own occupation, or for some profit-taking from an early resale; at any rate his lease had been purchased some time before 1817 by Sir Moore Disney, to whom a renewal was made in that year.[4] Admiral Disney lived there for a short time, but by 1828 the occupant of Rosslyn House was Henry Davidson, esquire.[5] Davidson bought the residue of the lease from the admiral,

---

[1] CC File 45820, South End Farm, Cluttons to George Pringle, Secretary of the Eccles[iastical] Comm[issioners], 7 February 1872, 20 February 1872, announcing that they had discovered that the last life had died on 17 June 1868.

[2] Ibid., 8 June 1872, Jennings, White and Buckston, Solicitors to the Eccles. Comm., to Geo. Pringle.

[3] See above, pp. 32–3.

[4] DCW RCO 32, H. E. Oliver to G. Vincent, 21 March 1846, sending Abstract of Title to lease of 1817 to Sir Moore Disney.

[5] *Pigot's Commercial Directory of London for 1828–29*, p. 443; Barratt, op. cit., II, 92.

and when the next life dropped, in 1845, the lease was renewed to him.[1] Davidson was still in possession of the lease, and in actual residence in the house, when building estate operations were started in 1853; it had been kept as a country-style property throughout the period, and no fresh development had taken place since 1808.

One of James Abel's prizes in the 1808 share-out was the plum property of the estate, Belsize House itself and its 45 acres of grounds and park, then still let to Spencer Perceval for £237. 10s. 0d. a year.[2] This was also preserved untouched, as the most eminent park on the Northern Heights after Ken Wood, for the next fifty years, passing through the hands of a number of tenants and owners. Martinez, a wealthy wine merchant, was one tenant; and another resident, Henry Wright who was one of the London private bankers, seems to have been the owner as well as the occupier in the 1830s. At any rate when Wright & Co failed in 1840 Belsize House was among the properties from the bankrupts' estates auctioned by Farebrothers in May 1841; it is probable that the purchaser was Charles J. Palmer, a Bloomsbury solicitor, who was the owner in 1853 when the park was put into the hands of builders.[3] Abel's other new property, a 19-acre field fronting the Hampstead road and lying on the south-east side of the grand avenue leading to Belsize House (later to become Belsize Avenue), had a more active history. There was a modest gentleman's house here, which was sold to Abel's tenant, Francklin, for £3,850 in 1822 after Abel's death, the proceeds going to wipe off Abel's debt of £4,000 to the widow of Thomas Forsyth, one of the members of the 1807 syndicate. The property changed hands again in 1834, when it was sold for £5,000 to John Wright, another member of the Henrietta Street banking partnership and possibly Henry Wright's brother or son. John was also pulled down in the 1840 failure of the bank, and the Wright family banking façade on Haverstock Hill vanished when his land was bought by Basil George Woodd in 1841 for £4,600.[4] Woodd was a man of means, a wine and

---

[1] DCW RCO 32, H. E. Oliver to G. Vincent, 18 December 1845, reporting the death of Duncan Davidson Milligan, one of the lives in the 1817 lease, and requesting the insertion of a new life, selected by Davidson. Milligan was probably inserted during the tenancy of Rosslyn House by Robert Milligan, West India merchant and founder of the West India Docks: Barratt, op. cit., ii, 92.

[2] See above, p. 37; and Barratt, op. cit., i, 98.

Barratt, op. cit., ii, 240, 270, records Henry Wright's residence, and selling
[3] up as a bankrupt. Further details of the failure of Wright & Co, bankers, of Henrietta Street, in December 1840, are given in another connection in DCW RCO 32, Abstract of Title of B. G. Woodd, 1857.

[4] DCW RCO 32, Abstract of Title of B. G. Woodd, 1857.

FIGURE 1 Belsize House in the mid-nineteenth century: last days

brandy merchant in New Bond Street, where he had been in business since before 1828.[1] It seems to have been Woodd who then took the house in hand and either rebuilt it entirely or greatly enlarged it so that it could well support the style and dignity of Hillfield House, the name which he gave it. For by 1857 its current value was put at £250 a year, and the freehold value of the whole little property was assessed at £18,000; even allowing for the fact that by this date the grounds and paddock had a building-land value, £500 an acre was reckoned a full building price for the locality at the time, so that the mansion and its coach-houses, stables, and outbuildings was being valued at something like £8,500, which gives a fair indication of what Woodd must have spent on his place.[2]

A similar development took place across the Hampstead road, almost opposite Hillfield House. Here the carve-up in 1808 gave Thomas Forsyth 45 acres of empty meadowland; at some date between then and 1851 the lease of this was bought by John Lund, who then built himself a mansion there called Haverstock Lodge, and turned 8 acres of the meadows into his pleasure grounds and park.[3] It is likely that Lund set up his seat here in the 1820s, since in 1828 he bought the adjoining 3 acres of copyhold land, at the smart residential price of £700 an acre, and threw them into the grounds of his Lodge; a large house was said to be 'now building' on the east side of Haverstock Hill in 1820, and most likely this was the Lodge.[4] There were no other substantial houses on the Belsize estate on this north-eastern side of Haverstock Hill; but a little further up from Haverstock Lodge towards Pond Street another large house, the Bartrams, was put up at about this period. The south-western side of the road was clearly the most favoured. Here, adjoining the Rosslyn House lands to the north, was George Todd's share of the 1808 division, bisected by the old Belsize Lane. North of the Lane there was an early-eighteenth-century house, standing in 16 acres of land. Todd demolished this, if it was not already in ruins, and by 1820 had

[1] *Pigot's Commercial Directory of London for 1828–29.*
[2] DCW RCO 32, H. A. Hunt's surveyor's report on the Hillfield estate, 4 April 1857.
[3] CC File 7142, Proposals for a building lease to W. T. B. Lund, 14 November 1851. No records of dealings with this estate between 1808 and 1851 have come to light.
[4] GLCRO E/MW/H/III/38/15, Case of Sir T. M. Wilson as to value of lands required for the Finchley New Road, November 1828; see also Tithe Apportionment, Hampstead, 1838. The large house building on the opposite side of Haverstock Hill is referred to in E/MW/H/III/38/17, Min. H. of C. Cttee on Hampstead Road Bill, evidence of Henry White, surveyor, 1 June 1820.

'built a magnificent mansion at a cost of upwards of £15,000'.[1] It was known, rather confusingly, as Belsize House, but was later renamed Belsize Court. Todd later sold off this half of his property and in 1841 it came into the hands of B. G. Woodd, the owner of Hillfield, who bought it as an investment: Matthew Forster, to whom Todd had leased the mansion in 1833 at £350 a year, was still the tenant in 1857, at the same rent.[2] On the other half of his land, the 14 acres between Belsize Lane and Belsize Avenue, some under-lessee from Todd built himself a fine new house, Ivy Bank; and in the angle formed by the sharp corner in Belsize Lane Todd provided the site for a large *cottage orné* in castellated gothic with little turrets, which has been variously known as Belsize Cottage, Belsize Lodge, Langwathby, and Hunters Lodge since it was built; this cottage, opposite Todd's new mansion, was built by another merchant, William Tate, 'at probably £3 or £4,000', some time before 1820.[3]

In many ways, however, the most interesting of all the sub-estates was the 38-acre piece taken by Edward Bliss, and lying between the southern boundary of the Chapter's estate on Englands Lane and the Abel-Woodd estate of Hillfield. When Bliss took this in 1808 it was a simple hay farm with two large meadows, and a small farmstead on the corner of Englands Lane and Haverstock Hill.[4] Of all the new owners Bliss was the real entrepreneur, intent on developing his property not for personal residential convenience or aggrandisement, but for whatever financial returns could be gained. Bliss, the son of a doctor, became a man of property, to whom his Belsize interests were a useful but not an essential addition. How he made his money remains a mystery; possibly it was in Anglo-Portuguese trade, or perhaps more plausibly in finance occasioning special services to the Portuguese court, for his heir received steps in the Portuguese nobility first as Baron de Bliss and then as Baron Barreto shortly after he died. Wherever it came from, there was certainly a lot of it. By the time he made his will in 1839 he had acquired Brandon Park in Suffolk and Northcomb Hall in Devon, each set in an estate of 1,000 acres or so, another country retreat in

[1] GLCRO E/MW/H/III/38/17, loc. cit.
[2] DCW RCO 32, Tenancy of Belsize House for a term of three years, B. G. Woodd to M. Forster, 25 July 1856; Agreement for Exchange, Dean and Chapter with B. G. Woodd, 23 June 1857. The high rental may imply that the house had been enlarged considerably by, or under, Todd.
[3] CC File 38689, Proposals for a Building Agreement with George Todd (junior), with map, 11 December 1867; GLCRO E/MW/H/III/38/17, evidence of Henry White, 1 June 1820.
[4] DCW 12451, Map of lands held by Edward Bliss, 1815.

Sussex, The Elms, without any estate attached to it, and a town house, Berkeley House, Hyde Park, in a fashionable aristocratic quarter. All this can hardly have come to him by marriage, since the second daughter of a country parson was scarcely a profitable match.[1] Moreover this may not have been the end of his land purchases, since he felt able to charge his freehold estates with a jointure of £1,400 for his prospective widow, and with annuities that totalled £935, and assumed that there would still be sufficient income left over to support his heir, his nephew Henry Aldridge (who took the name of Bliss on inheriting), in the style of a landed gentleman.[2] This was without bringing his leasehold estate at Belsize into the reckoning, and implied that his freeholds alone must have yielded something of the order of £4,000 a year at the very least.[3] His style of living is revealed by some of the annuities set up by his will; after the expected bequests to a string of nephews and nieces, he saw that his London hatter, his Suffolk wheelwright, his coachman, his gamekeeper, and a couple of his servants were provided for with annuities of £20 to £50 apiece. Altogether he emerges as a man of considerable means who had established himself as a member of the landed classes.

Bliss began development of his Belsize leasehold very soon after 1815, making his Haverstock Hill frontage available for a piecemeal and individualistic assortment of mansions, lodges, villas, and terraces, and leaving the remains of his two fields, some 24 acres in all, in the rear as back-land. In this back-land the Homefield ran up to Englands Lane which gave direct access; but in order to keep Pitfield in use either for pasture or as accommodation land he had to leave a way through to it from the high road, and this field access lane became in due time Belsize Grove. The Grove also served as a drive to Gilling Lodge, one of the

[1] Burke's *Landed Gentry* (1871 ed.), I, 114.
[2] DCW RCO 32, Abstract of Title of Devisees in Trust named in the Will of Edward Bliss made in 1839.
[3] If so, they must have been dissipated after his death in 1845, since in 1873 the estates of Baron Barreto were (exclusive of any freeholds in the metropolis):

	Acres	Annual Value (£s)
Devon (Northcomb Hall)	1,227	401
Suffolk (Brandon Park)	920	753
Sussex (The Elms)	1	116
Westmorland	625	98
	2,773	1,368

Source: *Return of Owners of Land, 1873*, Parl. Papers, 1874, LXXII.

more imposing houses to appear on the property, which was built on
the north side in 1826; in 1825 and 1826 a small stuccoed terrace in the
Grecian mode was built on the south side, and this, originally known
as Haverstock Villas, still survives as nos 26–38 Belsize Grove.[1] The rest
of the houses all fronted on Haverstock Hill, though some of them were
set well back and had long drives. The first went up in 1820 and 1821,
plain suburban villas, singly and in pairs and without any carriage
facilities, but nevertheless of a sufficiently superior type to have their
full rental values put at £100 for the cheapest and £160 for the most
expensive in 1872, rents which imply that they were suitable for pursy
gentlemen with incomes of over £1,000. Later in the 1820s some big
houses were built, with stables, coach-houses, large gardens, and names
calculated to impress in the pages of the directories. One of them,
Devonshire House, seems to have been built by Basil Woodd in 1826,
and was his first stepping-stone in Hampstead before moving on to
grander things at Highfield. By the end of the 1820s there were, besides
Devonshire House, running from Englands Lane northwards as far as
the present Howitt Road: Gifford Lodge, The Grange, Chestnut House,
Hillfield House, Haverstock Grange, Oak Lodge, Bedford Lodge, and
Bellaport House. Not all of these were as grand as their names; but
discarding the shams, there were still five of them with rents set at
£250 or more in 1872, a level which entitled the occupant to feel that
he was indeed living in a big house and was a person of consequence.
The area was virtually all parcelled out by 1826, only one or two villas
going up later, in the 1840s. When it was all covered there were thirty-
eight houses on the fourteen acres; and three of these acres lay empty
and inaccessible at the back of the houses, let as market garden ground
to a nurseryman. The development, though spacious, was therefore at
recognisably urban density, and even the best of the big houses had
scarcely more than an acre of grounds to stand in. Nevertheless there
was stabling for all, in their own grounds for the larger houses and
tucked away separately at the back for the terraces and lesser villas, and
it was definitely a colony of carriage-folk, less affluent no doubt than
their neighbours on the Belsize mini-estates but still persons of quality,
who had settled in Bliss territory.

[1] These and the other Bliss houses can be identified only from later documents:
CC File 42263, Particulars of Baron Barreto's estate, February 1872; and
Schedule of Baron Barreto's estate, 2 October 1890. Both of these documents
tabulate the separate houses and plots, the terms of their under-leases, names
of the under-lessees, and the rents payable to Barreto, and the second includes
a large-scale map. The dating of the buildings depends on assumptions regarding the under-leases, which are discussed below.

This high-quality islet, this advance guard of the wealthy bourgeoisie, was of immense benefit to the Dean and Chapter when Belsize
came to be opened to large-scale organised building development in
the 1850s, for it contained visible evidence of the class of people who
wished to live in the district. It is, however, extremely doubtful if the
Dean and Chapter ever appreciated the magnetic services rendered to
them by Bliss, for once they noticed that the development had occurred
they treated it as nothing but a headache. It was a trouble to the authorities because it had taken place on land held on a lease for lives, and this
came to seem administratively untidy and financially irregular once it
was established as received doctrine that all building should occur under
99-year leases held direct from the Dean and Chapter. The irregularity
was put into isolation in 1854, when on the occasion of the insertion of a
new life the old Bliss lease was split into two and the renewal was conceded only for the undeveloped 24 acres, the developed section being
left in a kind of limbo to be ignored while it struggled on, subsisting on
those lives which were already there without benefit of any further ac-
cessions of new blood into the lease.[1] But it could not be ignored for
ever, and the headache over ownership was removed only in the 1890s,
by the Ecclesiastical Commissioners buying out Barreto's interest and
agreeing to honour the unexpired terms of his under-leases.[2] It was
not until 1854 that the Dean and Chapter woke up to the implications
of their complete ignorance, both official and practical, of the kind of
development which Bliss had been contriving since 1820, and took
steps to put matters right for the future by requiring Henry Bliss to
inform them at ten-yearly intervals of the number and location of all
new-built messuages upon the 24-acre piece. But this was bolting the
stable door after the horse had fled, for the 24 acres was all back-land
which could not be developed without some essential preliminaries such
as the making of new roads, and in practice no new building took place
on this land before it became the subject of a regular building agreement, not with Bliss, in 1864.

The Dean and Chapter, indeed, did not receive their first detailed
and accurate information about the older Bliss doings until 1872, and
it is only from this document and an even later schedule of the properties prepared in 1890 that any impression can be gained of Bliss's
way of setting about exploiting his estate. To begin with, he was not at

[1] CC File 30177, Lease to Henry Bliss on two lives only (Octavius Greene and
the Prince of Wales) of such parts of Pitfield and Homefield as are not built
upon, 12 July 1854.
[2] CC File 42263, Cluttons to A. de Bock Porter, Secretary to the Eccles. Comm.,
13 March 1891, reporting agreement to buy out Baron Barreto.

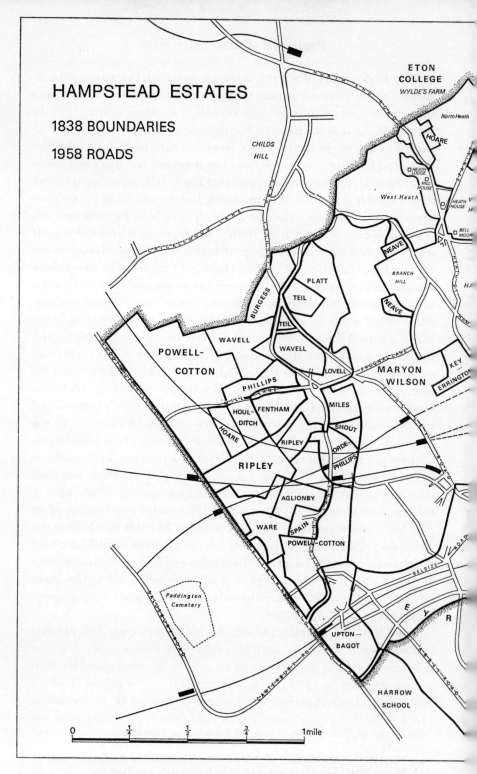

HAMPSTEAD ESTATES

1838 BOUNDARIES

1958 ROADS

ETON COLLEGE
WYLDE'S FARM

North Heath

HOARE

CHILDS HILL

HEATH LODGE
HILL HOUSE

HEATH HOUSE

West Heath

BELL MOOR

NEAVE

BRANCH HILL

NEAVE

PLATT

TEIL

BURGESS

TEIL

WAVELL

WAVELL

POWELL-COTTON

LOVELL

MARYON WILSON

KEY

ERRINGTON

PHILLIPS

MILES

HOUL-DITCH

FENTHAM

HOARE

SHOUT

RIPLEY

ORDE

RIPLEY

PHILLIPS

AGLIONBY

WARE

SPAIN

POWELL-COTTON

BELSIZE

E Y R E

Paddington Cemetery

UPTON—BAGOT

HARROW SCHOOL

0   ¼   ½   ¾   1mile

MAP 4 Hampstead estates: 1838 boundaries, 1958 roads

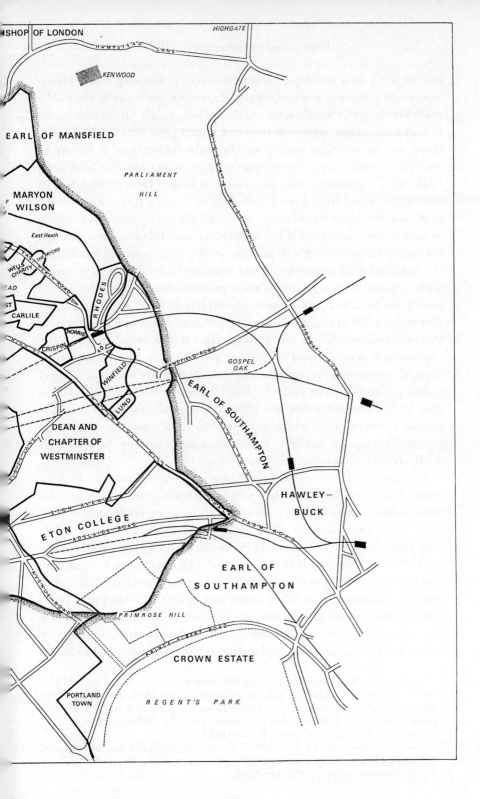

any expense as a developer in such matters as forming roads, laying sewers, or providing a water supply. He simply made use of the public road, Haverstock Hill, for access to the houses, or left his under-tenants to make what they pleased of the track which grew into Belsize Grove; there was no drainage system for the little district, and it was up to each householder to arrange his water supply as best he could by sinking wells or by negotiating with the tenant of Belsize House which had its own supply piped from a pond at the foot of Rosslyn Hill. All he needed to do as a developer was to make sites available to any who were willing to take under-leases from a life-leaseholder, and this was done through his Bedford Row solicitor who possibly acted as estate agent in publicising the availability of sites to let. These building under-leases were apparently granted for a term of 99 years provided the lives in Bliss's head lease from the Dean and Chapter should live so long; with a provision that when a life in the head lease dropped, and a new one was inserted, the under-tenant would pay Bliss a renewal fine equal to twice the current rack rent value of the property.[1] This way Bliss could recoup from his under-tenants the whole of the renewal fine which he himself had to pay to the Dean and Chapter; by shifting the burden the price paid by the under-tenants was effectively a good deal more than the annual reserved rents which they paid to Bliss, and these rents represented pure profit for Bliss, for he then had virtually no outgoings at all save for an occasional solicitor's fee.

It is nowhere directly stated that these under-leases were for 99-year terms. But when they first surface in the ground landlord's records the peculiar terms which were then stated to be unexpired, such as '$60\frac{1}{2}$ years from 25 December 1858', '$62\frac{1}{4}$ years from 25 March 1858', '$66\frac{3}{4}$ years from 25 December 1859', or '$61\frac{1}{2}$ years from 25 December 1858', strongly suggest that this was so.[2] The alternative is to assume that this rum collection of terms in fact records the original full run of years in a number of building leases first granted in 1858 and 1859. A mad hatter wanting to introduce some variety into the drabness of a lease-drafting office might perhaps have dreamt up such bizarre multiples, but the simplest explanation is that the leases had to be re-

---

[1] The payment of the renewal fines by the under-tenants, on the basis of two years' full annual value, is not documented before 1884; but the context indicates that this had been the practice since the particular under-lease had been granted, in Edward Bliss's lifetime: CC File 42263, Grane & Son, solicitors, to the Eccles. Comm., 9 May 1884.

[2] These examples from CC File 42263, Particulars of Baron Barreto's estate, February 1872, are repeated in precisely the same terms in the Schedule of Baron Barreto's estate, 2 October 1890.

issued in 1858 and 1859 because this was the earliest they could be re-drawn after the last insertion of a new life into Bliss's head lease, and that whatever portion of an initial 99-year term was then unexpired was written into the re-issues. The actual houses in the case did not exist when Park's map of Hampstead was surveyed in 1813, but were clearly shown on Greenwood's map of London in 1827, so that the cartographical evidence supports the interpretation of the documentary evidence that takes the granting of the building leases back into the 1820s.

Bliss did not build any of the houses himself, not being inclined to become one of the resident Belsize gentry. This was made clear when his heir, Baron Barreto, was pestering the Ecclesiastical Commissioners in the 1870s over the distressing consequences of their refusal to insert any more new lives into his lease. As he wrote in 1870:[1]

> The leases have been renewed from time to time for one hundred years and more, and upon the assurance of the good faith that the Dean and Chapter would so continue to renew their lease a great many persons were induced to expend all the money they had for years saved, in building houses upon this land, and if not again renewed many families will be utterly ruined, and therefore the Lessee hopes that the Ecclesiastical Commissioners will take their case into their consideration that the property may be enfranchised to the Lessee in order that he may be allowed to arrange with his respective under-tenants for a continuation of their leases to prevent their ultimately losing the money so expended by them, which will be the case unless the present Lease be renewed or enfranchised.

He made the same point again in 1875, dwelling with even more eloquence on the imminent ruin of innocent and deserving families:[2]

> It is a very distressing case for the lessees who have built upon these lands under the supposition that as the Church had renewed the Leases for Lives for hundreds of previous years, that they would always continue to do the same, and therefore depending that such good faith would be hereafter preserved induced many families to expend the chief part of their fortune in building upon these lands, intending to leave to their children hereafter a property in perpetuity, whereas now in the present state of

1 Ibid., Baron Barreto, Berkeley House, Hyde Park, to the Eccles. Comm., 31 January 1870.
2 Ibid., same to same, 7 May 1875.

affairs the good faith is being broken, and these families will at the expiration of the Lease for these lives become deprived of all their sunken Fortunes.

It was of course natural that Barreto should attempt to put his case as strongly as he could by trying to excite sympathy for the plight of hapless householders suddenly faced with the prospect of the value of their property entirely vanishing. By 1870, however, these house-owners had already, most of them, enjoyed the fruits of their initial investments for forty years and more; their under-leases depended ultimately on the lives of the Prince of Wales and Prince Arthur, Duke of Connaught.[1] Though of course they were not to know it in 1870, the longer-lived of these royal princes, the Duke of Connaught, did not die until 1917, so that as it turned out they did have the same period of tenure as 99-year lessees all but a few years; though as the princes grew older the suspense of not knowing how much longer they might live would undoubtedly have rendered their houses unmarketable from about 1900 onwards. Though by the same token, if they had initially held cast-iron 99-year leases they would not, by that time, have been able to secure much of a price for the short unexpired terms of 20 years or less. The actual investors, therefore, were not all that hardly done by. Moreover, though they did not know exactly where they stood in regard to security or permanency of tenure when they began, they did know that they were embarking on building under a rather strange tenure and a sharp ground landlord, and many of them embarked on their ventures as pure speculations rather than for their own personal shelter.

The ground rents charged by Bliss were ample, though not extortionate. When the ten or eleven acres had all been taken up, Bliss's income came to nearly £700 a year from the ground rents, plus some £90 a year for the buildings and about four acres of land let on a succession of short leases to a market gardener. A ground rent of between £60 and £70 an acre was on the high side, for building land where the ground landlord undertook no expense for roads and sewers, even in the 1850s and 1860s, and must have been all the higher when it was fixed in the 1820s for what was then a venture into unknown territory of as yet unproven values. It is of course quite possible that Bliss used a common developer's device for stimulating similar pioneering ventures, and granted under-leases where the ground rents were purely nominal for the first few years, the full agreed liability starting only when the houses had been up, and occupied, for a few years. Even so, the rates of

[1] The lives in Barreto's lease, named by him: ibid., 31 January 1870.

ground rent in which Bliss dealt ran very close to the maximum which prudent ground landlords considered advisable, which was one-sixth of the full annual value of the houses: in 1872 Barreto, making the most optimistic valuation he dared of the possible rack rental of the properties in order to boost his claim to the reversion of the houses when the under-leases should finally fall in, put the total at £4,426 a year, and some of the occupiers thought his figures were very rosy.[1] Still, some of the big houses were under-let in their turn by their builders, on medium-length tenancies for periods such as fifty years, at perfectly genuine rents of £250 and £230; such tenancies no doubt provided scope for the construction of several more layers of subletting before one could be certain of reaching the actual occupying tenant. For example, in 1855 a Henry Brown was living at Gilling Lodge, but its owner was George Grane; Charles Adams lived at Haverstock Grange owned by George Wood; and Farrow owned Chestnut House which was occupied by John Rawe. On the other hand John Maples was then the owner-occupier of Bedford Lodge, which he had acquired from George Grane.[2] It looks as if most of the big houses were originally built for personal occupation, while the terrace in Belsize Grove and a couple of smaller groups on Haverstock Hill were the work of speculative builders. The largest speculator who took a lease from Bliss, however, was George Grane of Cheltenham, who as well as being responsible for the Belsize Grove terrace seems to have entered the mansion market by running up Bedford Lodge, Oak Lodge, and Gilling Lodge at the same time.

It is somewhat surprising that the Bliss example of the successful introduction of a superior and elegant style of building and a group of select carriage-folk to Haverstock Hill was not followed, or indeed preceded, by something similar on the Eton College estate of Chalcots which lay immediately to the south of Englands Lane. William Driver had suggested the possibility when he reported on the estate to the College in 1796, remarking that:[3]

a considerable part of this Estate is very eligibly situate for build-ing, being within 3 miles of London and adjoining the Turnpike Road for a considerable extent, and provided sufficient encourage-

[1] Ibid., Particulars . . . February 1872. One under-lessee estimated the annual value of one of his houses at £160, whereas Barreto had put it at £260: Grane & Son, solicitors, to the Eccles. Comm., 9 May 1884.
[2] P.O. London Directory, 1855, sub Haverstock Hill.
[3] Eton, College Records, XLIX, No. 19, Survey and Valuation by Abraham and William Driver, 1796.

[107]

ment could be given to the tenant with respect to the length of the term, which should be 61 years and a fine upon renewal estimated upon the land only, we have no doubt it might be easily accomplished, in which case the land contiguous would be considerably increased in value, and of course the College would ultimately derive great advantage probably doubling the present Fines.

Nothing came of this, because Eton's indifference towards the management of its estate was at least equal to the Dean and Chapter's towards theirs, amounting to sloth tempered by some liveliness in anticipation of the goodies which the seven-yearly renewal fine brought to the Fellows; and Eton's lessees, Giles Earle and after him Thomas Clarke of Russell Square and St Leonards, Earle's solicitor, were equally unenterprising, being content to leave the farm entirely to Thomas Rhodes the under-tenant. In 1796 there were three houses and a cottage on the farm, used as five separate dwellings; in 1811 there were six dwellings, and in 1832 nine, so that there was virtually no development.

Apart from the old farmhouses of Upper Chalcots at the end of Englands Lane, and Lower Chalcots across the lane and the parish boundary from the Chalk Farm Tavern, and Steele's Cottage, the houses such as they were seem to have been flimsy affairs, little more than summer-houses. When estimating the rack rent value of the estate in 1832 in order to fix the renewal fine the College's surveyor, John Shaw, tried to blow up the houses into something considerable: 'there being nine in number of one sort or other, and some of them very substantial and respectable', Shaw thought that for their rack rents 'I presume to think about £400 per annum may be obtained'.[1] Clarke scoffed at this suggestion, holding that the houses were insignificant in appearance and as sources of rent. He wrote to the Provost:[2]

> I beg to observe that the buildings are of little value, but have been occupied by Tradesmen who have been induced to render them pretty *Villakins* as the late Mr Earle used to call them, but the retirement and the scenery which were the chief beauties are now to be destroyed by your Building plans and by the Railroad, and if the land should be taken away it could not be worth while to continue to hold these buildings.

[1] Ibid., No. 43, John Shaw to George Bethell, Provost of Eton, 14 March 1832.
[2] Ibid., No. 42, Thomas Clarke to George Bethell, 7 March 1832.

Clarke was so incensed by Shaw's talk of respectable and substantial houses that he obtained a full description from the tenant farmer Rhodes, and forwarded it to the Provost. Rhodes reported that:[1]

> The houses are, the two original farmhouses ['a third built by Mr Adam I think', Shaw pencilled] and Steele's Cottage [two distinct houses], a cottage which I built of two rooms and a lean-to, a house built by Mr Lloyd now occupied by Mrs Godsman whose husband built a two-roomed cottage and has formed a room in a shed where some person lives [this is now a common labourer's cottage]. [Total 9 distinct residences] . . . I have never received £300 a year for them including 19a. 3r. 35p. of land [on which the houses stand].

The argument was perhaps drawn. There were nine residences of a sort. The tenant farmer did receive rents for them. But at an average rent of little more than £30 apiece they could only by the wildest stretch of the imagination be called substantial and respectable. Shaw's fanciful idea of the qualifications required for this dignity may be gauged from the fact that he graced a cottage on Haverstock Hill with a rent of £13 a year with the style of Eton Lodge, and when it fell into ruin he regarded the undertaking of its owner-occupier, a cowkeeper called Richard Pritchard, to spend £300 in erecting a new cottage as being a proposal 'to erect a substantial building'.[2] In all this John Shaw might be doing the best he could for his employers' interests, but no special pleading could make this 'lodge' on Haverstock Hill and the few huts on the south side of Englands Lane into anything remotely in the same class as the Bliss developments of the 1820s. For Chalcots the consequences of Bliss were not to produce a similar kind of big-house colonisation, but to encourage a direct move from farm to building estate in a single step in the 1830s, which raised the tone from the petty shopkeeper and cowkeeper level to something decidedly more middle-class.

If Chalcots was a case of an estate on which there were no precursors of the building-estate stage, no preparations beyond a passive waiting for the impact of events on neighbouring properties, its neighbour to the west, St John's Wood Farm, was an illustration of the exact opposite in the way of active estate management. The St John's Wood and Chalcots estates were professionally advised by a form of

[1] Ibid., No. 50, same to same, 3 May 1832.
[2] Ibid., No. 62, John Shaw to George Bethell, 1 January 1833; No. 63, Agreement between John Shaw and Richard Pritchard, cowkeeper, 30 March 1833.

family agency. The John Shaws father and son acted severally as surveyors to the two estates, and their periods of service overlapped from 1825 onwards. As the son consulted his father from time to time on the best course of action which he should recommend Eton to follow, and as the father was intimately concerned in the whole opening-up of St John's Wood to villadom, it is unlikely that responsibility for the contrast in the vitality of estate policy can be laid at the doors of the agents.[1] By the same token, if in the one instance the absence of any policy was due to the landowner, Eton College, it follows that in the other it was also the landowner who was the main source of energetic initiatives in estate development. In the dealings which affected the Hampstead part of his property Henry Samuel Eyre, backed by his solicitor brother Walpole, is certainly revealed as an active man of business who was personally engaged in planning and scheming and fighting for the fullest exploitation of his estate, impatient to become a wholly urban or suburban landowner as quickly as possible and anxious to help this process along, within the limits imposed by his vision of creating an attractive, gracious, and prosperous district.

The part of St John's Wood Farm which lay in Hampstead was never eligible for the intermediate or semi-rural stage of development into mansion grounds, since it was entirely inaccessible except by footpaths and a special private bridleway which Spencer Perceval had been permitted to tread out when riding from Belsize House to Westminster across the Eyre fields to Baker Street. Without a public road at hand, whether a turnpike or simply an ancient lane, no gentleman had ever been likely to seek to seat himself anywhere in these fields, which were in any case rather low-lying and unattractive. But once Eyre had begun to lay out his own private roads further south, springing from Park Road and Lisson Grove, to provide himself with his first building frontages, he determined to secure the future development of his entire estate by running a public turnpike road through its middle. Not only was this cheaper, from his point of view, than relying exclusively on privately made roads, but it was also far more effective in promoting the whole development since a true thoroughfare served as much more than a convenient spine for residential communications: it was an artery which carried prestige to the district and brought extra value to the riparian lands. This was the origin of the Finchley Road,

[1] John Shaw, junior, seems to have been appointed surveyor for Chalcots immediately after making a rough survey of its potential in 1825: ibid., No. 22. Consultation with his father is reported for example in ibid., No. 28, John Shaw (junior) to George Bethell, 2 August 1831, and in several later letters.

one of the few major new roads in north London produced in the last, intensive, phase of carriage travel before railways rendered such things outmoded. Nothing comparable was seen again in north London until motor transport called forth the North Circular and the Barnet Bypass section of the old Great North Road in the 1930s.

Other new main roads were built in the 1820s by the Metropolitan Turnpike Commission, under which all the metropolitan turnpike trusts north of the river were consolidated; these included the Caledonian Road, and the new road linking Camden Town to 'a clump of trees called the Seven Sisters near Tottenham', both of considerable importance, but neither equalling the Finchley New Road in length, cost, or permanent usefulness. The Finchley New Road, though not built until the end of the 1820s, was the last major venture to be undertaken by an individual turnpike trust; it escaped the Metropolitan Commissioners because it had been promoted initially in 1819, while the Commission was not formed until 1826.[1] The Finchley Road would certainly never have been built as a public road under statutory turnpike powers unless it had been possible to make out a plausible argument claiming that such a road was needed by the general travelling public and would be of public utility. This indeed could be done, in terms of showing that the distance between Finchley and the West End would be cut by $1\frac{1}{2}$ miles by a road from St John's Chapel to the ancient Ballards Lane and thence to its junction with the North Road (the future Tally Ho Corner), when compared with the usual route from Westminster to the Bank, and thence up the North Road. The shorter distance, moreover, was strongly buttressed by the claim that the proposed new route would avoid the sharp gradients of Highgate Hill and substitute a much gentler rise and lower summit level, a telling point with coach and carriage owners and even more with the waggon men, who sometimes took the best part of a whole day negotiating Highgate Hill with a heavy load. All this was quite true, and after it had been built there is no doubt that at least from the later nineteenth century the public found the Finchley New Road a great convenience. At the time, however, there was very little traffic originating in Finchley itself. Before the road was built there was only one short-stage coach, making one daily journey, between Finchley and the Bank; when the new road had been open for nearly ten years this short-stage had been joined by a single omnibus, and its route via Charing Cross to the Bank suggests that it made use of the Finchley

---

[1] This explains the 'remarkable' jurisdictional situation of the Finchley New Road noted by T. C. Barker, op. cit., p. 13.

Road; but in 1856, when the new road had been available for nearly thirty years, there was still only enough local traffic to support this solitary omnibus.[1] As for the through traffic passing through Finchley on its way north, the stage coaches and waggons alike all ran from the City and collected the bulk of their traffic there; for them the new road meant weighing the saving to their horses of a heavy drag up through Highgate against the extra distance involved. In the short time when the alternative routes were available before railway competition began to kill off this long-distance road traffic it was not possible to tell in which way the traffic flow was adjusting itself. But it was at least clear that the anonymous 'man at Archway' who had gloomily forecast 'that Archway would lose £1,000 a year by the new road' in lost tolls, had been very wide of the mark.[2] Private carriage traffic from the north, however, may well have switched at once to the new road, since most of it was headed for the aristocratic town houses of the West End.

It was thus rather doubtful whether either the existing traffic or the potential traffic justified the construction of the new turnpike. But the arguments of public interest were sufficiently credible to lend the necessary colouring to Eyre's schemes and enable him to get his way; though only at the fourth time of asking, which shows that the benefits to the public were not overwhelmingly self-evident. The advantages to Colonel Eyre and one or two other Marylebone landowners, by contrast, were glaringly obvious. The disadvantages to the Maryon Wilsons of Hampstead, though not immediately so apparent, were keenly felt by the Sir Thomases father and son, and they resisted all the projects proposed by the ingenious and dogged colonel, strenuously and successfully in 1820, 1824, and 1825, but to no avail in 1826, when the colonel's political manoeuvring at last pushed an Act to establish the new turnpike through Parliament. The Wilson case, that he was defending the beauties, the privacy, and the exclusiveness of Hampstead against an unwarranted, noisy, and altogether intolerable intrusion, was rather overdone. It also casts a curious light on the same Sir Thomas Maryon Wilson who was so soon to become, and remain until his death in 1869, Hampstead's favourite enemy, accused of plotting almost unimaginable despoliation and desecration of Hampstead's beauties.[3] But it is not difficult to credit the burden of the Wilson argument, that Eyre and his associates were trying to feather their own

[1] T. C. Barker, op. cit., App. 1, p. 391 (short-stage routes in 1825), App. 2, p. 397 (omnibuses and short-stages in 1838–9), and App. 3, p. 412 (omnibuses acquired by LGOC in 1856).
[2] GLCRO E/MW/H/III/38/15, Memo. on Finchley Road Bill, 1824.
[3] See below, ch. 4.

nests by getting the travelling public at large to pay for the basic needs of their private building schemes. Eyre after all practically said as much when he first mooted his road plan, and it was perfectly normal for men of position to make use of the legislative process for purposes of private profit. The abnormal feature was that Eyre miscalculated in supposing that Wilson too would see the scheme as one which would promote his own private profit and would be keen to participate.

Colonel Eyre began in December 1819 with a proposal for a number of purely local roads designed to open up his estate and others in Hampstead, and to provide a road system for the parish's future internal needs rather than for any through traffic. The new Artillery Barracks alongside the St John's Wood Farmhouse was the centre of this scheme. Here a major road junction was planned, reached by a westerly road from the Yorkshire Stingo on the New Road (Marylebone Road) by way of Lisson Grove and the old lane to the St John's Wood Farm (Grove End Road), and by an easterly road from the St John's Chapel (Wellington Road). From the Barracks one road went north-west to Kilburn, meeting the Edgware road at the West End Lane junction, and another went north-east to meet Belsize Lane, roughly on the site of the later Swiss Cottage. Here another junction was to be formed, with a link road straight across to Kilburn, and a branch road direct to Hampstead Town (with the function, though not the precise alignment, of the later Fitzjohn's Avenue). The attractions of this scheme for the public were also put in purely local terms, that $1\frac{1}{2}$ miles would be saved on the journey from the Yorkshire Stingo to Church Row, and that the drag up Haverstock Hill would be avoided.[1] This scheme produced such a violent reaction that within ten days of launching it the Colonel's solicitor, his brother Walpole, wrote to Sir Thomas Maryon Wilson's solicitor: 'On 3rd December I left a Plan with you of several proposed new roads. I find there is likely to be so much opposition that I have abandoned them all except the road from the Yorkshire Stingo to the north-east end of Belsize Lane.'[2] He went on to point out the effects this road would have in creating building values: 'This road which I propose making will make an excellent communication from Sir Thomas Maryon Wilson's property to this part of Town, and will be of infinite benefit to his property.' At the same time he approached Sir Thomas himself, informing him that:[3]

[1] DCW Map 12538, Proposed Turnpike Roads in Marylebone and Hampstead, n.d. (refers to scheme of 1819–20).
[2] GLCRO E/MW/H/III/38/15, Walpole Eyre to John Stride, 13 December 1819.
[3] Ibid., Walpole Eyre to Sir T. M. Wilson, 6 December 1819.

My brother Colonel Eyre proposes to make a Turnpike Road from the New Road in St Marylebone opposite the Yorkshire Stingo, to the north-east end of Belsize Lane—he will need to obtain an Act, and before application to the House of Commons he must apply to the owners and occupiers of lands it is intended to cross, for their assent or dissent. This road will pass along a lane or occupation road which leads from my brother's estate to Belsize Lane . . . if this road is made, in my opinion it will considerably benefit your property and will be of great convenience to the public, and will make a ready access to Hampstead from the west and north-west parts of the Metropolis. When poor Mr Perceval lived at Belsize House he applied for and had permission to ride to Town along the very line of road my brother now proposes to make. I mention this circumstance to point out to you the convenience this road will offer . . . It is a long time since you and I met—my brother informs me he saw you at Cheltenham in the summer . . .

The opposition, however, was even stronger and better organised than Eyre had expected, and it defeated his whittled-down proposal for the single Yorkshire Stingo–Belsize Lane road at the private bill committee stage in the House of Commons. Sir Thomas Maryon Wilson marshalled his objections under four headings. First, the road would damage his Manor Farm, which used Belsize Lane as one of its access roads. This farm had been rather neglected, but had just been let to a new tenant, William Baker, from Michaelmas 1819 on a 14-year lease at the high rent of £5 an acre, and Baker had spent a lot of money in putting up new fences. Already, though 'there is no public way which would attract the Inhabitants of the Metropolis to the neighbourhood, he [Baker] and his servants are obliged to be on the alert to prevent persons breaking over the hedges and fences and trespassing on the lands and treading down his crops.' A public road would expose the farm 'to the depradatory practices of dishonest people, both as to cattle and as to fences, and also as facilitating great and serious annoyances trespasses and injuries which are likely to be committed by idle and disorderly persons of both sexes whom such intended Road might induce to that quarter.' Second, Sir Thomas's tenant farmer, other tenants on his demesne lands in Hampstead, the copyholders, and the inhabitants of Hampstead generally, would find their highway rates increased, for the repair of a road none of them wanted. Third, the Bill contained powers for the new road trustees to take road-building materials from the Heath, to which Sir Thomas objected most strongly, because he argued that he ought to be paid for all sand and ballast removed from the Heath, and because there was in any case, by his account, a shortage of materials so that the parish surveyor of highways could not always find enough for the repair of the parish roads. Finally, the road would ruin Hampstead's special charm, on which the value of his lands depended:[1]

> Hampstead is a very eligible situation from its nearness to the Metropolis. It has enough publicity at present. It is desirable, in order to meet the taste and choice of the Residents there for privacy, not to put in practice any measure to make it more public. The Gentlemen there who fill official situations, or are in professions, or are Merchants of the first rank in the Metropolis, wish to preserve about their Dwellings the quiet and privacy which the Country should secure for their refreshment and necessary retirement from active duties and pursuits daily prosecuted in the Metropolis. This quiet and privacy will be disturbed and diminished if, by a new Road, as designed, the idle, or pleasurable (not to say the vicious) members of any portion of the Metropolis are to be drawn to Hampstead for objects of pleasure or crime. The advantage of more direct communication with Hampstead is urged by the Projectors of the road, as a reason for its being formed. It is far over balanced by the multiplied disadvantages which we show will flow from it. And to give due effect to the remarks lastly advanced, it is to be observed that the proposed Road will run just the distance that persons would stroll, in order to get to an elevated situation.

Not content to rest on his own objections alone, Sir Thomas took care to marshal the complaints of the top-rank officials, lawyers, and merchants of Belsize Lane as well, to speak up in defence of their cherished privacy. As Sir Thomas's solicitor pointed out, 'the Dean and Chapter of Westminster are also opposing the Bill; but their tenants, who are Gentlemen and Merchants of the first respectability, are more strenuously opposing it, as their privacy will be destroyed, and the value of their interests be greatly reduced.'[2] These gentry accordingly presented their own petition against the bill, stating that they were 'lessees for lives or subtenants of different mansions and premises

---

[1] GLCRO E/MW/H/III/38/17, Petition of Sir T. M. Wilson against the Bill for a new road to north-east end of Belsize Lane, May 1820; Statement of Grounds of opposition of Sir T. M. Wilson to the Road Bill, prepared by Stride and Lyddon, solicitors, May 1820.

[2] Ibid., Stride and Lyddon to Bilton Jolliffe, MP, 2 June 1820.

in the Manor of Belsize, on which they have expended very large sums of money, and their properties are of great value particularly from the seclusion and privacy they enjoy, equal if not superior to any Country Seats within the same distance from the Metropolis.' They went on to deny that the proposed road would be of any public benefit, and claimed that 'the only person who will derive any benefit is its promoter, H. S. Eyre, esq., who has proposed himself to be at the entire expense of making the road under the direction of the Trustees to be appointed by himself, without the said road being of any public utility whatsoever.' Belsize Lane, they said, was a mere cartway at its south-western end, used by William Everett, the tenant of Belsize House. While the part of the lane nearest the High Road 'is the only road to the mansion house of petitioner George Todd and to the new-built house occupied by petitioner William Tate, and the coach-houses and gardens occupied by the several other petitioners. The lane is not used in any other manner or for any other purpose save by the carts passing through the first 10 chains . . . and is totally unfit to be made a public highway.' In fact, it could not be improved to turnpike standard 'without pulling down part of their houses and outbuildings.' Repeating that 'the sole object of the projector is to make a public access to Hampstead from his own land . . . so as to make it fit for buildings', they ended by a clear statement of the high value of inadequate communications, an application at the highly local level of a theme which governed much of Hampstead's wider status and desirability: 'the seclusion and privacy' of their valuable properties, they stated, 'is now effectually protected by the narrowness and inconvenience of Belsize Lane, and by the use thereof being restricted and confined as before mentioned. Indeed were the said Lane to be made a public Turnpike Road, the houses of many of your petitioners would become of little or no value.' The lane was only fifteen feet wide between the hedges, and Todd's coachman admitted that he could not pass haycarts which he met coming from Manor Farm fields from time to time, but there could be no clearer illustration of the very high value which could be attached to keeping a really bad bit of road.[1]

[1] Ibid., Petition of Belsize Lane owners and residents against the Bill, May 1820. The petitioners were: Thomas Roberts of Belsize; William Everett of Belsize House; George Todd of Belsize Court; William Tate of Belsize Lane (Hunters Lodge); Richard Power, Josiah Messer and Charles Beazley, who occupied a row of three new houses on Rosslyn Hill with gardens and coach-houses in Belsize Lane; and George Harvey of Lawrence Lane in the City, who had purchased the head lease of Belsize House from James Abel. See above, p. 95.

London going out of Town — or — *The March of Bricks & Mortar!*

PLATE 4 *London Going Out of Town* by George Cruikshank, 1829. A comment on Sir Thomas Maryon Wilson's 1829 Estate Bill in particular, as on the march of bricks and mortar in general: the signpost, top right, reads 'Hampstead' and the adjoining caption: 'Our fences I fear will be found to be no defence against these Barbarians, who threaten to enclose & destroy us in all "manor" of ways. Detachments are on the Road already' (see pp. 145 and 296)

PLATE 5 Happy Hampstead in 1856; the People's Holiday on the Heath (see pp. 154 and 169)

These forces, aided by one or two of his friends in the Commons whom Sir Thomas asked to attend the hearings to support his case, were enough to see the bill lost in committee. Sir Thomas, besides briefing counsel to attend the private bill committee at fifty guineas, and finding his own solicitors' fees, was also at the expense of bringing up a couple of Hampstead auctioneers and surveyors as witnesses. Naturally enough they confirmed the views advanced in the petitions. But in the course of showing that there was no need for the road they cast an interesting sidelight on Hampstead's commuting habits in 1820. The most explicit witness declared:[1]

> Not one in twenty of the Gentlemen in Hampstead would have any occasion for professional pursuits or objects of business to go along the proposed road; their business or concerns lie in the City or about the Inns of Court, and not westwards of Tottenham Court Road . . . The tradesmen of Hampstead of every description draw their goods and commodities from those parts of the Metropolis which the present roads to Hampstead are most convenient for them to be drawn by. . . . Some few of the families resident in Hampstead do occasionally in the season go to Brighton or other places next the sea, but would not pass along the proposed road.

The point perhaps was too true, and made too forcibly, for Sir Thomas's best interests. For if the Hampstead gentry were mainly lawyers and merchants who wished to get to and from Holborn and the City and had no call for an easy route to the West End; and if on top of this the wealthy and influential residents of Belsize Lane had rooted objections to having the lane improved; then the obvious course for Colonel Eyre was to jettison the Belsize Lane scheme and go for a quite different alignment for the northerly passage of any new road after it left his estate. When he did this, aiming now for a connection with Finchley rather than Hampstead, Sir Thomas was naturally deprived of his powerful Hampstead–Belsize allies who were no longer threatened, and became much more exposed in the fight against road schemes, any and all of which he regarded as pernicious.

When Colonel Eyre returned to the attack in 1824 with a road bill proposing substantially the same line as the eventual Finchley Road his opponent was the younger Sir Thomas Maryon Wilson, who had succeeded his father in 1821. Colonel Eyre himself also no longer appeared

[1] Ibid., Resumé of evidence to be given on the Road Bill, May 1820; evidence of George Paxon of Hampstead, auctioneer.

as the individual promoter of the bill, the earlier experience having taught him the political wisdom of staying in the background as the power behind the scenes, leaving the apparent conduct of the affair to confederates and front men. Nevertheless the Wilson son, taking on his father's cause with a will, was not far wrong in his surmise that 'if the present [1824] Bill has not originated with Colonel Eyre, yet he is a supporter of it', adding that Mr Portman who was just beginning to develop his land north of the Marylebone Road, which ran with Eyre's estate, was also closely associated with the promotion.[1] The chief financial backers of the road were, indeed, Colonel Eyre, Edward Berkeley Portman, and Augustus Hoffmann who owned land in Hendon parish near Golders Green, which it was intended to cross.[2] There was just as good ground in 1824 as in 1820 for the suspicion that the measure was one of private profit more than of public good, and the young Sir Thomas minced no more words than his father had done in saying so. It was, he said, merely designed to advantage Colonel Eyre and Berkeley Portman in their building schemes; they were quite welcome to build as much as they pleased, but ought to keep themselves to themselves. 'Let each individual scheme and execute plans on his own land', said Sir Thomas, 'but not seek to change the condition of the land of the next proprietor.' He urged them to follow the example of their neighbour Colonel Howard, and obey the rules of the private property game like gentlemen. Howard 'has without the aid of Parliament made a new road [Greville Place] on part of his land to create building frontage, and has many buildings erected thereon. The same mode is open to Colonel Eyre and Mr Portman to follow.' He capped this advice with a homily on the iniquities of using a specious plea of public good as a cloak for private interests:[3]

> It may be admitted that every Road may to some persons and under mere local circumstances, afford some particular, and as to a few persons, great advantage and convenience; at the same time the community may derive no advantage from it. The public good, or the public convenience, is often held out as a lure to the minds of MPs to win their countenance and support to a project, when, in truth, matters being truly seen into and ascertained, the measure is a scheme for ensuring individual advantages and benefit or convenience.

[1] GLCRO E/MW/H/III/38/15, Case of Sir T. M. Wilson against the Finchley Road Bill, which was read a second time in H. of C. 17 May 1824.
[2] Ibid., List of Subscribers to the 1826 Finchley Road Bill.
[3] Ibid., Case . . . against the Finchley Road Bill, 1824.

It was a courageous statement. But over the next forty-five years his enemies would have been more than a little intrigued to learn that the young Sir Thomas had once nailed his colours to this particular mast.

Deprived of his former Belsize allies by the new line of the road, Sir Thomas found new ones among the copyholders of West End, and the residents in the few select mansions which stood on his own freehold lands at Frognal. He also made the most of the annoyance and damage which would be done to the Manor Farm by a public road, which now threatened to sever the farm in twain. Already there were 'some public paths through the land of this farm (increased through the negligence of former tenants), and Mr Baker has used every means to confine persons to such paths; in order to which, he has a person on the farm almost constantly to check and prevent straggling.'[1]

> Now, if the projected road is made, the tenant will be put under the expensive burden of maintaining nearly one mile and a half of additional fencing . . . and so near the Metropolis it is well known how difficult it is to maintain fences, the lower classes of the Inhabitants not being restrainable from various acts highly injurious and destructive to hedges, banks and other descriptions of fences. This evil is the more likely to be occurring continually when a population is brought upon Colonel Eyre's land contiguous to Sir Thomas Maryon Wilson's. In fact, there is a mass of new and inferior buildings near to Colonel Eyre's land in Marylebone, which are called Portland Town, and are inhabited by persons of the lowest orders, on which account it is spoken of as the St Giles of Marylebone parish.

On copyhold lands on either side of West End Lane, close to the tiny hamlet of West End, one or two imposing houses had been erected, and their residents were easily induced to see that the proposed road came uncomfortably close to their grounds and ornamental plantations. In 1824 John Miles, the owner and occupier of Canterbury House which lay on the east side of West End Lane, came forward to say that the road would almost pass through his shrubbery, and 'would take off much of the beauty of the view'. And he was joined in 1825, when the scheme was renewed, by S. H. Binns of the even grander Treherne House standing immediately to the north of Canterbury, who was 'anxious to oppose the Road in every way, or otherwise in my opinion the Beauty and Privacy of Hampstead will be totally destroyed'.[2] Of

[1] Loc. cit.
[2] Ibid., Evidence against the Finchley Road Bill, on behalf of Sir T. M. Wilson,

greater, or at least more eloquent, assistance to Sir Thomas were the residents from big houses on his own estate, of which there were two or three off the Frognal–West End track. Should the lower-lying ground traversed by the proposed road become a built-up area it would utterly spoil[1]

[the] few houses, which have been preferred and selected by Gentlemen both for their privacy and the great beauty of the extensive scenery of which a view is commanded either from the houses or the lands held with them. This would be the case with reference to the houses now occupied by Thomas William Carr esq. (Solicitor to the Excise), Joseph Blunt esq., solicitor,—Innes esq., and John Thompson esq. (who has expended about £ ,000 [*sic*] in erecting a Gothic Residence and offices on an elevated part of the demesne land, and near to which the intended road is proposed to be carried).

John Thompson emerged as the star witness from this select band, thus bringing his bizarre structure of Frognal Priory to bear in defence of Hampstead against an unwelcome intrusion. To call this 'a Gothic Residence' scarcely does justice to the weird fantasy which Thompson himself designed, or rather assembled, as a fitting home for his collection of antiques. 'On a rough new Tudor foundation he erected old-fashioned features of every sort—Gothic, Norman, Early English—anything that was typical of ancient days', was Barratt's description.[2] Illustrations of the Priory, which was demolished in the 1880s, show that revivalism and antiquarianism ran riot in such eclectical profusion that it is a wonder that the building ever stood up. There was an enormous porch in an imaginary renaissance-baronial vein, there were mullioned windows, round-headed windows, and pointed windows, there were Dutch gables as well as parapets, and a plethora of turrets, pinnacles and towers, and twisted chimneys, with a low Grecian wing with portico and pilasters thrown in for good measure. Stunned by every architectural fad of the time, Thompson erupted in a crazed pot-pourri of them all, which if it had but survived would be beyond price as a storehouse of the styles. This strange house stood just south of the junction of Frognal and the present Frognal Lane, and, summoning all his authority as an eminent valuer of brewery properties

May 1824 (John Miles, Esq.); S. H. Binns, Treherne House, to W. Lyddon, 16 May 1825.

[1] Ibid., Case . . . against the Finchley Road Bill, 1824.
[2] Barratt, op. cit., II, 273.

and a connoisseur of good taste, Thompson stood forth to defend the integrity of his dream. He declared that he was:[1]

> eminent as a valuer of effects in the brewery line, and has had considerable practice in the valuation of estates. He is considered to possess much taste as regards the eligibility of situations for country residences. The superiority of Hampstead led him to select a commanding spot at Frognal—part of the Manor Farm, at a little distance from West End Lane . . . He has at an expence of £ ,000 [he never did divulge the figure] built in the Gothic Stile a Mansion and attached offices, and some detached, to which he has a private road. From the elevated position of this Residence, and the lawn and pleasure grounds formed around it, there is a most extensive view over a great part of the Metropolis, including the north-west end of it, and into Kent, Surrey, Berkshire, and a part of Hertfordshire. The near view . . . is the well-cultivated Manor Farm land spreading down near to Kilburn Wells and to Colonel Eyre's land to the south-west and south . . . To any person whose professional engagements place him in that part of the day usually devoted to business in situations of bustle and noise, the relief which must be experienced on returning to a house retired and undisturbed must be highly valued. The estate of Colonel Eyre in the valley or flat southward of Mr Thompson's house is wholly or nearly so, overlooked from it . . . Mr Thompson's view would be interrupted, certainly stripped of much of its near beauty, by any public or other road carried through Colonel Eyre's lands, especially if buildings be made on the side of it.

Considerations of John Thompson's private view prevailed in 1824, and again in 1825 when a similar bill was rejected. But in rehearsing his arguments for the 1825 session Sir Thomas Maryon Wilson overreached himself, and his subtlety laid himself open to defeat in 1826. Hoping to kill off the proposals for good, Sir Thomas produced a counter-suggestion in 1825 showing that the most direct, shortest and hence cheapest route would be to prolong Colonel Eyre's Wellington Road in a straight line to the north-west until it met West End Lane just to the south of the hamlet; if it was desired to continue the new road further, the existing West End Lane, Fortune Green Lane, and Platts Lane could be widened and improved, thus bringing the through road as far as Childs Hill, after which it might continue to Temple

[1] GLCRO E/MW/H/III/38/15, Evidence against the Finchley Road Bill, May 1824.

Fortune Farm and Ballards Lane as Eyre had planned. All this was fine; the alternative route only just touched the most south-westerly fields of the Manor Farm, instead of cutting right across its heart; and since it only went through the most western of Colonel Eyre's fields instead of crossing through the centre of his estate, his hypocrisy might be exposed and he might be forced to abandon all proposals.[1] Sir Thomas would have done better to have kept clear of the game of suggesting public schemes which he did not intend to execute as a means of protecting private interests. For his alternative route roused the alarm and anger of prominent West End residents, who now turned out in their turn to defend their privacy. It crossed two paddocks belonging to General Orde, which were held with his large West End House on the far side of West End Lane. The General, and his resident tenant the Marchioness of Headfort, 'strenuously object to the line of road as interfering with the privacy of the residence and depreciating the value . . . Lady Headfort says the present road is ample for two carriages to pass, from the Lodge Gate of Westend House to the full extent of her premises, and does not require any widening.'[2] The new line also touched a field belonging to John Powell on Orde's south-western boundary, and although Powell was out of reach, 'he being out at sea cruising in his yacht', his solicitor entered a decided opposition.[3]

All passed off successfully for Sir Thomas in 1825, but in the following session Colonel Eyre and his associates exploited the chink in the Wilson armour to good effect. As the Wilson side remarked in April 1826, 'the measure is now revived in slightly altered shape, and with some art.'[4] What the road party had done was to stand by their proposed line, and add two new branches. The first ran in a direct line from the Macclesfield Bridge in Regent's Park to join 'the originally projected line upon an elevated part of Colonel Eyre's land' (this was the future Avenue Road). It had the low cunning of meeting part of Sir Thomas's new fondness for straight roads and shortest routes by putting his lands in absolutely direct touch with the dreaded Portland Town. The second was a branch to West End precisely on the line which Sir Thomas had proposed the year before. The effect of this was to get General Orde and Lady Headfort to exert all their considerable political influence to prevent the branch; but in order to make quite

---

[1] Ibid., Map accompanying Sir T. M. Wilson's opposing statement to the 1826 Finchley Road Bill, respecting his 1825 counter-suggestion.
[2] Ibid., Fowke and White, Orde's solicitors, to W. Lyddon, 26 May 1825.
[3] Ibid., Mr Deane, Powell's solicitor, to W. Lyddon, 24 May 1825.
[4] Ibid., Brief for counsel to oppose the Finchley Road Bill, April 1826.

sure that it was abandoned, they were ready to let the main road go through. It was only too true that 'there is an awkwardness attending the opposition which Sir Thomas and General Orde are giving to the Bill. The General would preserve his fields inviolate—so that he must wish that the easterly line be taken; Sir Thomas is desirous that as few of his fields should be disturbed as may be, and he would prefer the westerly line.'[1] With the resistance hopelessly split the bill sailed through the committee stage, and the chagrined Sir Thomas was left merely to ask his friend Sir Edward Knatchbull to excite the sympathies of the House on the third reading by pointing out that General Orde's two copyhold fields, through which the lower, more westerly, road would have passed, had been more respected than Sir Thomas's six freehold fields, through which the upper and more easterly route sanctioned by the committee was to go.[2]

As a final blow in what had become a losing battle Sir Thomas procured a clause in the Finchley Road Act compelling the trustees of the road to start construction from the Finchley end, and not from Marylebone, to make sure that the road should not be made simply for its building frontages and then never completed.[3] Thus, through the persistence of Colonel Eyre and the afterthought of the defeated Sir Thomas Maryon Wilson, the Finchley Road was built; terminating, as an urban road, for forty years and more at the Swiss Cottage Tavern, which was very soon built at the new road junction of Finchley Road and Avenue Road; and barred by a new turnpike gate in the direction of Belsize Lane, against those Belsize gentry who had said they never had occasion to travel towards the West End. Having been overpowered, Sir Thomas was nevertheless put in the long list of local property owners who constituted the trustees of the new turnpike, as a matter of course. And he took some pleasure in forcing his fellow trustees to go to the expensive and irritating length of a jury case to settle the compensation due to him for lands taken for the road. Then, having protested to the end that his Manor Farm was simply fine farmland, a rural foreground for select mansions at Frognal, and in no way eligible as building land, Sir Thomas savoured the *volte-face* of making the trustees smart under a stinging building price of £600 an acre for his land, while they had obtained the rest of their needs at the

[1] Loc. cit.
[2] Ibid., W. Lyddon to Sir Edward Knatchbull, 20 April 1826.
[3] Ibid., Case on the part of Sir T. M. Wilson as to value of lands required for the New Road, as a Brief on Inquest before the Sheriff of Middlesex to assess compensation, November 1828; and see HLRO Private Acts, 7 Geo. IV, c. 137.

agricultural price of £150 an acre.[1] It no doubt assuaged Sir Thomas's bruised feelings to scare Colonel Eyre with the prospect of having to pay through the nose for his road; the fright did not last, for unhappily the jury awarded compensation only at the rate of £200 an acre.[2] But once more the road made Sir Thomas give a dangerous hostage to fortune, when the time came to judge his own good faith and integrity over building plans and the Heath a few years later.[3]

With this ultimate success in 1826 Colonel Eyre's efforts for his Hampstead property in its pre-building estate years were complete. The Finchley New Road was open by the early 1830s; the new Swiss Cottage Tavern rapidly became a favourite resort on the edge of the country, a place for refreshment before and after making sallies against the hedges or the proprieties of Manor Farm; and with this fine wide road through its heart, the building future of his land was assured whenever the time should become ripe. On the Maryon Wilson estate, as the opposition to the Finchley Road had partly revealed, the attitude towards the pre-building estate stage had been very different. It was, in short, an attitude which looked out with hostility and fear on the Metropolis from the Hampstead heartland; but while it sought to protect this from encroachment and preserve a green belt between Hampstead Town and London, it was not in the least averse to developments, on what was considered a fitting scale, within Hampstead Town itself.

The elder Sir Thomas Maryon Wilson and his mother Dame Jane, who ruled as lady of the manor between her husband's death in 1798 and her own in 1816, appear to have evolved a general policy for steering the development of their Hampstead property. The freehold estate was by and large to be kept as farmland, permitting the establishment of a very few, very discreet and substantial residences, on the Frognal side of the slope. On the copyhold lands, on the other hand, where they lay next to the old town, building development was to be encouraged as soon as a healthy demand arose. This strategy, which looks so like a piece of private town planning, in fact seems to have been dictated purely by financial calculation. The assumption was that the building demand was by no means unlimited, and that there was not enough of it to spread over both freehold and copyhold lands. The copyholds were seen as perhaps the less attractive, tenurially, for building purposes, and certainly as the trickier from the point of view of

[1] Loc. cit.

[2] The jury award is recounted in E/MW/H/III/38/14, Memo as to the Estate Bills of 1829 and 1830, 23 June 1843.

[3] His greatest hostage to fortune, luckily for him undisclosed throughout the rest of his life, is discussed below, pp. 135–7.

securing a share of their building value for the lord of the manor. If building were allowed on the freehold it was expected that it would starve the copyhold lands and perhaps sterilise them for ever because developers and builders were expected to prefer leases of the freehold whenever they were available. Hence it was held to be imperative if any building revenues were ever to be secured from the copyholds, to arrange for them to be taken up first, before considering the release of any freehold land on to the building market. The policy was firmly restated in 1824:[1]

> Building on the demesne land of the Manor of Hampstead, would, we say, prejudicially affect the income derivable by the fines receivable in respect of the Copyhold Estates held of the Manor. The fines are arbitrary. The increase of buildings on the Customary Estates necessarily enhances the manorial profits. If buildings were to be made on the lord's demesne land, for them he would be receiving only small ground rents, and such buildings affording habitations for many persons, none, or few, buildings would be made upon the copyhold estates. Not only that, but the erection of any number of houses on the part of the demesne land comprised in the farm, will have the effect of diminishing the yearly value of other parts . . . near whereon are a few houses, which have been preferred and selected by Gentlemen.

The great obstacle to development on the copyholds was the arbitrary fines which were due to the lord of the manor on every death or alienation; amounting to two years' full current annual value of the lands, these fines were considered far more inhibiting to building, because liable to arise with greater frequency, than the renewal fines under leases for lives. The way round this was for the lord of the manor to agree to a fixed level of fines for a specified term of years, well below the anticipated improved annual value of the houses to be erected, and thereby give developers and builders something of the security and certainty that they could enjoy under an ordinary building lease. The most important opportunity for implementing the Wilson policy came in 1812, when a developer named William Coleman[2]

> conceived a plan to purchase about 14 acres of copyhold land . . . for a building project. An agreement was made between Dame Jane Wilson, then lady of the manor and her son the late baronet

---

[1] GLCRO E/MW/H/III/38/15, Case . . . against the Finchley Road Bill, 1824.
[2] Loc. cit.

. . . [and William Coleman] for fixing the rate of fine to be taken in respect of such land and the buildings to be made thereon during a period of 63 years. From the time of any such land being let to be built on, when a fine should accrue to the lord . . . on death or alienation, it was to be estimated upon a rent of £100 per acre. . . . One acre thus yields to the lord a fine of £200 upon admission. . . . Upon these 14 acres there have been erected upwards of 60 dwelling houses, and others are now [1824] building thereon, and there remains room for more to build. Several of these houses let as high as £70, some £60, some £50, some £40, some £35. A very few small ones probably between £20 and £30. If we take the average of the rents at £40 per house, the income from 60 houses is £2,400. To which is to be added the rent of a large new-built chapel let for £300 p.a., and the total yearly income amounts to £2,700. The 14 acres of land, before the agreement was made . . . were assessed at £5 per acre rent, or £10 per acre fine, and the fine on the whole 14 acres if remaining in grass would be only £140. . . . Taking the yearly income of the 14 acres and the buildings thereon at the expiration of the 63 years at only £2,700 (there is no doubt but it will be greater), this part of the manor will yield a fine of £5,600. . . . What may be received by fines occurring on changes of parts of this 14 acres during the residue of the 63 years may be equal to (if not exceed) what Sir Thomas might obtain by ground rents from an equal quantity of demesne land.

This was the Downshire Hill and John Street (renamed Keats Grove) development, whose architectural charm no less than its financial success was covered by Wilson's observation that 'there can be no doubt but it was the proximity of Hampstead Heath to the 14 acres of copyhold land which induced the erection of so many houses thereon.'[1] The houses were by several hands, some for personal occupation and some for letting, and this produced a street of villas in pleasantly varying styles, held together by their characteristic stucco exteriors, the leafy appearance of the road, and the prospect of the Heath opening out at the foot of the Hill. The whole was set off by the proprietary estate chapel of St John, which helped to make the whole venture a social success. Keats's friends the Dilkes and Browns were among the very first to build in John Street, and it was in their pair of new Regency-style villas called Lawn Bank that Keats lived in 1818–20;

[1] Loc. cit.

and it was there that he met Fanny Brawne, whose parents took the Dilke half of the villa for a season, and then moved to another new house on the Coleman estate at the top of Downshire Hill.[1]

The same copyhold policy was applied with equal success in a number of lesser cases. In 1811 Thomas Gardnor, who held a couple of acres of garden ground off Flask Walk worth in their existing use £10 a year, arranged that he could build on it or let it for building, and have the entry fines restricted to the £10 a year value during his lifetime. Here Gardnor House had stood since 1736, in which the Gardnors themselves lived; and some small plots were carved out of the gardens to form the small houses of Gardnor's Place. In 1815 a similar agreement was made with William Woods, a carpenter, who proposed to build two houses on his small copyhold, and in 1816 with John Fildes, an upholsterer, who wished to put up a substantial house for himself; both were granted fixed entry fines for terms of 63 years.[2] This piecemeal infilling on the copyhold lands to the south-east of the old town, between Flask Walk and Pond Street, sometimes in tiny blocks and sometimes in large pieces capable of forming neighbourhoods on the Downshire Hill pattern, might well have continued without pause into the 1820s, and have given this large quarter of Hampstead a complete stucco covering. But the elder Sir Thomas Maryon Wilson died in 1821 and his will left the younger Sir Thomas holding the Hampstead properties as a simple tenant-for-life with powers to make leases and agreements of no more than 21 years' duration. This put a stop to the method of fixing the entry fines on copyhold building lands, and unless any copyholder or builder holding under him was willing to face the prospect of paying two years' full improved rents for every fine all further development was halted. The chief copyhold estate to be hung up in this way was the Carlile property, 11½ acres lying between Downshire Hill and the present Gayton Road. This was effectively sterilised by the legal difficulty for fifty years, fields with nothing on them except the family seat, Carlile House, when every other ground, above all its frontage to Willow Road and thus to the Heath, suggests that it was tantalisingly ripe for building by the 1820s. Other properties which

---

[1] Barratt, op. cit., II, 147–61. Barratt's statement that Lawn Bank 'belonged to Charles W. Dilke, who held it on a 130 years' building lease which expired in 1911' must be incorrect as to the implied date of the building, 1781. The style of Lawn Bank, with its low-pitched roof and deep eaves, is decidedly nearer to 1812 than to 1780; and in any case no John Street (Keats Grove), on which it faces, existed before 1812.

[2] GLCRO E/MW/H/III/38/14, Brief to Mr Bollard to appear at the House of Lords Cttee hearing on Sir T. M. Wilson's Estate Bill, May 1829.

appear to have suffered from this freeze, though there is no conclusive evidence that they also were copyholds, were Nathan Best's four acres, on which Gayton Road and Crescent were eventually built in the 1880s, and George Crispin's five acres, on which Hampstead Hill Gardens was formed in the 1870s. With the partial exception of this last, which was finally built in a reasonably spacious and pleasing manner, those who imagined that they were so stoutly defending the Heath and the beauty of Hampstead by denying leasing powers to Sir Thomas Maryon Wilson, might profitably have paused to consider that they were thereby denying Hampstead the pleasures and glories of a series of Downshire Hills for the sake of inflicting on her the postponed dreariness of Gayton Roads and Rudall Crescents.[1]

The contrast between the relatively intensive developments which the Wilsons were ready to encourage on the south-western side of the town, and the highly privileged park-like ventures which were all they would permit on the northern and western sides, demonstrates the way in which the dictates of a private landowner's financial advantage could lead to the adoption of a most sensible town and country planning policy. In this way the fringes of the West Heath were reinforced by a discreet force of private mansion-grounds, which not only improved the quality of the rural background which was raised far above the level of bare farmland by the labours of small-scale landscape gardening, but also made the permanent preservation of the Heath itself much more probable, since these big houses constituted a powerful vested interest in the protection of the surroundings from which their charm and value derived. The most costly if not the most attractive of these new mansions was no doubt Thompson's Frognal Priory. Close by was the large eighteenth-century house, Branch Hill Lodge, which had been the home of the line of eminent lawyers ending with Lord Loughborough.[2] This stood in nine acres of grounds, all of which were copyhold. It had been acquired by a wealthy merchant, Thomas Neave, before 1807, in which year Dame Jane Wilson sold to him 'as a great favour, some portions of the demesne land of the manor lying before and near to the House . . . The object of the purchases was to acquire an extent of land to protect the House from any annoyance to be experienced from any buildings which might otherwise be erected near thereto.' Neave gave £1,924 for these 4½ acres, which at the time was a high amenity price. And shortly afterwards he paid £1,000 for a long

[1] See below, pp. 141–2, for the frustration of Sir T. M. Wilson's efforts to obtain legal powers to deal with copyhold building land.
[2] See above, p. 30.

lease of another $2\frac{3}{4}$ acres of copyhold adjoining his grounds to the north-west, opposite Prospect Walk (or Judges Walk), because Dame Jane had agreed to lease it to someone else to build a small cottage residence.[1] Neave before long succeeded to a baronetcy and the Dagenham Park estate in Essex which went with it, and retreated from Hampstead to something more completely rural, turning his defensive purchases for his own personal green belt to good account as he went. Branch Hill itself he sold to Roberts, perhaps the Thomas Roberts who took part in the Belsize property deals. On his $4\frac{1}{2}$ acres of freehold he built Oak Hill House and leased it to a John Bates, later adding a second big house, Oak Hill Lodge; and on his north-western buffer he built Sandfield Lodge, leasing that to Cunnington.[2] He could scarcely complain when one more large house appeared next door towards West Heath Road, The Grange. It was smart work for a man who had bought the lands in order to prevent any building. The Wilson family feeling that they had been made the victims of sleight of hand if not sharp practice was heightened when Neave turned up in the guise of an aggrieved copyholder menaced by Wilson extortion in 1829, and abundantly confirmed when later on Neave calmly developed the Oak Hill park enclave as a little building estate. But it all showed that with proximity to the Heath so prized by the few wealthy residents that land hereabouts was worth £400 an acre and more to them simply to lay down to lawns and plantations, housing demand would need to grow immensely before it became worth anyone's while to consider this area as anything like ordinary building land.

What would have been interpreted in retrospect as the finishing touch to a masterpiece of planned development of resources in this post-Napoleonic burst of expansion fell victim to the elder Sir Thomas Maryon Wilson's will, and never materialised. Over on the Kilburn side of the parish Samuel Ware of the Adelphi, who was surveyor and architect to the Duke of Portland's London estate, began to lay the grounds for an ambitious speculation after 1815. He started to buy up land, and assembled a copyhold estate of about fifty acres, lying between the Edgware Road and West End Lane, aiming at a mixed development of big houses and more closely-built villas. Unfortunately for his plans, he was not ready to apply for an agreement to limit the level of entry fines to be taken on the building land until after July 1821; Sir

[1] GLCRO E/MW/H/III/38/15, Case . . . against the Finchley Road Bill, 1824; Case . . . as to value of lands required for the New Road, 1828.

[2] [Sir] Thomas Neave became a large landowner in Essex, and in Anglesey. The owners and tenants of the Hampstead grounds are in Tithe Apportionment, Hampstead, 1838.

Thomas was dead, and his son, though willing, was powerless to make an agreement. Ware hung on for a while, hoping that Sir Thomas would quickly remedy the omission in his father's will and procure the needful legal powers. But he could not afford to wait more than a few years—as it turned out, Sir Thomas failed to secure the powers within his lifetime—and by 1828 Ware had sold off piecemeal the major part of his copyhold, retaining only 12½ acres in his own possession. The opportunity for coherent treatment of the large area—roughly bounded by the present Gascony Avenue, West End Lane, the railway land, and Kilburn High Road—was thus lost. Instead a new tribe of small land-owners was created by Ware's sales, and at Ware's expense, since he received barely £200 an acre for what he sold, which was only a little above agricultural value; and he had bought with building potential in view. On the land he retained Ware built Kilburn Grange, whose memory survives in the Grange cinema; and five acres which he sold to Charles Spain was used by him for the grounds of the very large Oaklands Hall, with its drive from West End Lane, which he at once built for himself. These two houses conferred some distinction on the district; but the remainder of Ware's old estate stayed as a jigsaw of grazing grounds and laundry grounds until engulfed by indifferent and awkwardly sited housing in the late nineteenth century.[1]

There are ample grounds, therefore, for arguing that until it was halted in its tracks by the terms of Sir Thomas Maryon Wilson's will in 1821, the Wilson estate was set on a course of estate management which was both profitable to the family in realising the gains to be made from building and amenity values, and beneficial to Hampstead's future as a pleasant place to live in and its Heath as an open space to enjoy. The will changed many things. It may have furnished the occasion and opportunity to preserve the Heath for ever, for perhaps without this impediment and the attempt to remove it by private estate bills Sir Thomas might have contrived to obliterate the Heath by stealth; the evident appreciation, both before and immediately after 1821, of the pecuniary advantages which flowed to him from keeping the Heath as heath, must however render this a doubtful proposition. The will definitely kept the Wilson freehold lands out of the building land market for fifty years, and the absence of competition from this quarter was of great service to the orderliness and quality of development on the neighbouring Belsize, Eton, and Eyre estates. It is equally certain that the will deprived both the town and Kilburn of potentially

[1] GLCRO E/MW/H/III/38/15, Case . . . against the Finchley Road Bill, 1824; Case . . . as to the value of lands required for the New Road, 1828.

interesting and agreeable building schemes in the 1820s, which could conceivably have been important enough to cast their influence forward and, as it were, hampsteadise the whole of Hampstead parish. Whatever the balance of the arguments, this accident of family history not only put the Wilson family off stroke for a generation, but also cast a sizeable spanner into the workings of urban development.

Four

CHARACTER ASSASSINATION
Hampstead Heath and Sir Thomas Maryon Wilson

Much of Hampstead's fate in the nineteenth century was settled by a couple of family decisions by the Maryon Wilsons, taken no doubt for sound family reasons, but deflecting the course of urban growth in an entirely unpredictable and capricious manner: except, of course, that since in England that growth took place under, and was moulded by, the institution of private property in land, it was only to be expected that in some places and at some times it would be influenced by the form of the arrangements which private landowners were in the habit of making to provide for their families. The first decision was a matter of routine among landed families. In 1806 the elder Sir Thomas Maryon Wilson, being entitled to the fee simple in reversion of the family estates in Middlesex, Kent, Sussex, Hertfordshire, Essex, Suffolk, and Cambridgeshire whenever his mother Dame Jane should die, made a will settling all the property so as to make provision for his seven children. Under this will his eldest son, Thomas, was to inherit the Middlesex, Kent, and Sussex property, but as tenant-for-life of an estate in tail male with remainders over to his brother John and his sons, if any. This was an almost entirely standard form of strict settlement, a form under which the great majority of the landed classes held their estates. It was hardly less common for the powers over his property of a tenant-for-life, established by the deed of settlement, to be rendered insufficient or inappropriate by changing economic circumstances; practically all the numerous private estate bills which were regularly before Parliament in the eighteenth and early nineteenth centuries were concerned with remedying precisely this type of situation. The second Sir Thomas tried this course, and repeatedly failed to obtain his estate Act, which was unusual to the point of being unprecedented. At this point the second family decision, or lack of it, became crucial. The second Sir Thomas remained a bachelor all his life. Normally a tenant-for-life, if he could afford to hold his horses until his eldest son came of age, could join with his heir to break the family settlement, remove the troublesome provisions and remedy the deficiencies, and re-settle the property in the same line of succession as before. For Sir Thomas not to have married turned out to have been a grievous omission, for it denied him this escape route through the law of real property. These two circumstances between them, the will and the bachelorhood, provided Hampstead with a cliff-hanger which lasted almost without pause from 1821 to 1869.

The nub of the matter was that when he made his will in September 1806 Sir Thomas omitted to give anything much in the way of special powers to the tenants-for-life whom he proposed to create. The family estates were to be split into two roughly equal halves, the eldest son getting the principal seats of Charlton, near Woolwich, and Searles near Uckfield in Sussex with surrounding 1,600 acres, as well as Hampstead; and the second son inheriting the second country seat of Fitzjohns at Great Canfield in the Rodings country of Essex with its supporting 1,500 acres, together with detached farms in Hertfordshire, Cambridgeshire, and Suffolk. The family trustees appointed by the will were charged with raising portions of £5,000 for each of the five younger children who did not inherit any land, and were given the necessary powers of mortgaging to do this; £20,000 could be borrowed on the first group of lands, and £5,000 on the second. But apart from this, the only way in which any of the lands could be dealt with in any manner that might still affect them after the lifetime of the designated heirs was by the granting of ordinary agricultural leases of not more than 21 years' duration. Even this limited leasing power did not automatically belong to tenants-for-life, and its inclusion in the will was a sign of enlightenment and of progressive agricultural views. Just a few months before he died the elder Sir Thomas enlarged these powers, but only in a highly specific fashion. Noting that his lands at Woolwich and Charlton already contained many houses, and concluding that it would be desirable to have them tenanted under repairing leases and to get more houses erected on the unbuilt lands, he made two codicils bestowing the power to grant 70-year building leases on these two properties.[1] Having done this, he died. In 1821, therefore, the younger Sir Thomas inherited the Middlesex, Kent, and Sussex estates as tenant-for-life, with power to grant 21-year leases of any parts of them, and power to grant 70-year leases in the Charlton and Woolwich section; beyond that, in selling, mortgaging, or leasing, he could not go.

[1] The will of 5 September 1806 is given in full in HLRO, Maryon Wilson Estate Bill 1829, Petition and Judges' Report on Sir T. M. Wilson's Bill, 28 April 1829; and Judges' Report on John Maryon Wilson's Bill, 1 May 1829.

The usual course for a landowner in this predicament, once it became apparent that the deficiencies in his powers as life-tenant were losing him more than the £500 or so which it would cost him to get a private estate Act, was to promote a private bill setting aside the awkward parts of the settlement or will under which he held his estate, and enacting whatever leasing or selling powers were felt to have become desirable. It was, to be sure, not quite as simple as this to get Parliament to set aside the wishes of testators on the mere whim of one individual. Others besides the tenant-for-life of the moment were likely to be interested in the future of the estate and to have claims on it contingent on his death. It was thus necessary to obtain the consent of all the remainder-men to any alterations proposed by the life-tenant before Parliament would agree to pass an estate bill. But since these alterations were generally designed to increase the value of the estate and thus of any claims on it by the remainder-men, they were usually most happy to give their assent. In any case this small circle, largely made up of other members of the family, were the only group with any legal standing in the matter, the only people who could possibly advance valid and sustainable objections to a life-tenant's proposals. There was no opening, and no occasion, for ordinary tenants on the estate, let alone the public at large, to influence the proceedings; and in the ordinary case there was no reason why parties outside the family should consider themselves as being affected in any way by what was contained in an estate bill.

Maryon Wilson and his estate bills turned out to be the one colossal exception to this rule, an exception written in enormous letters across the history of private bill legislation. Continuing to protest right up to his death that he had been persecuted and victimised as the one private landowner who had ever been denied the customary facilities of private legislation and made to suffer heavy financial loss as a result, Sir Thomas became the exception because his estate bills seemed to affect the rights and properties of Hampstead copyholders, and through them to threaten the Heath. To decide whether they actually did so, and if they did whether this was illegitimate in terms of the rights of manorial lords or merely contrary to the public interest in open spaces, was a question on which skilled nineteenth-century conveyancing barristers and judges hesitated to pronounce, and it may seem presumptuous and unnecessary to pass retrospective judgment. The main historical fact is that the belief in the threats was so intensely felt that a long succession of Maryon Wilson estate bills from 1829 to 1865 were rejected, and Hampstead Heath was preserved. The grounds for this belief, however, must be investigated in order to understand the motives of the preservationist forces, without which the means of achieving Hampstead's chief glory cannot be appreciated. The uncovering of these grounds in turn depends on unravelling the legal tangle, on whose intricacies the contemporary pundits, after all, had good reason not to commit themselves simply because the implications of any definite statement touched a sensitive and explosive area. It was, in other words, politically unwise for them to make pronouncements, because the Heath issue was one of the hottest metropolitan potatoes of the century.

Sir Thomas Maryon Wilson began simply enough in 1829 with an estate bill which sought to give him powers to grant 99-year building leases on his Hampstead property, and to extend from 70 to 99 years the leases he could grant at Charlton and Woolwich. He argued that it was only by a mere slip, an oversight, that his father had given the leasing powers over Charlton and Woolwich but not over Hampstead, and that hardly more than a legal formality was involved in remedying the old man's mistake.[1] Unfortunately for this otherwise credible story, Sir Thomas had been rash enough to commit to paper a very different version when he had been in the thick of his fight against the Finchley New Road four years earlier. Then his statement of his case against the road had contained a crucial passage:[2]

> Under the Will of his late father, he is merely Tenant for Life (not without impeachment for waste) with a power to grant leases for 21 years in possession only. If building on the freehold or demesne land was desirable and beneficial (which we shall presently endeavour to point out it is not)—he must incur the expence of from £3 to £500 in obtaining an Act to be empowered to grant building leases . . . The late Sir Thomas made his Will in 1806 . . . and during his last illness, viz. 14 April 1821, he by a codicil empowered his son to grant building and repairing leases for long terms of his freehold property in Woolwich; and by another codicil made 20 April 1821 he extended this power to grant building and repairing leases over his freehold estate at Charlton, Kent; *but upon his being asked if he would do the like as to the Hampstead Property, he said no; and expressed his sentiments for leaving that as it was.*

[1] HLRO, Sir T. M. Wilson's petition for his estate bill, 28 April 1829.
[2] GLCRO E/MW/H/III/38/15, Case . . . against the Finchley Road Bill, 1824; my italics.

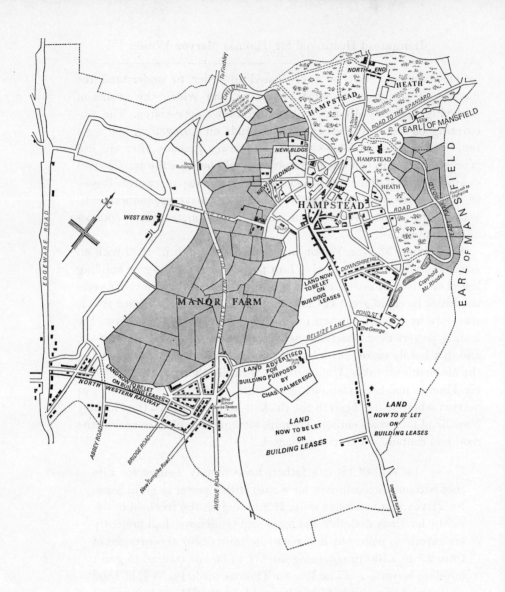

MAP 5 The Maryon Wilson estate in Hampstead, showing its relation to the Heath and to adjoining building estates, in 1853. The estate, comprised the shaded portions. HLRO House Bill, 1853, Maryon Wilson Hampstead Estate Bill (see p. 135)

In many ways this is the single most important document in Hampstead's modern history, since it shows in a convincingly circumstantial way that old Sir Thomas had a clear wish to prevent, or postpone, any building development in Hampstead. In private bill legislation Parliament would never flout the testator's expressed wishes and intentions. If this document had been generally known, the law lords on whom responsibility for vetting all private bills rested and who had to report on each particular estate bill that it was a proper bill which it was reasonable to pass, would never have allowed any Maryon Wilson estate bill through their net. Thus a proper interpretation of the practice of the law ought to have held all Sir Thomas's efforts out of order as involving direct contravention of his father's explicit words; in which case no occasion to mount an agitation to save the Heath would have arisen. As it was, young Sir Thomas chose to forget and suppress what he had so firmly recalled in 1824, and from 1829 onwards stoutly maintained that his father had never desired to prevent or delay building operations in Hampstead, sometimes going to the length of avowing that his father had wished to give positive encouragement to such development. A modest white lie, perhaps, rather than culpable perjury; and one which his brothers and sisters never challenged, since what was at stake was a vast increase in the value of the Hampstead property. Nevertheless it was an inexactitude which caused a lot of trouble to a lot of people, and cast a curious light on the character of a man who spoke easily of the dishonourable conduct of others.

It was a much lesser matter that by bringing in his bill in 1829 Sir Thomas contradicted himself and the stand which he had maintained consistently from 1821 to 1826 in his opposition to the Finchley Road proposals, that he had no desire to build over his Hampstead lands and that they were in any case not suitable for any form of intensive development.[1] This personal inconsistency was the small change of estate policy anywhere. The fact that the road, in spite of his resistance, was being built altered the whole economic circumstances of the estate, and by splitting the Manor Farm in two made the lower-lying land adjoining the new road highly suitable for building in the immediate future. There was thus every justification for Sir Thomas changing his mind about the desirable exploitation of part, at any rate, of his Hampstead property. And since he had to be at the expense of a private bill in any case in order to open up this section of near-ripe building land, it was natural that he should use the occasion to obtain powers over the entire estate, which might be useful in the more distant future. The bill

[1] See above, pp. 115, 125.

therefore contained clauses to give building lease powers over the whole of the Hampstead freehold lands; to grant licences to copyholders empowering them to grant 99-year leases of their copyholds, to commit 'waste' in the legal sense by digging up parts of their copyholds to form roads or to make bricks, and to make agreements fixing the entry fines on copyhold building lands; and, finally, to grant building leases 'on such part of the Heath and other waste land or ground in the manor of Hampstead . . . whether occupied or not, and which may hereafter be approved or otherwise exonerated or discharged from the customs of the said manor, by or for the sole use or benefit of the lord or lady thereof for the time being.'[1]

The 'Heath clause' was the most obviously threatening and controversial part of the bill. Though even if it had meant what the words, in their widest construction, appeared to say it would not have been unusual then, and was not unusual in the generation after 1829, for manorial owners, especially those on the fringes of expanding towns, to appropriate the whole or the main part of their manorial wastes and heaths. Indeed if this had not been done practically every erstwhile village which is now part of Greater London would still possess its own version of Hampstead Heath, which would be a highly common common. In truth, however, the clause required careful interpretation in the light of the law and customs of manors, and of this particular manor above all, before its likely effects could be assessed. And it implied something far less than an instant appropriation of the entire Heath to be followed by its death by building. The clause started from the universally true assumption that the actual soil of waste and heath land belonged to the lord of the manor; but it was only his subject to the continued enjoyment by the copyholders of the manor of their rights of user for such matters as pasturing, digging turf, and collecting furze. Subject to these superior rights, which depended on there always remaining an adequate area of waste and heath to support whatever copyholder use continued to be effectively exercised, the custom of the manor of Hampstead permitted the lord, with the consent of the homage in court baron—and this meant in effect with the consent of the chief copyholders—to 'approve' or in other words to appropriate and enclose, small parcels of the waste or heath, and grant them to be held by copy of court roll. This process of approvement from the Heath had been going on constantly through the eighteenth century, and right up to 1829. It could not take place through the unilateral action of the

[1] HLRO, Judges' Report on Maryon Wilson Estate Bill, and Schedule to the Bill, 28 April 1829.

lord of the manor; but as well as approving parcels to the benefit of copyholders, the lord could, and did, approve parcels to himself by using the device of inserting a nominee, usually his steward, into the court roll to hold on his behalf.[1] The clause dealt solely with the possibility of building leases being granted on these latter parcels which might be taken from the Heath in future. It was indeed argued, much later, that under this customary system Sir Thomas could slowly and painfully convert the whole Heath into his own freehold, nibble by nibble, and then build on it.[2] But this salami technique could work only if the copyholders became supine, meekly consented to endless piecemeal approvements, and neglected to exercise their rights on the Heath. Once concern had been aroused in 1829, and indeed well before that since the body of copyholders contained many wealthy and influential men who were highly conscious of their rights and of the cash value of their properties which depended on those rights, it was inconceivable that anything of the kind could happen. For the disappearance of other metropolitan manorial commons was due either to a complete desuetude of common rights and practical vanishing of copyholders leaving a manorial lord in undisputed possession of the field, or to agreement between a manorial lord and surviving copyholders to carve up the common and share the spoils. So long as a sufficiency of Hampstead copyholders did not allow their common rights to fall into disuse, and resisted any temptation to concur with Sir Thomas in an enclosure of the Heath, the Heath must have remained safe from any loss save for a few inconsiderable trifles taken from the edges. The bill was not a major threat to the Heath. The security for its survival depended on the behaviour of the copyholders, and on their continuing to put out their cows to pasture—it was never altogether clear whether donkeys or horses would do equally well in asserting common rights.

From a pure preservationist point of view the effects of piecemeal grants from the waste, over the years, should not be written off as completely insignificant. When the Heath was finally purchased for the public in 1871 the steward of the manor prepared a list of all grants

[1] The customs of the manor were set out at length in HPL Documents in the case of Hoare *v.* Wilson, Chancery 1866 H No. 273. Although this case was never settled, the Master of the Rolls directing certain issues of fact as to the precise nature of common rights to be tried before a special jury, which never sat because of the intervention of Sir T. M. Wilson's death, the actual nature of the customs, especially the manner of making approvements from the Heath, is sufficiently clear.

[2] GLCRO E/MW/H/III/38/16, Hampstead Heath Purchase Bill, in Parliament, evidence to be given by Alfred Clark, Steward of the Manor, 1864–9, in 1871.

made from the waste, in order to bolster up the purchase price. This showed that between 1799 and 1870 there were 219 separate grants, amounting in all to 37½ acres. Only one individual grant was of more than one acre, and that was a 2½-acre piece of manorial waste at the junction of Edgware Road and Shoot-Up Hill lane (now Mill Lane) granted to John Powell in 1833. Nevertheless a multitude of penny packets, the vast majority of which were less than one-eighth of an acre each, could add up to rather more than a slight dent in the Heath; although some proportion of these grants concerned, like Powell's, bits of the manorial waste at Shoot-Up Hill, West End, South End, or Fortune Green, which were far removed from the essential Heath.[1] Nor, from the preservationist point of view, could it be assumed that all the copyholders would be ready to go to the stake for their common rights. There was in any case a social division in the ranks of the copyholders, between the gentry who set great store by their big houses and grounds and the scenery and open space which contributed so much to the value of their properties, and the 'peasant' copyholders who were tradesmen and shopkeepers who tended to favour anything which might create more business for themselves. On top of this there was an incipient geographical division among the gentlemen copyholders, between those whose properties lay near the Heath, and those which were at a distance. Copyholders in the western parts, men like Samuel Ware with his schemes for developing Kilburn, or John Powell who had a freehold estate at Shoot-Up Hill Farm but a copyhold estate on West End Lane, might well be lukewarm towards the defence of the Heath if there was a chance of making a profitable bargain with the lord of the manor which would release their Kilburn estates for building land.[2] Hence it could have proved an insecure foundation for the preservation of the Heath to rest it entirely on the will of the copyholders and the assumed coincidence of their private interest with the public good, even though it was an impregnable legal position. But with public opinion aroused a possibly frail and vulnerable cause was rendered invincible.

[1] Loc. cit. Indeed in grants of 1832, 1833, and 1841 Powell received over 4 acres of the total of 37½ acres of waste granted, and they all lay at Shoot-Up Hill.

[2] There is a full list of the major copyhold properties in GLCRO E/MW/H/III/38/14, Statement of copyholders having land—titheable—not built on, 24 June 1843. There were 34 individuals holding 326 acres; the total number of copyholders was thought to be between 250 and 300; the 250 or so 'peasant' copyholders held between them, as sites of their houses, about 130 acres. For Samuel Ware, see above, p. 129.

If the Heath was not directly endangered by the bill, but only remotely so through some future disintegration of copyholder solidarity, public opinion was aroused under false pretences. The cry was that the Heath was in danger. The reality was that the copyholders were alarmed by the 'copyhold clause', which they wrongly imagined was going to force them to pay a fine to the lord for a licence to do what they had formerly done as of right and without payment. The copyholders had always been able to deal with their properties as they pleased, building on them if they chose, without needing the lord's permission. They imagined that the bill sought to prevent them doing this any more by obliging them to buy a licence to build from the lord. In fact the bill merely proposed that a copyholder could if he chose obtain a licence from the lord, from which he would get the benefit of fixed entry fines for a 99-year period; but he would still be at liberty to use the traditional system, of building without the special licence and running the risk of paying full fines on every death or alienation. Knowledge of the 'copyhold clause' leaked out just before the bill came up in the Lords, and it was in defence of the imagined attack on these rights that the copyholders swung into action. A meeting of the Committee of Hampstead Copyholders, which had ironically been set up in 1819 to help the Maryon Wilson side against the Finchley Road project, was called; it passed a petition against the bill, and began anti-Wilson publicity, dragging in an alleged threat to the Heath in order to give their case wider appeal.

The sequence of events was that the petition asking for the bill was presented in March 1829, whereupon it was referred in the ordinary way to two law lords. These two, Barons Park and Littledale, reported on 28 April that the bill was a proper one to be passed, and the Lords gave it a formal first reading the same day and a second reading on 2 May, committing it for 27 May. Thus far it had been a purely private and family affair, but after the second reading someone, suspected to be Lord Mansfield who did not want to have any buildings anywhere within sight of Ken Wood, divulged its contents. On 3 May a notice was read out after service in Hampstead church calling a public meeting of the copyholders and inhabitants, which met on 6 May and again by adjournment on 13 May, when under the leadership of two gentlemen copyholders, Charles Holford of Hampstead Terrace and Henry White, surveyor, of High Street, a petition against the bill was drawn up for presentation to the House of Lords. This petition dealt only with the point concerning the injustice of asking copyholders to obtain building licences from the lord. The petitioners were heard at the committee hearing on 27 May, through their solicitor and counsel, and were propitiated by the insertion of a clause saving the existing rights of copyholders without prejudice. This seemed to remove any possible legitimate grievance, and by making it plain that the bill could not alter the property rights of other parties but dealt only with an internal rearrangement of the property rights of the Maryon Wilson family it emphasised that it was truly a private measure and not one with which the public had any call to be concerned.[1]

The bill accordingly passed the House of Lords on 1 June, and that should have been the end of the matter; the parliamentary practice was for any substantive consideration of private bills to take place in the Lords, and for the stages in the Commons to be purely formal. But when the bill had been read twice in the Commons, and committed for 12 June, and just as Sir Thomas's solicitors were relaxing, thinking themselves home and dry after the nasty shock in the Lords, the totally unexpected happened. A part—Sir Thomas naturally said it was the more respectable part—of the copyholders were satisfied by the concession made in the Lords, and withdrew any further opposition. But a rump took over the Copyholders' Committee, determined to use it to stop the passage of any bill at all, however amended. They got up a petition to the Commons, alleging that the bill would take away their rights of digging sand, gravel and other building materials from the Heath, and that the lord was trying to usurp a unilateral power to approve parcels from the Heath. Neither allegation was correct. Their petition arrived at the Commons only on 12 June, when the committee stage was actually being taken, and was too late to affect it. But before the third reading, set for 19 June, the rump of twenty-four second petitioners called a further public meeting for 16 June, and advertised it in several newspapers. This meeting seems to have been very thinly attended, only eight voting for the resolution to continue opposition to the bill, but still being enough to carry it. Sir Thomas's solicitor might disparage these eight as men of no consequence, but they had done the trick:[2]

The persons who made up the majority to carry the resolutions were:

George Paxon—auctioneer and undertaker [he had been glad

---

[1] GLCRO E/MW/H/III/38/14, Dates of proceedings on this bill, to refute the allegation of its being hurried through the Houses of Parliament, 8 June 1829.

[2] Ibid., Draft brief for attending House of Commons on the petition of some of the Copyholders presented on 12 June, 17 June 1829.

enough to have his evidence to support the case against the Finchley Road]

John Kelley—a retired shoemaker from Fleet Street

Reverend Allaton Burgh—(who is sometimes spoken of by a nickname)

Thomas Finden—a builder near Tottenham Court Road

William Clews—believed to be a tailor in a small way

Samuel Nightingale—a carpenter in a small way

William Alexander Ambridge—a shoemaker in a small way

Edward Rushbrook Sutcliffe—a minor, the son of a deceased surgeon, who was only admitted [as a copyholder] on 1 June.

Thus the opposition of '80 of the Copyholders comprising many of the most wealthy and most intelligent' [the description in the petition], is dwindled down to the small number of 8 comprising some not very competent (from their mental endowments) to act, and perhaps some others acting under a pique arising from past occurrences—as a difference of religious profession, etc.

However correct this analysis of the calibre of the surviving opposition may have been, and however true Lyddon's further surmise about William Ripley, a considerable gentleman-copyholder who 'was at the meeting, addressing it, and shewing that his pique against the Steward of the Manor was one great point for him to gratify himself in', the eight carried the day. Not by their own weight, but by public opinion. 'In order to give more weight to the Petition to the House of Commons', as Lyddon reported, 'and to excite a bias in the minds of Members against the Bill, it has been called—and the public press joined in the wilful misnomer—an Enclosure Bill.'[1] This cry, that he was pushing through a bill to enclose Hampstead Heath, in the guise of an estate bill, was Sir Thomas Maryon Wilson's undoing. Once raised, it was never forgotten. Whether or not it was justified by the actual provisions of this or any subsequent bill the public was not competent to decide, and did not care to inquire too closely. But on the principle that there could be no smoke without a fire the public were inclined to believe the repeated accusation; and for the next forty years all those who wished to thwart Sir Thomas, either from genuine apprehensions or from selfish interests, had but to repeat the cry and he was brought to a halt.

[1] Loc. cit. The cause of Ripley's pique is not revealed; but he was a Roman Catholic and may well have been involved in the unspecified 'religious differences'.

The Times had carried a letter on 'The Bill to enclose the Heath' on 30 May, and this also helped to sound the alert.[1] Lyddon did what he could to prepare for the storm which suddenly threatened to break when the Report on the bill was brought up from committee to the House on 19 June, and warned Sir Thomas's most reliable political friend, Perceval the member for Newport, to turn up to counter any attack.[2] The preparations were to no avail; yet another parliamentary precedent was broken, and a debate took place on the report stage of the bill, remarkable also for being the first occasion on which the 'lungs of the metropolis' arguments for open spaces received a public airing. Gordon, the member for Cricklade, who had already interested himself in the case when he presented the petition of 12 June, arguing that 'it was a great hardship to many poor copyholders residing on the manor to be deprived of the advantages they derived from it', took the lead on 19 June, placing his objections on wider grounds of public policy.[3] He repeated that the bill was a threat to the rights of the copyholders, but continued:[4]

> even if all the copyholders had consented to the measure, he should object to it on the behalf of the public. It was not the fashion of the day to think much about the amusements or comforts of the poorer classes of society; but he nevertheless contended, that the House was bound not to do anything that might tend to abridge those comforts or amusements. Besides, it was not merely the poorer classes of society that were interested in this question; for he would venture to say that there was not a gentleman who resided in the vicinity of Hampstead that did not derive a benefit, either for himself or for his family, from having access to the Heath. If the lord of the manor already possessed the right of building there, let him have it; but he must protest against any further facilities being afforded for the prosecution of so undesirable an object.

Gordon was backed by John Stewart, who brought the health of Londoners as well as their recreation into the argument:

> The inhabitants of London had also a right to oppose it. No place was so advantageous to them for the restoration of their health as

---

1 *The Times*, 30 May 1829, p. 6, stating that 'enclosing of the Heath will be a serious deprivation to the inhabitants of the Metropolis'.

2 GLCRO E/MW/H/III/38/14, Draft brief for attending House of Commons... 17 June 1829.

3 *Hansard*, N.S. xxi, H. of C. 12 June 1829, 1771–2.

4 Ibid., 19 June 1829, 1814–18.

the heath at Hampstead. It was a common source of good to all classes in the metropolis (hear); and even artists were in the habit of going to Hampstead Heath to draw sketches of the metropolis.

Sir Joseph Yorke clinched the matter, by harking back to old fears that London was becoming ungovernable, a potential revolutionary menace, by reason of its enormous size. He proposed, in effect, to begin a policy of restriction by obliging Sir Thomas Maryon Wilson to keep his estate empty of people, which he presented as a small sacrifice of private gain in the wider interest of the defence of private property everywhere against becoming a breeding ground of disorder and violent revolution. 'For the sake of the public', he opposed the measure.

There were already 1,200,000 people in London. The right hon. Secretary [Peel] had been obliged to bring in a new police Bill to govern them; and he believed he was not mistaken when he said, that the government looked with alarm at the daily increase of their numbers. It was because he did not wish the metropolis to become larger, that he voted for Sir T. Wilson remaining where he was; and he hoped that gentleman, by endeavouring to grasp at all, would not endanger what he already possessed.

In was in vain that Perceval tried to point out the illogicality and injustice of basing a general policy of restricting London's growth on the mere accident that one fringe landowner out of dozens had been obliged to come to Parliament to obtain building powers; and as to the value of open space to the general public:

He begged to deny distinctly that there was one syllable in the Bill which would enable the lord of the manor to inclose any portion of the Heath . . . He was quite prepared to go with those who wished to preserve the Heath for the recreation of the public; and if the present Bill would interfere with the Heath, it would be easy to strike out from the schedule that part which referred to the waste of Hampstead.

Although apparently no vote was taken, the sense of the House was so definitely against the bill, and the agitation outdoors so vociferous, that Sir Thomas's advisers promptly withdrew the measure, hoping that it could be reintroduced when passions had cooled and reason, legally-informed, could prevail. *The Times* celebrated a notable victory editorially:[1]

[1] *The Times*, 20 June 1829, p. 5.

> The Bill for enclosing the Heath has been withdrawn. We agree with Sir Joseph Yorke, that public convenience is a fit and excellent ground for rejecting a measure of this kind. Mr Littleton will see . . . that the rights of private property are always subordinate to the rights of the public. The whole doctrine of nuisance . . . rests on this principle.

The whole episode, for pre-Reform 1829, represents an astonishing trouncing for the sanctity of private property and shows that Parliament's extreme tenderness towards landowners and their rights to do what they liked with their own had at least one limit. It is, to say the least, curious that this limit should be reached in terms of a metropolitan open space, desirable though that is in itself, at a time when no question was entertained of the pre-eminence of the public interest over private property in such favourite areas of radical attack on 'landlord oppression and corruption' as the game laws, nepotism in the public service, pluralism in the church, or sinecure-holding by the aristocracy. In truth the Heath case was not a triumph of the champions of the propertyless public over the selfishness of an individual landowner, as it seemed to be; rather, it was the victory of one set of property owners over one of their own class. It was those 'gentlemen who resided in the vicinity of Hampstead' who had carried the day, however much they had used small tradesman-shopkeeper copyholders as their stooges and 'healthy open space' for their propaganda.

In August 1829, when the dust had settled, another public meeting was called in the Assembly Rooms at Hampstead. At it, William Ripley complained that he had borne most of the expense of the opposition to the Wilson bill, and asked for a public subscription to be raised to carry on the opposition in the future. He announced that Lord Mansfield had already agreed to subscribe £50. The meeting was thinly attended —only twenty-two copyholders plus six journalists being present— and Paxon the auctioneer held that the proceedings were unconstitutional, and that the proper course was to convene a general assembly and appoint a representative Copyholders' Committee as had been done with the original Committee of 1819; hence this meeting dissolved without passing any resolutions.[1] It sufficed, however, to reveal the real manipulators of the agitation, both of whom had stayed well in the background. William Ripley, a substantial copyholder beyond West End and a partner with his brothers in a firm of City solicitors, apparently footed the bill in furtherance of a personal vendetta against

[1] Ibid., 6 August 1829, p. 2.

[146]

the steward of the manor. Lord Mansfield promised some money, and leant his considerable political weight against Wilson, because he did not want any rash of houses to spoil the foreground of Ken Wood.

The key to Mansfield's position and indeed to a great deal of the subsequent campaigns which were ostensibly concerned solely with the Heath, was not in fact the Heath itself but the sixty acres of freehold land which Wilson owned on the east and north-east side of the Heath, and which Wilson later on christened East Heath Park. The only existing access to these fields was across the Heath, which separated them from Spaniards Road on the north-west, and the Vale of Health and East Heath Road on the south-west. But access to the outside world across non-Heath land might be made through Rhodes's copyhold on the South (the present South Hill Park Road and Gardens) and so to South End and Pond Street. While in any case there was already access to East Heath Park by footpaths and cart-tracks across the Heath from the end of Well Walk and from the Vale of Health. The development of East Heath Park was thus an eminently feasible proposition, so soon as Sir Thomas Maryon Wilson should obtain leasing powers over his own freehold lands. No amount of protection of the Heath or of the copyholders' rights could ever prevent his building on it. Yet on the north-east and north, East Heath Park ran with the grounds of Ken Wood; and the Hampstead residents were in the habit of regarding East Heath Park as indistinguishable from the Heath when it came to walking, riding, or admiring the view. It was therefore of the utmost importance to Lord Mansfield, and to the lovers of open views, to prevent Sir Thomas gaining full control of his own freehold estate. But because this was too monstrous an object to avow openly, since it amounted to a complete denial of the accepted rights of private property, it was in the interest of this group to ensure the continuation of the maximum amount of confusion between the issues of copyhold, Heath, and freehold estates, which were in reality easily separable and perfectly straightforward.

This was all made clear to those who cared to read about it when Sir Thomas returned to the attack in 1830. An estate bill was introduced on the lines of that of the previous session, but omitting any clauses for granting licences or making agreements with copyholders for the encouragement of improvement of their copyholds by building, and omitting from the schedule of Wilson freehold lands all mention of the Heath and parcels of it which might be approved in the future.[1] These

[1] GLCRO E/MW/H/III/38/14, Print of the Maryon Wilson Estate Act [sic], 1830.

crucial amendments rendered the bill perfectly innocuous, and should have removed all grounds for the previous objections so far as they had derived from honest misunderstanding of the bill's purposes and probable effects. This time the Wilson forces took care to run their own publicity and not leave their opponents to make the pace. On overhearing a remark on his way from depositing the bill at the private bill office, to the effect that it was a bill for the enclosure of Hampstead Heath, Lyddon drafted a long letter to the *Morning Herald* which pointed to the East Heath Park angle of the business:[1]

> The powers to grant building leases and make contracts for the granting of building leases will apply to the inclosed properties enumerated in the Schedule, and *to none other* . . . To such an Act Sir T. M. Wilson conceives there cannot be any *fair* or *reasonable* objection. 'A Solicitor' whose letter you published on 28 April, has used a subterfuge to mislead those who do not see the Schedule to the Bill . . . Parts of Sir T. M. Wilson's *old inclosed freehold lands* are situate on the east side of Hampstead Heath; other parts on the south-west side . . . Need I add that inclosed lands on the one and the other side of Hampstead Heath do not form any part of that Heath . . .

Lyddon went on to reveal one of the motives which had operated in 1829, when some copyholders saw the value of their properties being sharply depreciated unless the bill was stopped.

> A Baronet who is the Proprietor of Freehold Houses and Land in Hampstead, and a small Copyholder [Sir Thomas Neave, owner of Oak Hill House] in the last session strenuously opposed the Bill, under the imperfect impression wrought upon his mind, and through a person who was in treaty for part of his land to build on declining it in consequence of the report that Sir T. M. Wilson was obtaining an Act to enclose and build upon Hampstead Heath. The Baronet alluded to was not rightly informed . . . This year a print of the present form of the Bill was submitted to him, and upon seeing it, he felt that, though not without fear of the Act affecting his Freehold Property in Hampstead . . . he cannot *as a Gentleman* desire that Sir T. M. Wilson should not have an Act to enable him to improve his estate. You will view this as honourable and therefore praiseworthy conduct, which deserves

[1] Ibid., Draft letter from W. Lyddon to the Editor, *Morning Herald*, 29 April 1830.

mention by me. [And he added a note in pencil:] If any other person follows this honourable course, I will publicise their names.

None did. Instead when the bill, which had once more received a favourable Judges' Report, came up for second reading in the Lords it was strongly opposed by Lord Mansfield backed by Lord Tenterden. Mansfield objected because 'it would prove exceedingly injurious to the town of Hampstead and to all who held property in its vicinity', adding to please the lawyers that to grant the leasing powers would be to overturn the deliberate terms of the 1806 will. Tenterden rested himself entirely on this legal ground; neither, of course, knew that they were perfectly correct. Only Lord Arden, better known for profligacy than probity, spoke up for Maryon Wilson on grounds of equity, since the House had always consented before to this kind of estate bill and ought not to make an exception. Probably for the first time in its history the House divided on an estate bill, and defeated it by 23 to 7.[1] Sir Thomas Maryon Wilson's recollection of this incident painted in the personal motives involved:[2]

> On the second reading of the Bill of 1830, the late Earl of Mansfield offered an opposition by himself, and Lord Tenterden, and other peers, and on a division the Bill was stopped. That opposition has been considered unfair, as it was based upon a pretence that the House of Lords had been acting erroneously in passing Acts of the like nature, and ought to change its practice; whereas, as to Lord Mansfield, it was a mere personal apprehension that Caen Wood might be less agreeable if buildings should arise near its boundaries, and as to Lord Tenterden it might be also a personal concern, as his lordship traversed Hampstead Heath in his way from and to Hendon, and he may have willingly credited the falsehoods which had been propagated of the intended enclosure and building upon Hampstead Heath; though as a Judge, his lordship might have been expected to have ascertained the truth of the representation.

Sir Thomas was even more explicit in accusing Lord Mansfield of highly self-interested motives, when he drew up a statement with which to launch his third attempt, in 1843:[3]

[1] *Hansard*, N.S. xxiv, H. of L. 5 May 1830, 423–4. Lord Arden was Sir Thomas's first cousin.
[2] GLCRO E/MW/H/III/38/14, Memo as to the Bills of 1829 and 1830 NOT to inclose the Heath, 23 June 1843.
[3] GLCRO E/MW/H/III/38/14, Draft statement by Sir T. M. Wilson to the Copyholders, 1843.

The Bill was again introduced in 1830, and having found how strong and obstinate was the opposition of Lord Mansfield, I obtained after some difficulty an interview with him at his house in Portland Place. When he talked about Entailed Estates, I asked why he did not oppose other Private Estate Acts (there were then about 20 before Parliament) and why he did not assist me in opposing the New Road made through my estate which my father as well as myself objected to. But, and this was his answer, the other Estates for which private bills come before Parliament are not at Hampstead, and the new road through your property does not come near Caen Wood. I own that it is hard that you cannot by law do that which you are not by law forbidden to do. I oppose you on private grounds, I will put it on public ground and I know I can beat you, I know the ways of the House. And he did beat me —for on the second reading of the bill when he knew there would be but a thin house he took with him a few Scotch lords as honest as himself, and the bill was thrown out for that session. Since then I have not renewed my application to Parliament because for the last ten years there has been no certainty of the House sitting out a session.

There is little reason to doubt Sir Thomas's account, and every reason to understand his sour tone; though it may be observed that Lord Mansfield's evident personal interest in preserving open land on the park boundaries of Ken Wood did not preclude a genuine sympathy with those who wanted to keep open land all round the Heath, since the two purposes coincided. Given these objectives, the tactics of presenting their case in terms of the Heath alone, knowing that it was not actually threatened, were obvious and highly effective. For once the Wilson side had made the blunder of mentioning the Heath in the 1829 bill, no one afterwards was inclined to believe that the Heath was beyond the reach of all the later versions of the bill.

The only remarkable feature, perhaps, is that as early as 1829 the Heath had become an object of sentimental attachment for many people who had no property interests at stake, and the idea of its enclosure had become powerfully emotive. It had not always been so. It may be hard to imagine that there ever was a time when the Heath was not regarded as a thing of beauty and a joy for ever, but until the late eighteenth century there is little sign that it was regarded with anything but utilitarian eyes, as the source of so much sand, or fearful eyes, as the refuge of so many footpads. It is true that Defoe had noticed the

Heath and found it agreeable, in the early eighteenth century. 'On the Top of the Hill indeed', he commented, 'there is a very pleasant Plain, called the Heath, which on the very Summit is a Plain of about a Mile every way; and in good Weather 'tis pleasant airing upon it.'[1] After his time it is possible that some of the locals may have taken the air on the Heath occasionally, but there is no record of people making a special journey from London just to visit the Heath; and it is significant that so exact an observer as Daniel Lysons, writing in 1795, commented that there was a fine view of the metropolis from Hampstead, but found no occasion to say more of the Heath than that 'the waste is 273 acres.'[2]

The first local historian, J. J. Park, was certainly interested in the Heath when he wrote in 1813, but chiefly from the point of view of its geological composition and of the wild flowers and herbs found there by a succession of dedicated botanical collectors since the early seventeenth century. He was careful to inquire into the number of loads of sand which were taken from the Heath daily, it being prized as a building material.[3] And he was curious about the legal technicalities governing appropriations from the waste for building plots and garden grounds.[4] But he found no occasion to mention that the Heath was admired for its beauties or wildness, or was a favourite resort for pleasure and recreation, presumably because the Heath was little used for such purposes. Even the fair on the Heath, which seems so traditional, appears to go back no further than the early nineteenth century. Park knew of only one earlier fair, advertised in 1712: 'This is to give notice, that Hampstead Fair is to be kept upon the Lower Flask tavern walk, on Friday the first of August, and holds for four days', the notice ran. His comment was that he did not know when it was put an end to, 'but it is not within the memory of any person of whom I have enquired.'[5] The regular local fair, in Park's time, was held at West End: 'Here is a Fair for toys, gingerbread, &c. held on the 26th July and two following days.'[6] It was held on the small West End Green, with an overflow into a field belonging to General Orde, now the site of West End Lane station. Traditionally it had been a very small affair of four or five

---

[1] Daniel Defoe, *Tour through the Whole Island of Great Britain*, I, 383.
[2] Daniel Lysons, *The Environs of London* (1795), II, 528.
[3] J. J. Park, *The Topography and Natural History of Hampstead* (1818), p. 45.
[4] Ibid., pp. 92–6.
[5] Ibid., p. 246.
[6] Ibid., p. 256. The fair had been held at West End in July since the early eighteenth century at least; Edward Walford, *Old and New London* (6 vols, n.d. [1877]), V, 503.

booths only, but early in the nineteenth century it began to attract crowds of roughs from London, and grew to alarmingly riotous proportions. The local magistrates made an unsuccessful attempt to suppress it as a nuisance in 1812; then the 'enormous outrages' committed at the fair of 1819 spurred Germaine Lavie, J.P. and West End resident, to more forceful efforts. He reported to the Home Secretary that the mischief was increasing every July 27th, as more and more people swarmed across the fields to West End from the north-west end of London, mainly undesirables 'productive of drunkenness and debauchery, and the practice of every species of vice and immorality'; the inhabitants were appalled by 'the daring depredations and atrocious outrages committed at the last fair by large gangs of desperate thieves.' Since the fair was an informal one in the sense of not resting on any charter or special grant, it was relatively simple to suppress, and it ceased very soon after 1819.[1] Until it disappeared this was the annual Hampstead fair. It might well be that the annual fair on the Heath took up where West End left off, to provide in a somewhat less outrageous way for the new taste of the London populace for an annual expedition to Hampstead.

One would expect that the beginnings of truly popular use of the Heath by the populace—which despite magisterial depositions must have consisted of more than just riff-raff since there had to be some law-abiding pockets for the criminal elements to pick—would have been preceded by some attentions from the more refined classes. But again there is little evidence of any explicit appreciation of the Heath on aesthetic or therapeutic grounds, as a place of particular enchantment and beauty or as an invigorating exercise ground, until romanticism began to make a cult of nature and the outdoor world in the very late eighteenth century. The eighteenth-century authors, poets, and artists who had been connected with Hampstead had not drawn their inspiration or subject matter directly from the place, however much the atmosphere of their Hampstead houses had contributed in the way of quiet working conditions. The landscape painters arrived in Hampstead in the early 1820s: John Constable came to live at 2 Lower Terrace, in 1821; John Linnell took Collin's Farm—the Wyldes Farm belonging to Eton College, which provided the land for the Hampstead Garden Suburb—near North End, in 1822; and William Collins took a cottage at North End in 1823. Though Linnell was also a portrait painter of note, all three were landscape artists, and all three painted many

---

[1] T. J. Barratt, *The Annals of Hampstead* (1912), II, 244–5; GLCRO E/MW/H/III/38/15, W. Lyddon to Sir Edward Knatchbull, 20 April 1826.

Hampstead pictures, particularly pictures which show the central importance of the wildness and naturalness of the Heath to their artistic vision. The poets anticipated the artists by a few years in recording their appreciation of the Heath. Mark Akenside, it is true, had commemorated the curative powers of the greenery of Golder's Hill in his 'On Recovering from a Fit of Sickness in the Country' of 1758, written when he was living in Golder's Hill House just over the border into Hendon parish beyond North End; but this was scarcely appreciation of nature of 'lakeland' style or quality. The true application of the poetry of the countryside to Hampstead and the Heath came with the sonnet on Hampstead by the local man, Thomas Park, father of the local historian John James Park, published in 1818; and with the association of Leigh Hunt and his circle with Hampstead which began in 1812.

Leigh Hunt's first sonnet to Hampstead, written in Surrey Gaol in 1815, marks the arrival of Hampstead in romantic literature with its opening lines:

> Sweet upland, to whose walks with fond repair
> Out of thy western slope I took my rise
> Day after day, and on these feverish eyes
> Met the moist fingers of the bathing air;

While his later sonnet captures the romantic view of Hampstead in verse as Constable captured it on canvas:[1]

> A steeple issuing from a leafy rise,
> With farmy fields in front and sloping green,
> Dear Hampstead, is thy southern face serene,
> Silently smiling on approaching eyes,
> Within, thine ever-shifting looks surprise,
> Streets, hills and dells, trees overhead now seen,
> Now down below, with smoking roofs between,—
> A village, revelling in varieties.
> Then northward what a range—with heath and pond
> Nature's own ground; woods that let mansions through,
> And cottaged vales with billowy fields beyond,
> And clumps of darkening pines, and prospects blue,
> And that clear path through all, where daily meet
> Cool cheeks, and brilliant eyes, and morn-elastic feet.

Returning from gaol to live in a cottage in the Vale of Health—Vale

[1] Quoted in Barratt, op. cit., II, 139–40.

Lodge being his home for a time—Leigh Hunt drew a poets' circle to Hampstead, including Keats, Shelley, Byron, Lamb, and Hazlitt among his frequent visitors. In the years after 1816 the country-lovers and the nature-lovers in this set made the Heath into their wilderness on the doorstep, their 'prettiest walk in England' across to Highgate, perhaps to meet Coleridge, and the backcloth for the 'Ode to a Nightingale'.

It is, therefore, legitimate to suppose that it was only from about the early 1800s that the Heath began to have a cultural history and a cultural importance, and that the great divide between sandpit and cattle run, and beauty spot, is relatively recent. As for pure conservation, or rather carefully controlled and contrived wild-landscape gardening, and suppression of the ancient workaday use of the Heath for digging ballast and sand, and grazing cattle, that was much more recent still, and dates only from 1871 and the subjection of the Heath to municipal park management. Moreover, the Heath seems to have entered into the cultural experience of the middle and intellectual classes only a few years before it became associated with popular culture: the one in pursuit of the elevating effects of natural solitude so close to teeming multitudes, the other in pursuit of enjoyment, entertainment, and relaxation. The most remarkable feature of all this is not the apparent lateness of the change in the Heath's status, for this was perfectly in step with the nationwide alteration in attitudes towards rugged and untamed countryside; it is that the new development of both cultured and popular taste was noted and acted upon politically so very rapidly. The little debate in the Commons in 1829, infinitely remote from the staples of party controversies and the great issues like representation or emancipation, is an astonishing vindication of the sensitivity to changes in people's attitudes and concerns which was possible in the unreformed Parliament.

After 1830 Sir Thomas Maryon Wilson's concern was to obtain control over his estate so that he could start cropping it with houses instead of hay. As far as can be judged he was completely sincere in his repeated disclaimers of any intention to do a building damage to the Heath as properly defined and bounded, and his lawyers were equally honest in their statements that as a matter of law nothing in any of the Wilson estate bills could possibly confer any power to build upon the Heath. Besides, whatever hidden thoughts he may have entertained about his ownership of the residuary rights in the soil of the Heath, it was absurd to imagine that as a pure matter of estate policy and building economics Maryon Wilson could ever contemplate starting any building schemes with the Heath. Despite Defoe's impression of a large 'Plain', the local topography and the irregularity of the ground made the Heath very far indeed from ideal building land. While Sir Thomas's own freehold estate of over 400 acres was more than enough to keep the market for building land supplied for a very long time; when this land did eventually become available for building after his death it in fact took sixty years and more for it all to be taken up, even allowing for the 'loss' of sixty acres which was purchased and added to the Heath. If his land had been developed at the same standards and densities as Chelsea, then the whole of Hampstead's population in 1871 could have been accommodated on the area of Sir Thomas's freehold estate. To aim first at the development of his freeholds, while much copyhold land yet remained uncovered, admittedly went against Sir Thomas's preferred policy for gaining the greatest possible income from property; but after the row in 1829 this seemed to him a necessary sacrifice because people were wilfully incapable of seeing that his scheme for granting licences to copyholders for building purposes was not a device for grinding the faces of the poor. But quite understandably he entirely failed to see why he should not cover his freehold property with houses, if it was profitable for him to do so, just as every other landowner was at liberty to do. The Heath, the wider and legally pseudo-Heath which included his 60 acres of East Heath Park, stood splendidly and irrationally in his way. Unreason, prejudice, hypo-critically disguised self-interest, and unjust persecution of a single individual rode roughshod over all the rules of the property game, and presented to posterity the priceless gift not of the legal mini-Heath surrounded on three sides by rows of houses, but of the greater Heath, wider yet and wider, wide open to Parliament Hill Fields and beyond to the Highgate Road, a continuous open space not of some 80 or 90 acres which was the size of the East Heath *de jure*, but of over 350 acres.[1] With every year that passed after 1830 the Heath became more prized by the intellectuals and more embedded in the Londoners' folk culture, and neither of these interests was inclined to be bothered by legal fuss over boundaries and extents. The increasing attractiveness of the place, which anywhere else would have made it irresistibly ripe for building, simply doomed the luckless Sir Thomas to perpetual failure.

Immediately after his disappointment in the Lords in 1830 Sir

[1] 350 acres refers to the area bounded by East Heath Road–Spaniards Road–Ken Wood park–Highgate Road–North London Railway. If the Ken Wood estate is included, the modern East Heath comprises nearly one square mile of open space. The North Heath (between Spaniards Road and North End Road) and the West Heath (between North End Road and West Heath Road) contain, together, about 150 acres.

Thomas's advisers tried on one of those ingenious devices for out-flanking the provisions of the law and the legislative process which real property lawyers have ever excelled in producing. The nature of the proposal to abuse the trusts of the 1806 will was a piece of legal machinery almost as intricately beautiful to a conveyancer's eye as the original work of the Restoration lawyers in evolving the trustees to preserve contingent remainders, which now constituted the chief cause of difficulty. The will had given the first estate in the Maryon Wilson properties to trustees for a term of 500 years with the duty of raising and paying portions to the younger children, and subject to that trust had given the second estate to the eldest son, Sir Thomas, for his life. As soon as all the portions had been paid, the term of 500 years would cease and become void. Of the elder Sir Thomas's five non-landed children, two had died, unmarried, in the 1820s; his three surviving daughters were due to share £25,000 in portion money, of which £20,000 was to be raised from the younger Sir Thomas's estates. By 1830 some £4,800 of this sum still remained to be raised, the rest of the £20,000 having already been found by the sale of timber from the Sussex estate and by borrowing £11,000 in 1829 from the Union Assurance Society on the security of part of the Hampstead property. The proposal now was that the term of 500 years might be kept alive for a guaranteed 99 years by getting the 'portion trustees' to grant 99-year leases of the remaining unmortgaged 300 acres in Hampstead, taking a premium at the rate of about £15 per acre from the lessees so as to make up the £4,800 of capital to discharge the portion; but reserving in the leases a full building rent to be paid to Sir Thomas, and inserting in the leases the usual covenants for getting the land built upon in an approved fashion. Unluckily for the ingenuity of this scheme, when the kite was flown before two leading conveyancing barristers their conservative instincts rebelled against the monstrosity of using a portion trust as the vehicle for issuing building leases. Their answer was uncompromising:[1]

The proposed plan is wholly impracticable. Such leases would in fact amount to sales of part of the Estate for part of the term of 500 years, and the testator has expressly prohibited a sale—even if that prohibition did not exist, we think that the proposed leases would be inconsistent with the trusts . . . and that no purchaser

[1] GLCRO E/MW/H/III/38/14, Case for the joint opinion of Mr Preston and Mr Rudall, May 1830, and Opinion of Richard Preston and John Rudall, 21 May 1830.

could be advised to accept a title under any such lease. An Act of Parliament is the only means by which the wishes of the parties can be carried into effect, and we think Sir Thomas ought not to despair of being successful on a future application to Parliament.

Richard Preston and John Rudall, the two conveyancing counsel, may therefore rank among those who played a part in preserving the greater Heath from the builder.

From 1830 to 1843 Sir Thomas remained quiet, partly no doubt for the reason he gave that the duration of parliamentary sessions became erratic, so that an expensively prepared private bill might easily be killed in mid-course by an unexpected closure; though such a situation did not inhibit the passing of a great many other private acts in this period. The dormancy was mainly caused, it seems likely, by the prolonged building recession which meant that there was very little activity anywhere in Hampstead during these years; equally, the revival of operations, chiefly on the Eyre and Eton estates, was the signal for Sir Thomas to make his third attempt. His 1843 Estate Bill followed the pattern of 1830, carefully excluding all mention of the Heath or any parcels taken from it, and including a general saving clause saving the rights of all persons except the Maryon Wilson family in the scheduled lands 'as they might be before the passing of this Act'. It gained a favourable Judges' Report in the Lords, but after reaching the stage of a second reading without a debate was withdrawn because of the uproar from the Hampstead residents and copyholders.[1]

The Copyholders' Committee was re-activated and joined issue under the lead of their secretary Thomas Toller, a solicitor residing in Hampstead who was also the clerk to the Vestry and chief representative of such municipal life as there was. Sir Thomas then bombarded the copyholders with printed circulars explaining his case and the distinctions between his freeholds, the copyhold lands, and the Heath; but the resistance, naturally, did not want to hear. On 8 May Sir Thomas wrote:[2]

Hearing that my Estate Bill now before Parliament has caused great and unnecessary alarm, I am solicitous that you should understand that it relates only to my Freehold Houses, Buildings and inclosed Lands in Hampstead, which are specified in the first

[1] HLRO, Maryon Wilson Estate Bill, 1843, Judges' Report, 1 May 1843, second reading, 26 June 1843, withdrawn, 29 June 1843.
[2] GLCRO E/MW/H/III/38/14, Letter from Sir T. M. Wilson to the Copyholders of the Manor of Hampstead, 8 May 1843.

Schedule to the Bill; and does not interfere with any of the Copyhold Properties in the Manor.

If inquiry be made of Mr Thomas Toller, he will satisfy you
that a Bill could not, with propriety, be introduced into the House
of Lords . . . which is to interfere with the interests and privileges of Copyholders, unless they were jointly with me petitioners
for the Bill . . .

I submit, that so legitimate an object as the improvement of my
old inclosed Freehold lands is not one which should be sought to be
frustrated by false representations, or through the impulse of
erroneous apprehensions; the more so, as it is evident that considerable local benefits and advantages will be the result of the
improvement.

It was naïve of Sir Thomas to place any faith in Thomas Toller's
straightforwardness, for he promptly issued his own disingenuous
circular implying that the Heath was in danger. So after a week Sir
Thomas fired his second shot:[1]

The letter addressed to the Copyholders by Mr Thomas Toller,
their clerk, shows that I relied too much on the candour of that
gentleman in referring them to him (as their legal adviser). The
drift of Mr Toller's Circular is to induce the Copyholders to
believe not only that the Bill *does* seriously affect their interests
and privileges, but that a purpose exists in my mind ultimately to
enclose Hampstead Heath.

That any such purpose ever existed in my mind I utterly dis-
avow, or that I have ever asserted 'my right to inclose the Heath,'
in the general and unrestricted sense of those words by which
Mr Toller seeks to mislead the Copyholders. It may be true, that I
have on occasions by myself, or my Agents, asserted my right, as
an abstract legal question, as Lord of the Manor, and Owner of the
Soil, to approve small portions of the Waste, under specific and
peculiar circumstances. But that I ever thought of claiming a
general right to inclose Hampstead Heath, is an assertion groundless and preposterous, that nothing but a malicious determination
to oppose my reasonable and well-defined Petition to Parliament

[1] Ibid., second letter from Sir T. M. Wilson to the Copyholders of the Manor
of Hampstead, 15 May 1843. Thomas Toller's letter to the Copyholders, 12
May 1843, simply said that the 'Present Bill is identical to the Bill of 1830
and therefore is open to the same objections'.

for an aid, I believe, never refused by the Legislature in analogous cases, can account for.

. . . The only definite allegation of any possible injury to the Copyholders is, that the Heath must be cut up in order to form Roads to the intended buildings. That a single road on some part of the Heath would be required, is not impossible. But any person acquainted with the locality must see the absurdity of the assertion, that such road 'must cut up the Heath to the destruction of all Manorial Rights.' No one can have so great an interest that the Heath should not be destroyed, or even disfigured, as myself.

As for the allegation, that 'your Estates would be greatly depreciated in value, if the Meadows skirting the Heath were built upon'—it is so vague and indefinite that it is impossible to meet it, otherwise than by a remark, that it would be strange indeed, if an outlay of capital, tending to the increase of the most respectable population, the extension of trade, and the diminution of parochial rates, could possibly be prejudicial to the general value of Property within the parish.

Sir Thomas accompanied this rather tardy exercise in public relations with a printed map, sent to every copyholder, showing very plainly the boundaries of his freehold lands and the boundaries of the Heath. But already the press had taken up the case again, with the *Morning Herald* as the main vehicle for reporting the public meetings and the organisation of opposition. It did little good to Sir Thomas that Henry White, of The Mount, a prominent surveyor, was brought to acknowledge that he had been misreported by the *Herald*:[1]

I did not call your Bill a Bill to enclose Hampstead Heath. I said, that if the Bill passed without any clause for the protection of the rights of the Copyholders, I was apprehensive it would give you an exclusive right to such parts of the Heath, for making roads etc., as you might think proper, and there was no knowing to what extent it might be carried, to the injury of the Copyholders and the public at large.

Nor did it improve Sir Thomas's chances significantly that the *Herald* published a leader setting out the legal position and the immunity of the Heath, though Lyddon felt this was 'the commencement of the breaking forth of truth, which will disabuse the minds of the Copyholders', and consoled himself with the thought that there was 'a

[1] Ibid., Henry White to Sir T. M. Wilson, 17 May 1843.

change in the minds of the people, which is supposed to have resulted from the truth now spreading by your letters'.[1] The determination to prevent building, not on the Heath, but anywhere near the Heath, was too strong to be diverted by argument.

It was also too strong to be defeated by an appeal to the self-interest of the Hampstead traders and shopkeepers who could be expected to welcome more new residents on their doorsteps as that much more trade for themselves. Sir Thomas got up a public petition in favour of his bill, but it was supported only by a score or so of the locals, though it was felt that many more shopkeepers had been afraid to sign for fear of losing the custom of the resident Hampstead gentry. A letter from Daniel Smith, a hairdresser in High Street, was typical of the shopkeeper support which Sir Thomas did receive:[2]

> With great pleasure I signed a Petition this morning *in favor* of the Bill now before Parliament, by which you seek to obtain the power to improve your enclosed property at Hampstead by granting building leases . . . I believe, Sir, this is the only thing that will be of real benefit to the tradesmen of this place. I have been in business here 27 years, and have long seen the necessity of that description of detached Villa, or Cottage, that is to be met with in every other direction; and often have to regret the loss of a good customer because no such thing is to be met with here, and I am sure, that so far from being an injury, it would be of general advantage to the inhabitants, as it would cause a revival of trade, and greatly reduce the rates which are now tremendously heavy in consequence of the comparative few that have to bear the burden. Hampstead is not what it was when I first came to it—a village at a distance from London, but London is brought all around us without giving us the advantage of an increased population. I would take the liberty to suggest that, the greatest improvement (if practicable) would be, to continue the Road from the Swiss Tavern, through Shepherds Fields, to Church Row; this would bring the very heart of the Town into immediate connexion with the West End of London, and this would give us the advantage of getting to Hampstead without hills, which are so generally complained of: others may, and perhaps I should argue differently if I had an estate on the Heath; but in all other cases

[1] Ibid., W. Lyddon to Sir T. M. Wilson, 19 May 1843; W. Lyddon to the Editor, *Morning Herald*, 22 May 1843.
[2] Ibid., Daniel Smith to Sir T. M. Wilson, 24 May 1843.

the private good gives place to the general weal, and so it should be here. I sincerely hope you will succeed in your undertaking.

Hairdresser friends cannot have been congenial to the proud Sir Thomas, but in any case there were not enough of them. The Toller party got up a petition against the bill, and obtained well over 400 signatures. These included only 40 copyholders from the current total of 327 on the court rolls, the rest of the supporters being residents with no landownership status. Moreover, among the 40 copyholders who did sign there were only 7 who owned sizeable properties which themselves could become building land; 6 of these owned and resided on properties facing the Heath, and only one, Ware, who came from the Kilburn side could be considered disinterested. The absence of the signatures of the other 28 considerable copyholders who owned the rest of the 326 acres of potential copyhold building land was conspicuous. The non-landowning majority among the petitioners could not, however, be written off merely on that account. It might include lesser men who had earlier supported the 1829 petition, like Ambridge 'a shoemaker in a small way' and Clowser 'a bricklayer and reversioner in 2 or 3 small copyhold houses'; but it also included many men of distinction, wealth, and influence. There were: Thomas Sheppard, M.P. for Frome, who lived at Upper Heath; Sir Francis Palgrave, historian, Keeper of the Records, and father of the *Golden Treasury*, who lived at The Green, Pond Street, which became the site of the Hampstead General Hospital and the new Royal Free Hospital in turn; Archdeacon Philip Jennings, who lived in another house also at The Green; Martin Burgh, son of the rich clergyman Allatson Burgh who gave the name to Burgh House in New End Square; and his neighbour H. L. Baxendale, owner of Weatherall House in Well Walk, the converted Assembly Rooms; Colonel Charles Bosanquet of The Firs, by The Spaniards, to represent the old order; and Basil George Woodd, the wealthy wine merchant of the new Hillfield House, to represent the new; and many more besides.[1]

---

[1] Ibid., Petition of the Owners, Leaseholders and Occupiers of Houses and Lands in Hampstead against the Bill, June 1843; Statement to show the total acreage of Copyholds in the Manor in 1762 and in 1843, and of Copyholders having land—titheable—not built upon, 24 June 1843. The six substantial copyholders living near the Heath were: John Gurney Hoare of The Hill, North End; his neighbour John Powell who had Heath Lodge—which his son lived in—though his main copyhold estate was at West End and Kilburn; Ann and C. H. Winfield of Belle Vue and The Bartrams (in grounds opposite the future Vestry/Town Hall); Sir Thomas Neave of Oak Hill House (late of Branch Hill Lodge); and James Emlyn Carlile of Carlile House (opposite

The weight and respectability of this body of local opinion could not be gainsaid. Sir Thomas made a third and final appeal to reason, submitting the draft bill to the Attorney-General, the Solicitor-General, and John Rudall, and circulating to the copyholders their unanimous opinion that there was nothing in the bill which could lead to the enclosure of the Heath.[1] It was like so much water off a duck's back. The residents' petition rested only partly on the allegation that enclosure of the Heath would be aided by the bill; it made a far more telling point than it knew in claiming that the 1806 will, by preventing Sir Thomas granting leases for more than 21 years, had been deliberately framed to prevent his Hampstead freeholds being built over; and it made effective use of recent history by showing that in 1826 Sir Thomas had resisted the Finchley Road by arguing that a large part of his Manor Farm lay in a valley and was ineligible for building, and that it was important to him not to increase building on any of his freehold lands. But its most revealing points were that 'the demesne lands adjoining the Heath cannot be built upon without making roads across the Heath, thus destroying it and injuring your Petitioners', and that the erection of houses there 'would destroy the natural beauties of Hampstead and would greatly depreciate the value of your Petitioners' property.' That the only object which really counted was the preservation of the greater Heath by fair means or foul was made completely explicit in a letter to *The Times* under the signature of a personifier of Hampstead Heath. This admitted that the point was not whether the bill gave any direct power to enclose the Heath, dismissing the opinions of the Law Officers on this matter as true but elementary; the point rather 'is that your building will spoil all my beauty, and I can then be thrown away as worthless—preserved just as a thoroughfare, like Highgate Hill. If you had a son', the letter ended by taunting Sir Thomas, 'and that son 21 years of age, you would not want an act at all. Then why are you a bachelor?'[2]

Sir Thomas prepared more material to put his case to the general public, and to members of the House of Lords, paying particular

---

the Soldiers' Daughters Home, where Kemplay Street now runs). Thomas Sheppard knew all about the East Heath Park at first hand, since he held three paddocks there, of 11 acres, as a yearly tenant of Sir T. M. Wilson; Thomas Toller was also a yearly tenant of a 4-acre field in the same vital area.

[1] Ibid., Letter from Sir T. M. Wilson to the Copyholders of the Manor and the Inhabitants in the Parish of St John, Hampstead, 24 May 1843.

[2] Ibid., Letter from 'Hampstead Heath' to the Editor, *The Times*, 27 May 1843.

attention to the need to counter the suggestion that his father had a
positive wish to deny him building powers over Hampstead, by pointing
out that all the leases of lands and fields in Hampstead made by his
father contained a clause providing for the resumption of any part
wanted for building purposes at short notice to the tenant. Less in-
sincere was his view that general social and economic circumstances
had altered greatly since his father's death, and that what had been
suitable for the Hampstead estate in 1821 was not necessarily still
appropriate in 1843:[1]

> The testator has been dead nearly 22 years. Since his death great
> alterations have taken place in the outskirts of the Metropolis;
> and the mode which for many years past has been adopted by
> Merchants, Professional Men, and superior Tradesmen in the
> Metropolis, of having their Families in a residence at a short
> distance therefrom, has brought into use land in most of the
> parishes adjoining thereto, or at a few miles distance therefrom,
> for the erection of Villa and other superior Residences. A very
> considerable part of the lands of the Testator in Hampstead is
> particularly eligible for the erection of superior Residences, to
> which the appendages of gardens, lawns, and paddocks may be
> attached; and the natural beauties of the locality may be aided in
> their effect by a judicious selection of positions for Villas, and their
> usual adjuncts. Besides the comfort to be enjoyed by the occupiers
> of such pleasantly arranged abodes, there will be local benefits
> resulting to the Tradesmen in the parish; and other advantages
> will arise from the improvement by building.

He capped this alluring prospectus with his account of what had happened in 1829 and 1830, with its implication of Lords Mansfield and
Tenterden, which has already been quoted. For good measure, to show
how unjustly he had been treated, this returned to his discomfiture
over the Finchley Road. He took some pleasure in showing that although 'this Turnpike Road was pretended to be considered as needed
by the Public, and as a material one for saving the ascent of the
Highgate Archway', it had in fact turned out to be no more than the
private accommodation road he had predicted. He was still owed some
of his compensation money for lands taken, and 'this sum has not been
paid to this day and never will be' because the road was bankrupt
through the thinness of paying traffic; 'the Metropolitan Commissioners
[for Turnpikes]', he said, 'are understood to have abandoned the road;

[1] Ibid., Draft for a public statement on the Bill, June 1843.

a mortgagee has taken possession of the toll gates and tolls; and the parish is to be subjected to the cost of repairing the road.'[1] His cup was full, and he demanded justice. But he did not get it by talking to the lords like an estate agent; being advised that the House was likely to defeat his bill, it was withdrawn before any debate could arise.

In 1844 Sir Thomas tried yet another tack, this time trying to put through an estate bill authorising him to sell off his Hampstead property lock, stock and barrel, and to re-invest the proceeds in other estates which would be settled to the same uses. This again was a standard procedure, adopted by scores of tenants-for-life without a murmur from Parliament. Only if it should be sold, the Hampstead estate would naturally fetch a building price, and the purchaser, since he would acquire the fee simple of the estate completely unencumbered, would be at liberty to proceed to the fell deeds of building which Sir Thomas had not been permitted to perpetrate. Sir Thomas took this scheme sufficiently seriously to scan the market in estates and settle on Holm Lacey in Herefordshire, then in the market at £220,000, as the place to which he would transfer his affections. His Hampstead property, manorial rights as well as freehold, was valued at £180,000, which was in the region of three times its agricultural value but not a very stiff building price.[2] Though his brother John, whom he jovially called 'the future Duke of Hampstead', consented to this arrangement, the House of Lords did not. One of Sir Thomas's friends, the Earl of Egmont, moved the second reading for him, and was supported by a lawyer, Lord Colchester, and by the Earl of Wicklow. But Lord Mansfield weighed in against the bill, claiming that his property near the Heath, and that of many other copyholders, 'would depreciate in various degrees, from 30 to 50 per cent' as a result of any sale; which was a novel argument for placing a legal veto on a neighbour selling his own property. And he was joined by Lord Chief Justice Denman, who managed to conceal the lively personal interest he had in the issue deriving from his residence at Wyldes Farm behind an eloquent plea for a little personal sacrifice—to be undertaken by Sir Thomas—for the welfare of the general public:[3]

> It had been said this was a Bill to inclose the Heath. It was not, but it would give power to grant to any builder 400 acres of that land which now made Hampstead such a healthy and happy place

[1] Ibid., Memorandum as to the Bills of 1829 and 1830, 23 June 1843.
[2] Ibid., Memorandum on the Bill for the sale of Hampstead, March 1844.
[3] *Hansard*, 3rd ser. LXXV, H. of L. 6 June 1844, pp. 312–18.

—where thousands of persons from the metropolis daily enjoyed themselves during the fine period of the year, in a manner they could not do elsewhere. Surely that consideration ought greatly to outweigh any small advance in value—any small improvement, in a pecuniary point of view—that might be effected by devoting the ground to building purposes. The copyholders too would be greatly annoyed by the proposed disposition of the property. At present they enjoyed a most beautiful view, open to Harrow, open to the west. But, if this Bill were passed, they would soon have a row of houses bounding their view, and surrounding these 400 acres.

This piece of fraudulent rhetoric was enough to procure the rejection of the bill by 31 votes to 20. It was a sham because if there were public grounds for preserving the whole of the Maryon Wilson property as open country—and this would have been most delightful—then all the rules of property rights then, and since, dictate that the public should pay the owner for this benefit, and not expect him to provide it free.

It was at this period, probably in anticipation of a success for his 1843 bill, that Sir Thomas built the handsome little viaduct across one of the upper Hampstead Ponds which were leased to the New River Company as one of their water sources. Nowadays enjoyed as part of the Heath scenery and a convenient bridge on one of the paths across the Heath, this viaduct in fact lay fairly and squarely on Sir Thomas's private property, and was built in preparation for opening out his East Heath Park building scheme, forming part of the spinal road which he named East Park Road, that was to run from a point opposite Jack Straw's Castle along the line of an ancient path across a few yards of the Heath north of the Vale of Health, and then down the length of East Heath Park until an exit should be formed by the lower Hampstead Ponds and across another short stretch of the Heath to link up with the foot of Downshire Hill. It is indicative of the highly-charged emotions which lingered round this viaduct until well into the present century that the local historian Barratt, although he quite correctly placed it within the Maryon Wilson property—purchased in 1889 and only then thrown into the ancient Heath—on his map of the Heath, still blandly discussed the viaduct as evidence of the nefarious plans of the 'self-willed and pertinacious' Sir Thomas to enclose and build on the Heath. Speaking of resistance to 'further encroachments' by Sir Thomas, Barratt says that 'the situation became more acute when . . . [he] constructed a new road across the valley, bridging the deeper part by a viaduct which still stands as a memorial of an ill-considered project. His idea was to build villas, but the opposition was too strong for him and he was not allowed to go on.'[1] The amount of confusion in these pronouncements is astonishing, unless indeed Barratt believed that the £100,000 which the public paid to Sir Spencer Maryon Wilson in 1889 for the 60 acres on which the viaduct and East Park Road stood, had been given under false pretences, and that this land really already belonged to the 'public'—or at least the copyholders of the manor—as an ancient part of the Heath long ago stolen from it by some pre-decessors of the Maryon Wilsons. But such a careful historian could not have entertained such a crazy notion; for all the documentary evidence, stretching back for centuries, showed that this land never was any part of the Heath and had always been private property. Neverthe-less, building over it, though permissible within any normal inter-pretation of the law, would still have been ill-considered from the viewpoint of public interest in a matchless piece of metropolitan scenery. To expect one individual, Sir Thomas Maryon Wilson, to bear the entire cost of forebearing to do the permissible so that the public might enjoy themselves at his expense was an outrage on the Victorian conscience. An outrage which millions must be grateful it was willing to bear.

[1] Barratt, op. cit., II, 205, and Map of Hampstead Heath, facing II, 196.

Five

THE HEATH ACQUIRED

In the 1840s it was virtually unthinkable that public money, taxpayers' and ratepayers' money, should be spent on anything so frivolous as the acquisition of land for open spaces or parks. Virtually, but not quite unthinkable. In 1846 an Act was passed to enable the Commissioners for Woods and Forests to form a public park in Battersea Fields, and an expenditure of £200,000 was authorised for the purchase of land, laying out a park, and forming an embankment along the Thames. The operation could be excused to some extent, as not being quite such a startlingly new form of government expenditure as it appeared, since it was intended to be self-financing in the long run: out of the 320 acres which was acquired, only 198 were retained for the new park, and the remainder was let for building sites. It could also be excused, as being a regrettably necessary measure of moral policing, to suppress the notoriety into which the previously unregulated Battersea Fields had fallen—'if ever there was a place out of hell that surpassed Sodom and Gomorrah in ungodliness and abomination, this was it'—by substituting a decorously controlled environment where shameless dancers, foot-racers, and other forms of sin would be prohibited.[1] Such was the genesis of Battersea Park; though it was more than a decade before the enabling Act was translated into achievement, under the aegis of the newly-established Metropolitan Board of Works, and the Park was opened in 1858. The gross expenditure, disregarding any future income that might come in, had been £312,000, all charged on the Consolidated Fund.[2] It was a notable, and successful, departure from the rules of economy in public expenditure and from the doctrine that local improvements should be paid for by the local beneficiaries and not out of general taxation. But it exhausted the willingness of the government to support such extravagances.

In the 1850s it became rather more thinkable that public money

[1] S. E. Rasmussen, *London: the Unique City* (Penguin ed., 1960), p. 234.
[2] E. Walford, *Old and New London* [1877], VI, 477.

might be spent on open spaces for large towns, though in the fine youth of Gladstonian finance it became if anything less conceivable that the Treasury should be the one to find the money. Municipal enterprise municipally supported could be tolerated and even positively assisted by enabling legislation, but to ask the general taxpayer to foot the bill with any sort of subsidy so that part of a Manchester man's pleasures and comforts might be paid for by a Birmingham taxpayer was asking too much. Where some recognisable sense of belonging to a true urban community developed, and with it the beginnings of civic pride, as it did in many provincial cities, this emphasis on local self-reliance had its virtues and did work. But in great amorphous London with no structure of metropolitan government and no corporate existence it was a policy calculated to stimulate and aggravate parochial squabbling rather than to produce any visible results. When the conversion of Hornsey Wood into Finsbury Park was discussed in 1857—the Park was not opened until 1869—it was typical that the MP for Lambeth should object to any arrangement which might involve Lambeth ratepayers contributing towards the cost of a park for Finsbury people.[1] Though one of the very first enlargements of the scope of the Metropolitan Board of Works, which had been designed in 1855 as little more than a superior sewer authority for greater London, was to give it powers to acquire and manage public parks, the parochialism of its constituent vestries and district boards made them almost ineffectual.

In this climate, where taxpayers and ratepayers could not or would not pay to buy out the owner of any private grounds wanted for a public open space, it was perhaps inevitable that if the Maryon Wilson grounds in Hampstead were to be preserved at all as open country they had to be preserved by the deceit, fraud, and misrepresentation which portrayed these grounds as being public property already. Whether the deceit was practised with honest intentions, as it were, as the only practicable means to hand for securing a genuine public benefit, or whether it was a truly deceitful deceit calculated to advance the private interest of a few individuals under the cover of a public cause, it may not now be possible to determine conclusively. But that the men on the spot who were the stage-managers of all the anti-Wilson manoeuvres knew that it was a deceit, and that they were attempting to sterilise large tracts of privately-owned ground as permanent open country without having to pay for it, there is no doubt whatever. Those who

[1] *Hansard*, 3rd ser. CXLI, H. of C. 23 June 1857, p. 239. W. Williams was the MP for Lambeth. On this occasion the proposal to make a grant of £50,000 towards the cost of creating Finsbury Park was defeated.

entered into the Hampstead Heath affair from a distance, such as the metropolitan MPs and from the 1860s the Commons Preservation Society, probably did not know that they were having wool pulled over their eyes, and fought the more strenuously because they remained free to believe that they were engaged in a wholly righteous struggle against a wicked and grasping landowner. But while this group, the press, the wider public, and the local historians after them, all shared a feeling of outrage at the knavery of Sir Thomas Maryon Wilson, the actual documents serve rather to excite understanding that Sir Thomas should have become increasingly incensed by the shameful and shabby treatment meted out to him. Indeed, his behaviour was remarkably restrained in view of the provocation he received, and it is a wonder that he did not completely devastate and disfigure the Heath in a peevish rage.

The main development in the saga of the Maryon Wilson estate bills after his fourth failure, in 1844, was that the MPs for the metropolitan constituencies became interested in blocking the passage of subsequent attempts. They may well have been put up to this, as the Maryon Wilson side alleged, by the ring-leaders of the Hampstead gentry, Hoare, Powell and Turner; and it was through these three and their propaganda that the MPs learnt to accept without investigation that any and every estate bill emanating from Maryon Wilson must imply building over the Heath whatever the clauses in the bill might say to the contrary. But their eagerness to take up this cause was not due to old-fashioned patronage politics or personal friendship with the Hampstead gentry; it was rather a matter of necessary political and electioneering tactics, rendered necessary by the growing popularity of the Heath among the general body of their constituents. Particularly after the opening of the Hampstead Junction Railway in 1860 the Heath became easily accessible to East-Enders, and estimates of the size of the holiday crowds arriving at the Hampstead Heath station rapidly climbed into the 50,000–100,000 region. Mass enjoyment of the Heath on such a scale was not something which any MP with London electors could afford to see endangered if he had any ambitions of remaining in the House. A second new development, a consequence of this widened political concern, was of absorbing and painfully-surprised interest to constitutional lawyers: Maryon Wilson was made an exception, almost literally by name, to the applicability of an ordinary public Act of Parliament, a piece of personal discrimination never before or since made part of a statute.

Before this, however, the resumption of active building on the Eyre lands adjoining his south-western boundary at the end of the 1840s, and the first signs of building estate operations on the Belsize lands to the east and south-east at the beginning of the 1850s, inspired Sir Thomas to another bout of parliamentary activity on the same lines as before. He fired off estate bills in quick succession in 1853, 1854, and 1855. And in 1850 he whetted the appetites of speculative builders, and further alarmed the Hampstead gentry, by publishing a prospectus called *Sketch of the Plan proposed for the erection of Villas at Eastpark, Hampstead, the freehold property of Sir Thomas Maryon Wilson,* which showed villas standing in one-acre grounds arranged on either side of East Park Road. A few years later he had a model constructed of this proposed development and put it on show at his Hampstead estate office, where most observers apart from the gentry party agreed that it showed how 'a few handsome villas . . . will add to the beauties of the Heath [and that] their value will depend on keeping the Heath as a heath'.[1] It is indicative of the pervasive influence of the anti-Wilson rumours that one local historian, after having looked at this prospectus, thought that it showed 'a road previously constructed by him [Maryon Wilson] down the middle of the East Heath' and concluded that this offer to sell building plots on the Heath could not have been wholly serious. Whereas in fact the prospectus, as well as all other maps including the cadastral Tithe Apportionment map of 1838, show conclusively that this 'Eastpark' was not part of the Heath.[2] Clarity of exposition, of draughtsmanship both legal and cartographic, and patience in explanation of intent, were no manner of use to Sir Thomas. The 1853 bill went to great lengths to spell out the extent of building frontages to the Finchley Road, to Belsize Lane, and to West End Lane which were at stake, as well as the frontages to Childs Hill Lane (Hermitage Lane) adjoining the West Heath and to East Park Road adjoining the East Heath. The bill was defeated on second reading debate in the Lords.[3]

In 1854 Sir Thomas leant over backwards, swallowing his pride in the process, and produced a bill, significantly entitled the Finchley Road Estate Bill, which sought building powers only over his frontages to the Finchley Road and carefully omitted to seek any powers whatever over his lands adjoining the West and East Heaths. This time the

[1] GLCRO E/MW/H/III/38/16, *Sir T. Maryon Wilson and Gurney Hoare, Esq.* (*Hampstead Express*, 1862), a pamphlet reprinting articles and correspondence on *The Heath in Danger* from the *Hampstead Express.*
[2] E. F. Oppé, *Hampstead, a London Town* (Hampstead, 1951), p. 12.
[3] HLRO Bill to enable Sir T. M. Wilson to grant building leases of his estate in Middlesex, 1853.

Judges' Report to the Lords was extremely guarded. Pollock and Vaughan Williams stated:[1]

> We feel great difficulty in certifying our opinion that it is reason-able that the Bill . . . should pass into a Law. It may well be that the Testator abstained from extending the leasing power to the lands in question for reasons which could have operated in his mind with equal force even if the lands had been as valuable for building purposes at the date of his Will and Codicils as they are now . . . But supposing your Lordships not to adopt these scruples, We think the provisions of the Bill are proper for carrying its purposes into effect.

Sir Thomas thereupon sent some 'Observations on the Judges' Report' to members of the Lords, in which he perjured himself by affirming that his father had never intended to deny building powers to him.[2] This apart, his arguments were unanswerable. The Finchley Road running through his estate from south to north, and the Hampstead Junction Railway running across (in fact mainly under) it from east to west, were two major innovations since his father's day which had made the estate valuable 'for building and not any longer for farming'. He continued:[3]

> The presumption of the Judges that he [his father] might intend it rather to become a waste for the Metropolitan public to ramble over, must be disregarded by Parliament, for Parliament is always ready to make such additions and alterations in deeds and wills and in private Acts as the changed character of the properties to which they relate require for the benefit and protection of the rights of those in possession. If the Testator had declared that his son should *not* grant leases for 99 years, it would have been a grave question whether changes in circumstances warranted the grant of such powers by Parliament . . .
>
> The opposition to this Bill has been put upon the ground that the Metropolis should not be extended. Parliament should not listen . . . unless the opponents are ready to compensate Sir T. M. Wilson for the enormous loss he is to sustain . . . Tyburnia and Belgravia have been added to the Metropolis within a few

[1] GLCRO E/MW/H/III/38/15, Finchley Road Estate Act [*sic*], 1854, and copy of Judges' Report, 29 May 1854.

[2] See above, p. 135.

[3] GLCRO E/MW/H/III/38/15, Observations on the Judges' Report, June 1854.

years under powers granted by Parliament [Marquess of Westminster's Estate Act, 1845, for Belgravia, and several Acts from
1794 to 1825 granted building lease powers to the Bishop of
London for Tyburnia].

He failed to see why he was not entitled to the like treatment.

These arguments were sufficient to ensure that their lordships did
not adopt the scruples of the Judges, and the bill went through to the
Commons. There it met the full opposition of the metropolitan MPs
led by Lord Robert Grosvenor and Bernal Osborne, and being held in
some entirely unspecified way to constitute a danger to Hampstead
Heath, it was defeated on second reading by a crushing 97 to 43.
The short debate was marked by the first suggestion that if the public
wanted to keep the Heath and its surrounds as an open space, then the
public ought to buy it; it was made by Robert Lowe, not a politician
given to advocating new forms of public spending.[1] The draft for the
bill of 1855, prepared in unflagging pursuit of Sir Thomas's rights,
contained an even more explicit self-denying clause:[2]

> It is hereby declared that nothing in this Act shall in any wise
> empower, or be construed to empower, the said Sir T. M. Wilson,
> to enclose, or build upon, or let for building purposes, any part or
> parts of Hampstead Heath, or to build upon or let for building
> purposes any part or parts of the lands on the east or west sides
> of the said Heath in the said map coloured yellow, or any other of
> the lands in the parish of Hampstead save and except the said
> lands in the said map coloured green and marked A and B [these
> were the lands on either side of Finchley Road].

This, however, was overtaken by a general measure to deal with the
problems of 'limited owners' or tenants-for-life who did not possess
adequate powers over their estates for ensuring the full development
of their economic potential. This measure, which finally became the
Leases and Sales of Settled Land Act, 1856, was the first small step in a
general revision of the land law designed to meet, or at least to draw
the sting of, the radical campaign to 'unfetter the land' from the
constricting effects of the practice of strict settlement—popularly
referred to as entail—which had been under way since just before 1832
and which promised to become, after the achievement of the repeal of
the Corn Laws, the main staple of radicalism. The evil effects of strict

[1] *Hansard*, 3rd ser. cxxxv, H. of C. 27 July 1854.
[2] GLCRO E/MW/H/III/38/15, Finchley Road Estate Bill, 1855.

settlement which were the ground of the complaints had been ex-
cellently illustrated by the story of the Maryon Wilson estate. Where
the owner of an estate was not in fact its absolute owner but only a
tenant-for-life it could well happen that he did not possess the necessary
legal powers of disposition, whether by leasing or by selling and re-
investing, for facilitating the development of the resources of that
estate. In the normal case everyone agreed that it inflicted losses on the
community and the economy if forms of development which were
economically justified, say in mining or in housing, were prevented
simply because the land required could not be made available. The
terms of deeds of settlement and wills, which set up limited owner-
ships, could be altered only by legislation; and in the 1840s and early
1850s private estate bills conferring powers of granting mining leases,
building leases, and of making exchanges of land with other owners
were being passed at the rate of fifteen a year. This way of procuring a
supply of land needed for industrial and urban development, however,
was inefficient and expensive for the tenants-for-life, to whom the
average cost of an estate bill was £1,270. The remedy now proposed for
liberalising the land supply was to substitute a somewhat cheaper and
more expeditious—though still cumbersome—Chancery procedure for
the estate bill; some official supervision of alterations in the provisions
of deeds and wills still being felt essential, to prevent unscrupulous
tenants-for-life rigging things so that remaindermen and other residuary beneficiaries were cheated of their expectations. Whenever some
act was not expressly forbidden by a settlement or a will, then a
Chancery judge should be able to make a simple order on the application
of any tenant-for-life, conferring whatever powers of leasing or ex-
changing were requested.

This somewhat modest piece of law reform slipped through the Lords
easily enough, encountering no more than the expected opposition of
the reliably traditionalist ex-Chancellor Lord St Leonards, abetted by
the highly conservative Lords Bath and Derby who feared that this
measure would lead to a general dispersal of settled estates and hence to
the undermining of the entire aristocratic order.[1] When the bill
reached the Commons, however, it was at once noticed that Sir Thomas
Maryon Wilson would be as much entitled to make use of the new
procedure as any other tenant-for-life; and since his abortive estate
bills had been judged reasonable by a variety of law lords in their
Judges' Reports, and had been rejected only by politicians, it was a fair
assumption that under this bill a Chancery judge would automatically

[1] *Hansard*, 3rd ser. CXXXVIII, H. of L. 11 May, 22 May, 11 June 1855.

grant the order for which he would at once apply. The friends of
Hampstead Heath or enemies of Sir Thomas, led by Sir John Shelley,
the member for Westminster, therefore proposed a clause providing
that no person who had previously applied to Parliament for the
powers covered by the Act and had them refused should be eligible to
make use of the provisions of the Act. This was resisted by the lawyer-
MPs Whiteside and Malins on the grounds that it was blatant and
unconstitutional discrimination against Sir Thomas, who was the sole
individual who would be affected by the new clause; and by Sir James
Graham, who sympathised with the desire to preserve Hampstead
Heath, but felt that it ought to be purchased by the public at a fair
price. The feeling in the committee stage was so strong, however, that
the passage of the bill was endangered, and the government was
obliged to withdraw it altogether.[1]

The same bill was reintroduced the following session, and, sur-
mounting a petition against it from the Islington Vestry who wished to
protect the Heath, once more reached the Commons. Once more the
special clause to debar Sir Thomas was proposed by Sir John Shelley
and seconded by Lord Robert Grosvenor; Whiteside and Malins again
protested against the scandal of deliberately excepting one single individual from the operation of a public Act, and defended the principle of
one law to apply to all citizens without exception; and the member for
Norwich joined in by attacking the clause as 'an attempt aided by a
newspaper cry to obtain Sir Thomas Wilson's property with or without
his consent'. But by 84 votes to 42 the clause was added to the bill, and
with reluctance the Lords accepted the Commons' amendment; what
became the notorious Section 21 of 19 and 20 Victoria cap. 120 reached
the statute book.[2] It was equally notorious, in Hampstead at least, that
Section 21 was introduced only because of the frantic exertions of
John Gurney Hoare in lobbying and wire-pulling.[3]

Stymied by Section 21, for a few years Sir Thomas hoped that his
cause would be rescued by a constitutionalist revulsion against exceptional legislation. Whiteside and Malins persevered with attempts
to repeal the offending section in 1857, 1859, and 1860, but on each
occasion the metropolitan MPs—Shelley and Grosvenor as before,

---

[1] Ibid., cxxxix, H. of C. 16 July, 8 August, 9 August 1855.

[2] Ibid., cxl, H. of L. 5 February, 10 March, 17 June 1856; cxliii, H. of C.
15 July, 18 July 1856.

[3] GLCRO E/MW/H/III/38/16, *Maryon Wilson and Gurney Hoare*, 14 May
1862. Hampstead Vestry lobbied Lord Robert Grosvenor to ensure that
Section 21 was inserted in the bill: HPL Vestry Min[utes], 18 April, 8 May
1856.

assisted by Cox of Finsbury, Byng the second Middlesex member, Alcock of East Surrey, and Lord Fermoy and Edwin James the two members for Marylebone—turned up just as regularly in its defence, and succeeded in retaining it.[1] It was only at this point, having been thwarted for more than thirty years in his endeavours to turn his private property to profitable uses, that Sir Thomas did begin to contemplate milking his manorial rights over the Heath itself for whatever he could get, at the cost of destroying its prettiness if necessary. Previous grants of parcels of the waste, at least since 1820, had invariably been made with strings attached which prohibited building on them; the beneficiaries had been gentry-residents like Hoare, who wished to extend their gardens. Now, Sir Thomas seriously threatened to make such grants without the restrictive covenants, and by making them to his nominees who, since they would be copyholders, he would then enfranchise under the general Copyhold Enfranchisement Act, he would gain possession of the freehold in the parcels, which could then be sold off as building plots. The legal technicalities of such an operation were involved but workable, and would suffice to produce sound marketable titles to plots carved out of the Heath. Observing due manorial formalities and customs, no wholesale appropriation of the waste could be contemplated with this machinery; it would rather be a slow attrition. Sir Thomas also proposed, therefore, to go in for systematic exploitation of his other manorial rights. He would go into the sand and gravel business on a commercial scale. And he would commercialise the traditional use of the Heath by the Hampstead washerwomen for their laundry posts by negotiating with the London Dyeing Company for the erection of large-scale carpet-beating grounds on the Heath; these required several acres of unsightly wooden beating-frames, and created a great deal of dust and annoyance to nearby residents. He would even turn a penny from the mounting popularity of the Heath and license an Italian ice-cream vendor and caterer to erect a temporary wooden refreshment room, called the Rotunda, on the Heath at the foot of Downshire Hill.[2] He hoped this would annoy the local gentry by

---

[1] *Hansard*, 3rd ser. CXLVII, H. of C. 5 August 1857; CLV, H. of C. 1 August, 5 August 1859; CLVI, H. of C. 5 March 1860.

[2] Of all these ways of exploiting and laying waste the Heath only the refreshment room actually materialised, the licence to erect it being granted to Alesandrio Buicchi, confectioner, of Battersea, in August 1861 and renewed in 1865: GLCRO E/MW/H/III/38/16, Agreement between Alfred Clark (Steward of the Manor) and Buicchi, 26 May 1865. Part of the lands on East Park were indeed leased as a brickfield, to John Culverhouse, who may have poached some of his brick earth from the Heath itself.

encouraging further vulgarisation of the Heath; and he would compound the annoyance by exploiting the adjoining East Park lands as a brickfield, it being easy to find a brickmaker who would take it under the 21-year lease which he did have the power to grant. By crying 'wolf' often enough the pretended defenders of the Heath had at length succeeded in provoking the very danger which they claimed to have been warding off all these years.

The first rumblings that Sir Thomas might at last turn to building on the Heath in earnest, if his hopes for the repeal of Section 21 were not kept alive, appeared in the local press in the summer of 1861. Then at the annual Court Baron held at Jack Straw's Castle and followed by a dinner for the copyholders the Steward, George Loaden, made an effort to persuade the Hampstead gentry to use their influence to get the repeal of Section 21 in return for the abandonment of Sir Thomas's designs on the Heath. The *Hampstead Express* reported:[1]

> The Steward referred to our recent statements, that Sir T. M. Wilson could build on the Heath by making grants to nominees, and that in fact in all grants of the waste made by him he had inserted a condition prohibiting building. He confirmed what we had written, and described the plans formed by Sir T. M. Wilson many years ago of beautifying the Heath, all of which had been thwarted by certain persons owning property on the Heath who feared it would become a spot of choice public resort, and thereby their privacy would be disturbed . . . These persons had not scrupled to spread a report that Sir T. M. Wilson sought to enclose Hampstead Heath and build upon it, and to assert that they were the guardians and preservers of the Heath, and to call upon the Metropolitan public to oppose the wicked designs of Sir T. M. Wilson. The Steward owned that these persons had succeeded to the utmost of their wishes and far beyond their expectations; but that the inhabitants of Hampstead and the Metropolitan public had sustained great injury from the success of these few, and that Sir T. M. Wilson had been imbittered instead of being encouraged. That encouragement and co-operation would by this time have made Hampstead Heath everything that could be desired, as a Heath.
>
> We gather from the Steward that it is not improbable Sir T. M. Wilson might make grants of the Heath for building, as his

---

[1] *Hampstead Express*, 18 December, 25 December 1861; reprinted in *The Heath in Danger* (Hampstead, 1862), a pamphlet in GLCRO E/MW/H/III/38/16.

last chance of making the Wilson Hampstead Estate profitable. It is true that he is a man of taste, and as we understand, an amateur artist; but will such accomplishments alone preserve the Heath? . . . A strong pecuniary interest not to make such grants would . . . be a valuable addition to such preventives.

This marked the opening of a local press campaign to disabuse the London public of the deception which had been practised on them, and thus liberate the metropolitan MPs from their belief that the Heath was entrenched behind Section 21. The argument was that if only Sir Thomas Maryon Wilson could be allowed to build select and ornamental villas on East Park 'then their value will depend on keeping the Heath as a heath, and there will be security that Sir T. M. Wilson will never try to destroy the Heath.'[1] The finger was pointed very plainly at Hoare and Powell as the men who could save the Heath, because they had been the culprits in endangering it:[2]

As to the powers of the lord of the manor to grant plots of the Heath for building, we are informed that the copyhold property of Mr Gurney Hoare consists wholly of such grants, making together about 4 acres . . . and likewise the copyhold property of Mr Powell . . . These gentlemen exerted themselves, among others, to shut the doors of Chancery against Sir T. M. Wilson. Gurney Hoare and Powell are the first people the people of Hampstead should look to for aid in repealing Section 21, which would make it Sir Thomas's interest not to grant plots of the Heath for building . . . because they know best how to unravel the combination which they assisted in weaving for the introduction of the Section.

As a result of this a public meeting of the inhabitants of Hampstead was held in April 1862 at the Caxton Institute in Holly Mount, with Donald Nicoll of Oaklands Hall in the chair. It was stated that Sir Thomas had laid out many thousand pounds in preparing the 60 or 70 acres of his East Park for building fifty superior villas on it; but that because he was unable to grant building leases, he was preparing instead to carve building plots out of the Heath. Thereupon Gurney Hoare moved a resolution, which was carried unanimously,[3]

1 *Hampstead Express*, 28 May 1862.
2 Ibid., 26 February 1862.
3 Ibid., 14 April 1862.

That if Sir T. M. Wilson should take steps for obtaining a private Act to grant building leases over his Finchley Road estate, and pledge himself not to seek further building powers, this meeting will not oppose such application.

In other words, Gurney Hoare would withdraw his opposition provided Sir Thomas agreed never to build on East Park. This was a form of blackmail under which Sir Thomas contemptuously refused to bend. On receiving a copy of the resolution from Donald Nicoll, Sir Thomas replied that he had read the pamphlet *Hampstead Heath in Danger*, which had occasioned the public meeting, and that it was a substantially correct statement:[1]

> I have abstained from exercising the power I possess of building on the Heath itself until lately; but no sooner do I entertain the project than the local newspaper is made use of to raise a party to deter me, by recommending that my hope of obtaining the extension of the power of leasing the freehold lands . . . should be sustained, because it would then be in my interest to preserve the Heath as a heath.
>
> The Leases and Sales of Settled Estates Act passed in 1856. Section 26 declares that if an express declaration or manifest intention be contained in the instrument under which the applicant applies to the Court, or may be reasonably inferred therefrom, or from extrinsic circumstances or evidence that leasing powers shall not be given, then the Court shall be powerless. The Act also contains Section 21, to exclude me from the Court of Chancery.
>
> I require no private Act and do not intend to seek any. I am content to apply to the Court of Chancery on the same terms that all other persons must apply; and if the people of Hampstead, through the members who represent them in Parliament, amend the Public Act by permitting the Court of Chancery to hear my application in common with all other landed proprietors, Hampstead Heath will not be in danger.
>
> Do Mr Hoare and Mr Le Breton [a barrister living in Milford House, John Street; Hampstead's representative on the Metropoli-

[1] Ibid., 23 April 1862. The 'bribe' required Sir T. M. Wilson to do only a little more than he had voluntarily proposed to do in his 1854 Finchley Road Estate Bill which had sought building powers only over the Finchley Road lands; the little more, however, amounted to a permanent renunciation of building powers in respect of East Park and of his lands adjoining the West Heath, without compensation.

tan Board of Works; as prominent as Hoare and Powell in defence of the Heath] know by experience that members of Parliament can be deceived into doing an injustice, while the Court of Chancery cannot? And does this knowledge lead them to demand a bribe from me, of the sacrifice of 60 or 70 acres of freehold land to serve some end they have in view? I am ready to meet them, on oath, in Chancery; but I am not ready to pay a bribe.

In this letter Sir Thomas himself confirmed that he had been driven to the point of embarking on building on the Heath itself. But more important than this confirmation was the open accusation of Gurney Hoare. The *Hampstead Express* was dismayed, and called on Hoare to clear himself:[1]

The letter of Sir T. M. Wilson has taken almost everyone by surprise. It accuses Hoare, a magistrate, of demanding a bribe, and requires an answer from him. The letter implies that Hoare has systematically made false statement to members of Parliament whereby he has deceived them into sustaining Section 21. [Hoare kept his silence, so the editor tried again.] We have urged the people of Hampstead to stir for the repeal of Section 21, but none seemed to come forward. How different this refusal from the exertions used by Mr Hoare to introduce Section 21! Cannot any persons be found to undo what Mr Hoare did? We hoped to find in Hampstead some who would be equally active in producing a right, as a magistrate has appeared to be in perpetrating a wrong.

The evidence as to Hoare's complicity in this plotting and this deliberate distortion of the facts is purely circumstantial, but his failure to answer the public challenge tends to confirm Sir Thomas's interpretation. It could be argued in Hoare's defence that he was all along engaged in a perfectly disinterested campaign to *extend* the Heath by keeping its eastern and south-western borders as open country; but if so, the surreptitious and dishonest means used to further such an admirable end were scarcely those which a man of property, a highly respected banker, and a magistrate, would have used. They are more like the means which a householder would use to preserve, by hook or by crook, the privacy and pleasant surroundings of his own residence. In any event, neither he nor anyone else came forward to engineer the repeal of Section 21. Grants from the waste of the manor, of which

[1] Ibid., 7 May, 14 May 1862.

there had been none since 1844, were resumed in 1864, 1865 and 1866; and on one of them, beside the flagstaff near Jack Straw's Castle, Sir Thomas began to build a new estate office in 1866, while on another, a small detached triangle of manorial waste on the south-west side of East Heath Road and north-west of Well Road, the building of The Logs was started 'a formidable atrocity by J. S. Nightingale [exhibiting] yellow, red, and black brick, excrescences in all directions, arches pointed and round, motifs Gothic and Frenchified.'[1]

This was the occasion for Gurney Hoare, presumably with his tongue in his cheek, to suggest to Sir Thomas that there should be a friendly suit in Chancery to determine once and for all the precise nature of manorial rights in the Heath. He wrote on 6 December:

> Dear Sir,
> My neighbours as well as myself much regret that you should have commenced building on the Heath. Several gentlemen interested in the matter met last night, and were advised that the only course open to them was an appeal to law. I can assure you that they will do this with reluctance, as they have no hostile feelings towards you, and it would give great and general satisfaction in this place if you would consent to stay all proceedings and obtain a legal decision on the real or supposed rights of yourself and the copyholders by an amicable suit. In this manner a long and costly litigation, as well as much irritation, may be avoided. Believe me, your very obedient servant,
>
> J. Gurney Hoare.

Sir Thomas's reply on 7 December, whose brusqueness has usually been taken to show his unreasonable incivility and to reveal his turpitude, was perhaps called for by the history of the case: 'Sir, Take your own course.'[2]

So the case of Hoare v. Wilson came before the Master of the Rolls in Chancery, and while the suit was being heard Sir Thomas was obliged to give an undertaking to suspend all building operations. The case was never settled, because after it had gone on for nearly two years Lord Romilly pronounced that he could not decide the matter of the manorial rights until a special jury had tried a long list of particular

---

[1] Pevsner, *The Buildings of England: London, except the Cities of London and Westminster* (1952), p. 196. The Logs survives as a grisly memorial to these events; but the estate office near the Flagstaff never got beyond the foundations.

[2] Exchange of letters published in *The Times*, 15 December 1866.

issues, at common law and not in Chancery, relating to the facts of copyholders' and lord's rights.[1] Before these specific issues came on for trial, Sir Thomas had died in May 1869. Since the whole issue had been about the nature of the manorial rights, it seems curious that after listening to arguments and evidence for practically two years Lord Romilly decided he was unable to decide the matters of fact involved, but had to direct someone else to answer such question as:

> Whether the copyhold tenants of the manor of Hampstead from the time whereof the memory of man runneth not to the contrary, have been accustomed in right of their copyhold tenements to enjoy common of pasture upon the Heath and waste lands of the Manor for all manner of cattle, levant and couchant on their tenements or belonging to them. [And] Whether by the custom of the manor the lord could dig for and carry away sand, gravel, and loam, or brick-earth, in quantities more than sufficient for the use of the demesne lands of the lord.

The answers to all the queries were clear enough from the documents already before him. Romilly's parade of making the law even more obscure and intricate than it really was can only have been a deliberate delaying tactic, trusting that something would turn up before he was forced to issue his decision.[2]

[1] HPL copies of documents in Hoare v. Wilson, in Chancery, 1866 H No. 273.
[2] Lord Romilly's opinion is in *Minutes of Metropolitan Board of Works* [MBW Min.], 6 November 1868. The full list of points sent for decision by a common law judge and jury were:
  1. As quoted in the text.
  2. Whether the copyhold tenants have been accustomed, in right of their copyhold tenements, to cut heather, gorse bushes and fern, or any one or more of such things for cattle levant and couchant on their copyhold tenements, or for fuel, or for the purposes of agriculture.
  3. Whether copyhold tenants have been accustomed . . . to dig in different places, and carry away sand and loam for the repair of their lands, houses, and gardens belonging to and within the said copyhold tenements.
  4. Whether copyhold tenants have been accustomed . . . to use the Heath for recreation by walking and riding thereon, and also carrying on lawful sports and pastimes on the said Heath at seasonable times.
  5. If any such customs be found to exist, whether they or any and which of them are in respect of ancient copyhold tenements only, or whether they are in respect of both ancient and new copyhold tenements.
  6. Whether according to the custom of the Manor of Hampstead the assent of the homage is necessary in order to make valid a grant, by the Lord of the Manor, of any new copyhold tenement . . .
  7. Whether the homage in such cases have been accustomed, from any

It was not Sir Thomas's death which Lord Romilly hoped would relieve him of the embarrassment of making a decision, but a hope that public action might remove the problem by taking over the Heath. Since the first tentative suggestions in 1854 and 1855 that the public should buy the Heath there had been a good deal of talk and framing of motions, but precious little progress. The main trouble was that when it came to applying the fine-sounding idea to any particular instance no one was anxious to foot the bill, and everyone prevaricated by producing differing definitions of who the 'public' might be in such a context. Perhaps it should properly be some group of public-spirited persons assembled for the occasion, who would raise the purchase money through voluntary contributions, as some new form of charity; but, it was argued, a local asset which would be used and appreciated by local people, and which would raise the rateable values of favourably situated properties, ought to be paid for by the local community through its vestry and its parish rates; on the contrary, came the reply, this was an asset for London at large, and London as a whole should pay, through its properly constituted authority, the Metropolitan Board of Works; and this argument in turn was easily side-stepped, by the claim that a major metropolitan improvement amounted to an adornment of the capital city, for the benefit of all the empire, and therefore the nation as a whole should pay, through the central government—moreover, was there not a precedent from the 1840s in the acquisition of the neighbouring Primrose Hill by the crown?[1] And over all these possible positions there loomed the radical view, imbued with anti-landlordism and grossly inaccurate both legally and historically, but of no less appeal on that account with its stark simplicity and complete economy: that since the commons already belonged to the people, there was no need for the people to pay anyone for them. The welter of debating points, and the

---

and what time, to impose conditions, and if any, of what nature . . . upon the grant of such copyhold tenements.

8. Whether by the custom of the Manor the Lord could, without the assent of the homage, enclose any part of the waste, leaving sufficient common for the copyhold tenants.

9. As in the text.

10. In case any one or more of the customary copyhold privileges described in the first six issues should be found to exist, then, whether sufficient common has been left for the due preservation of such customary privileges, or of such of them as shall be found to exist, and to which any of the copyholders of the Manor are found to be entitled.

[1] For Primrose Hill see below, pp. 220–2; the crown in fact acted as the agent for its acquisition as an open space, but the transaction involved little, if any, of the taxpayer's money.

great scope for shifting any financial costs on to someone else's shoulders, offered delightful opportunities for delay.

The opportunities were fully indulged. The proceedings were so prolonged and the manoeuvres so intricate that when, at the end of the day, the Metropolitan Board of Works took possession of the Heath on behalf of the public, in December 1871, it is difficult to say with utter certainty whether the bargain was either a good or a necessary one. Two matters are certain. First, that it was forty-two years since Sir Thomas had made the first of what in the end became a series of no less than fourteen attempts to gain full control of his Hampstead estate; and more than seventeen years since the first suggestion that the public ought to pay something to acquire the Heath. Second, that the 1871 acquisition was at best a compromise, at worst a costly defeat, for the Heath party, since all that was acquired was the Heath and nothing more than the Heath, while all along the key to the affair had been the desire to preserve the adjoining lands of East Park. In some respects, indeed, the 1871 arrangement was an unmitigated disaster for the Hampstead gentry, for it explicitly reserved to the Maryon Wilson family the means of building upon East Park by providing for the necessary access roads across the Heath. Those who had successfully thwarted Sir Thomas thus had the bitter satisfaction of knowing that their efforts had simply increased the probability that they would reap the whirlwind and live to see their fine views curtailed by rows of villas across a narrow tongue of heath. There was, to be sure, the lesser satisfaction of knowing that the Heath itself was for ever secure from the threat of building and spoliation. But it was extremely doubtful whether they had not themselves called this threat into being purely by their frustration of Sir Thomas's more legitimate designs. In the end, of course, East Park was never built over; it was purchased for the public at a full freehold building land price, at the same time as Lord Mansfield's Parliament Hill Fields, and thrown together with the Heath to form the magnificent modern open space. In this lies the retrospective justification for all the preceding actions of the Heath party. It is, however, a justification which does no credit to them as individuals, for it depends on a series of developments after 1871 which they could not have foreseen and which therefore could not be used to excuse their pre-1871 conduct. In the first place the later purchase rested on a greater willingness to use large amounts of ratepayers' money, and a greater willingness on the part of wealthy individuals to make donations, in the later 1880s than had existed fifteen or twenty years earlier. Undoubtedly there was this greater willingness; but it had not been predictable, and had not been predicted, at any time before it was actually put to the test. Second, the later purchase was only possible at all because East Park had not in fact been built over, although the legal capacity to do so, on the part of Sir Thomas's successors as owners, had existed for over fifteen years. It had been the essence of the case against Sir Thomas that at any time since 1829 the builders would move in the minute he should obtain powers to grant building leases. No one had dreamt that there were economic factors involved in the potential development of his estate, as well as legal factors; and no one had so much as hinted at a possibility that legal powers might remain unused for years at a stretch. It was certainly no thanks to any prescience on the part of the Heath party that it turned out to be undesirable on economic and financial grounds to take East Park as the first building estate on the Maryon Wilson lands. As far as the achievements and calculations of the Heath party were concerned, the stay of builders' execution over East Park was entirely fortuitous. The most that can be said for their efforts is that having created their own mess over the Heath proper, they succeeded in extricating themselves from it at a price; and that by accident they managed to help preserve for the future an opportunity of muddling through to the attainment of their real objective, the establishment of the greater Heath.

The Heath produced one of the earliest signs of life in parochial government when that was reformed in 1855 as part of the Metropolis Management Act setting up the Metropolitan Board of Works, introducing Hampstead in common with the other London parishes and districts to the novel experience of administration by an elected vestry. The first meeting of the new Vestry was in January 1856, and within a month it was sending out its first deputation on the matter of the Heath. The deputation was led by Thomas Turner of Fenton House, barrister and JP, and the Vestry's nominated representative on the Metropolitan Board of Works, who had been active in the cause at least since the days of the 1843 petition to the Commons.[1] The Vestry was entirely open about its aim: the deputation was to impress upon the Board the urgency and importance of securing 'the Heath *and the adjoining lands*' as a place of recreation.[2] There was nothing underhand here, no suggestion that the neighbouring lands might somehow be sterilised and preserved as open country under the pretence of preserving the Heath; there was merely naïvety, for the Vestry forbore to say how much of the 'adjoining lands' ought to be secured—it might have

[1] See above, p. 161.
[2] HPL Vestry Min., 22 February 1856. My italics.

been a few fields, or several square miles between the Heath and Hendon and Finchley, for all the resolution said; they all adjoined and they were all as yet unbuilt—or what price should be paid for them, or who should pay it. Yet, coming from a body which included several barristers, solicitors and JPs, the extreme vagueness of the 'adjoining lands' phrase which turned up in most subsequent resolutions as well as in this initial motion can but have been deliberate, an attempt to foster the impression that the Heath was indissolubly coupled with certain adjoining lands which by inference were so well known that they did not need to be specified, and that it was impossible to treat of the Heath in isolation from them. Such would have been an almost routine forensic trick. As with most such tricks, it was likely to be more successful in gulling the general public than in hoodwinking fellow experts. And sure enough the Metropolitan Board of Works made short shrift of Hampstead's proposal, ruling that it was worthy but hopelessly extravagant in relation to more pressing mundane matters of sewers and public health. It went on record with the view that:[1]

> This Board acknowledges the importance of retaining open spaces in the Metropolis, and the great permanent advantage which would accrue to the northern suburbs by the preservation of Hampstead Heath, and its appropriation as a place of recreation for the public; but is of opinion, that improvements of much greater necessity and advantage to the general public are more urgent and desirable, and therefore resolves not to entertain the question of the purchase of land for the purposes of a park.

Rebuffed in this quarter, the Vestry determined to approach the government directly, and in conjunction with like-minded delegations from Marylebone and St Pancras its deputation managed to obtain an interview with the Chief Commissioner of Works and Public Buildings, Sir Benjamin Hall. Sir Benjamin was tactfully sympathetic towards the project of securing the 'Heath and some adjoining land as a place of public recreation', and put in a word with the Chancellor of the Exchequer, Sir George Cornewall Lewis. Sir George in turn played it cool, knowing that the metropolitan MPs were likely to take a lively interest, and received the deputations in order 'to unfold the Government's proposals for preserving the Heath without any need of additional taxation.' The proposals, however, were simply that the government should make a loan which the Metropolitan Board of Works

[1] MBW Min., 4 June 1856, pp. 227–8.

should service; so the Vestry's effort to bypass that body was politely but firmly deflected. Back in the Board's court, sundry motions to open negotiations 'to ascertain on what terms Sir T. M. Wilson will relinquish his rights as Lord of the Manor, and the price per acre of other land that may be required or considered necessary' were resolutely ruled out of order. Thus the campaign of 1856 was blunted by shuttlecock tactics, and the Vestry turned to the more promising business of helping to insert the discriminatory Section 21 into the Leases and Sales of Settled Estates Act.[1]

The momentum of this initial spurt of activity by the new-broom Vestry carried over into the two following seasons, after which the public authorities remained inactive for nearly a decade. In 1857 the Vestry coupled its contribution to the movement to resist the repeal of Section 21 with renewed pressure on the Board to set about acquiring the Heath 'and certain adjoining land'. Defence of Section 21 was simple, since it involved no expenditure by the Board, though the Vestry splashed out on 250 copies of a petition against the Wilsonian amendment. Acquisition either of manorial rights, or of freehold adjoining lands, was another matter; and the Board thankfully postponed any consideration of the 'proposal to form a park at Hampstead' on receiving a lengthy assurance from Sir Thomas's solicitor that 'whether the Bill [to repeal Section 21] pass or not, the relation between Sir Thomas Wilson and Hampstead Heath will be unaffected', and that his rights over the Heath 'will neither be increased or decreased by the Bill.' The solicitor, William Loaden, went on to tell the Board:

> I am honestly bound to say that the expenditure of public money in the purchase of Hampstead Heath will be a fraud upon the public, until the lord of the manor for the time being shall apply for an Act of Parliament to enclose the Heath . . . Sir T. M. Wilson does not wish to enclose it; he is desirous that the Heath should remain in its present state, and does not wish it to be made into a prime park, and that the public need not fear any enclosure of the Heath until a Bill for that express purpose shall be brought forward.

This was an amply emphatic and irrefutable statement of the legal position, as well as of Sir Thomas's personal intentions, to convince all the members of the Board—except for the minority who were really

[1] HPL Vestry Min., 25 March, 18 April, 8 May, 26 June 1856; MBW Min., 4 June 1856, p. 229, 8 August 1856, p. 439.

interested in 'the adjoining lands' rather than the Heath itself—that there was no danger to the Heath, and that to acquire it would be a waste of public money.[1]

Acknowledging that the Board had seen through the attempt to use the Heath proper as a stalking horse for larger ambitions, and that it was in no mood to raise the large sums of money which would be needed to make a fair purchase of the 'adjoining lands', the Vestry had one more shot at outflanking the Board, by promoting its own private bill to preserve the Heath and adjoining lands as an open space. The Vestry spent several hundred pounds in preparing and launching its 1858 Heath Bill, but although it was introduced as a simple preservation bill it was impossible to suppress the fact that it was also a finance bill, and that it entailed considerable financial commitments which were aimed at the Metropolitan Board of Works as a whole and not simply at the Hampstead Vestry. The London authorities lined up in a neat north–south division for and against the bill; and the Board as such added its official weight to the opposition, with the result that the Private Bill Committee threw out the bill on the grounds that it sought to usurp powers and responsibilities which properly belonged to the Metropolitan Board of Works. The Committee reported, however, that:[2]

> they are strongly impressed with the public utility of the proposed purchase of Hampstead Heath for the purposes of the recreation and health of the labouring classes of the Metropolis, [and] they wish to impress upon the Metropolitan Board of Works the urgent necessity of taking the matter into their serious attention with the view to securing Hampstead Heath for the public without any unnecessary delay, as owing to the peculiar circumstances of the case, the Committee much fear that the selling price of the property will be largely increased if deferred much longer.

The Board, however, paid no attention to this exhortation; not because it was indifferent to the interests of the labouring classes in

[1] HPL Vestry Min., 19 June, 25 June 1857; MBW Min., 3 February 1857, pp. 82–3, 26 June 1857, p. 480, 29 June 1857, p. 486.
[2] HPL Vestry Min., 30 October, 20 November 1857, 22 January, 5 February 1858; MBW Min., 29 January 1858, pp. 108–10, 26 February 1858, p. 177, 12 March 1858, pp. 194, 210, 19 March 1858, pp. 216, 218–20, 7 May 1858, pp. 319–20. The vestries which supported the Hampstead Vestry's bill were Marylebone, Islington, St James's Westminster, and St Pancras; those which opposed it, on grounds of its needless extravagance and local irrelevance, were Clerkenwell, Woolwich, and Wandsworth.

recreating themselves on the Heath, but because it felt utter confidence in the view that the Heath itself was in no danger; only the 'adjoining lands' might conceivably disappear under houses at some time—though the Board did give its support to resisting the attempts to repeal Section 21, in 1859 and 1860, which would have made such building probable—and the Board had no stomach for getting involved in any proposals to purchase them.[1] This reasoning, entirely justified at the time, accounts for the complete absence of any official discussion of the purchase of the Heath between 1858 and 1866.

In the interval the situation changed, both legally and practically. The legal change was not of much moment as far as Hampstead Heath was concerned, since it largely gave explicit statutory confirmation to a position which had already existed for many years. In the early 1860s the threatened loss of several metropolitan commons at the same moment—either through the complete disappearance of copyholders to keep up the exercise of common rights and thus restrain the lord of the manor, as in Peckham Rye and Morden Commons; or through the possibility of the lord of the manor and the copyholders striking a lucrative bargain to share the benefits of an enclosure, as with Lord Spencer and Wimbledon Common—impelled an increasingly sympathetic public and political opinion into legislative action to preserve open spaces. An inquiry into the extent of surviving commons in the metropolitan area was rapidly followed by the Metropolitan Commons Act of 1866, which prevented the Inclosure Commissioners from entertaining any applications for the enclosure of a metropolitan common, and which together with the amending Act of 1869 enabled the Inclosure Commissioners (and their successors, the Land Commissioners) to approve schemes for the management of commons as public open spaces when agreed proposals were put forward by the lord of the manor, the common right holders, and the local vestry, of any particular common.[2] It was the situation leading up to the 1866 Act which gave birth to the Commons Preservation Society, under the leadership of George Shaw Lefevre, strongly supported by most of the metropolitan MPs, and counting among its original members such Hampstead campaigners as Gurney Hoare and Philip Le Breton, barrister and Vestryman living at

[1] MBW Min., 15 July 1859, p. 481, 5 August 1859, p. 572, 2 March 1860, p. 161, 9 March 1860, p. 179.

[2] SC on Open Spaces (Metropolis), Parl. Papers, 1865, VIII; Return of Commons and Open Spaces (Metropolis), including maps, of all commons and open spaces within a radius of fifteen miles round London, Parl. Papers, 1866, LIX; Metropolitan Commons Acts, 29 and 30 Vict. cap. 122, 32 and 33 Vict. cap. 107.

Milford House in John Street (Keats Grove). This Society played a large part in obtaining the 1865 inquiry into metropolitan open spaces, and in passing the 1866 Act. Its energies were mainly devoted in its early years to such vast open spaces as Wimbledon Common and Epping Forest, both the subject of prolonged agitation and litigation at this time. But it was also on hand to advise local residents and local preservation societies on suitable campaigns to protect lesser commons, and it no doubt played a part in getting Gurney Hoare to start his Chancery suit against Sir Thomas in December 1866, just as it influenced the foundation of the Hampstead Heath Protection Society as a sub-committee of the existing local cultural group, the Kyrle Society.[1]

The 1866 Act was largely a statutory long-stop for the Heath, there being no possibility that Sir Thomas could promote an ordinary enclosure measure since that required the consent of at least three-quarters of the commoners, and there being even less likelihood that he would come up with an agreed scheme under the Act for dedicating the Heath to the public, in view of the forty years' souring of his relations with the commoners. The Act itself, however, was partly responsible for changing the practical situation of the Heath. For it brought to a head the latent conflict between those lords of manors who held that the commons had become virtually their private property because the rights of the commoners had vanished by non-use, and the open-space advocates who argued that the common rights of the owners of adjoining properties, though admittedly little used because of encroaching urbanisation, were dormant rather than extinct and could be upheld at law for the desired purpose of abating any enclosures. The legislation invited, and almost obliged, both sides to put their claims to the test. In Shaw Lefevre's words:[2]

> [it] was followed by important consequences, and led to a course of litigation respecting the London Commons without parallel for its duration, the importance of its issues, and its historical interest. Each party to the great controversy before the committee proceeded to act upon its views. The lords of manors of numerous commons round London commenced a wholesale course of enclosure, which put in issue their contention as to their rights in the most practical manner, and which, if uncontested, would have

[1] *The Times*, 25 January 1866, reporting an early meeting of the Commons Preservation Society.
[2] G. Shaw Lefevre, *English and Irish Land Questions* (1881), pp. 211–13; the whole of his essay on Common Lands is of interest in this context.

speedily led to the disappearance, not only of Epping Forest, but of all the most valued commons near London. Within a short time, nearly three thousand acres of the forest were abstracted from it, and enclosed with fences. The Commons of Berkhampstead, Plumstead, Tooting, and Bostall, were wholly, or in great part, enclosed; Hampstead Heath and many others were threatened, and would, doubtless, soon have been engulfed. The opponents to this view of the right to enclose were equally determined to resist, in the interest of the public. In the autumn of 1865, I formed a Society for the Preservation and Protection of the Commons in the neighbourhood of London, with the object of resisting, or advising and assisting in resistance to their enclosure . . . As each Common near London was enclosed or threatened, local opposition was aroused, which only needed the advice and assistance of the parent society to commence active proceedings against the wrong-doers. In most cases the resident owners of villas adjoining the common formed committees and raised funds to oppose the aggressors in the law courts, or public-spirited men took upon themselves the burthen of resistance. In the case of Berkhampstead, where six hundred acres were enclosed by the late Earl Brownlow, and added to his park, the late Mr Augustus Smith, well known as the Lord of Scilly, vindicated his right as a commoner, after the manner well recognised by the law as a legitimate method of dealing with an illegal encroachment. He sent down two hundred men to Berkhampstead, who in one night removed the iron fences which engirdled the stolen common. At Plumstead, Sir Julian Goldsmid took the leading part against the enclosure. At Hampstead the late Mr Gurney Hoare joined with his neighbours in organising resistance. At Tooting, Wimbledon, Wandsworth, and other suburban places committees were formed for protecting the Commons.

This account, in the stirring tones of a general reliving the incidents of a recent victory, gives a vivid picture of the place of the local Hampstead skirmish in the wider metropolitan battle; it is characteristically partisan in attributing all the black wickedness to the defeated foe and all the virtue to the friendly troops. In fact the lord of the manor was driven to entertain sinister designs on Hampstead Heath only in the year or two before 1866, since up to that time he had had a stronger vested interest than anyone else in keeping it as an open space in order to sustain, and raise, the value of his own adjoining lands. The 1866

Act no doubt seemed to oblige Sir Thomas to make a formal and overt assertion of what he held to be his rights over the Heath, and thus it may have been the proximate cause of those symbolic acts of building on plots taken from the Heath which triggered off the Hoare litigation. But the really serious threat to the Heath arose from the explosion of Sir Thomas Maryon Wilson's long pent-up exasperation over the endless frustration of his entirely legitimate aspirations for developing his freehold estate. This explosion amounted to a determination, only partly feigned, to exploit his manorial rights over the Heath as ruthlessly as he could, if necessary leaving the land a torn and scarred wreck behind him. There may have been little real prospect of Sir Thomas carrying out a threat to turn the Heath into another Agar Town by granting the short leases for 21 years, which he was competent to do; these were certainly the tenures with which William Agar had produced his crop of shanties, but Sir Thomas's leasing power, such as it was, was applicable to his freeholds and not to the Heath. But that he might literally carry away the Heath and sell it piecemeal as ballast was a very real prospect indeed.

The apparently precise threat to turn the Heath into an instant slum, however, did come straight from the horse's mouth. In the course of the inquiry into metropolitan open spaces in 1865 Sir Thomas gave evidence to the Select Committee. His crucial exchange with the chairman, John Locke, ran as follows:[1]

6068. We were informed that you were willing to dedicate a certain portion to the public upon obtaining the right to build upon another part?—No, I make no compromise and no promise. In the year 1829, my intention was to have laid out Hampstead Heath with ornamental walks; but I lost my Bill for building on other parts of my property, and having always been thwarted, I must now see what I can do to turn the heath to account, and get what I can. By the outcry that has been made against me, I am deprived of about 50,000*l.* a year. My property would have produced me that without the slightest injury to the public, if any of my Bills had passed. There were other parties who wanted to possess my property. Mr. Samuel Hoare wanted it, and offered a price for it; and Lord Mansfield was also anxious to have it, and so they wanted to come poor Poland over me.

6069. Is there nothing that you wish to do with it now?—Only to turn it to account.

[1] *SC on Open Spaces (Metropolis)*, 1865, Q.6068–71.

6070. What do you mean by turning it to account?—I might build an Agar Town there upon 21 years' lease.

6071. Will you explain what you mean by an Agar Town?—I have never been to Agar Town, but we know very well that some property has been turned to account there by building cottages for poor people upon short leases.

The alarm sounded by S. Barber of The Grange (West Heath Road) in November 1866 was thus perfectly justified. He wrote to *The Times*:[1]

Building has now actually commenced on the Heath. The first house is in course of erection by the lord of the manor at the flag-staff—the very point which commands the most magnificent of our views. Brickmaking is to be extended over a considerable portion of the Heath, and the rest is to be covered with cottages and huts; in fact another Agar or Kensal Town is to occupy this splendid site. I do not write to cast blame on Sir Thomas Wilson. He is in a difficult position, and as his Bill for building on the Finchley Road estate was again rejected last Session, he has now resolved (perhaps not unnaturally) to make the most of the heath itself, whether by building himself, or by granting leases for his limited term of 21 years, or brickmaking, or selling the sand, of which enormous quantities are being daily removed for railway contractors. I have been with a deputation from Hampstead, Marylebone, Islington, and St Pancras Vestries to urge the Metropolitan Board of Works to make some arrangement with Sir T. M. Wilson, whether under the 1866 Open Spaces Act or otherwise, which would preserve the park here as expressly recommended by the House of Commons Committee in1858, and at the same time enable the owners to deal with their detached property. But the Metropolitan Board of Works is evidently fearful of being thought extravagant if they do anything. In fact, there has been no great pressure on them from the public to carry out the Report of the Select Committee [of 1865, on Metropolitan Open Spaces].

The construction of the Midland Railway extension to St Pancras opened the way to the desolation of the Heath. As with all major railway works, the construction was divided into sections on which work went ahead simultaneously; and until the tunnels at Belsize and at Elstree were open the London section and the Hampstead–Mill Hill section remained landlocked and isolated from the abundant supplies of railway building materials which lay to the north. This was Sir

[1] *The Times*, 28 November 1866, p. 4.

Thomas's opportunity, for while the tunnels were being pierced he had a temporary monopoly in the supply of sand and gravel. In 1866 and 1867 a quarter of an acre of sand and ballast from the Heath was sold to the Midland Railway for £1,500, at the high price of 1s. 6d. per yard. This quarter-acre lay in a strip on either side of the Spaniards Road, where the sand could be won with minimum trouble, and it was excavated to a depth which in places reached 25 feet. Such was the origin of the causeway-like appearance of the Spaniards Road, which now looks as if it had been raised on an embankment many feet above the level of the land on either side. The Maryon Wilson surveyor estimated, a few years later, that there were up to 120 acres of workable sand on the Heath extending in many places to a depth of 60 feet. This was the measure of the ravaging to which the Heath could be exposed if ever the commercial contractors were unleashed; the bite taken by the Midland Railway was a mere nibble beside the quarrying which might have been in store.[1]

However much Sir Thomas may have been provoked by the selfishness of others over the years into starting to tear up the Heath in a profit-making rage, it was still painfully true that in 1866 the Heath was, for the first time, really in danger. Hence, while Gurney Hoare put a temporary stop to the danger by taking Sir Thomas to Chancery, the Metropolitan Board of Works moved cumbrously to the longer-term defence of the Heath and set in motion the moves which led finally to its public acquisition in December 1871. In December 1866 the Board reversed its decision of 1857, and resolved that its chairman should find out whether Sir Thomas was ready to negotiate for the dedication of Hampstead Heath to the public—to which the famous 'adjoining lands' were added on amendment—and to ask for his terms.[2] There followed some prevarication and protocol sparring before the two men actually got together. At first the Chairman of the Board, Sir John Thwaites, wished to argue that he need do nothing until the Chancery suit was decided, but he was pressed by public opinion to make some move. Then he wrote suggesting that Sir Thomas should call at the Board's office in Springfield Gardens, which was not an auspicious beginning since it rubbed up Sir Thomas quite the wrong way. As soon as he had heard of the December resolution, it appeared, Sir Thomas had decided to stay on at Charlton House at considerable inconvenience, instead of going to 'Searles where I usually spend the winter', awaiting

[1] GLCRO E/MW/H/III/38/16, Purchase of Hampstead Heath by MBW, evidence of F. J. Clark, surveyor, 1871.
[2] MBW Min., 21 December 1866, pp. 1600–1.

an interview, which ' I shall be happy to [give]. But I must decline the privilege you have accorded me, to wait upon you at your office.'[1] When these ruffles had been smoothed down, Sir John made the journey to Charlton House, and had a long and highly unproductive interview with Sir Thomas, who indicated that he was willing to sell out only at an astronomical price.[2]

> The question of the purchase of the Heath was discussed at considerable length, it was reported to the Board, and Sir Thomas at first stated that until Section 21 . . . was repealed, he would not be able to sell, or even to treat for the sale, of it. He then observed that he supposed he was asked to sell his freehold property at Hampstead. [Which indeed, in respect of the 'adjoining lands', he was.] The Chairman reminded him that up to the present time he had been treated as the Lord of the Manor, and not as the Freeholder of the Heath [a confusion between the Heath and the 'adjoining lands'] . . . The extent of his rights in the Heath need offer no interruption to the progress of negotiations for its sale to the public, since the question of his rights was at present before the Master of the Rolls and would in due course be determined. The Chairman distinctly stated to Sir Thomas that provided an arrangement could be come to between the Board and himself, for the purchase of the Heath, they would be willing to join him in an application to Parliament for the purpose of obtaining the necessary powers to enable him to grant building leases of such portions of the adjoining lands as the Board might not require for the purposes of the public, and that in all probability Parliament, having regard to the fact that such an arrangement would secure the Heath to the public in perpetuity, would accede to the request. Sir Thomas, however, did not appear disposed to agree with that suggestion, but argued that he saw no reason why he should sell his property at Hampstead for the purpose, as he alleged, of gratifying and benefiting certain parties, who had for years opposed him in obtaining his rights. Upon being urged by the Chairman to favour him with his views as to the value of his interest in the Heath, Sir Thomas stated that having regard to the price which he obtained for some land at Charlton, sold by him to the South Eastern Railway, he was of opinion that the property on Hampstead Heath was worth from £5,000 to £10,000 per acre.

[1] Ibid., 11 January 1867, p. 48.
[2] Ibid., 1 February 1867, pp. 142–3.

The Chairman expressed his astonishment at the amount mentioned by Sir Thomas . . .

And there the interview ended, as well it might. For not even the Board could be accused of its usual parsimony if it declined to start talking in terms of giving £1¼–2½ million for the Heath alone; though it may be that Sir Thomas intended his price to include the 'adjoining lands', even those were being put at five to ten times their current value. The figures were so completely ridiculous that Sir Thomas clearly intended to show that he was not prepared to enter into negotiations. Presumably he wanted the pleasure of watching the Board, and the public, sweat it out while the extent, and hence the market value, of his manorial rights was determined in Chancery. The Board, naturally, fell in with this design, and determined to await the result of the Chancery action before doing anything more about the Heath.[1] There the matter rested until after Sir Thomas's death in May 1869. Within a few weeks informal soundings took place between 'a gentleman of great influence with the Metropolitan Board of Works' and F. J. Clark, the estate surveyor, and as these at once showed a willingness to make a reasonable bargain, formal talks were arranged in July 1870.[2] After Sir Thomas's death the entire Maryon Wilson property was inherited by his brother, Sir John, as tenant-for-life subject to the same limitations under the 1806 will as had applied to Sir Thomas. But Sir John had a son, Spencer, already 41 years old in 1870. Father and son acting together could break the restrictions of the will, by ordinary land law procedure, and obtain full powers of granting building leases over the freehold estate. Section 21 of the 1856 Settled Estates Act therefore at once became irrelevant, and the legal disability which had prevented building operations on the estate was instantly removed. No one appears to have paused to consider the implications of this completely altered situation for the Heath. For it could well have been argued that it had become Sir John's own private interest to preserve the Heath as an attraction to confer value on his adjoining building lands, and that there was therefore no longer any case for spending public money in acquiring his manorial interest in the Heath. It was certainly the case that the 'adjoining lands' had all at once been turned into fully ripe building lands, and that the ruse of sterilising East Park

[1] Ibid., 8 March 1867, p. 280, 11 October 1867, p. 1201, 3 July 1868, p. 875, 6 November 1868, pp. 1224–5, 12 February 1869, p. 260.
[2] GLCRO E/MW/H/III/38/16, F. J. Clark to Alfred Clark (Steward of the Manor), 5 July 1870, reporting the chain of events since May 1869. MBW Min., 14 January 1870, p. 33.

under the pretence of protecting the Heath had now run its course. Feeling about the Heath was running so high, however, that it never occurred to the Metropolitan Board of Works that there might be no risk in sitting it out with Sir John without offering to acquire the Heath at all, leaving Sir John to preserve it as a matter of self-interest. Instead, since he was offered hard cash for rights which were still of indeterminate extent, Sir John could hardly be expected to refuse.

Starting from the supposition created by the Board, that the public must acquire the Heath by purchase, the negotiations simply concerned the price which should be given. Sir John and his son Spencer very rapidly agreed to sell, since in effect any price was so much extra money in hand for doing what they would have been likely to do in any case. But since it was purely a matter of financial bargaining, they or their agent made sure that they received the best price possible, by pretending to put an extreme value on the manorial rights. The Board at first suggested £25,000 for the lord's rights, an offer which F. J. Clark would not consider. Then at a meeting in July 1870 between F. J. Clark and Sir John Thwaites, P. Le Breton, and the Board's solicitor and surveyor, agreement was reached on £45,000 plus costs. The really significant point, however, was not the price, but the fact that the agreement dealt only with the Heath; the 'adjoining lands' were not merely ignored, but their ultimate sacrifice was positively encouraged by the express reservation of access roads to East Park. What was celebrated as a triumph for the Heath party and a vindication of years of struggle was in fact a resounding defeat, an acknowledgment that the large expanse of open country might indeed shrink to a narrow strip and that the views might be curtailed by rows of villas on East Park. After noting the agreed price, that the Board would compensate the copyholders for any rights they might claim in the Heath, and that there would be a joint approach to Parliament for the private Act which would be needed, the heads of the agreement continued:[1]

3. No portion of the Heath to be let for building purposes, ever.
4. Land originally proposed to be reserved for an Estate Office on the site of the Flagstaff, marked A on the Plan, to be included but not built upon. The alternative site from 4 to 6 acres at point

[1] Ibid. The North Metropolitan Railway, approved in 1866 but luckily never built, would have entered Hampstead at the northern end of the Hampstead Ponds and run through the whole length of the Heath from there to Golders Hill, then proceeding by way of Childs Hill to cross the Midland Railway at Cricklewood.

B near the Reservoir to be included, except for 1 acre to be reserved to Sir John Maryon Wilson for the erection of a Residence
and Estate Office.

5. M.B.W. at spots marked C and D, the Donkey Stations, to enclose plant and maintain as ornamental grounds.

6. At points E, F, and G, being site of driftways footways and
roadways which must eventually be utilized as the approaches to
East Park, Sir John M. Wilson and his successors to have the right
of extending these Roads 60 feet wide.

7. All rights under the North Metropolitan Railway Act for
making a railway through Hampstead Heath from H to K—H to
I in tunnel, and I to K in open cutting—to be reserved to the
executors of the late Sir T. M. Wilson, and also to Sir J. M.
Wilson.

8. All solicitors' and surveyors' costs, not exceeding £1,000 [later
amended to £2,000], to be paid by the M.B.W.

Whether this was a good bargain for the public or not, it was certainly a good one for the Maryon Wilson interests, and was made even
better before the formal contracts were signed. For in addition to the
reservation of the roads across the East Heath to East Park, a strip of the
West Heath was also retained by Sir John: this was a strategically important slip of land at the foot of Telegraph Hill, where the Heath
extended to the south side of West Heath Road, and by the acquisition
of this couple of acres the Maryon Wilson estate obtained a vital length
of building frontage. The Chairman of the Metropolitan Board of
Works sensed that the bargain might favour the lord of the manor, for
'he wished me [F. J. Clark] to understand that practically this was the
first and last proposal that would emanate from him [Sir John
Thwaites]. That the meeting itself must be taken as confidential between Gentlemen because he would have very strong opposition on the
part of some who believed that the Lord's rights were of little or no
value'.[1] His fears were real enough. They harked back to views
expressed in 1865, when Le Breton had put forward the opinion that
'in valuing the Lord's rights in the Heath, the sole issue of substance is
whether he could, under any conceivable powers, build upon it. . . .
In my view, his profits from it must be trifling (chiefly for sand, sold
off in great quantities), and £30 an acre would be ample compensation.'[2] On that basis £7,000 or so would have been a generous price.

[1] Ibid.
[2] SC on Open Spaces (Metropolis), 1865; a copy of the evidence on Hampstead
Heath was kept in the Maryon Wilson files: E/MW/H/III/38/16. Le Breton

Moreover, with the 1866 Metropolitan Commons Act at its back, the Commons Preservation Society took the line that it was both unnecessary and positively harmful to the general cause to go through any form of purchase of the lord's rights whatever, since this would gravely compromise the principle that surviving commons could not in any circumstances be enclosed and were already adequately protected by law as permanent open spaces.[1] Finally, Sir John Thwaites's apprehensions anticipated the lively local objections to the various small exceptions from the surrender of the lord's interest in the Heath, which predictably erupted when the details of the agreement became public. The opposition to the act of purchase, though it was all pilloried as the mean-minded parochial unwillingness to put Hampstead's pleasures on everyone's rates which did indeed form a part, was therefore in some measure informed by a more high-minded and wider outlook than that of the supporters of the purchase.

The confidential negotiations and undertakings were made public in October 1870, when its Works and General Purposes Committee reported to the full Metropolitan Board of Works. The report was couched in terms which showed that the committee believed that they, and the public, had come very well out of the protracted Heath affair. 'Your Committee cannot refrain from expressing the great satisfaction they feel', ran the peroration, 'at having been enabled to bring this important matter to what they venture to hope will be considered a satisfactory issue.' The price, of £45,000 for the lord's rights in the Heath, plus £2,000 for lawyers' and surveyors' costs, they presented as a great bargain: 'Although a long period has elapsed since the attention of the Board was first called to the subject, the difficulties to be overcome fairly account for the time consumed, and if regard be had to the value set on the land by the late Lord of the Manor, it will be seen that, in a pecuniary point of view, the ratepayers of the metropolis have not been losers by the delay.'[2] The self-congratulatory tone rested in good part on self-delusion and ignorance of the history of the issue. The main count was the bland retreat to the little Heath, the legal Heath, without so much as a passing acknowledgment that the long struggle to

did go on to admit that Sir T. M. Wilson could certainly enclose parts of the Heath, with the consent of the homage, and build on them, provided sufficient of the Heath always remained for the effective exercise of the commoners' rights. This admission might indicate a potential cash value for the lord's rights of rather more than £30 an acre.

[1] MBW Min., 25 March 1870, p. 343, letter from Commons Preservation Society.

[2] Ibid., 21 October 1870, pp. 482–4.

achieve the greater Heath of the 'adjoining lands' had been abandoned
and cast to the winds. The lesser count was financial, the complete
failure to see that, if the public could really rest content with the lesser
Heath and had never needed more than that, then it may be that the
'ratepayers of the metropolis' ought never to have been asked to pay
anything at all for the preservation of this smaller open space.

The project of the great Heath was not merely postponed to some
future occasion, it was written off for ever so far as it lay in the power
of the Metropolitan Board of Works to achieve this. The Committee,
in recommending the terms of the agreement made with F. J. Clark,
went out of its way to state that 'the reservations are only such as are
proper under the circumstances of the case.' These reservations included the all-important reservations to the lord of the manor of full
liberty to make access roads across the Heath to the 'adjoining lands' in
order to make possible their residential development. Whoever were the
victors in the struggle, they were certainly not the Hoares, Turner, Le
Breton, Lord Mansfield, or the rest of the local notables, all of whom
had always looked on the preservation of the 'adjoining lands' from the
builders as the prime object to be achieved. Even on the Maryon Wilson
side it had long been acknowledged that the ideal open space, from an
aesthetic and recreational point of view as distinct from a legalistic
application of ancient rights, ought to be a good deal larger than the
legal Heath. F. J. Clark, who had been the Maryon Wilson land agent
for a quarter of a century, put this view very plainly, in answer to Shaw
Lefevre:[1]

> I quite agree with some of these gentlemen who have been called
> [he stated, referring to Turner and Le Breton] that it would be an
> advantage to keep the Heath open; it is probably one of the most
> popular places in the vicinity of London, and its popularity will be
> further increased by the railways. There is a Bill now before
> Parliament for a railway up into the town, and one or two will
> come close to it. I think, in the acquisition of the Heath, a great
> deal more land ought to be acquired for by forming a frontage to
> the common which would be always preserved by the Act of Parlia-
> ment for the use of the public; I think the whole expense might
> be covered by the portions which might be sold off round the
> Heath.

His syntax becoming a little muddled, Clark's meaning was not

[1] *SC on Open Spaces (Metropolis)*, 1865, Q.3063.

altogether clear to the Committee; in a later answer he managed to be more explicit.[1]

> But I understood you to say [John Tollemache interposed] that you think a portion, I suppose by far the larger portion, could be secured to the public if a certain other portion were sold and allowed to be built upon?—No; my answer went to this, that in purchasing Hampstead Heath it should not be confined to Hampstead Heath proper, but that a much larger area of land, whether of Sir Thomas Wilson or anyone else's, should be acquired, and then the Heath being preserved for ever to the public by Act of Parliament, there would be a security which would so far increase the value of the adjacent land which had been acquired, that I thought the re-sale of that property would probably go a great way towards recouping the purchase money of the property.

Clark's plan clearly contemplated that the strategically vital non-Heath fields of East Park and Telegraph Hill, both belonging to the Maryon Wilson estate, ought to be purchased, as also should Lord Mansfield's lands in Hampstead which were then used as Ken Wood's kitchen gardens, and probably Rhodes's copyhold estate at South End which was then still unbuilt. All these extra lands should be thrown together with the Heath proper to form a single, viable, open space. Further than this, Clark was proposing that other fringe lands, which he did not specify, ought to be acquired so that they—perhaps with some fragments of the enlarged open space—could be laid out for high-class building development, and could be re-sold in order to cover the costs of the entire operation. This was an imaginative scheme, and could if required have been supported by appealing to the precedent of the financing of Battersea Park by precisely the same kind of real estate dealings. It is true that if it had been implemented the resulting open space would have been different from and smaller than today's continuous open stretch: the Parliament Hill Fields frontier would probably have been sealed by building; but against this, the Rhodes 'invasion' of the South Hill Park estate would never have occurred, and the West Heath would have been greatly improved through the retention of Telegraph Hill. In terms of fresh air the balance of public advantage would not have been heavily against the Clark plan; in terms of cost the balance of advantage would have been overwhelmingly in his favour. The extended Heath as ultimately achieved cost the public in its various guises as ratepayers, taxpayers, and voluntary subscribers,

[1] Ibid., Q.3096.

about £500,000 for land purchase; the Clark plan, if the development and re-sale had worked out as envisaged, might ultimately have cost the public nothing at all.

The plan, of course, was not implemented. It was not implemented because it required a large initial outlay by or for the public. The large initial outlay was not even contemplated, because the Metropolitan Board of Works was frightened of its ratepayers and was dominated by the representatives of civic parsimony. Among these, Le Breton of Hampstead could pass for a generous and liberal-handed man, because he did not stand for complete and total resistance to using ratepayers' money for such objects, but regarded a carefully controlled minimum expenditure as laudable. Greater open-handedness than his, however, was perfectly conceivable in the contemporary situation: he merely had to observe the activities of Manchester or Leeds in purchasing land to form parks to see the lengths to which municipal activities and finances could be stretched. Behind his narrowness of vision on the particular Hampstead issue, and that of many like him, there lay the long history of attempting to get something for nothing, of trying to sterilise Maryon Wilson's estate by legal dodges and political tricks. These had worked, until Sir Thomas's death in 1869. After his death it was impossible for such men to adapt quickly enough to the new situation where the old dodges no longer had the quirks of the land law and the restrictions of limited ownership to bite upon: the new situation, with the Maryon Wilson estate in the hands of an owner with full powers to lease, and therefore to build, meant quite simply that if it was desirable to preserve any part of the estate as open space then such lands had to be purchased at a fair price. It is understandable that neither the Hampstead men nor the Londoners at large, among the governing circle, were capable of making this sudden *volte-face* from preserving without expense to preserving at vast (initial) expense. But since it was the Hampstead party who had been responsible for creating the belief that the large open space could be preserved without cost and simply by defending rights and manipulating the law, it was primarily the Hampstead party which bears responsibility for the poverty of imagination and enterprise shown in 1870. The narrowness of the 1870 Heath acquisition is a monument to London's civic meanness in general, and to the Hampstead gentry's long career of pettiness and distortion in particular.

Nevertheless, hoist with their own petard, the friends of the Heath did not have an easy passage in gaining acceptance of the limited agreement and small outlay of 1870. The Commons Preservation Society weighed in with an objection on principle, writing to the Metropolitan Board of Works 'deprecating the course taken by the Board in paying to a lord of the manor so large a sum as that agreed upon, as tending to prevent the general preservation of Metropolitan Open Spaces; and also expressing regret at portions of waste land in the neighbourhood of Hampstead being sacrificed for private purposes.'[1] The 'portions of waste ground' referred, among other grants, to a series of grants to prominent Hampstead residents who readily obtained from the new lord of the manor small pieces of the Heath which they coveted as embellishments for their private gardens, in an undignified scramble to have one final nibble at the Heath before it passed into public control: the largest and most widely resented of these was the grant of Lovers Bank to Powell, for adding to the grounds of Heath Lodge.[2] Less high-minded objections came from the really narrowly parochial vestries, such as Battersea, Lambeth—which later changed its mind and decided to remain neutral—and, at least at first, Islington. Islington's memorial to the Metropolitan Board of Works took its representative on the Board completely by surprise, and he refused to move its reception 'as he was ashamed of it'. The Board gracefully resolved that 'it would be too cruel to place the memorial itself on the minutes as a lasting record of Islington's disgrace.'[3] Against this background muttering the bill incorporating the terms of the 1870 agreement passed through Parliament in June 1871; the Metropolitan Board of Works, having paid over the £47,000 in purchase price and costs, formally took possession of the Heath at the beginning of December 1871, though the ceremonial entry was postponed until 13 January 1872, when Colonel Hogg, the Chairman of the Metropolitan Board of Works, walked from Hampstead Heath railway station up to Jack Straw's Castle for a celebration lunch, in the company of F. J. Clark, Richard Ware, Thomas Turner, Philip Le Breton, S. Barber (a churchwarden), and others.

If one takes the view that by the late 1860s, whatever may have been the case earlier in the century, the fate even of the Heath proper had been brought into serious question as a result of a whole complex of

[1] MBW Min., 25 November 1870, p. 667, letter from E. W. Fithian, Secretary of the Commons Preservation Society.

[2] GLCRO E/MW/H/III/38/16, F. J. Clark to Sir John Maryon Wilson, 18 January 1872; *The Times*, S. Barber of The Grange, Hampstead, to the Editor, 23 December 1871.

[3] *The Times*, 25 February 1871. Islington Vestry thereupon sent in another petition, this time in favour of the purchase: MBW Min., 3 March 1871, p. 389.

misunderstandings, obstinacy, irritability, profit-seeking, and plain dishonesty, then the 1870 solution may be held to have been necessary to the survival of the Heath. And by rather similar reasoning, emphasising the political and financial constraints of the time, it may be held that realisation of the larger Heath was not on the cards in 1870. In which case, on the general principle that half a loaf is better than no bread, and ignoring questions of individual responsibility for making the half loaf all that was practically attainable, the local feting of Philip Le Breton as the hero of the hour and chief benefactor of Hampstead was entirely justifiable. In the public eye he was the figure, even more than Hoare, who had campaigned longest, loudest, most persistently, and ultimately most successfully for the preservation of the Heath from threats which the public had been persuaded were real, sinister, and perpetually imminent. For such services the presentation of a silver tea and coffee service, a gold watch, and a purse of £500 by the grateful inhabitants of Hampstead and neighbourhood was but a fitting reward.[1] Looking behind the scenes, however, and making the same assumptions about the necessity of public acquisition by 1870, it may appear that the true architect of victory was Frederick James Clark. Clark was not only the land agent for the Maryon Wilson estate, responsible for its management—as distinct from the Steward of the manor of Hampstead, who for a short while chanced to be Clark's brother, but who was concerned purely with manorial and therefore largely legal matters; but also he was a local resident, living at the large mansion of Oak Lodge in the Edgware Road, Kilburn (opposite Willesden Lane), and had a sincere wish to see the Heath permanently preserved as a public open space, and moreover as a piece of 'natural' country and not as a formal park. In Sir Thomas's later years, when his whole lifetime of frustration and gross misrepresentation fed upon his pride and obstinacy to produce a state of advanced irascibility, Clark had an exceedingly difficult brief. On the whole, Clark's performance in balancing between advocacy of his employer's interest and legal rights, and regard for the public's interest in the Hampstead scenery, was exemplary. If any one individual was responsible for keeping the option alive, of the eventual dedication of the Heath to the public, by ensuring that a heath capable of being dedicated did survive Sir Thomas's anger, it was Clark.

In the public prints it was Hoare, with his Chancery action, who was cast in this latter role. But not only were Hoare's motives tarnished, but also the ultimate success of his move, should Sir Thomas have lived,

1 *The Times*, 11 December 1871.

must be doubted. Considered purely as a matter of law, and of the backing which the law was bound to give to the custom of the manor of Hampstead, it seems practically inescapable that Lord Romilly would have been obliged to acknowledge that while those copyholders who could establish that theirs were ancient copyholds of inheritance—and it seems that there were no more than three or four of these extant—possessed undoubted rights of pasturage on the Heath, it was equally the case that the lord of the manor had the right to appropriate portions of the Heath, provided only that sufficient always remained to enable these copyhold rights to be exercised. The custom would also have been shown to be that such appropriations had in recent times always been made by the lord 'with the consent of the homage', and that if there ever had been a custom for the lord to do this *proprio motu* it had long been disused. 'The consent of the homage', however, was not a clearly defined process; and the evidence of actual nineteenth-century practice by the Hampstead court baron and court leet was that any dozen 'good copyholders' who chanced to be summoned to attend by the steward, constituted 'the homage'. The copyholders eligible for attendance for this purpose were, perforce, by no means confined to the tiny band of 'ancient copyholders', but could be drawn from the entire group of some 250 copyhold tenants of the manor. It would have been simple to select a dozen men from this large body who, because they were local tradesmen and shopkeepers, were in favour of the greatest possible amount of new housing in the district to bring the most rapid possible expansion of trade. Some pretty elementary politicking could, therefore, have ensured that 'the consent of the homage' would have been forthcoming for whatever fell designs the lord might choose to entertain. It follows that, from a preservationist point of view, the Chancery suit could never have been more than a delaying action. And insofar as it would, if completed, have resulted in a clearcut decision on what, to this point, many people had held to be indistinct and obscure, it would necessarily have led to an acceleration of the very process—with no possibility of legal resistance—which it was designed to avoid.[1]

Clark, on the other hand, while firm in his interpretation of the extent of the legal rights of the lord of the manor, was equally firm in his advice that it was against Sir Thomas's interest to attempt to exer-

[1] It is courting disaster to offer such firm opinions where a Master of the Rolls declined to pronounce: but they appear to follow from the evidence of the court rolls; from GLCRO E/MW/H/III/38/16, F. J. Clark's evidence on the valuation of Hampstead Heath to determine the value of the lord's interest, 1871; and his evidence to *SC on Open Spaces* (*Metropolis*), 1865, especially Q.3053.

cise them. It may be conceded that this advice was very largely an expression of a view of his employer's enlightened self-interest, that any notional pecuniary sacrifice involved in retaining the Heath as an open space would be more than compensated by the extra building values attaching to the riparian sites and near vicinity by virtue of the attractions of proximity to an open space. Which is no more than to say that, given the existence of a large estate adjoining the open space, the largest slice of the social benefits of having an open space could be internalised by the machinery of the real estate market and turned into direct cash benefits for the landowner. Enlightened self-interest, however, is not in itself a mean or despicable concept; and this particular line of advice was not rendered any less in the public interest because it also happened to make shrewd business sense. There are, moreover, grounds for believing that Clark found that his business judgment was buttressed by a concern for scenery and for public welfare; though had these considerations pointed in opposite directions rather than run in harness, there is no reason to suppose that the latter would have come out on top. Both in 1865 at the time of the Select Committee, and in 1870–2 in the course of the negotiations for the acquisition, he showed considerable personal concern for the natural beauties of the Heath and for the need to enhance them by carefully controlled 'wild' landscaping and planting, avoiding the formalising effects of regimented 'park' gardening. He acknowledged that the general public had a right, in practice if not in law, to walk and stroll over the Heath, even though the lord of the manor could, and did, charge tolls for the use of the Heath by particular individuals or organised groups such as the Marylebone schools which brought up vanloads of children for an occasional day's outing. Admittedly this acknowledgment was less a matter of public spirit and generosity than of simple expediency, since in the face of the holiday crowds of 50,000 people and upwards it would have been physically impossible as well as dangerously provocative to attempt to charge for admission to the Heath. Nevertheless there was nothing grudging about the way in which this right of access was admitted, and there was indeed a hint of pleasure in Clark's explanation of how in practice there was a rough discrimination between purely individual and recreational use of the Heath, whether on foot or on horseback, which was free, and organised or commercial use for which charges were collected from the owners of tea-tables, booths, donkeys for hire, and such like.[1]

[1] SC on Open Spaces (Metropolis), 1865, Q.3052–3, 3071–5, 3191–8; GLCRO E/MW/H/III/38/16, F. J. Clark to Sir J. M. Wilson, 18 January 1872.

Behind Clark was his employer, and if any medals are to be awarded for the preservation of Hampstead Heath the claims of Sir Thomas Maryon Wilson should at least be considered. After all, if the lord of the manor did possess any powers to dismantle the Heath and build upon it, these had certainly not come into existence only in the mid-1860s but must always have been present. In which case the physical existence of a heath which could be acquired in 1871 ought to be attributed mainly to Sir Thomas's forbearance in not exercising such powers, at any time after it could be held that the growth of housing demand had reached such a point as to make the development of the heathland a practical proposition. Certainly his own land agent did recommend that such forbearance was prudent and profitable. But because of Sir Thomas's peculiar position as a life-tenant holding his property under exceptional restrictions, this course was profitable for the estate as a continuing concern rather than for him as an individual. Hence Sir Thomas's acceptance of his agent's advice cannot be taken to have been automatic; for that the twin factors of his sense of family pride and continuity, producing a trustee-like attitude of responsibility for husbanding the family estate for the benefit of future generations, and his own personal attachment to the Heath for its own sake, were also necessary. Being a colonel of the Sussex yeomanry and an admirer of the military life, Sir Thomas had some tendency to look on the Heath as a valuable exercise ground, and of all requests acceded most readily to that of the Marylebone Rifle Volunteers to drill on the Heath. When the civilian public swarmed over the Heath he tolerated but did not welcome them:[1]

6174. Are you aware that many thousands of people frequent Hampstead Heath on holidays? [Shaw Lefevre asked him]—They go there on holidays.

6175. Have you ever treated them as trespassers?—When there are fetes, and people go up there to amuse themselves, they pay an acknowledgment.

6176. But I suppose that is only when they bring horses and carts on the common. You have not treated pedestrians as trespassers?— No; I do not know that I have; it is uninclosed land, and I could only bring an action for trespass, and should probably get 1*d.* for my damages.

6177. You never have treated the public as trespassers?—Some

[1] *SC on Open Spaces (Metropolis),* 1865, Q.2185 (Col. Wood) and Q.3063 for military drilling on the Heath.

people imagine that persons go to Hampstead Heath to play games, but it could not be done; part of the heath is a bog; and there are cases of horses and cows having been smothered there.
6178. But people go there and amuse themselves?—Just as they do in Greenwich Park, but they have no right in Greenwich Park.
6179. You have never treated people as trespassers?—No; are they treated as trespassers in Greenwich Park?

On the other hand, his appreciation of the scenery was far from grudging, and he may, even though a non-resident, have had a genuine affection for the place. Sir Thomas was being perfectly accurate when he said, in 1865, that 'it never entered into my head to destroy Hampstead Heath at all until I found that I was thwarted in every Bill that I brought into Parliament.' From 1829 onwards it had been his intention 'that if I had the power of building on the inclosed land, I should lay out Hampstead Heath as a place of recreation for my own houses.' When plans were made in 1858 for creating a Hampstead Park, 'the plan which Mr Cockerell, the architect, drew [for landscaping] was, so far as Hampstead Heath was concerned, very much my own.' In preparation for improving the beauty of the Heath 'I had a very large collection of cedar trees and curious oak trees raised at Charlton, in order to place on Hampstead Heath, but they have all died, or become too old to transplant.' But even with all the frustrations and disappointments, Sir Thomas had still made some new plantations on the Heath, chiefly some tree belts near the Vale of Health 'for a screen to some linen posts in the grounds of some laundry people.' While both he and Clark bitterly resented, though they were powerless to prevent, the conversion of the Vale of Health from a few peaceful cottages into a raucous mini-town with gin-palace-style hotel and vulgar amusement gardens, this desecration of the atmosphere of the Heath by building development took place on copyhold land, compulsorily enfranchised at the demand of the copyholder.[1] The record of concern for the Heath is not unimpressive, particularly since the general public had been trained to regard Sir Thomas as public enemy No. 1 ever since 1829.

It may be thought, however, that in the final analysis the preservation of the Heath had no heroes, and also no villains. All the actors in the drama may have been sincere and upright men, Sir Thomas and F. J. Clark no less than Gurney Hoare, Thomas Turner and Philip Le Breton. Maybe no one of these was any more wicked, selfish and scheming than any other; and no one of them any more public-spirited,

[1] Ibid., Q. 6087, 6135, 6140, 6142, 3099.

honest and plain-speaking than any other. The duplicity of Hoare in pretending that he was fighting to preserve only the Heath when in fact he was trying to preserve its non-Heath surroundings without cost to himself or the public, was perhaps matched by a duplicity of Sir Thomas in pretending that he was going to desecrate the Heath when in fact he really wanted powers to develop his own free-hold estate. The possible hypocrisy of Le Breton in accepting the plaudits of the public for an action which undoubtedly contributed to his private pleasure and his private profit in terms of the value of his house, was perhaps matched by the possible hypocrisy of Clark whose arguments for the public benefits of open space and fresh air were clearly based on calculations of the resulting private profit for his land-owning employer. The lies of Sir Thomas, who had in 1824 firmly recalled that on his death-bed his father 'upon his being asked if he would do the like [in making a codicil conferring building lease powers] as to the Hampstead Property, he said no; and expressed his sentiments for leaving that as it was', but who in 1865 recalled that his father on that occasion had made the entirely opposite reply, 'I am too tired to do it now; I must put it off until tomorrow',[1] were perhaps no different from the lies of Donald Nicoll of Oaklands Hall, who in 1862 chaired a meeting to organise resistance to the Danger to the Heath, but who at the same moment was busy demolishing a small cottage in the Vale of Health and building the Suburban Hotel on its site, a corner of the new hotel being in fact an encroachment on the Heath;[2] or those of David Powell, who sided with the anti-Wilson party on high grounds of public interest, but who took care to appropriate for himself as private property the high ground of Lovers Bank in 1871, thus taking in part of the Heath and stopping up a public footpath from North End on to the West Heath.[3]

In fact all the actors pursued their own interests, and dressed up their actions in whatever raiment of principle could be made to fit. That the play turned out to be a limited success, and not a disaster, may perhaps be laid more to the credit of market forces than to the posturings and follies of any individuals. The arguments of the market place for preserving this particular piece of open space were indeed particularly

[1] GLCRO E/MW/H/III/38/16, Case . . . against the Finchley Road Bill, 1824; see above, p. 135; *SC on Open Spaces (Metropolis)* 1865, Q.6107.

[2] Ibid., Q.3110; GLCRO E/MW/H/III/38/16, report of public meeting on the Heath in Danger, 14 April 1862.

[3] Ibid., copy of Memorial from Hampstead Vestry to MBW objecting to the exclusion of certain portions of the Heath from the purchase agreement, December 1871; and ibid., F. J. Clark to Sir J. M. Wilson, 18 January 1872.

strong, though probably not strong enough to ensure that a continuous stretch of several hundred acres should be preserved, rather than a spacious housing layout with many, but individually small, squares and gardens on the West End pattern. It was more important that the market forces which dictated in general terms the degree of ripeness for building development of different localities were still relatively weak when they reached the vicinity of the Heath. In other words, the area was not yet ready for building operations in terms of the state of demand for building land. Not yet ready, luckily for the cause of the greater Heath, not merely in the late 1860s but also in the next dozen years. The Heath proper remained, legally secure after 1871, and able to have been legally secured because it had not previously been practically threatened. The improper Heath, of East Park and Parliament Hill Fields over into Highgate, also remained as open country after 1871, because the interplay of ownership structure and building demand had not yet brought it within the ambit of development. It remained outside just long enough for the tactics of estate development policy to be played out and for public and private opinion to swing round to the necessity of footing the bill in hard cash for the sake of creating an exercise ground and viewpoint of unsurpassed magnificence.

Six

THE BUILDING
FIELDS OF ETON
Chalcots, 1825-71

One consequence of the legal and political steps which were conceived to be necessary in order to protect the Heath was the sterilisation of the Maryon Wilson estate during the whole of Sir Thomas's lifetime. Or rather, Sir Thomas himself believed that this was the consequence, and his view has been accepted by historians.[1] Certainly, no building took place on his estate before his death in 1869, and this absence of development had considerable local effects on the nature and success of development which did take place on neighbouring estates. Though the area which was kept off the building market for this long period was large— 416 acres, enough for the potential sites of anything from 2,000 to 5,000 houses on reasonable hypothetical densities—it may be doubted whether land starvation on this scale had any more general, metropolitan, effects. The reason is the simple one that although the demand of greater London for new houses was in aggregate very large, so also was the area of potential building land over which this demand might exert itself, so that the withholding of any particular supply of land was unlikely to make very much difference. Thus while the Maryon Wilson houses which were conceivably foregone in the years before 1869 could have amounted in physical terms to anything between half and the whole of Hampstead's actual stock of houses in 1871, the total number of these non-houses at the uppermost estimate would not have exceeded one single year's addition of new houses in greater London as a whole. Hence, unless we conceive of a locationally specific housing demand which insisted on houses in Hampstead and would not accept any substitute locations, the Maryon Wilson deprivation was of no more than local and family significance.

This situation means that the nature of the sterilisation from which Sir Thomas's estate suffered requires definition. His legal disability was

[1] H. C. Prince, 'North-west London: 1814–1863' and 'North-west London: 1864–1914', in J. T. Coppock and H. C. Prince (eds), *Greater London* (1964), pp. 84, 130–1.

plain enough. The inability either to grant building leases or to sell building sites outright meant that he was powerless to use the two main methods by which landowners got other people to cover their estates with houses. In the London area in particular, any landowner who was unable to enter into building agreements or building leases under which developers or builders could conduct building operations in return for paying ground rents naturally felt that he was denied the normal means of urban estate development. But in such a condition of legal incapacity abnormal means still remained a possibility. The only real alternative for such a landowner was to develop out of his own resources. Direct enterprise of this sort was certainly uncommon, but it was not unknown, and therefore was not ruled out on any grounds of incompatibility with the social position and dignity of a landowner. It demanded finance as well as managerial expertise; it may well be that Sir Thomas was short of the first, though the second could always be hired. But even if Sir Thomas had no savings which he could have devoted to getting a snowball of building operations in motion, it would still have been quite possible for him to have borrowed the necessary initial capital. Perhaps £10,000 or so would have sufficed to set works going, after which the normal revolutions of building finance would have taken care of the enterprise by financing further houses on the profits, and security, of those already built. In the light of the enormous sums which other life-tenants managed to borrow at this time, on the flimsiest of securities and for the most frivolous and totally unproductive purposes, it cannot be argued that Sir Thomas would have been unable to borrow if he had wanted.[1] A man of his position and property, with such a productive object in view, could probably have raised the money from his bankers on a simple personal bond at comparatively low interest; but failing them, there were plenty of insurance offices who would have considered him a good risk, provided he offered the additional security of taking out a life policy.

A direct building enterprise would therefore have been perfectly feasible. No doubt the main reason that Sir Thomas apparently never even contemplated such an activity was one of temperament: a feeling that he ought to be granted his rights as every other incapacitated landowner was, and an aversion to being compelled against his will to suffer the worry and bother of conducting business affairs and taking risks. Quite so; but his failure to show sufficient enterprise to find a way

[1] For one of the most notorious cases of massive borrowing on a life-interest, see F. M. L. Thompson, 'The end of a great estate', *Econ. Hist. Rev.* 2nd ser. VIII (1953).

out of his predicament indicates two things. Firstly, that his own circumstances were sufficiently comfortable as they were for the thought of the extra income lying locked up in undeveloped Hampstead not to have enticed or provoked him into any effort to unlock it. Secondly, that if unlocked it might not have turned out to be large enough or reliable enough to take care of the costs and risks entailed. Sir Thomas professed to believe, by 1865, that 'by the outcry that has been made against me, I am deprived of about 50,000*l*. a year. My property would have produced me that without the slightest injury to the public, if any of my Bills had passed.'[1] This implied a belief that by 1865 every one of his 416 acres could have been successfully let at building rents, if it had not been for his legal incapacity; this was so absurd that Sir Thomas can only have been bluffing. Between 1821, when he inherited the estate, and his death in 1869 about 3,000 houses were actually built in Hampstead. In 1869 much other land besides Sir Thomas's was still vacant, some of it nearer to the City and West End than his and some of it just as close to Hampstead Town. It is therefore reasonable to suppose that under any conditions of land supply the number of new houses going to Hampstead in these years would still have been about 3,000. Hence the most that Sir Thomas could have expected, either if if he had obtained full leasing powers or if he had gone in for building himself, would have been a redistribution of this almost finite number of new houses. Broadly, some of them would have been built on parts of his estate which were easiest to develop, alongside the Finchley Road, and some on parts closest to Hampstead Town, at the expense of roughly equivalent parts of other estates which would have suffered from the competition of Maryon Wilson sites. It would be idle to attempt to estimate the likely extent of this hypothetical redistribution with any precision. But the likelihood that in real, as distinct from legal, terms only some small fraction of his estate stood any chance of becoming ripe for building within his lifetime meant that Sir Thomas's lack of enterprise, no doubt based on inertia and gentry conventionality at the conscious level, had a sound rational basis.

It also meant that in tolerating the sterilisation of his estate Sir Thomas was in effect tolerating the exclusion of the builders only from some unknown, but small, fraction of it. Viewed from the angle of the entire 416 acres, in other words, the sterilisation down to 1869 was perhaps rather less a matter of legal incapacity and rather more a matter of the weakness of market forces than might at first be imagined.

[1] *SC on Open Spaces* (*Metropolis*), 1865, Q.6068.

After all, once the Maryon Wilson estate was legally open to development under building leases it took a further sixty years before all the
building land was taken up. The impatience of landowners to start
milking the urban cow as soon as they saw it making across the fields
towards their own fences, and their dreams of sudden riches from
ground rents, were matched only by the long-drawn-out slowness with
which building estates actually progressed and the many *longueurs*
when building plots hung fire and failed to find any takers. It may well
be that by declining to become an entrepreneur Sir Thomas avoided
burning his fingers. And it could even be that the period of enforced
idleness for the estate was ultimately to the advantage of the family, by
making the post-1869 development more compact in time, and more
certain in its rewards, than would otherwise have been the case.
Whether the delay was of ultimate benefit to the Hampstead community depends in large measure on questions of architectural taste,
and the view which is taken of the actual Fitzjohn's Avenue,
Redington Road, or Goldhurst Terrace, in comparison with the
pre-1869 houses and streets which might have been, but were not,
built.

Calculation of the social benefit or loss occasioned by the Maryon
Wilson sterilisation also depends on the view taken of the merits of the
roads and streets which were built up between 1821 and 1869. For the
character of such districts as Adelaide Road and College Road, Belsize
Square and Belsize Park Gardens, Parkhill Road and Lawn Road,
Alexandra Road and Boundary Road, or Thurlow Road and Lyndhurst
Road, owe much to the fact that for nearly fifty years their development
was able to go ahead without the interference of Maryon Wilson competition. In broad terms this meant that the remaining estates—Eton,
Dean and Chapter, Eyre, and Howard (Upton)—had collectively a tight
grip on the Hampstead land supply, and were thus able to concentrate
building in time and place in a much more compact and orderly fashion
than might have been the case if all Hampstead had been in the market
all the time. It would be a mistake to attribute any complete restraint
on sporadic, haphazard, scattered, and piecemeal development to this
single cause: the four estates which were legally free to supply builders
with sites did not form a local land monopoly, since they acted in competition with each other rather than in collusion; each of them followed its own local variant of the principle of ribbon development, with
short fingers of residential streets poking out into its fields; and a glance
at the 1873 map will show that there were still at that date large
amounts of vacant 'back-land' on the Eton and Dean and Chapter

estates, indicating that there was no question of achieving an entirely compact and continuous mid-century development of uniform character before the frontier was breached and the builders could fan out into the open country of the Maryon Wilson lands. Nevertheless, reinforced as it was by the peculiarities of the internal tenancy arrangements of the Dean and Chapter's estate, it can be argued that the fortuitous sterilisation of this large slice of Hampstead had the effect of bottling up mid-century building in a much more confined space than would have happened in 'normal' conditions of land supply. The earlier argument leads to the suggestion that there was little demand for sites specifically in Hampstead as distinct from demand for sites somewhere within the contemporary greater London, and hence the fact that the choice of sites within Hampstead was restricted is unlikely to have given the ground owners of available sites any premium, and developers choosing Hampstead plots were unlikely to have had to pay any more for them than for comparable plots elsewhere in London. The whole situation therefore probably did not lead to the final consumers, the new Hampstead house-owners and residents of the period, paying any more for their houses than in any other district; though, on the other hand, it almost certainly did present all the other ground owners except Maryon Wilson with a steadier income from ground rents, starting from earlier dates, than they could have expected had the Maryon Wilson lands been available. Hence the only significant financial costs of the affair seem to have been a redistribution of property incomes amongst the small group of ground owners, leaving the general public unaffected. On the positive side of this balance sheet, we can infer substantial social benefits, in terms of the emergence of blocks of residential property of reasonably uniform and harmonious character larger in extent than normal, and in terms of the enjoyment of access to unspoilt and uncluttered farmland by nearly two generations of settlers on the Maryon Wilson frontier.

Such reflections would, no doubt, have brought little comfort to Sir Thomas, and might not have sounded very convincing to the managers of the other estates, who were so much impressed by their day-to-day difficulties that they may be excused for never dreaming that they were enjoying a comparatively easy run for their money before 1869. The most vivid impression conveyed by scrutiny of the immediacy of the estate documentation is of the slowness with which building went forward and of the problems and troubles involved in getting a building estate launched and in keeping it on the move; it is only in retrospect that the blessings of an artificially rigged market become apparent.

Nevertheless the landowners and their agents became increasingly aware from the 1820s onwards that:[1]

> The richest crop for any field
> Is a crop of bricks for it to yield.
> The richest crop that it can grow,
> Is a crop of houses in a row.

And although the crop may not have turned out to be so quick-maturing and trouble-free as it seemed in anticipation, it was still most ample, and opportunities for its cultivation were not likely to be neglected.

The first to perceive the opportunities in Hampstead were the private landowners, Eyre and Howard, and the private owners of the sub-estates on the Belsize property; the corporate owners were either power-less or indifferent or both.[2] After 1825, however, and no doubt because of the financial crisis of that year and its aftermath, development on the Howard estate came to a halt and nothing much happened for twenty years; similarly, on the Belsize estate, although some further country-mansion creation continued, the more intensive building on the Bliss sub-estate petered out after 1825. Samuel Eyre does not seem to have been put off stroke by the crisis, but his builders probably were; although his northward expansion of St John's Wood into Hampstead went forward along the lines of the new Finchley Road and Avenue Road converging on the new Swiss Cottage Tavern, the pace of the advance seems to have been much slowed down in the 1830s and early 1840s. It was not until the end of the 1840s that his operations began to quicken once more. In 1848 Boundary Road extended only one block to the west of Finchley Road, there was no Loudoun Road, and the triangle of Eyre land to the west of the Swiss Cottage bounded by Fairfax Road (at first called Victoria Road), Belsize Road, and Hillgrove Road (at first called Adelaide Road North) was still a field; by 1853 Boundary Road had been pushed right across to Abbey Road, and the present Fairfax, Harben, Belsize, and Hillgrove Roads were in full building spate.[3]

While the private owners were quiescent for a couple of decades after 1825, and apparently did not embark on any new, ambitious

[1] Anon. quoted in Tarbuck, *Handbook of House Property* (1875).
[2] See above, ch. 3.
[3] Inferred from a comparison of the following detailed maps of the district: O.S. six-inch street outline of London, surveyed 1848–51, published 1857; *P.O. London Directory*, three-inch London map, 1850; Maryon Wilson Hampstead Estate Bill, four-inch map, House Bill, HLRO 1853.

schemes, it was left to a corporate owner to attempt the difficult exercise of trying to launch a brand-new project against the tide of the market. It was perhaps typical of the sluggishness and unworldliness of corporate landowners that Eton College got wind of what was going on in the vicinity in the building line only after the housing boom of the 1820s had already been pricked. It was equally typical that once the College had got it into its head that building estate development on its Chalcots estate was possible, it kept doggedly on its way through the 1830s and 1840s without paying any attention to the general state of the building industry and of the demand for housing. Hence came a block of development in the triangle of Adelaide Road–Eton Road–College Road of housing of an otherwise uncommon date in these parts. Hence also the great problems at Chalcots, problems which were very much interconnected, both of conceiving any grand design or master plan for the development of the estate as a whole, and of finding any developers or builders in a large enough way of business to undertake building except in penny packets. In time, as demand strengthened, the second problem was indeed overcome, and the eventual covering of Chalcots which stretched out into the 1890s was largely the work of just one or two big builders. The first problem, however, was shelved; and when more rapid development did become possible the College and its advisers had no spirit for ambitious planning, and instead allowed development to drift along its own channels, with only the minimum of direction needed to create Adelaide Road as the spinal cord of the estate's communication system.

It was, indeed, early in 1825 that Eton's London solicitor, William Tooke, first noticed the building potential of Chalcots. He was impressed, no doubt, by the activities in Regent's Park immediately to the south and the fact that this development was finished. The immediate occasion, however, was that the beneficial lease of Chalcots was coming up for one of its regular renewals at Lady Day 1825, and if the College was to go in for any building it was necessary to seize this chance to insert a new clause into the lease enabling the College to resume possession of earmarked lands at any time. Tooke thought that there might be some pickings for the College from development of the frontages on Haverstock Hill and on the lane to Chalk Farm, which would be inexpensive since no road-forming would be required. But he also noticed that the Duke of Portland had just begun to create what became his slum of Portland Town on the northern edge of Regent's Park, centred on Charles Street (now Charlbert), and the thought occurred to him that Eton's eighteen-acre field called Rugmoor (now the southern part of Primrose Hill park) was highly eligible for a continuation of development of the Regent's Park class.[1] Rugmoor, and indeed the whole 50 acres of Primrose Hill, were preserved as open space not because Eton was in the least squeamish about covering them with streets and houses, but because no developers were forthcoming at this particular time.

The immediate result of Tooke's appraisal was to prepare the ground, both legally and administratively, for action. On his advice an 'able surveyor' with knowledge of building estates was engaged to act as the College agent: this was John Shaw, son of the surveyor and agent of the Eyre estate in St John's Wood. The Chalcots' lease was renewed, to the widow Margaret Earle, of Penningborough Hall in Yorkshire, with the new resumption clause. Finally, Eton obtained a private estate Act in 1826 giving the College powers to grant building leases of 99 years on the Chalcots estate and to raise up to £20,000 on mortgage to pay for roads, streets, squares, drains, and sewers should these be provided by the College. Significantly, the College's petition in support of this Act emphasised that the lands 'abutting . . . Regent's Park from their situation are particularly eligible for the Scites of Buildings.'[2] Although the decks were swiftly cleared, no action followed. It was not until 1829 that John Shaw was ready to issue a printed prospectus advertising the attractions of[3]

this very desirable Property, which is too well known to render necessary any description of its eligibility in all respects, for Villas and respectable Residences, combining the advantages of Town and Country. It is proposed, in the first instance, to offer to the Public that part of the Estate adjoining the Hampstead Road at Haverstock Hill . . . containing about 15 acres, in lots of not less than half an acre, for the erection of single or double detached Villas. Two roads, with proper drainage, will be immediately formed by the College . . . and are intended hereafter (should the Buildings go on) to be continued and connected with other Roads, particularly with the new Turnpike Road from Marylebone to Finchley, now in progress; but if not so continued, the Roads at present proposed will afford very desirable Frontage for Buildings, having the advantage of adjoining the main Hampstead Road, and being at the same time secluded from its publicity.

[1] Eton, College Records, XLIX, No. 22, Notes and rough survey of Chalcots estate, 1825.
[2] The Act is 7 Geo. IV, No. 237, Original Act H. of L. supported by the Petition of Provost of Eton, H. of L. 13 March 1826: HLRO and Lords Journal, LVII, 388, 552.
[3] Eton, Chalcots Box 1, Proposals for Building, 1 May 1829.

The estate development plan marked out the general line of what eventually became Adelaide Road as the proposed axis of advance, but the circumspect tone in which this through route was presented was amply justified by the lukewarm response to the 1829 flotation. It was to be twenty-five years and more before this road was actually driven through to make its connection with Swiss Cottage, so that the tentative nature of John Shaw's first proposals did much to establish his reputation for prudence and caution. 1829 was not a propitious year in which to make a start, for money was tight and speculators were disinclined to commit themselves: the prospectus produced a few nibbles from individuals who put up villas for their own use on the Haverstock Hill frontage, but no bites from any developers prepared to take on large-scale speculative development. The 1829 street plan did not, however, remain an entirely paper scheme, for in 1830 the College formed the first hundred yards or so of the new road, at its own expense, and named it Adelaide in honour of the new queen. This, as it turned out, was virtually the sole piece of direct development cost ever undertaken by the College, necessary as initial bait to attract developers to a new area, who could then be expected to shoulder, as lessees, the work of subsequent street formation. It was also a most timely investment, for almost at once talk began of running a railway across Chalcots, on its way to Birmingham; having a short section of Adelaide Road actually on the ground gave credibility to Eton's case that the railway proposed to cut through valuable building lands. The episode of the London and Birmingham Railway in itself accounts for much of the further delay in the Chalcots development, for it was such a novel and unknown quantity that until it had settled into its stride it inevitably cast such a spell of uncertainty along its course that builders hesitated to run the risk of putting up houses anywhere within sight or sound. The line was actively canvassed in 1831, promoted an abortive bill in 1832, obtained its Act in 1833, and was not opened to traffic until 1838: so that the best part of a decade was swallowed up by railway interference.

The lessee of Chalcots reacted vehemently to the early railway talk, naturally enough since his only interest in the estate was in its profitability as a grass farm—it was actually farmed by his sub-tenant, Thomas Rhodes, a very large-scale stock and dairy farmer both here and in St Pancras—and he had no prospect of benefiting from its building value. He told the Provost:[1]

[1] Eton, College Records, XLIX, No. 32, Thos. Clarke to Rev. G. Bethell, 23 January 1832.

The measure [for making a railroad] is viewed by most of the landholders as fraught with bad consequences to their interest, and the Middlesex farmers who have already suffered so much by the Canal consider this Rail-Road as likely to produce their utter ruin. It is hardly possible to let a Farm in Middlesex *now* but upon most deteriorated terms. I hope the College will not only withhold their consent but contribute their powerful aid to the opposition which is making to the Bill and that it will ultimately be thrown out.

The 1832 bill was indeed thrown out, on the ground that the promoters had not 'made out such a Case as would warrant the forcing of the proposed Railway through the Lands and Property of so great a proportion of dissentient Landowners and Proprietors.'[1] But Eton had not contributed to the landowners' opposition. Shaw's 'first impression is', it was reported, 'that so far from injuring the Estate it [the railway] will ultimately prove of benefit to it.'[2] This was carrying optimism to extremes, since it would be difficult to argue that this particular railway, that is the Euston main line, has ever been of any benefit to the Eton estate—though its later branch, first to Fenchurch Street and later to Broad Street, no doubt was. Acting on his faith, however, Shaw persuaded the College to use its influence to extract the best possible terms from the railway, rather than to try to prevent it altogether; in this he was helped by the fact that the College solicitors were also the London agents for the London and Birmingham Railway. The result was that the Railway bought off any possible College obstruction by agreeing to put the line in a tunnel through the Chalcots estate, although this was rather unnecessary from an engineering point of view since the rails of the original Primrose Hill Tunnel were never more than 50 feet below the ground surface. Moreover, the tunnel might well have been shallower still, as the promoters were also obliged to give the College power to require the line to be carried aloft on arches on its approach from Camden Town: it being thought that railway arches were more decorative than railway embankments, less land-consuming, and that an elevated railway was less of a nuisance and a hazard than one on the flat. The tunnel, of course, kept the unfamiliar thing out of sight and therefore made it less likely to scare off potential builders; it also had the merit of using no land, the surface being carefully preserved for building by a special provision in the Act that 'the

[1] HLRO, London and Birmingham Railway Bill, 1832, Parchment Collection R 16, Mins of Evidence, v.
[2] Eton, College Records, XLIX, No. 31, Tooke to Bethell, 6 December 1831.

Tunnel shall be constructed of sufficient strength to admit of buildings being erected thereon, except where the crown of the Tunnel is within 15 feet of the surface.' To make doubly sure, it was also provided that the tunnel had to be made by tunnelling and not by 'cut-and-cover' methods. Finally, in order to ensure the minimum interference with building values, Eton insisted that 'the mouth of the Tunnel at the eastern end shall be made good and finished with a substantial and ornamental facing of brickwork or masonry to the satisfaction of the Provost and College so as effectually to prevent the soil immediately above or round such mouth from giving way or slipping.'[1]

When it was opened the Primrose Hill Tunnel became a great attraction for sightseers, who flocked to see the latest marvels bursting out of its baronial mouth in all their hissing splendour; until the Great Northern line was built out of King's Cross, it was the only railway tunnel in London, and its fascination may conceivably have served to introduce some early train-spotters to the idea that Chalcots was a place to live in or build on. Otherwise the line did practically nothing to stimulate local development. It was conceived as a through route for long-distance traffic, and it was operated as such, local suburban traffic being notoriously neglected, even actively discouraged, at least until the end of the century. It is true that a station was opened at Kilburn, but not until 1852, and then only with prompting from the Howard estate; while South Hampstead did not gain a station—initially under the name of Loudoun Road station—until 1879, a quarter of a century after that neighbourhood had been built up. Eton College could thank the Railway for a handsome tunnel, a handsome price for the land taken—at £600 an acre, about six times its agricultural value—but precious little else.[2] While the railway was building nothing else was; the Chalcots lessee protested on behalf of the established residents that 'the retirement and the scenery which were the chief beauties are now to be destroyed by your Building plans and by the Railroad', but the plans very much hung fire.[3] For a brief moment in 1831 it looked as if it might be possible to negotiate a building lease of the Rugmoor field

---

[1] HLRO, London and Birmingham Railway Bill, 1832, Parchment Bill, f.34. Contrary to some accounts, Eton College was returned as 'neuter' in the Book of Reference to the Railway's deposited plan; Thomas Rhodes, the occupying tenant of Chalcots, entered his 'dissent'; Lord Southampton, the adjoining owner in St Pancras, and Col. Eyre, the adjoining owner to the west, both gave 'assents'.

[2] Eton, College Records, XLIX, No. 64, John Shaw to Geo. Bethell, 23 April 1834.

[3] Ibid., No. 42, Clarke to Bethell, 7 March 1832.

at Primrose Hill to a solicitor who wished to establish a botanical institution there, in emulation of the successful new Zoo just across the
road; but this fell through. John Shaw's father had felt 'that the
successful establishment of a great public institution on the College
estate must add very greatly to its value'; but when the next application
for Rugmoor came along, in 1836, from the London Cemetery Company, this was not thought to be the type of public institution which
respectable future neighbours would find acceptable.[1]

Preserved from corpses in the interests of future building development, Primrose Hill was preserved from houses in the interests of the
general public by the unusual determination of the government to
acquire the area as an extension to Regent's Park. In 1838 the Commissioner of Woods and Forests approached the College asking to buy
Primrose Hill and 50 acres of ground to be 'dedicated to the use and
recreation of the Public.' In view 'of the public object to which the land
is intended to be dedicated', Eton was willing to part with it at what
was regarded as the give-away price of £350 an acre; but the Crown's
valuer, William Driver, advised against the purchase since he held
£300 an acre to be its utmost value 'considering the purpose to which
it was to be appropriated and the benefit thereby to the rest of the
Estate', and the negotiation was dropped. John Shaw, however, felt
that the College ought not to try to screw the last farthing out of
Primrose Hill, for although it had great future value at present there
was 'the long continued liberty or rather trespass of the Public over it
in all directions [which] would render an exchange perhaps desirable;
and if it were beneficial to the College in its more local interests, some
sacrifice might perhaps be advisable as regards this property.'[2] So it
fell out. Shaw ferreted out some crown land adjoining the College in
Eton, and proposed that this should be exchanged for Primrose Hill,
advancing important educational reasons for the proposal:[3]

> That it is highly desirable for the good discipline health and recrea-
> tion of the youth educated at the College that the Buildings and
> land in its immediate vicinity should be under the control of your
> Memorialists so as to preclude the risk of additional buildings
> being erected or trades or businesses carried on there which might

[1] Ibid., No. 28, Shaw to Bethell, 2 August 1831; No. 77, Shaw to Thomas
Batcheldor, College Registrar, 7 May 1836.

[2] Ibid., No. 78, Tooke to Driver [1838]; No. 80, Shaw to Bethell, 15 March
1839.

[3] Ibid., No. 86, Draft Memorial to the Commissioner of Woods and Forests
from Eton College, 4 February 1840.

by the noise and traffic attending the conduct of them prove of annoyance to the College by disturbing the attention and interfering with the orderly rules and regulations of the Establishment.

After considerable delay in agreeing the values of the two pieces of property it was eventually agreed that the College should take 32 acres in Eton and the Crown should take 53 acres at Primrose Hill as a clean swap, each parcel being put at £15,112; as Eton was surrendering part of its ancient endowments a special Act was needed to effect the exchange, and this was passed in 1842, a Whig gesture towards the fondness of the public and of radical orators in particular for Primrose Hill being thus completed by the succeeding Tory government.[1] Thus secured as an open space, Primrose Hill remained extremely popular for radical meetings, demonstrations, and ceremonial tree-of-liberty plantings through to the late 1860s; for it was remote from police control in comparison with Hyde Park, and anything like a right to hold protest meetings in Hyde Park was not established until after 1866. Thereafter, encircled by governesses and prams, it became even more popular with them. Perhaps the Whigs in 1838, and the Tories after them in 1842, were thinking less of the health of the public than of the preservation of order and the protection of property, when they took steps to preserve Primrose Hill: they succeeded, at any rate, in preserving a stamping ground for the crowds at a safe distance from the centre of property and fashion, one where authority could avoid provoking awkward disputes about rights of public meeting and free speech because it could afford to ignore what was going on.[2]

Elsewhere on the Chalcots estate very little was going on. In the early 1830s Mortin, a plumber from Holborn, was building villas on two lots he had taken on Haverstock Hill, one Wilkins had taken three lots there, and a local cowkeeper replaced his ruinous cottage by a substantial 'lodge', and this was pretty much the sum total of activity.[3] It

[1] Ibid., No. 87, A. Milne, of the Commissioners of Woods and Forests, to the Provost, 24 March 1840; No. 98, Draft Agreement for Exchange with the Crown, 1841; No. 104, Tooke to Bethell, 24 March 1842; No. 107, same to same, 18 April 1842; No. 108, Bill for effecting an Exchange between H.M. and the Provost and College of Eton, 24 May 1842 [5 and 6 Vict. cap. 78].

[2] Exceptionally the police took a lively interest in a Garibaldi rally on Primrose Hill, during his visit to London in 1864, and this elicited accounts in the columns, e.g. of the *Beehive*, of the supposed prescriptive right of holding public meetings there.

[3] Eton, College Records, XLIX, No. 48, Shaw to Bethell, 23 April 1832; No. 63, Agreement between Shaw and Richard Pritchard of Haverstock Hill, cowkeeper, 30 March 1833.

was as well for John Shaw's pocket that he had other work—as Surveyor to Christ's Hospital, and for the Ramsgate Harbour Commissioners, for instance, as well as being in the front rank of minor architects[1]—for his income from the Chalcots estate, for setting out plots and as a commission on ground rents collected, barely came to £20 a year at this time. When the railway had been running for less than a year, however, the developers began to emerge from their cover. In March 1839 Henry Bassett, the manager of the Southampton Estate Office in Camden Town, made an offer to take 380 feet of Haverstock Hill frontage stretching up the hill from some houses built by Wynn in 1830 to Steele's Cottage, at the rather satisfactory rent of 4s. per foot which was the equivalent of £43 an acre. 'This offer appears to me very desirable to accept', Shaw advised, 'especially as Mr Bassett will be likely to set an example on the Estate of a superior and more elegant style of building than can be expected from a mere Builder', such as Wynn.[2] Then, only a few days later, came a really attractive proposition from William Kingdom, one of the large-scale property developers of the day, who had just completed a large development on Lord Holland's Kensington estate, a man of large ideas and large means.

If Kingdom's initiative had come to anything, it would have altered the entire character of the district, for he proposed to drive the road linking Haverstock Hill to the Eyre estate at Swiss Cottage straight through, starting building operations at each end simultaneously, and he intended to do this in an altogether more formal and imposing style than that of semi-detached villadom, for, as he wrote,[3]

> I propose adopting a style of Building somewhat similar to the Terraces of the Regent's Park, or of the Oxford and Cambridge Terraces; there can be little doubt of the new Road becoming a splendid addition to the projected improvements of the neighbourhood, and with the permission of the Provost and Fellows, I should propose to name it Eton Terrace.

Shaw was most enthusiastic at the prospect opened up, but it all fell through on the question of rents. His enthusiasm is understandable: it

---

[1] Pevsner, *The Buildings of England: London*, II (1952), identifies Shaw as the architect of Goldsmith's College, New Cross; Christ Church, Stepney; and Wellington College, Berks: pp. 106, 417. Other buildings are identified as his in Pevsner, *The Buildings of England: London*, I (1962 ed.), but apart from the Law Life Assurance Office in Fleet Street, and the Infants School in Fetter Lane, pp. 321, 323, these are probably by John Shaw senior, his father.

[2] Eton, College Records, XLIX, No. 79, Shaw to Bethell, 9 March 1839.

[3] Ibid., No. 81, W. Kingdom of 3 Charles Street, St James's Square, to Shaw, 22 March 1839.

was not every day that someone came along willing and able to negotiate for a single take of 40 acres which could be treated as a single, coherent, piece of building, and moreover a take which would forge the highly desirable mile-long lateral link with the St John's Wood estate at one stroke and under the management of one single developer. It would even do this in a fashion which appealed to the architect-surveyor's sense of symmetry and planning, by paralleling the line of the railway and tunnel as the axis of advance. As he admired 'the proposition . . . to form a wide and handsome road with a sewer under it, from the eastern to the western boundaries of the Estate', Shaw had no time to comment on the difference between high-class terrace development and villa development, though it clearly implied a differ- and better, class of residents. He saw clearly that the main road and sewer, provided they were constructed at Kingdom's expense, 'would so materially advance the value of the Estate generally, that it is deserving of much consideration how far it will be desirable for the College to moderate their demand for the land in question', and he pressed for a decision:[1]

> What I wish principally to be informed upon, is the lowest rent per acre at which they [the College] will let the land, subject to Mr Kingdom's making the Road and Sewer. So important do I conceive this to be that I should suggest from £20 to £25 as the maximum.

This was the stumbling block, and to understand why the College was so apparently short-sighted as not to accept a slightly low ground rent for the enormous advantages of letting building land in bulk, and attracting a pioneer high-class development to their estate, it is necessary to probe the idiosyncrasies of college finance. As a purely business proposition Kingdom's case, backed by Shaw, was excellent. The College had come to expect something in the region of £35 to £45 an acre in ground rents, but this related to small takes of an acre or two at a time in which the whole piece of ground was available for houses and their gardens and none had to be used for roads. Kingdom estimated that not only would he have to devote about one-sixth of his take to road formation, but that forming the road and a main sewer would cost him nearly £10,000. He was used to paying ground rents of less than £35 an acre for takes from Lord Camden and from Lord Holland where these owners had themselves been at the expense of constructing the roads and sewers. Hence he expected a much reduced rent, and Shaw

[1] Ibid., No. 82, Shaw to Bethell, 28 March 1839.

agreed that £20 to £25 an acre was reasonable, since the College was opposed to making any outlay itself on road-making. From the point of view of the Provost and Fellows, however, such a reduction in ground rents made building development scarcely worth while. They were accustomed to receiving from Chalcots, as a grass farm, purely nominal annual rents which were counted as endowment income to be appropriated to the school, and large fines when the lease was renewed every seven years—charged as a multiple, latterly of $1\frac{7}{8}$ times its full rack rent value—which by custom were regarded as a personal perquisite of the Provost and Fellows to spend as they pleased. These windfalls had amounted to £2,794 in 1825 and £2,500 in 1832.[1] As land passed out of farmland and under houses, however, it passed out of the lease and the system of renewal fines, so that every grant of building land meant a reduction in the next fine even if it also meant an increase in overall income. The accounting conscience of the College, moreover, insisted that all regular annual receipts, such as ground rents, had to go into the general pool of College income and could not be regarded as part of the personal fortunes of Provost and Fellows as the fines were. Since only a portion of the general pool of College income went to Fellows' stipends, their personal interests were against covering Chalcots with houses unless the resulting ground rents were really high. It was on grounds such as these that the College declined to entertain Kingdom's application, and this opportunity of impressively imposing development was turned down.

With it went the last chance of any systematic and comprehensive treatment of the urbanisation of Chalcots. The urbanisation which it did in fact receive in the course of the remainder of the century was not imposed upon it by any master plan or any dominant developer; rather it just happened, piecemeal, in response to demand for suburban housing or more directly in response to speculative builders' ideas of what the demand for suburban housing was likely to be. The total effect was highly successful: a pleasantly leafy, prosperous but not ostentatious, middle-class district, with varied architectural styles which were in the main modest and unpretentious, which escaped the rigidity and monotony of a single-handed operation or an estate-office development. The pleasing features of the result owed only a little to estate management, which concentrated on seeing that the vital link road to

[1] Ibid., No. 44, Notes by Bethell on the renewal of Chalcots and Wyldes, 25 March 1832; No. 60, Clarke to Bethell, 20 June 1832. The figures in the text relate to the renewal fines for Chalcots only; Wyldes Farm was always included in the same renewal, but a separate, even larger, fine was paid for it.

Swiss Cottage was attained, and apart from that was content merely to see that road lines were laid out to make the fullest use of the College property and provide the maximum amount of frontages; they owed much more to the fortunate selection of builders who came on to the estate; and perhaps most of all to the persistent desire of middle-class families to live near the royal parks and among their own kind.

John Shaw continued to make efforts to assert a positive controlling rôle, but they were to little avail. His heart did not seem to be in it, and he was largely at the mercy of whatever builders might come forward and make offers. To be sure, when offers did come he could, and did, steer them in appropriate directions of street layout; but, as an architect himself, it was somewhat surprising that he made no efforts at all to dictate or suggest designs, contenting himself with the standard and universal building-lease formula that the plans of each house were to be subject to the estate surveyor's approval. As soon as the Kingdom bid was rejected, indeed, Shaw made a general appraisal of the position of the estate. He reported early in 1840:[1]

> The frontage of the Estate next the Hampstead Road, to the extent of the private road parallel in its rear [Eton College Road], being now built upon, I take the liberty of calling your attention to the circumstance, and of making some suggestions with reference to the Property generally . . . before making any further advance it is highly important to consider not only this point [the precise line for the extension westwards of Adelaide Road], but further what will probably be the most beneficial mode of appropriating the Estate generally to the purpose of building, so that whatever may be done shall be upon a definite plan.

It is astonishing that Shaw should not have begun thinking about his general building strategy until 1840: less astonishing when it is appreciated that his notion of the proper content of a strategy was scarcely any more precise or detailed in 1840 than it had been in 1829 or was to be another dozen years later. By 1840 he had moved far enough to lay down that the centre line of the future progress of Adelaide Road should be plumb over the Primrose Hill Tunnel, thus displaying lack of confidence in the ability of Robert Stephenson to make the tunnel strong enough to support houses on top of it; and he felt that it was about time to get in touch with Colonel Eyre to make some definite arrangements for the ultimate access to the St John's Wood Estate. It is indicative of the generally leisurely approach to managerial duties

[1] Ibid., No. 84, Shaw to Bethell, 14 January 1840.

that this arrangement was not in fact made until 1845.[1] Also by 1840 Shaw was impressed by the need so to order the lines of any new roads as 'to secure double frontages to each line as far as practicable'; this sensible resolve was, as it happened, a criticism of his own early mistake in setting out the road behind Haverstock Hill, Eton College Road, merely as a service road for the villas which fronted the Hill, so that this road created only one set of building frontages, on its south-west side. It was this piece of extravagant land use which gave these early villas of the 1830s a secluded gentrified look, as they were set back 150 feet from Haverstock Hill; and, when their leases fell in during the 1930s, it created at a century's remove the opportunity for the comparatively spacious redevelopment of the mansion flats of Eton Place, Eton Hall, and Eton Rise on a 'double-block' scale at the cost of replacing only a single block.

Finally in 1840, but only on the prompting of the most considerable builder on the estate up to that time, who was also resident in one of his own houses in Adelaide Road, Shaw took up the notion that a church or chapel was a necessary part of the equipment of successful middle-class estate development, likely to promote the material welfare of the College even more than the spiritual welfare of its tenants.[2]

> I find that there is a general demand for a Chapel on the Estate, there being no place of worship within a very considerable distance; Mr Wynn the builder of many of the houses, and other persons, have led me to believe that it would be profitable even as a speculation to establish one, and that if the object could be entertained or promoted by the College, such a subscription would be made by the neighbourhood as would with their aid accomplish it. Undoubtedly the existence of such a building on the Estate would most materially lead to the formation of a neighbourhood around it.

The sentiments and the business sense were sound, but here again the thought was but tardy father to the deed, the more surprisingly since Eton College was supposed to be something of a religious foundation. By 1846 a residents' association had been formed, calling itself The Inhabitants of Haverstock Hill and Neighbourhood, and its secretary, a surgeon named Henry Bird living at Milan Cottage, one of the Haverstock Hill villas, once more raised the question of a church. The patron of the chapel of Tailor's Almshouses, which lay behind the Load

[1] Ibid., No. 114, same to same, 14 July 1845.
[2] Ibid., No. 84.

of Hay on what later became the Maitland Park Estate, had declined to contemplate any extension of that chapel to accommodate Chalcots' residents, and the residents' association therefore threatened to go over Eton's head and appeal direct to the Metropolis Churches Fund for assistance, at the same time making one more appeal to Eton's financial interest in the matter. Henry Bird stated:[1]

> The population of this place is rapidly increasing, and the want of Church accommodation is severely felt by those residing here, and operates greatly to the disadvantage of the neighbourhood by keeping away families who would otherwise become residents.

The College did indeed reserve a site for a church in that year, limiting its support simply to the gift of the ground and leaving the residents and builders to raise the money for the building by their own devices. But in 1847 Bird continued his pressure, pointing out that the rector of St Pancras was starting a scheme for nine new churches in his parish, and intended[2]

> to place one of them close to Haverstock Hill, and for fear his parishioners should subscribe towards the church to be built on the College Estate we are informed that Mr Dale [the St Pancras rector] proposes to erect immediately a wooden church at Haverstock Hill in his own parish. The Committee are therefore anxious to begin before Mr Dale is able to proceed with his intentions.

Dale probably did not fulfil this plan, for no contemporary map shows any temporary church on the St Pancras side of Haverstock Hill, and the nearest permanent church built at this time, Holy Trinity in Clarence Way which was put up in 1850, is a fair step away; St Silas, in its own private cul-de-sac off Prince of Wales Road, is indeed close to Haverstock Hill, but it was not built until 1912, and far from being on the site of an earlier wooden church its site was cleared from slum property, and a whole street, Preston Street, disappeared to make room for it. Meanwhile building started on the island site provided by the College at the junction of Eton Road, Provost Road, and Eton Villas, and by 1856 St Saviour's was finished. Coming nearly thirty years after the start of building development, and when some hundreds of houses were already occupied on the estate, it was more of an afterthought than a magnet for further residential expansion. With the

[1] Ibid., No. 128, Henry Bird to Bethell, 7 September 1846.
[2] Ibid., No. 130, Tooke to Bethell, reporting Henry Bird's observations, 10 July 1847.

PLATE 6 The viaduct built by Sir Thomas Maryon Wilson on his East Park estate, and now on the Heath (see pp. 165 and 309)

PLATE 7 Digging gravel from the Heath beside the Spaniards Road; photograph taken about 1867 (see p. 193)

PLATE 8 Fashionable admirers of the new Chalk Farm Tunnel on the London and Birmingham Railway, 1839 (see p. 220)

PLATE 9 Working-class housing: terrace houses in Fleet Road, built in the 1860s, being demolished in 1961 (see p. 270)

PLATE 10 Middle-class housing: the dining-room of a house in Thurlow Road in the 1870s (see p. 292)

only other church built on the Chalcots estate, St Mary's in King
Henry's Road, the College moved much more in keeping with progressive estate enterprise in putting up this church as early as 1873,
when this area of the estate was just starting to be developed. Two
churches on an estate which eventually carried a population of about
10,000 may not be considered bad going, and was only a little worse
than the average rate of provision for Hampstead as a whole by 1901;
but for a respectable middle-class area it was distinctly poor, and for a
religious foundation distinctly stingy.[1] The College relied, in fact, on
neighbouring estates to provide a good part of this essential service for
successful suburban settlement.[2]

The other essential of a good building estate was a good public house,
and here again the College had to have its elbow jogged by the builders.
In 1842 William Wynn tried to get the College registrar to use any
Eton influence with the Metropolitan licensing justices to press for the
grant of a licence on the Chalcots estate. A memorial should be presented, Wynn suggested,[3]

> stating the quantity of houses that I have built, the houses that
> are now finishing will make 41. Also state the number of acres of
> land that you have got there, and not one public house there,
> and taking the improvement altogether with the new park and
> Adelaide Road being a principal thoroughfare to the park the
> house will be an improvement to the estate.

As Thomas Batcheldor was an impossibly unbusinesslike registrar—one
solicitor once had occasion to write to him to observe that 'I appear to
be very unlucky in writing to you as I never obtain a reply at anything
like a reasonable date'; and another, the College's own solicitor, was
provoked to exclaim, in March 1842, that 'since May last I have been
in constant correspondence with Mr Batcheldor [about the production
of title deeds] . . . but the necessity for an early compliance with
which I could never sufficiently impress on the mind of Mr Batcheldor'[4]
—it is most unlikely that he did anything to help Wynn obtain a

---

[1] *1901 Census*, Parl. Papers, 1902, cxx, Table 5.

[2] At the peak, before conversion and demolition set in, there were 38 places
of worship, of all denominations, in Hampstead; that is one to every 2,240
people. There were four on the College estate, or one to every 2,500: LCC
Municipal Map, 1913.

[3] Eton, Chalcots Correspondence, Box 1, Wynn to Thos. Batcheldor, 12
December 1842.

[4] Ibid., William Wyatt to Batcheldor, 4 November 1844; College Records,
xlix, No. 103, Tooke to Bethell, 17 March 1842. The Adelaide Hotel is
opposite the present Chalk Farm tube station.

licence. Fortunately, however, licences were easily come by at this period, and Wynn's superior-class public house, the Adelaide Hotel, was opened shortly afterwards. A start having been made, this essential attraction for obtaining a good class of resident was not neglected in the future; by 1846 provision was being made for a second good-class hotel further along Adelaide Road. This became the Eton Hotel, on the corner with Elsworthy Rise, and was built to the standards of the 'first-rate' category under the London Building Act. Its builder, Samuel Cuming, vouched for its utter respectability, and 'thinks such an house essentially necessary for the convenience of the large neighbourhood which will be established.' Interestingly enough, his request for the tavern was directly coupled with a request for a church, for in the same letter he told Shaw 'there is very great want of a place of worship.'[1] Perhaps, in the end, the College got its priorities right. Residents in a new district, before they could be tempted to settle there, needed to be assured that they could both pray and drink. Drinking needs, however, were rather more demanding than praying needs, since a supply of drink had to be close at hand while a supply of pews was not strictly necessary for prayer itself, only for its public manifestation.

Samuel Cuming, of the Eton Hotel, came to Chalcots in 1844, and from then on became its chief creator. Until then Shaw had to be content with the slower progress of lesser builders, whose resources allowed them to undertake just two or three houses at a time. William Wynn was one of these, whose 41 houses in Adelaide Road had taken him more than a decade to build, along the first few yards of the road which the College had made at its own expense. Another was Thomas Mortin, the Holborn plumber and glazier, who pushed on slowly up Haverstock Hill, crossing to the north of the line of the later Steele's Road in 1841.[2] With these houses, indeed, and giving a wide berth to Steele's Cottage—a plain, low, whitewashed cottage—which was allowed to stand until 1867, Mortin completed the ribbon of development up Haverstock Hill to link up with the Bliss enterprises on the other side of Englands Lane. Northall Lane, as Englands Lane was then called, was a narrow way leading to Northall House, The Elms, a couple of other less grand houses, and the Chalcots farmhouse; Shaw decreed that there should be no interference with this little settlement, which was to remain the centre of the farmland even though the farm itself was to be split in two by the line of Adelaide Road. Wynn, who wanted to push

[1] Ibid., No. 119, Shaw to Bethell, 8 January 1846.
[2] Eton, Chalcots Leases, Box 1, leases of four villas on Haverstock Hill to T. Mortin, 20 December 1841.

up towards Steele's Cottage from his earlier building on Adelaide Road, was frustrated in this intention by the difficulty of resuming possession of a small parcel of land from the farm lessee; so instead he pushed Adelaide Road out a few hundred feet further on its way towards Swiss Cottage. His application in 1840 is important for having elicited a statement of new estate policy on road construction costs from Shaw:[1]

> A commencement having been made by the College [in making the initial bit of Adelaide Road] it will I conceive be desirable in future lettings that a part of the consideration shall be that the lessees form Roads and Sewers to the extent of their respective frontages, it will be more desirable to let the ground upon lower terms on this condition, than that the College should embark on this expence.

This policy certainly saved the College from making any capital investment in development, and the direct money cost of this capital-saving made it seem a reasonable course. Wynn offered a ground rent of £45 an acre if the College would make the road and sewer, or £35 an acre if he was to bear the cost of making them; moreover, in the first case he was willing to become the College's sub-contractor and perform the actual construction of a 50-foot road, and sewer, at £1 per foot.[2] At these rates the sums indicated that by passing responsibility on to its lessees for road construction which would cost about £200 per acre, the College would sacrifice £10 an acre in income; at 5 per cent on the outlay, this looked fair enough. There were many snags, however, which Shaw did not trouble to explain to his employers. Putting this burden on to lessees was bound to put a strain on builders' finances, and would mean that builders had less cash and credit to devote to building houses, or skimped on both roads and houses, or were forced to make slower progress, none of which could be in the best interests of the ground landlord. By surrendering the work of road formation to the lessees the ground landlord weakened or abandoned altogether the power of supervision and quality control, and poor, messy roads were not a good advertisement for a building estate. Finally, the costings were mischievous: £1 per foot was only barely enough to pay for the construction of a tolerable road surface—made up of a 12-inch layer of rubble, brick rubbish, or dust pickings, 4 inches of gravel, and a topping of 4 inches of pit flints; it could not cover the more hard-wearing finish of granite chippings needed for a thoroughfare with continuous traffic

[1] Eton, College Records, XLIX, No. 84.
[2] Ibid. No. 92, Shaw to Bethell, 19 August 1840.

(which Adelaide Road was meant to become); and it left nothing at all to pay for making a sewer.[1] It is, therefore, scarcely surprising that the College was shortly receiving complaints from the residents. Captain Kelly Nazer, RN, wrote from Chalcots Villas in 1847:[2]

> Adelaide Road being the property of Eton College, I beg leave to acquaint you with its dreadful state; the lower part of that Road is full of deep holes and its surface covered with thick mud; recently several carts have stuck fast in it, and nothing but the assistance of an additional horse was able to extricate them: I verily believe there is not a Road in any part of England in a worse condition, and therefore trust you will cause an inspection of the same to be made in order that it may forthwith be put into proper repair.

It was a perfect case of penny wise pound foolish. The College was saved from the worst consequences of this short-sighted policy by the advent of Samuel Cuming. A carpenter from Devon who had come to try his luck in the Great Wen, Cuming was a real-life model of the founder of the Forsyte family fortunes. By the 1840s he was a man of substance, combining in his own person the roles of property developer with wide vision and of speculative builder of middle-class housing. He did not have grand ideas or the itch to build great vistas all at once, as Kingdom appears to have done or as Nash certainly did for Regent's Park. Rather, he was a sober and cautious businessman who proceeded step by step within a sensible idea of the limits of his capacities, careful never to bite off more than he could chew. He was also a man who came on to a property meaning to stay, and who knew that his business would be as solid as the quality of his work, and that his success as a developer depended on the good reputation of his handiwork. So he built well and he made his roads properly; for his kind of speculative building gimcrack, fly-by-night, jerry-building was quite simply bad for business and he therefore had no truck with it. His houses were built to last, perhaps more soundly built than his church, St Saviour's, since people were paying good money to buy his houses; that many of them, along Adelaide Road, have not lasted longer is due more to the accidents of bomb damage and to the social deterioration of property fronting a busy traffic artery causing redevelopment opportunities in

[1] Road making costs were given in the Parish Surveyor's reports, e.g. HPL Vestry Min., 21 October 1856, 13 February 1857.
[2] Eton, Chalcots Correspondence, Box 1, Capt. K. Nazer, 3 Chalcots Villas, Adelaide Road, to the Provost, 13 December 1847.

the 1950s and 1960s, than it is to any structural deficiencies. Roads made by Cuming, also, were no disgrace to the district for he knew that a good-looking road was a necessary introduction to get the right class of house-hunters. When his roads were adopted by the parish only very minor repairs, or perhaps the paving of the footpaths with York stone, were required in order to bring them up to the Vestry's standard of acceptability. By this acid test Cuming was a more thorough and reliable worker than even such a reputable architect and builder as Richard Batterbury, whose Church Road on the Eton estate needed almost complete reconstruction in 1857 before the parish surveyor was prepared to accept it as a public road.[1]

Samuel Cuming was a godsend to the Eton estate; but he arrived on it quite by accident, as it were, unannounced, uninvited, and as far as one can see unvetted by the agent. Though it is fair to add that, within a year or so of his coming, he was not unappreciated. He first emerges early in 1844, operating as a builder from an address in Cirencester Place, Marylebone, building five houses in Adelaide Road as a sub-tenant under Wynn's 1842 building agreement; hence his introduction to the estate rested entirely on his dealings with Wynn, and involved no direct contact with Shaw or the College. Indeed, the first they ever heard of Cuming was when Wynn requested that the actual leases of these five houses should be granted to Cuming.[2] On the day that he finished these first five houses, however, Cuming moved up into the position of a principal and negotiated his own building agreement with the College.[3] This was a take of some $5\frac{1}{2}$ acres on which Cuming was to build forty houses paying a ground rent rising progressively from £7 an acre in the first year to the full College norm of £35 an acre from

---

[1] HPL Vestry Min., 5 September 1856, for the acceptance of the final 708 yards of Adelaide Road; 13 February 1857 and 14 April 1857 for refusal to accept Church Road (later called Eton Road) until the College and the lessee, Batterbury, had spent £428 on making it up to standard.

[2] Eton, Chalcots Correspondence, Box 1, Shaw to Batcheldor, 22 July 1844. The usual arrangement on building estates was for the chief developer or builder to operate each 'take' under a building agreement, which provided that the actual leases should be granted when each house or small group of houses was completed (technically, when the carcase was complete and covered), and should be granted to whomsoever the developer nominated as lessee. This nominee was normally either the actual builder of the house, or the first purchaser of the house from its builder. If the actual builder was not the holder of the initial building agreement, he would pay to him, i.e. the developer, either an 'improved ground rent' or, occasionally, a lump sum; as these transactions did not concern the ground landlord, they did not find their way into estate records.

[3] Eton, College Records, XLIX, No. 111, Draft Building Agreement with S. Cuming, 5 August 1844.

the fifth year. It involved an extension of Adelaide Road in its destined course, not directly over the Tunnel as Shaw had once wanted, but sufficiently to the north of it to allow the Tunnel to lie under the back garden fences of the new properties, as Cuming more cautiously desired; and it involved the formation of a new road, Provost Road, and a start on a connecting lateral which eventually became the jumping-off point of Fellows Road and Eton Road. It was provided that 'no house [is] to be built inferior as respects materials and workmanship to those now building by Mr Cuming on the estate', but apart from this no attempt was made to influence the designs of his houses, so that both the late classical of Adelaide Road and the Italian-rustic of Sir John Summerson's No. 1, Eton Villas, may be regarded as all Cuming's own work, which is to say his own medley composed from the builders' manuals of the day.[1]

Cuming was well pleased with the district on which he had alighted, less pleased with the administration which he encountered, its incompetence rapidly driving him to despair. By October 1844 his solicitor was getting restive because the building agreement made in August had not yet been signed by the College: 'Have you prepared this Contract?' he asked the College Registrar.[2]

If yes, please let me have it for perusal that it may be finally settled in ample time for the next College [the formal meeting of Provost and Fellows]. Do not let us be again driven into a corner by delay. I believe the next College will be held in December next. Time is on the wing.

It was indeed. Wyatt, the solicitor, did not yet know his Batcheldor. A month later he was writing:[3]

I appear to be very unlucky in writing to you as I never obtain a reply at anything like a reasonable date. It is a month since I last wrote to you about the Contract you were to prepare relative to the land recently taken by Mr Cuming of Eton College, there can be no good reasons assigned why my Client is to suffer by such delay and which he is likely to do, nor that I as his solicitor should not have ample time to peruse and advise on the Draft after I receive

---

[1] Pevsner, op. cit., II (1952), p. 201; Sir John Summerson's foreword to H. J. Dyos, *Victorian Suburb: a Study of the Growth of Camberwell* (1961), pp. 8–9.

[2] Eton, Chalcots Correspondence, Box 1, William Wyatt, Cuming's solicitor, to Batcheldor, 3 October 1844.

[3] Ibid., same to same, 4 November 1844.

it and before it is to be executed. I should like to avoid all inconvenience to you, at the same time I am entitled to some consideration. I trust you may be induced to take some notice of this letter that I may know your intentions; it is nearly three months since you promised to send the Draft in a few days.

Batcheldor, however, declined to believe that the matter was of any moment, driving Cuming to a protest which also explained the importance of legal documents of title in a builder's credit arrangements:[1]

> You say you cannot conceive what inconvenience the delay of the agreement can have put me to. In answer to which I beg to ask what is the position I am in either as regards the sale of houses or the letting of any portion of the ground without having the precise terms of the contract before me . . . I have put a large number of houses on the ground considering the short time I have had possession and have hitherto been confined to my own resources whereas had I the agreement on which to form a basis I might have had the combined efforts of my friends and perhaps have put twice the number on the ground that I have now done, making the College more secure and diminishing my own responsibility as to the ground rent. I have sufficient confidence in the College myself as may be seen by what I have placed on the ground, but it is difficult to instill that confidence in the minds of others. Everyone wants (and very properly too) to know something of my holding with the College before they will enter into an agreement with me. . . . I am exceedingly sorry to be obliged thus to write as I would be the last to complain without cause or to give any reason for unpleasantness. But I must say I like to be treated with some little civility however insignificant I may appear to those with whom I have transactions . . .

By his dilatoriness Batcheldor was depriving Cuming of the only negotiable instrument available to him to offer as security for loans with which to finance his house building; the fact that in spite of this restriction Cuming had been able to get on with the building of eight houses financed entirely out of his own resources indicates that he was a substantial man for the trade, able to commit £2,000 or more of his own money to this part of his business.

The incompetence was not enough to discourage Cuming from increasing his stake on his faith in the great promise of the district.

[1] Ibid., Cuming to Batcheldor, 5 December 1844.

Before his first agreement had even been executed he settled the terms, in January 1845, of his second building agreement with the College, for a take of $3\frac{1}{2}$ acres in a strip between Adelaide Road and the railway on which sixteen houses were to be built. This time the superior class of the houses was underlined by a new provision, that there should be a minimum gap of fifteen feet between the outside walls of each pair of semi-detached villas.[1] Cuming, who had begun by envisaging a rate of output of eight houses a year on the Eton estate, had now raised his target to twelve a year; soon he had increased it still further, and in the three years 1849–51 his own production averaged twenty-four houses a year, and there were several more built on his takes by other builders holding plots under him. By this time he had clearly concentrated the bulk, possibly the whole, of his building activities on the Chalcots property, since in 1846 he moved into one of his own houses in Adelaide Road and gave up his Marylebone interests. Troubles with Batcheldor were by no means over, for he was incapable of learning how the finances of a builder's business worked and could never see the need to bother himself with drawing up proper contracts or issuing leases of finished houses with any promptitude. At the end of 1845 Wyatt was once more trying to impress on Batcheldor the extreme importance of documentary proofs of title for Cuming's financial arrangements, and suggesting that if he could not bring himself to face the trouble of anything else Batcheldor should at least send Cuming a letter stating 'Batcheldor now thinks the expense of a formal Contract is needless. If you desire to underlet part of the ground, and deem it necessary to have a formal Contract under seal for this purpose, the College will draw such a Contract on your request'.[2] Such a bit of paper would be better than no paper at all. It is doubtful if Batcheldor ever mended his ways. In 1851 Cuming was still writing in exasperation that:

> I have just come from Mr Shaw's office and am sadly disappointed in finding the Skins are not yet sent for the Leases when you promised me faithfully they should be sent off the same day I was last with you. Will you do me the very great favour of sending them to Mr Shaw immediately, and when returned to you to get them sealed as soon as possible . . .

[1] Eton, College Records, XLIX, No. 112, Draft Building Agreement with Cuming, 1 January 1845. The ground rents were at the same rates as in the first agreement.

[2] Eton, Chalcots Correspondence, Box 1, Wyatt to Batcheldor, 31 December 1845.

No doubt he still felt, as in 1846, that 'my future credit is solely dependant on it.'[1]

In fact as his operations gathered momentum and the wheels of building finance began to turn more quickly, enabling Cuming to finance further building with the proceeds of completed houses which he had sold, he may have been in less need of obtaining outside credit. Certainly by July 1845 he had already become a favourite with Shaw, who saw the estate at last beginning to 'go' with a swing. He reported to the Provost:[2]

I passed some hours yesterday in going over [Chalcots], and was very much pleased with the new line of Road which is now complete up to Mr Cuming's last take, and with the houses he has built and is building, which are of a superior description as he proceeds: the branch road is also formed into the Hampstead Road [Eton Road] at the north end of the row of houses fronting the Hampstead Road, and the other valuable entrance is made into the Estate by the Road from the bridge over the railway at Chalk Farm Lane [Regent's Park Road and Bridge Approach]; it would be a great satisfaction to me before any conclusion is come to, to have the opportunity of attending you or any other members of the College over the Estate, or more fully to explain its present circumstances, and to show the Plan of the St John's Wood Estate adjoining, which is now nearly complete and forms one of the most important and valuable properties connected with the Metropolis, especially that part which adjoins Chalcots, the Roads being wide and the houses of a very superior class; this is also the case with the approach to the Estate from the Regent's Park.

The reason for singing the praises of St John's Wood was that the moment of decision had been reached; Adelaide Road had become a long finger stretching 500 yards into the estate, Cuming wished to push through a further 700 yards at once to link up with Swiss Cottage, Shaw was generally in favour, but the College hesitated to sanction such an ambitious single piece of development. Shaw set out the possible alternative:[3]

Should there be . . . an objection to so large a measure as the

---

[1] Ibid., Cuming to Batcheldor, 3 January 1851; earlier delays in preparing leases were the subject of complaint by Cuming to the Provost: College Records, XLIX, No. 133.
[2] Ibid., No. 116, Shaw to Bethell, 22 July 1845.
[3] Ibid., No. 115, same to same, 16 July 1845.

continuation of the Road through the Estate westward, it may be also well to consider the alternative of continuing it only as far as the mouth of the Tunnel of the Railway, and thence to branch off southward to the Regent's Park and northwards to Northall Lane, so as to effect a Thoroughfare, as the Road now extends so far into the Estate without an exit.

This alternative, Primrose Hill Road, was indeed constructed, and has been made into a thoroughfare by commuting motorists; but it was a purely subsidiary project, for in the end the College was persuaded to screw up its courage and take a chance on Cuming's major scheme. Shaw himself thought that it was risky to put so many eggs in one basket. He liked the idea of making the through route

> at once and not progressively, as thereby the best security would be given for the fulfilment of the Agreement by the Lessee, and in this condition Mr Cuming acquiesces; indeed it is to his interest with reference to his selling or letting the houses now building upon the land he has taken, as there naturally exists a feeling in the Public, either that the Road may not be continued, or that many years may first elapse.

But he was still suspicious that:[1]

> it may not be advisable to let to one Tenant the whole of the land in question [though] at the same time it would be inexpedient that the College should embark in the speculation of any portion of the Road and Sewer, which it is most desirable, and indeed the first object with Mr Cuming in making a Proposal, to form completely through the Estate, so as to obtain an important thoroughfare; I have therefore considered the alternative of his making the Road and Sewer throughout, and of his taking the plots only coloured dark red upon the terms proposed, making an abatement therefrom for the interest of his expenditure on that portion of the Road and Sewer where the frontage would be retained by the College, and in this case one side only of the Oval portion of the Road need be formed [the other side of the 'oval' was to provide a root for the future King Henry's Road]. Supposing the land to be so reserved by the College and that with the Road and Sewer it would command a rental of £50 per acre, it will not I apprehend realize more than I have before stated [i.e. £35 per acre net], when the interest on the outlay of the same is

[1] Ibid., No. 114, same to same, 14 July 1845.

deducted, but there is the chance of a higher rental being obtained, as there is no doubt but that the new Road will excite much competition among Builders, not only for the frontage in question, but for other portions of the Estate in connection with it.

Cuming was no less aware that the interest of other builders might be excited once such a long stretch of territory was opened up, and if he was going to shoulder the risk and cost of opening it by road-building he was not ready to be elbowed out of any of the possible profits. So Shaw, and the College, had to accept his terms: he built the entire road and sewer, and he received the entire take, to build on himself or to underlet to other builders, as he chose. For such a large slice of development the College indeed accepted slightly lower terms than for the lesser nibbles of previous years: 28 acres were involved in all, but Cuming paid the usual ground rent of £35 an acre only on the net building area of 22¼ acres, after being allowed to deduct as 'dead' ground the land to be used for roads.

Faith in Cuming was not misplaced. He worked on the road with a will, and at the same time Colonel Eyre began building Tunnel Road [later taken in as part of Hillgrove Road] at his end, reaching his estate boundary in front of the present Swiss Cottage Library and Swimming Bath, at which point Cuming arrived from the Eton direction in the course of 1850. By 1853 houses lined both sides of Adelaide Road, with very few remaining gaps, and almost all of them had been built by Cuming himself. By 1856 the 'thoroughfare' concept had been hallowed by the establishment of an omnibus service along Adelaide Road.[1] The arrival of the horse-drawn buses, indeed, produced a profound modification in the entire character of the development, and made it into an even more powerful instrument of social segregation than was all along implicit in the over-riding aim of tapping the market for middle-class family housing. The builders had assumed that this market consisted of carriage-folk of some description, that the professional men, City gentlemen, and other men of means whom they hoped to attract to the area would all run some form of private transport, and that building plans needed to take notice of this. The early villas up Haverstock Hill were in the class with their own coach-houses and stabling; it was assumed that the later, more closely spaced semi-detacheds of Adelaide Road would require mews to be associated with them, placed on convenient back-land, and it was the intention to

[1] HPL Vestry Min., 25 July 1856.

squeeze these in between Adelaide Road and Fellows Road to the north and King Henry's Road to the south. In the event a few, but only exceedingly few, mews were ever built on the Chalcots estate, perhaps in all enough to cater for less than one-twentieth of the private houses. The answer was that if there was a horse bus service within easy reach a private carriage was no longer a necessity. Already in 1849 Cuming had discovered that there was no call for the land which he had ear-marked for stabling as the tenants did not require it.[1] Private carriages remained, of course, a valuable status symbol as well as a convenience; and the other part of the answer was that the Chalcots estate attracted a slightly lower rung of the middle class than had once been hoped for, consisting of highly respectable middle-class families which could afford to keep their two or three domestic servants, but which could not afford to keep carriages and the outdoor servants who went with them. They were from the younger and less affluent reaches of the professional classes, the higher reaches of the clerical workers and shopkeepers, rather than from the successful mid-career professional men and the top layer of the City. Stables and mews, however, implied the working-class population of grooms, coachmen, and stable-boys—the outdoor servants—to run them, and this was a section of the servant class which was not directly and continuously under the supervision and control of its masters, and which therefore was able to behave with a freedom that earned it a reputation for immorality, drinking, swearing, and irreli-gion. Charles Booth found in the 1890s, for instance, that mews could often be pockets of poverty and poor living conditions in the midst of wealthy neighbourhoods.[2] Because it came just below the carriage-owning income and social level the Chalcots estate was, in time, able to make a virtue of bourgeois respectability out of its deprivation, and to adopt a positive policy of keeping mews off the property in order to keep the poor off the estate. In this way, precisely because it was at the middle of the middle class rather than at the top, or in the upper class, Chalcots developed in social terms as a much more purely segregated and single-class district than other, more wealthy, environments.

The social unity, or exclusiveness, of a residential district at this level of completeness was plainly the consequence of the demands of the group of house purchasers and occupiers over-riding the initial intentions of the builders to supply a more varied range of buildings,

[1] Eton, Chalcots Correspondence, Box 1, Shaw to Batcheldor, 27 February 1849.
[2] Charles Booth, *Life and Labour in London*, Map of London Poverty, 1889, north-west sheet.

even though the proposed variations were purely derivative from the supposed service needs of what were thought to be the prospective residents. Whether the forces working from the demand side were equally dominant in bringing about the social segregation of complete residential districts in a more general sense is a much wider question, which can be more fruitfully considered when other examples of building estates have been examined. At this point it is sufficient to observe that the landlord's agent to some extent, but the speculative builders above all, were insistent on the desirability of building virtually one single type of house on the estate, once the early days of piecemeal ribbon development along existing public roads had been left behind. The houses might vary in appearance and design, either radically or merely in cosmetic details; but inside they provided very much the same amount of accommodation, the typical mid-century middling-sized family house which could, if required, be run with just a single general servant, but which had enough room for two or three domestics if the family could afford them. They were solid, respectable, comfortable, unexciting; nothing grand or imposing. If the ambition had been to reproduce St John's Wood, the achievement was more middle-brow Finchley Road than smart Avenue Road. The builders having created a supply of a particular kind of houses, the district was peopled by social groups suited to that type by their means, way of living, and aspirations. From the side of housing demand there was a very powerful urge for people of like condition to want to live in the same neighbourhood with their kind, to decline to be mixed up with their inferiors, or at the very least to keep away from noxious, unhealthy, or otherwise unpleasant areas. These were strong tides making for segregation. But it does begin to look as if the actual decisions as to where the socially-differentiated demand was to come to roost, which districts were to be appropriated to which groups, were taken by the providers of the houses, and rested upon geography and topography to some extent, but even more upon the activities of the landowners and builders.

Some such thoughts could have been in Shaw's mind when he reflected on the satisfactory state of affairs and prospects for the future, at the close of 1850. In the next few years, he thought,[1]

the lettings of ground will much increase—there has been generally a cessation of building during the last two years [which was not altogether true], but what has been done at Chalcots I am

1 Eton, College Records, XLIX, Shaw to Bethell, 16 November 1850.

happy to say has been well done, and the houses are of a respectable class and character.

Twenty-one years after the first building proposals Chalcots had at last got under way, and had established itself as one of the active growth points of north-west London. In the same letter Shaw unconsciously revealed how little this gratifying outcome owed to managerial enterprise:

> The Estate having now so much increased in importance, I have thought it desirable to have proper books for the Plans, Lease Roll, and Rent Account with reference to each other so that the management of the Estate may be simple and intelligible to anyone.

The implication is that up to this time the management had been so rudimentary that it did not matter whether it was intelligible or not, and this is supported by the evidence.

What had grown had been dictated by the logic of social and economic opportunities, and of topography, and Shaw was well aware of its requirements. It made good sense to open up the estate by driving an east–west link from the Hampstead Road to Swiss Cottage, for this promised to put the more westerly parts in more direct contact with the professional areas of Holborn and the commercial areas of the City, as well as grafting Chalcots on to the residential image of St John's Wood. Further, it made sound engineering sense to choose the line of Adelaide Road for this link, for it followed easy gradients along the path of an undulation which divided the higher ground of Primrose Hill to the south from the steady rise to Rosslyn Hill and the Hampstead Heights to the north. When this great first step was complete Chalcots lay split into two unequal parts by this band of housing. The larger portion lay to the north of Adelaide Road, well over 100 acres lying in nine sizeable fields, served as farmland by Englands Lane, and crossed by footpaths, one leading to Hampstead village by way of the Belsize Park walls and Shepherd's Well, the other branching off at Chalcots Farm to join Haverstock Hill by way of Haverstock Terrace [Belsize Grove]; it was the first of these paths which had been used for the line of Fellows Road where it left Adelaide Road. The smaller part lay to the south, nearly 40 acres lying in four fields which ran up to the new Primrose Hill Park and to the old Chalk Farm Tavern, also crossed by paths leading from Swiss Cottage to the Hill and from Adelaide Road to the Tavern.

[242]

By the middle 1850s a decision had to be made whether to wheel the building march north or south. The early inclinations on the estate, in the 1830s, had been to inch northwards towards old Hampstead; but different considerations ruled when it was a matter of forming great new roads across the fields, and Cuming swung the direction of advance to the south. This seemed the more promising area for the developer, as it offered the attractions of placing houses close to Primrose Hill Park, and calling in the influence of proximity to Regent's Park to reinforce the spillover of estate agents' promotion of the charms of St John's Wood. It was also highly acceptable from the angle of farm management, for although the southern fields had once been the most valuable by reason of their closeness to manure supplies and to market, once the unity of the farm had been destroyed they became, as detached lands, something of a nuisance to farm and much subject to the nuisance of rambling by the surrounding townspeople. Hence from 1856 Cuming made a start on King Henry's Road, attacking it simultaneously from the eastern and western ends, and on the several link roads, King's College Road and Merton Rise; his last operation on the estate seems to have been to start on Primrose Hill Road, in 1858, with the intention of driving it through to Queen's Road [Regent's Park Road] and thus opening up the boundary of Primrose Hill. This was not achieved, however, until the 1870s, long after Cuming had gone.[1]

Cuming had become a respected local citizen, and was elected to the reformed Vestry at the initial elections of November 1855. But he did not stand for re-election in 1857, and by then his zest for building also seems to have been on the wane. His new venture may not have been going as briskly as he had hoped, for among his last acts was the creation of a cricket ground on the northern edge of Primrose Hill; this, the Eton and Middlesex Cricket Ground, lay at the end of the short spur of Eton Place [Elsworthy Rise] and athwart a line joining the two ends of King Henry's Road. Cricket definitely added to the amenities and attractive power of the district; but playing it across a main building line showed a certain scepticism about the speed with which the houses were likely to bowl. His last act was to arrange to hand on the developer's baton, by introducing Robert Yeo to the estate. Yeo had been busy building on the northern section of the Eyre estate, to the west of the Finchley Road, operating in Belsize Road and Fairfax Road in the early

[1] HPL Vestry Min., 19 March 1858, which stated, in relation to Cuming's application to form new streets and sewers, that the land between Primrose Hill Road and Queen's Road, Chalk Farm, was intended to be let on building leases in 1860: this road, and Oppidans Road, were in the event not formed until 1868.

1850s from one of his own houses in Adelaide Road North [Hillgrove Road].[1] He was in a substantial way of business, like Cuming, and sat as a fellow-Vestryman from November 1855. He moved across to the Chalcots estate on an underletting from Cuming, and then blossomed into the principal undertaker of King Henry's Road, submitting a scheme for fifty-six houses there in 1856.[2] Taking a small slice off the cricket ground, he pushed this road through in the course of the 1860s, though by 1871 he had not filled up all the frontages. He kept the Chalcots estate on the move, but that is about all that can be said for Yeo, as his ideas for semi-detacheds were a good deal more skimped and debased than Cuming's had been, even though they were apparently found perfectly satisfactory by much the same kind of middling-middle-class purchasers and tenants.

Such was the state of play at Chalcots in 1871. John Shaw had just been succeeded as agent by another architect-surveyor, George Pownall, who had an altogether brisker and more efficient approach to his managerial tasks. Pownall had schemes for pushing ahead much more rapidly, both north and south, and in 1868 put in an application for a quiverful of new roads—to be named Oppidans, Scholars, Bursars, Adamson, Fontaine, Crossfield, and Elsworthy—but none of these had yet been formed.[3] The only new road of Pownall's regime which had actually been laid out, though not yet much built on, was Steele's Road, which in 1867 had swept away Steele's Cottage.[4] The Chalcots estate, therefore, may have been poised for extensive expansion in the 1870s, but it still had getting on for 120 acres lying under grass. Much of this, moreover, was potential building land not merely in the optimistic terminology of an estate agent, but in the practical vocabulary of the builder and developer, its ripeness ensured by the many access roads giving directly on to the fields and offering sewer connections all ready to be made. There is no evidence to be found here that the abstraction of the Maryon Wilson estate from the market had caused the slightest twinge of shortage of building land in Hampstead.

[1] Ibid., 6 June 1856.
[2] Ibid., 21 November 1856.
[3] MBW Min., 31 July 1868, p. 1007.
[4] Ibid., 7 June 1867, p. 731.

Seven

MIDDLE-CLASS COLONISATION
The creation of Swiss Cottage and Belsize, 1850-71

The best testimony to the quality of the houses which Samuel Cuming built along Adelaide Road came, perhaps, from the Engineer of the LNWR. When the Hampstead Junction Railway was being proposed, in 1853, he argued that it was in large measure a means of effectively quadrupling the tracks on the LNWR's approach to London, and that the alternative way of doing this would be to make a second Primrose Hill Tunnel. But to do this would involve taking down a whole row of new houses 'of a very good class indeed, let at £100 to £150 a year. Our line involves removing no more houses, and of a different class, let at £25 to £40 a year [in the Buck estate in Camden Town].'[1] A second and a third Primrose Hill Tunnel did, of course, have to be built eventually, and it was indeed necessary in the end to demolish a whole block of Cuming's houses on the south side of Adelaide Road. But until this became inescapable because of the growth of traffic, the railwaymen naturally sought out the route where property acquisition was cheapest even if the actual work of construction might itself be more costly and more extensive. So, for a time, these good houses were allowed to remain. When the pace of development on the Chalcots estate slackened off from the middle fifties, and other parts of Hampstead took up the running, it might have been expected that this very line was at the root of the switch. For the other avowed aim of the new line, which may indeed have been the chief aim in the minds of some of its promoters, was to expand the highly successful suburban services of the E & WID & BJR (renamed the North London Railway in 1853) by opening up the territory to the north and west of Camden Road station for building. All its supporters emphasised this point. The tunnel, from the proposed Heath station to the Finchley Road, said the same George Berkeley, 'is all under property which is laid out for building, and therefore the line is perfectly unobjectionable and it is

[1] HLRO SC (Commons) Hampstead Junction Railway Bill, Vol. 81, Evidence 1853, George Berkeley, 8 June 1853, ff. 70-1.

[245]

most convenient for that large class of building which is going on . . .
It is proposed to work the line by omnibus trains at a distance of a
quarter of an hour apart at low fares, so as to give the suburbs of
London the same accommodation as is given to the north and west
suburbs.' Robert Stephenson argued that the line would give 'accommodation to Hampstead and the vicinity'; while the architect, William
Tite, related somewhat untruthfully how 'this line will develop the
ground there [in Hampstead] for building purposes. Sir Thomas Wilson,
who has property there, upon which he has built, first appeared as a
Petitioner against this Bill, but when I disclosed to him the real state
of the case, he has withdrawn his petition.' It was left to a surveyor,
Charles Lee, appearing for the opponents, to assert that 'the line has
not been asked for by the Hampstead people—I know three or four
Hampstead people who say they do not like it.'[1]

Of all these witnesses, Charles Lee seems to have been nearest the
truth. On the immediate issue of the attitude of the Hampstead property
owners affected by the route, there were only four owners of small and
old houses at South End—one of which, interestingly enough, was
occupied by a builder who years later was active in putting up terrace
houses in that district—who were in favour of the project, and also one
more substantial figure, the Reverend William Dunbar who owned
West End House, though its lessee, Admiral Sir George Sartorius, was
more understandably non-committal. Most of the rest of the owners
and head-tenants, if they answered the notices from the railway company at all, were opposed to the scheme; among them Sir Thomas
Maryon Wilson, the Dean and Chapter of Westminster, the Norris
executors who were the copyhold owners of the site of the tunnel
entrance at South End, and Thomas Rhodes who was the copyhold
owner of the lands immediately to the north of this. Over the parish
boundary, Lord Mansfield returned a similar dissent.[2] Hampstead
people of this kind clearly did not like it. In the short term, moreover,
none of the residential development which was foreseen as a consequence of building this railway in fact took place. The project was
generally known about from 1853 onwards; the line was opened to
traffic in 1860; and yet by 1871 no development had even started in the
vicinity of the three stations which were initially opened, at Hampstead
Heath, Finchley Road, and Edgware Road. In the world of railway

[1] Ibid., George Berkeley, 8 June 1853, ff.10, 22–4; Robert Stephenson, 7 June
1853, f.10; William Tite, 8 June 1853, f.130; Charles Lee, 8 June 1853, f.186.
[2] HLRO Hampstead Junction Railway, Session 1852–3, Plan and Book of
Reference.

promoters and traffic managers, property developers, and speculative builders, this was more like a lifetime than the 'short term'.

If the tide of development receded somewhat on the Eton property it was not the new railway which pulled it away but the horse. The horse with its buses shifted the attractions to areas which were in direct competition with Chalcots but which succeeded either in offering something rather cheaper in the way of houses, as in the northern end of the Eyre estate, or in providing rather better value for money, as on the Howard estate; while the horse with its private carriages led the way to areas in the Dean and Chapter's estate where something of a better class than Chalcots was put on offer. It is not that building on Chalcots came to a standstill in these years. It went on, at a slower pace, but was overshadowed by these three districts of Kilburn Priory, South Hampstead, and Belsize, which made the major contribution to Hampstead's growth by some 2,600 houses between 1851 and 1871.

True to the over-riding principle of economy in property costs, the LNWR managed by 1879 to fit in its second Primrose Hill Tunnel, when its traffic bottleneck on the approach to Euston made it impossible to postpone it any longer, without having to gobble up any expensive property. Taking the bore to the south of the original tunnel, the approach lines were squeezed into the back gardens of houses at the corner of King Henry's Road and Primrose Hill Road at the entrance, and of those on the corner of Alexandra Road and Hillgrove Road at the exit; it was only at the entrance that half-a-dozen houses themselves had to be demolished. When the third tunnel became necessary, in the 1900s, this delicate feat could not be repeated, and taking this one to the northern side involved the LNWR in considerable and expensive destruction of houses in Adelaide Road at the entrance and in Belsize Road at the exit. By then, however, it was a relatively less expensive operation than George Berkeley had feared in 1853; for in the interval the Adelaide Road property had deteriorated from its pristine value, shaken down by half a century of backing on to a busy main line, while Belsize Road had been developed with an altogether poorer class of housing from its very beginning. The initial development of the northern, or Hampstead, section of the Eyre estate had been carried on as a direct extension of St John's Wood in style and value of houses and the class of housing demand in view. This was in the sub-district round Swiss Cottage, with Finchley Road as its axis, and bounded by Avenue, Boundary, Loudoun, and Belsize Roads, which was developed under building agreements of 1838 and 1845 with the main weight of actual building taking place in the late forties and early fifties, in which

Richard Thomas of Circus Road and Robert Yeo were among the active builders. The most imposing villas, some of them standing on their own and with their own coach-houses, were in the eastern part of this area, on Avenue Road, St John's Wood Park, and the Finchley Road itself; moving west the gardens became rather narrower, the pairs of semi-detacheds less grand, but the entire district nevertheless had the authentic 'St John's Wood' air.[1]

When the estate began to roll westward, however, on lines parallel with the railway—Boundary Road, west of Loudoun Road, from 1853, Alexandra Road from 1858, and Belsize Road, west of Fairhazel Gardens–Loudoun Road from 1853—to link up with its own western artery of Abbey Road, the character of the housing was tuned to a lower social and income level. In Boundary Road the density of the semis was almost doubled and their frontages were only half the length of those in Avenue Road; it is hard to believe that the stabling provided in the Boundary and Loudoun Road Mews was ever intended to be used by the tenants of the front houses; it was destined, rather, to service their more wealthy neighbours to the east. Both Boundary and Alexandra Roads still preserved the idiom of the semi-detached villa, though in debased and cramped form with extremely narrow gaps between the pairs; in Belsize Road, for the first time for very many years on the Eyre estate, blocks of terrace housing appeared, almost the complete antithesis of the spacious, leafy, semi-rural illusion which St John's Wood had created as its image. Admittedly, this terrace housing might still be termed middle-class housing, but only precariously so, suited to the lesser clerks who were far removed in income and social standing from the prosperous lawyers and merchants, or even the legendary officers' mistresses, of St John's Wood proper. The change in social and architectural character was partly a matter of local topography, with Loudoun Road marking a frontier beyond which the land sloped gently down into a shallow trough before rising again to a slight ridge along the line of Greville Road. But it was much more decisively a matter of chronology, the break coming quite cleanly in the middle of Fairfax Road, between numbers 25 and 27; here again, the fifty-seven stables built in Fairfax Mews at the end of the 1850s were plainly designed for the convenience of residents further afield than the front houses.

[1] This account of the Eyre estate can be pieced together from one of the very few documents surviving in the Eyre MS., Particulars of Leases in force on 25 March 1903, supplemented by the twenty-five-inch O.S. map in use as the current Eyre estate map, and by references, under London Building Act applications, in MBW Min.

In the absence of the records of either the estate or the builders it is difficult to be certain of the reasons for this surprisingly abrupt decline from grace and space on the Eyre estate. One reason, in Belsize Road, appears to have been sheer lack of space, for when the road had been driven through between the railway and the estate boundary to the north there was so little depth left in the building plots that the back gardens of the houses in the middle of the terrace were barely ten feet long. The wavy line of the estate boundary between Eyre and Maryon Wilson can still be seen in the fences dividing the gardens of the Belsize Road houses from those of the Goldhurst Terrace houses. To face a builder with such narrow sites was to face him with a strong temptation to go in for terrace-housing with its 'back yard' associations. A constricted site, which in this instance was up against the boundary with the Howard estate, may also account for the high-density, cramped building in Bolton Road, which was started in 1858 and finished by 1865; though in this case the narrow sites were self-imposed, since there was no necessity to lay out the road on the precise line which was adopted. In other instances of similarly close-packed building, however, there was no lack of space to inhibit a different policy: in the triangle of the Eyre property formed by Belsize Road, Abbey Road, and the backs of St George's Road were packed no less than twenty-seven terrace houses, eight mews in Abbey Mews, and a corner pub, on an area on which the adjoining Howard estate, in St George's Road, put only seventeen houses, and moreover put them there at the very same time. It may be that by the late fifties the estate surveyor, and the builders, had decided that some of the building land was too close to the tracks for comfort and was suffering from a railway blight which made anything but lower-middle-class housing out of the question. This is an explanation which could cover Belsize Road and Alexandra Road, but could scarcely be stretched to take in the Abbey Road triangle, or the complex of Bolton Road, Holtham Road (also built between 1858 and 1866), and Alexandra Mews. Lax estate management, allowing the builders to slip out of control, is a possibility even if it seems unlikely on an estate which was otherwise so well ordered and so much under the constant eye of its owner. It is noticeable, however, that in all the roads mentioned the builders had succeeded in discharging their ground rent obligations to Eyre when less than half the eventual number of houses had been finished and leases for them had been granted, and the remainder were all leased at peppercorn ground rents. This was generally held to be bad management, for if a builder could secure the entire ground rent stipulated for a take when he had only partly covered it with houses it was felt that it could be difficult to supervise the way in which he subsequently built on the uncovered part, and that these remaining houses, which would have to be leased at peppercorns, might tend to get lost to sight before their remote reversion to the estate at the end of their 99-year leases.

In all these roads, however, the houses were all of a piece; so that there is no visible mark of difference between those on ordinary cash ground rents and those on peppercorns. Moreover, if it is to be argued that the natural inclination of builders when they escape from the leading reins of an estate office is to pack in as many houses as they can, however small and mean, then the entire basis of low-density, superior, suburban villa development is called in question. For if it was true that builders found it more profitable to run up the greatest possible number of houses on the smallest area, then presumably ground landlords would have found it more profitable too, since builders would naturally have offered the highest ground rents per acre for the more profitable mode of development; it would then become difficult to see why there should be any economic reasons for any high-class residential development ever occurring at all. It could have occurred only if landowners felt the social pressures to create desirable residential neighbourhoods, or the administrative pressures to have fewer and larger ground rents to collect rather than more numerous small ones, or the municipal pressures to create high rateable values and thus keep the rates down, sufficiently strongly to compel builders to accept restrictions forcing them to build houses of a better class than they wanted to. All of these non-economic, or only indirectly economic, motives did affect landowners in some degree; and some builders did need keeping up to the mark, in terms of the quality of houses they built, by the power of landowners to insert conditions into building agreements. But although we may suppose that many builders, if not adequately controlled by the landlord, might try to cut corners, skimp on materials, and generally dress their houses up on the cheap, it is ridiculous to suppose that builders did not know their own business; they built for a particular market, for people of quality if they thought they could get them to purchase, for people of lower station if they thought otherwise, and they built willingly for whichever market they expected to be most profitable in a particular locality.

Hence both on general grounds and on the particular grounds of the normal competence of the Eyre estate management it must be presumed that these developments were undertaken with the consent of the landowner and the willing co-operation of the builders. Somewhat paradoxically it may even have been the case that the tight-packed, poorer houses were more profitable to Eyre and less profitable to the builders than the typical St John's Wood villas. In Bolton Road, for instance, the ground rent was of the order of £100 an acre or more, at least double and probably nearly three times as much as the ground rents received for the villas of Avenue Road, Finchley Road, or Abbey Road.[1] A glance at the 25-inch map gives a strong impression that Eyre and his builders decided to make the entire north-western part of the estate into the service area for the rest of the St John's Wood community. This could not have been as literally true as with Nash's Cumberland Market and Albany Street market and service area for the Regent's Park terraces, for north-west Eyre-land did not attempt to go in for shopping and market facilities and was in any event too distant from most of the wealthier part of the estate for such a purpose. Moreover, the sheer numbers of small terrace houses, and mews, built in this quarter were greatly in excess of the direct requirements of the wealthier inhabitants of the near vicinity for housing for their own out-door servants and private carriages. Nevertheless the notion is not so far-fetched as it appears at first sight. Laundering, for one thing, was a necessary by-product of a middle-class residential district; and although much of the dirty washing which was sent out from the homes of the better-off may have gone further afield—to old Hampstead, for example, where the Heath was found highly useful as drying grounds by the washerwomen—some of it may well have found its way to these more humble quarters nearer the doorstep. It could also be that some of the other 'polite' home industries of a suburban community found their home in this quarter: demand for a great range of work was generated by a suburb to cater for its own needs in repairing and servicing its clothing, its furniture, and its household equipment, not to mention the fabric of the houses themselves, while the labour force engaged in building the houses for the middle-class employers of this miscellany of occupations was frequently itself housed pretty well on the building sites.

Above all, however, it seems as though this quarter was called into existence by the needs of the horse bus services, whose provision was crucial to the mid-century development of the whole area of southern Hampstead—not merely to the Eyre estate—as a residential district for the carriageless middle classes. The detailed chronology of development

---

[1] Eyre MS., Particulars of Leases in force on 25 March 1903. The paradox of higher ground rents per acre for cheaper houses is discussed more fully below, pp. 365–70.

shows that the initial activity in the Fairfax Road area was the building of the Victoria Mews (as Fairfax Mews were originally called) for bus horse stabling, the construction of an access road to them, known for many years as North End Road (and eventually used as the opening stretch of Fairhazel Gardens), and the provision of housing for the bus stable staff and probably for the bus drivers and conductors in Britannia Terrace along part of Belsize Road and Victoria Road (Fairfax Road).[1] It was only after this, some time between 1863 and 1873, that the rest of Fairfax Road, from the Britannia Terrace northward to its junction with Finchley Road, was developed with pairs of ample middle-class villas. A similar sequence seems to have been followed in the neighbourhood of Bolton Road, where the first development was of a complex of stabling and associated terrace housing in Belgrave Gardens, Bolton Road, Alexandra Mews, Holtham Road, and the short stretch of Boundary Road involved, the whole little area being mainly devoted to horse bus needs. The building of the chief residential stretches of Springfield Road, Boundary Road, and Alexandra Road followed later, between 1856 and 1873, and, at any rate in their middle reaches, attained the lower rungs of rather close-packed middle-class villadom. The location of these bus stables at the same time met the needs of the bus traffic and suited the logic of the Eyre estate. They were on the edges of the extremes of the built-up area, allowing space on their Londonward side for future residential expansion by infilling, and they formed the rational termini for the bus routes starting from Swiss Cottage and going down Finchley Road, and shortly going across Adelaide Road, on the eastern side, and for the route down Abbey Road on the western side. They were also, from the estate's point of view, tucked away on the periphery of the property and therefore out of harm's way in respect of exerting too much of a baleful influence on the rest of the estate. In other words, in so far as the whole north-western part of the Eyre estate suffered a lowering of social tone as a consequence of 'blight', the villain was not railway blight at all, but horse bus blight deliberately introduced on to the estate and not in-flicted upon it by sinister outside forces.

By 1873 the Eyre estate was virtually completely built up, with just a couple of vacant plots left in Alexandra Road, and the extreme north-western tip by the Abbey Road 'triangle' and St Mary's Church still to

[1] Postal District map of London issued by the *Illustrated Times* (n.d. but from internal evidence 1856 or 1857); *P.O. London Directory*, 1863, map; HPL Vestry Min., 25 July 1856, referring to North End Road as 'the only means of approach to Victoria Mews, and [it] is subject to the whole of the Omnibus Traffic to and from the Stables'.

receive its final instalment of terraces.[1] Twenty years later, when the building frontier had moved a long way further north, the service areas which had been tidily planted on the edge of open country found themselves in the centre of a vast urban area instead. This did no harm to the prospects of the estate on which they stood, since it had no further prospects until the 99-year lease mechanism should bring round the opportunity of re-development, which indeed was duly taken with the LCC and Borough Council acting as joint re-developers of the 'triangle' and Bolton Road complex in the 1960s.[2] Whether it harmed the prospects of the estates to the north is hard to tell; these certainly did develop as middle-class residential districts, but it is possible that the proximity of the one-time stabling depots denied them a chance of aiming at the wealthiest end of the middle-class market, and served as one ingredient in setting the social tone of West Hampstead. What is certain is that when the horse bus routes were pushed farther out and these ceased to be useful as terminal depots other semi-industrial uses were sucked into the vacant stabling and other working-class inhabitants, albeit of the superior and 'comfortable' working class, came to the terraces, so that the quarter remained a permanent island of a species generally foreign to the Hampstead middle-class sea.

At the time, however, these developments on the Eyre estate do not appear to have influenced in any way the simultaneous development of its immediate neighbour to the west, the Howard estate, which proceeded more or less in isolation with its own estate policy although it tied itself in to the Eyre communications system on the Greville Place–Boundary Road line, the prolongation of Alexandra Road to join Kilburn Priory, and the similar continuation of Belsize Road. These lateral links were a matter of convenience; the main axis of advance on the estate was quite different, along a new road driven due north from the Edgware Road, Kilburn Priory and its two arms of Priory Road and St George's Road (Priory Terrace), which made the maximum use of the shape of the estate. After the initial opening up of Greville Place with gentlemen's villas in the 1820s this estate remained quiet for twenty years, perched on the very edge of civilisation.[3] It came to life

---

[1] Six-inch O.S. map (1st ed., 1873). These last few gaps had been filled by 1880: GLCRO MBW map of Railway and other proposals deposited at the Private Bill Office, 1880.

[2] This redevelopment has obliterated Holtham Road and Alexandra Mews, the greater part of Bolton Road, and the prolongation of Alexandra Road which formerly linked it to what is now Langtry Road on the Howard (Bagot) estate.

[3] See above, p. 87; it was half a mile further up Edgware Road than Pineapple

again in 1845 when Fulk Greville Howard made a building agreement with James Carter, a local builder from Manchester Terrace in Maida Vale, for a small parcel of land on the high road, on which Springfield Lane was laid out at the back. Once more horses provided the main drive. Carter built a considerable livery stable on much of the land (Greville Mews), most of which was bought by a City upholsterer in 1848; and surrounded this by appropriately modest two-storey tenements backing the stables and two inns, the Bell and the Red Lion.[1] Howard's aim, however, was not to appropriate all his property to such commercial uses, and the same James Carter made a start on some more classy houses in what became Kilburn Priory, which he called Springfield Villas. The opposite side of Kilburn Priory was started a few years earlier by William Cullum, a china manufacturer, who built four substantial houses under an agreement made in 1843. He had finished them and the leases were all ready for sealing when Howard died on 4 March 1846. The Hampstead property was inherited by Howard's nephew, Colonel Arthur Upton, and Upton had to be taken to Chancery in 1850 in order to be compelled to grant the lease to Cullum.[2]

Colonel Upton was not exactly trying to wriggle out of honouring his uncle's commitments, but felt it necessary to get plain orders from Chancery to overcome a scruple which he had developed. Under his uncle's will he had been left the Kilburn property with an express power to grant 99-year building leases, but with no power to make building agreements by which he contracted to grant building leases at some future date. Chancery settled the particular case for him, though it took over two years to do it, on the elementary grounds that the building agreement in question had been perfectly validly made by his uncle. For the further development of the estate, however, it was necessary to remove this legal impediment, and the slight hiatus in building between Howard's death in 1846 and 1851 is accounted for by this process. Upton promoted a private estate bill for the purpose, and it was passed without difficulty in 1851. It is noticeable that in this

Place, the local bus terminus in 1838: T. C. Barker, *History of London Transport* (1963), p. 401.

[1] Bagot MS., Lease No. 89, 8 September 1847, recites the building agreement of 3 September 1845 with James Carter; Lease No. 133, 22 September 1848, recites sale of the stables to Thomas Paul of Mansion House Street, upholsterer.

[2] Ibid., Lease No. 112, 30 May 1849, of pairs of villas, with basement and three storeys; Lease No. 109, 31 December 1852, Upton to William Cullum of 13 Cockspur Street, china manufacturer.

BELSIZE ESTATES

	Name of sub-estate	First building lessee
A	ROSSLYN ESTATE	DAVIDSON 1853
B	BELSIZE HOUSE	WOODD *surrendered lease 1857 in exchange for freehold of E*
C	IVY BANK	BARKER 1868
D	BELSIZE PARK	PALMER 1853
E	HILLFIELD	WOODD *purchased freehold 1857*
F	BLISS'S BACKLAND	TIDEY 1864
G	BLISS	BLISS-BARRETO
H	HAVERSTOCK LODGE	LUND 1851
J	SOUTH END FARM *(part)*	GIBB 1881
K	SOUTH END FARM *(part)*	PICKETT 1878

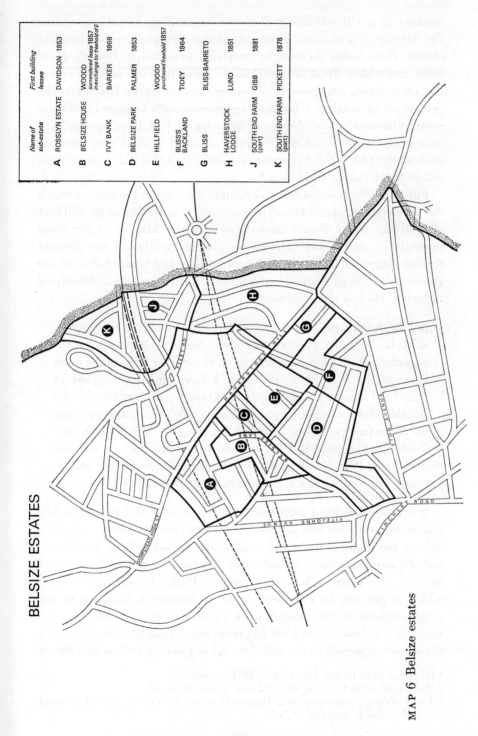

MAP 6 Belsize estates

[255]

instance of a will which was defective for building operations, unlike the Maryon Wilson case, no opposition was whipped up: but then, of course, there were no wealthy residents overlooking Upton's Hilly Field and Abbey Field and anxious to preserve them as open spaces and open views. Just prior to obtaining this Act Upton had taken the precaution of making a building agreement with George Duncan, a substantial builder and developer from Grove End Road on the Eyre estate, who with his son was the chief architect of the Upton development of the 1850s; this agreement naturally provided that Upton would obtain legislation to validate it.[1]

Fulk Greville Howard had had definite ideas about the way in which the development should be carried on, down to providing in his will that all building leases should have 'drawn in the Margin of the same respectively, or by way of Schedule thereto, a Plan of the Ground therein comprised, together with an Elevation and Ground Plan of the House or Building erected', an excellent device for the architectural historian. He had also expressed[2]

> my Wish (though I do not intend such Wish to be imperative, or to be regarded as a positive Direction or Obligation) that as regards the Buildings to be erected on any Part or Parts of the same Premises in Middlesex, the Plan I have hitherto adopted of detached Cottages or Two adjoining Cottages, and not more, with suitable Garden, shall be pursued as nearly as may be, and that no Manufactory, Shop, or other Building for carrying on any Trade or Business shall be permitted on any Part of the last mentioned Premises, except for a Public House or Livery Stable, when required for the Convenience of the Inhabitants.

It was as well for Upton that this was a wish and not a binding instruction, since his first act was to encourage Duncan to cover the area nearest the high road with 'close adjoining houses', of the fourth-rate and of a minimum value of £200 each, in which 'there might be carried on . . . any trade or business (except a Public House or Beershop) which might not be offensive, or be or become a nuisance to the neighbourhood or the tenants upon Upton's estate.'[3] To be fair, the major part of Duncan's take of $15\frac{1}{2}$ acres was developed in keeping with the wishes expressed in the will, in pairs of good-class villas in Kilburn

[1] HLRO, Upton Estate Act, 14 and 15 Vict. cap. vii.
[2] Ibid., where the Greville Howard will is recited in full.
[3] The building agreement with George Duncan, 19 February 1851, is cited in full in the Upton Estate Act.

Priory, Priory Road, and St George's Road; the two public houses which Duncan was permitted to erect were reduced in the event to one, kept discreetly out of the way in West End Lane; the 'close adjoining' or terrace housing was confined to the Kilburn end of Belsize Road, and used to serve the shopping needs of the new estate; and Duncan set aside a site from the beginning, close to the northern boundary of the property, for a church. This, St Mary's, rather hazily associated with the original site of Kilburn Priory, was built in 1856 to Horace Francis's comfortably conventional design, setting the seal of respectability on the district while it was still in the midst of development.

In most respects this Duncan enterprise was typical of a well-regulated and successful small building estate. It was covered with its complement of some 200 houses with great despatch between 1851 and 1857, so that it was all of a piece in general appearance; it had shops close at hand but not intruding; and it had its church. Typically also, George Duncan, and his son John Wallace who succeeded him in the family business in 1854, were not able to attain the building output of over thirty houses a year by themselves, and about one-third of the houses were actually built by other and smaller builders on under-leases from Duncan: George Robinson from the Harrow Road built six houses in St George's Road in 1851, William Bricknell and George Miller, both from Camden Town, built one apiece in the same year, while in 1852 Thomas Parnell from the Harrow Road was responsible for four houses in the same road; in Priory Road William Green, also from the Harrow Road, put up six houses in 1852, and George Ireland, of 7½ Old Church Street, Paddington, contributed two houses.[1] It was not quite so typical that the landowner, Upton, was himself at the expense of forming the major new road, Kilburn Priory, as far as the bridge over the railway, from which point further new residential roads became Duncan's affair. Perhaps partly in recognition of this landlord's outlay, Duncan paid the very satisfactory ground rent of £40 an acre on his take. Perhaps least typical of all was not merely the closeness of the railway, but the fact that the developer made great efforts to have a station built to serve his estate. Duncan was empowered to dispose of a strip of land up to 100 feet wide, without any

[1] Bagot MS., leases of various months: George Robinson, Nos 198, 200, 202, 204, 206, 208, of 1851; William Bricknell, No. 205 of 1851; George Miller, Nos 207, 209, of 1851; Thomas Parnell, Nos 211, 210, 212, 213, of 1852; William Green, Nos 155, 157, 159, 161, 163, 165, of 1852; George Ireland, Nos 156, 158, of 1852. All these were granted by Upton 'at the nomination of George Duncan'.

reduction in his total ground rent, to help in the formation of a station, siding, and station approach, and Upton undertook to convey the freehold of this strip to the LNWR. The railway did indeed open a station at Kilburn in 1852, using some of this land, but, as the company's engineer reported, 'the length of the through traffic rendered it very difficult to carry out',[1] and there was no more than a sketchy and inconvenient suburban train service to stimulate the settlement of the Duncan houses.

All these Duncan houses, built in the Old Abbey Field to the north of the railway, were substantial three-storey affairs with their porticoes, front steps, and basements, architecturally nondescript no doubt in their builders' Italianate with trimmings, but costing rather more than the minimum £400 prime building cost which Duncan was contracted to expend. They were, no doubt, good value for servant-keeping families who did not aspire to their own carriages. For no individual stabling was provided, merely a very small run of ten stables in Wavel Mews on the estate border to the north of Abbey Road, to serve the needs of 150 family houses. The breadwinners, if they travelled far to work, were much more likely to rely on the horse buses than on the vestigial suburban services of the LNWR. The Kilburn Gate on the Edgware turnpike was only a few minutes' walk; in 1838 only one omnibus had run from there, to the Bank; by 1856 there were at least twenty, running through to London Bridge, or to Whitechapel.[2] The higher-class development on the Upton estate was reserved for the land south of the railway and adjoining the earliest building, in Greville Place; here, appropriately on its little eminence of Hilly Field, Greville Road and Mortimer Road were laid out from 1853 onwards. These larger houses were developed partly by Ferdinand Ball, a gentleman who came to live in Greville Road himself and acted in partnership with Isaac Coney, a mason from Douro Cottages in St John's Wood, and partly by the Duncans. Most of them were simply larger versions of semi-detached villas—one, pretentious enough to be named Milford Cottage, sold for £750.[3] One or two stood in their own grounds of a quarter-acre

[1] The measures to encourage the establishment of Kilburn Station were in the building agreement of 19 February 1851; the LNWR Engineer's statement in HLRO Hampstead Junction Railway Bill, George Berkeley, 8 June 1853, f.29.

[2] Barker, op. cit., App. 2, pp. 393–403 for services in 1838–9; App. 3, pp. 404–12, for omnibuses acquired by the LGOC in 1856.

[3] Bagot MS., Lease No. 74, 12 October 1854, of 37 Greville Road to Thomas Enbery Rees of Islington, gentleman, who had paid £750 to Ferdinand Ball, the builder.

or so, and had their own coach-houses and stables; one such was Loanda House in Greville Place, built by Duncan in 1855, and subsequently occupied as the convent of St Peter's Harbour.[1] Not surprisingly it was Greville Place and Greville Road which supplied the touch of gold (the colour used to denote the 'upper-middle and upper classes') for the Upton estate on Booth's 1889 map; all the rest was solid red for the 'well-to-do middle class', except for the pockets of the 'fairly comfortable' working class in Greville Mews and Springfield Lane, and Wavel Mews from the 1850s, and in Kilburn Vale and Abbey Lane from the earlier development of the 1820s.[2]

By 1860 the Upton estate was practically complete; there remained just one or two gaps in St George's Road and Alexandra Road, which were filled in 1867 by the builder on the abutting Eyre property, David Tildesley of Irongate Wharf, Paddington, who appropriately enough was an ironmonger by trade.[3] Thereafter there was no room for any more building until some small pieces of redevelopment became profitable. In 1887 Richard Bristow, a builder from Stroud Green financed by Fisher, a draper in the Kilburn High Road, put up eight houses in Kilburn Priory in the back gardens of the High Road houses; and in 1900 the triangle of land at the junction of Kilburn Priory and the High Road which had initially been developed as a florist's business with its own nursery ground was redeveloped as the five shops of The Parade and the Kilburn Empire music hall (later the Essoldo cinema).[4] The whole little estate was a compact and successful venture, especially in its sustained phase of development after 1851, its social symmetry interrupted only by the deliberate introduction of a tiny commercial and working-class fringe fronting the main road, and by the careless creation of a poor quarter in Kilburn Vale in the 1820s. It was, perhaps, wholly unremarkable save for the circumstance that the estate was bisected by a railway and the tracks failed to form anything of a barrier or social dividing line. All in all the estate contributes in its modest way to raising some doubts about the role of the railways as an all-powerful force in the moulding of the urban environment.

[1] Ibid., Lease No. 82, 30 April 1855, and later endorsements.
[2] Booth's Map of London Poverty, 1889, north-west sheet; for Kilburn Vale see above, p. 86.
[3] Bagot MS., Leases Nos 18, 20, 21, 8 April and 20 September 1867.
[4] Ibid., Lease No 75, 13 February 1855, to the florist, and surrender in 1887 with regrant by Nos 220-8, 27 August 1887-8 September 1893; and Nos 230-9, 26 June 1899-24 December 1900. The Kilburn Empire was not built until 1907.

Such doubts are strongly re-inforced by an examination of the way in which the Belsize estate lurched into action in the 1850s. This large area, stretching from Swiss Cottage to the Heath and from Englands Lane to the High Street, occupied a commanding position on the middle uplands of Haverstock Hill. When it was discreetly sprinkled with mansions, lodges, and little parks it formed the centre of the merchants' country-estate Hampstead; when it had been laced with streets, avenues, and crescents and covered with brick and stucco it became the heartland of professional middle-class Hampstead. No one planned this transformation, no one intended it, no one controlled it. It was a response to the elemental forces of urban expansion, and it is tempting to visualise this response as being set in motion by a dramatic event, the arrival of a railway to open up a new residential area, or the removal of some awkward legal or personal obstacle. Belsize did not conform to any such pattern. Its development, started for minor reasons, shows rather the enormous importance of the details of property rights and arrangements, and the almost indelible impression on contemporary urban living of tenancy agreements made nearly two hundred years ago. A housing estate began to be laid out on the first of the gentry estates in 1851; but the last of them to pass to the developers, Ivy Bank, was kept up in style as a gentleman's establishment until the eve of 1914, a survival which accounts for the pocket of modern inter-war houses in the area of Perceval Avenue. Between these dates the half-dozen or so mini-parks which had been carved out of the original Chesterfield property in 1808 were themselves parcelled out, at intervals, into building plots.[1] Much of the street layout was dictated by the boundaries of these parks, just as the different layers of development and of styles which are spread over Belsize as a whole were determined by the intervals at which different owners embarked on building and by their different ideas of taste. These intervals, on which so much depended, were in their turn very largely determined by the internal mechanism of the leases under which the owners held, a mechanism which was not especially responsive to the broad general impulses towards urban expansion. Without these general impulses, without the growth of London's population in general and the growth of demand for good middle-class housing in particular, there would indeed have been no housing estates on Belsize at all. When the force of these large external factors had been filtered through the meshes of the estate and lease system, however, it was translated into actual roads and houses

[1] See above, p. 91, for the 1808 division.

at a pace which had a weak connection with the pressures of demand. In the specific local situation it was the supply of building land which appeared dominant, and the character of new residential districts was moulded by whoever and whatever controlled the release of land on to the building market.

The Dean and Chapter of Westminster were the owners of the Belsize estate but there was little they could do on their own to control its release for building purposes, since they had surrendered the bulk of a freeholder's managerial and proprietary rights to the holders of the leases for lives on the estate. The strong convention of perpetual renewal of these leases, founded on the Dean and Chapter's keen appreciation of the fat fine they received for each new life inserted when one 'dropped', made these lessees into virtual owners of their sub-estates. In law they remained leaseholders, but in the ordinary language of society, the press, or local directories they were indeed referred to as owners; their leasehold interests were so extensive that they changed hands in the property market at only 10 to 20 per cent less than equivalent freehold estates.[1] They remained undisturbed and unchallenged as reputed owners until the Dean and Chapter could see some alternative form of income to the large, but irregular, renewal fines: for the only way of winding up the leases for lives, apart from a freely negotiated treaty between lessee and Dean and Chapter, was for the Dean and Chapter to sit it out until each named life had died off, refusing to insert any new lives and receiving only the nominal fixed annual rents the while, paltry sums of the order of 3s. to 5s. an acre. Building rents furnished the alternative income, and once these began to flow the Dean and Chapter could make credible threats to refuse to add any more new lives to leases. By 1857 they were doing precisely this, 'having in view the ultimate appropriation of the land to building purposes'; though the refusal to add a new life could achieve no more than the presence of the lessee Basil Woodd at the negotiating table, since with two lives in his lease still surviving, even if on the old side, he retained valuable bargaining counters.[2] The difficulty was to get the flow of building income started.

As soon as one of the reputed owners noticed the potential building value of his property and became anxious to exploit it, the weakness in his legal powers became a serious inconvenience. He was unable to

[1] DCW RCO, 32, sale particulars of Abercrombie Villa, held on lease for three lives, 6 August 1856.
[2] Ibid., C. St John Bedford, Clerk to the Dean and Chapter, to J. J. Chalk, Secretary to the Eccles. Comm., April 1857.

grant sub-leases for a longer term than that of his own title, which ran for the no doubt considerable but still unpredictable term of the natural life of the longest liver of three named persons. The uncertain and possibly precarious nature of any building leases that could be granted under such a tenure had not bothered Edward Bliss in the 1820s.[1] It is virtually certain, however, that imperfect building leases of this kind were tolerable only for specialised, piecemeal development of the Bliss type in individual grand houses for owner-occupation or large houses put up in twos and threes as a speculative sideline; people were extremely chary of undertaking the risks of a large-scale building estate except with the security of a definite and reliable agreement such as a conventional 99-year building lease. As it happened, it would have been futile for Bliss to bother about such matters in the 1820s, for the Dean and Chapter did not then have any power to grant long building leases for any specified term of years. It was not until 1842 that this defect in the legal capacities of the holders of church lands was remedied by a leasing Act, which formed part of the administrative and financial reforms in church affairs associated with the establishment of the Ecclesiastical Commissioners.[2] This new power to grant 99-year building leases gave the Dean and Chapter an extremely important advantage in relations with their lessees, since they now had something to offer of great value in opening the way to development and its riches. But although the Dean and Chapter held the key which would unlock the treasure chest of building values, the treasure chest itself remained firmly in the possession of the lessees. The question was how, and on what terms, the two parties would agree to open it up.

In spite of the 1842 Act the first move still had to be made by one of the lessees; the Dean and Chapter might dispose, but one of the reputed owners had to propose. The first proposition did not come until 1851, and the delay suggests not only that the leasing powers were created well in advance of any practical call for them in this district, so that the incapacity had no effect in retarding development, but also that the availability of the powers was not by itself a decisive influence on the release of land for building. William Lund of Haverstock Lodge, lessee of the 45 acres which had originally gone to Forsyth in 1808, had his own independent reasons for choosing to turn his fields into a building estate in 1851. He was perhaps influenced by the beginnings of the Maitland Park development just down the road from his estate (and the parish) boundary at The Load of Hay, whose attractive leafy

1 See above, pp. 98–107.
2 Act giving leasing powers over church lands, 5 and 6 Vict., cap. 108.

villas might well have suggested the possibilities of his own property.[1] The spacious layout of Maitland Park could easily have convinced him that it was perfectly possible to mobilise an income from housing development and yet by discreet management continue to enjoy his own residence and its large grounds without interference or annoyance, an ideal way of having his cake änd eating it. The new E & WID & BJ Railway certainly weighed heavily in his decision that his property was ripe for building, for he made his proposals to the Dean and Chapter in November 1851 when the line had been open for only four months; and his building prospectus, issued early in 1852, made a particular point of the fact that the St John's Park Estate was 'close to the Hampstead Road Station of the Blackwall & Fenchurch St Railway.'[2] In this first building speculation on the Belsize estate, indeed, the opening of London's first commuter railway did play a decisive part, in the first rush of incredulous enthusiasm and optimism created by the astounding figures of its passenger traffic.[3]

Nevertheless, although the unexpected popularity of this particular railway, pouring clerks and City gentlemen in their thousands on their roundabout way to Fenchurch Street, and creating out of a line intended for the goods traffic of the docks the very concept of the suburban commuter railway, launched a wave of high expectations for the power of railways to tap a cornucopia of building values, such visions of rich new possibilities were not the only element in Lund's decision. He held the Haverstock Lodge estate under a lease for three lives granted in 1808, which his father had bought from Forsyth probably in the 1820s. In 1851 one of the three had just died, leaving the lease dependent on the lives of Sir Gilbert John Heathcote and his brother, by then aged 56 and 54 years and actuarially with only a short further expectation of life. Lund, therefore, was securely in possession but had a weak title in sore need of strengthening; otherwise the investment in his family mansion with its fine gardens and ornamental lake might shortly slip out of his hands. The Dean and Chapter, on their side, were in a position to reap financial advantage from whatever strengthening they granted but not in a position to dictate its form. It was a chance, momentary, balance of power conducive to an agreeable settlement. Instead of asking for the insertion of a new life in his lease and paying a

---

[1] The Load of Hay is now called The Noble Art, but its original name is preserved on a plaque recording its rebuilding in 1863.

[2] DCW Map 12534, The St John's Park estate, Haverstock Hill, 1852.

[3] Nearly 1·5 million passengers were carried in the last six months of 1851: Michael Robbins, *The North London Railway* (1967 ed.), p. 2.

renewal fine in the usual way, Lund proposed to turn himself into a building developer by surrendering the residue of his lease for lives in exchange for a 99-year building lease of the estate. Under this he could either build himself, or more to the point he could arrange a series of agreements and sub-leases with speculative builders who would undertake the actual construction. His offer of £500 a year as the ground rent for this lease was accepted. It was a very low ground rent, averaging only £11 an acre and not more than a third or a quarter of the going market rate in the neighbourhood, but even when their foregone future receipts from renewal fines are discounted it gave the Dean and Chapter an immediate increase of income that was perhaps tenfold. The bargain may have favoured Lund unduly; but the Ecclesiastical Commissioners, whose approval of the terms was necessary, were assured by their experienced consultant surveyor, John Clutton, that 'the proposition is an advantageous one to the Chapter and that the rent is fair taking into consideration the existing interests of Lund in the property.' That being so, the low rent is a fair indication of the surrender value of Lund's existing lease with its two surviving lives. He could look forward to clearing at least £1,000 a year for himself as his share of an ordinary ground landlord's rents, quite apart from the income he could make out of a developer's profits from the under-letting of 150 or so building plots.[1]

In addition to the building ground of 38 acres Lund retained Haverstock Lodge and about 8 acres of grounds annexed to it effectively rent-free; indeed in 1879 the fee simple of the mansion and grounds was conveyed to him in exchange for two large detached houses on Haverstock Hill, Sycamore Lodge and Anchmore, which had been built in 1872 and carried ground rents of £38.12s.0d. payable to Lund.[2] The Lodge continued as an urban country seat until the 1890s, when it was demolished and Downside Crescent was laid out in its grounds.[3] From it Lund watched over the growth of his houses, kept largely out of sight by the fall in the ground towards the Fleet valley. He intended that he should have complete control over this growth, suggesting that he should 'not be restricted in the class or value of the houses beyond a provision that he shall expend a sum of at least £ [blank] in building within the next 7 years', subject to the approval of

[1] CC File 7142, Proposals for a Building Lease to William Thomas Buller Lund, 14 November 1851; John Clutton to J. J. Chalk, 8 December 1851.

[2] Ibid., Exchange between Eccles. Comm. and W. T. B. Lund, 10 June 1879.

[3] Haverstock Lodge appears in the 1894–6 ed. of the O.S. six-inch map; by the time of the *P.O. London Directory* 1902 map Downside Crescent had been formed, but was not yet fully built up.

house plans by the Chapter's surveyor. Though unwilling to allow him quite so much freedom to do as he pleased, the conditions eventually imposed at Clutton's suggestion were so minimal as to be practically inoperative. He was required to ensure that no detached or semi-detached residence was built of less than £40 annual value, and no other dwelling house, for instance in a terrace block, of less than £20 annual value, figures which implied prime building costs in the region of £400 and £200 a house at the most. He undertook to expend at least £5,000 on building within the first seven years of the lease, and a total of £20,000 within twenty-two years.[1] For a developer with ideas of creating a distinctive and modish neighbourhood these were almost meaningless lower limits, since only houses of two to three times these values were contemplated. The one restriction which might have had a real bite was a product of the moment, when the pother over the Papal Aggression in re-establishing a Catholic episcopacy stirred the Dean and Chapter to look to their religious responsibilities: Lund covenanted that no buildings should ever be used 'for the ecclesiastical, collegiate, or other purposes of the Church of Rome.'

With this wide freedom of action Lund aspired to create a high-class district, starting by publicising the project as the St John's Park Estate, a title intended to appropriate some of the allure of St John's Wood. His plans were not particularly imaginative, and there was nothing park-like about the layout except for the views of his own Lodge grounds reserved for the houses on the east side of the future Lawn Road. But, by the simple device of using the existing field hedges to set the lines for the new roads, he avoided dull rigidity and obtained interesting informality in the curves of Parkhill, Upper Park and Lawn Roads.[2] These roads, occupying the higher ground, were intended for good-class villas on generous fifty-foot frontages with ample gaps between the pairs. The low-lying seven-acre field running up to the Fleet brook on the north-ern edge of the estate was set aside for the service area, to accommo-date 256 close-packed terrace houses and shops, and a mews of twenty stables and coach-houses, in a group of new streets. It was a not unattrac-tive venture, which perhaps deserved rather more success than it ever achieved; for after fifteen years or so of fair prosperity and impeccable reputation the district began to become rather tattered at the edges and slipped into anonymity, a decent and respectable anonymity to be sure, but one in which St John's Park was completely unremembered

[1] CC File 7142, Clutton to Chalk, 8 December 1851.
[2] DCW Map 12533, giving a slightly different layout from Map 12534, shows the close connection between field boundaries and the road system.

as any sort of definite neighbourhood with an identity of its own.

The start was propitious enough. Lund laid out the line of his new roads and made sewers, and there was a keen demand for his sites so that within less than ten years sixty or more houses had been built—reaching roughly the line of the first cross street, Tasker Road—which were more than enough to secure the whole of the ground rent due to the Chapter, leaving the entire profits of both ground landlord and developer from the remaining vacant land to be reaped by Lund. This was rapid progress for a small estate.[1] It was also substantial progress, for although the houses jostled each other on less generous plots than at first planned they were still comfortable family houses, in pairs of unobtrusively classical villas, which fetched £1,000 and more apiece.[2] Many of them, especially in Parkhill Road, were built by Richard Batterbury of Camden Town who emerged as the chief speculative builder of St John's Park with an output of around ten houses a year in good years; later on Batterbury was associated with building elsewhere in Hampstead of some architectural interest, in Hampstead Hill Gardens and in Steele's Road, but these first efforts were more solid than notable. He played some part too in Upper Park Road and Lawn Road, though here there was a medley of building interests involved, James Copp and Thomas Crofts apparently in partnership as investors, Richard Wood and William White as builders of several houses each.[3] The trouble came not from this part of the estate, but from its bottom end. Here a short stretch of estate road was constructed on the line of an ancient footpath, designed to form part of a new through road from Kentish Town to South End in the future. This, the first section of Fleet Road, was destined for a shopping street by geography, for in due course it would become a thoroughfare, and by topography, for the land was too low-lying, ill-drained, and unhealthy for the middle classes.

[1] CC File 7142, Thomas Calthorp, solicitor, to the Eccles. Comm. 29 February 1864; Clutton's report on the estate, 24 July 1871; *P.O. London Directory* 1863 map.

[2] CC File 7142. Each assignment of the head lease of a house, made on its transfer, had to be registered with the Dean and Chapter (after 1866, with the Eccles. Comm.). The assignments sometimes, but not in all cases, mention the purchase price; moreover it is not always clear if the head lease was being bought subject to an existing under-lease to the actual householder, or was being bought with vacant possession, a difference which would have affected the price paid. The figures in the text, therefore, are no more than rough guides to real market prices. In the late 1850s, and in the 1860s, assignments of houses on the Lund estate register prices in the range £850–£1,300.

[3] Ibid., various assignments. HPL Vestry Min., notices from builders of intention to make drains and to start on new buildings, 1856 onwards. Pevsner, *The Buildings of England: London*, II (1952), pp. 200–1.

The natural destiny of Fleet Road was, however, all too definite. The Fleet brook, flowing out of the Hampstead Ponds, was an open sewer used by Downshire Hill, Pond Street, and South End, and was becoming steadily more noisome when the Metropolitan Board of Works took over responsibility for London's drainage in 1856. For several years after that the Board was too preoccupied with more pressing needs for

FIGURE 2 Middle-class housing: a doctor's house in Hampstead Hill Gardens by Batterbury & Huxley, 1877

main drainage works elsewhere to have time to turn to the Fleet, so that it was not tidied away into pipes until after 1860. Meanwhile the Board endured complaints from the Mansfield Road residents in Kentish Town at the foul condition of the Fleet Sewer, and the one person who seems to have enjoyed its resources was Batchelor who happily diverted the waters over his watercress beds at Mansfield Place for an hour every morning.[1] Fleet Road, therefore, got off to a poor start with the area too smelly and unpleasant to attract the better class of shopkeepers aiming at a middle-class trade, and little demand for inferior shops since the poorer-class neighbourhoods on the old Southampton estate already had their own provisions. The street seems to have fallen at once, in default of any other demands, into tenement and lodging houses, which gave it social links with Southampton Road and Malden Road rather than with the rest of St John's Park. Having started off on the wrong foot, events conspired to push this little area downhill, not merely preventing it from becoming the useful dependency of the wealthy end of the Lund development which had been planned, but also making it into a positively baleful influence on the rest of the estate. As a start the St Pancras extension of the Midland Railway cut through the corner of the estate for the approach to the Hampstead tunnel from Gospel Oak. This inevitably cast a damper on building operations near by while there was uncertainty about the effects, between 1862 when the scheme was announced and 1866 when the line was finished. Moreover, with the tunnel starting right beside Parkhill Road, building values in the vicinity were more permanently damaged since builders still believed that better-class people would never consent to live on top of a railway, even if the houses could withstand the vibration; where one railway company gave promise of riches another took away.[2]

Much worse was to come. Lying between Lund's section of Fleet Road and Pond Street, and stretching up to the Haverstock Hill road, were several fields belonging to the Winfield family, about sixteen acres altogether, known as the Bartrams. At the junction of Pond Street and Haverstock Hill there was a small open space, Hampstead Green, and near this village green on the London side were several large Georgian houses which were perhaps the most desirable residences in

---

[1] MBW Min., 22 May 1857, p. 246; 14 May 1858, p. 482; 17 August 1860, p. 622.

[2] HLRO Midland Railway London Extension, 26 and 27 Vict. cap. lxxiv, Plan and Book of Reference, Session 1863; Batterbury, as a lessee, returned his 'dissent' to the scheme.

the whole of Hampstead at this period for people of unostentatious quality. The residents at the time included Sir Francis Palgrave, the Keeper of the Records; Sidney Godolphin Osborne, nephew of the Duke of Leeds, Dorsetshire parson, and sympathetic observer of the hardships of agricultural labourers who publicised their case from the 1840s through to Joseph Arch's 'revolt of the fields' in the 1870s; and Sir Rowland Hill of the penny post. There were no other men of such public distinction in the Hampstead of the middle years of the century, and they made the Green into the centre of local excellence.[1] Behind them, however, lay the Bartrams in four or five untouched paddocks and meadows; in 1869 the recently formed Metropolitan Asylums Board cast its eye on this handy open space and obtained leave to erect three large fever wards and some administrative offices, all in wooden buildings, as part of its preparation of temporary accommodation to deal with epidemics.[2] The emergency came all too quickly with a serious outbreak of small pox in the autumn of 1870; the sheds at the Bartrams were hastily extended, and were reinforced by the removal of similar huts from the Fever Hospital in Liverpool Road, Islington, until the fields were crowded with fever sheds and their hundreds of smallpox patients from all parts of northern London.[3] Apart from the initial step in 1869, when no time limit was imposed on the permitted stay of the temporary wards, all the sheds were put up on condition that they should be removed within twelve months. But when the time came all the beds were full, all the Asylums Board's other smallpox hospitals were overcrowded, and the wards at the Bartrams had to be allowed to stay.[4]

Parochialism inevitably rose to the occasion, for although Hampstead residents could appreciate as well as anyone that smallpox had to be dealt with and that its victims had to be isolated and looked after, they could not see why they should harbour pestilential fellow-Londoners in their midst. Local committees were formed to obtain the removal of the smallpox hospital, pressure and influence were applied, alternative sites more remote from habitation, or at least remote from residences

[1] Ibid., for residents in 1863. Palgrave was there in 1838, holding a lease from Samuel Ware: GLCRO Hampstead Tithe Apportionment. For S. G. Osborne's activities see *Report of the Special Poor Law Commissioners on the Employment of Women and Children in Agriculture*, Parl. Papers, 1843 (510), p. 76.

[2] MBW Min., 17 December 1869, p. 1316.

[3] Ibid., 9 December 1870, p. 723; 13 and 27 January, 5 May 1871, pp. 58, 174, 627.

[4] Ibid., 22 December 1871.

of quality, were suggested. All to little avail. What had begun as a temporary overflow hospital became a permanent hospital area, its use for smallpox patients restricted after 1881 but nevertheless the site for the North-Western Fever Hospital, and in the 1970s the site for the new Royal Free Hospital.[1] The panic and dread aroused by smallpox, and the not unfounded fears that a fever hospital would infect the local inhabitants, make the vehement reaction perfectly understandable. Since it was widely believed to be a threat to the reputation, amenities, and health of the district, the hospital was a bitter blow to the building prospects and property values of the neighbourhood. The very real shanty town of sprawling fever sheds on the Bartrams was a much more serious threat to Hampstead's attractions than the non-existent phantom shanty town on the Heath which excited so much attention at the same date.[2] Lund was the first to feel smallpox's withering effects, as its presence at once threw a blight over the whole northern end of his estate and cast its damaging influence back up Lawn Road and Upper Park Road. As Fleet Road was still a private estate road he built a barrier across it to stop the pox waggons coming that way to the hospital; it succeeded in annoying everyone else by forcing the fever traffic to use the far smarter Haverstock Hill, but it was completely ineffectual in keeping the property-contamination at bay.[3] All fresh building stopped because the scare made houses unsaleable, until the smallpox patients were removed in 1872. Their replacement by imbeciles made only a marginal improvement in the situation, and in any case the smallpox cases were back again in 1876 in the next outbreak. This made a complete mess of the plans for the Fleet Road end of Lund's estate, and effectively kept the Dean and Chapter's adjoining estate to the north, South End Farm, out of the building market for nearly twenty years. It also undermined the standing of a fair portion of the existing development of the St John's Park estate, and by pushing it out of middle-class acceptability ensured that residents, house agents, and proprietor all preferred to forget the by then embarrassingly pretentious title.

The highly sensitive nature of the status of the estate, and the shifts which were suggested to preserve it from sliding downhill, were clearly shown in a complaint to the Dean and Chapter from a householder in Upper Park Road, on the eve of the smallpox invasion in 1869. Having

[1] See below, pp. 357–9, for the Smallpox Hospital agitation.
[2] See above, pp. 191–2.
[3] CC File 62499, T. E. Gibb to Eccles. Comm., 6 June 1885, discusses the history of Lund's barrier. It was removed in 1881.

bought his house in 1865 as a family residence in a respectable middle-class road he was outraged to find that:[1]

> Recently there has been erected a few hundred feet lower down this Road some houses of an inferior description with shops . . . and within sight of a flaring Public House or Gin Palace, and to make matters worse the parochial authorities have named the part of the road in which these wretched shops are erected, '*Upper* Park Road', thus identifying us in name. I have written to the Vestry urging it being called *Lower* Park Road or any other name than the present, but as yet without result. I have also asked Mr Lund . . . to assist me, but he does not seem disposed to do so. I therefore as a last resource apply . . . to the Dean and Chapter and ask them . . . to have these shops converted into private houses or the name changed . . . The older houses are already greatly deteriorated in value and will be still more so if these shops are opened as being in Upper Park Road, and after expending a large sum of money in purchasing, furnishing, and fitting up this house it will be very annoying to be driven away.

The Dean and Chapter took no notice of this, since there was nothing they could do to halt a slide which had evidently already begun. It shortly became much steeper, with lower-middle- and working-class multiple occupation of many of the villas towards the northern end of this and Parkhill Road, as the family men were scared off by the hospital. Another Upper Park Road resident recorded the bottom of this slide in 1893:[2]

> The whole of this road has been greatly lessened in value by the abominable way in which the houses at the north end have been let, viz. in tenements to dirty and objectionable people. [On which an office note commented:] The E.C. cannot in a building lease stop the letting of houses in lodgings . . . Probably the Smallpox Hospital close by is responsible at any rate in part for the depreciation of the neighbourhood.

What had started with high hopes in 1851 ended, not in disaster, but in an untidy confusion as the popular dread and mistrust of smallpox and hospitals allowed some lower-class tenants to infiltrate some middle-class housing.

[1] CC File 7142, N. S. Steinberg, 52 Upper Park Road, to C. St J. Bedford, 22 October 1869.
[2] Ibid., H. W. Wreatmore, solicitor, 27 Upper Park Road, to Eccles. Comm., 9 May 1893.

The next couple of mini-parks on Belsize to be transformed into building estates, by contrast, never faltered in their status. Started in the same year, 1853, Rosslyn Park and Belsize Park followed very different paths and styles but reached the same goal of undisputed acceptability, and more than a touch of luxury and charm. The palm perhaps belongs to Belsize Park, the very centrepiece of the Dean and Chapter's estate; but together the two ventures dominated development in the 1860s and—if it was ever in doubt—set the whole course for the growth of modern urban Hampstead into a prosperous community and coveted postal address. The two mini-parks were tenurially alike, and in both cases Lund's example was followed by the existing lessees using the leverage of their lifehold stake to convert themselves into property developers. One, however, was a non-resident who decided to pull down his mansion house forthwith and go straight ahead with the comprehensive planning of his estate as a unified housing development. The other decided to keep his residence, either for himself or for letting, and to proceed gradually with more piecemeal exploitation of the fringes of the property. From these decisions sprang the divergence in the histories of the two districts.

Charles Palmer, a solicitor practising in Bedford Row, had bought the head-lease of Belsize Park in 1841; in the next few years it was apparently impossible to find a suitable tenant for Belsize House, so that by 1853 he was anxious to turn his investment to account and get rid of the old house which had become a white elephant. He, at least, seems to have been quite indifferent to the arrival of railways to serve Hampstead. For although the old grand avenue to the House was preserved, to become much later the modern Belsize Avenue, possession of it was resumed by the Dean and Chapter and Palmer put a temporary barrier between his new roads and the avenue. The avenue, however, was the link with Hampstead Road and the railway station. Palmer chose to turn his back on this, and to take instead Spencer Perceval's old route across the fields towards Westminster as his line of advance, grafting his road structure into the railwayless Finchley Road and Swiss Cottage, where, however, horse bus services were to hand.[1]

It is impossible to say why his plans came to the surface at this precise moment, apart from speculating that both the local and the general metropolitan situation, with building activities booming, made this a good time to launch a building scheme. But although he was not pushed into making his proposal by the mechanics of his lease, as Lund had been by the dropping of a life, they certainly contributed both to the

[1] See above, p. 252.

timing and to the terms of the proposal. All the three lives in Palmer's lease who had been selected by James Abel in 1808—Henry and Edward Harvey, and young Henry Perceval—were still living in 1853; but with ages of 61, 54, and 54 there was a high risk that any or all of them might drop very shortly. Palmer was firmly in possession of his estate and no one else could have developed it without first buying him out; but at the same time its value was being rapidly eroded as the lives became increasingly frail, and it was very much in Palmer's interest to convert his tenure into something more durable and marketable. The short expectation of the three ageing lives accounts also for the relatively high ground rent of £1,100 which Palmer was ready to offer for a 99-year building lease of the forty acres which he proposed to take. At £27.10s.0d. an acre this was not far short of a full market rate, and was at the least three-quarters of the going price. Accepted without comment by the Ecclesiastical Commissioners' surveyor as a fair offer, it represented a surprising advance on the ground rent given by Lund when his vested interest, with only two surviving lives in his old lease, had been much weaker. Either the Dean and Chapter had been tricked by Lund, or their initial building agreement had been a form of loss-leader whose early success made a smart increase in rent possible from the next agreement.[1]

This explanation is rather blown upon, as will be seen, by the low ground rent of about £10 an acre which was settled for Rosslyn Park later in the same year; but Palmer was still well satisfied with his bargain. His original plans, though greatly modified in the execution, were much more ambitious, and more formal, than Lund's ideas for St John's Park; and many traces of them survive in present-day Belsize. Within the confines of the old park walls and the neck of fields which joined them to Swiss Cottage alongside the New College (opened in 1851 as a pioneer training college for Dissenting ministers) he planned to plant a self-contained community of the highest quality. The central feature was to be a secluded, elongated, square leading to ornamental lakes at the south-eastern end, on the site of the present Lancaster Drive, thriftily preserved from the grounds of the old park. The garden island of the square was to house those essential features of a socially and commercially successful estate, a church and a public house. The approaches to the square from the outside world from College

[1] CC File 7143, Heads of Proposed Agreement with Palmer, 17 January 1853; Report by Cluttons, 17 March 1853. The original, 1808, Belsize Park estate was 45 acres, but in 1853 the Dean and Chapter resumed possession of 5 acres along with the Avenue.

Crescent were to be developed in blocks of terrace housing with stabling behind, to provide for the service and commercial needs of the residents. Otherwise the outside world was to be kept at arm's length, the seclusion of the residents in the square being guaranteed by sealing them off with mews blocks along three sides of the old boundary walls; on the fourth side, to the north-west, the boundary was Belsize Lane, but although this ancient way could not be blocked off it was but a farm track and lovers' lane which would not seriously compromise the peace of the square. Exclusiveness thus secured, graciousness was to be attained through well-spaced development at a density of about five houses to the acre.[1]

Twentieth-century Belsize residents may well regret that the original plan to have no through communications on the estate was quickly abandoned, though for the building prospects of the rest of the Dean and Chapter's lands in the nineteenth century it was fortunate that this was so: for the price of excluding modern traffic might well have been the sterilisation of much adjoining 'back-land' through lack of access roads. Deviations from the plan were chiefly the work of Daniel Tidey, who emerged as the master builder and main creator of Belsize. Acquiring the main takes under Palmer's agreement, he modified much of the strategy and the detail of the scheme during the 1850s. Above all however, Tidey himself became the titular developer of the adjoining fields to the south-east, once part of Bliss's Haverstock Hill estate, in 1864, whereupon it became his interest to extend the Belsize Park roads and connect them with Englands Lane.[2] As a consequence Belsize Park Gardens (called St Margarets Road when first built), instead of being a cul-de-sac forming an arm of an outer square enclosing the inner Belsize Square, was extended to the Dean and Chapter's boundary and an agreement was made with Eton College to carry it on for a few hundred yards to join Englands Lane; and the northern leg of Belsize Square itself, instead of ending in a lake, was projected, as Lambolle Road, right up to the Chapter's frontier demarcated by the handsome news of Lambolle Place. The result of these radical changes in the intended layout is that although the boundaries of the Chapter's property can still be clearly detected—in the line of Lancaster Grove and Lambolle Place, and in the sharp kink in Belsize Park Gardens where it crosses into Eton territory—the once sharp outline of the original Belsize Park can be only faintly discerned underlying the modern map: the back fences of the gardens on the north side of Belsize Park Gardens and the

1 Ibid., Plan 215 of land agreed to be leased to Palmer, January 1853.
2 See below, p. 286.

south side of Lancaster Grove, and the line of Lancaster Drive, are all that survive of the park walls and ha-ha.

Belsize House itself left no imprint on the urban landscape. Standing in the northern corner of the park, on the axis of the avenue, it got in the way of the designs for the district and was speedily demolished. Its site became the road junction of Belsize Avenue, Belsize Park, and Belsize Park Gardens; and it was not inappropriate that the new village of Belsize developed hard by, as the shopping centre of the neighbourhood. By the time this happened, in the 1860s, Daniel Tidey had pretty much taken control of the physical development of the estate and imposed his commercial modifications on Palmer's first designs, among which was this relocation of the service quarter. No building could begin until late in 1854 because the lawyers' work in preparing the head-lease took an unusually long time. By then, since he had become liable to pay the full ground rent of £1,100 a year from Lady Day 1853, Palmer was exceedingly anxious to find some builders and get some houses on the ground as rapidly as possible in order to begin to cover his outgoings.[1] Hence he was in no position to press his notions against those of the builders, whose business sense indicated that in the short run the quickest and largest gains were to be got from starting good-quality building at the Swiss Cottage end, building their way villa by villa towards the projected square. By the summer of 1855 Palmer was nearly £2,000 in arrears with his rent, and was happy to have fourteen houses practically finished and bringing him some income, even though they used the existing Belsize Lane for their frontage.[2] Financial pressure therefore forced the abandonment of the plan to put the service quarter of the estate in this section, and Belsize Lane and Belsize Park (originally called College Road) were launched as streets with sub-

---

[1] CC File 7143, G. G. Vincent, Chapter Clerk, to J. J. Chalk, 4 September 1854, with the draft of the lease. In their early building leases the Dean and Chapter exacted the full ground rent from the first day, unlike later practice, and practice on other estates, under which the rent due increased in annual instalments over the first five or more years of the agreement until the full agreed rent was reached. This initial liability to full rent meant that lessees like Lund or Palmer were in effect paying a higher ground rent than that indicated by a simple calculation on the basis of acreage.

[2] Ibid., Murray & Calthorp, solicitors to the Eccles. Comm., to J. J. Chalk, 9 August 1855. One of the legal difficulties in this early building agreement was that the Dean and Chapter proposed to grant a formal 99-year lease to Palmer of the entire area in a single document. This was an inflexible arrangement, and Palmer's title was made more readily negotiable with builders by a Supplemental Agreement in 1855, which converted his lease into the more usual form of building agreement, under which the Dean and Chapter undertook to grant a separate formal 99-year lease for each individual

stantial middle-class villas. It was a lucky twist of fortune for the Maryon Wilson property which ran up to Belsize Lane, for it meant that a quarter of a century later Fitzjohn's Avenue could start from a solidly respectable base when its prospects might otherwise have been jeopardised by taking its departure from a lower-class district.

Several builders were involved in these early operations, and among them Daniel Tidey made his entrance to Belsize with a couple of houses in College Crescent. He quickly found that the area answered well, and in 1856 he began to form Buckland Crescent, where his Buckland Villas earned him a reputation as a builder of large town houses of inoffensive classical form, with porticoes which were just showy enough to indicate the status of the residents in the carriage class, and of reasonably sound construction. With this start he found that he could quite readily raise the credit for the expansion of his operations, and within another year or two he had become the principal undertaker of all works under Palmer's lease, the true architect of Belsize Park. As with so many of the nineteenth-century builders, many of them wealthy and important men in their day, Tidey remains unknown and virtually unknowable, coming from nowhere and, when he went bankrupt in 1870, going to nowhere, leaving no trace at all save for the most lasting and visible trace of all, his houses. He moved at once, as was the habit of many of the big speculative builders, into one of his own houses, and conducted his business from Buckland Crescent. He gained sufficient standing as an entrepreneur for the Dean and Chapter to make agreements direct with him as principal in 1864 and 1865. He operated largely on credit, as was usual, secured by mortgages of the houses as each was completed to the bare carcase stage. His chief creditors were Palmer, Palmer & Bull, the firm of Bloomsbury solicitors to which Charles Palmer belonged; Bowker, Peake & Bird, another firm of Bloomsbury solicitors which developed extensive Hampstead interests; and Farebrother, Clark & Lye, one of the largest firms of surveyors and estate agents in London, and the home of F. J. Clark who became agent for the Maryon Wilson estate. It is impossible to say whose money these were lending, but it is likely that a high proportion of it was for clients, who found such firms in the property professions useful financial middlemen when the means of investment in property were only just beginning to be institutionalised through building societies and property companies. Tidey's borrowings

---

house as it was completed, to whomever Palmer should name as lessee (the actual builder, or the builder's mortgagee), with the 99 years counting from March 1853 in every case.

were extensive, so extensive that he failed in 1870, when he allowed his position to become too illiquid. So extensive also that he must have been building in several other districts as well as Belsize; for against his debts of £341,136 he held assets in houses with an estimated value of £509,141, and it would be a generous estimate which put as much as two-fifths of these in Belsize.[1]

A business of this magnitude lifted Tidey clean out of the class of petty builders who ran up two or three houses in a street and then moved on. In the second half of the 1860s, when he was operating on two adjoining takes in his own name as well as on Palmer's tract, he was able to organise the building of as many as fifty houses in a year; and there were few years after 1856 when his annual output fell below fifteen houses.[2] This, moreover, was presumably only a portion of his total building business in London, though it is not at present known where else he had interests. Activities on this scale were some guarantee of quality, for it was only the small men in the building trade with their one-man firms who could afford the fly-by-night tactics of shoddy work and manage to scrape a living by palming off jerry-built houses on unsuspecting purchasers. A man like Tidey, staying in business in the same district and same street for year after year, had to establish and guard a reputation for providing an article of reasonable reliability and workmanship, and value for money. He may not have indulged in frills, and he may not have been adventurous, but the solid quality of his work made his houses popular at the time and ensured the continued attraction of Belsize stucco-land more than a century later. The market he aimed at was the wealthy professional and commercial middle class, wanting 8- or 10-bedroom houses of proven acceptability, and able to pay £1,000 to £1,500 or rents of £100 to £150 for them.[3] Commonly, indeed, such families rented their houses on 5- or 7-year leases, and the actual house-owners were absentee landlords who bought the long

[1] Ibid. Tidey's activities, and the identity of his creditors, can be reconstructed from the details of the leases granted; and from occasional letters from his solicitors, e.g. Langley & Gibbon to Eccles. Comm., 8 June 1866. Reports of his bankruptcy, *The Times*, 12 February and 11 March 1870. By then he had perhaps built over 250 houses in Belsize and his cumulative investment might have totalled a quarter of a million pounds; but he had already parted with all his interest in many of these houses on outright sales, though in many others he retained an interest as sub-lessee in receipt of an 'improved ground rent'.

[2] CC Files 7143, 33405, 32878, record of leases granted to Tidey and his creditors. It is more than likely that he did not build all 'his' houses with his own labour force, but sub-contracted an unknown proportion.

[3] Ibid., figures for purchase prices and rack rentals from assignments registered.

leaseholds of single houses or groups of houses as investments, some-times buying outright and becoming direct lessees from the Dean and Chapter, sometimes buying an under-lease from Tidey and paying him an 'improved' ground rent which might be several times the ground rent owed by Tidey himself. The base of the pyramid of legal and financial interests in any house was, however, the occupier who paid the full rent from which each person further up the chain deducted his share.

These residents were from a slightly higher and smarter layer of the middle class than that catered for by Samuel Cuming's scheme on the Chalcots estate, as befitted the greater elevation of Belsize: the houses were rather larger, in room size more than in numbers of rooms, and rather more horses and carriages were expected. They were not, how-ever, from the very smartest layer, witness the subdued convention-ality of the classical shapes, large porticoes, pedimented windows, and lavish stucco which were Tidey's stock-in-trade. This, by the 1850s and 1860s, was the taste of the previous generation and its continued em-ployment was a form of safe conservatism appealing to those who were not secure enough socially to dare to risk being fashionable by using their houses to set a trend, but who needed their houses to confirm their own status. Gardens and horses clearly show the limits of gran-deur. In 1857 Tidey tried to raise the attractions of Buckland Villas to West End standards by setting aside a couple of acres which the lie of field boundaries south of Lancaster Grove made awkward for other uses, as an ornamental garden for the residents. But the residents saw no benefit in having such a garden and were unable to agree on any arrangements for sharing its upkeep, so that this piece of upper-class embellishment was quickly allowed to lapse.[1] More telling was the abandonment of the original intention of the 1853 scheme to provide stabling on a lavish scale, the plan allowing for enough mews blocks to supply one stable or coach-house for every pair of villas. The people who moved into Belsize turned out to have far more modest needs. In terms of wealth many of them must have qualified as members of the carriage trade, with incomes topping £1,000 a year; but comparatively few seem to have belonged to the carriage-owning class. Until 1864, by which time there were more than 100 families living on the Belsize Park estate, only a single block of a dozen or so stables, on the south side of Belsize Lane had been built on the property, and the land initially

---

[1] CC File 7143, Murray & Calthorp to J. J. Chalk, 21 January 1857. Much of this garden was later used for Crossfield Road and Strathray Gardens, pro-viding connections with the Eton estate.

earmarked for mews and quarters for horse servants had largely been appropriated for villas. The great majority of the residents, in other words, must have relied on hiring their horses and carriages at need from jobmasters, of whom there was a colony outside the estate on the far side of the Finchley Road.

The developers had plainly been taken by surprise by the appearance of affluent householders who were not carriage-owners. In part this suggests that the residents who materialised were not quite so wealthy as had been hoped. In the main, however, it suggests that at a given income level and social level carriage-ownership was becoming less feasible and less desirable as a result of the increasing unpleasantness of traffic congestion in London on the one hand, and the increasing convenience of commercial transport by bus, cab, or private hire on the other. After 1864 the ratio between households and stabling shifted in favour of the horses as Tidey increased the proportion of building land which he used for mews. He did this on his two new takes. In 1864 the Dean and Chapter bought out Bliss's remaining lifehold interest in the two fields which lay behind his Haverstock Hill houses, and then granted these twenty-four acres to Tidey on a 99-year building agreement.[1] In the narrow Home Field, abutting on Englands Lane and squeezed between Bliss on one side and Eton College land on the other, he just managed to fit in the elongated oval of Primrose Gardens (originally called Stanley Gardens), connecting them with an extension of Bliss's Haverstock Terrace, renamed Belsize Grove. The Englands Lane frontage was devoted to shops and a public house, and immediately behind them was built the considerable range of Elizabeth Mews, clearly intended to serve houses farther away than Primrose Gardens since these were not so grand as the Belsize Park Gardens. The larger Pit Field stretched across to the old park boundaries and supplied the space for the extension of Belsize Park Gardens, Lambolle Road, and Lancaster Grove, which were terminated by the extensive Lambolle and Lancaster Mews running along the estate boundary.

Ultimately, though not all within Tidey's time, these two areas provided more than fifty sets of stables. Many more again were eventually built on the north-western edge of Belsize Park. Here, in a complicated exchange with Basil Woodd of Hillfield House in 1857, the Dean and Chapter regained full possession of the 14-acre Belsize House estate to the north-west of Belsize Lane. Most of this continued to be tenanted as a large mansion and park, but a triangular meadow of $4\frac{1}{2}$ acres was

[1] CC File 30177, Report by H. A. Hunt, surveyor to the Dean and Chapter, 7 January 1864. And see below, p. 286.

detached and let to Tidey on a building agreement in 1865.[1] Partly because of the irregular shape and cramped nature of the site, and partly because he needed to develop a small commercial area for his building estate somewhere, Tidey used this piece of land for some tightly packed work. One reasonable street, Belsize Crescent (originally Prince Consort Road) was fitted in, a curve leading only to a footpath behind Rosslyn House for many years; though even here the houses were below his usual standard of finish, and were cramped. For the rest, the curving boundary against the Maryon Wilson estate was used as the line of Daleham Mews, leaving a space which was filled in with Baynes and Belsize Park Mews; and the footpath from Belsize Lane to the Conduit Wells, which divided Tidey's field from the Belsize House grounds, was used unaltered and unwidened as an alley leading to Princess Mews, though it was dignified with the name of Upper Belsize Terrace. The little complex was completed, again not all under Tidey, with shops on part of the Belsize Lane frontage and in Belsize Place (originally Prince Arthur Road), and more stabling in Belsize Mews. It was no doubt a useful village for the customers and employers coming from the grand houses, handy without being obtrusive. But it was nevertheless an untidy, crowded, messy little complex, smelly to boot with all the horses, and it introduced a pocket which has always remained an alien element in the sedate residential roads surrounding it.

When Belsize village was finished, in the 1870s, it contributed another 50 or 60 stables to the resources of the enlarged Belsize Park or Tidey Town, so that there were eventually nearly 120 stables in all. This was a ratio of nearly one stable to every four houses, well below the original target it is true but still far above the rate on the Chalcots, Eyre, or Upton estates; it was indeed the best-horsed part of Hampstead outside the country seats and gentlemen's houses of the old town. The odd thing was that it became so only when the best part, getting on for two-thirds, of the residential development had already been finished. Yet the purchasers and tenants kept on coming, unchecked by the prospect that they would be extremely unlikely to find any private stabling to go with their houses; indeed in the first decade of Belsize Park it would have been literally impossible to find a private coach-house on the estate. Clearly the residents did not belong to the class which demanded that its houses have mews attached; and, when the stabling was built, it is hard to believe that this was a response to an upgrading of the district into the carriage-owning class. When it was

---

[1] CC File 32878, J. Clutton's report to J. J. Chalk, 11 April 1865. And see below, p. 287.

provided some of the stabling, it is true, in Lambolle Mews, was available for private occupation by neighbouring householders; but the major part seems always to have been let to commercial users in the horse trade. The residents, it seems, relied on hiring from jobmasters; what happened was not an improvement in the wealth and class of the Belsize citizens, but the crossing of a threshold in their total numbers, beyond which it became inconvenient to have to hire at a distance and profitable for jobmasters and cab owners to have premises on the spot.[1]

In Charles Booth's time, nevertheless, everything that Tidey had built, apart from the stable areas, naturally, was coloured pure gold to denote the wealthiest quarters inhabited by the upper and upper-middle classes; the only exception, curiously enough, was Belsize Square itself, which was in red for the simply 'well-to-do middle class'.[2] There is no reason to suppose that the social character of the district had altered between the time of its building and 1889; certainly any detectable change had not been upward. Hence here was proof that a housing project for the wealthy by the 1860s no longer needed a private stable to go with nearly every house, indeed no longer needed much in the way of private stabling at all. It was among the first rich neighbourhoods in London to show this; Belgravia, Bayswater, and Kensington which developed just before or at the same time as Belsize were all equipped with extensive stabling attached to every square, place, terrace, or crescent. Belsize marked the beginning of a period in which the private transport of carriage-owning was no longer a requisite of high social standing. It was a change in social habits which decreased the opportunities of employment for male servants at the time, and diminished the nuisance of flies and the problem of fly-borne diseases in the curtilage of the homes of the wealthy; while it increased the problems of street-parking for future generations, when they found few stables to convert and no space to add garages to their houses.

Although the development ultimately brought ruin to its chief creator, Tidey, it also brought gold to its passive developer, Charles Palmer. Such rapid progress was made that by early 1862, after little more than six years of actual building, enough houses (93 of them) had been erected and disposed of on under-leases to secure all but £5 of the total ground rent of £1,111 due to the Dean and Chapter. The remaining £5 a year was due from uncovered land which Palmer reckoned was sufficient for a further 100 houses, which would thus carry an average ground rent of a shilling a house. His firm, 'without dwelling on the

[1] *Hampstead and Highgate Directory*, 1885.
[2] Booth's Map of London Poverty, 1889, north-west sheet.

many inconveniences and waste of property to all interests from nominal ground rents', proposed to purchase the reversion to the uncovered land, that is its freehold, for £300 'equivalent to about 60 years purchase'.[1] This would have been a bargain for the Dean and Chapter, but it was declined; houses continued to go up with ground rents of one shilling, and from 1868 of twopence, awkward trifles which the Chapter tolerated out of sloth rather than any premonition of the unimaginable value of the reversion of the houses themselves in 1952. It was, whichever way it went, a bargain for Palmer and his partners. Houses in Belsize Park Gardens built in 1864, for which sixpence a house ground rent was paid to the Dean and Chapter, were underleased to Tidey, their builder, at 'improved ground rents' of £30 a house.[2] At that sort of rate the 130 or so houses which were in the event built after 1862 yielded Palmer and his associates an income of nearly £4,000 a year for which they had no outlay to make at all; their developer's profit on the first 93 houses—the difference between the 'improved ground rent' they charged for the site and the 'head ground rent' due to the Dean and Chapter—seems to have been in the range £5 – £10 per house, perhaps £700 or so a year.[3] The developer's income from the forty acres of building land thus in the end reached something like £4,500 or more a year, though it was not until the last house was finished in 1880 that it reached the full amount. To earn this Palmer probably needed to make a relatively small investment in laying out the roads and sewers, since part of this expense was likely to be borne by Tidey; he may have contributed to the costs of the estate church; and for the first five or six years of his lease he had to find the Dean and Chapter's rent while little income was being earned by the estate. It was a small price to pay; the rewards of an intermediary in the property business were handsome indeed.

Few perhaps would say that St Peter's Church was handsome, an example of suburban gothic so undistinguished that it is not so much as noticed by Pevsner.[4] Its chief merit was that it went up rapidly, started almost as soon as the first houses and consecrated in 1869; the

[1] CC File 7143, Palmer, Palmer & Bull to J. J. Chalk, 27 March 1862.

[2] Ibid., leases granted in 1864, for a total of 37 houses in Belsize Park Gardens; assignment of 8 of these, quoting the 'improved ground rents', 27 June 1870.

[3] Evidence is scanty, but a Statement of ground rents held by Samuel Lahee deceased, 3 February 1877, ibid., details the 'improved ground rents' of 29 houses in Buckland Crescent at £10–£19 a house, where the head rents were £2–£10; and of the Belsize Park Tavern (head rent £10, 'improved ground rent' £40). The estimate in the text is a conservative one.

[4] Pevsner, op. cit., II, 185–9. The architect was J. P. St Aubyn; the church cost £9,000.

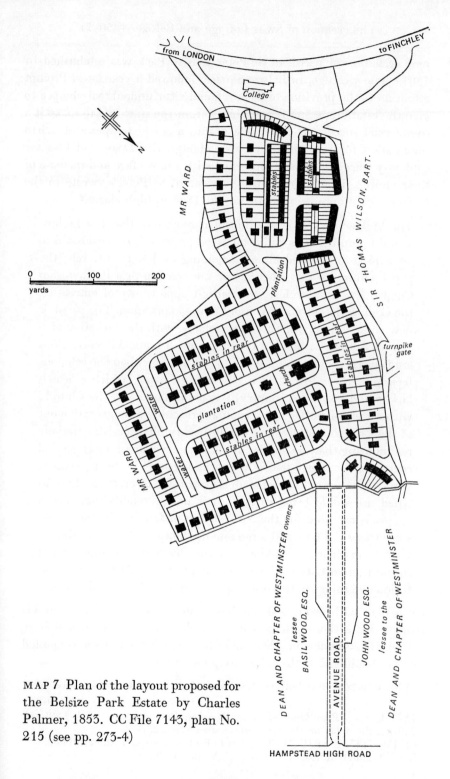

from LONDON

to FINCHLEY

College

MR WARD

stables

stables

stables

SIR THOMAS WILSON. BART.

plantation

turnpike gate

stables in rear

water

stables in rear

plantation

church

stables in rear

water

stables in rear

MR WARD

0   100   200
yards

N

DEAN AND CHAPTER OF WESTMINSTER owners

lessee
BASIL WOOD, ESQ.

AVENUE ROAD.

JOHN WOOD ESQ.

lessee to the
DEAN AND CHAPTER OF WESTMINSTER

HAMPSTEAD HIGH ROAD

MAP 7 Plan of the layout proposed for the Belsize Park Estate by Charles Palmer, 1853. CC File 7143, plan No. 215 (see pp. 273-4)

new ecclesiastical parish of St Peter Belsize Park was established in 1861.[1] The vicarage, in Belsize Square, followed a year later. Prompt attention to the provision of a church and vicar undoubtedly helped to give the estate tone and respectability from the start and to make it a commercial success. It also made it into a successful piece of urban colonisation for the Anglican cause, though the Dean and Chapter evidently were not greatly concerned with the welfare and increase of their church. F. W. Tremlett, the vicar of St Peter's, wrote to the Ecclesiastical Commissioners in August 1868 in high alarm.[2]

> The builder on this estate informed me today that the Ecclesiastical Commissioners had been asked to grant him permission to let a piece of ground almost adjoining St Peter's Church (the parish church of this District) for the erection of a Presbyterian Chapel. I take, therefore, the earliest opportunity of entreating the Commissioners not to consent to the application. The parish is now most united. All the householders, with the exception of 6 Jews, 2 Roman Catholics, 1 Congregationalist, and 3 Presbyterians are Church people, and it would be an outrage upon the religious feeling of these to put up a Dissenting Chapel (which a Scotch kirk would be in this country) 9 doors distant from the Church, with a view of gathering by popular preaching a congregation out of the Church and dividing our bitherto united parish—the sole reason being that the builder might get a few pounds more ground rent than the 5 or 6 houses which he is bound by his agreement with the Dean and Chapter of Westminster to erect on the proposed site would bring in . . . It is not pretended that such a chapel is required for the 3 Presbyterian families in the parish since there is a new and large one in Hampstead not 10 minutes walk from their doors. Moreover the Presbyterians might let it to the Roman Catholics or to the Mormons, and very great confusion and injury to this essentially Church parish would ensue.

For a man with about 300 families in his parish Tremlett knew his people with a thoroughness which an election manager would have envied. He also knew his Dean and Chapter, for when it was suggested that he should look to them for action he countered:[3]

I have no reason to believe, however, that the Dean and Chapter of

---

[1] *1871 Census, Population of New Parishes*, Parl. Papers, 1872, LXVI (1), 240; cf. the delay on the Eton estate, above, pp. 227–8.
[2] CC File 7143, Revd. F. W. Tremlett to Eccles. Comm., 5 August 1868.
[3] Ibid., Tremlett to Eccles. Comm., 13 August 1868.

Westminster feel any interest in the welfare of the Church in this parish, notwithstanding they are the owners of the land and the patron of the living. More than three years ago I wrote a letter to the Chapter asking whether they could grant a site for an additional church seeing that they had built a much larger number of houses than was at first contemplated; because if so, I would make arrangements to get one built. I have received no answer to that letter yet, but this is not a matter of surprise to me as I am not without some previous experience of the alacrity of the Chapter's officials . . . It is therefore to the Commissioners that we must look for protection for the interests of the Church . . .

The Commissioners made no more reply to this entreaty than the Dean and Chapter had done, apparently holding that zeal for the Church did not require them to go to the length of denying space for other Protestants to profess their faith. As it happened no chapel was built in Belsize even in the absence of a landlord's veto, presumably because the demand for one was so small; and Tremlett's lively fears of his own inability to withstand the competition of some 'popular preaching' were not put to the test. Belsize managed very well, also, without an additional church; the enlarged congregation was accommodated by additions to St Peter's, made in 1875.[1] The Maryon Wilson estate, however, found a site at the foot of the Conduit Fields, on the spot where Fitzjohn's Avenue now meets Belsize Lane, for a temporary church in a wooden hut which was replaced by Trinity Church, Finchley Road, in 1872; its informal 'parish' must have lain in Belsize and Swiss Cottage, since the Maryon Wilson estate had no residents at all. It may have been a pity for Belsize Square that it did not become the scene of sectarian rivalry, for some such spark of life might have preserved it as a true square with central gardens, as a meeting place and focal point for the new community. As it was the idea of formal public gardens clearly did not answer any better here than at Buckland Crescent, and Tidey very soon built over the south-eastern end of the square, leaving only a small open patch between the church and vicarage.

Business rather than religious considerations were uppermost in the

1 DCW RCO 32, F. W. Tremlett to Dean and Chapter, 28 June 1875. The additions were by the original architect, J. P. St Aubyn. The cost of £2,500 was largely met by subscriptions from the congregation, which spread outside Belsize Park to Alexandra Road, Fairfax Road, Adamson Road, Adelaide Road, Lawn Road, and Upper Park Road. The parish, of 114 acres, was not exclusively Dean and Chapter land.

minds of ground landlords, developers, and builders alike. The growing expertise and acuteness of the Dean and Chapter in handling the building market is well illustrated by the two agreements with Tidey in 1864 and 1865. After several years of negotiations designed to free Bliss's two fields behind Haverstock Hill, Home Field and Pit Field, for building development the Dean and Chapter's surveyor, Henry Hunt, at length persuaded Henry Bliss in 1864 to sell back his remaining lifehold interest. Bliss had the misfortune to lose one of the lives on which his lease depended in the Indian Mutiny when Octavius Greene, a lieutenant in the Bengal Army, was killed at Seetapore at the early age of 29. In face of the Dean and Chapter's by then settled policy of refusing to insert any more new lives in existing leases this mishap left Bliss with only one surviving life. To this, the Prince of Wales, he clung tenaciously, and between 1857 and 1864 steadfastly refused to surrender his lease in exchange for the grant of a building agreement.[1] In the end Hunt concluded that the only way of realising the building value of the property was for the Dean and Chapter to buy Bliss's interest, for which they agreed to pay £8,000, precisely one-third of the valuation of the fee simple of the 24 acres. This was a high price to pay, for £1,000 per acre was an extreme value for building land and one-third was a generous allowance for a lease hanging on a single life, albeit a royal one. But Hunt had at the same time agreed terms with Tidey which were a keen bargain for the Dean and Chapter, for Tidey offered an ultimate ground rent of £1,200 a year, at the rate of £50 an acre; as Tidey was to meet all the costs of making roads and sewers, this constituted a high rent for the area. Since the Dean and Chapter's income up to this time, averaging out the lump-sum receipts from renewal fines, was reckoned to have been about £300 a year at the most, the arrangement gave them an increase of £900 a year which was an excellent return on an investment of £8,000.[2]

1 Ibid., Certificates of lives being in existence, Bliss lease, 1848–58.
2 CC File 30177, H. A. Hunt's report on negotiations with Baron de Bliss, 7 January 1864; H. A. Hunt's report on building agreement with Tidey, 7 January 1864. Hunt put the annual value of the 24 acres under existing use at £150, and its fee simple value at £24,000: 24 January 1864. Besides the £8,000 purchase money the Chapter had to hand over £4,000 to the Eccles. Comm. 'to represent the excess of income accruing to a corporation from bringing a property into possession, over and above the amount which such corporation might have expected to have received in the shape of fines and reserved rent had the property not been dealt with . . . In the present instance the receipts of the Chapter will . . . for the second year [£254 ground rent] be only just below those of former years.' Eccles. Comm. to C. St J. Bedford, 5 May 1864. This reduced the rate of return to the Chapter, but not the rate of return on the transaction as such.

Tidey's second new take, made in 1865, was of the $4\frac{1}{2}$-acre field on the north-west side of Belsize Lane which formed part of the Dean and Chapter's share of an exchange with Basil Woodd in 1857. Woodd, the Bond Street brandy merchant, had acquired by purchase two mini-estates on the Belsize lands, held under different leases taking their roots from the 1808 division. On one of these, fronting Haverstock Hill and running between Bliss's land on the south-east and Belsize Avenue on the north-west, he lived himself in his large Hillfield House and its 19 acres of grounds. On the other stood Belsize House in 10 acres of gardens and parkland, as well as the $4\frac{1}{2}$-acre field; it had been occupied at least since 1833 by Matthew Forster, an MP, who began his residence as George Todd's under-tenant and continued, as sitting tenant, when Woodd became his immediate landlord. In 1857 Forster was paying a rent of £350 a year for Belsize House, an aristocratic sum.[1] One of the lives in the Hillfield lease, William Bliss, died in 1857 leaving Woodd with two lives aged 53 years each. His request for the insertion of a fresh life was refused, because of a newly formed determination to get the whole of the Belsize lands into building leases as occasion offered. Woodd, however, was in a reasonably strong position, since all three of the original lives of the Belsize House lease were still surviving, though getting on in years, so that he had a strong title there to trade.[2] An exchange was therefore agreed the way he proposed, though this gave him the freehold of his own residential estate which was the one ripe for building with its frontages to Haverstock Hill, while the Dean and Chapter resumed full control of Belsize House which was mainly 'back-land' in builders' estimation. The valuations for the exchange reflected this difference: £18,000 for the 19 acres of Hillfield and £10,000 for the $14\frac{1}{2}$ acres of Belsize House. The division of these fee simple values between the two parties is, however, somewhat mysterious: the Dean and Chapter's share of Hillfield was put at two-thirds, £12,000, while their share of Belsize House was just less than one-half, £4,750. The disproportion in relation to numbers of lives surviving seems to have been

[1] See above, pp. 95–8, for the origins of Woodd's estates. DCW RCO 32 contains details of Forster's tenancy in Hunt's report, 4 April 1857. This Belsize House was also known at different times as the White House and Belsize Court.

[2] Ibid., Abstract of Title of B. G. Woodd, 1857. The lives chosen by James Abel in 1808 (Hillfield lease) and by George Todd in 1818 (Belsize House lease) were all local people or relatives. The William Bliss was the son of John Bliss, Hampstead surgeon; he may have been a relative of Edward Bliss (Haverstock Hill and Brandon Park, Suffolk) and such a connection would help to explain Edward Bliss's presence in the 1808 division. Edward, however, was the son and grandson of other Edwards, and hence not a member of John Bliss's family.

expected and was accepted by Woodd. In the end he paid rather more, £7,755, for the equality of the exchange, and in return received outright possession of Hillfield which as a result was held off the building market for a further thirty years.[1] Belsize House also remained a country seat for many more years, until 1880. But although receipt of the full building value of their acquisition was thus postponed, the Dean and Chapter enjoyed some consolation from the $4\frac{1}{2}$ acres let to Tidey, since his ground rent was fixed at £328. The very high rate of over £70 an acre reflected partly the smallness of the area and the fact that Tidey was anxious to have it, and partly the inferior class of development which he proposed. There appeared to be an inverse relationship between the quality and price of the houses proposed, and the size of the ground rent per acre.[2]

Tidey had by no means covered all his ground with houses before his bankruptcy in 1870. After reaching up to Belsize Square by Buckland Crescent and Belsize Park he concentrated partly on the Belsize village, and partly on pushing his stucco down his new through route of Belsize Park Gardens which he brought close to the boundary with Eton. Elsewhere he went slowly, and the limits of his activity can still be clearly seen in the sharp frontier between squarish stucco buildings and stockbrick or red-brick with round-arched windows or prominent gable ends which marks Lancaster Drive and Lambolle Road. Before he failed he had introduced William Willett to the district, building five houses in Belsize Crescent in 1869 on an under-lease.[3] The Willetts, father and son, were to become the largest builders in Hampstead in the later nineteenth century, responsible for a greater acreage of the final borough than any other firm; but they did not get into their stride until the 1870s. Meanwhile at the end of 1870 much of Tidey-town, about a third of the 70 or so acres with room for nearly 150 more houses, remained uncovered.

Tidey's development, nevertheless, had been rapid, orderly, and compact. Almost the reverse was the case on the Rosslyn Park estate which

[1] CC File 11684, C. St J. Bedford to J. J. Chalk, 17 April 1857; J. Clutton to J. J. Chalk, 13 May 1857, putting the renewal fine which the Dean and Chapter could have received on Hillfield at £1,000; same to same, 21 March 1859, discussing surveyors' fees for the transaction, and basing them on the fee simple valuations.

[2] CC File 32878, J. Clutton to J. J. Chalk, 11 April 1865, reporting terms of the building agreement with Tidey.

[3] Ibid., Leases for five houses in Prince Consort Road (Belsize Crescent) granted to W. Willett, 2 August 1869.

was let to Henry Davidson in 1853 on a building agreement in much the same circumstances as governed Palmer's lease. The lease of Rosslyn Park had passed swiftly from Thomas Roberts through the hands of Robert Milligan and Admiral Sir Moore Disney until it was bought by Henry Davidson, a City merchant, some time before 1828.[1] Davidson came to live in Rosslyn House, one of the most coveted mansions in Hampstead, elegant and commodious without being over-large, and enjoying a favoured prospect over Maryon Wilson's Conduit Fields and more distant views to the west. He was lucky in the lottery of the leases for lives, for two of the original lives dropped of old age in 1845 and 1846. At the time he grumbled mightily at the heavy fine of £1,700 which he had to pay for the insertion of two new lives—two young girls, one of them his own daughter Georgiana aged 7—maintaining that because of 'the serious drawbacks to which [these premises] are liable they cannot in justice be estimated at a higher rental than £150 a year'; a rack rental which would yield £600 as a reasonable fine for two lives.[2] He paid up, however, and in June 1846 received one of the very last regrants with new lives which the Dean and Chapter were prepared to make, giving him an excellent position entrenched behind lives aged 48, 21, and 14 when he came to make building proposals in 1853. He made these proposals because the time seemed ripe for profiting from the building potential of part of the 21-acre property, while retaining Rosslyn House and its immediate grounds as his own residence for the time being. The time seemed ripe not because of any fresh accessibility to his part of Belsize, for it was on the edge of the old town and remote from the new railway a mile away down a steep hill; railways, indeed, turned into nothing but a nuisance for Davidson's plans. If anything it seems to have been the 'serious drawbacks' from which he conceived Rosslyn House to suffer which made Davidson choose this moment to initiate building. He had felt in 1846 that the snag about Rosslyn House was that 'Thomas Wilson's land runs into the very heart of these premises—almost touching the principal rooms, and that that land is shortly to be built upon.'[3] In 1853, with another Maryon Wilson estate bill pending, he undoubtedly sensed that building would begin behind him any minute and that it was necessary for him to try to get in first before the local market was saturated; Thurlow Road and Lyndhurst Road thus appeared to meet an anticipated competition from Maryon Wilson which never materialised.

[1] See above, pp. 94–5.
[2] DCW RCO 32, H. Davidson to H. E. Oliver (his solicitor), 11 June 1846.
[3] Loc. cit.

Davidson surrendered his lease for lives in exchange for a 99-year building lease at a ground rent, payable in full from the start, of only £220 a year. The low rate of scarcely more than £10 an acre certainly reflected the great strength of his existing tenure, for if it had been allowed to run its course Georgiana Davidson might easily have kept the old lease going for a further forty or fifty years. But this hardly seems sufficient to explain all the difference between his ground rent and Palmer's, and it is possible that some of the difference was due to an expectation that Davidson's houses would be of lower quality. For although both leases had the same formal clauses providing that 'each detached house shall be of the cost value of at least £600, and semi-detached houses of at least £1,000 the pair', it was only in Davidson's lease that further provision was made that 'in the event of houses being built in terraces or rows, the cost value is not to be less than £400 for each house.'[1] If so, Davidson was dissembling, for he had quite different ideas for such a choice situation next to the old town and never intended to appropriate it to cheap and inferior terrace housing. His plan was to develop a good-class extension of the town with large three- and four-storey houses standing in a secluded quarter enclosed by his property boundaries of Shepherds Walk on the north-west, the field path dividing him from the Conduit Fields on the south-west (preserved as Spring Path), and the new Lyndhurst Road on the south-east. The north-eastern frontage on Rosslyn Hill was indeed used for similar houses, but larger and more sheltered ones were to be placed well back on the new road, Eldon Grove, running parallel to it. Privacy and quiet were to be assured by building all round the boundaries and deliberately preventing any link with the Maryon Wilson land; the extension of Lyndhurst Road through to its junction with Fitzjohn's Avenue and Akenside Road came much later, and was an emphatic breach in the original layout.

The houses which did go up were rather larger and a great deal less uniform in design than those being built by Tidey further south at the same period, suggesting that a number of different builders took part, with ideas ranging from the faintly classical with quoins and porticoes to the faintly gothic in stock-brick with occasional decorated courses and pointed windows; only one builder, a William Munt, seems to have been responsible for a reasonable group of houses, on Rosslyn Hill and in Thurlow Road. The chief trouble was that the houses did not go up at all quickly, and the project dawdled and hung fire. Davidson himself put most of this down to the railway, with a certain amount of justi-

[1] CC File 7141, Terms of proposed lease to H. Davidson, 8 March 1853.

fication. He had no sooner signed his lease than he discovered that the Hampstead Junction Railway was proposing to tunnel under Rosslyn. Fearing the effect which this might have on timorous builders above, Davidson petitioned against the company's bill and succeeded in introducing new clauses into the Act securing the company's liability to support the surface and to construct the tunnel in arch-work 'of sufficient strength and depth to admit of buildings being erected and ever after maintained above the said tunnel.'[1] This precaution was of little avail, according to Davidson, for although the tunnel was safely buried 75 to 100 feet below the surface of his land builders were apparently most reluctant to risk placing houses on top of it. Explaining how, eleven years after the start of his lease, there were still only about forty houses on his estate, Davidson ascribed this to:[2]

> One unexpected drawback [which] has occurred—namely the Tunnel made by the L.N.W.R. under the very centre of the Estate, after sewers had been put in, and roads made, and some houses built. I opposed this, and secured the trifling compensation of £500 awarded by arbitration . . . The Plan, which I beg to send, shows the roads made, the sites of houses built, and the line of the Tunnel—and it will be observed that as yet, after a lapse of many years, no houses have been built over the Tunnel, all builders considering it so hazardous to erect houses in that part of the property—latterly I have induced one builder, Mr Watt, by offering him very easy terms of rent, to try the experiment in that part of the Estate, viz. Thurlow Road, where the Tunnel is deepest from the surface—and I have also myself, as I could find no one else willing, ventured to speculate, and am now building a pair of houses in Eldon Road—but practically the surface over the Tunnel is almost useless for building purposes.

Although he supplied evidence for this unreasonable prejudice on the part of builders, Rosslyn Park suffered from more than tunnel-disease; for there were many empty plots in Eldon, Lyndhurst, and Thurlow Roads which were not directly over the tunnel, and Davidson was engaged in some special pleading in an abortive attempt to get the Dean and Chapter to sell him the fee simple of the estate in preparation for selling out himself. The sluggishness, in truth, was probably more fundamentally due to a rather limited demand for large houses in

---

[1] Ibid., Baxter, Rose & Norton (Davidson's solicitors) to J. J. Chalk, 25 May 1857. Hampstead Junction Railway Act 1853, secs 32, 33 and 34.
[2] CC File 7141, H. Davidson to Eccles. Comm., 9 January 1864.

this part of Hampstead near the old town. Demand picked up in the later 1860s and most of the rest of the new roads was filled up notwithstanding the tunnel. Nevertheless at the end of 1870 there were no more than seventy houses on the estate, and the entire south side of Lyndhurst Road, recently laid out in building plots, was still unbuilt. The houses were large, and those in Rosslyn Terrace (later named Lyndhurst Terrace) were detached houses standing in ample gardens; though the builder did not provide stabling, at least one of the residents, who bought his house in 1857, at once added a coach-house and stable at his own expense.[1] All in all, it was an example of the comparative slowness with which a housing estate for the wealthiest of the new suburban rich was taken up.

The southern part of Rosslyn Park remained undeveloped, however, because it remained a private residence. Davidson himself tired of Rosslyn House quite soon after the building started, and sold it in 1859 to Charles Henry Lardner Woodd, Basil Woodd's son and successor in the wine trade. Charles Woodd lived in the house until his death in 1893, keeping up Rosslyn House and its grounds in style. He bought further pieces of the estate from Davidson in 1863 and 1869, partly to preserve his private drive, whose entrance from Lyndhurst Road is marked by a surviving gateway, but partly in order to develop with houses and mews himself, which he did in the 1870s and 1880s.[2] The mews were built on the site of Rosslyn Lodge, a substantial building which was still standing in 1873; and in 1883 the curiously hexagonal Congregational Church in purple brick and majolica work, by Alfred Waterhouse, rose on the site of Rosslea Grove, another small villa in the Rosslyn grounds—despite the fact that Davidson's building agreement had contained a covenant prohibiting any 'chapel or meeting house . . . of persons dissenting from the Church of England.'[3]

The whole venture, though neither a dramatic nor an instant commercial success, served Davidson most comfortably in the end. He received about £12,000 for the various pieces of his lease which he sold to Woodd, amounting to some eight acres in all, and the House. Then in 1869 he sold the remaining part of his lease, about thirteen acres covered with houses, for £30,000 to W. J. Blake. The underleases of these houses produced an income in 'improved ground rents'

[1] Ibid., H. Harris, of 5 and 6 Rosslyn Terrace, to Eccles. Comm., 23 February 1893, detailing his purchase in 1857 and subsequent additions.

[2] Ibid., assignments to C. H. L. Woodd, 21 November 1859, 5 March 1863 and 8 February 1869; leases and under-leases of houses on Woodd's section of Lyndhurst Road, 1870–89.

O.S. six-inch map, 1873 ed., for Rosslyn Lodge and Rosslea Grove.

of £1,153, while the share of Davidson's original ground rent to the Dean and Chapter attributed to them was £130; he had thus worked up a developer's net income of £1,000 a year out of the thirteen acres and then succeeded in capitalising it at thirty years' purchase, a most satisfactory state of affairs.[1]

The final piece of building development on the Dean and Chapter's estate which was launched before 1871, but not yet physically started, concerned the tract lying between Belsize Lane and Belsize Avenue. This was the half of George Todd's original share of the 1808 division which he had detached from the Belsize House estate, and on it stood the two large houses, Hunters Lodge and Ivy Bank, which in the 1870s were known as Belsize Cottage and Elm House, that had been built early in the century.[2] Todd's lease, with the three original lives still just keeping going aged 69, 67, and 60, was bought in 1868 by Richard Pierce Barker who at once applied for a building agreement, clearly suggesting that the district had only just become of interest to developers. The two large houses, standing in five acres of grounds between them, had been sub-leased on terms not due to expire until 1884, and therefore had to be left out of the building agreement for the time being. Their garden fences formed the line of the future Ornan Road, leaving a strip of 7½ acres between Ornan Road and Belsize Avenue which Barker took on a building agreement from 1868 at a ground rent of £380 a year, a full rate of £50 an acre being appropriate, as the lease for lives which he surrendered was deemed to be almost defunct anyway. The agreement envisaged top-class development, making particular provision to preserve all the existing trees in the Avenue and to ensure that houses were set back fifty feet from the centre of the road; and the minimum cost values prescribed for the houses on the main frontages were higher than any previously used in Belsize, £1,000 for a detached house and £1,600 for a pair of semi-detacheds. In due course William Willett moved in to take most of the Belsize Avenue frontage under Barker, and more than fulfilled the spirit of the agreement by building very substantial houses which sold at £2,400 to £3,100 and commanded rents of £180 a year upwards. But he did not begin building until 1873.[3]

[1] CC File 7141, Clabon & Fearon (Blake's solicitors) to Eccles. Comm., 27 April 1876, reciting the sale by Davidson to Blake on 18 July 1869. W. J. Blake, who had been MP for Newport 1837–41, was a country gentleman with his seat at Danesbury, Welwyn, in Hertfordshire.
[2] See above, p. 98.
[3] CC File 38689, C. St J. Bedford to J. J. Chalk, 10 January 1868, enclosing

As the jigsaw puzzle of property interests in the Dean and Chapter's Belsize estate composed itself into a pattern of building estates it is apparent that several pieces were still being withheld from the building market in 1871 because the Dean and Chapter were powerless to act, held at arm's length by their lessees. Resident gentry, protected by long leases, still occupied Rosslyn House, Belsize House (otherwise known as Belsize Court), Hunters Lodge, Ivy Bank, and Haverstock Lodge, while the Dean and Chapter had parted with the freehold of Hillfield to Basil Woodd, who had built in its grounds a second large house, Woodlands, for one of his sons, Robert Ballard Woodd. As long as these gentry chose to remain, balancing the attractions of their fine houses and small parks against the unpleasantness of encirclement by new streets—or if they were sub-tenants, until their leases expired—all these grounds could not be released for building. Elsewhere the Smallpox Hospital cast its baleful spell and effectively sterilised the part of South End Farm next to Fleet Road as well as stunting the development of the St John's Park estate. Even so there were substantial areas of the Belsize estate which had been released into the building market but had not yet been built upon. The building sites which were still empty in 1871 on the lands already let on building agreements to Lund, Palmer, Tidey, Davidson, and Barker were ample to provide at the least for a further 300 houses in the new roads which had already been formed, so that the building estates which had been started were only a little over two-thirds of their final completed size. The very first building development of all, Bliss's administratively piratical venture on Haverstock Hill, was the most completely settled district; but even there, although at the time Bliss was held up by his tenure, there was room on the land devoted to market gardens and nurseries in 1871 for the later Antrim Road. Most telling of all, however, was the part of South End Farm lying to the north of the Hampstead Junction Railway, adjoining the Heath, and but a couple of minutes from Hampstead Heath station, which had been opened in 1860. There was no country seat here, no residential or tenurial obstacle to making the area available for building; yet in 1871 it was still ordinary farmland, neglected by developers and speculators quite as much as it was neglected by the Dean and Chapter who had no idea who the lessee was or whether any of the lives named in the 1808 lease to Thomas Roberts were still surviving. The negligence of the lessee was equally surprising, for he allowed the last

Hunt's report of 11 December 1867 on proposals for a building agreement for Todd's lease; Jennings, White & Buckston to Eccles. Comm., 1 November 1869, completing the agreement with R. P. Barker. And see below, pp. 344–5.

surviving life to die in 1868, thus letting his lease run out and enabling the Dean and Chapter to assume outright possession of the farm, without making any efforts to obtain the insertion of new lives. That he thus suffered potentially valuable property rights to disappear without trace and without payment suggests incompetence possibly mitigated by a lower value for the area than its position would seem to indicate. This suggestion tends to be confirmed by the fact that although the railway company had been compelled by its 1853 Act to provide access to the severed lands of South End Farm and had done so to the extent of roughly forming the future South Hill Park road, this had failed to excite any building proposals.[1] It is evidence which not only confirms that new railway access was by no means invariably a spur to suburban growth, but also supports the impression that the supply of building land from within the Dean and Chapter's resources was more than adequate to meet the effective demand.

[1] CC File 48520, J. Clutton to George Pringle, Secretary to Eccles. Comm., 7 February and 20 February 1872. These reports suggest that Thomas Roberts was still the lessee in 1868 and had not sold his estate.

Eight

SMART HAMPSTEAD AND POPULAR HAMPSTEAD
Fitzjohn's Avenue and the greater Heath, 1871-89

After the issue of the Heath had been temporarily laid to rest in 1871 the Maryon Wilson estate was free to turn its attention to prospects of development; under Sir John it was in the hands of an owner with the necessary legal powers for the first time since 1821. The half-century of enforced abstinence, however, had deprived the estate of far less refreshment than either Sir Thomas or the public had liked to think. The large amounts of undeveloped but fully available building land on the Chalcots and Belsize estates suggest that there was a plentiful supply of land locally, and that if there had been any building assault on Maryon Wilson territory before 1871 it could not have been on the massive scale—terrifying or mouth-watering according to interest—frequently imagined by contemporaries.[1] What was true in general of unused supplies of building land in the southern parts of Hampstead was equally true in detail of the old town, where the position of the Maryon Wilson lands gave them an advantage over Chalcots and Belsize. Here also there were many properties which were not part of the Maryon Wilson estate, which remained as fields, paddocks, allotments and market gardens in 1871. There was indeed so much of this open land in and immediately around the old town that the very delights of its village atmosphere, with every town street giving on to grass or gardens at every turn, seem to argue that there was no great pressure to enjoy them. Had there been such pressure the delights would surely have dwindled away under a steady nibbling at the village fields by those anxious to live among them.

The tally of open spaces in the heart of the town is impressive. It is, of course, not surprising that many of the old-established large houses

---

[1] See, for example, the cartoon by George Cruikshank, 'London going out of Town' (1829), in which the general comment on the 'March of Bricks and Mortar' in terms of the battlefield and military operations also contains a specific comment on Sir Thomas Maryon Wilson's 1829 bill and the impression that it was a proposal to enclose Hampstead Heath (Plate 4).

continued to survive in their settings of extensive grounds: the prospective profits from building on the lawns and in the shrubberies were not yet so huge as to tempt owners to sacrifice their pleasant spaciousness. At Sunny Field, indeed, just over the edge of the borough boundary on West Heath Road, the temptations of building in the back garden proved resistible until 1970; Branch Hill Lodge and The Grove survive precariously as shrunken examples of large establishments on the fringe of the town. More in the centre was such a place as Gardnor House, owned by the Gardnor family since the eighteenth century, whose grounds fronted on to Flask Walk; in 1864 one or two building plots had been tentatively marked out here, but it was not until the 1880s that the lawns were cut up to form Gardnor Road.[1] Much less immune to building seduction, however, was the considerable area adjoining Gardnor House to the south, with frontages to Willow Road and stretching to the old White Hart Yard on High Street. In the 1830s this plot of four acres had been a single paddock, but subsequently it was divided up into some forty or so garden allotments. This was a use undoubtedly appreciated by the assortment of High Street shopkeepers, tradesmen, doctors, and other residents who tilled the gardens. But as the land continued in single ownership and the allotment tenancies could be ended at short notice, it is apparent that the impulses which turned the area into Gayton Road and Gayton Crescent in the 1870s had not existed any earlier.[2] Further to the south-east was the larger area lying between these allotments and Downshire Hill, which formed the Carlile family estate. Here stood Carlile House, just behind the King of Bohemia's brewery; but apart from providing a site for the Presbyterians, who replaced their old chapel with a new church in 1862, and for the Unitarians, the Carliles allowed their land to remain in meadows until well into the 1870s, when the estate road system of Willoughby, Worsley, Kemplay, Carlingford, and Denning Roads, and Rudall Crescent, was laid out. Smaller pockets also remained on this side of High Street and Rosslyn Hill, which would have tempted any builders should there have been any to tempt. There was, for example, Crispin's field round which Hampstead Hill Gardens subsequently curled its way; and more tempting still, Norris's field opposite the

[1] For the position in 1864, HLRO Metropolitan and St John's Wood Railway, extension to Hampstead, Session 1864, Plan and Book of Reference. Francis Lowe was the lessee and occupier of Gardnor House.
[2] Ibid. In 1864 this land was owned by the trustees of the will of Margaret Merry. For 1838, see Hampstead Tithe Apportionment, when it was owned by G. N. Best and Rev. D. Williams as trustees.

Hampstead Heath station, where Heath Hurst Road was not built until the 1890s.[1]

Hampstead Heath station, immensely popular with holiday crowds from the moment it was opened in 1860, clearly did not attract regular commuters so quickly; for Thomas Rhodes kept his fields as grazing ground and did not begin to develop his South Hill Park estate until 1871.[2] Similarly on the south-west side of High Street the town continued to end at the old Church Lane (renamed Perrins Lane) with its eighteenth-century cottages and the William IV on the corner; beyond them lay the Greenhill. This was a small grass farm of about fifteen acres with its farm buildings, Mount Farm, at the end of a short farm lane known as Field Place leading out of Church Place; Church Place became part of Heath Street when that was driven through a mass of old buildings to the junction with High Street in the 1880s, and Field Place furnished the line for the start of Fitzjohn's Avenue (this section being originally known as Greenhill Road). The only considerable houses on this property were on High Street: the Rookery, demolished to make room for the Wesleyan chapel on Prince Arthur Road opened in 1872, where the publisher Thomas Norton Longman lived in the 1830s; and on the opposite side of Prince Arthur Road the old house where the fashionable landscape and seascape painter, Clarkson Stanfield, lived until 1865, giving his name to the house which was subsequently preserved as the Hampstead Subscription Library. Prince Arthur Road itself did not exist at the time, for it was not until 1871 that the first steps were taken to lay out the Greenhill estate for building, with Greenhill, Arkwright, Ellerdale, and Prince Arthur Roads, the last named after Prince Arthur because he had come to open the new Sailors' Orphan Girls' Home there in 1869.[3]

There were indeed very few new developments in the old town in the middle years of the century. Cooper's triangle of gound bounded by

[1] HLRO Hampstead Junction Railway, Session 1852–3, Plan and Book of Reference. O.S. six-inch maps, eds of 1873, 1894–6, and 1920 (surveyed in 1912); *P.O. London Directory* map, 1902.

[2] CC File 45820, J. Clutton to G. Pringle, 20 February 1872, reporting on South End Farm, adjoining South Hill Park. MBW Min., 17 March 1871, noting that the sewers sanctioned for the South Hill Park estate in March 1870 had not yet been constructed.

[3] Hampstead Tithe Apportionment 1838, when the estate was owned by Sir John Key, a Lord Mayor, and tenanted by Thomas Norton Longman, publisher; Metropolitan and St John's Wood Railway, Hampstead extension, 1864, when the owner was George Henry Errington, with several tenants, including Clarkson Stanfield; E. Walford, *Old and New London*, v, 483; GLCRO E/MW/H/III/26/19, F. J. Clark to W. W. Knocker, 16 April 1872, discussing the sale of plots on Errington's estate of Greenhill.

Well Walk, Willow Road, and Christ Church Hill was built over, mainly by barracks for the militia. There were new public buildings, like the new workhouse in New End where the vestry held its meetings and conducted its business until the 1870s, and the new church of Christ Church built in the perpendicular style in 1852 for the first of the new ecclesiastical parishes to be carved out of the ancient parish of St John's. The sole venture on any scale, however, was Oak Hill Park. Here Sir Thomas Neave, while continuing to live in the neighbouring Branch Hill Lodge where he amassed a vast collection of stained glass largely liberated by the French Revolutionary armies, got a local builder, Thomas Clowser, to lay out a small and secluded close of villas which were started in 1856.[1] It was not exactly a large contribution to the expansion of the town, and suggests that there was no strong demand from newcomers to settle in the town, in contrast to the Londonward fringes of the parish. What was done at Oak Hill Park was neatly done, a grouping of houses compelled by the geography of Neave's fields to adopt a retiring privacy which brought no offence to the picturesque collection of eighteenth-century houses and villas at the front in Frognal Grove (renamed Montagu Grove to commemorate the residence of an eighteenth-century Master in Chancery, Edward Montagu).

Practically all of these fields which were later to house the growth of the town were, it is true, copyhold lands. It is possible that they remained as fields not because of lack of initiative by the owners or lack of demand from new residents, but because of the imperfections of the copyhold tenures for building purposes which Sir Thomas Maryon Wilson had pointed out in the 1820s.[2] The continuing inability of the lord of the manor to grant building licences to copyholders under which their entry fines would be fixed for 99 years at a figure agreed in advance must have placed a severe damper on building enterprise. To be sure, the customary alternative still existed, under which a copyholder was at liberty to develop his lands, accepting that on every transfer the entry fine would amount to twice the current full annual value. But even if lawyers could find devices to prevent every disposal of a house counting as a transfer for these purposes, the liability to pay tribute to the lord of the manor on this scale and at unpredictable intervals was enough to keep outside finance and speculative builders away from such tenures. Houses certainly grew only sparsely and with difficulty on copyhold land. After 1841, however, the situa-

[1] HPL Vestry Min., 20 and 26 June 1856. And see above, p. 129.
[2] See above, p. 141.

tion changed with the first Copyhold Enfranchisement Act. This Act enabled limited owners such as Sir Thomas to carry out enfranchisements, under the control of the Copyhold Commissioners who had to approve the valuations and compensation payments; but proposals for enfranchisement still required the voluntary agreement of both lord and copyholder, and it is extremely likely that Sir Thomas took what revenge he could on his tormentors by rejecting any requests he received. Then in 1852 the second Enfranchisement Act made enfranchisement compulsory on the application of either lord or copyholder, and Sir Thomas's powers of obstruction were at an end.

It was generally held that under this Act the scale of compensation was usually too high for tenants of purely agricultural copyholds to think it worthwhile to remove the tenure, though most experts held it to be obstructive and injurious to efficient farming; but for copyholds with building value the acquisition of the freehold made the compensation to the lord well worth paying. The copyholders of Hampstead seem to have been of this mind. Between 1853 and his death in 1869 Sir Thomas was obliged to accept the enfranchisement of 88 copyholds, the compensation being fixed at either four years' or five years' purchase of the full annual values. The annual reports of the Copyhold Commissioners record only the number of cases settled each year, and there is no way of identifying the particular copyholds treated; and it is true that the eight years of Sir John's lordship saw a sharp rise in the rate of enfranchisements, 114 cases being dealt with between 1870 and 1877.[1] It is just conceivable that the holders of the largest and potentially richest copyholds held off during Sir Thomas's lifetime, fearing unpleasantness and hard bargaining over compensation terms, and then came forward in a rush after his death. It is, however, most improbable; for any copyholders could invoke the compulsory powers, the Copyhold Commissioners always had to be satisfied of the fairness of the compensation terms, and these in any case remained the same under Sir John as they had been under Sir Thomas. It looks very much as though any copyhold obstruction of development in the town could have been removed at any time after 1852 so soon as a copyholder decided that building was desirable and profitable.

The rush to turn copyholds into freeholds may be dated from 1866, when enfranchisements exceeded ten in a year for the first time; it was

[1] *The Annual Reports of the Copyhold Commissioners*, Parl. Papers, from the 13th Report (1854/5, xv) list the names of parishes and lords of manors in enfranchisement cases. After 1877 the enfranchisements in Hampstead began to fall off, there being 24 in the years 1878–3, by which date the process was almost complete.

associated, not with any change in the law or any softening in the disposition of the lord of the manor, but with some shift of circumstances that began to make expansion of the old town seem profitable where it had not been before. Just what this shift was it is hard to say. Probably no single event, incident, or development was responsible, but rather a general sense that Hampstead's detachment from the metropolis was coming to an end. Physically this could be seen with the Rosslyn Park and St John's Park developments almost joining parts of the old town to the main mass of London; socially it could be seen in the vast crowds which swarmed on to the Heath from the Hampstead Junction Railway on holidays, taking over South End and turning its inns and tea-rooms into a miniature resort industry. Certainly old Hampstead continued to preserve its distinct character and style of living for many decades after this, refusing to become socially, as indeed it never could become topographically, just one more anonymous and featureless wealthy London suburb. This, however, was not an argument available to prevent contemporaries lamenting the beginning of the passing of the old, slow, friendly Hampstead they had known all their lives, and its invasion by metropolitan bustle, sharpness, and commercialism. Just as Clarkson Stanfield moved away from the Greenhill in 1865, fearing disturbance of his peace and quiet even though no actual building had started anywhere near him, so others may have decided that they could not maintain their village ways and that it was time to move out and take what profit they could from their gardens and fields.[1]

Lucy Aikin, one of Hampstead's literary figures of the middle years of the century, who lived in Church Row while writing her *Memoir of Addison*, and who after a spell of desertion to Wimbledon returned to live with her niece and her husband Philip Le Breton, caught the peculiar social charm of the Hampstead of the 1830s and 1840s as being in but not of London:[2]

> Several circumstances render society here peculiarly easy and pleasant. In many respects the place unites the advantages and escapes the evils both of London and provincial towns. It is near enough [to London] to allow its inhabitants to partake in the society, the amusements, and the accommodations of the capital as freely as ever the dissipated could desire; whilst it affords pure

[1] Stanfield moved to one of the new houses in Belsize Park Gardens, preferring a fully urbanised setting where the builders' rubble had at least been cleared away, to the agony of watching the fields behind him turn into a building site.

[2] Letter to Dr Channing, quoted in Walford, op. cit., v, 476–7.

air, lovely scenery, and retired and beautiful walks. Because everyone here is supposed to have a London set of friends, neighbours do not think it necessary, as in the provinces, to force their acquaintance upon you; of local society you may have as much, little, or none, as you please; and with a little, which is very good, you may associate on the easiest terms. Then the summer brings an influx of Londoners, who are often genteel and agreeable people, and pleasingly vary the scene. Such is Hampstead.

Walford added, but with some hesitation: 'And such, to a certain extent . . . is Hampstead in the present day [1877]; for as yet it is quite distinct from the great metropolis, and has quite a character of its own.'[1] The more timorous and apprehensive, however, or the more profit-minded, could well have reasoned that the old order was passing by the late 1860s, and that the moment had come when spacious living had to be abandoned as no longer proof against invasion. It needed, after all, only one or two copyholders owning key sites near the town centre to decide that opportunities for exploitation should be seized, to upset the whole ecology of the town and force the others to follow suit because the attractions of their properties were being spoiled.

Some such process may well have been triggered by a non-event, the proposal to build a surface railway into the heart of the old town. The Metropolitan Railway had no sooner been opened between Paddington and Farringdon Street in 1863, the world's first underground railway, than an independent company was promoted to provide a feeder line from Finchley Road (where it intended to make a connection with the Hampstead Junction) to Baker Street. This company, the Metropolitan and St John's Wood Railway, always acted in close association with the Metropolitan, depending on it both for finance and for the engineering services of John Fowler, and was formally absorbed by the Metropolitan in 1883 when it had emerged as the parent company's most valuable asset, the tunnel leading out to the fresh pastures of Willesden, Harrow, and Pinner, and the real open country of Aylesbury and Quainton Road. The Metropolitan and St John's Wood may lay claim to being the world's second underground railway, beating the Metropolitan District (the southern arc of the Inner Circle) on to the statute book by a short head in 1864, and struggling to its opening at Swiss Cottage in April 1868 a few months before the District could run its first train.[2] Before any work on the Swiss Cottage tunnel had even

[1] Ibid., p. 477.
[2] The Acts were: Metropolitan and St John's Wood, 27 and 28 Vict. cap. 203; Metropolitan District, 27 and 28 Vict. cap. 312.

started the new company showed its high hopes by obtaining powers to extend its line to Hampstead. Token opposition to the proposal was offered by an assortment of affected interests: the New College at Swiss Cottage; Hampstead Vestry and the Metropolitan Board of Works, who wished to see their sewers properly protected; and the other railway companies who wished to insert clauses to safeguard their interests— the LNWR, the Midland, and the Metropolitan itself. All these were satisfied by technical clauses in the Bill, withdrew their petitions, and the Bill passed unopposed, somewhat to the chagrin of Sir Thomas Maryon Wilson who had been sheltering behind them, although his hostility to this extension was softened by an offer of large compensation for the use of his land to dispose of the spoil from the original Swiss Cottage tunnel.[1]

The plan was for the extension to surface in College Crescent, cross Maryon Wilson's Conduit Fields roughly on the line of Fitzjohn's Avenue, enter a short tunnel directly after passing over the Hampstead Junction's tunnel, from which it would emerge in the Greenhill to sweep round to cross High Street by a bridge from the King William IV to the Hampstead vicarage on the opposite side, which would be demolished for the run through to the terminus on Willow Road beside Gardnor House.[2] It was a steep line, with a gradient of 1 in 27 throughout, but it would not have been unworkable. Its arrival would certainly have brought violent changes to the old town, and wrenched it uncompromisingly into the middle of the nineteenth century. The proposal was exactly the kind of opportunity, and of shock, that would start off building schemes in the town. In the event, of course, the line was never constructed, for the company found its first section from Baker Street to Swiss Cottage almost cripplingly expensive and only just managed to scrape together enough money to build this even as a single-track line. But the Hampstead extension was not abandoned until 1870, when the company first began its moves for extending in a different direction, although for a time its aim shifted uncertainly between Kilburn and Willesden. For half a dozen years, therefore, between 1864

[1] The Act for the Hampstead Extension was 28 and 29 Vict. cap. 31; and see HLRO Evidence, 1865, XLIV, for the petitions and their withdrawal. The Maryon Wilson estate appears eventually to have received £24,000 for the spoil heaps of the Swiss Cottage tunnel: GLCRO E/MW/H/III/26/18, Notes of the history of Wilson and the Metropolitan and St John's Wood Railway, 1873.

[2] Metropolitan and St John's Wood Railway, Hampstead Extension, 1864, Plan and Book of Reference. The old vicarage was demolished later, the unusual depth of its site making a large yard for the present Blue Star Garage.

and 1870 it was reasonable to hope, or fear, that the railway was about to come to Willow Road, thus setting building plans afoot. It may well be that when the railway failed to materialise these plans had to be revised to aim at a less wealthy market than that of the anticipated upper-class commuters. In which case what a non-event began, a non-railway consummated in the inferior housing of Gayton Road, and the squandered opportunities of the Carlile estate.

The only other event which may have set off building in the old town was the death of Sir Thomas Maryon Wilson himself. For this meant that his brother Sir John who succeeded him would very shortly have the power to grant building leases, and the imminence of effective competition from the Maryon Wilson estate would be a powerful spur to others to get their land to the builders first. Whether released by this, by the abortive railway, or simply by a general feeling of London's approach, it is apparent that there were supplies of land in the town available for release to building when the owners felt so inclined and when the demand seemed to them to justify it. Looking at the town of Hampstead, therefore, just as when looking at the southern and south-eastern parts of the parish, it appears difficult to make a convincing case for attributing any effects to the long sterilisation of the Maryon Wilson lands during Sir Thomas's lifetime. Yet even if other lands were available locally, the map of 1871 conveys a powerful impression that there had been some effects; for the clean, sharp line of the frontier of the built-up area, running along Belsize Lane, College Crescent, Fairfax Road, Belsize Road, and Abbey Road until it reached West End Lane, followed the Maryon Wilson estate boundary with absolute precision.[1] The character of these effects is vividly sketched in a letter from a Kilburn resident in 1869 supporting a shortlived scheme to form a new park between Finchley Road and West End Lane:[2]

All who have enjoyed a stroll on summer evenings through the green fields occupying the area between St John's Wood and West End Lane will feel deep regret at the prospect of losing this recreation ground. It is certainly the most rural spot—indeed the only rural spot—which we Londoners possess within $2\frac{1}{2}$ miles of Oxford Street. At no other part of the suburbs of London is there to be found, as here, a distinct line of demarcation between town

[1] O.S. six-inch map, 1873 ed. A map revised literally in 1871 shows precisely the same urban frontier: GLC Members' Library, Map of proposals for Metropolitan Railways and Tramways deposited at the Private Bill Office, 30 November 1871 for 1872 Session.
[2] *The Times*, 22 November 1869, letter from 'K' of Kilburn.

and country. In all other parts the approach of building operations is announced for two or three years previously by the disappearance of the farmer, and the arrival of brickmakers, roadmakers, ballast-burners, carpet-beaters, dust collectors, and other industrious members of the community, who are deadly enemies to hedges, trees, and everything green and rural. But wherever the buildings have reached the boundary line of the late Sir Thomas Wilson's estate, the destroyer has thrown down his weapons . . . Hence it may be said that along the line of this estate London ends and the country begins . . . The immunity which this favoured territory has enjoyed from being swallowed up by the metropolis is now at an end . . . By virtue of his ancestor's will we have hitherto been able to use his land freely as a place of exercise and recreation. Our nursemaids and babies have found health and amusement in his hayfields on summer afternoons; our boys have played cricket and football and flown their kites in his meadows, and innumerable young couples from our crowded houses have rambled by moonlight along his footpaths or spent their pleasant hours of courtship under the shade of his trees. The time has now arrived for showing our appreciation of these privileges [by purchasing this land for a public park].

The delightful way in which the public made itself free of the farmer's fields for frolics in the hay is sufficient explanation for the way in which the farm rents for this land had fallen from £5 an acre in 1819 to under £3 an acre in 1870. But it was not entirely true that the dust collectors had been kept at bay. John Culverhouse rented the farm, which by 1870 had been split into two: Belsize Farm of 77 acres with a cottage and farm buildings alongside Daleham Mews; and the Manor Farm of 133 acres with a substantial farmhouse and range of barns and cowsheds at Frognal. Culverhouse, besides running the farms, was a general contractor and brickmaker; he rented the nine acres to the west of Finchley Road hemmed in by the Midland and the Hampstead Junction Railways at over £10 an acre, and had already turned this triangle of land into a twilight zone of dust heaps and brick-burning. He also carried on brickmaking in a different quarter, on part of the East Park fields to the east of the Heath.[1] With this qualification—and the Finchley Road rubbish tip was well out of sight between two railway lines—the Kilburn resident's description fitted exactly. A clear

[1] GLCRO E/MW/H/III/28/19, Schedule of tenancy agreements on the Hampstead estate, 1871. And see above, p. 175.

frontier between town and country was most unusual, and that is what the artificial restrictions on Sir Thomas Maryon Wilson had achieved. Without them it is highly likely, not that there would have been more building in Hampstead by 1871 in total, but that it would have been more untidy and ragged with odd ribbons and fingers of houses poking out into the Maryon Wilson fields to produce the messy boundary zone of unfinished streets, half-formed roads, and forlorn, weed-grown back-land between the ribbons of earliest development which was typical of London's periphery elsewhere.

The public did not, of course, get their new park in the area now occupied by Priory Road, Compayne Gardens, Goldhurst Terrace, and other streets, for the likely purchase price of between £100,000 and £200,000 meant that the idea was never more than a pipe dream.[1] No more did the public obtain a new park in the Conduit Fields on the east side of Finchley Road, though a rather more determined effort was made to acquire and preserve them in 1875, when the construction of Fitzjohn's Avenue was about to start. Octavia Hill gave her support to this scheme, in the interests of the poor of Lisson Grove; though it was hardly in the minds of the chief promoters of this preservationist move that indiscriminate gaggles of the poor should be invited into the bosom of Hampstead. They were out to preserve, rather, their exclusiveness and their isolation from the crowds: 'to keep up the character of Hampstead as a healthy place of residence and holiday resort' as one put it, or as another said, to stop the loss of 'the last piece of green grass which separates Hampstead from London.' The bid failed, not only because subscriptions showed no sign of raising the purchase money, but also because some felt that a park was not needed and would be a positive waste. 'The Conduit Fields are comparable to Hastings and Ventnor', one resident claimed, 'in being sheltered from east winds by being on a western slope, and therefore suitable for people with pulmonary complaints.' His conclusion was that they should be used for residences for the wealthy weak, and 'not be wasted as a mere day-time park.'[2] The area did indeed become a wealthy quarter, though more notable for its successful artists than for its bath chairs. Failure to secure either new park was probably just as well, for Hampstead could have become outrageously over-privileged in relation to other boroughs; and as it was, energies and cash instead of being frittered away were conserved

---

[1] Letters to *The Times* on the scheme for a Finchley Road Park, 18 and 20 November 1869.

[2] *Hampstead and Highgate Express*, 10 July, 24 July, 21 August, 4 September 1875.

for the much more momentous efforts a decade later which led to the extension of the Heath.

It was indeed a fortunate accident of the mechanics and capacity of the building industry that anywhere still survived in the mid-1880s for the Heath to extend into. After Sir Thomas's death it was generally assumed that market forces would speedily take their course and that the entire Maryon Wilson estate would be covered with streets and houses in a trice. This seemed to be confirmed by reports that by the autumn of 1869 the Maryon Wilson fields were already sprouting hoardings advertising that they were to be let for building.[1] Preservationists no doubt felt powerless in the face of the juggernauts of private property and speculative building enterprise once these had been set in motion, and were in any case priding themselves on a triumph over the Heath. At any rate, apart from the whimpers over the Finchley Road and Conduit Fields there were no moves from this quarter, and most notably there were no squeaks of protest when Thomas Rhodes proceeded to lay out his curious 'lollipop' or 'squash racket' formation at South Hill Park. Unless it is assumed that the earlier outcry against Sir Thomas's schemes had been motivated by personal spite, which is entirely possible, it can only be that by 1871 the preservationists had lost heart and abandoned hope of being able to halt development on private property. For Rhodes's building at South Hill Park was just as much an encroachment on and desecration of what was popularly thought of as 'the Heath', as anything which Sir Thomas had ever proposed to do on his East Park. To make matters worse, Rhodes perpetrated an outrage on a magnificent location. His road layout was understandable, the lozenge and its stalk creating the maximum amount of building frontage within the confines of the shape of his field; but it was decidedly unfriendly in deliberately denying any future access to roads on the Maryon Wilson fields to the north, strongly contrasting in this with the scheme on the adjoining piece of South End Farm where Parliament Hill and Nassington Roads were aligned to make connections with future developments on Lord Mansfield's estate. The houses which he allowed builders to put up were inelegant, tightly-packed, and tasteless for such a fine situation; but no worse than most other unambitious middle-class suburban housing of the period. The real crime was to make the whole estate inward-facing to his dismal oval, so that the houses turned their ugly backsides to the Heath like so many rude apes. Quite apart from the pain inflicted on sensitive walkers on the Heath, it showed total lack of imagination and complete indifference to

[1] *The Times*, 18 November 1869.

the locality; a piece of standardised routine suburbia was slapped down without thought, when houses turned outwards with their fronts to the Heath would have fetched more as well as looked better. At least it can be said that in all the Maryon Wilson schemes to build on the East Park enough business sense was shown—leaving aside any deference to aesthetic niceties—to shape the proposed road plan and style of houses to extract maximum advantage from the splendid situation commanding the Heath.

Far from dying with Sir Thomas, schemes for turning the East Park into a building estate came very much alive with the prospect that the owner was now free to act. The power to make access roads across the Heath had been carefully reserved in the agreement with the Metropolitan Board of Works, and a provisional road layout was shown in a plan outlining the general development of the entire Hampstead estate submitted to the Vestry in 1873.[1] In the 1870s the estate received good offers for sites on East Park almost every year, but these were always offers for individual houses and estate policy was firmly set against piecemeal development which could prevent the future letting of complete building estates as entities. Other features of general estate policy fortunately relegated the exploitation of East Park to a low priority in relation to other parts of the Maryon Wilson property. It was realised that 'this is no Ordinary Estate, and its magnitude renders every care in the outset necessary so that no mistake should be made which its owners might hereafter regret.' One chief care was to divide the whole 400 acres or so into a series of potential building estates which could each be treated in an orderly and systematic fashion, mainly in order to ensure that the local land market was not ruined by a glut of building land appearing simultaneously in every direction. As the land agent for the estate, F. J. Clark, put it:[2]

If roads and sewers are to be made over a series of building estates in Hampstead it will ruin any man even with a stronger back than Mr Spencer Wilson's. I have never yet seen any plan shewing how it is proposed to lay out the Estate [this was in 1871], but I should think beyond the frontages to the Finchley New Road and the frontages to one new Road direct to Hampstead, no more building

[1] See above, pp. 196–7 GLCRO E/MW/H/III/26/54, Bell & Steward (Spencer Maryon Wilson's solicitors) to W. W. Knocker, Dunmow (Sir John Maryon Wilson's solicitor), 19 September 1873.

[2] Ibid., Bell & Steward to Knocker, 6 December 1873; F. J. Clark to Knocker, 30 November 1871.

land will be required for many years, especially as we have other land adjacent in competition with it.

This linked with the other main plank of general policy, that the owners should themselves make the initial investment in forming the principal roads and sewers for each building estate. This contrasted with the practice on the Chalcots and Belsize estates where the builders or developers holding the chief leases had been left to finance all road construction, but it was quite normal for private landowners with large developments in prospect to undertake these outlays. The arguments were firstly, that in this way the ground landowner exercised the most direct and reliable control over the broad disposition of his property to its best advantage, while it might prove impossible to compel a lessee to make roads that were not of immediate benefit to his own particular take; and secondly, that in the long run the estate would produce larger returns. Clark demonstrated the advantage to the family in terms of an offer to lease 33 acres at either £45 an acre ground rent with the builder making the roads or £60 an acre with Wilson making them, estimating that the roads and sewers would cost £8,000. After deducting the interest which the estate would have to pay on the capital the net income would only begin to show an advantage at the higher ground rent after seventeen years; but besides that future benefit 'I should certainly recommend the larger ground rent', Clark advised, 'Mr Wilson making the roads, as in the event of his ever being asked to sell the ground rent the number of years purchase upon the larger rent would be considerably in excess of the cost of making the roads and sewers.'[1] Assuming that ground rents fetched twenty years' purchase on a sale, which was a low figure, the difference of £15 an acre in rents could be capitalised at £9,900 showing a capital gain of £1,900 on the outlay. It was such a combination of the comparative remoteness of any income advantage and the prospect of capital appreciation only if the property could be sold, which made development investments unattractive to corporate landowners but attractive to private landowners with future family interests at heart.

It was this road-making policy as much as anything else which reprieved East Park from early attention. The shape and topography of the fields which made up the 60 acres of East Park was such that any main estate road (using the viaduct built by Sir Thomas, which still stands) would create a small amount of building frontage and of openings for subsidiary residential roads in comparison with equivalent

[1] E/MW/H/III/26/19, Clark to Bell & Steward, 2 March 1872.

lengths of new road anywhere else on Maryon Wilson property. On top of this, main drainage for the area would be difficult and expensive to provide because of the lie of the land, all the more so because the studied unfriendliness of Rhodes's disposition of South Hill Park made it difficult if not impossible to take any sewer along the line of natural fall, which lay through his property.[1] As South Hill Park went up in all its selfish ugliness between 1871 and 1877 it may have performed the priceless service to posterity of tipping the scales against any early development of East Park. In any event, for whatever reasons this area, which for situation and visual appeal was the gem of the entire estate, was placed low on the list of priorities for opening up to building, and once Wilson resources had been committed to road building in other parts of the estate there was nothing to spare for investment here.

Quite apart from the rational calculations of estate management and economics which preserved East Park in open fields until the preservationists could set about preserving them permanently as an addition to the Heath in the 1880s, there were irrational factors undreamt of by contemporaries which delayed the mobilisation of any of the Maryon Wilson property for years after Sir Thomas's death. At times it seemed to the professional advisers concerned with the estate 'as if the development of the estate, which may require many years and almost generations, was never to be accomplished', and that it was becoming a somewhat pious hope that Sir John, through his indifference, 'will not willingly by inattention to these matters be the one who unconsciously will be giving effect to the unjust decision of Parliament against building on this estate. He now has it in his power to do what Parliament most arbitrarily told Sir Thomas he should not do, and we feel sure he will use this power.'[2] To the solicitors, land agents, and surveyors retained by the family further delays seemed quite unnecessary after Sir Thomas's death and doubly vexatious because the family appeared bent on ignoring all that he had striven for. The delays arose out of one of those father-and-son quarrels which were typical in landed families, occasioned perhaps by disapproval of the son's marriage though more likely by his extravagant demands for money.

In order to get any building going it was vital for Sir John and his eldest son Spencer to act together, partly because their agreement was needed in granting building leases, and partly because Sir John was an old man disinclined to take any financial risks and adamant that since

[1] E/MW/H/III/26/54, Clark to Sir John Maryon Wilson, 30 March 1874.
[2] Ibid., Bell & Steward to Knocker, 6 December 1873; same to same, 20 November 1871.

his son would be the one to inherit all the increased income he should be the one to make the initial outlays. When he inherited, Sir John was already 67 years old and well set in his ways as an Essex country gentleman living quietly on his modest but comfortable estate at Great Canfield, content to leave its management and that of all his affairs in the care of his father-in-law, an exasperatingly slow-moving Dunmow solicitor. He had six sons and three daughters to launch in the world, and Spencer may well have been a drain on his purse in his young days in the Navy or if he expected his father to support his wife and his own six children. At any rate when Spencer wrote to his father in 1872 that: 'All I can now assuredly say is "that your interests are mine" and that my hands need not approach your pockets under any circumstances, and I am prepared to put as much the past as the present in the "broadest light"', he was plainly hoping to bury some past money trouble which still rankled with his father.[1] Sir John in his turn made it absolutely clear to the surveyor whom his son employed to prepare schemes for Hampstead that 'he did not intend at his time of life to sink any property there; that his present income must be wholly uninterfered with, that he was ready to talk matters of principle with me, but that all detail must be settled with Mr Wade [Sir John's father-in-law and man of business] who he should instruct on his recovery.'[2]

Relations between father and son were distinctly prickly, and for half-a-dozen years one or other had no difficulty in discovering insuperable objections to anything that was proposed for the Hampstead estate. Sometimes it would be Sir John who 'was so annoyed at cold water being thrown upon everything for the improvement of the estate that [he threatened] he would at once grant 21 year leases of the whole of it.' 'Pray do not let us come to this pass', Clark besought Spencer's solicitors, for Sir John could grant such leases on his own without any need for his son's concurrence, and they would sterilise the property for another twenty-one years.[3] At other times it would be Spencer chafing at the endless delays and prevarications of his father through Wade and his successor Knocker, who out in the country at Dunmow did not notice and did not care that building season followed building season with not a sod cut. 'Time is pressing or another year will be lost', Clark was moved to plead in the spring of 1874, taking Spencer's part for once.[4] The year was lost, frittered away as much in the torpor of the

[1] Ibid., Spencer Maryon Wilson to Sir John, 7 February 1872.
[2] Ibid., Henry R. Newton to Spencer Maryon Wilson, 13 November 1871.
[3] E/MW/H/III/26/19, Clark to Bell & Steward, 3 December 1872.
[4] E/MW/H/III/26/54, Clark to Knocker, 28 May 1874.

Dunmow solicitor's office where it was seldom thought proper to answer letters, as in active disagreement. After all the lost opportunities and lucrative negotiations which had fallen through it seemed scarcely credible when the contract for Fitzjohn's Avenue was actually let in the summer of 1875 and road-making at last began.

From the early 1880s onwards Fitzjohn's Avenue became widely admired as 'one of the most handsome thoroughfares in all London'. 'Its tree-planted roadway', it was said, 'and the artistic houses on either side, give the avenue a unique appearance worth a journey to see', and it was hailed as London's answer to the Parisian boulevards. Whether or not, after half a jaded century of traffic, dust, and changing tastes, 'this commanding, tree-beautified avenue of stately dwellings' is thought to deserve such a rapturous welcome, its creation has some-times been quite wrongly attributed to an act of imaginative municipal enterprise of a quality and far-sightedness far in advance of its period.[1] The contribution of the Vestry was, indeed, important; but it was limited to giving the northern end of the new road a direct access into the old town, and was made only after much dithering and haggling. The road itself was the achievement of private enterprise, and, what is more, the personal achievement of Spencer Maryon Wilson in the teeth of his agents' professional advice. Since his father insisted that all the responsibility and worry of making decisions about the Hampstead estate should be taken by his son, Spencer determined that the Conduit Fields should be opened to luxury development in the grand manner, by making 'a truly imposing road, 50 feet wide with 10 foot paths, planted with alternate red and white chestnuts, and with the houses set back a further 15 or 25 feet'. Neither the land agent, F. J. Clark, nor the building surveyor retained by Spencer, H. R. Newton, thought anything of this idea which seemed to them an extravagant and showy gesture, a waste of money and of precious land which would rapidly degenerate into a strip of real waste land through inevitable neglect. Clark commented on Spencer's 'wish that the main road leading to Hampstead should be made into a kind of Boulevard planted with trees' that:[2]

I agree with Mr Newton that it becomes a nuisance if left open, and I doubt if the Parish would be content if the onus of maintain-

[1] *Hampstead and Highgate Express*, 1 January 1881; T. J. Barratt, *The Annals of Hampstead*, III (1912), p. 312; E. F. Oppé, *Hampstead a London Town* (1951), p. 28.

[2] E/MW/H/III/26/54, Clark to Knocker, 6 October 1874; E/MW/H/III/26/19, Clark to Bell & Steward, 7 May 1872.

ing these trees were thrown upon it, neither do I think it will be worth while to sacrifice so much land . . . I presume Mr Newton would insist upon the houses being put back some 15 or 20 feet, and this intervening space between the houses and the road would form the forecourts and gardens and would necessarily be planted by the lessees, and so form the Avenue, but to add 10 feet more as an enclosure would entail expense, always have a ragged appearance as it is next to impossible to get all the occupiers to contribute equally to the maintenance, and lastly none of the occupiers would be grateful for having so much additional expense thrust upon them coupled with the extra distance from the road in case of wet weather.

Spencer got his way, and when the contract for making the road from the iron church at College Crescent to a meeting with Greenhill Road in the rear of the Soldiers' Daughters Home was let to Culverhouse in 1875 the price of £8,987 included planting with ornamental trees.[1] The road, of course, never achieved the formality and regularity of a city boulevard; but the liberality of its leafiness was undoubtedly a major reason for its success as the principal drive in a wealthy, and for a while highly fashionable, district whose residents possessed sufficient servants and umbrellas to mitigate the rigours of long front paths. While Spencer was responsible for the concept of a grand avenue, the exact alignment was left to Newton to settle. Here the views of the Vestry, or rather of its surveyor, did have some influence; for although Newton was chiefly concerned to choose a line that would be of greatest advantage to the estate in giving convenient access to all the potential building land between Swiss Cottage and the town, it was also important not to antagonise the Vestry. This was partly on the general ground that although it was not necessary to obtain a vestry's approval for building a private road 'practically they [the Vestry] are the masters of the situation, for they can at a future date refuse to take to a road [adopt it as a public highway] without material alteration in its structure'; and partly on the particular ground that the new road involved 'obliterating the footpath' from College Crescent across the fields, by the Shepherd's Well to Shepherd's Walk, 'and sooner than risk an unnecessary collision with the Vestry we submitted plans of the road to the Parish Surveyor.'[2] Moreover, in order to avoid problems of

[1] *Hampstead and Highgate Express*, 21 August 1875.
[2] E/MW/H/III/26/54, Bell & Steward to Knocker, 1 September and 6 December 1873.

short-term finance, the estate hoped at one stage that the Vestry might be persuaded to construct the new road on sub-contract, being repaid when it was finished; given luck, the first receipts from sales or leases to builders might then come in in time to pay off the Vestry, so that Spencer would not need to find any ready cash. This move to work on credit unwittingly provided by the ratepayers did not come off, but it was an added reason for readiness to make the route of the new road a matter of negotiation with the Vestry.[1]

The footpath across the Conduit Fields, which was a right of way, ran from the iron church on College Crescent to a ventilating shaft of the Hampstead Junction tunnel, now in Netherhall Gardens, where it made a sharp turn north-eastwards to join Shepherd's Walk. Newton wished to abandon the line of the path and take the road further down-hill to the west to link up with Frognal Lane, which he held would give the best gradients for a 'new lower Heath Road' and be 'the most serviceable to the estate.' Douglas, the parish surveyor, also wished to abandon the path, but to deviate to the east in order to produce a new main road aimed at the centre of Hampstead by joining the existing spur of Greenhill Road. To this Newton cogently objected that 'if a new line of Main Road is laid down in the direction the Vestry wish, there is no proper termination to it at the Hampstead end.' He concluded:[2]

> The only suggestion I can make that would enable me to put the matter before Mr Spencer Wilson for his personal decision, is if the Vestry would undertake to remove the block of houses between Church Row and Heath Street, the glaring defect of the line which the Vestry wish to see carried out would as a public road be then obliterated.

In the event, under pressure from Clark who wanted to avoid any new grounds for ill-feeling between the Vestry and the Maryon Wilsons, the Vestry's wishes for a dead straight road from the iron church to the corner of Errington's land, joining Greenhill Road by a pronounced bend, were followed without securing any binding undertaking to remove the maze of old buildings and tiny courts which lay between Church Row and Heath Street. The Vestry's officer had successfully used his influence to bend the private purposes of estate development to

1 E/MW/H/III/26/19, Clark to Bell & Steward, 7 May 1872; E/MW/H/III/26/54, Clark to Knocker, 27 July 1874; *Hampstead and Highgate Express*, 14 August 1875.
2 E/MW/H/III/26/19, Newton to Clark, 30 July 1872; Newton to Douglas (Vestry Surveyor), 30 July 1872.

suit the public interests of a major improvement in metropolitan communications. But although the Vestry was ready to see this major improvement peter out for another decade in the awkward turnings of Prince Arthur Road or Perrins Lane which took any traffic from Fitzjohn's Avenue–Greenhill Road into High Street, the action which it ought to take to complete the improvement had been plainly indicated by the Maryon Wilson men.

The parish surveyor, to be sure, went ahead with drafting schemes for the municipal contribution to the exercise; but even the cheapest alternative which he suggested, involving simply the widening of Perrins Lane, foundered on resistance to the cost of acquiring buildings for demolition.[1] For a while the Hampstead public and the Vestry became happily absorbed in the connected issue of footpaths in the Conduit Fields, where local rivalries could be forgotten in a common suspicion of the Maryon Wilsons. With some reluctance it was agreed that the main path to Swiss Cottage should be surrendered, since Fitzjohn's Avenue itself provided an alternative and more direct way for the public. But there were two lesser paths: one had come across Rosslyn Park to the Shepherd's Well, and a short section still survived as a path on Maryon Wilson land, from Windsor Terrace to the Well; the second ran from Belsize Crescent to the Well, and formed the boundary between Maryon Wilson and Dean and Chapter lands. The Vestry had a good record in looking after footpaths, keeping stiles repaired, and providing benches at attractive spots; but it had also been sensible in agreeing to abandon them when streets and houses arrived, as had happened with this second path which had formerly run on across Dean and Chapter and Eton College fields to link Hampstead to Chalk Farm and Primrose Hill.[2] With the Maryon Wilson estate, however, there was a much more tenacious attitude to the literal preservation of public rights and the Vestry insisted on retaining the two vestigial paths, encapsulated on the building estate as Shepherd's Path and Spring Path, for no better reason than that these sections ran across Maryon Wilson land. Alderman Ralph Ellis, one of F. J. Clark's business partners, argued the Maryon Wilson case, pointing out that new roads would provide perfectly good substitutes and that in particular it would be possible to continue Thurlow Road through to the new Avenue, from where a future road was planned in a direct line to the Midland station on Finchley Road. In any case, Ellis argued, if forced to keep the paths the estate would simply encase them between

[1] *Hampstead and Highgate Express*, 4 November 1876.
[2] HPL Vestry Min., 27 March and 17 July 1857.

walls, leaving narrow unlit passages; to which, the local paper added, there were the gravest possible moral and sanitary objections, envisaging much urination if not copulation in the midst of a respectable neighbourhood.[1]

In the paths issue neither middle-class morality nor the utilitarian convenience of pedestrians was the effective consideration. A coalition of those who could not bear to acknowledge that the beautiful Conduit Fields were to be built over, who dreamt that Hampstead could be rural forever, with those who could not bear to miss a chance to inflict some pinpricks on the Maryon Wilsons, carried the day. In the more weighty matter of the street improvements, however, the clash of local interests and overtones of class divisions prevented agreement. As a start the estimated cost, running from £23,000 up to as much as £90,000 according to the scale of improvements contemplated, not only alarmed ratepayers who were at the same moment finding £18,500 for a new Vestry Hall, but also caused the ratepayers of Kilburn, Adelaide, and Belsize Wards to protest that the whole thing was no concern of theirs since the improvements were calculated to benefit only the old town; an argument of extreme sub-parochial self-interest curiously at odds with the parish surveyor's contention that what was involved was of metropolitan significance as a new outlet from the West End to the Heath which on that ground ought to attract assistance from the Metropolitan Board of Works. Within the old town, however, the proposals brought the slumbering tensions between tradespeople and gentry into the open. The shopkeepers in the High Street feared loss of trade if any traffic was diverted to a new route, and held out for a scheme which would debouch Fitzjohn's Avenue into High Street at the King William IV; while the gentry wanted the direct route to Heath Street and the Heath, arguing that this gave a bit of slum clearance of Bradley's Buildings, Yorkshire Grey Yard, and Bakers' Row as a bonus. The dissension continued when the scheme was revived with a number of public meetings in 1881, dominated by the gentry element which was increasingly exasperated at having its carriages bottled up in Fitzjohn's Avenue without any proper exit. The High Street traders rallied, under Richard Hackworth, one of the longest-serving Vestrymen, and with the cry that the parish should not make a fine new roadway simply for the carriages of the rich to roll along, succeeded in forcing a compromise. To preserve the attractions of High Street to traffic and trade it should be widened by demolitions on the west side from Crockett's Court to the Black Boy public house; then at the same time Fitzjohn's Avenue could

[1] *Hampstead and Highgate Express*, 3 June and 8 July 1876.

be driven straight through from Church Row to Heath Street. Thus it fell out that this side of High Street displays the same style of liverish red-brick shop buildings of the late 1880s and 1890s as does the new section of lower Heath Street. The cost of these street improvements entailed loans which exceeded the normal borrowing powers of a vestry, and the authorisation of a special local improvement Act was necessary, obtained in 1883 in the Metropolitan Board of Works' annual instalment of legislation. The main work on the Town Improvements, as they were called, started in 1886, and the new roads with the modern intersection of Heath Street–High Street–Holly Hill were opened in 1888.[1]

The local authority, it seems, moved a good deal more slowly than the private landowners, and had great difficulty when it came to spending money in deciding where the public interest lay. Several hands contributed to the shaping of the new road, among them those of the Vestry; but it is proper that the main stretch of it should be known after Spencer Wilson's house in Great Canfield, Fitzjohn's, as his was the chief part in the ruling concept. The grandness of the avenue was rapidly rewarded by the grandness of the houses which were built on it as soon as Culverhouse finished the road-making in 1876. A few of these were architect-built for individual clients who acquired plots, most notably by Norman Shaw who provided several versions of his red-brick Queen Anne–Dutch gabled composite revivals for prosperous Royal Academicians, as well as one for himself in Ellerdale Road on the adjoining Errington estate. The bulk, however, were by speculative builders, of whom Herbert and Edward Kelly were the chief, who saw the opening for providing large houses for the very wealthiest class.[2] The individual plots, indeed, were one of the causes of family dispute which held up the Maryon Wilsons for several years. Spencer, when he realised that if anything was to be done in his father's lifetime it had to be done by himself, was anxious to find as much of the road-building money as possible without having to borrow it: one way he favoured was the sale of some of the plots, for which offers were frequently coming in naming tempting prices of £1,000 to £2,000 an acre.

While he wished to accept such offers, his father's advisers held by the enduring benefits of developing only under building leases, and warned against the folly of selling. The leasing of considerable tracts of

[1] Ibid., 1 January, 8 January, 15 January, 18 June and 5 November 1881; F. E. Baines (ed.), *Records of the Manor, Parish and Borough of Hampstead* (1890), pp. 192–4.

[2] Norman Shaw houses are nos 6 and 61 Fitzjohn's Avenue, and 6 Ellerdale Road: Pevsner, *The Buildings of England: London*, II (1952), p. 202.

building land was preferable, it was argued, because by selling it was more than likely that only the choicest plots would be taken, leaving awkward and irregular gaps hanging fire. Moreover, Clark advised, 'unless an absolute necessity arose I should prefer letting to selling, because the owners of the estate can then entirely control the class of buildings and prevent any nuisance, and the reversion in the third generation would make the Wilson Family one of the wealthiest in the kingdom.'[1] Builders, on their side, were most reluctant to purchase building land because of the cost of finding the purchase money for any large area, and much preferred to rent.[2] It seems likely that the solution on the Fitzjohn's Avenue development was a compromise between the two positions, with the main part of the initial building estate on either side of the road let under a single building agreement, but coupled with the simultaneous sale of a few separate plots.[3]

The solution to Spencer's problem of road finance was found mainly not in the sale of land, but in his father's agreement to drawing on the family's capital funds from the sale of the manorial rights in the Heath and from copyhold enfranchisements. The accumulated copyhold moneys alone amounted to at least £23,900, and like the land itself could only be dealt with by Sir John and Spencer acting jointly, though the income from the fund belonged to Sir John alone. The eventual agreement was that Spencer could draw on this fund for road expenses, paying his father 3 per cent for the sacrifice of interest, well below the 5 per cent which Spencer would have paid if he had borrowed on the open market.[4] This agreement followed from a formal treaty between father and son, signed in 1873, which if it did not restore family unity at least put relationships on a definite business footing. This concordat provided that Sir John would permit Spencer to take possession of specified parts of the Hampstead estate in order to turn them into building properties, guaranteeing his father a minimum rent of £5 an

[1] E/MW/H/III/26/19, Clark to Bell & Steward, 7 May 1872. Small pieces of the Errington (Greenhill) estate were sold by auction at £1,800 an acre; but this was after hanging about with no takers for three or four years, and in any case it was the price fetched by one acre, which would not have been reached for large parcels.

[2] Ibid., Clark to Knocker, 22 April 1872, reporting the refusal of the Yeo brothers to consider purchasing 33 acres in Conduit Fields, for which at a minimum price of £33,000 they would need to find £1,650 a year to cover the interest.

[3] The Maryon Wilson estate documentation unfortunately ends before the conclusion of the final building agreements for this, or any of the other, building estates.

[4] E/MW/H/III/26/54, Bell & Steward to Knocker, 3 June 1874.

acre all the time so that at no point should he suffer a drop in income; that Spencer would provide all the money needed for making plans, roads, and sewers, and for paying agents; that the resulting ground rents should be divided fifty-fifty between father and son; that mutually agreed sales of building land should be permitted, the purchase moneys being also shared, with the father receiving as a capital sum the value of his life interest, this being valued at the end of each year by an actuary; and that all plans for roads, and for every house, should be subject to Sir John's approval.[1]

It was in this stiff and formal way that preparations were made for breaching the tight urban frontier which ran across south Hampstead, father and son behaving like nothing so much as a pair of thoroughly distrustful eighteenth-century allies endlessly raising real and imaginary difficulties before committing troops to battle. In this instance the advance troops were the turf dealers with whom all arrangements were made 'to cut and remove the turf [for the new road] the instant the agreement is signed.'[2] The new road in question here was on the Kilburn boundary of the estate, where it marched with Colonel Cotton of Quex Park in the Isle of Thanet, who had inherited both the West End Lane and the Shoot-Up Hill Farm properties owned by John Powell in 1838.[3] Cotton owned about 60 acres lying on either side of West End Lane, stretching from Upton's part of Abbey Road up to the present West Hampstead station on the east side, and from Kilburn to Oaklands Hall (with its fence on the line of Messina Avenue) on the west; well-situated for a building estate, but coming within the pull of the market only in the 1870s. The boundary between Maryon Wilson and Cotton land was a footpath which Spencer and the Colonel agreed to straighten out by an exchange of small pieces of land and use as the line of a new road, Priory Road, each meeting half of the cost. This road, started in 1874, became the first development on the Maryon Wilson estate.[4] Cotton set out to make something good-class of his estate, or at least of the section to the east of West End Lane, where Acol, Woodchurch, Cleve, and Chislett Roads were formed and supplied with large and

1 E/MW/H/III/26/19, Bell & Steward to Knocker, 26 February 1872, 26 December 1872, 10 January 1873, 12 February and 27 February 1873, and 19 April 1873; Instructions to Counsel (Eyre Foakes) to settle an Agreement, 12 March 1872.

2 Ibid., Bell & Stewart to Knocker, 10 January 1873.

3 HLRO Midland Railway London Extension, 1863, Plan and Book of Reference, for H. P. Cotton's ownership of Shoot-Up Hill Farm. And see above, p. 83.

4 HPL Vestry Min., 30 April 1874, notification of the starting of Acol Road and Canfield Road.

well-spaced houses in the next dozen years; Cleve Road, indeed, was found by Booth in 1889 to be an upper-class road in the same class as Fitzjohn's Avenue. His land to the west, with Birchington and Quex Roads, Smyrna Road, Gascony and Messina Avenues, and Kingsgate Road, was set aside for lower-quality development in terrace houses, some large enough for middle-class occupation, some more suited to artisans. For Spencer Wilson, however, this area constituted 'the worst part of the Estate, namely the Kilburn end', destined by its lack of elevation for respectable middle-class development maybe, but development of a decidedly more skimped, crowded and altogether less expensive character than the uplands. It was perhaps intended as a comment both on the intended social level of the district and on his relations with his father that the principal road into this new quarter, now known as Priory Road, was the one at first chosen by Spencer to carry the name of Canfield, after Sir John's Essex seat.[1]

For this less-favoured part of the estate Spencer was well content to look forward to ground rents at the rate of £60 an acre, with himself finding the roads; and on some such terms this part of the estate began to move briskly in the second half of the 1870s, with Canfield and Broadhurst Gardens following close on the heels of Priory Road. Compayne, Greencroft and Fairhazel Gardens came mainly in the decade after 1885, while Aberdare Gardens and Goldhurst Terrace rounded off the development in the later 1890s. All this was essentially housing for the middling middle classes. The provision of stabling was, significantly, kept to a bare minimum, with a small range in Coleridge Mews opposite Fairfax Mews. At the start there had been two or three dozen more in Canfield Place backing on to the Finchley Road station, where Ernest Estcourt and James Dixon, the builders of Canfield and Greencroft Gardens, placed premises for a riding school, livery stables, workshops, and privately-tenanted coach-houses and stables; but when the whole of Canfield Place was demolished to make way for the Great Central Railway's extension to Marylebone in the 1890s there was felt to be no call to replace these.[2] The higher ambitions of Colonel Cotton's development are to be seen in his provision of the same amount of stabling, in West Hampstead Mews behind the West Hampstead police station, for a quarter of the number of residences.

[1] E/MW/H/III/26/19, Bell & Steward to Knocker, 26 February 1872. Chislett Road was the original name of Cotton's part of the present Compayne Gardens.
[2] HPL Vestry Min., 24 September 1885; HLRO Manchester, Sheffield and Lincolnshire Railway, London Extension, 1891/2, Plan and Book of Reference, Railway No. 8.

Built for this particular layer of middle-class families, which had maybe three or four domestic servants but no carriage, 'the worst part' of the Maryon Wilson estate was in competition with dozens of other areas elsewhere on the fringes of London offering the same kind of streets and houses, and it is not surprising that it took the best part of a quarter of a century for the supply of sites to be taken up. Matters were different on the other side of the Finchley Road, where the whole of the Fitzjohn's Avenue neighbourhood was developed within ten years after 1876. Netherhall and Maresfield Gardens, named after a manor and a parish of the family's Sussex estate, and Daleham Gardens (known for a few years as Akenside Road, before the present road of that name was made along the Maryon Wilson–Dean and Chapter boundary) followed within a year or two of the first arrival of the contractors. Here, with plenty of trees and large building plots, the fashionable appellation of 'Gardens' for new residential roads was better deserved. Many large detached houses were built, set well back from the road; and many of them had room for their own carriage drives, albeit they were highly abbreviated versions of the original article, while Tidey's earlier development of an inferior commercial quarter on the south-eastern border, at Belsize Village, was turned to good account in providing the estate with one bank of Daleham Mews. The whole became a very wealthy, indeed a luxury, quarter; and the rapidity which which the sites were filled indicates that the Conduit Fields had few competitors as living space for London's new wealthy of the 1880s. It is the successful artists who are best remembered as setting the tone of the district, with their weekly 'Sunday parade' on the Avenue: Frank Holl, the society portrait painter, living at the Three Gables which Norman Shaw built for him; John Pettie at the Lothians close by; Paul Falconer Poole at Uplands, a house in 'crude, elephantine Gothic' by T. K. Green; Edwin Long at Kelston, in Netherhall Gardens, another Shaw house; and in Maresfield Gardens, Henry Moore and Sir Ernest Waterlow.[1] This was a passing phase, however, and as intellectual and artistic society moved on to something more intimate and less ostentatious it was the solidly rich businessmen and retired people of private means who sustained the district's character.

While such success and renown had yet been but a possibility Spencer had been dismayed when Robert Yeo, a builder in a large way of business, had offered no more than £60 an acre to take the first 33 acres of this choice land. To Spencer's mind it seemed that an area of such attraction and potential ought to command a much higher price

[1] Pevsner, op. cit., II, 202; Barratt, op. cit. III, 312.

than flat, low-lying land over towards Kilburn of indifferent aspect. F. J. Clark, however, pointed out that this was a reasonable offer which the estate ought to accept, 'as these builders are A1 men and it would be the means of showing that the estate can be developed and the other land would then go off more rapidly and of course at a higher price.' Moreover the lower density at which Yeo proposed to build meant that he could not afford a higher rent; he would put up houses worth about £180 a year, and 'no builder would of course take such a large area as this with loss of interest arising from the financing unless he saw that he could double the ground rent', while in practice such houses would not be marketable with 'improved ground rents' of anything over £30 a year. At four houses to the acre, this put a ceiling of £60 an acre on the basic ground rent.[1] Practical experience was brought in to confirm the reasoning of the property market, for, as Clark reported later,[2]

> Messrs Yeo are very candid. They were with me yesterday, and stated they could not give more rent, but brought with them 7 Building Agreements extending from 1851 to the present time, shewing that they had covered nearly 100 acres [in Hampstead] and that the ground rents payable to Col. Eyre, Eton College, N.W. Rly and others varied from about £35 to £43 per acre.

Spencer declined to let Yeo on to his best land on these terms, and since Yeo was most anxious to get his men to work he took a lease on the Kilburn side instead, where he became the principal builder on both the Cotton and the Maryon Wilson sides of Priory (Canfield) Road. When Fitzjohn's Avenue was opened to builders a couple of years later the main speculative take, after the road had been given a start by one or two directly commissioned architect-designed houses, went to Herbert and Edward Kelly, who quickly moved up from Camden Town to operate from a new estate office on the corner of Nutley Terrace, and became the main builders of the Avenue. It is possible that the Kellys offered a higher ground rent, but it is unlikely; for they built large detached houses of the value which Yeo had contemplated, and Clark's reasoning must still have applied.[3] This showed that there was no immediate advantage in income to the ground landlord from more

[1] E/MW/H/III/26/19, Clark to Knocker, 5 March 1872.
[2] Ibid., Clark to Knocker, 16 April 1872.
[3] HPL Vestry Min., 12 October 1876, 14 November 1878, for Yeo in Canfield Road; 4 October, 13 December 1877, 21 February, 6 June, 10 October 1878, for H. & E. Kelly and their estate office in Fitzjohn's Avenue; 7 May 1885 for H. & E. Kelly in Maresfield Gardens. *Hampstead and Highgate Directory*, 1885, shows H. & E. Kelly's estate office still in action.

expensive rather than medium-quality development, the higher cost and rental value of larger houses being balanced by the fact that there were fewer of them. The advantages came, though uncertainly, from the prospect of somewhat higher rents from later takes, and the chance that a really wealthy development might fill up rapidly if it was lucky enough to become fashionable; rather more certain were the correspondingly slighter advantages that the ground rents would be better secured the more wealthy the occupants, and that the value of the ultimate reversion would be greater. In selecting the broad type of development there would not seem to have been much in it financially either way, for the landowner, leaving the personal, social, or aesthetic preferences of either the owner or his agent to sway the decision.

In this instance the owner's personal wishes carried much weight in determining the form of the development. It was as well, however, that his enthusiasms and his anxiety to mobilise his urban wealth as fast as possible were restrained by the prudent counsel of Clark:[1]

> If there were only 33 acres he might stick out for price, but where 33 acres is only a small portion of 500 acres belonging to the Wilson family, and there are nearly 500 acres also adjoining which can be brought in competition, it makes a very material difference.

Clark believed in making haste slowly, in not starting too many separate building ventures at the same time but rather in concentrating on getting just one or two properly launched and progressing steadily; the essence of good estate management was to contrive a controlled release of building land so that good builders were neither scared off by fearing there would not be enough space to keep their resources fully employed for a period of years, nor tempted to hang back expecting a glut of land and falling rents. The launching of the two major enterprises of Priory Road and Fitzjohn's Avenue, with a smaller but profitable development of the Finchley Road frontages from the North Star public house to the Midland station, were sufficient to meet these objectives in the later 1870s and beyond.

When Sir John died in May 1876 and Spencer gained sole control of the estate Clark could not prevent some dispersion of activities, with a small start being made to the future Redington Road. But when the new Sir Spencer's solicitors informed the Vestry later in 1876 that they had been inspecting the East Park estate to consider the best mode of developing it, and that this would involve using the powers to make roads across the Heath, one of which would mean the removal of 'some

[1] E/MW/H/III/26/19, Clark to Knocker, 5 March 1872.

erections for the bathing pond', the purpose was more to remind the Vestry and the public that the right to make roads across the Heath did exist than to announce that the builders were about to start.[1] Although the prospect of an abrupt end to public bathing in the Hampstead Ponds would have gratified the prudish ratepayer who had been 'more shocked and disgusted than I can find words to express [on seeing] some 50 perfectly naked men and boys bathing in the Pond, and running about the banks among the bystanders in a state of absolute nudity', there was little chance that it would be in the interests of the estate to oblige before the mid-1880s.[2] The movement to extend the Heath by acquiring for the public the adjoining fields of East Park and Parliament Hill was started early in 1884 on a note of urgency because the Maryon Wilson estate was thought to be making ready for the builders by staking out roads and building plots. But even this was probably a mistake, although East Park was inevitably much closer to the point of building ripeness in 1884 than it had been in 1869–70 when the negotiations for taking over the Heath were completed. In 1884 the Maryon Wilson estate was busy getting a sewer laid down West Heath Road in preparation for developing that area; and while this no doubt revived some bitter memories of the surrender of a strip of Heath here to Maryon Wilson as part of the 1870 bargain, giving him a potential building frontage to this road, and excited well-grounded fears that a barrier of houses might shortly divide the West Heath from the commanding local eminence of the privately-owned Telegraph Hill, thus destroying one of the favourite walks in this part, all this had no immediate connection with the East Heath and East Park.[3] There is no sign that Sir Spencer had designs on East Park precisely in 1884, though he certainly had it in mind to develop at some stage.

The other evidence used to stress the urgency of the task of saving the open fields was equally misleading. The lines of the probable roads on East Park had long been marked out, since Sir Thomas's day; and the presence of a brickfield not far from the bathing pond was of equally long standing, where Culverhouse's brickworks and the four cottages of his workers were no doubt an unpleasant and a menacing sight, but not a new one.[4] Indeed if, as seems likely, Culverhouse held this brickfield on a 21-year lease from 1866 his presence provided some slight dis-

---

[1] *Hampstead and Highgate Express*, 10 June 1876. And see above, p. 197.
[2] Letter to *The Times* from 'Ratepayer', 24 July 1872.
[3] Baines (ed.), op. cit., p. 193.
[4] HPL Vestry Min., 2 July 1874, report on sanitary state of these cottages.

incentive to any building development before 1887. In truth it seems that the movement to extend the Heath simply needed some respectable and roughly plausible reason to get started, a reason which would serve to divert attention from the awkward point that the traditional efforts of the Hampstead gentry to appropriate the 'adjoining lands' as public property on the cheap, or indeed without any payment, were being abandoned in favour of a straightforward attempt to purchase them at a fair market price, which was the procedure that the Maryon Wilsons had always been prepared to follow. It was a favourable moment, in terms of Hampstead personalities, to launch a campaign: the veterans of the contests with Sir Thomas—Hoare, Le Breton, Turner—had all gone, and there were new local leaders on hand unembarrassed by associations with the wild and often mendacious claims of the past. In January 1884 C. E. Maurice, who had arrived in Hampstead only in 1873 when the Heath passions were already cooling or turning towards asserting rights to take donkey rides or play cricket, against the new custodians the Metropolitan Board of Works, inspired the group of local notables in the Kyrle Society to convene a meeting in the Holly Bush Assembly Rooms to consider taking action to extend the Heath by buying lands before the builders got them. Supported by Cornelius Walford, barrister and cousin of Edward Walford of *Old and New London*, and H. M. Bompas, another barrister then fresh from struggling against the Smallpox Hospital, who were both relative newcomers to Hampstead and its public life, the Kyrle Society set up an Open Spaces Committee with Maurice as its secretary and were in business in the property market, without funds but with a popular idea.[1]

It was a favourable time, also, for arousing an influential public opinion in the cause of open spaces for the masses. The idea of providing 'lungs for the metropolis' as a measure variously of physical, aesthetic or social health had been circulating in progressive circles off and on for more than half a century. Since 1865 the Commons Preservation Society had provided an organised outlet for such views, and its activities no doubt helped to increase interest in the question. In the eighties the dedicated minority of open-space enthusiasts was caught up in a much wider movement of upper-class concern for the plight of the urban working classes mingled with fear of their capacity for violence. The

---

[1] *The Times*, 2 February, 5 February 1884. Barratt, op. cit., II, 219, misdates this inaugural meeting as in July 1884. C. E. Maurice was the son of F. D. Maurice, a prominent mid-Victorian Anglican theologian, who came to live on Rosslyn Hill in 1873.

conscience of the comfortable classes was stirred by the *Bitter Cry of Outcast London* and the publicity it received on its appearance in 1883, with its searing revelations of slum conditions; and it was fanned by the stream of information on housing conditions flowing from the Royal Commission on the Housing of the Working Classes of 1884–5. Upper-class panic is generally held to have been aroused when windows in Pall Mall were smashed by a procession of the unemployed organised by the Social Democratic Federation early in 1886, when for the first time since Chartist days the property of the wealthy was exposed to physical danger. At the same time the working-class vote was becoming increasingly significant and was increasingly courted by politicians. These were the ingredients of a climate of opinion in which support for the welfare of the working classes could be expected, whether this was regarded as a necessary concession, a contribution to social reconciliation, or a step in the direction of physical and moral improvement.

It was in terms of the welfare of the common people of London that the cause of the wider Heath was presented, and it was this concern which eventually generated sufficient support, both in political pressure and in money, to carry through the extension. First and foremost it was seen as a question of health, almost as a sanitary measure, with the Heath acting as a gigantic ventilator, cleanser, and purifier of the crowded, foetid, noisome districts of working-class London lying below it: 'from the high ground, the Heath pours into the town volumes of fresh air such as cannot come from the valley of the Thames or the low lands of Essex', wrote Baroness Burdett-Coutts in advocacy of the enormous importance of preserving this public-health bellows. And she went on to stress the vital contribution which this grand stretch of fresh air also made to the physique of the poor children and invalids who visited it for exercise.[1] The second string to the arguments for treating the wider Heath as a public concern was that as a playground it provided pleasure and enjoyment for London artisans and East End slum-dwellers for whom it was an easily and cheaply accessible tract of open country whose delights did something to relieve the dismal poverty or misery of their personal living conditions. All this was undoubtedly true. The crowds which came swarming to the Heath, particularly on bank holidays, were largely lower-middle and working-class; though with their patronage of the booths and stalls, the donkey men, the Italian refreshment kiosk on the lower Heath, and the tea-rooms, pubs, and hotel in South End it may be doubted whether they came from the slums and the poverty-stricken groups. Octavia Hill testified that 'on

[1] Letter to *The Times* from Baroness Burdett-Coutts, 30 October 1885.

bright Sunday and Saturday afternoons hundreds go to see the hay made [in the fields alongside the Heath] and I have seen the Heath black like an anthill on a Bank Holiday,' and contemporary pictures of Happy Hampstead amply bear her out.[1]

Hampstead Heath was extremely popular, and the interests of the masses provided one good reason for wishing to extend it by acquiring East Park and Parliament Hill Fields. But it was only one reason, and it could hardly be denied that when the talk was of how 'the prospect from the Heath would be spoiled and the sense of freshness and freedom . . . would be dispelled' if these fields were to be covered with houses, causing the Heath to 'lose much of its charm and descend to the level of an ordinary park or recreation ground', the appeal was to sentiments mainly held by the middle and upper classes.[2] More was at stake, of course, than the visual appeal of the scenery, the woods, and the view. For many years the public had been in the habit of walking over these fields and had beaten out many paths, though from the legal angle this was done on sufferance by the owners and not by right; the public, for this purpose, was much more likely to be drawn from nature-lovers, artists, and walkers from the higher ranks of society than from the toiling masses. Above all, perhaps, it could hardly be denied that the main benefit of the enlarged expanse of open space, in terms of opportunities for year-round enjoyment, would go to the residents of Hampstead and Highgate; among these, members of the working classes were not prominent, nor was the presence of roughs from the lower orders especially welcomed by many of the gentlefolk who liked to regard the Heath as their own preserve. In other words it was a matter of tactics to emphasise the popular motives for acquiring the new lands, and to keep the other motives in the background; for the way to attract support and loosen purses outside the locality, and to enlist public money in the scheme, was to stress the benefits to the working classes, not the protection of beauty or riparian property values which it promised. Among themselves, however, some Hampstead residents were ready to acknowledge that there was rather more in it for them than for the broad masses. At a meeting of the local Liberal Club in 1884 C. E. Maurice was concerned to wipe out a general impression of Hampstead's selfishness held by 'some people in London [who] looked on Hampstead residents as a selfish people, who were

[1] Letter to *The Times* from Octavia Hill, 9 October 1887. An annual fair had long been held on the site between East Heath Road and the Ponds, and by the 1880s was becoming increasingly elaborate with steam roundabouts and steam organs: Barratt, op. cit., II, 232.
[2] *The Times*, 2 February 1884.

FIGURE 5 Municipal strangulation of the Heath: riders foiled by the Board's regulations, 1883

trying to drive away now smallpox patients, now tramways,' by emphasising the altruism of the drive to enlarge the Heath. But G. W. Potter brought matters nearer home when he asked the meeting to 'try to imagine what a narrow brown strip the East Heath would appear, as looked at from the end of Well Walk, if the East Park were built over.' And Maurice's chairman, Cornelius Walford, clinched the argument by supporting the health reasons for enlarging the Heath 'not so much on account of the working classes as of the brain workers, who derived so much benefit from the invigorating air of Hampstead.'[1]

It was in this situation that the local initiative quickly attracted influential support for the formation of a metropolitan Heath Extension Committee with the Duke of Westminster as its chairman and Shaw Lefevre, the leading champion of open spaces, as its chief man of action, and the philanthropists Baroness Burdett-Coutts and Octavia Hill among the members. Initially the Committee saw itself as publicising the case sufficiently forcefully to persuade either the government or the Metropolitan Board of Works to take over the actual business of negotiation and finding the purchase money. After some preliminary discussions which established that Sir Spencer Maryon Wilson and Lord Mansfield were willing to sell their lands for an open space, if the price was right, the Committee staged its big promotional set-piece of a lavish garden party on the top of Parliament Hill, complete with the band of the Coldstream Guards, with the area to be acquired marked out with red flags for the guidance of the 1,000 guests from Parliament, London government, and top society.[2] It was a colourful social occasion but it failed to achieve its main purpose, for although the chairman of the Metropolitan Board of Works, M'Garel Hogg, was sympathetic to the need for public open spaces if they did not cost too much, the Board itself thought that this particular space would be far too costly to justify the use of ratepayers' money, and declined to take up the cause.[3] Faced with close-fisted municipal non-cooperation the Committee found itself obliged to take responsibility for the main negotiations and financial arrangements if the cause was to be kept alive. Shaw Lefevre attended to the landowners, and to the parliamentary strategy; the local members, Highgate as well as Hampstead men, took care of most of the administrative work.

[1] *Hampstead and Highgate Express.*, 26 January 1884. By the 'tramways' Maurice was referring to the determined, and successful, resistance of the old town to every proposal to bring trams up Haverstock Hill to the High Street: see below, p. 364.
[2] *The Times*, 28 July, 30 July 1885.
[3] Ibid., 29 October, 3 November 1885.

Money was the nub of the matter. To Sir Spencer and Lord Mansfield the future use of their lands was a matter of some indifference so long as they got a good price. This was perhaps less true of Lord Mansfield, who had shown no previous signs of being anxious to turn Parliament Hill into building land, as he liked the prospect from Ken Wood and could afford to indulge this taste as he was plentifully supplied with income from other parts, not least from neighbouring Gospel Oak and Kentish Town; even he, however, never contemplated accepting anything so base as a mere agricultural price for the fields. Sir Spencer, on the other hand, was non-resident and contemplated a housing estate on East Park, or its value, with no qualms about disturbing his own repose; moreover he was fully aware that 'this property is the key to the whole proposal, indispensable to the scheme' from the preservationist point of view, for it commanded the scene and could be be used to drive a broad wedge of town houses between the Heath and Parliament Hill.[1] He was likely to want a full building price, and to be in a position to get it. He did. When the Board turned down the proposal in 1885 it had a clear offer from Sir Spencer to sell his 56 acres for £100,000, and he adhered to this price through all the later moves; £1,800 an acre was a full price, very full for what in building terms was a large tract of land, though it fell well short of being extortionate. When the Board declined to move, Shaw Lefevre's task was to get Sir Spencer to stand by his offer, and to get Lord Mansfield to name his price. This, as expected, turned out to be £1,000 an acre for the 200 acres which Mansfield was willing to sell; it could be argued that when account is taken of the differences in situation, access, degree of readiness for building, and size of tract, Mansfield's was the smarter price. The problem, then, was to find £300,000. Shaw Lefevre's solution managed, very slowly, to prise the Board's hand half open.

The scheme he propounded was an enabling bill, which for very shame at seeing a voluntary body taking responsibility for London's affairs was taken under the Board's wing in its passage through Parliament, that authorised the purchase of the lands and the provision of funds by a number of public authorities. The Act was passed in 1886. The next and most difficult step was to persuade everyone to put its provisions into effect, for it empowered the Metropolitan Board of Works, London Vestries, and the City Parochial Charities to apply their funds to the purchase but did not oblige any of them to do so. It was, apparently, Shaw Lefevre who then settled the terms of purchase with Sir Spencer and Lord Mansfield, and floated a plan for the City

[1] Letter to *The Times* from Shaw Lefevre, 3 November 1885.

Parochial Charities to provide £50,000, the Hampstead and St Pancras Vestries another £50,000 between them, and for the Metropolitan Board of Works to put up the balance of £200,000. A year of discussion and manoeuvring followed while these bodies tried to make up their minds whether to make any promises, and who should commit themselves first; the steady support of *The Times* all the while kept up the pressure of influential opinion in favour of the scheme. Hampstead was the first to act to prevent 'Hampstead Heath, the one open space of North London, [being] reduced to the insignificant proportions which are all that it can claim as its own', and to stop 'the clear open views which it now commands [disappearing] from the eye.' A public meeting, supported by H. H. Asquith among other local residents, was held within weeks of the passing of the Act, and adopted the target of a contribution of £20,000 by the Hampstead Vestry.[1] In the Vestry it was not such plain sailing, and at the first attempt a Kilburn bloc led by Richard Hackworth, a local builder living in Loudoun Road and one of the longest-serving Vestrymen, successfully argued that it was the owners of the immediately riparian property who stood to benefit most and that they ought to match in private contributions any amount the Vestry raised from the rates. When, however, it became clear that the Metropolitan Board of Works was dragging its feet and was never going to make an opening move itself, the Vestry changed its mind and voted to contribute the £20,000.[2] A week later the St Pancras Vestry agreed 'to follow in the footsteps of that noble little army at Hampstead' by providing £30,000.[3]

The Metropolitan Board of Works proved to be the hardest to shift. For a long time it seemed impervious to the pleadings of Shaw Lefevre who appeared with a deputation to explain the terms which his Committee had negotiated, and to a drubbing by *The Times* which delivered a sharp lecture to the Board on its duty concluding that 'it might have

[1] Ibid., 2 December 1886. *The Times* gave full reports of the progress of the campaign, as well as supporting it in many leading articles. The City Parochial Charities Fund had been formed under an Act of 1883 merging the management of parochial charities in the City of London; the Act had specified the provision of open spaces as one of the purposes for which the funds could be used. The activists in Hampstead, besides those mentioned in the text, included F. E. Baines, E. Bond, Miss Buss, Miss Davenport Hill, E. Gotto, Dr E. Gwynn (the Medical Officer). Prof. Hales, H. Harben and Sir Spencer Wells.

[2] Reports in *The Times*, 15 January and 15 July 1887. Hackworth was, at this period, building in Ornan Road.

[3] Ibid., 21 July 1887. Baroness Burdett-Coutts addressed a public meeting of St Pancras ratepayers the evening before the Vestry meeting; and a petition in favour of the scheme collected 3,000 St Pancras supporters.

been expected that the body which claims to represent London and to understand its wants, would appreciate the great importance of the rescue of these open spaces, and would take the initiative in propounding a scheme by which so desirable an object should be attained upon equitable terms. If the Metropolitan Board of Works will not move first, others must be found to open the game.'[1] The opening moves by Hampstead and St Pancras did the trick, to the extent of prompting the Board to promise to find half the purchase price, £152,500, if the other half could be found elsewhere. Taking it for granted that the City Charities would chip in with their £50,000, the Committee calculated that when all expenses were met £52,500 was still needed, and in November 1887 launched an appeal to the public to subscribe that amount.[2] £43,500 was quickly promised, and Octavia Hill hoped that the last £9,000 might be given by some rich man at Christmas who would be flattered to feel that his gift would secure the nine acres of the Elms estate opposite The Spaniards, from which Lord Mansfield had always excluded the public. No kind fairy appeared; but the Committee had the luck to secure an unscheduled contribution of £5,000 from the Marylebone Vestry.[3] Following this new vein proved unrewarding when the Paddington Vestry flatly rejected the suggestion that since parts of its parish were within fifteen minutes' walk of the Heath it might care to vote a sum. Inevitably it was hard going raising the last few thousand pounds from private subscriptions, but by July 1888 Shaw Lefevre and the Extension Committee were able to return to the Metropolitan Board of Works and announce that these subscriptions had reached £46,000, thus reaching the target and making £303,500 in all promised for the purchase.[4]

Prevaricating to the last, the Board felt that it could carry out the 1886 Extension Act only on condition that the Charity Commissioners first gave a formal undertaking that they would provide the £50,000 from the City Parochial Charities. This the Charity Commissioners could not do, since they were only empowered to act once the Board had formally resolved to enter into a contract to purchase the land. For a moment it looked as if the whole project would fall through at the last

---

[1] Ibid., 9 July 1887.

[2] Ibid., letter from the Duke of Westminster and Shaw Lefevre opening the appeal, 7 November 1887.

[3] Ibid., letter from C. L. Lewes, Hon. Sec. of the Extension Committee, 23 December 1887.

[4] Ibid., 7 and 8 March, 20 July 1888. C. L. Lewes must have been a fast walker, as the closest tip of Paddington is 3,000 yards from the nearest part of the Heath.

minute because of this absurd deadlock, and *The Times* entreated the Board to ignore these formal points and make its exit, before being replaced by the London County Council, with the thought that 'to enlarge the means of enjoyment open to the poorest will be an act gratefully remembered of a body of which both good and bad will be said, but which can never be ignored in the history of the metropolis.' Harben, the Hampstead Vestry representative on the Board, perhaps hardly needed the benefit of this moral lecture; he moved the crucial amendment that the Board should adopt the 1886 Act forthwith, relying on the subsequent receipt of the Charity contribution, which removed the procedural difficulties and permitted the Board to go ahead with the purchase.[1] The lawyers still took their time, and it was not until 6 March 1889 that the contracts were signed, 'almost the last important act of the Metropolitan Board of Works', and a few weeks later the Extension Committee was wound up, dividing its surplus funds of £660 equally between the two organisations which had played the largest part, the Kyrle Society and the Commons Preservation Society.[2] After five years spent largely in overcoming the pusillanimity of the Board in its characteristic reluctance to see London's interests reaching above sewers, it was a shade galling to find the Board taking pride in its tireless work for open spaces in its signing-off Report.[3] As recollection of its passing mulishness receded with the passing years, however, the Metropolitan Board of Works does perhaps deserve to be remembered for two main achievements: the Thames Embankment, under which its principal sewers run; and the wide expanse of Hampstead Heath, a truly outstanding and astonishing piece of wild country to find close to the centre of a capital city, whose expanse owes much to the Board's willingness, however grudging, to foot half the bill. Even its wildness might be claimed by the Board as an unintended benefit of its tight control of the ratepayers' purse strings, for after 1870 all thoughts of introducing shrubberies and flower beds in the customary regimentation of municipal park management were rejected on the grounds of cost, and the years of 'judicious neglect' under the understanding management of the Board's superintendent set the original Heath on the path of 'natural' rather than 'artificial' recovery. The Board scattered gorse seed rather than plant municipal dahlias because

[1] Ibid., 20 and 21 July 1888.
[2] Ibid., 25 March 1889, Report of Final meeting of the Heath Extension Committee.
[3] *Final Report of the Metropolitan Board of Works*, Parl. Papers, 1889, LXVI, sec. vi.

it was cheaper; posterity gained the most convincing illusion ever created of real country brought to the heart of a vast city.[1]

[1] MBW Min., 13 October and 15 December 1871, 15 March 1872, illustrate the early decisions of the Parks and Open Spaces Committee on the management of the Heath, which developed from a policy of economy into a conscious policy of gently assisted 'natural' wildness.

Nine

THE COMPLETION OF URBAN DEVELOPMENT, 1889-1914
Poor man's Hampstead

At the time of the Heath Extension in 1889 this great expanse was not an island of country surrounded by town, but was itself the frontier between town and country; or, to pursue the language of trench warfare, it was a salient with the town forces more or less occupying the eastern and southern flanks, but with the northern and much of the western sides firmly supported by the great mass of open territory stretching away to the villages of Finchley, Hendon, Edgeware, Kingsbury and Wembley. It was in the course of the next half-century that the Heath was encircled and the enormous contribution of the men of 1889 was made manifest in the ability of their creation to keep at bay the rows of houses in East Finchley, Golders Green, and Childs Hill. On the eastern or right flank the builders had already marched a long way, in Dartmouth Park, towards a continuous built-up stretch from Kentish Town to Highgate. But the right hook, to the north of the Heath and Ken Wood, was for long delayed by the Bishop of London's estate, where the first development of the grand houses in Bishop's Wood on The Bishop's Avenue—Dane Court, Kenmore, Barons Court, Glenthorne, Westwood, Bishop's Mead, and East Weald—did not come until the very end of the century; and the slightly more intensive but still very wealthy developments to either side of the Highgate Golf Course, linking with the most expensive part of the Hampstead Garden Suburb, came mainly at the same time as dense suburban growth in their rear at East Finchley starting just before 1914 and continuing in the interwar years. On the left flank the situation was a good deal more confused, and the 1889 battle map showed a number of isolated skirmishes in progress in advance of the main urban forces whose firmly consolidated base extended no further than the line of the Hampstead Junction Railway. The north-western axis of advance along the Kilburn High Road had breached this line; but Cricklewood was a completely detached railway settlement round the Midland Railway's yards, housing a large depot and stabling for the London General Omnibus Company as well as the railway workers; while Childs Hill had lately grown into a small urban-agricultural village as one of the centres in organising London's milk supply. Beyond this there were only the miniature country seats of the London plutocracy, pushed outwards from their earlier settlements in districts like Belsize. On West Heath Road, over into Hendon parish, were such large establishments as Sunnyfield, Beechworth, St Mary's, Westover, and West Heath House, and the Finchley Road could boast a few mansions and small parks in Fernside and Helenslea opposite the future Dunstan Road. But the extension of North End Road, now known as Golders Green Road, had become the favourite area for these mansions, and the stretch between Hoop Lane and the modern Highfield Avenue was a veritable gentry row shared by ten imposing houses—The Oaks, Ravenscroft, Elm Lodge, Kimbolton Lodge, Portsdown Lodge, The Elms, Elmer Lodge, Golders Lodge, Woodstock House, and Highfield—each with several acres of grounds. Otherwise all was farmland, and the left hook round the Heath did not begin to develop until after the tube was opened to Golders Green in 1907 and unleashed a rush of speculative development there, and the great social experiment of the Hampstead Garden Suburb.

This broad context suggests that the greater Heath was secured almost a generation in advance of any probable conquest of the area by builders, although their first arrival to open a campaign, had it been permissible, would undoubtedly have come much sooner. The suggestion gains support from the timing of the subsequent main additions to the Heath, when it spread over into the adjoining parish. The Golders Hill estate was put up for sale for building land on the death of its owner, Sir Spencer Wells, in 1897, and in a dramatic auction described by Barratt he secured the 36 acres of park next to the West Heath for £38,000, on behalf of a new Extension Committee once more headed by the Duke of Westminster and Shaw Lefevre (Lord Eversley), which transferred the acquisition to the LCC. In 1907 some 80 acres of Wyldes Farm were purchased from Eton College for £39,000, at the time when the rest of this farm was acquired by the Hampstead Garden Suburb Trust, and was dedicated to the public as the North Heath Extension.[1] For both these additions the recipe of 1889 was repeated: a mammoth garden party at Golders Hill to promote the project, and a mixture of public money, metropolitan and local, and private subscriptions to meet the costs; Hampstead, Vestry and Borough, laying out money beyond its borders for the general good as

[1] T. J. Barratt, *The Annals of Hampstead*, II (1912), pp. 221–8.

others had done before.[1] In both cases, though more noticeably with Wyldes Farm, the prices were easier than in 1889; this, coupled with the comparative slowness of the surrounding building progress, makes the undercurrent of objection in the 1880s to the successful appropriation of the 'unearned increment' by Maryon Wilson and Lord Mansfield for mere heathland understandable though not necessarily justifiable.[2]

Within the context of existing property laws and fiscal arrangements, of course, Maryon Wilson had received no more than his due in getting a building price for the heathland of East Park; and where one generation had been victimised by the unprecedented discrimination against Sir Thomas and his estate bills there was an added reason for not seeking to deprive the next generation of its rights. Sir Spencer received these in full measure. Although from the vantage point of today, no doubt, £1,800 an acre seems a ridiculously small price to pay for the immense benefits of the Heath and even for the quaint charm of the once menacing viaduct, it was a full value in 1889. In the short run it may even have been above an open market valuation, for the closing years

[1] Paddington Vestry redeemed its reputation by contributing in 1898, having failed to contribute to the 1889 Extension. The Golders Hill purchase was financed by:

	£
LCC	12,000
Hampstead Vestry	10,000
Marylebone Vestry	1,026
St Pancras Vestry	1,000
Paddington Vestry	500
Middlesex CC	500
City Parochial Charities	1,000
City Corporation	250
Private subscriptions	15,037
	41,313

which left a small balance after meeting the legal costs. The Wyldes Farm purchase was financed by:

	£
LCC	10,000
Hampstead Borough	5,000
Middlesex CC	2,000
City Parochial Charities	1,500
Private subscriptions	21,243
Deficiency provided by private guarantors of the Extension Cttee.	4,350
	44,093

[2] A criticism made for example by a MBW member in *The Times*, 16 November 1885, and endorsed by Barratt, op. cit., II, 220.

of the nineteenth century did not see a particularly brisk demand for high-class building on the Maryon Wilson part of Hampstead, so that the immediacy of the ripeness of East Park for development might have been overestimated. On the other hand it can be argued that the enlargement of the Heath brought no immediate advantages to the attractions of the remainder of the uncovered estate, which lay close to the West Heath whose status was already assured, so that a generous price for the surrender of development opportunities on the detached section of East Park could be viewed as a fitting compensation.

At all events the development of the section of the estate running northwards from West End Lane (renamed Frognal Lane) to West Heath Road moved sluggishly from the first start on Redington Road in 1877 and the laying of a sewer down West Heath Road itself in 1884. By the mid-nineties only the skeleton of a road system for this district, Redington Road and the link to Finchley Road, Heath Drive, had been laid out, and only the merest handful of houses had been completed. One other new residential road, Chesterford Gardens, was formed before 1900; but it was only between then and 1914 that this district took on its modern shape, with the making and rapid development of Bracknell Gardens, Oakhill Avenue, and Templewood Avenue in an Edwardian spurt. Even then many gaps remained, including most of the choicest frontage of all facing the West Heath, which were only filled by inter-war building whose most fanciful flights into Hollywood baronial and Elizabethan contrived, at last, to deprive the public of their view of Telegraph Hill; while Frognal Park and its grounds survived the First World War, until it was carved up into Greenaway Gardens. None of this suggests that this area, by nature the most attractive of the remaining undeveloped parts of Hampstead, had an irresistible appeal to wealthy late-Victorian Londoners; though when Hampstead residents still watched hay being made in the fields behind Spedan Tower and The Grange in the 1890s it was not for want of efforts by the Maryon Wilson estate to order matters otherwise.

At first sight it is rather remarkable that such a well-endowed district experienced apparently considerable difficulties in achieving its destined covering of high-class, expensive houses when the site, the height, and the scenery all seemed to conspire to make it a keenly-desired choice for residents seeking social elevation. Part of the explanation may be that upper-class and uphill Hampstead ran into a sort of twilight time towards the end of the century, becoming thought of as either too near or too far from central London by the kind of people who were in the market for really expensive houses. Certainly a second, and almost final, retreat of the gentry occurred at this time, as those who had survived into the 1870s from the early villa age decided that the time had come to sell up and move out into more rural settings. By 1900 all the earlier mansions and their mini-parks had disappeared, save for Ivy Bank, retained with shrunken grounds by a new developer, Alfred Ridley Bax, a barrister from Balham 'of very large private means' who had moved in in 1893 and used the house as both residence and his headquarters for managing the development of Ornan Road; and Frognal Park on the Maryon Wilson estate.[1] Charles Henry Lardner Woodd, one of the leading new gentry of Hampstead, an active Vestryman and local benefactor, held out in Rosslyn House until his death at the end of 1893, though he had already given up part of his grounds for William Willett to make a start on Lyndhurst Gardens. After his death the house was sold and demolished, Wedderburn Road was built and Lyndhurst Gardens was completed.[2] The main settlement of the Woodd clan, founded by Basil George Woodd, was further down the hill. Basil, born in Croydon in 1781, had seemed destined for a fruitful career in the Treasury since he had influential patrons in the Pulteneys and the Evelyns; instead he entered business and in time became 'the father of the London wine trade'. One of his first customers was Gardnor of Gardnor House, and it may have been on that account that he came to settle in Hampstead in 1826. He settled most comfortably, purchasing the lease of the Hillfield estate in 1841 from the bankrupt banking Wrights. In 1857, when the Dean and Chapter refused to add a new life to his lease, he was lucky enough to be able to acquire the freehold of Hillfield in exchange for his lease of the Belsize House estate which he surrendered to the Dean and Chapter along with the sitting sub-tenant of that mansion, Matthew Forster, MP. Before his death in 1872 Basil had built another large house, Woodlands, in the nineteen acres of Hillfield's grounds, for one of his sons, Robert Ballard, and amassed a fortune of £120,000 for the support of his twelve children.[3]

[1] CC File 38689, Rye and Eyre, solicitors, to Eccles. Comm., 3 Aug. 1893. Ivy Bank and its five acres had been let on a building agreement to Francis Const Barker, of Leigh, Essex, in July 1872; this was purchased by Charles Hill in 1878 for £11,180; on his death it was acquired by A. R. Bax at auction in 1893 for £10,075: CC File 38689, Second Agreement with Barker, 30 July 1872; Terms for 999-year lease of Ivy Bank, 24 March 1893. And see above, p. 293.

[2] CC File 7141, Application by executors of C. H. L. Woodd for a 999-year lease, 4 June 1894; Map 9614 of May 1872, with later amendments. *Hampstead Year Book for* 1894 (1893).

[3] DCW RCO 32, Abstract of title of B. G. Woodd to an estate at Hillfield,

When Basil Thomas Woodd, who took on the Hillfield house, is added there were thus three Woodd sons well heeled in the Hampstead of the 1870s and 1880s, though Basil Thomas operated on a rather wider stage: through his father's relations he inherited a comfortable country estate at Conyngham Hall in the West Riding and sat as Tory MP for the local borough of Knaresborough.[1] Hillfield supplied the site for the Vestry Hall in 1878, but otherwise the Woodd empire in these parts survived as parkland for as long as the younger brother's outpost at Rosslyn, although the frontage to Belsize Avenue was partly built up in 1883.[2] By the 1890s, however, Hillfield and Woodlands formed an island surrounded by the houses of Belsize Avenue, Belsize Park Gardens, and Belsize Grove, and their attractions as countrified seats had disappeared. Parts of the Hillfield grounds went first, to provide the sites of Glenloch and Glenilla Roads; then in the early 1900s Woodlands was demolished and Glenmore and Howitt Roads were rather awkwardly squeezed on to its site. Hillfield house itself survived the First World War shorn of its proper setting which had been reduced to the level of back-land and space for tennis courts, until a new speculative owner, Whipple Wheeler, erected blocks of flats on this site in 1928, commemorating its earlier grandeur in the name of Hillfield Court.[3] On the opposite side of Haverstock Hill the Lunds gave up Haverstock Lodge at very much the same time in the 1890s, and Downside Crescent was built over it. And it was at about this time also that this stretch of Haverstock Hill was developed as a shopping area, on frontages supplied from the Woodd freehold, since where they retained any control the Ecclesiastical Commissioners had set their faces against allowing any shops on this thoroughfare, most sensibly insisting that shops ought to be kept away from a main road.[4] At the beginning of the twentieth century, therefore, a few of the grand houses from the

1857; CC File 11684, H. A. Hunt's report and valuation of sale of the fee of Hillfield and surrender of the lease of Belsize House (Belsize Court), and map, 4 April 1857. *Hampstead and Highgate Express*, obituary of Basil George Woodd, 31 August 1872.

[1] J. Bateman, *The Great Landowners of Great Britain and Ireland* (1878 ed.), p. 455.
[2] CC File 11684, P. B. Matthews to Eccles. Comm., 30 March 1883, complaining that Woodd was building across a footpath (long disused) which ran through the Hillfield park.
[3] CC File 11684, W. J. Ross, estate agent of Haverstock Hill, to Eccles. Comm., 23 January 1928, putting Whipple Wheeler's proposal to erect blocks of flats on the tennis courts.
[4] CC File 38689, Eccles. Comm. to Daniel Smith & Oakley, surveyors, 15 and 23 May 1893, refusing permission to erect shops on Haverstock Hill.

PLATE 11 One of the country seats of West End Lane: Treherne House in the mid-nineteenth century (see p. 341)

PLATE 12 The Finchley Road station of the Hampstead Junction Railway, in 1860; a green field setting unexpectedly preserved for many years (see p. 343)

earlier phase of development still stood: Hillfield, Ivy Bank, Belsize House (Court), and the lesser Hunters Lodge. But they had lost their park-like settings, and were no longer to be classed as residences of the gentry.

West Hampstead had experienced a similar flight of the gentry, though in this area rather more of the original houses were still standing. In the 1820s and 1830s the stretch of West End Lane to the south of the old hamlet which lay by the junction with Mill Lane had become a veritable millionaire's row of grand houses: on the east side of the lane lay Canterbury House, Treherne House, and Westend Hall, and on the west Oaklands Hall, Westend House, Sandwell House, and Lauristone Lodge, together forming an almost unbroken belt of parkland from the present Smyrna Road to West End Green. A little further north, served by the new Finchley Road, a couple of the landowners at the time of the tithe commutation built themselves substantial houses: Henry Burgess made Burgess Park for himself, now occupied by Burgess Hill, Ardwick and Ranulf Roads; while Thomas Pell Platt built himself Child's Hill House, on the site of the present Rosecroft Avenue, and gave his access drive its name of Platt's Lane. A third owner of this period, John Teil, sold his twenty acres to Charles Cannon, who ran a highly successful business as a dyer just off Oxford Street; Cannon built himself a large house in the late Greek revival manner in the 1840s, which he named Kidderpore Hall after the good fortune which the India trade had brought him.

Cannon died in 1876, and soon after Kidderpore Avenue was driven through to the front of the Hall and the West Middlesex Water Company constructed a reservoir at the back. Little building followed immediately, and these signs of division of the property may have been due as much to the fact that Cannon left his estate to be split equally between his three daughters as to any loss of residential charm. Nevertheless building ripeness was approaching, and the consequent readiness to split up the park enabled Westfield College, started in two private houses in Maresfield Gardens with five students in 1882, to buy Kidderpore Hall and just $2\frac{1}{2}$ acres of grounds in 1890 to house an expansion to forty or fifty students.[1] As Kidderpore Hall succumbed to one movement of the times, the spread of higher education for girls, Westend House fell to another and more penetrating influence, that of the railways. Railway Hampstead, which burrowed underneath the

[1] *Hampstead and Highgate Express*, obituary of Charles Cannon, 19 August 1876. Anon., *Westfield College*, 1882–1932 (1932), p. 4; the College paid £12,000 for the house and grounds.

most superior areas, surfaced at the Finchley Road and bore down on West Hampstead with a full concentration of its forces. West End Lane was in due course served by three railways and three stations within a couple of hundred yards, and traversed by a fourth, the Great Central; to either side of what was a conjuncture rather than a junction, the gathering and dispersing lines cast their influence on a broad band of territory stretching between the Finchley Road and Kilburn High Street and at least a third of a mile deep, leaving a waste land of stone yards and rubbish tips to the east of West End Lane, and so cutting up the district to the west that it was rendered unfit for anything approaching high-class development.

The first line through was the Hampstead Junction Railway, authorised in 1853 and opened in 1860. At the time Westend House was owned by the Reverend William Dunbar, leased to Rear-Admiral Sir George Sartorious, and sub-leased to William Morris, who understandably disliked the project since the line ran along his southern hedge. Dunbar, who was an absentee landowner living at Thornhill in Dumfriesshire, quickly sold his property hereabouts, the chief purchaser being Charles Bischoff, a speculator who acquired land on both sides of West End Lane at this time, and who was the owner when the next railway blow was delivered in 1863, with the Midland Railway's proposal for its extension to London. This line when it was opened in 1868 passed along the northern boundary of Westend House, leaving it so hemmed in by trains that it was ruined as a residence for any family of means. It passed its final years as a Girls' Laundry Training School, not unsuitably in view of its grimy surroundings, and was then sold by Bischoff to the British Land Company, which had laid out a building estate on the large triangle of land between the Hampstead Junction, the Midland, and the Edgware Road just before the third railway onslaught was made in 1873 with the proposals for the New Lines of the Metropolitan and St John's Wood Railway which were to take the Metropolitan out into the open country. Iverson Road, running through the centre of Westend House, had by then already been laid out; but although much of its frontage had been divided up into building plots few houses had been completed, and most plots simply had a shed on them for use while the individual purchasers from the land company got ready to build.[1]

[1] HLRO Hampstead Junction Railway, Plan and Book of Reference, Session 1852–3; Midland Railway London Extension, Plan and Book of Reference, Session 1863; Metropolitan and St John's Wood Railway, New Lines, Plan and Book of Reference, Session 1873. *P.O. London Directory*, map, 1863.

Of the three lines which crossed West End Lane only the last, the Metropolitan, placed a station there at the time of its opening; and indeed West Hampstead was for a short time after 1879 the terminus of its trains, until the line was open through to Willesden and Harrow. The opening of this station, with its service to Baker Street and access to the City by the Metropolitan, undoubtedly acted as a powerful stimulus to the rapid development of the whole West Hampstead district in the fifteen to twenty years after 1879. It was, nevertheless, hardly a station set in green fields with all the work of attracting passengers lying ahead after its opening. For apart from the Iverson Road estate of the British Land Company which was already under way before the line was projected, another developer, Donald Nicoll, had acquired the land immediately to the south and had prudently laid out his estate roads and building plots before the New Lines were proposed, in order to inflate his compensation claim. One of his roads, slightly diverted to accommodate the line, became Sherriff Road, which with its links to Hemstall Road formed the Nicoll development. At that point he marched with the Cotton estate, whose development had been proposed well before 1873, and had been delayed in part because of intervening uncertainty over the exact line the railway would take, while further to the west the development of the Netherwood Street estate, under the United Land Company, was well advanced by 1873.[1] Both the Hampstead Junction and the Midland no doubt had more than enough experience of 'green field' stations with their Finchley Road stations, both of which remained without any residential hinterlands for years after their openings because of the peculiar situation of the Maryon Wilson estate. In any case neither company constructed a station on West End Lane until long after their services had begun and until West Hampstead had had a chance to develop a sizeable potential passenger traffic without benefit of their trains. The Hampstead Junction opened its West End Lane station in 1888, surprisingly late for a line which lived by commuter traffic; while the Midland, in spite of its general neglect of its suburban services, was a little earlier off the mark in putting in a West Hampstead station in 1880, its services to St Pancras and the City being perhaps in more direct competition with the Metropolitan than those of the Hampstead Junction to Broad Street.

The Sumatra Road development, to the north of the Midland, began in the 1880s and swept away Sandwell House and Lauristone Lodge; but on the other side of West End Lane Canterbury House, Treherne

[1] HLRO Metropolitan and St John's Wood Railway, New Lines, Session 1873. And see above, pp. 319–20.

House, and Westend Hall survived until the late 1890s. The first two then gave way to Lymington Road surviving only in the name of Canterbury Mansions; but Westend Hall, occupied by the Miles family from 1813 to 1889 during which time they produced an early tennis champion, Eustace Miles, lived on to receive a visit from Edward VII when it was occupied by Major-General Sir C. Crauford Fraser, before being demolished to make way for Fawley Road. He was, however, the last resident of high social pretensions in these parts; Oaklands had been razed to the ground, like so many other mansions; Child's Hill House, though still standing until 1904, did not long survive the death of its later owner, Joseph Hoare, in 1886, as a gentleman's residence; while Burgess Park had followed the same path as Kidderpore Hall, at a lesser level, and become the home of the Anglo-French College.[1] By about 1900 West End Lane, once one of Queen Victoria's favourite country drives near London, had practically seen both country and gentry depart.

The disappearance of the gentry, however, was by no means the sole explanation of the sluggish development of the potentially very choice part of the Maryon Wilson estate by the West Heath. Of equal importance was the competition of William Willett and the high reputation of his 'Willett-built' houses for the custom of a necessarily limited number of purchasers and tenants who were in the market for good-class suburban housing rather than on the climb towards family seats in miniature. Willett had begun building in Hampstead in 1869 when he took a large number of plots in Belsize Crescent on a sub-lease from Daniel Tidey just before Tidey went bankrupt. Willett was an extremely ambitious builder, looking for openings for large-scale operations, and he did not find either the cramped houses he had to build in Belsize Crescent or his subordinate status there much to his liking. He was in course of becoming the chief builder of Kensington, with extensive developments on the Cadogan and Holland estates which shortly led him to open his principal estate offices in Sloane Square and Kensington High Street, and he was not content to continue in Hampstead except as a principal. This he became in 1873, and setting up a branch office in Belsize Court he proceeded to put up large houses on the north side of Belsize Avenue, houses which let for up to £200 a year and were sold mainly for £2,400 apiece.[2]

[1] *London School Board Map*, 1889; *P.O. London Directory*, map, 1902; O.S. six-inch map, 1920 ed. (surveyed 1912).
[2] CC File 32878, Lease to W. Willett of five houses in Prince Consort Road (renamed Belsize Crescent), 2 August 1869. After Tidey's bankruptcy Willett became the chief lessee for the remaining Belsize Crescent develop-

The Avenue was at the height of its popularity in the late 1870s and 1880s, with a sprinkling of carriage-folk among the residents, in houses which had their own stabling attached. Several, passing through the hands of Willett's financiers to large property investors, were quickly re-sold to their occupiers, an assortment of businessmen and wealthy widows, at prices which in some cases topped £3,000.[1] By the 1890s, however, the district had begun to fall out of favour as taste turned against the great tall houses stretching from basement to third floor, and began to prefer more compact homes whose management was less labour-intensive. Rents, and rateable values, were reduced by up to a quarter, and by 1894 Cluttons were telling the Ecclesiastical Commissioners that 'the property in the Avenue has deteriorated in value considerably during the last few years.' Ten years later several of the once desirable family residences had found new uses as boarding houses, frequently skipping the formality of the ground landlord's permission which was strictly necessary. It was a development closely paralleled on the Rosslyn Park estate, where the equally large houses became equally difficult to let or sell as private houses, and a veritable rash of discreet girls' schools broke out in the 1890s. Though no doubt these were quiet and unobtrusive establishments, their coming was a good deal bolder than that of their forerunner, Mrs Coghlan's school, which was allowed to set up in Thurlow Road in 1877 only as a special favour because of its religious connections, having previously been conducted in the vicarage of Christ Church, and because 'all the children [are] of the upper classes of Hampstead.'[2] Cluttons drew the line at a

---

ment: ibid., Cluttons to George Pringle, 29 July 1872. For Belsize Avenue development, and house prices, see CC File 38689, especially assignment of seven houses by Willett to Henry Sargant, 15 March 1877. And see above, pp. 288, 293.

[1] CC File 38689, assignments 1873–85. £3,100 was paid for 63 Belsize Avenue in 1876 by Eugene Mason, buying for his own occupation, and £3,150 for 51 Belsize Avenue in 1883 by George Clulow, also for his own occupation. Owner-occupiers, though rather more common than in most middle-class districts, were still only 15–20 per cent of the residents, it being normal for middle-class families to take their houses on 5- or 7-year tenancies. £3,000 represented a very expensive house, at a time when 6- or 8-bedroom houses in good districts could be had for £1,000 and under.

[2] Ibid., Cluttons' report on terms for granting a 999-year lease of 37 Belsize Avenue, 19 April 1894. Solicitor's report on application to use 13 Belsize Avenue as a boarding house—'we understand that many houses in the neighbourhood are used for a similar purpose'—3 August 1905. By 1911–13 houses in Belsize Avenue could be bought for £650–£860. CC File 7141, William Ambrose, Northcote House, Hampstead, to Eccles. Comm., concerning request to open Mrs Coghlan's school in Thurlow Road, 10 October

hospital, however, because the surrounding property was still 'of a high class character' in 1899 which would suffer from the presence even of guaranteed non-infectious patients.[1]

Willett was ready to move with the shifts in fashion, and on the Dean and Chapter's estate his work in Lyndhurst Gardens and Wedderburn Road from the late 1880s onwards showed his ability to adapt to lower profiles and steeper pitched roofs. But the new Willett really came into his own when he established a connection with the Eton College estate in 1881, and moved in to resuscitate the flagging Chalcots development and complete with a triumphant flourish the covering of what had lain for years as unloved back-land. It may literarlly have been a new Willett who was responsible for the transformation of Eton Avenue, for although William senior does not appear to have made over the family business to his son William junior until 1903, junior entered the firm as a young man, and 1881, when he was 25, very likely saw his start.[2] The young William Willett is best known as the originator of the notion that Greenwich Mean Time could be manipulated to produce 'daylight saving', an idea which he propagated with indefatigable single-mindedness between 1907 and 1914 with nineteen editions in almost as many languages of his pamphlet on *The Waste of Daylight*, meeting with much ridicule in peacetime but posthumous success in wartime when 'summer time' was first introduced as a war economy in 1916. His more durable, or at least less changeable, achievement was to create, in partnership with his father, the particular brand of 'Willett-built' houses which acquired an outstanding cachet and reputation in late-nineteenth-century London, Chislehurst, and Hove as something special and out of the ordinary in the way of speculative building, comparable to the earlier 'Cubitt-built' or later 'Wates-built' brand images.[3]

The typical Willett house differs from the ordinary stucco-fronted London dwelling in the use of good bricks, tiles, and Portland

---

1877. Schools were opened in Windsor Terrace (letter 7 August 1891), Thurlow Road (letter 23 November 1897), and Windsor Terrace (letter 27 June 1898).

[1] CC File 7141, Cluttons' report on application made by Wilfrid Parker, 19 Hampstead Hill Gardens, on behalf of the Hampstead Hospital, 13 July 1899.

[2] CC File 32878, Indenture of 26 June 1919 in the process of reciting the wills of the Willetts, father and son, recites an Agreement of 21 August 1903 by which the father sold all his house property to his son.

[3] This and the following passage are from the entry in the *Dictionary of National Biography: Twentieth Century. 1912–1921*, for Willett, William, (1856–1915).

stone, giving to the exterior an effect of warmth, colour, and interest. Variety of elevation was aimed at and achieved. Great care was devoted to internal planning, ample window light, domestic convenience, and good craftsmanship. Although an architect was constantly employed in the firm's office, and others were commissioned from time to time, much of the credit for the success of these houses was due to the Willetts themselves, father and son, who took great pains to make every detail satisfactory.

Which being translated means that the Willetts in effect put Norman Shaw on the production line, going in for gables, tiled roofs, bay windows, red brick exteriors, and above all abandoning decisively the near-uniformity of town housing, which had permitted only minor variations in ornamental detail, and going in for deliberate contrasts in shape and elevation between adjoining houses. It was the effective beginning of twentieth-century suburban architecture, on a grand scale and for wealthy customers, producing houses which offered great comfort without compelling the stiffness and formality which mid-Victorian household management had had to provide in order to make the mid-Victorian house function.

The start was made in July 1881 when William Willett the elder made a building agreement with Eton College to take the fifteen acres bounded by Belsize Park Gardens, Lancaster Road, Winchester Road, and Fellows Road, on which a tentative start had been made with the outline of a road christened Bursars Road, which Willett quickly had renamed Eton Avenue. He agreed to pay an ultimate ground rent of £900 for this area, and since he was to make up Eton Avenue and the new link roads—Adamson, Crossfield, and Fontaine (renamed Strathray Gardens)—at his own expense, the rate of £60 an acre was not cheap. His original idea was to build 200 houses, to be completed by 1900, but in 1885 the target was reduced to a total of 140 houses, shops, and stables to accord with the concept of grander and more spacious development which he had evolved.[1] In 1883 he took into the agreement The Elms and West Croft, two large houses standing on the site of the original Upper Chalcots Farm on the corner of Belsize Park Gardens and Eton Avenue, undertaking to put up not less than six new houses in their place when he had pulled them down.[2] At first Eton's

[1] Eton MS., Building Agreement with William Willett of Cornwall Gardens, South Kensington, 27 July 1881.
[2] Ibid., Agreement with Willaim Willett, 5 December 1883. The Elms and West Croft were substantial establishments with their own coach-houses and stables, originally in seclusion at the end of Englands Lane.

surveyor had in mind a conventional building estate and reserved a site for a church at the junction of Eton Avenue and Lancaster Road, but by 1895 Willett had convinced him that times had so far changed as to make this symbol of respectability unnecessary for the success of a top-class development, and he was permitted to build on the church site if it had still not been 'definitely appropriated for a Church' by 1905; in the event this corner plot was at first appropriated for a saw mill, presumably used by Willett in his operations, and then more permanently as a fire station.[1]

Eton Avenue and its link roads went ahead rapidly in the 1880s, one or two of the houses being architect-designed but the majority of the gable work, tile-hanging, and bay windows flowing from Willett's own speculations, and finding purchasers and tenants in the wealthiest class. In the 1890s progress was interrupted, leaving the centre section of the avenue to be filled in the first decade of the twentieth century, with more definitely neo-Georgian porchwork and more assistance from an architect, A. F. Faulkner.[2] The early residents were definitely in the carriage class, but George Pownall's estate policy, as Eton College surveyor, ensured that they had to keep their horses and carriages a little distance away. Pownall felt that mews quarters introduced pockets of poverty into the estate and created a need for providing elementary schooling at public expense which would not otherwise exist at all on an estate of the Chalcots character, and he was therefore determined to keep the horses at arms' length as much as he could. Willett was thus forbidden to erect any stables (or shops for that matter) except on the very short frontage to Belsize Park Gardens; he therefore moved over the property frontier and took sites on the Dean and Chapter's estate, where he built the fine range of Eton Stables in Lambolle Place for the service of Eton Avenue, adjoining the Lancaster Stables which served residents on the Belsize estate.[3] For shops recourse had to be made either to Englands Lane, where both Eton and Westminster sides were available to trade, or to Swiss Cottage.

Having launched his Eton Avenue operations Willett took on a new area in 1890 when Eton decided to make the Eton and Middlesex Cricket Ground into building land. This cricket ground had been shifted

[1] Ibid., Agreements with William Willett, 23 July 1889 and 14 December 1895. By 1889 Willett's permanent address was at West Brighton. See also O.S. six-inch map, 1894–6 ed.

[2] Stanford's *London School Board Map*, 1889. Pevsner, *The Buildings of England: London*, II (1952), p. 201.

[3] Eton MS., Agreement with William Willett, 31 December 1885. CC File 33405, Willett to Eccles. Comm., 30 January 1883.

a few hundred yards to the west from its first site, when King Henry's Road was completed in the 1870s and Elsworthy Road was started. When it went in 1890 Hampstead lost its last privately owned pitch, for the St John's Wood Cricket Ground, off West End Lane, had been turned into Priory Road fifteen years earlier.[1] For many years Elsworthy Road, Harley Road, and King's College Road had ended at the boundary of the Eton and Middlesex club. When the ground was handed over to Willett these roads provided ready-made access, while the shape of a cricket ground furnished him with an opportunity to produce a layout which was nevertheless almost self-contained. Rising to the occasion he designed the irregular, elongated oval of Wadham Gardens and an extension of Elsworthy Road, joined to an extended Harley Road and with a connection punched through to Avenue Road. The curving line of the road made possible a more free-flowing use of the same kind of ingredients—gables and porches of Dutch or Queen Anne influence, tile-hung gable-ends, bay windows, and comparatively low elevations—as had gone into Eton Avenue. With the use of privet hedges in place of the traditional brick or stucco walls of town streets, and small front gardens instead of the area steps leading down to the now vanished basement kitchens, the leafiness of Wadham Gardens made a greater visual impact than an equal square footage of leaves in one of the stiff, straight residential roads of mid-century, and earned it the reputation of being among the first, if not the very first, propagator of the 'garden suburb' concept.[2] Although it was eventually an attractive development which went extremely well in the house market its early years were disappointing, for by the end of 1895 no houses had been finished and leased off, so that Willett had paid five years' rents without receiving any return. Recognising his difficulties, Eton agreed to revise the terms of the 1890 agreement, with the result that the 99-year terms of the Wadham Gardens houses all run from 29 September 1895 instead of from 1890. Thereafter matters moved very briskly indeed, and the whole district was completed before 1902.[3]

Willett put more than 100 houses on to the old cricket field in little more than five years, a pace of development which shows that in Wadham Gardens he had found a more sure key to success than in Eton

[1] Stanford's map of Metropolitan Railways, Tramways, and Miscellaneous Improvements for the Session 1878. And see above, p. 243.

[2] DNB, loc, cit. Eton MS., Agreement with William Willett, 18 December 1890. His ground rent for the cricket ground, about 11 acres, rose to an eventual £650 a year.

[3] Ibid., Agreement with William Willett, 14 December 1895. P.O. London Directory, map. 1902.

Avenue, and demonstrates the stiffness of the competition for high-class custom from which the West Heath portion of the Maryon Wilson estate suffered. Willett had found in this location the perfect recipe for the 1890s: a secluded situation, bordering on the open space of Primrose Hill and away from main thoroughfares, where he could develop an exclusive estate of the most modern type of luxurious family houses; but a location which had the advantage, before the coming of tubes and motor buses, of being reasonably close to central London and within easy reach of the established horse bus route on Finchley Road, and the Metropolitan station at Swiss Cottage. It seems that the empty Maryon Wilson lands were just a little too far from any form of public transport to be able to compete against these advantages; they would have been suitable largely for two-carriage families, to cope with the necessary reliance entirely on personal transport, and the type of houses which Willett did build and which failed to get built on Redington Road were never intended to be in the two-carriage class. There was never any doubt that residents in Willett houses were among the most affluent of late-Victorian Londoners; they quickly abandoned their carriages in the earliest days of motor cars when these were very largely confined to the luxury trade as direct carriage substitutes, and by 1913 Willett was successfully applying for leave to convert his stabling into motor garages because the horses had all departed.[1]

The Willetts also made a fortune out of their building businesses, the father spending the last dozen years or so of his active career in the stately semi-retirement of The Drive House at Hove, where he also lived on for ten years of complete retirement until his death in 1913. In 1903 he transferred a large part of his house property to his son for over half a million pounds, subject to outstanding mortgages of about a quarter of a million; by 1906 William junior had paid over £210,000 to his father in cash, whereupon his father made over to his son the £367,112 which was still owing; although this was charged with mortgages amounting to £249,112, it still left a clear fortune of £128,000 for his son and his trustees to enjoy. It is by no means clear whether these transactions related to the whole of the Willett enterprises, or only to those in London; but in any event they show that by 1906 the family had accumulated a combined fortune of at least £338,000 clear of all

[1] CC File 32878, Cluttons' report on Willett's application to convert stables into garages, 26 April 1913. This application covered the Williams and Princess Mews off Belsize Lane, as well as the Lancaster Stables. At the same time 3 Belsize Place, Belsize Lane, became one of the earliest motor repair works in Hampstead.

liabilities.[1] It was quite ample to support young William in style as he cantered over Pett's Wood near his Chislehurst home early in the summer mornings and launch him, on noticing how many blinds were still drawn in the large houses he passed, on his campaign for daylight saving.

While the Willetts made their pile the growth of the Maryon Wilson fortune was only slightly retarded by the hiatus in development in the West Heath section, for the run-of-the-mill building for the less affluent or fashionable middle classes in Greencroft Gardens, Aberdare Gardens, and Goldhurst Terrace was going forward on the estate without a break right through the last two decades of the century. In Hampstead generally there was some further activity at this period aimed at this part of the middle bracket of the middle classes, but it was dwarfed in scale by the earlier building on the Eyre, Upton, Chalcots, Belsize, and Maryon Wilson estates of housing in this size and price range, and over-shadowed at the time in terms of bulk by new housing going up elsewhere in Hampstead for the lower middle class and upper working class. This tendency for new development towards the end of the century to cater for lower social levels than before, and indeed to create the first sizeable working-class quarters in Hampstead, forms the third leg in the explanation of how it came about that choice sites were still vacant in the West Heath district and able to embrace Hollywood Tudor in the inter-war years: the final retreat of the gentry, the superiority of the Willetts in competing for a limited smart clientele, and the general shift in the social balance of Hampstead as a whole, all contributed towards the same result.

The hitherto neglected South End (or Holylands) Farm on the Dean and Chapter's estate was one of the districts which became active in the 1880s and 1890s. Eight acres of this 40-acre farm, including the original farm house, had been taken by the Hampstead Junction Railway in 1854 for £7,105, completely severing the farm into two blocks each of about 16 acres. Apart from pocketing the compensation money, which in due course went towards the purchase of a new estate in the country

---

[1] Ibid., Indenture of 26 June 1919 reciting Agreements between the William Willetts father and son of 21 August 1903 and 1 December 1906. The detailed figures were: in 1903 son agreed to pay father £584,390; in 1906 son still owed father £367,112, the residue having been paid, and £239,112 was required to discharge mortgages on the properties sold to the son. There is no complete schedule of the properties covered by the 1903 intra-family sale, and although it is clear that the sale covered all the Willett houses on the Dean and Chapter estate, and probably all those on the Eton estate, it may well have excluded part or all of the Willett properties elsewhere in London, in Chislehurst, and in Hove.

at Ashleworth in Gloucestershire, the Dean and Chapter and their surveyor apparently took no notice whatever of this event, and allowed the sitting farm tenant, Joseph Pickett, to continue with his farming as best he could. Eventually in 1872, stirred by the fact that Rhodes had just started building on his adjoining South Hill Park estate, Cluttons began to show interest in the farm and discovered that the last surviving life in the lease for three lives granted to Thomas Roberts in 1808 had expired in June 1868, so that the farm had unexpectedly and gratifyingly fallen into the possession of the Ecclesiastical Commissioners.[1] Pickett had meanwhile continued to farm without paying rent to anyone, and Cluttons shamefacedly patched up the negligent estate management by agreeing that Pickett should pay £150 for his $3\frac{1}{2}$ years without a known landlord, and for the immediate future should stay as a yearly tenant at a rent of £64 a year.[2] With this loophole plugged Cluttons turned to the building possibilities of the farm, and discovered that the Hampstead Junction Railway had never fulfilled its obligation to make new access roads, on the north and south of the line, to the two halves of the farm. Attention was first turned to the southern half and negotiations with Joseph Salter, a surveyor from Kentish Town, who owned a strip of land separating Chapter land from Fleet Road and wanted to exploit it as a speculation. Agreement was reached with Salter in 1872 for an exchange of small parcels of land on either side of the old Fleet brook to straighten boundaries, and for the joint construction of Cressy Road, starting through Salter land, as the main access to the Chapter land. The railway access road, intended to go through the smithy at South End Green, was therefore abandoned, and after prolonged negotiations the LNWR paid £650 in 1882 instead of constructing this road. The arrangement with Salter took an equally long time to come to anything, and he had died, in 1876, before any development had started; in 1880 a sale was made to his wife, but the real purchaser was T. E. Gibb acting as guardian for the twelve Salter children. It was Gibb also who took the sixteen acres of Chapter land on a building agreement in 1881, but for a variety of reasons it was 1889 before building began in earnest on this property.[3]

[1] CC File 45820, Cluttons' survey and report on South End Farm, 20 February 1872; Cluttons to George Pringle, 7 February 1872.

[2] Ibid., Eccles. Comm.'s solicitors to George Pringle, 8 June 1872. The rent of £2 an acre shows how far the value of grass farms had fallen since the early nineteenth century: see above, pp. 11–13.

[3] Ibid., Cluttons' report on South End Farm, 20 February 1872; Cluttons to George Pringle concerning sale to Mrs Salter, 24 May 1880; Cluttons to George Pringle concerning LNWR's obligations, 29 November 1882; T. E. Gibb to Eccles. Comm., 3 July 1883.

Contrary to Cluttons's expectations, the northern half of the farm was the first to become a building estate, although with its better elevation and proximity to the Heath, not to mention its greater distance from the baleful influence of the Smallpox Hospital, it might have been foreseen that this was the more attractive locality of the two. Here Joseph Pickett took a few more crops of hay and then performed the feat of converting himself from a farmer into a speculative builder. He found a Kentish Town builder, John Ashwell, to come in with him and they jointly took a building agreement for this northern part in March 1878 at a ground rent building up to £700 a year. The first houses, in South Hill Park Road (renamed Parliament Hill Road), were finished by the end of 1880 and building went forward steadily at the rate of about ten houses a year until by 1894 only two vacant plots were left; these were not filled until 1899. The two principal roads of this development, Parliament Hill Road and Nassington Road, were laid out in 1878 and designed to form future connections with possible residential roads on Lord Mansfield's Parliament Hill Fields, which at that time were expected to be developed in due season; their abrupt termination at the edge of the enlarged Heath is a permanent reminder of how the ordinary course of property development was halted in its tracks in 1889. In return for their ground rent of £45 an acre, which was comparable to the rates which were expected for well-situated parts of the Maryon Wilson estate at the same date, Pickett and Ashwell undertook to build respectable but by no means expensive houses for the middle classes; on the frontages to Parliament Hill Road they contracted to put up houses of not less than £60 annual value, while on the back-land of the later Nassington and Tanza Roads they were allowed to fall to the £50 annual value range, figures which implied houses of only a third to a quarter of the value of the best ones in Belsize, Chalcots, or the Fitzjohn's Avenue district.[1]

Pickett and Ashwell, and later Pickett alone after Ashwell had given up in 1881, were largely financed by their solicitor, William Reeve, and clearly operated on a slender margin, being anxious for a rapid turnover and as low costs as possible. Pickett's continual deferment of the construction of proper sewers for Nassington Road; the arrears of rent due to the Ecclesiastical Commissioners which accumulated periodically; his eagerness to create 'improved ground rents' and sell them in small packets to the Ecclesiastical Commissioners from time to time, as one method of raising extra funds and clearing off his arrears; and his

---

[1] CC File 57425, Pickett & Ashwell's building agreement, and Cluttons' report, 21 March and 29 April 1878.

near bankruptcy in 1887; all these point in the direction of an under-financed builder struggling to keep his head above water.[1] When he purchased the hay crop on Clissold Park from the Ecclesiastical Commissioners in 1886 there is some suggestion that he was extending his speculations to that part of London.[2] Hence it is not surprising that, although he does not seem to have exploited his power to differentiate between the quality of the houses put on the front and the back-land, all his houses should have been built as close to the limits imposed by the ground landlords, and as cheaply, as possible. The normal price for his houses, both when new and on early re-sales in the late 1880s, seems to have been about £900; though a few sold for as little as £750, and some for as much as £1,125. They were very ordinary semi-detached houses, large enough for servant-keeping families, with their basements and three other floors, respectable enough for professional men, and cheap enough to be snapped up by those who wanted to commute from Hampstead Heath station, or to live near the Heath on modest means. At this price they attracted a high proportion of owner-occupiers, well over a quarter of the residents, who were an assortment of widows, doctors, civil engineers, surveyors, customs officers, and printers; the great majority of the houses, however, were occupied by tenants and owned by those who went in for house property as an investment, chief among whom in this development were Joseph Elliott of Warwick House, South End Green—he later moved into one of his own houses in Parliament Hill Road—who bought up over a dozen of the houses; and Robert Thorpe, a Hampstead builder, who invested in half a dozen; most of the remainder were bought individually by a solicitor or two, an engineer, a hat maker, a few clergymen, a few widows, and a larger number of unspecified gentlemen.[3]

The Ecclesiastical Commissioners thought at one time of reserving a site for a church on the Pickett estate, but this turned out to be unnecessary for the creation of a lively community, brought together by their comparative isolation and as a result of Pickett's parsimony. The

[1] Ibid., J. Ashwell to Eccles. Comm., 8 December 1881; William Reeve, Gray's Inn Square, to Eccles. Comm., 17 October 1882; Eccles. Comm.'s solicitors to George Pringle, advising that Pickett had at last completed the sewer from Nassington Road under the railway line, 21 September 1885. Pickett first sold some 'improved ground rents' to the Eccles. Comm. in 1886, and despite the start of bankruptcy proceedings in 1887 he continued to do so until his death in 1893: Cluttons to George Pringle, 24 June 1886; Eccles. Comm.'s solicitors to George Pringle, 22 March 1888; same to A. de B. Porter, 31 July 1894.
[2] Ibid., Eccles. Comm.'s solicitors to George Pringle, 26 July 1886.
[3] Ibid., assignments 1881–91.

Parliament Hill Road residents formed a residents' association at the end of 1884, and were active in the protection of their interests, in particular getting the Vestry to press for the construction of a proper sewer for Nassington Road whose drains 'had previously overflowed on the adjoining field and had become a serious nuisance.' The association was less successful in getting anything done about the annoyance caused 'by the habitual throwing of house refuse into the ditch on the railway bank', though convinced without any evidence that no 'householder would permit such a practice on the part of his servants.' They were least successful of all in making representations to the Vestry about 'the nuisance created by the Fleet Road and other brickfields, and the dangers of the Smallpox Hospital.' Their main effort for 1886, how-ever, was to plant trees along Parliament Hill Road, which they rightly argued 'in any case is desirable [but] would be absolutely called for should Parliament Hill and the adjoining property be made, as is hoped, into a Public Park, as our road would, of course, be one of the principal approaches to the Park.'[1] The trees were planted, and the association then turned its attention to planting up the railway embankment 'at present in a most disgraceful condition and quite an eyesore to the road and in consequence prejudicial to the property.' The point is that in most other developments the developer would have considered it well worth his while to create a bit of leafiness himself, expecting that attractiveness would more than repay his trifling costs; in this case Pickett not only provided no leaves but also declined to contribute to the residents' fund.[2] An interlude in 1891 saw the first two residents in Tanza Road—both owner-occupiers—acting on their own to try to persuade the Ecclesiastical Commissioners to use their influence to alter the name, stating that:

> No name has been put up as yet, and the road is not taken over by the Vestry—but it has become known to a certain extent as Tanza Road—which name would appear to have some reference to the German word for Dancing. The Secretary of the Nomenclature Department of the L.C.C. suggested that we should ask your selec-tion of a name more in keeping with the character of the Free-holders.

But in spite of Cluttons' backing for the name Holland Hill, the LCC

[1] CC File 57986; CC File 57425, William Hart, Secretary of the Parliament Hill Road Residents' Association, to Eccles. Comm., enclosing 1st Annual Report of the Association, 16 December 1885. The Eccles. Comm. gave £5 to the tree planting fund.
[2] Ibid., W. Hart to Eccles. Comm., 25 September and 11 November 1886.

ruled that Tanza Road it should remain.[1] Then in 1892 the residents' association gave a final sign of life, taking up the question of closing a public footpath which ran alongside the railway line to Parliament Hill Fields:

> Until Nassington Road was formed, this footpath formed the only access to the fields, and being then a field path was quite unobjectionable. Now however that it is fenced on one side by the L.N.W.R. and on the other by the garden fences it has become a nuisance not only by the filthy state in which it generally is, but because it is used only for purposes not decent and for pleasures not innocent.

Though Cluttons agreed to help towards the costs of petitioning to have this footpath closed and diverted to Nassington Road, some of the Vestrymen who were members of the Public Footpaths Association stood out in defence of rights of way even when they involved unmentionable passages, and the path continued for another year or two before succumbing.[2]

By this time the annoyance from the Fleet Road brickfield had been abated. It had been one of the expedients to which T. E. Gibb had been driven in an effort to raise some income from his building land while it lay idle through his inability to get any building started and his outgoings in ground rent payments continued to mount. Another device for making a little income out of an investment which continued to disappoint was to allow Lord George Sanger's Circus to perform on the site of what is now Lisburne Road, though the storm of protest because 'the property will be overrun by the roughest and most undesirable class from the surrounding districts, and the fact of so many people camping without sanitary and other conveniences is likely to leave traces for some time' made the small rent from Lord George scarcely worth the fuss.[3] Gibb was a developer in a large way of business on his own account, from a base in Kentish Town, besides being a friend of the Salter family, and after Joseph Salter's death in 1876 he arranged to take over the Salter freehold fronting Fleet Road. In 1880 he agreed, using Mrs Salter as his nominese, to purchase the freehold of some $3\frac{1}{2}$ acres immediately to the east of South End Green, from the Ecclesiastical Commissioners, paying £5,155 for this land which he hoped

[1] Ibid., J. H. Cocksedge, 3 Tanza Road, to A. de B. Porter, 2 September 1891.
[2] Ibid., G. H. Steinberg, Secretary of the Parliament Hill Road Residents' Association, to A. de B. Porter, 6 April 1892.
[3] CC File 62499, Cridland & Nell, solicitors, to Eccles. Comm., complaining about the circus, 2 November 1891.

would enable him to start on the future Constantine Road.[1] This left the Ecclesiastical Commissioners with just over 11 acres still in hand, and they were delighted when Gibb, again through Mrs Salter, offered to take this on a building agreement in 1881, hailing it as 'an important Building Letting, the residue of the Hampstead building land.' Up to this point nothing at all had moved on this part of the estate, except for the sale of the Fleet Road school site to the London School Board, and this no doubt had been made available most willingly because builders and developers were so uninterested in the district. Gibb, moreover, offered the very high ultimate ground rent of £835, or £75 an acre, while he was to bear the cost of road making and, even more important, the cost of an outsize sewer for the drainage of Pickett's houses in Nassington Road north of the railway. He was to build smallish houses, of not less than £42 annual value, which would just about make the lower end of middle-class respectability.[2] All now seemed set for a routine and uneventful completion of the conversion of the last corner of the old Belsize Estate into a built-up area.

Gibb had reckoned without the Smallpox Hospital; or rather he had badly miscalculated its future and its effects on the property market. By 1885 the only development achieved was the establishment of a steam laundry on land behind the school, producing a ground rent of £25 as the sole contribution towards the £835 which Gibb had to find in the end and the £440 which was his contracted rent for the fifth year of his lease, 1885–6.

Gibb was in bad trouble and was obliged to appeal to the good nature and liberality of his ground landlord to help him out. His account of the recent history of Fleet Road, which moved the Ecclesiastical Commissioners to grant him some relief, can hardly be bettered:[3]

> Some years ago the late Joseph Salter was the owner of about 2½ acres of land . . . [abutting] upon Fleet Road. A slight exchange of land was made to improve the boundary between that land and your Estate and to form Cressy Road into your Estate. For some

[1] CC File 45820, Cluttons to George Pringle, concerning two separate sales to Mrs Salter (T. E. Gibb), 24 May and 27 November 1880; T. E. Gibb to Eccles. Comm., 3 July 1883. Gibb finally settled this purchase in 1883: letter from Eccles. Comm.'s solicitors, 8 August 1883.

[2] Ibid., letter of 24 May 1880 for grant to London School Board. The School Board purchased the freehold of this site in 1888, and obtained an extension of their site under lease in 1891, of which they also later purchased the freehold, in 1892: CC File 62499, letters from Eccles. Comm.'s solicitors of 22 March 1888, 26 July 1892. Ibid., Building Agreement with Mrs Salter (T. E. Gibb), 14 July 1881.

[3] Ibid., T. E. Gibb to Eccles. Comm., 6 June 1885.

years this land was unprofitable owing to the establishment of the Smallpox Hospital on the opposite side of Fleet Road, and houses partly built were then taken down and the materials sold.

Mr Salter died in 1876 and I took possession of the land under an arrangement for the benefit of his large family of twelve children to whom I have since acted as guardian.

Subsequently the Hospital was closed for smallpox by order of the High Court of Justice and it was then generally believed that the place would never again be used for smallpox, but might be used by the Metropolitan Asylums Board for fever or imbecile cases. Under this view of things the neighbourhood began to improve and the portion of the Estate of Lord Mansfield close by was let and building operations commenced there and upon other building estates in the neighbourhood.

At that time one of the greatest opponents of the Hospital was Mr Lund who was owner of the soil of part of Fleet Road and maintained a barrier there which prevented patients to the Hospital being admitted from Fleet Road. Another active opponent of the Hospital was Mr Hill the owner of a residential estate adjoining the Hospital property at the west end of Fleet Road.

It then appeared that the Estate in Fleet Road in which I was interested might be brought into the market, especially if laid out with the land belonging to the Commissioners, so that Fleet Road should be made secondary to a road agreed to afterwards as Agincourt Road.

It was under these circumstances that I arranged in 1880–1 to purchase from the Commissioners the land on the west of Cressy Road, and take a building lease of that on the east for the purpose of laying out the whole as one Estate.

Within a short time after this another threatened epidemic of smallpox gave the Asylum Board grounds for proceeding with their appeal to the House of Lords, which it was hoped and expected would have dropped. All the old fears and agitations against the Hospital were revived with greater vigour. Building soon stopped in the neighbourhood and the number of empty houses increased. When the decision was given in favour of the Asylums Board many still however hoped that they would not take advantage of it, as members of the Board had publicly stated they would not, except in the case of urgent need. This hope was soon lost by alterations being made to divide the Hospital into two—one for smallpox and the other for fever.

Mr Lund sold his right to maintain the barrier and to pacify the residents on the Haverstock Hill side of their Estate the Asylums Board arranged that the small pox cases should enter the Hospital from Fleet Road. Mr Pearson Hill sold his estate to the Asylums Board and they immediately built a boundary wall including the new estate which had been looked upon as an oasis between Fleet Road and Pond Street and the Hospital Grounds.

The position of my Estate with its new liabilities has therefore become much worse than before. There has been the loss of income on about £12,000 invested in purchasing freehold, and there has been a loss of the amount heretofore paid as progressive rent on the portion taken under the building agreement; beyond this there has been about £2,000 expended upon roads and sewers from which no return has been received.

Three years ago I arranged to find plant, etc. for brickmaking— the brick earth being taken from the freehold portion which needed to be lowered for improving the levels. The local Vestry took proceedings against the brickmaker and recently an injunction was granted to restrain him from making in the ordinary mode. Hitherto there has been very little profit and now there must be a loss whether the brickmaking is continued under a more costly mode of manufacture or stopped, and the plant and prepared materials thus thrown out of use.

I have shown on the plan the roads which have been formed and under which sewers have been built. The construction of the large sewer [under Lisburne Road] was made so large as it is, and at the time that it was, only for the sake of the Commissioners' Estate on the north side of the Railway and in which I have no interest.

I have tried to sell or let, but there does not seem at present to be any prospect of either, and even if the Smallpox Hospital were removed it would take a long time to restore the character of the neighbourhood. The neighbourhood has so deteriorated that I do not think under any circumstances it would be advisable to build houses so large as was contemplated when the agreement was made with the Commissioners four years go.

Under the circumstances stated I trust that the Commissioners will see that I have suffered great loss through circumstances over which I have had no control and which could not have been foreseen, and that I am still called upon to pay a progressive rent on land agreed to be taken under lease but which is unproductive.

[359]

The interest on Capital and the Rent together make a loss of £1,000 a year and under the present arrangement this must increase. It is therefore absolutely necessary that other arrangements should be made. It has been suggested to me that the whole Estate—freehold and leasehold—might be laid out for workmen's cottages to be let at from eight shilling to twelve shillings per week, and in such a manner as to make Fleet Road a back road, and this is perhaps the best suggestion for utilizing the land.

Gibb made various suggestions for ways in which this revised scheme, for creating a working-class quarter, could be achieved. He was ready to buy the freehold of his leased land, offering to pay £1,000 an acre and stating that 'Sir Spencer Wilson's land by Hampstead Heath can be purchased at £1,000 an acre' as evidence for current market values. He was ready to sell his own freehold land to the Ecclesiastical Commissioners and leave them to make new arrangements for its development. Or he wanted a cancellation of his 1881 building agreement and a renegotiation of terms. The Commissioners declined either to sell or buy the lands, but Cluttons regarded it as only fair and reasonable that the building agreement should be modified. The new terms made the ground rent start from Midsummer 1884 instead of 1881, allowed Gibb to build 215 houses instead of 120 on the 11 acres, of a minimum annual value of £30 instead of £42; the ultimate ground rent, however, was increased from £835 to £860.[1]

Gibb was undoubtedly right to lay the major part of the blame for the social down-grading of this district at the doors of the Smallpox Hospital; but it should be remembered that a lower class of development had been spreading from Malden Road and Gospel Oak in any case, and that it was in many ways simpler and tidier to draw the frontier between this and better-class Hampstead at the railway line, rather than to try, as Gibb and the Commissioners had initially done, to draw it at the property boundary. Furthermore, in so far as Gibb's troubles were temporary rather than ineradicable they may have been due almost as much to unfortunate timing in trying to start a new development at the wrong moment in the building cycle when the house market and the building trade were entering a slack period after the boom of the late 1870s, as to the unpredictable twists and turns of the Asylums Board and smallpox outbreaks. In any event the next five years after 1886, although the hospital question had ceased to excite and

[1] Ibid., Cluttons to George Pringle, 23 March 1886.

alarm the neighbourhood, did not witness any strong return to favour; the first house, on Agincourt Road, was completed in 1888, but by 1891, when his full rent of £860 became payable, only a quarter of the proposed 215 houses had actually been built. Gibb thereupon made another request for alteration of his rent, asserting that he had been held up because he had been unable to settle the exact lines of roads and sewers to link with Lord Mansfield's adjoining estate, and because 'generally the drawback to development has been the proximity of the Smallpox Hospital and the general depression of building operations in the neighbourhood for years past, and the competition with better sites.'[1] In return for a further £43 increase in the rent ultimately due, to £903, its payment was postponed for a further four years to 1895.[2]

Gibb died in June 1894 with the estate still far from complete. Seventy-five houses had been built, in Agincourt Road and Lisburne Road, most of them by Robert Thorpe, who was much engaged in building in Nassington Road at the same time, and the rest by John Sanders, who lived in one of his own Lisburne Road houses. In addition a second industrial site near the school, on the east side of Cressy Road, had been most favourably let to a factory making 'articles in paper for the serving of food and decoration of the table' at a ground rent of £65. Thanks partly to the fact that industrial premises contributed £90 to the ground rents, as well as to the comparatively high ground rent of £7 secured on each house which had been built, £626-worth of ground rents had already been secured on completed buildings even though much less than half the estate had been completed; indeed only £277 of ground rent was left to be secured by some 130–140 houses which remained to be built. At this rent the rest of the vacant land was taken over by a Hampstead surveyor, Francis Thomas Binnington, whose sub-tenants—Thorpe and Sanders, as before, joined by John Pavier, a builder living in Lower Lawn Road, and G. D. Barns, one of the builders of Nassington Road in which he lived—went ahead so rapidly with the rest of Agincourt and Lisburne Roads, and with Constantine Road, that by the end of 1896 all the rest of the ground rent had been secured on completed houses save only for £2. Binnington then obtained a lease of all the remaining empty land, about three acres of it, for a ground rent of £2, and on this residue he developed Cressy Road and Mackeson Road, all of whose rents were

[1] Ibid., letter from Eccles. Comm.'s solicitors, 22 June 1891. Constantine Road was re-aligned to link with Savernake Road, on the Mansfield estate, to form a new direct thoroughfare from Gospel Oak and Kentish Town to Hampstead Heath.

[2] Ibid., Cluttons to A. de B. Porter, 17 December 1891.

clear profit for him. Gibb had been right to suppose that there were good development profits to be made out of the Fleet Road district; but he had started ten years too soon and had the bad luck to die too early.[1]

The houses of Gibb's enterprise were certainly of a lower class and quality than anything else on the Dean and Chapter's estate, but they were tawdry rather than mean, and if not conclusively on the lowest of middle-class rungs then decidedly at the most respectable end of the working class, rather than in the category of mere 'workmen's cottages' which Gibb had contemplated in the depth of his despair. Admittedly they had no basements, which meant that they could hardly cater for the usual domestic arrangements of servant-keeping families; and they were in terrace blocks of half-a-dozen or so houses at a time, which made them not genteel enough for those who regarded occupation of a semi-detached house as essential for the maintenance of middle-class pretensions. At the same time they were not in continuous street-long terracing; very few indeed had merely a ground floor and one bedroom floor, the usual house having two upper floors, though their 18-foot frontages made the rooms fairly small; and the elevations rose a little above stark utilitarianism by incorporating flimsy false gable-ends of vaguely Dutch derivation, which by the 1970s looked extremely perilous for passers by but in the 1890s were no doubt a comfort to those for whom a house in Agincourt Road marked a step in social advancement. The somewhat ambiguous social position of the new district is brought out by the social mixture of the new owners. Almost precisely a quarter of the houses in Agincourt, Lisburne, and Constantine Roads were purchased for owner-occupation; among these about a third came from somewhere in the middle classes—a couple of 'gentlemen', the wife of a doctor, a dentist, a commercial traveller, a chemist, and several commercial and solicitors' clerks; two-thirds were members of the working classes, albeit well-paid and prosperous workers able to afford the £400–£500 which the houses cost. They ranged from members of the building trades—builders' foremen, plasterers, carpenters, and plumbers—through the railways—a couple of engine drivers, and four railway

---

[1] Ibid., Leases granted 1883–94. Thorpe also lived in one of his own houses in Agincourt Road, the large corner house called, and still called, Sunnyside. Mansell, Hunt, Catty & Co., the paper makers, to Eccles. Comm., 13 October 1893. Letter from Eccles. Comm.'s solicitors, 27 November 1894; the same, 8 January 1897. Leases granted 1894–7. In all 145 houses (70 since Gibb's death) were built on the estate with ground rents payable to the Eccles. Comm. Binnington built a further 70 or so, at nominal or peppercorn ground rents sufficient to produce £2 a year to the Eccles. Comm. and had the opportunity to create an annual income for himself of £500 or more, in addition to any profits from the sale of the houses themselves.

foremen—to an electrical fitter and a solitary piano maker. Perhaps it is not surprising that many of those purchasing the houses as investments came from much the same kind of class; for someone with savings he wished to put into house property it would be natural to choose as securities houses like his own since he would be familiar with their qualities, their snags, and their values, and moreover he might intend to move into his investment himself sooner or later. To be sure, the investors included a goodly number of the more affluent men and women of property who clearly did not dream of regarding Agincourt Road as anything more than a source of steady income: such clearly were the solicitor—Reeve, Pickett's solicitor, and much involved in building finance—who took five houses, the City man who bought nine, and the several spinsters with fashionable Hampstead addresses who bought singly. But among those who bought single houses not for personal occupation were several obvious workers—coachman, postman, engine driver, railway foreman, foreman horsekeeper, carpenter, joiner, and builder's foreman—while other purchasers, though employers, were very little removed from labouring themselves—several cab proprietors, and gardeners, and a printer and a jobbing master fall into such a group. There were a number of clerks, a large group of very local tradesmen and small shopkeepers—photographers, bakers, grocers, greengrocers, drapers, a wine merchant, a confectioner, a china seller, and a bookie—all of whom, with varying degrees of certainty, belonged to the lower middle class.[1]

One stimulus to the development of the Fleet Road area, and towards its development with a working-class character, was the opening of the London Street Tramway's extension to South End in 1887. The London Street had been one of the earliest in the horse tram business, opening its line from the Euston Road through Camden Town to Kentish Town in 1871. In 1880 the company made a branch along Prince of Wales Road and up the length of Malden Road to a temporary terminus at the junction with Southampton Road; and in 1887 it made a dash to the Heath with one new branch up Highgate Road to the foot of the hill, and the extension from Malden Road up Southampton Road and then round Fleet Road and Agincourt Road in a loop which neatly solved any turning and reversing problems. By this time

[1] Ibid., analysis of assignments made between 1889 (the first) and the end of 1898, covering a total of 135 houses. None of the houses erected after 1897 in Cressy and Mackeson Roads were subject to recording in the Eccles. Comm.'s files, but it is very probable that house ownership there showed a similar social distribution. A jobbing master hired out horses and carriages.

the trams were firmly established as a decidedly working-class form of transport because the low fares at which they were able to operate meant that working men could afford tram rides, and once working men were inside all other classes decamped to avoid contamination with the dirt, smell, and social degradation which it was assumed must follow from close contact with the lower orders. Hence the strong resistance to all tram projects by better-class Hampstead, with the High Street shop-keepers in the lead, anxious to defend their high-class trade against any threats of working-class intrusion. The tradesmen made common cause, for once in a while, with the local gentry, a combination which was more than a match for every attempt to lay tramways up Haverstock Hill. The most ambitious project proposed, in 1883, to take trams right up to Jack Straw's Castle, hauled by a continuous cable running in a slotted groove. Despite the support which this proposal received from the editor of the local newspaper, who was in favour of lessening the 'suffering now experienced by horses bringing passengers up the cruel Hampstead hills', and who argued that it was more important that the industrious middle classes of Hampstead 'should have increased facilities [of transport] than that the seclusion or privacy of a few idle persons should not be interfered with', it was defeated along with the rest. A permanent committee had been formed 'to oppose Tramways through Haverstock Hill and High Street'; it had an influential membership, including Francis Hoare, Charles Woodd, and George Gilbert Scott from the gentry, Henry Bompas the QC who had led against the Smallpox Hospital, Edmund Gwynn the medical officer of health, and Hack-worth and Clowser who were prominent local builders. Most of these were also Vestrymen, and they carried the Vestry with them in the anti-tram cause. The lobby was still just as powerful in 1899, perhaps more powerful than ever, for it then defeated the last tramway scheme ever proposed, for lines up Haverstock Hill to Jack Straw's Castle and thence down East Heath Road to Hampstead Heath station; the sponsor who was forced to abandon the scheme in face of the Vestry's veto was the LCC itself.[1]

In the light of this determined and sustained defence of Hampstead's middle and upper-class virtue against tramway penetration it is not sur-prising that the one and only place at which the dreaded lines were allowed to cross the border was in a neighbourhood already irretrie-vably ruined from an élitist point of view by the baleful influence of

[1] *Hampstead and Highgate Express*, 17 December and 24 December 1881, 21 January and 2 December 1882. Hampstead Vestry, *Annual Report for* 1899, p. 27. And see above, p. 329.

the Hospital.[1] The influence which the London Street Tramway Company brought with it up Fleet Road was much more decisive than that of a simple tram route. For the Company took the opportunity to close down its small stable on the corner of Malden Road and Southampton Road, and to construct a large depot and stables at its new terminus, on the large area of back-land of Gibb's freehold property, bounded by Fleet Road, Constantine Road, Agincourt Road, and Cressy Road. A large commercial stable cast its own aroma and influence over its neighbourhood; but at least it could be said that it was a more predictable and respectable influence than that of smallpox. Employment on the trams was the dominant feature in the peopling of this working-class quarter, even if tram workers were not well enough paid to figure among the house-owners. In his second survey, undertaken in 1897–8, Booth found that 'in the working-class streets near Fleet Road many drivers, conductors, and horse keepers live, besides railway men and labourers.' The map of social conditions accompanying this survey shows all the streets of the Gibb and Binnington development in the working-class categories of 'poverty and comfort (mixed)' or 'fairly comfortable'; the poorest houses in the district, classed as 'moderate poverty', were however in the northern end of Lund's estate, in Upper Park Road and his side of Fleet Road, a small patch of earlier pre-tram development.[2] The whole district, indeed, and its eastern extension on the Mansfield estate in St Pancras, made a convenient home for transport workers by horse and steam, being both an offshoot of the railwaymen's quarter in Kentish Town and Gospel Oak and a colony with its own source of employment.

It may well be that small pox, trams, and trains between them settled the social character of the Fleet Road district, thereby confirming the general proposition that the working classes were permitted to set up house where no one else wanted to live; the development, nevertheless, makes the ground landlord's exercise of overall control seem somewhat puzzling. Within the broad limits imposed by the individual features of particular sites which determined the range of groups to which they might appeal for residence, it is clear that the ground landlord wielded great power in settling the specific type of building which was carried out, through his control of street layout, individual plot sizes,

---

[1] F. E. Baines (ed.), *Records of Hampstead* (1890), p. 222, presents this 'as a great concession'.

[2] Charles Booth, *Life and Labour of the People of London*, 3rd ser. *Religious Influences*, I, *Outer Ring North* (1902), pp. 213–15 and Map G. And see above, pp. 268–71, for the deterioration of Lund's St John's Park estate.

and minimum value of houses to be erected, and through his ability to prohibit certain kinds of premises which might annoy residents and damage the character of the rest of the property. All these powers were used by the great ground landlords of Hampstead. It might have been expected that financial controls, through the ability to charge differential rents for sites destined for different types of development, would have been the most powerful instruments at the ground landlord's disposal. The standard contemporary handbooks on the development of building estates certainly assumed that because houses of the most superior type for 'mansion people' were the most valuable, they were also the most profitable for builder and landowner alike; and they took it for granted that there was a descending scale of profitability through all the possible gradations of house size and social class until with workmen's cottages the lowest level of profit was reached, so low that the opportunity cost in terms of the rents of market gardens which might be sacrificed might make such low grade building completely undesirable.[1] In such a situation a ground landlord should have secured the highest rents from land leased for the most expensive housing, and his interest in maximising his income should have ensured that he would always seek the highest possible rent each building property would bear; in this way the level of ground rents—rather than the physical controls of restrictive clauses in building agreements—ought to have seen to it that each property was covered with houses of the best class which its particular situation allowed. The experience of the Dean and Chapter of Westminster's Hampstead estate suggests, however, that things did not necessarily happen like this in practice, and that the descending scale of rents might be, in social terms, topsy-turvy.

The Belsize Estate was the only one of the large estates in Hampstead which came to include a sizeable working-class district, as distinct from the small pockets of poorer housing clustering round the mews and stables on the other estates. It is thus the only estate where the range of ground rents received provides some test of contemporary estate management techniques and rent theory. When development was completed the estate formed four main blocks: the wealthy upper-class district around the original Belsize Park where houses sold for £2,000 to £3,000; the well-to-do middle class district of the initial Rosslyn Park estate around Lyndhurst Road, where houses were worth

---

[1] A typical example is R. Scott Burn, *The Practical Directory for the Improvement of Landed Property, Rural and Suburban* (2 vols, Edinburgh, 1882), II, ch. V, 'Land on the property suitable for suburban domestic structures—the position, setting off, and laying out of the plots', especially pp. 343–4.

£1,300 to £1,500 (the St John's Park estate was of the same character, the houses there being a shade cheapter in the 1880s); the more middling middle-class district around Parliament Hill Road, where the houses changed hands at £900; and the working-class district of Fleet Road, where the houses sold at £400 to £500.[1] At first sight the ground rents received from these different districts do not follow any coherent pattern: in the first district successive agreements were set at rents of £28, £50, £77, and £50 an acre; in the second the rent was £10 an acre; in the third, £46 an acre; and in the fourth, £82 an acre. The lowest rents, however, may be disregarded because they concerned the earliest agreements in which the lessees had substantial previous property rights of their own in the areas leased to them; for the second district the rent of £50 an acre, paid for the land on which the good middle-class neighbourhood of Stanley Gardens was built, may be substituted. The rents of ordinary commercial building agreements thus run: £50, £50, £46, and £82. Admittedly they were fixed at different times over a rather long period, from 1864 to 1891, and it is possible that the entire scale of building values shifted upward in this time. On the other hand, there is the evidence from the Eton estate that land was let for the highest-class development, on the old Eton and Middlesex Cricket Ground, as late as 1890 for £50 an acre, while the way in which Cluttons dealt with the rent of Gibb's agreement for the Fleet Road district, raising it every time the quality of the proposed houses was lowered, seems to clinch the apparently perverse argument that if there was any notion of progressive rates in ground rents it was one in which the rents became higher as the houses became poorer and cheaper.[2]

Any simple conclusion that it paid landlords best to get their building land covered with as many cheap houses as possible undoubtedly ignores the complexity of a land agent's calculations of the proper level of rent to charge. There may have been a carry-over into the urban setting of the precept from the conduct of agricultural estates that a multitude of small rents were harder to collect and carried a higher risk of defaults than a small number of sizeable rents; in which case a higher rent per acre for the large number of working-class houses per acre would furnish a cushion for any such difficulties. There may have

[1] The prices were established from assignments and applications for 999-year leases, and all relate to the period 1885–95.

[2] All figures of ground rents are taken from previous detailed discussion in the text; all are comparable in the sense that they are rents paid by developers who were responsible for constructing all roads and sewers at their own expense.

been a simple rough-and-ready calculation that since each house would bear its share of the ground rent, and since each rent should be for some proper sum in pounds, then where there were going to be more houses to the acre the ground rent per acre had to be larger in order to be divisible. Against this explanation there is the evidence that ground rents were not visualised as some constant sum per house irrespective of its value, but care was taken to insist that they should never exceed one-sixth of the full annual value of a house.[1] Finally, if the land agent was sophisticated in his methods, there is the possibility that he fixed the ground rent in relation to the expected value of the reversion when the 99-year lease expired, moving one up as the second fell so that the ground landlord's ultimate profit from the land should always remain approximately the same.

A comparison of the values of the bricks and mortar put on each acre in the different grades of housing does suggest that this last consideration was indeed important. In the wealthiest district the houses may have been comparatively sparse, but they were also comparatively expensive, so that there was something like £12,500 worth of building on each acre; this was the top value, the other three districts supporting £10,000, £8,000 and £7,500 on each acre. The actual cost of the buildings put on each acre obviously bore little relation in practice to the value of the reversion to the ground landlord 99 years later, since urban land values had undergone such immense and unforeseen upheavals in the interval. But it is fair enough to assume that at the time of building it was supposed that when the time did come for the leases to fall in the value would be closely connected to what had gone up. Using this rough assumption an equally rough-and-ready calculation can be made of the total benefit to the ground landlord over the entire 99-year period, ignoring such matters as reduced ground rents payable in the first few years of each lease and the theoretical option which the landlord had of investing his rents at compound interest, which should be incorporated in a precise comparison: on the upper-class district rents plus reversion would reach about £17,500 per acre over the 99 years, and on the working-class district about £15,600. It is therefore quite probable that the much higher rent per acre charged in the latter was an attempt to ensure that what the ground landlord lost on the swings in a lower-

[1] When the Eccles. Comm. offered to convert their 99-year leaseholds into 999-year leaseholds in the 1890s, at increased ground rents, these were normally fixed at 20–25 per cent of the full annual value of the houses: CC File 7142, 20 February and 9 May 1893 for examples in Upper Park Road. Many leaseholders regarded these increased ground rents as extortionate and declined to take up the offer of a 999-year lease.

class development, in house values, he won on the roundabouts from ground rents. The argument cannot be pressed too far, for on the one hand the two districts of middle-class housing showed a larger gap below the wealthiest area, in rents plus reversionary value, than did the working-class district; and on the other hand when the ground rent of the Fleet Road district was raised in 1885 the value of the reversion was also increased since so many more of the cheaper houses were permitted that the cost of buildings per acre went up, a movement in the opposite direction to that expected. In this particular instance it is likely that the ground rent was increased at least partly to make Gibb pay some price for the changes in the terms of the agreement, which he had requested.[1]

The experience of the Belsize estate suggests, therefore, that the agent made an effort in fixing ground rents to see that different districts produced in the long run roughly similar levels of total profits for the ground landlord, although even so it is clear that the most superior type of housing was also the most profitable. The houses themselves were built in the short run, however, and the annual rents were the only immediate returns which the ground landlord saw; accepting lower rents for better houses was a case of sacrificing present income for the prospect of future capital gains, behaviour more likely from a corporate landowner like the Dean and Chapter or a semi-corporate landed family confident of unbroken succession and inheritance in the future than from a mere individual property-owner without an inkling, maybe without a thought, of who might own the site 99 years on. Hence it seems that the landowner may have had no more than a slender and remote incentive, in hard financial terms, for procuring the development of his land with the most superior residences; although it should be admitted that he probably had a very strong disincentive, which perhaps could be measured in terms of a money cost, against permitting development of neighbourhoods way below the class of Fleet Road, where all manner of damage, deterioration, dilapidation and defaulting could be expected to accompany housing for the poorest sections of society or for the Victorians' favourite social peril, the criminal classes. The landowner's motive in hedging himself round with restrictive clauses in his building agreements intended to ensure an exclusive and homogeneous class of building, it might be thought, was less to protect his pocket than to preserve his self-esteem, by creating respectable communities and if possible socially elevated communities on his property.

[1] See above, p. 360.

The developer or builder, it seems, was the person likely to reap in his own lifetime the extra profits from better-class development, on the reasonable assumption that building profits per acre were directly related to building costs per acre. If that was so, then a builder did not need to be compelled to build as expensive houses as possible by a landlord's physical controls, since business sense would lead him to do just that in any case. The function of these controls was merely to guard against the odd chance of a stray builder falling on hard times, running short of cash and credit, and being driven to seek a rapid turnover by running up cheap, small and lower-class houses which might foul up an entire neighbourhood that had been launched as a high-class estate; such a fall-back function for the minimum-value clauses would explain why they were seldom if ever actually invoked, and why the houses actually built were almost invariably considerably more costly than the minimum value stipulated in the agreement.[1] For the developer who embarked on a venture aimed at a particular social group the landlord's physical controls could indeed be seen as a form of protection for his investment, a pledge that the landlord would apply similar conditions to any adjoining takes and thus ensure that property values on the earliest development were not damaged by any intrusion of poorer-class elements subsequently.

If the Fleet Road area came to form a working-class district as an extension into Hampstead of Gospel Oak and Kentish Town, the fully indigenous working-class quarters of Hampstead grew in the west in the tangle of land left by the railways. By 1901 this large triangle of ground bounded by West End Lane, Kilburn High Street and the parish boundary with Hendon on the north contained nearly 27,000 people, one-third of Hampstead's total population, on rather less than one-fifth of Hampstead's total area; since a fair slice of the 435 acres of the two wards involved, West End and Kilburn, was eaten up by the railways and particularly by the Midland's West End Sidings, the disproportion was greater than the bare figures suggest. It was the fastest-growing

[1] Comparison of minimum values for houses stipulated in building agreements, and costs of those in fact built:

	Minimum value £	Actual cost £
Belsize Avenue	1,000	1,500
Lyndhurst Road	500	1,000
Stanley Gardens	800	1,000
Parliament Hill Road	750	800
Constantine Road	360	360

part of Hampstead in the late nineteenth century, more than doubling its population in the 1880s and growing by 50 per cent in the 1890s. In these two decades it made up for a late start, overtaking in a great spurt the old-established districts of the Town, Belsize and Adelaide wards, and crossing the finishing line, as Hampstead's general urban development reached its limits, with a frenzied gallop of building operations which gave it a handsome lead in numbers and a poor reputation as the ugliest part of the borough.[1] By Hampstead standards people were packed in. By 1901 Kilburn ward housed 79 persons to the acre, more than twice the population density of the borough as a whole and nearly three times as many to the acre as in the leafy spaces of the Fitzjohn's Avenue district of Central ward; it had risen to 83·7 people to the acre by 1921, and remained at about that level throughout the inter-war years. No doubt the East-Ender, accustomed to population densities of well over 200 to the acre in Bethnal Green, would not have considered the Kilburn levels at all remarkable. But for Hampstead they pointed to a large area of development of a considerably lower class than was altogether comfortable for its social standing, and to a degree of populous vulgarity which tarnished its reputation for exclusiveness.[2]

It is tempting to argue that things went that way because railway laceration so mutilated and disfigured this tract of country that it was unfitted for any better class of development. There is indeed much to be said for such an argument, and an inspection of Ravenshaw Street, Sumatra Road, Maygrove Road, Iverson Road, Netherwood Street, or Sherriff Road says it with all the force which can be mustered in any large town by the rows of tiny back yards and the ranked backsides of terrace houses thrust close against a railway line. Moreover, the first true building estate in the area, as distinct from the building of isolated houses, was laid out in the open fields between the Hampstead Junction and Midland Railways in 1869, as soon as the latter had been built and

[1] Hampstead parish was divided into four wards in 1873, and then rearranged into seven wards in 1900. In the 1881 and 1891 Censuses the western lay within the Kilburn Ward; in the 1901 Census it was divided between Kilburn and West End Wards. The new wards of 1901, Central and Priory as well as West End, were mainly carved out of the old Kilburn Ward; though Central Ward (the Fitzjohn's Avenue district) also contained part of the Town Ward. It is thus not possible to make exact comparisons of ward populations in 1891 and 1901. See *1881 Census*, Parl. Papers, 1883, LXXIX, p. 33; *1891 Census*, Parl. Papers, 1893/4, CV, pp. 40, 43; *1901 Census*, Parl. Papers, 1902, CXX, p. 17.

[2] Population densities calculated from *1901 Census*, loc. cit., and from *1931 Census* (repeating 1921 figures), County of London Table 3, p. 6.

alongside the Edgware Road station, opened in 1860, of the former.[1] This, the Kilburn estate of the British Land Company, was at once followed by the Netherwood Street and Palmerston Road development immediately to the south of the Hampstead Junction Railway, by the United Land Company.[2] These two developments, still surrounded by fields and connected to the general built-up area only by the railways which determined their own street lines, set the tone for the entire district and formed the centre of a miniature suburban planetary system exercising its influence on the character of the surrounding small estates as they were built over in the following thirty years. The full potential of this influence was released by the arrival of the Metropolitan Extension in 1879 with its stations at West Hampstead and Kilburn (on the Edgware Road, and initially known as Brondesbury), and with its highly convenient commuter service. The nature of the influence can be seen both chronologically in the dating of building as it moved away from its Netherwood Street–Iverson Road epicentre, and socially in the gradually ascending size of the houses and standing of the streets as they move away towards West End Lane on the east and Fortune Green on the north-east.

Before concluding that this was an entire sub-district whose fortunes were settled by the geography of railway layouts, however, it should be acknowledged that other features contributed to the end result. The most obvious of these was that the initial developers were land companies, and land companies generally put a highly distinctive stamp on the estates which they developed. The land companies, a mid-century product of the drive to institutionalise thrift and the urge to stabilise society by creating a large body of small property-owners, usually worked alongside parent or associated building societies and towards the end of the century had largely merged with them. During the period of their independent existence the function of the land companies was to act as middlemen in the market for building land, acquiring estates in small parcels of a few acres at a time, laying them out with roads and sewers, and then selling off building plots on mortgages which they provided; the associated building society would then normally finance the actual house building. The whole system was geared to the needs of the small man with small savings, ambitious of becoming the owner of his own house, and although the system was sometimes

[1] MBW Min., 29 October 1869, p. 1128 for the approval of the formation of Iverson, Loveridge and Maygrove Roads, and Ariel Street.

[2] HLRO Metropolitan and St John's Wood Railway, New Lines, Session 1873, Plan and Book of Reference, for the Netherwood Street development, and the projected extension (Sherriff Road) by a speculator, Donald Nicoll.

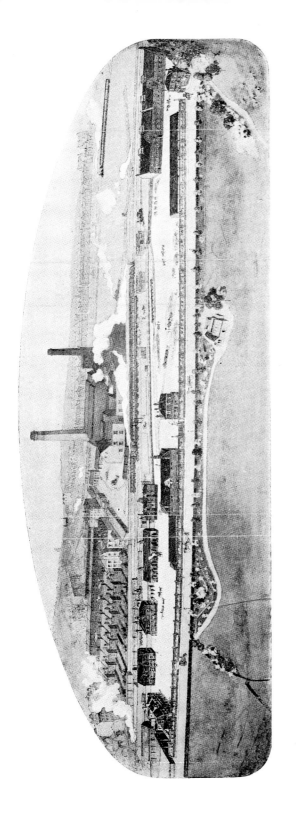

PLATE 15 Municipal electricity: the power station at Lithos Road in 1906 (see p. 415)

PLATE 14 'The Harrow of the Board Schools': the Fleet Road School, opened in 1880, photographed in 1965 (see p. 416)

exploited by speculative builders for whom it was not intended at all, its main stream of customers did indeed consist of individuals building single houses for their own use. These people formed a fairly well-defined layer of the housing market, in the region of the upper levels of the working class and the lower end of the middle class, naturally well above the bread line since there had to be some savings in the kitty, but also well below the affluent, let alone the fashionable, middle classes whose tastes did not run to home-ownership especially if achieved through financial institutions which retained from their origins more than a whiff of radicalism and vulgarity.

The housing on land company–building society estates, therefore, tended to conform to a pattern of respectable but modest and inexpensive homes, rather closely packed and frequently in terraces, usually well cared for by the artisans or clerks who might be their original owners, but also not uncommonly slipping rather rapidly if the owner found that he had over-reached himself and had to take in lodgers to help foot the bills. Within Hampstead the only other area in which land companies seem to have been involved in development was on the Carlile estate in the old town; and the result in Kemplay, Carlingford and Denning Roads was to produce a district of terraced lower-middle class which Booth, in 1898, found no different in standing from the better bits of the Fleet Road district.[1] Similar physical and social results were, of course, easily supplied by other means of development, by speculative builders working on leasehold properties; but while other developers and speculators could supply a range of products, land companies appear to have been limited to this one type. They were also limited, by strong preference, to freehold land which could be acquired in the small parcels of half-a-dozen acres or so which it was financially and administratively convenient for them to handle. The freehold requirement necessarily meant that the land companies shut themselves out of the development of the estates of the larger urban landowners who generally clove to the leasehold system. For the British and United Land Companies one of the main attractions of the Kilburn properties undoubtedly was that they were available as small freehold estates.[2] Perhaps they were put on the market because railway interference made the previous owners abandon residence; but their

---

[1] It was again the British Land Company which was involved on the Carlile estate: *Hampstead and Highgate Express*, 3 June 1876. Booth, *Religious Influences*, I, Map G. This was surveyed in 1897–8.

[2] Strictly they were recently enfranchised copyholds. Changes of ownership between the Tithe Apportionment and purchase by the land companies have not been traced.

evident suitability for purchase by land companies perhaps influenced their destiny as much as their proximity to the tracks, as a blight on good-class residential development, or their proximity to the stations, as an incentive to intensive development for a commuting class.

The poor streets which Booth found in Kilburn in 1898—Palmerston Road, Netherwood Street, Loveridge Road, and Ravenshaw Street—no doubt represented decline and deterioration since their building twenty and more years earlier, decay at least partly induced by railway noise and grime but aided by the readiness and eagerness of the owners to take in lodgers. By 1898 lodgers were very common hereabouts; practically every house which had started life with a single family now contained at least two, and it was becoming quite usual to let out the houses of Palmerston Road in three flats: the two kitchen rooms in the basement let for 6s. a week, the three parlours on the ground floor for 7s. 6d., and the three top rooms for 6s. 6d. The occupants were mainly workers with local employment, bus drivers, cabmen, stablemen, workers in the building trades and the like; the accessibility of the trains to Baker Street or the City probably meant very little to them.[1] A little earlier, in 1885, the local directory gives a hint of the kind of people for whom the British Land Company's estate had been built. The residents—and there is, of course, no proof that they were also the owners—included many skilled craftsmen and workers, mixed with some professional people. Gasfitters, brass finishers, stained glass workers, gunmakers, watchmakers, coachbuilders, plasterers and carpenters represented the former; there was a dentist, a doctor, an accountant, an insurance agent, an architect, an auctioneer, a photographer, two music teachers (with a piano tuner to look after them), and three ladies' schools, all no doubt at the lower end of the professional middle class; and the shopkeeping middle class put in an appearance in the persons of a grocer, an ironmonger, a draper, several coal merchants, and an undertaker.[2] Those whose occupations or businesses were listed in the directory were there, presumably, precisely because their activities were local; but they formed about a third of the residents, so that the clerks and others for whom the commuter trains were important could have been only some fraction of the remaining unidentified two-thirds.

The influence of the social mixture and physical appearance of the land-company-style building estate on its immediate surroundings when

[1] Booth, *Religious Influences*, I, 213–15 and Map G.
[2] *Hampstead and Highgate Directory*, 1885, analysis of Iverson, Loveridge and Maygrove Roads.

they too became ripe for development can be readily appreciated; and in this instance it was strengthened by the presence of a third land company as a developer in the neighbourhood, on the small estate of Hillfield and Aldred Roads just to the west of West End Green.[1] Nevertheless it does not seem likely that railways and land companies alone can account for the eventually practically complete colonisation of West Hampstead and Kilburn by the petit bourgeoisie. Topography helped, since although this was no depressingly low-lying or unhealthy area it did lie at the western foot of the Hampstead heights whose elevation stood always close at hand as a visible reminder of where social superiority resided, and its very gentleness of gradient was the prime reason for railways seeking it out. The parish authorities also lent a hand by selecting twenty acres of land at Fortune Green in 1874 as the site of their new cemetery. This was chosen because it was remote from the wealthy part of the parish, reasonably well clear of any existing houses, and right on the parish boundary; the fact that it was acquired for £350 an acre at a time when any alternative land with an immediate building value was available only for three or four times as much, indicates that its ripeness for building was still some way off. None of this prevented objections, although they were overridden. The Cotton estate flourished plans for the development of the Shoot-Up Hill Farm that had been drawn up as much as nineteen years previously, only to be dismissed by the observation that not a single house had been built. The trustees of the Burgess estate, on which some building had started, objected that they had paid up to £832 an acre in purchasing much of their forty acres thereabouts, and that if a cemetery was formed builders would put up houses letting at only £25 to £40 a year, instead of grand houses at £200 or £300 a year which they had contemplated. The Principal of the Anglo-French College, on Burgess Hill, objected; and Cannon of Kidderpore Hall claimed that his mansion and park would be so injured that its value would drop from £1,000 an acre to £300.[2]

The objectors certainly had a point, even if this was indeed by far the best available site within the parish for a badly-needed new burial ground, and even if there were no solid grounds for a cemetery to discourage the building of good-quality housing nearby. Builders certainly did believe that the better-class residents would be scared away by the

[1] MBW Min., 17 July 1868, pp. 927, 1049; the owners are simply described as 'The Land Company'.

[2] HPL Vestry Min., 7 April 1874; *Hampstead and Highgate Express*, 21 March and 18 April 1874. The Cotton Estate was in two parts, on West End Lane and Shoot-Up Hill Farm.

imagined dangers to health and trials to the spirit, of life overlooking the gravestones, and at any rate in the early years felt that the vicinity could support only the lower-middle-class terraces of the somewhat lugubriously-named Achilles, Agamemnon, Ajax and Ulysses Roads.[1] It was extravagant to claim, however, that any possibly baleful and damaging aura could reach as far from the Cemetery as the Kidderpore property, whose development into the wealthy streets of Kidderpore and Ferncroft Avenues and Heath Drive was, in the event, entirely un-hindered. Perhaps the main effect of the Cemetery was to freeze development in the immediate area until there had been time for the timid to overcome the notion that it was not respectable or acceptable to live in the vicinity. Hence activity on this section of the Cotton estate was set back for over a decade; but when it came, the Gondar Gardens development of the 1890s, encircling the Grand Junction Waterworks Company reservoir, was of a fairly spacious comfortable middle-class standard. To the west of the Cemetery the rest of this estate had to wait much longer; Somali, Asmara, and Menelik Roads, conceived no doubt at the time of the Italians' humiliation by Abyssinia in 1896, were still not finished by 1914 and there was considerable building here in the 1920s; it was, however, rather expensive housing, and by the time the cemetery side of Menelik Road came to be com-pleted it had become a positive advantage to enjoy the seclusion and green outlook which the position afforded.

Behind or beneath all these factors of topography, railway layouts, land company estates, and the Cemetery lay a network of property rights, and the property boundaries were perhaps the most fundamental feature of all in determining the shape of the West Hampstead urban landscape. For in other parts of the parish very similar points of damag-ing influence, such as the Fever Hospital, the railways at Primrose Hill and the Heath, or the Workhouse at New End, were successfully absorbed into one vast, solidly and impeccably middle- and upper-middle-class district, with very much more circumscribed and localised degrading effects than in West Hampstead. Near the Workhouse, indeed, in old Hampstead, there were a few blocks of poverty, but they stretched no further than a street's width away in New End and Streatley Place; and if other circumstances were favourable it was more often than not possible to restrict the baleful effects of any particular activity which withered the prospects of high-class development to no

---

[1] These streets, on the south-east side of the Cemetery, were in Booth's third class, 'fairly comfortable', in 1898: Booth, *Religious Influences*, Map G.

more than the immediately adjoining street or two.[1] In West Hampstead, however, such influences seem to have run unchecked over field after field as it was turned into town, until reaching the line of West End Lane which became a marked frontier between the respectable and fashionable to the east and the socially mixed tending to lower class and poverty to the west. West End Lane, with its meandering course and puny width, was very far from an obvious or striking physical boundary; but it was, for most of its course, a very clear-cut property boundary. To the east lay large estates, Cotton and Maryon Wilson, whose owners and managers approached building development with an eye to distant future interests and benefits. To the west lay small fragmented properties, in some cases further subdivided between the time of the tithe apportionment and the beginning of building development.[2] Some of the individual properties were not large enough to be developed as superior building estates in any event; but it was more important that the greater part of the small owners lacked the sense of family interest or tradition which induced the larger owners to accept some sacrifice of present income for the prospect of greater gains in the remote future. The small men, intent on the largest immediate returns from either selling or leasing their building land, necessarily embarked on the most intensive development, which was the most profitable but which was also inferior in size, appearance and social standing.

Kilburn had once had its resident pseudo-gentry in their villas along the High Road, just like West End Lane and Haverstock Hill. Running northwards from the LNWR line in 1850 there had been Clarence Place, Oak Lodge (later known as The Grange), Bunder Lodge, Kilburn Lodge, Ryde Cottage, and Royston Hall, all on the Hampstead side of the High Road, before reaching the farmhouses of William Verey (close to where the Hampstead Junction line now crosses the road), and John Froggart of Shoot-Up Hill Farm (close to the junction of Mill Lane and Shoot-Up Hill).[3] But where their Haverstock Hill counterparts, and most of those on West End Lane, had been displaced by rows of houses for residents not much less well-heeled than the

---

[1] Loc. cit. Booth's general impression of Hampstead was that, with the exception of some long-established poverty in old Hampstead, 'the whole of this vast district is either middle or upper middle class' apart from the extreme west at Kilburn and West End: ibid., pp. 206–7.

[2] See above, pp. 75–81, for the Tithe Apportionment. Some of the subsequent changes in ownership are revealed by the Plans and Books of Reference of the Hampstead Junction, Midland, and Metropolitan New Lines already cited.

[3] Map of London and Environs by James Wyld (n.d. but c. 1850).

outgoers, the Kilburn villas were supplanted by the artisan rows of Palmerston Road and Gascony Avenue. The sole survivor was The Grange, and this together with the adjoining market garden became in due course Kilburn Grange Park.[1] Their different fates were no doubt swayed by location, but they were sealed by landownership: the first set lay on large estates, the second were in individual ownership or lay on petty estates. The steep descent of the Kilburn villas was a particularly striking and abrupt example of the social decay which Booth saw as West Hampstead's hallmark. Only at Kilburn and West End, he remarked of Hampstead at the end of the century, 'a working class population has come in and is very rapidly increasing in number, and becoming poor and crowded in places. But the increase happens everywhere, more or less', he continued in an irrelevantly prejudiced sociological aside, 'and with growth in numbers there is social decadence. The old families leave, the Jews come, the artistic and Bohemian element prevails.' Resuming the discussion of the district under consideration he observed that 'quite apart from the poor streets forming there, West End where the population is all new, is found by the Congregationalists to be a "strange and a difficult district". They think there is no place where people of a similar class are so slack'. The explanations offered were that 'the people came before the churches and so acquired habits of neglect', or that 'existence in flats, only one remove from hotel life, lacks the ties and responsibilities of domesticity'. The rage for cheap and showy flats was said to be attracting 'mixed classes bound to become poorer', reiterating the moral condemnation of flat-dwelling. Of West End he concluded that the population had increased twentyfold in the previous ten years and that as a result 'the place looks forlorn, and the people seem still unaccustomed to their surroundings'; while he returned to the point that Kilburn, through its growing population, 'is becoming poorer, owing to the increase of lodgers'.[2]

Although comparison of Booth's 'Poverty' maps of 1889 and 1898 does show a certain amount of downgrading in the status of some Kilburn streets, notably Eresby Road, Gascony and Messina Avenues, Palmerston Road, Netherwood Street, Iverson, Loveridge and Maygrove Roads, and Broomsleigh and Ravenshaw Streets, it is something of an exaggeration to speak of a general social decay in the neighbour-

[1] The five acres, then belonging to Samuel Ware, had been a market garden at least since 1838 (Tithe Apportionment Map, field 113) and were still a market garden in 1890 (Stanford's London School Board Map). The Borough purchased the land for a park early in the present century.

[2] Booth, *Religious Influences*, I, 207–8, 213–15.

hood.[1] The great majority of the inhabitants of 1898 were newcomers, first-generation settlers in brand new houses, not people taking over from previous occupants of higher status; Booth's description is essentially a picture of the initial character of West Hampstead and Kilburn as it left the hands of the builders, a place with an indifferent social standing to match its indifferent architecture. Also, despite the formation of three new ecclesiastical parishes west of West End Lane—Emmanuel (1885), St Cuthbert (1888) and St James (1888)—the building of churches for them—at West End Green (1898), Fordwych Road (1887) and Sherriff Road (1887)—the provision of a Roman Catholic chapel in Quex Road, three Dissenting chapels and a couple of corrugated-iron mission halls, it was apparently an irreligious place. Withal it was in the lump a valuable piece of property, and property rights had largely made it what it was: a district which the more refined part of Hampstead preferred to ignore, and which Pevsner remarked, in a different context, 'need be visited only by those in search of Victorian churches. The houses and streets require no notice.'[2]

[1] Booth, Map of London Poverty (1889), north-west sheet.
[2] Pevsner, op. cit., II, 199. Dates of formation of ecclesiastical parishes and districts are in the *1891 Census*, Parl. Papers, CIV, p. 225. The first (temporary) Emmanuel Church was built in 1882.

Ten

HAMPSTEAD COMMUNITIES, 1850-1964
Church and Chapel, Vestry and Borough

If the several members of the Hampstead urban parish and metropolitan borough of 1900, 'one of the largest and most prosperous of the well-to-do residential suburbs of London' which was 'solid and stolidly middle class', were held together by anything it was by religion, not by a sense of shared citizenship.[1] This was well-nigh inevitable in the atmosphere of headlong urban growth after the 1840s. Developers and builders created their several neighbourhoods, stamping them with the social character which they intended them to develop. But when they had done their work in shaping streets and houses they had created no more than receptacles ready to receive people. People pre-selected, no doubt, in terms of income, wealth, family size, social status and aspirations by the shape of the mould into which they chose to move; but still people who as residents could alone generate the loyalties, attachments and activities which could turn the developers' empty carcase of a neighbourhood into a living community. To the newcomers Hampstead meant little except as a place-name dispensing a coveted address; its administration barely touched them or involved them in any common activities, and if Hampstead did exist and function as an entity the fact escaped their notice. Where any civic presence or corporate life was hard to detect people naturally turned, if at all, to a much more local centre as the focus of a community. This was the church or chapel, forming social ties and bonds in the nineteenth century much as football clubs or constituency party associations do in the mid-twentieth century.

The prominence of the churches did not necessarily rest on particularly intense devotion and piety, though the traditional image of the mid-Victorian middle-class household assembling for daily morning prayer and bible-reading under the ministration of its master is prob-

---

[1] Booth, *Life and Labour in London*, 1st ser. II, 424; Booth, *Religious Influences*, I, 206.

ably not too wide of the mark. The Hampstead population, indeed, perhaps was notably zealous in its churchgoing at mid-century; the Religious Census of 1851 indicated that there were 8,298 attendances at worship in the course of the census Sunday, and the attempted elimination of the double-counting of the faithful who attended two or three services that day by taking two-thirds of attendances as the probable number of individual churchgoers suggests that they were half the total population. This was a high attendance record, since the census-takers themselves thought that after making allowances for children, invalids, and those properly absent about their household chores, no more than 58 per cent of the total population of the country were at liberty to attend service if they wished.[1] Regularity of attendance was, no doubt, a necessary prop for the churches; but it may well have been the result of non-religious motives which reflected the power of the local church to confer social acceptance and assist personal advancement, just as much as it was a manifestation of faith. That the church's ability to do this must have relied, in the last resort, on some form of religious belief on the part of the leaders of each social group, even if it might amount to little more than an unwillingness to challenge the traditional authority of the Christian teaching, is not inconsistent with the possibility that much, maybe the major part, of the congregations was there for essentially secular reasons.

These reasons, in the wealthier and comfortable districts, can be summed up as the drive to attain respectability and recognition. Recognition as an acceptable and equal member of a congregation was the very essence of absorption into a community of social kin, and it was through this function of a public demonstration of social affinities that the local churches were able to form communities out of the individual family atoms of a raw building estate. In the poorer areas members of the lower orders came to church, if they came at all, perhaps because they knew it would please their social superiors, perhaps out of fear of the displeasure which abstention could occasion, perhaps out of a desire to better themselves, sometimes to obtain solace. For the fortunate church had it both ways in the new urban areas of the nineteenth century: in the respectable parts new residents went out of their way to procure a church as a social necessity; in the poorer quarters outsiders felt that the new residents must have a church imposed upon them in the interests of social discipline, social control and, who knows, the salvation of souls. One kind of area had committees and bazaars and

[1] *1851 Religious Census*, Parl. Papers, 1852/3, LXXXIX, p. 4; W. L. Burn, *The Age of Equipoise* (1964), pp. 271–2.

ladies' teas to raise money for the building of a church; the other had mission halls, revivalist preachers, and soup kitchens.

Developers, and ground landlords, were well aware that a church was a necessary part of the equipment of any building development with pretensions to quality, and usually assisted in its establishment. The first new church of the century, of the Church of England, was a case in point: the chapel of St John in Downshire Hill, which began and remained as a proprietary, and unconsecrated, estate chapel, and which was built in 1818 while the new street was forming, as graceful and charming as the houses it was to serve.[1] Eton College, however, needed sharp prodding from its principal lessee and from the residents of its partly-formed Adelaide Road estate organised into a Committee of the Inhabitants of Haverstock Hill and Neighbourhood, before it thought of supplying a church. This was in 1846, and the College responded to the pressure; a site was provided, a temporary wooden church hut was erected, to serve while the church of St Saviour was building in Eton Road, which was ready in 1856. It was paid for by subscriptions from the residents' organisation, including £200 from Samuel Cuming the chief local builder, and a grant from the Metropolis Churches Fund which the energetic Bishop Blomfield had to support his drive for more churches; the College was content to contribute the site.[2] Other new churches followed the more regular, smooth course of the development of well-to-do suburban estates, with active participation and contributions from the three parties most interested in seeing a local church on the ground as soon as the makings of a new congregation had settled—ground landlord, developer, and the first batch of new residents. St Paul, Avenue Road (church 1864, ecclesiastical district 1860), St Peter, Belsize Square (church 1859, district 1861), St Mary, Priory Road (church 1856, district 1863), St Stephen, Rosslyn Hill (church 1869, district 1880), and St Mary, King Henry's Road (church 1873, district 1885) all followed this pattern. Each church, once established and vicared, naturally tended to acquire an individual reputation for the style, content and quality of its services, and the attractive or repelling powers of any particular church could be very strong indeed in an age when High and Low Church feelings were running high. But although a church might draw a few attenders from a distance for such reasons, it tended to remain serving an essentially localised, estate-based, congregation, a situation well illustrated by the distribution of

---

[1] See above, p. 126.
[2] Eton, College Records, XLIX, No. 128, Henry Bird to Bethell, 7 September 1846; and see above, pp. 227–8.

subscribers to the fund for enlarging St Peter's in 1875: all the subscribers of ten guineas or more lived on the Belsize Park estate, while the 31 lesser subscribers included 14 living off the estate in Adelaide Road or Lawn Road, and in one case as far away as Church Row from whence some acute difference with the vicar of the old parish church of St John, Beaumont Burnaby, must have shifted him.[1]

The building of Christ Church in Hampstead Square and the formation of its parish in 1852, like much else in which Sir Thomas Maryon Wilson was concerned, was far from smooth and regular. The very siting of this church, the second new Anglican building of the century, suggests that it had little connection with any recent growth of population or opening out of a new building estate. It stood close to the workhouse, surrounded by eighteenth-century buildings except to the north, where the grounds of Heathfield House and neighbouring allotment gardens remained devoid of parishioners until Cannon Place and Holford Road were built up from the 1880s onwards:[2] even the splendidly monstrous The Logs, on East Heath Road, could not disgorge its pewful of worshippers from their riotously assorted tower rooms and Gothic chambers for many years, since the mansion was not built until 1868. Christ Church was put there because John Gurney Hoare managed to find a site next the workhouse; and, Sir Thomas suspected, perhaps correctly, because Hoare and his friends wanted to promote their 'private or party purposes' and inflict a wound on the Maryon Wilson interests. The trouble was that Maryon Wilson had the advowson of the parish of Hampstead, and any diminution of the ecclesiastical territory of St John was only too likely to damage the value of the living and hence of the patronage. This was all the more so because the vicar of Hampstead drew no income at all from Hampstead tithes, but relied on an endowment of a moiety of the tithes of lands at Woodhorne in Northumberland, and surplice fees and offerings. The rub came with the fees, for 'on payment of fees the rich often give sovereigns in lieu of shillings' which were legally due, and the new Christ Church district would take many of the rich away from St John. Sir Thomas readily admitted that the growth of population made new church accommodation necessary; but he had a strong case in arguing that this ought to be provided where the new population was, and not in a long-settled spot,

[1] DCW RCO 32, F. W. Tremlett, vicar of St Peter's, to Dean and Chapter, 28 June 1875.

[2] William Shepherd, a local builder, purchased the Heathfield or Holford estate about 1875 and then began developing it; he was also the builder of the new Vestry Hall (Town Hall): *Hampstead and Highgate Express*, 24 June 1876.

and that if the St John's territory was to be carved up then St John itself should be left with the area of Old Hampstead as it existed in 1850.[1]

Sir Thomas, being obstinate and unpopular, was not heeded; and the parochial district assigned to Christ Church, with all the territory to the north and east of Flask Walk and Heath Street, did indeed take about half old Hampstead away from St John. A deft westward flick of the boundary at North End was all that was needed to put Hill House, Gurney Hoare's place, out of the spiritual reach of the Maryon Wilson church interest. Acting on his admission that new population meant new churches Sir Thomas had already, several years before 1850, 'selected a spot whereon to build a church, and [had] with the approbation of the Bishop erected near thereto a Temporary Church', himself paying the stipend of the officiating clergyman.[2] It was no fault of his that this wooden hut on Belsize Lane, at the bottom of the Conduit Fields, proved to be peripheral to the centres of new population, since it was intended to serve both the new estates on others' property and to be the focus for the development of his Finchley Road lands. When this failed to materialise, and three new churches were built close by—All Souls, Alexandra Road (1865, built at the cost of its first vicar, H. R. Wadmore), St Peter and St Paul—the temporary church was not very serviceable and lapsed into a schoolroom before ending its days as the plan and drawing office for the Fitzjohn's Avenue development.[3]

Thirty years after it had been run up, and after Sir Thomas's death, the Belsize Lane temporary spawned its intended permanent church, Holy Trinity on Finchley Road. Its building in 1872 in the field just beyond the North Star inn which had for so long marked the urban frontier of London was the first concrete evidence that that frontier had been breached. Concrete quite literally, for the architect Henry Legg prudently employed specially deepened concrete foundations under the steeple to guard against vibration from trains in the shallow tunnel which was expected any day to carry the Metropolitan's extension from Swiss Cottage; Legg's fears that in spite of this precaution his steeple might topple proved groundless.[4] Holy Trinity was an expensive church,

---

[1] GLCRO E/MW/H/III/38/15, Sir Thomas Maryon Wilson to the Church Commissioners, 8 April 1850, objecting to the application of John Gurney Hoare and others to build a new church.

[2] Loc. cit.

[3] E/MW/H/III/26/19, Bell & Steward to Knocker, 30 November 1872, seeking possession of the hut from the Trinity School Committee, for use as a plan room.

[4] HLRO Metropolitan and St John's Wood Railway, New Lines, Session 1873,

FIGURE 4 New churches for the new suburbs: Trinity Church, Finchley Road, architect Henry S. Legg, built in 1872

at £17,000, as befitted its service of an expensive catchment area in Fitzjohn's Avenue. In this instance the Maryon Wilsons were obliged to beggar the mother church of St John in drawing the bounds of a parish for their own new church, and arbitrarily chose the line of the Midland Railway and its tunnel as the dividing line between St John and Holy Trinity, producing a highly artificial parish boundary across the middle of Fitzjohn's Avenue and Maresfield and Netherhall Gardens of which the residents were probably quite unaware. Its western boundary became, in the course of time, equally artificial, though when it was chosen the line of the track leading from the Fairfax Mews to West End would have seemed natural enough; unfortunately building lines did not follow this path, and the parish boundary came to cut through the middle of Compayne, Canfield, Greencroft and Aberdare Gardens. Generally speaking, however, the boundaries of the new ecclesiastical districts conformed pretty closely to the property boundaries in comfortable and prosperous Hampstead, perpetuating their housing estate origins. Holy Trinity, of course, did not follow this rule very closely; even so, the overwhelming bulk of the Maryon Wilson lands ended up within that district and the residual St John's parish as finally shrunk to the area between Heath Street and High Street on one side and Finchley Road on the other. The boundaries of St Peter with St Saviour, and of All Souls with Holy Trinity, are particularly faithful reproductions of the estate limits of Dean and Chapter, Eton College, Eyre and Maryon Wilson properties.

Matters were necessarily different in West Hampstead since there were scarcely any individual estates large enough in the first place to sport their own church, and once they were developed most were of too low a social status to generate their own internal pressures for a local status symbol of this kind. The south and the north, the early and the late, flanks of West Hampstead were the exceptions: St Mary, Priory Road, certainly started life as the Greville-Upton estate church; and it is likely that St Luke, Kidderpore Avenue, began in 1898 as the centre for the projected expensive development on the old Cannon estate, though its parish beat included some socially indifferent streets at Fortune Green. Emmanuel, St Cuthbert and St James were the mission-type churches and parishes of West Hampstead, planted by

Mins of Evidence Vol. xxx, Henry Legg, 20 May 1873. Legg's particular fear was of the extra strong vibration which might be caused by heavy goods traffic, the prohibition of which was the great ground of local policy towards this and similar extension schemes in 1870, 1871, 1872 and 1873. As in the event goods traffic was not carried, these fears were never put to the crucial test.

evangelising clergy and laity intent on bringing the faith to the irreligious, and perhaps on encouraging some sense of community among the amorphous inhabitants of these mushroom streets.[1] Here the Anglican mission halls were to be found; and here too the Dissenters and Catholics flourished, cultivating a soil that was, unlike the rest of new Hampstead, not pre-empted by the established church acting through powerful Anglican landowners and exploiting the strongly Anglican directions of the socially ambitious.

Sir Thomas had imagined, in 1850, that 'a very large proportion' of the population was Nonconformist, growing with the growth in new inhabitants. In fact over three-quarters of the total number of places in Hampstead's churches and chapels, and over 80 per cent of actual attendances at them during Sunday 30 March 1851, were in Anglican churches.[2] Dissent was indeed quite strong, and well-established, in old Hampstead, and had been so since the seventeenth century; there were Unitarian, Baptist and Methodist chapels, and a Quaker meeting house, by the early nineteenth century. The old town, with plenty of small property owners able and perhaps anxious to flout the wishes of an Anglican overlord by granting sites for dissenting chapels, and with a mixed and cosmopolitan society, was a congenial environment for nonconformity. But the 1851 figures scarcely suggest that the newcomers moving into Hampstead in the first half of the century included any great number of Nonconformists. It was, after all, the deliberate policy of Eton College and the Dean and Chapter of Westminster to exclude them and to put their influence behind an exclusively Anglican urban colonisation. Such influence, and the prospect of social isolation and ostracism of non-Anglicans which it implied, may not have been able to prevent the arrival of some individual Nonconformists; though Tremlett could boast of his parish of St Peter in 1868 that it 'is now most united. All the householders with the exception of 6 Jews, 2 Roman Catholics, 1 Congregationalist, and 3 Presbyterians, are church people, and it would be an outrage upon the religious feeling of these to put up a Dissenting Chapel 9 doors distant from the Church.'[3] The three Presbyterian families could, in his view, perfectly well attend the

---

[1] Such missions did not always bring comfort only to the poor and deprived; the father-in-law of the vicar-designate of St James, Charles McAnnally, gave £2,000 towards the cost of this church: *Hampstead Year Book for 1889*, p. 27.

[2] Sir Thomas Maryon Wilson to the Church Commissioners, 8 April 1850, loc. cit. *1851 Religious Census*, p. 4.

[3] CC File 7143, Rev. F. W. Tremlett to Eccles. Comm., 5 August 1868. And see above, pp. 282–5.

new Presbyterian Church of the Trinity opened in the High Street in 1862. The landowner's power was quite strong enough, however, to prohibit the erection of any non-Anglican places of worship, a prohibition which would effectively discourage most Nonconformists and Catholics from taking houses on an estate, and one which was effectively enforced on both College and Chapter land until 1883. Then the Chapter let the Congregationalists have the four-acre Rosslyn Grove estate, and the Lyndhurst Road Congregational Church, a large dumpy Alfred Waterhouse building, was built on the site. Its size, architectural richness, and adventurous romanticism in any case made it a Nonconformist 'cathedral' for prosperous Congregationalists whose impeccable respectability forbad unseemly friction with the Anglicans. It was the one and only lapse from Anglican purity in the entire sweep of the Chalcots and Belsize estates, save only for the working-class quarter of Fleet Road where a Methodist chapel was deemed appropriate for Lisburne Road. The Maryon Wilson estate also relaxed its Anglicanism just once, to allow the building of St Andrew Presbyterian Church, Frognal Lane, in 1903.

Estate policies, reinforced by the inclinations of the inhabitants which those policies attracted, effectively confined the non-Anglican places of worship and hence the bulk of the non-Anglican congregations to the old town and to West Hampstead. Most denominations appeared in both places, perhaps with rather different kinds of members in each. This was most noticeable with the Catholics, whose exquisite little church of St Mary in Holly Place built in 1816 derived from an aristocratic French *émigré* community and its pastor, Abbé Morel; while the large church of the Sacred Heart of Jesus in Quex Road, built in 1879 with seating for 1,800 people, catered mainly for the Kilburn Irish. The Methodists also favoured Quex Road (1868), as well as Prince Arthur Road (1870), and made a second foothold in West Hampstead at Solent Road; while the Baptists became established on the Kilburn High Road, at Iverson Road, in 1879. Only the Jews, it seems, took up a truly middle position, with synagogues in the heart of West Hampstead on the Finchley Road at Burrard Road, and just off West End Lane at Dennington Park Road. Broadly, then, the religious map of Hampstead displays a solidly Anglican centre and south tapering towards the north-west into a wedge that just managed to keep apart the two quarters of mixed congregations, the old town in the north-east and Kilburn and West End over to the west. By Booth's time the religious cleavage that mattered was less between Church and Chapel, as this pattern might suggest, than between High and Low Church; and very friendly relations subsisted between Evangelicals and Nonconformists, who co-operated in a joint charity committee to share out the poor between them and prevent competition to dispense succour to what some found a distressingly small number of deserving families. By then, though churchgoing was still very active, it was coming to depend increasingly on the sideshows—especially good singing, or particularly stirring preaching. Maybe the shadow of Booth's dreaded social decay was beginning to approach the area, perhaps particularly at the weak spot where West End came right up to the Finchley Road and Anglican territory narrowed to a salient. Looking at the parts south of the Hampstead Junction Railway Booth saw that 'the district tends to a lower social level.' And he seemed to detect his law of decay in motion: 'the best families go to Hampstead [the old town area], their places being taken by well-to-do Jews, and a Jewish colony is rapidly growing here, and also in St Saviour's Paddington.'[1] Not everyone might recognise this as social decay; but many at the time certainly thought of it as social death.

The progressive subdivision of the original parish of St John, which started with the creation of the Christ Church ecclesiastical district in 1852 and was completed by the establishment of St Luke's in 1896, made fourteen parishes where there had once been one.[2] This complete separation between the civil parish and the religious organisation of its inhabitants both made the divorce between secular and ecclesiastical aspects of parish administration unavoidable, and in the long run helped to make it possible for some kind of municipal existence and sense of community to grow through the work of the civil parish. In the short run, however, until at least the closing years of the nineteenth century, it was the ecclesiastical districts which reflected much more closely the social realities of an area with a number of local communities that happened to lie in a single administrative jurisdiction. From outside the old town it seemed that civil government, in practice, was largely an additional arm of authority wielded by the old town for its own benefit, drawing to its aid the resources of its dependencies in Swiss Cottage or Kilburn.

---

[1] Booth, *Religious Influences*, I, 208, 210, 213. The poor were almost embarrassingly scarce in relation to the charitable machinery mobilised to help them. One clergyman contemplated regretfully 'a splendid soup kitchen not used for three years', and another said 'there are four churches after every poor family'.

[2] Including the new districts which were based outside Hampstead but had part of their areas within it (All Saints, Regent's Park; St Paul, Kilburn Square; All Hallows, Shirlock Road; St Augustine, Kilburn Park Road), by 1900 the ancient parish included 18 ecclesiastical districts.

Matters had been very different in the days before the new population began to arrive in numbers in the 1840s. The old open Vestry of Hampstead, which in form survived until 1856, had of course dealt indifferently with religious and civil affairs, church building as well as poor relief, sermons and highways. The indifference concerned the mixture of business more than the attitude of the inhabitants; whether it related to the quality of the work is hard to judge. In normal times the conduct of the Vestry seems to have fallen into the hands of a small group of regular attenders, usually chaired by the vicar, and controlled by some long-serving Vestry clerks—William Masters from 1799 to 1832, and Thomas Toller from 1832 through the reforms to 1868—who were highly respected solicitors; this was a normal pattern with open vestries, though there is no sign at all that Hampstead's local oligarchs were corrupt, incompetent or inefficient, as many others were. Thus there were only twelve people present in 1823 to discuss the introduction of gas lighting, or eleven in 1830 to fix the poor rate for the year. Nevertheless the 1823 Vestry acknowledged the general utility of gas lighting both for private purposes and for the public service, 'as the most efficient aid to the police in the repression and detection of offenders in the streets and highways', and encouraged the Imperial Gas Company to go ahead and bring its main up the hill from the Camden Town canal bridge; on its arrival in Hampstead gas was at once used by several of the High Street shops as well as for lighting the street itself.[1] This was hardly the act of a backward, slothful or obscurantist vestry.

Although routine parish business was conducted by a handful of regulars, generally respectable tradesmen rather than local gentry, anything exciting could always turn the open vestry into something like direct democracy in action. The parish boundaries were good for an outing, as when a good crowd turned up in May 1751 to beat the bounds, enjoy some refreshment, and settle disputes with St Pancras and St Marylebone by driving in fresh stakes.[2] Encroachments on public footpaths aroused considerable feelings, and forty attended a vestry in 1835 to hear the surveyor of highways report on the success of a mass expedition he had led to re-open the ancient path from Upper Chalcots Farm, Englands Lane, across the fields to the turnpike road near Haverstock Terrace (Belsize Grove) 'lately blocked by Mr Bliss by erecting houses in 1819 or 1820.'[3] But the most electrifying issues were faith and free-

[1] HPL Vestry Min., 21 August 1823, 23 September 1830.
[2] Ibid., 13 May 1751.
[3] Ibid., 22 September 1835.

dom. There were many packed meetings in the early years of the century to wrangle over the appointment of a divine to deliver the weekly evening lecture endowed by a Hampstead surgeon, William Pierce, in 1771; different doctrinal ideas were deliciously spiced by the vicar's bland assumption that he had the sole right to the patronage which many of his parisioners believed was rightfully theirs. The high-water mark came, however, in 1832 when 121 named persons 'and very many others whose names could not be taken' were recorded as present at a vestry which discussed, and rejected, plans of the vicar and Church Trustees to enlarge the parish church.[1] Liberty and the avoidance of expense ran religion close in popularity. Two meetings in successive weeks in November 1830 'to consider the utility of the new Police as applicable to this parish' were attended by over 100 named persons 'and many others' whose names could not be recorded. The meetings resolved that the Metropolitan Police 'is unnecessary and oppressively expensive'; but the second meeting found that disapproval had been an incitement to disorderliness and quickly resolved that it 'disavows all sympathy with the individuals who have been guilty of personal attacks on the New Police, and while in the strongest terms it condemns the System as unconstitutional and expensive with equal earnestness it desires that the men be treated with humanity and civility.'[2] After this outburst against Peel's instruments of authoritarian oppression Hampstead settled down to a century and more of well-policed orderliness and dutiful payment of the police rates: the common offences within its borders were drunken brawling, usually of strangers distracted on their way to or from the Heath; and 'furious riding', the driving offence of the horse age which was committed with particular ease by uncontrollable horses getting the thought of a good gallop on the Heath.[3]

As if to show that it was not only the issues which touched partisan feelings that drew the open vestry into full action, over 100 parishioners turned up to elect a new Vestry Clerk in 1832, attracted perhaps by the unfamiliarity of the business since it was thirty-three years since any such appointment had been made. The appointment of Thomas Toller, of Hampstead Square, turned out tolerably well.[4] Under his guidance

[1] Ibid., 4 April 1832.   [2] Ibid., 4 November and 11 November 1830.
[3] An impression of Hampstead's law-abiding character, and of the predominant types of petty offences, can be gained from the reports of Petty Sessions in the *Hampstead and Highgate Express*: all the cases of 'furious riding' in 1872 took place in Willow Road, Christ Church Road or Spaniards Road, that is near or on the Heath.
[4] HPL Vestry Min., 24 April 1832.

the Vestry met the beginnings of building developments on the Chalcots and Belsize estates with a prudent determination not to get involved in any rash expenditure. While the developers were left to get
on with it the parish was embroiled in more interesting matters. Under
the Poor Law Amendment Act of 1834 Hampstead was incorporated
from 1837 in the Edmonton Union, a loss of parochial identity and
independence which was strongly resented. Although the resistance to
this unionisation was led by Hampstead's own Board of Guardians—
which had been set up by a local Act in 1800 and had then moved the
parish Workhouse from a ruinous house in Frognal (later the site of the
Mount Vernon Consumption Hospital, itself converted into the home
of the National Institute for Medical Research) to an adapted mansion
in New End—the Vestry lent a hand in the struggle. A long campaign
of protests and petitions brought victory for parochialism, and in 1848
Hampstead became a separate Poor Law Union, containing just the one
parish. More than local pride was at stake in this fight; Hampstead had
a very small number of paupers, and a modest expenditure on poor
relief, and was apprehensive that association with other parishes in the
Edmonton Union would cause an increase in the poor rates.[1] Restored
to independence, Hampstead also found restored to its own control a
new Workhouse built at New End in 1845; in this the Vestry found a
committee room convenient for its meetings and the transaction of its
business. Business was certainly not so demanding as to prevent many
of the active parishioners spending much time on thwarting Sir
Thomas Maryon Wilson and his supposed designs on the Heath, which
was the other main public concern of the times.[2]

With responsibility for the administration of poor relief in the hands
of the Guardians of 1800 the unreformed Vestry took its remaining
duties very gently. These were chiefly concerned with the public
streets and roads, their maintenance, repair, paving, cleansing and
lighting; and although the Vestry provided a service through its un-
paid Surveyor of Highways and its two contractors for lighting which
made some show of moving with the times, it remained decidedly
sketchy. Gaslights were provided on the main roads, but hardly on a
lavish scale; 34 lanterns sufficed for the whole of Edgware Road and the
Finchley Road as far as the Swiss Cottage tavern. Elsewhere there were
only naphtha lights, few enough in number, and strictly confined to a

---

[1] GLCRO P81/JN/1/61, Petition requesting a separate Poor Law Union, c.
1844; P81/JN/1/36, Accounts of the treasurer of the Hampstead Guardians,
1824–37, which indicate an annual expenditure of between 10s. and 15s. per
head. In the event the poor rate fell after 1837.

[2] See above, chs 4 and 5.

winter lighting season from October to March. The streets were kept moderately clean, though not the courts and yards in the old town, and rather grudgingly the refuse contractors extended their collection to a selective list of household rubbish. But the parish possessed no sewers except for the natural streams which carried storm water and house drainage, and the new ones constructed by private developers and discharging almost where they listed. It was no part of the business of the Vestry to give thought to sanitation or public health, let alone to any amenities, and the Vestrymen were quite content to mind their own business. For many years the water supply remained rudimentary, a matter of private wells, a couple of parish pumps for the common people, and one or two private piped supplies drawing on springs at Shepherd's Well and in the Conduit Fields. The waterworks which used the Hampstead Ponds on the Heath as reservoirs—first considered in the early sixteenth century, and constructed in 1692—provided water for Holborn and later Camden Town, under the management of the New River Company, and did not supply Hampstead houses. The water mains were pushed steadily northwards to provide a piped supply for the new streets on the southern edge of the parish in the 1830s and 1840s; but it was not until 1853 that the New River Company extended its pipes from Highgate along the top of the hill to Hampstead, and followed by building a reservoir in 1856 on the crown of the hill at the top of Hampstead Grove, bringing a piped supply to the old town. This was the work of private enterprise and the Vestry gave no indication of believing in the importance of water.[1]

In truth a new Hampstead was being created by private enterprise and private developers while the old official Hampstead of the Vestry took little notice and made no effort to influence or supervise the process, contenting itself with passively notching up increases in its rateable value.[2] It was only the fortunate accidents of geography and natural social elevation, not any superiority of local administration, which spared Hampstead the catastrophic slaughter, especially of the cholera outbreaks of 1832 and 1849, that eventually led to the reform

[1] HPL Vestry Min., especially 8 May 1856 on gas lights taken over by the reformed Vestry. Semi-private public naphtha lights could be procured by people of influence, as by Cannon for the entrance to Kidderpore Hall, ibid., 27 February 1857. *Public Acts*, 35 Henry VIII, cap. 10 (1543) for the first project to bring water to the City from Hampstead. Vestries, far from encouraging water companies to extend their services, were normally at war with them over the constant breaking up of streets for laying and repairing pipes: F. Sheppard, *London 1808–1870: the Infernal Wen* (1971), p. 261.
[2] The rateable value grew from £27,317 in 1821 to £77,768 in 1857.

of metropolitan government. Hampstead escaped the deaths because it was too wealthy, too thinly populated and too high-lying, cholera being most dangerous when the disease became water-borne through infected drains discharging into the sources from which water supplies were drawn. It did not escape the reorganisation of London's government, or rather lack of government; long talked about, equally long resisted by the vast gaggle of vestries, improvement commissioners, lighting commissioners, paving commissioners and other vested interests, the reform was finally attempted as a measure to meet the appalling problems of disease and mortality. In November 1847, with another cholera outbreak known to be imminent, a bill was rushed through to establish a single Metropolitan Commission of Sewers in place of the seven existing commissions with their thousand members and complete lack of co-ordination, to take emergency action to cleanse and drain the metropolis. This Chadwickian Commission set to flushing out the sewers with Chadwickian zeal, to wash away the smells which were supposed to cause cholera; unwittingly the more they flushed the more they contaminated the Thames and the more they spread the disease. Utterly discredited, and moreover with no new sewers even started before the next wave of cholera threatened in 1854, the Commission was replaced, and replaced at a moment when Chadwick and his ideas of unified, centralised control were in full retreat. The result was that with the anti-centralists dominant the grand promise of giving London a municipal government ended up with the mouse of the Metropolis Management Act of 1855. This divided the metropolitan area—practically the same as that taken over by the LCC in 1888—into 38 administrative units consisting of the larger parishes and new district boards formed of groups of smaller parishes. The reconstituted vestries and the district boards elected members from their own ranks to the new central institution, the Metropolitan Board of Works. The Metropolitan Board of Works, thus indirectly elected, was given severely limited functions, initially indeed almost the single function of constructing a system of sewerage which would effectually keep sewage out of the Thames.[1]

Thus ended, for over thirty years, the high hopes of progressive and enlightened opinion for the creation of an effective and powerful system of metropolitan administration exercising control at least over all the sensitive health areas, paving, street cleansing and water supply, as well as sewers. Instead London got the Metropolitan Board of Works, kept at arm's length from any direct ratepayer involvement or control, and perhaps wisely so, given the ratepayers' penchant for avoiding

[1] Sheppard, op. cit., pp. 253–81.

spending any money; a Board which concentrated single-mindedly and with resounding success on its job of constructing London's main arterial drains, a system of lateral interceptor sewers at different levels which collected sewage from local feeders and carried it off to the great new Northern and Southern Outfalls at Barking Creek and Crossness. The Board, it is true, gathered many other functions by the accretion of duties which seemed appropriate to London's sanitary authority: the administration of the London Building Acts with their extensive powers for the regulation of building plans and structures and street widths, controlled by a separate Office of Metropolitan Buildings since 1844, passed to the Board by a separate Act of 1855; the Board acquired control of the fire brigade in 1866, and powers over parks and open spaces by Acts of 1857 and 1866; in the outbreak of cattle plague in 1866 it was the obvious body to enforce the measures of the Prevention Act in inspecting cattle and cowhouses and ordering slaughter and cleansing; and when petroleum spirit came into use in the 1860s it was convenient to make it the licensing authority for premises where this could be stored and retailed.[1] But the Board was still far from being regarded as London's municipality, and the tradition of establishing separate authorities for each large area of public activity persisted, with the Board acting simply as one such authority. Thus everything stemming from the administration of poor relief remained quite outside the Board's sphere, and when some of the problems of London's poor were at length treated as a whole the Metropolitan Poor Act of 1867 set up an entirely independent Metropolitan Asylums Board, whose functions grew from caring for the sick poor to providing a system of public hospitals for all Londoners. For public education an entirely separate London School Board was established under the 1870 Act, not surprisingly since throughout the country School Boards were quite distinct from all existing local authorities. As for water, it eluded everyone, Metropolitan Board of Works and LCC alike, so powerful were the vested interests of the water companies, nearly engulfed the politicians, and ended up in the hands of the Metropolitan Water Board only in 1902.[2]

[1] MBW Min., 1856–88, *passim.*

[2] The attempt by the Disraeli Government in 1879–80 to buy out the eight London water companies and form a London Water Trust collapsed in the face of accusations of stock exchange profiteering over negotiations promising an inflated compensation price, and was thought to have contributed to Tory electoral reverses in London in 1880: Paul Smith, *Disraelian Conservatism and Social Reform* (1967), pp. 294–9. Control of the police remained, of course, with the Metropolitan Police Commissioner, directly responsible to the Home Office.

All this left a great many of the services and facilities that determined the quality of life in the home and in the urban community to be provided by the vestries, by private enterprise, or not at all. The vestries, made into local sanitary authorities by the 1855 Act and obliged to appoint a medical officer of health and an inspector of nuisances, were all reformed on a uniform model as bodies elected by householders occupying houses with rateable values of at least £40; it was a much more restrictive and property-weighted franchise than that for parliamentary elections, where the £10 householder had the vote. In Hampstead, with an electorate of about 1,000, control of the new Vestry was assumed by the old-established elements without any contest. There were 33 Vestrymen in the new body elected in November 1855 and well over half of them, 19, came from the old town; the trouble then and later was to convince residents on the new estates that they were part of Hampstead, though significantly Adelaide Road did produce the couple of builders on the Vestry, aware no doubt that its proceedings might be important for the approval of new streets and houses. Although the butcher and the baker were there—in fact two of each, along with one draper and one plumber—the Vestry was in practice controlled by members of the established Hampstead gentry, a group of 13 Vestrymen headed by three magistrates, John Gurney Hoare, David Powell and Thomas Turner, and including Philip Hemery Le Breton who became the most active and influential Vestryman (and representative on the Metropolitan Board of Works) of the next thirty years.[1] Although the Hampstead gentry could not retain such a tight grip on affairs, later in the century, in the face of the great growth in population, and above all after the division into wards in 1873 which ensured that local men would represent each district, they withdrew only gradually from local politics and in favour of newcomers from their own social class, so that the local power continued to reside in the gentlemen of independent means and their close allies, the professional men.

There may have been a phase in the later days of the Vestry, in the 1880s and early 1890s, after the older generation of Hampstead notables from pre-reform times had either moved on or passed on, when local trading interests came close to gaining control. But, as Table 6 suggests, Hampstead never shared the lot of so many of the London vestries, which fell into the hands of the local shopkeepers and tradesmen, whose pursuit of highly local commercial interests, general

---

[1] HPL Vestry Min., 1856. For Hoare, Powell, Turner and Le Breton see above, pp. 177ff. Le Breton continued to serve on the Vestry until 1880.

meanness with public money, and blinkered indifference to municipal welfare, led to unimaginative and parsimonious administration which was much criticised at the time.[1] The compilers of the local yearbooks and almanacs were strangely reticent in informing their local public of the occupations or professions of their vestrymen or councillors, and for no clear reason included this information only between 1896 and 1914, so that there is no simple way of extending the social analysis of the council into the years of great population changes and movements since the First World War. There are some problems of classification in the data which are available, and the category of 'skilled tradesmen' may have been improperly swollen with men labelled as 'art metal worker' and 'printer' who perhaps would have been more at home in the ranks of the 'shopkeepers'; though for those described as 'bricklayer' or 'carpenter' the matter does not seem to be in doubt. Similarly it is possible that some of the 'clerks', who were described as such or as secretaries, were in fact people of some position who might be counted among the 'professional men'. The category of 'businessmen and employers' poses difficulties of another kind: some of these, such as the estate agents, the laundry owner, and the furniture manufacturer from

Table 6 Occupations and social status of Hampstead vestrymen and councillors, 1855–1914

Percentages of total membership, whose size is given in brackets

	1 Shop- keepers	2 Builders	3 Skilled trades- men	4 Business- men and employers	5 Clerks	6 Profess- ional men	7 Gentle- men
1855 (33)	18	6	3	0	0	30	43
1896 (72)	22	14	7	14	1½	25	16½
1900 (72)	15	15	8	10	4	28	20
1901 (49)	18	2	6	16	6	36	14
1908 (49)	12	2	10	14	2	38	22
1914 (50)	18	2	4	16	0	38	22

Sources: 1855: Hampstead Vestry Mins. and local *Directory*; 1896, 1908: *Hampstead Yearbooks*; 1900, 1901, 1914: Baines & Scarsbrook, *Local Guide and Almanac*. 1900 was the last Vestry and 1901 the first Borough Council; the mayor and aldermen are included in the analysis of the borough councillors.

[1] See Patricia E. Malcolmson, 'The Potteries of Kensington: a study of slum development in Victorian London' (unpublished M. Phil. thesis, Leicester University, 1970), ch. IV. In 1866 half the Kensington Vestrymen were local shopkeepers.

Parsifal Road, had local businesses; others who were merchants in the City, or company directors like Sir Henry Harben of Fellows Road, leading member of the last Vestry and first mayor of the Borough, clearly earned their livings elsewhere and had a purely residential interest in Hampstead. When it comes to deciding how many vestrymen and councillors depended for their livelihoods on local trading and employment, and how many were in the different and more detached position of residents and people of independent means (one female councillor, Mary Balkwill of Ellerdale Road, gentlewoman, was elected in 1912, top of the poll in the Kilburn Ward), this particular class should be divided into roughly equal halves.

It is true that among the professional men several of the solicitors and doctors, and possibly some of the architects and surveyors, may have had largely local practices; but on the whole this group, buttressed by the large contingent of barristers in its ranks, was generally assumed to have its detachment and independence of any corrupting influence from clients, customers or personal profit assured by its professional standards. Splitting column 4 of Table 6 in half, therefore, it is not unreasonable to think of columns 1, 2 and 3 as representing those with strongly local commercial and economic interests, and columns 6 and 7 with the dependent clerks of column 5 as containing those of independent position and generally higher social status. In class terms it could be said that this was the division between lower and middling middle class (with a trace of the labour aristocracy), and the upper middle class and gentry. Such a grouping suggests that the social superiors were decisively in command in 1855, had slipped until they formed perhaps a shade less than half the Vestry in 1896, and thereafter climbed back to practically their earlier position of dominance in the early twentieth century. It is quite likely that the 1896 position itself represented some recovery from an unrecorded low point in the 1880s.[1] Between the slide and recovery, however, the character of the municipal upper crust had been transformed.

[1] In reporting the Vestry's discussions of the proposed Town Improvements (the Heath Street–Fitzjohn's Avenue link) in the early 1880s the local paper suggested very strongly that there had been a marked decline from former days when 'a few families dominated the entire population', and that, in place of the sense of local cohesion which then prevailed, the Vestry had become disunited and overburdened with local tradesmen: *Hampstead and Highgate Express*, 15 January, 18 June, 5 November and 24 December 1881. Even an incomplete identification of the occupations of the Vestrymen of 1890, by reference to the local *Directory* (64 per cent identified) shows that 26 per cent of the total Vestry were local traders, and 10 per cent were builders.

The rise of the professional element, mainly from the legal profession, is plain enough from the bare statistics; but what these do not show is the shifting nature of the independent gentlemen. The families of the older Hampstead gentry, some but by no means all of whom had indeed left the district, had abandoned all interest in local government by the 1890s, and did not have a single representative among the Vestrymen or the later councillors. Their disappearance was most striking in Town Ward, which contained most of their seats; there, out of 18 Vestrymen in 1900, there were only 2 gentlemen, both relative newcomers, and no less than 10 shopkeepers and local businessmen, and 6 professional men. The main strength of the gentry group from the later nineteenth century, in other words, and much of the strength of the professional group, came from the newer residential areas, which were able to balance the High Street traders. Within the upper set control had shifted from the old Town to Belsize and Adelaide Wards. The change is epitomised by the dominant personalities: the long-serving Le Breton of the third quarter of the century, living in John Street, was matched by the even longer-serving Harben (1874–1901), who lived in Fellows Road and sat for the Belsize Ward.[1]

The rise and decline of the local builders in parish affairs is equally apparent from Table 6, and would seem to show eminently sensible behaviour on their part, in willingness to participate during the phase of highly active building activity and readiness to step down as soon as this phase neared its end. The builders were presumably not to know that they had practically withdrawn from municipal life at the very moment when ratepayers' money was about to be spent, for the very first time, on housing.[2] It is in any case hazardous to relate these changes in the balance of social forces in Vestry and Borough Council to any particular changes in the quality and direction of administration. It is quite possible that the impression of an initial spurt of activity by the new Vestry of 1856 giving way to a period of economy, prevarication and conservatism until the later 1880s, to be followed by renewed vitality and enterprise, derives from Hampstead's close dependence on the general tone set for London administration by the

[1] Baines and Scarsbrook, *Local Guide and Almanac for 1900*. Sir Henry Harben was chairman of the Prudential Assurance Company, in charge of its rapid growth in the late nineteenth century; besides being a Vestryman from 1874 to 1900 and first Mayor in 1901, he was one of the two Hampstead members of the LCC from 1889, having before that been the Hampstead representative on the MBW.

[2] The Park Dwellings improvement scheme, undertaken by the Borough in 1906 at a cost of £12,782, which provided 42 tenements: see below, p. 424.

Metropolitan Board of Works and then by the LCC. It is arguable, moreover, that there was a logical and necessary sequence about the order of municipal doings: that the major nuisances and menaces to public health had to be eliminated first before it was possible to go on to think of providing any amenities or frills. Although the definition of what was essential for securing public health proved to be elastic, the only major quarrel with this proposition must concern the timing and speed of the development from the municipality of drains to the municipality of drains and public libraries.

There was no room to doubt, at the start of 1856, that drains were the top priority and recruiting a staff to deal with them the first task for the new Vestry. Sir Henry Harben, indeed, in presenting the final meeting of the Vestry in October 1900 with a review of its achievements since 1855 rested his case entirely on the reduction of the death rate from 16·8 per thousand in 1851 to 11·4 in 1900, challenging any critics by asking 'do you need more proof of what the Vestry has done?'[1] With a death rate which averaged 18 per thousand in the decade 1841–50, Hampstead of course already in all senses lay well above the wretched cesspits of habitation which Chadwick and his colleagues were investigating and recording in the 1840s, and which had death rates rising to 40 or more per thousand in the worst spots. Hampstead, by contrast, was in the healthy league, and could look down on Kensington, St Pancras and Marylebone with their death rates of 20, 23 and 24.[2] Comparative salubrity, however, was no guarantee of sweet-smelling purity and no ground for complacence. The old town, in particular, had its fair share of noisome courts and alleys, festering middens, contaminated wells, and an assortment of pigs and cows living cheek by jowl with humans; while the new estates, though generally equipped with water closets and the drains to deal with them, not infrequently let their sewers discharge on to a field at the end of the street since there were no main sewers with which they could connect.

It was, therefore, to the sanitary state of the parish that the new Vestry turned its attention, strongly nudged by the law which directed it to appoint a medical officer of health and an inspector of nuisances. After a preliminary discussion of the organisation and duties of a new administrative staff, which indulged in the expansive idea of running the parish as two separate sanitary districts, the Vestry settled for economy and appointed just a single Medical Officer of Health, Charles

[1] Speech reported in *Hampstead and Highgate Express*, 27 October 1900.
[2] *Supplement to the 25th Report of the Registrar-General* (with historical retrospect), Parl. Papers, 1865, XIII.

Lord, who for his salary of £50 also doubled up as Sanitary Inspector. Similarly having at first resolved not to appoint a Surveyor but to put it into commission by getting a committee of vestrymen to discharge a Surveyor's supervisory functions, and having decided to appoint one Inspector of Nuisances and one Foreman of Roads to be the working officers of a surveyor's department, the Vestry drew back from the salary implications and appointed John Douglas at a salary of £200 to be Surveyor, Inspector of Nuisances and Foreman of Roads all rolled into one. Douglas was very quickly allowed to have two assistants, one to superintend sewerage works under construction, both public and private, and one to superintend all to do with streets, refuse removal and lighting, and an office clerk. With Thomas Toller at the head of the outfit as Vestry Clerk, starting at a salary of £250, and a Vestry messenger who was paid 10s. a week, that completed the establishment of the local civil service, responsible for spending £15,000 to £20,000 a year.[1] Business was not expected to be very arduous or taxing. The organising committee resolved that it was not 'advisable that the Vestry should at present incur the expense of erecting or hiring a building for the meetings of the Vestry and for the offices required by the Act', and accordingly for the next twenty years the Vestry met in the boardroom at the Workhouse. The Surveyor was also provided with a permanent office in the Workhouse, in a room providentially vacated by the Relieving Officer. It is hardly surprising that the Vestry's porter and charwoman were workhouse inmates, earning 1s. a week for their occasional duties.[2]

In these grim and unpromising surroundings the Surveyor planned his attack on Hampstead's sanitary problems with exemplary speed. By June 1857 Douglas had drawn up two connected schemes: the first for the construction of seven miles of public sewers, in six new drainage sub-districts serving the old Town and much of the Chalcots and Belsize Estates, which would act as feeders to the proposed arterial sewers of

[1] HPL Vestry Min., 16 January, 7 February and 22 February 1856. The officers' salaries were raised after eighteen months: Vestry Clerk £350; Surveyor £300; Medical Officer of Health £75: ibid., 3 July 1857. Thomas Toller was also Clerk to the Guardians (£175 a year) and Superintendent Registrar (for which he received fees). Charles Lord was also Medical Officer for the parish poor (£100 a year) and Medical Officer for the Workhouse (£40 a year); and as Public Vaccinator he received a fee of 3s. for each successful case (£55. 19s. 0d. in 1860); he also had a private practice.

[2] HPL Vestry Min., 16 January and 19 September 1856, 3 July 1857. In 1859 two rooms were hired in a house adjoining the Workhouse, for use as the Surveyor's office; and from 1871 the entire house was rented by the Vestry for its offices.

[401]

the Metropolitan Board of Works; the second for the paving and curb-
ing of the footways on all the parish roads.[1] Before Douglas retired in
1871 the whole of his original sewer scheme had been carried out,
including the construction of the sewer in Heath Street observed by
Ford Madox Brown from his lodgings and captured in his painting *Work*.
With the expansion of building development, although developers were
responsible for providing sewerage on their estates at their own cost, the
parish had necessarily to provide more public sewers wherever existing
public roads were involved—West End Lane, Fortune Green Lane,
Mill Lane and Edgware Road were the chief parish roads which had
not been included in Douglas's original scheme. By 1868, when the
first batch of sewerage works was completed, over ten miles had been
constructed, West End being the main addition to the planned mileage
of 1857, at a cost of £37,100. In the same period Douglas and his
assistant had also supervised and inspected the six or seven miles of
private sewers laid down by builders and developers; frequently
Douglas undertook the actual construction of these, on contract, with
the Vestry itself contracting out the work to private firms, since from
the developer's point of view it was important that new sewers should
pass the Surveyor's inspection so that the Vestry would agree to adopt
new roads without insisting on any alterations. In the course of his
drain-laying Douglas acquired a little modest fame by inventing a
special kind of street gully with traps that prevented 'the evils of the
practice of sweeping road refuse into the main sewers' and also 'the
escape of effluvia from the sewer into the street'.[2]

There was a certain amount of trouble over the new outfall sewers
on the Kilburn side, when the Vestry most understandably tried to shift
financial responsibility on to other shoulders. The Main Ranelagh
Sewer for which the Metropolitan Board of Works had responsibility in
succession to the Metropolitan Commissioners of Sewers ended thereabouts, and the question was where precisely it did end and cease to be
a Main Sewer and become simply a number of tributaries or District
Sewers which remained the responsibility of the parishes. Faced with
complaints in the early 1860s, from such knowledgeable persons as the
Kilburn Dispensary Board, about the offensive condition of open sewers
in Kilburn, the Vestry naturally tried to pass them over to the Board.

[1] Ibid., 29 February 1856, 5 June 1857.
[2] MBW Min. 7 June 1867 record the use of Douglas's street gullies since he
first designed them in 1856. All the sewer schemes are recorded in MBW
Min. since they required Board approval and loan sanctions. See also Hampstead Borough Council [HBC], *Abstract of Accounts* (1937), App. III, which
lists all loans raised by Vestry and Borough, 1857–1937.

The Board ruled, however, that the Main Ranelagh Sewer ended at Kilburn Vale as shown on the map prepared by Bazalgette in 1855, and from that point (near the LNWR crossing of the Edgware Road) the two connecting streams or foul open sewers belonged to the Hampstead Vestry: one ran northwards to its source near West End Green, and the second north-east and then north across the Maryon Wilson lands of Britannia Fields (near the line of Fairhazel Gardens) to an origin at Frognal.[1] Frustrated in this attempt, the Vestry did not find it necessary to be at the immediate expense of piping these open sewers, and contented itself with putting a few hundred feet of the Kilburn stream into pipes and providing a trap door to stop the smells drifting back to annoy the West End residents. It was not until 1876 that the stream across the Britannia Fields was put into a brick sewer, by which time the Maryon Wilson estate could be charged with nearly half the cost of £10,965 because the new streets around Canfield Gardens wished to make use of this outfall.[2] The Vestry tried once more, in 1870, asking the Board to extend the Ranelagh Sewer another 850 feet up the Edgware Road, to provide an outfall for the British Land Company's new estate at Iverson Road; meeting with no more success than before, the Vestry found it possible to postpone all major works for building its own main sewer for the upper section of Edgware Road until 1883.[3] The other appearances of the Ranelagh Sewer found the Vestry supporting the Board, for when it was discovered that a rank outsider was surreptitiously joining the drains for houses he was building on the west or Willesden side of the Edgware Road to that Board's main sewer, Vestry and Board had a common interest in sealing off the sewage of householders who were outside the metropolitan district and beyond the reach of the sewer rate.[4]

The main work of bringing Hampstead up to date with its sewers and remedying previous neglect was completed by 1868. Thereafter there was a lull with no further drainage works until 1875, when a new phase began of extending the parish collecting sewers, more or less in step with the progress of building development. This phase was completed by 1893, £31,850 having been spent on these works since 1875; the needs of virtually all the lands which still remained unbuilt in 1893 were within the scope of the parish system as it then existed, and there

[1] MBW Min., 27 March 1863. The text traces the course of these open sewers upstream from the point where they joined the (piped) Ranelagh Sewer.
[2] F. E. Baines (ed.), *Records of Hampstead* (1890), p. 191.
[3] Ibid., p. 192; MBW Min., 21 January and 18 February 1870.
[4] MBW Min., 14 February 1868, 19 March 1869. The Hampstead Surveyor reported this infringement to the MBW.

was no further expenditure on sewerage works subsequently, apart from a small group of minor schemes executed between 1911 and 1915.[1] By the end of the 1860s, therefore, Hampstead had been provided with its basic sanitary equipment and thereafter simply needed to extend it in tune with the spread of new houses and streets. It might be expected that once this backlog of essential works had been removed the Vestry would find some of its resources and energies released to devote to the less fundamental aspects of the welfare and amenities of its citizens.

Douglas and Lord had certainly found time to devote their attention to many things besides the chief business of the sewers. Lord, whose duties were advisory rather than executive, had the keen nose for unsavoury smells characteristic of Victorian Medical Officers, and was indefatigable in reporting overflowing cesspools, festering mounds of manure and night soil, choked house drains, and other such commonplace features of mid-century Hampstead; the owners of the affected properties were usually ordered to abate the nuisances within 48 hours, and if it was a matter of installing water closets were rarely given more than fourteen days to do so. The Vestry was free with its orders to instal water closets in the older houses and tenements, but rarely checked up to see whether its instructions had been obeyed, which was just as well since the use of closets before there was any water supply or any main drainage was apt to pose problems. Thus Mrs Stevenson did install three closets for her tenants in Crockett Court following a Vestry order in July 1856; by February 1857 these were 'choked up, the floors covered with soil, partly from the dirty habits of the occupiers, but chiefly from want of a water supply'.[2] Douglas, in the intervals of shoring up Holly Bush Hill whose banks were crumbling through being used as a children's slide, joined Lord in the campaign to close cesspools and adopt water closets. He shared with Lord the minor triumph of securing the first public lavatory in the town, which replaced the walls of Cock Alley, running from the Cock in High Street to the Yorkshire Grey Yard, which appropriately enough was 'resorted to as a public urinal'.[3] But to Lord alone belonged the glory of complaining to the Metropolitan Board of Works of 'the mischief to health around the Swiss Cottage Railway Station . . . [from] the hot water of the engine boilers being run off into the sewer, so that the foetid vaporized or volatilized malaria and steam rises up into the road, and even, it is said,

[1] HBC *Abstract of Accounts* (1937), App. III.
[2] HPL Vestry Min., 25 July 1856, 13 February 1857.
[3] Ibid., 5 June 1857, 26 February 1858.

tarnishes the furniture in some houses.' He expected this to cause an epidemic; the Board in its stolidly unimaginative way had never heard of malaria being carried in locomotive boilers and declined to take any action, without causing any noticeable harm to the residents.[1]

By the time Lord retired as Medical Officer of Health in 1879 most of the bad smells had been banished, mainly as a result of energetic official action but also partly as a consequence of economic changes which had made such businesses as cowkeeping in urban areas unprofitable.[2] Lord then proceeded to write his sanitary reminiscences, redolent with the odours of the slaughterhouses, bakeries, cowhouses and pigsties he had inspected, flushed out, and lime-washed. Pigs had been his greatest enemies, associated as they were everywhere in nineteeth-century towns with poverty, filth and disease, and the obstinate refusal of their owners to part with them. But his most vivid memory was of the opposition excited by his condemnation of Pickett's dairy farm at the bottom of Pond Street, held to be the most wholesome and best-ventilated in the parish. People found it incredible that it could be insanitary, he recalled, because they 'often come here and sit a long while in the shed on purpose to breathe the air and the breath of cows, which everybody knows is healthy.'[3] Both Douglas and Lord had good reason to be pleased at the results of their labours. Unluckily the arrival of the Smallpox Hospital in 1868 and of quantities of smallpox patients in 1870 deprived them of the satisfaction of seeing the proper fruits of their work. Deaths in hospitals were credited, or debited, in the registration statistics to the districts in which they occurred; and in any case the smallpox did spread to the surrounding streets as the protest committees had prophesied, there being over 100 cases during the epidemic of 1870–1. The result was that in the decade 1871–80 Hampstead's death rate actually rose, to 19·9 per thousand, and for the first and last time the parish slipped below Kensington in the mortality league table. The Vestry Officers might have taken comfort from the fact that this high death rate included a death rate from smallpox alone of 5·17 per thousand when for London as a whole this disease was responsible for only 0·44 deaths per thousand. If there was an 'artificial' excess of the order of 4 deaths per thousand at least, then the measure of the success

[1] MBW Min., 12 February 1869.
[2] The decline of the town cowhouses was hastened by the cattle plague of 1866 and the sanitary and veterinary controls imposed in consequence; but they were extinguished by the competition of rail-borne fresh milk from the country. See MBW Min., 1866, *passim*.
[3] HPL, C. F. J. Lord, 'Records of sanitary experience, 1827–89' (unpublished MS.).

of sanitary undertakings might be presented as a reduction of the 'true' death rate to around 16 per thousand.[1]

It is true that in the 15–20 years after laying the foundations of urban health the Vestry did cultivate new activities; but the flowering did not start until the end of the 1880s. From 1870 the Vestry took a prominent part, either on its own initiative or in association with local movements, in first the acquisition and then the extension of the Heath, in the fight against the Smallpox Hospital, and in the resistance to the threats of invasion by trams. Its co-operation with local protest movements and campaigns showed indeed, the strength of the Vestry's identification with local public opinion; though, with the possible exception of the Heath, the popularity of the causes taken up was regarded by many of the ratepayers as more evidently connected with the self-interest of the old town than it was enthusiastically shared by the newer districts. Again with the notable exception of the Heath, whose extension cost the Hampstead ratepayers £20,000 in 1889, these efforts re-required the exercise of political skills rather than expenditure of the rates; and none of them created new functions for the parish officers or entailed any expansion of the local civil service. The efforts of the officers in these years between 1870 and 1890, and the most considerable new capital expenditure by the Vestry, lay in more routine directions which were mainly a development and extension of health measures and their administration: the acquisition of a cemetery, the establishment of a parish works depot or Stone Yard, the building of the Vestry Hall, and the road improvements known as the Town Improvements.

A new parish cemetery where corpses might decompose in peace without afflicting the living had long been regarded as essential by Lord. A true Chadwickian, he had always paid close attention to corpses as a source of infection, had been dismayed by some of the shifts to which the poor were obliged to resort because of the problems of securing early burial—'recently a man died in Heath Street', he reported in 1858, 'the front room being an open shop, and was kept there seven days'— and had persuaded the Guardians to circulate all poor families 'offering the gratuitous use of the Dead House at the Workhouse for the deposit

---

[1] *Supplement to the 45th Report of the Registrar-General*, Parl. Papers, 1884/5, XVII. The local triumph over the Asylums Board in 1881 was soon reversed, though the Board agreed to restrict the North Western Fever Hospital to not more than 30–40 smallpox cases at any one time. See above, pp. 269–70 and 357–9. In the decade 1881–90 Hampstead had a slight excess of smallpox deaths, 0·28/000 compared to London's 0·12/000, and thereafter smallpox deaths were nil.

of corpses.'[1] Lord was mainly responsible for getting the Vestry to set up a separate Burial Board in the early 1870s, and steered this Board to the acquisition of the cemetery at Fortune Green in 1874; when the Burial Board was re-incorporated in the Vestry in 1896 its outstanding loans were £12,650.[2]

For a long time the parish managed to function without any proper place to keep its equipment and materials for road repairs, street cleaning, sewer flushing, and the like. When a steam-roller was acquired in 1877 the storage problem became acute. At first the Surveyor had managed to keep his modest equipment of a couple of horses, a cart, sundry shovels, wheelbarrows and 'an invert sewer fork' in stabling in High Street rented a trifle suspiciously from Hazard, the Vestry's foreman of roads and lighting.[3] From 1857 a slightly larger yard was rented in Holly Hill, which was razed in the Town Improvements of 1885–8 and became the site of the model working-class tenements of Bradley's Buildings. C. H. Lowe, who became Surveyor in 1871, persuaded the Vestry that the parish needed something better for a works yard, and in 1881 the triangular area between the Midland and the Hampstead Junction Railways on the west side of the Finchley Road was purchased from the Maryon Wilson estate and equipped as the parish Stone Yard, for £8,000, a development which naturally clinched the lowly character of Lithos and Rosemont Roads which were the access roads.[4] Public ownership of the Stone Yard was before long to prove extremely useful.

The parish had also managed to function without any proper offices for nearly as long, operating either from within or in the shadow of the Workhouse as though the Vestry's services were a mere adjunct of poor relief. It was not any rejection of the derogatory associations of this situation, nor yet any growth in the administrative work of the parish, which brought a change; it was the division of the parish into wards in 1873, and the consequent doubling of the number of vestrymen to 60, who could not fit into the boardroom at the Workhouse, which made the provision of a separate Vestry Hall unavoidable. In 1874 the Vestry resolved to look for a site and build, and fierce wrangles followed over

[1] HPL Vestry Min., 26 February and 19 March 1858.
[2] See above, p. 375.
[3] HPL Vestry Min., 1 May 1857, 22 January 1858.
[4] F. E. Baines (ed.), op. cit., pp. 189–90. The Stone Yard site had previously been used as a dustyard and brickfield by Culverhouse, one of the regular dust contractors to the parish. He had made singularly unsavoury bricks from a mixture of his dust collections and sewage water: HPL Vestry Min., 19 March 1858.

the choice of a location. It was admitted that a public hall should be conveniently placed for the whole parish and that the old town would have to abandon its claims to dominance; but the group of High Street traders were unwilling to relax their hold further away than a site on Hampstead Hill Gardens, where building was just starting, holding that the (obviously unacceptable) alternative was the site of the old vicarage in Heath Street. The press thought, with reason, that there should be a little delay until the proposed Fitzjohn's Avenue had been made, since that seemed certain to become the central artery of the parish. But in the end the majority settled on the site on the Haverstock Hill–Belsize Avenue corner, where a quarter of an acre was purchased for £2,800 to the accompaniment of rumblings of discontent from the High Street traders who pointed out that the site was directly above the Midland Railway tunnel, and that there was something distinctly fishy about the price of more than £11,000 an acre paid to Robert Woodd of Hillfield. At the time, 1875, the chosen site was roughly central in relation to the inhabited parts of the parish; but it could easily have been foreseen that later developments in the emptier lands of the centre and west were bound to make the new Vestry Hall increasingly inconvenient and eccentric for the majority of inhabitants. Any schoolboy geographer could have pointed out that a position of the foot of Fitzjohn's Avenue or close to the present Swiss Cottage Central Library would have placed the Vestry Hall conveniently near the centre of its area and its ultimate population; but he would not have been able to persuade the strongly entrenched interests of the High Street traders of the wisdom of accepting such a site in 1875. Hence the Vestry and after it the Borough Council and its officers and departments had their being on Haverstock Hill, increasingly out on a limb, because in the 1870s it was the best compromise which the then balance of local interests and forces would allow.[1]

Much local opinion felt that the chance should be taken to provide Hampstead with a public building which would be 'an ornament to the parish', and which should make a substantial contribution to its upkeep through receipts from the hire of the hall for meetings, entertainments and receptions. There was doubt on the second score, since 'pleasant but drowsy Hampstead' was felt to be far too somnolent and apathetic to support any large number of lectures or concerts, the existing functions at the Assembly Rooms being in advanced decline through public

[1] *Hampstead and Highgate Express*, 18 April and 11 July 1874, 3 April, 17 April and 18 September 1875. HPL Vestry Min., 23 March and 3 June 1875.

FIGURE 5 The Vestry Hall, architects Kendall & Mew, 1878

indifference.[1] Although the Vestry resolved not to look at any designs for the hall which were likely to cost more than £10,000 it was thought at the time that this proper spirit of economy had in no wise prevented the achievement of a public building worthy of the parish. The design, chosen in competition, was by Kendall and Mew, H. E. Kendall being the District Surveyor: it was built by William Shepherd, who put in the lowest tender of £10,520, although when it was completed in 1878 it had cost altogether, including the land, £18,500. Its first use was for the Cambridge Local Examination for women, in June 1878. It was considered admirably adapted for this and other public purposes, as well as for its primary municipal role. Its style and appearance were widely admired by locals, and the design was hailed as 'the free common sense style of Classic suitable for the official departments of a parish vestry' by the *Builder*. It did not occur to anyone at the time that the red brick and stone Italianate building was 'crushingly mean; a disgrace to so prosperous and artistic a borough', not so much because Italianate was then fashionable, nor because Hampstead was not prosperous, but perhaps because it was not particularly artistic; in the 1870s it was a community of City merchants, lawyers, businessmen and shopkeepers, and other such philistines.[2]

If the Borough was lumbered with a Town Hall which became something of an embarrassment it also inherited a set of road improvements from the Vestry which had been ambitious in their time and coped tolerably well with the traffic of the next half-century. The great scheme of Town Improvements involving the extension of Fitzjohn's Avenue from Church Row through a mass of old buildings to form a connection with Heath Street was discussed from 1876, put in hand in 1883, and finished in 1888, at a cost of £120,000 of which the Vestry found half and the Metropolitan Board of Works the other half. This was the largest and most costly project in which the Vestry had engaged. It was so expensive because of the large amount of demolition involved. In spite of the fact that the Metropolitan Board of Works acknowledged that the new thoroughfare which emerged was of genuine metropolitan importance, and therefore agreed to put up their half of the cost, many local ratepayers felt that it was precisely the slum clearance and re-housing aspects of the scheme which made it one of concern to the old town rather than the whole parish. It was fortunate for the acceptance of the scheme that the Vestry did not itself carry out any of the re-

[1] Ibid., 15 April 1876.
[2] Loc. cit.; Baines (ed.), op. cit., pp. 196–7; Pevsner, *The Buildings of England: London*, II (1952), p. 189.

housing; even though much of it was done by the local charity, the amalgamated Wells and Campden Charities formed in 1880, which put up the 65 tenements of Campden Buildings in Holly Bush Vale in 1887 at a cost of £13,500, this charity was effectively beyond the reach of ratepayers' anger.[1]

With capital expenditures approaching £100,000 on these four main projects of cemetery, stone yard, vestry hall and street improvements, it seemed that the Vestry was not short of achievements in this period. Yet Hampstead was still without such things as public baths and public libraries, although it had been permissible to provide these on the rates since the new Vestry was set up in 1855. Already in 1860 the Vestry of St George's Hanover Square, for instance, had been employing a Clerk of the Public Bathhouses with a staff of attendants, firemen and cashiers which included a laundry money-taker, a towel-washer and a swimming instructor.[2] In 1874 the local paper reprinted strong criticisms which had been made by the *Pall Mall Gazette* claiming 'there are few places in the world more behindhand in everything than Hampstead. Situated at the top of a hill, and practically inaccessible by any other means than a broken-winded bus-horse, it is not surprising that in spite of its natural beauties it is but half civilized.' Though the criticism was directed at the deficiencies of Hampstead's schools and the lamentable ignorance of its schoolchildren, in accepting its justice the local editor broadened the accusation to include most of Hampstead's public life. 'Compared to other metropolitan parishes', he agreed, 'Hampstead is decidedly behindhand. It has proved itself unable to keep a literary and scientific institute a-going; it will not support those who as private speculators attempt to amuse or instruct it; it has no baths or washhouses for the use of its population; it has a model Vestry, but not a Vestry Hall; and it has a Board of Guardians, fatherly kind, but unable to conceive why the light of public knowledge and public opinion should penetrate into its deliberations.'[3] Since the editor was normally a loyal not to say partisan local citizen he was in effect saying that Hampstead was a comfortable and healthy backwater, a well-run backwater to be sure within rather narrow limits, but a backwater lacking in enterprise and apparently without any intellectual or cultural life to speak of.

[1] *Hampstead and Highgate Express*, 22 April and 29 April 1876, 4 November 1876, 1 January, 8 January, 15 January, 18 June and 5 November 1881. Baines (ed.), op. cit., pp. 192–3. *Hampstead Year Book for 1889*, pp. 77–8.
[2] *Return from each Vestry and District Board*, Parl. Papers, 1862, XLVII, 3–14.
[3] *Hampstead and Highgate Express*, 1 August 1874.

The sea-change came in the later 1880s when the Vestry began to play a more positive role in caring for the welfare of its inhabitants; it was not a change associated with any fresh faces among the chief officers—Lowe who had been appointed Surveyor in 1871 continued through to the days of the Borough, as did Gwynn who had become Medical Officer of Health in 1879, while Thomas Bridger was Vestry Clerk from 1879 to 1894. The new activity was associated, in so far as it had strictly local origins, with the period in which Sir Henry Harben rose to dominate the Vestry and act as its normal chairman (though the titular position belonged *ex officio* to the vicar); in more general terms it marked the period of the ascendancy of the professional and gentry elements from the newer residential areas and the containment of the power of the old town. The first new enterprise to be undertaken was the washhouses, and these were done in the grand manner to make up for their belatedness. Hampstead's great unwashed were left to the care of the Wells and Campden Charities, which erected its first set of baths and washhouses in Palmerston Road in 1887 and its second set in Flask Walk in 1888, containing a washhouse, laundry, and set of nine baths (three 1st class and six 2nd class). The Vestry could thus confine itself to providing a superior establishment of swimming baths and private baths, 'no washhouses being necessary in this part of the parish, it not being the centre of a poor neighbourhood'. The part was Swiss Cottage, the site in Finchley Road acquired by the special Commissioners of Baths set up by the Vestry being that of a roller-skating rink of the 1870s whose popularity had faded. The Finchley Road Baths were opened in 1888, three swimming baths (men's 1st and 2nd class, and ladies' and twenty-four private baths enshrined in a splendid brick and stone Gothic building adorned with carved brick capitals and wreathed in an entablature of fruit and flowers, all for £20,000. The Baths were a great success, and very soon a second women's bath had to be added to permit them to swim with the same class distinction as the men. The swimming class structure was indeed the cause of one of the stormiest episodes in the history of the Baths Committee when a special investigation had to be made in 1899 of public complaints of mismanagement that included allowing both 2nd class bathers, and beetles, into the women's 1st class bath.[1]

---

[1] Ibid., 3 June 1876, for Bird's Skating Rink; Bird was in trouble for using Spiller's skates, which infringed Plimpton's patent. For the public baths, *Hampstead Year Book for 1889*, pp. 28–9. The Campden Charity was founded by Lady Campden in 1642, endowed with 13¾ acres of land at Childs Hill which was sold between 1870 and 1880 for £15,000 in all; the Wells Charity was founded by Lord and Lady Gainsborough in 1698. Both

Having looked to the cleanliness, and leisure, of its citizens it was natural that the Vestry should decide to bring them light. It was not quite so natural that this light should be not that of knowledge in public libraries, but electric. The first proposal to bring electric lighting into Hampstead was made in 1884 when a Hampstead Electric Light Company announced itself; nothing came of it.[1] Interest revived in 1891 when several private companies applied for Board of Trade permission to light the parish; the Vestry opposed them all, fearful of indiscriminate tearing up of its streets and of discriminate and partial lighting in them, and all fell through. Instead the Vestry obtained its own order from the Board of Trade, intending to use the powers to exercise close control over whatever company should be allowed to supply electricity. Instead it was convinced by expert advisers that electricity supply could be profitable and might contribute to parochial income, and resolved to build and run its own undertaking. A site was to hand in the Stone Yard at Lithos Road, and the Vestry's own power station complete with 140-foot chimney and the latest generators by Siemens was opened there in 1894.[2] From the start the intention was to supply private consumers as well as public street lamps, and the private consumers at once established themselves as the major users. A municipally owned commercial undertaking of this sort was not unusual elsewhere in the country, though less usual for electricity than for gas or water supply; neighbouring St Pancras also decided to provide municipal electricity, but London as a whole was supplied by company electricity just as it was supplied with company water and company gas. In the 1870s and 1880s the whole question of municipal ownership had acquired at the hands of Joseph Chamberlain in Birmingham and of the Fabians an advanced radical reputation as the instrument of 'gas and water socialism'. It was a reputation which excited few beyond the ranks of politicians and journalists, and had not penetrated to the solid Vestrymen of Hampstead, who entered on the adventure of municipal enterprise as practical men of business unaware that what they were doing could have any doctrinal implications.

The electricity supply was a great success, as a public utility. The demand, 80–90 per cent of it from private consumers, grew from a

---

were for the benefit of the poor of Hampstead, and in the 1880s applied their income to providing apprenticeships, scholarships, pensions, and outfits for children entering domestic service. For the 1899 complaints, Hampstead Vestry, *Annual Report* (1900), p. 35.

[1] *Hampstead and Highgate Express*, 5 January 1884.
[2] *Hampstead Year Book for 1892*, p. 26; *Hampstead Year Book for 1895*, p. 27.

quarter of a million units in the first full year of operation, 1896, to one million in 1899, five million in 1918, ten million in 1923, twenty million in 1928, and forty million in 1936. It was, however, expensive to supply. The original power station had cost about £30,000; already by 1897 it was necessary to borrow a further £30,000 to extend the generating capacity and lay more cables, and two years later £67,000 more was laid out. The Vestry, sensing that it had to use good salesmanship to make the venture pay, was on the point of offering to carry out the wiring of private houses on deferred payments when it handed over to the Borough.[1] The Borough was not dismayed by the huge initial expense of the business, and borrowed £90,000 in its first year and £78,000 in its second to keep up the momentum of growth. It also carried on with the Vestry's policy of stimulating consumption, purchasing and installing slot meters from 1903 onwards for the poorer houses with weekly tenants and for flat dwellers. The assumptions behind such policies—that there were economies of scale to be found in electricity generation, and that spreading the classes of consumers was likely to spread the load more evenly throughout the day and therefore more profitably—were doubtless entirely correct. It did not make them any less voracious in their appetite for capital during the early stages of building up the generating plant and transmission system. By 1914 Hampstead had committed getting on for £500,000 to its electricity system. In return it enjoyed a supply which was probably at least as cheap and efficient as any that could have been provided by a private company, and the Borough's own consumption in street lighting probably came significantly cheaper. But electricity's eagerly anticipated contribution in aid of the rates, though it did manage to materialise after 1900, never managed to struggle above £2,000 in a good year; by 1914 the accumulated credits to general municipal expenditure had reached £19,000, and that remained the sum total of such appropriations from electricity profits in the entire life of the municipal undertaking. Without exactly meaning it the Vestry had stumbled into running a non-profit-making public utility.[2]

Nobody had ever expected a library service to make profits, at least in cash terms; it was simply a form of expenditure like drains or refuse

---

[1] Hampstead Vestry, *Annual Report* (1900); HBC *Abstract of Accounts* (1937), Electricity Statement A.

[2] Harben, for one, expected large profits once the initial investment was completed: *Hampstead and Highgate Express*, 26 October 1900. Accounts and output figures in Hampstead Vestry, *Annual Reports*, and HBC *Abstract of Accounts* (1937), Electricity Statements A, B and C. The costs of production, and charges to consumers, moved as follows:

collection—though not like baths or cemeteries since the individual user did pay something for those at the moment of use—even if on a different intellectual plane. It was a form of expenditure which the Vestry had long felt able to avoid, secure in the knowledge that all of Hampstead that mattered was wealthy enough to make its own arrangements for books and libraries. To be fair, the wealthy did so sufficiently handsomely to leave something over for the poorer folk. What Baines in 1889 called the 'Hampstead Public Library' was in fact the Subscription Library; but it did by then lend to the working classes without charge and provided them with a free reading room. Moreover both reading room and library were open free to all-comers every Sunday evening. Baines concluded with some complacence that 'Hampstead has therefore practically a Free Library without burdening the rates.'[1] This was only a recent development, probably undertaken at least in part in order to postpone a little longer the day when the rates would have to be burdened with a proper public library. The Subscription Library had been founded in 1833 with the support of the eminent—Lucy Aikin, Constable, John Murray and Norton Longman were among the early shareholders, and Philip Le Breton was the secretary—and in its first two homes in Flask Walk and in High Street it was exactly what it set out to be, a library serving those who chose to subscribe to it who were necessarily the comfortably-off and well-educated. It was only when the patronage of genuine readers wore thin and the institution faced collapse

	Prime cost per unit[a] (pence)	Gross cost per unit[b] (pence)	Charges to private consumers per unit (pence)
15 months to end 1895	6·87	9·25	6
Year to Lady Day 1897	3·42	4·87	6
Year to Lady Day 1900	2·43	3·58	6 for 1st hour, 2½ all rest
Year to Lady Day 1914	1·43	2·68	Fixed charge and ¾

[a] Fuel, oil, labour, maintenance and management.
[b] Including interest and depreciation, which was provided for by loan repayments spread over 25 years.
Source: Electric Lighting Department, Statement of Accounts, 1914, pp. 20–5.

[1] Baines (ed.), op. cit., pp. 282–3.

that the philanthropic note was introduced, and with sufficient effect to keep the library going; this coincided with the move to Stanfield House in Prince Arthur Road, which did not take place until 1885. In 1884 there had been but 200 subscribers; by 1889 there were 1,100.[1]

When it did come, however, the free reading for the poor served only to emphasise how the benefits of enlightenment and charity tended to enhance the privileges of the old town, and to draw attention to the neglect of the rest of the parish. It was a neglect which shamed the Vestry into action. It had been permissible ever since William Ewart's Free Libraries Act of 1850 to build and run libraries on the rates, and elsewhere in the country, even if not at all extensively within London, public libraries had been growing in the cause of improving the minds and morals of the lower orders.[2] By the 1890s it was too late for libraries to act as an educational spearhead in Hampstead, since popular elementary education reinforced and vastly expanded by the energetic London School Board since 1871 had already annexed that position; indeed the Fleet Road Board School had already established its reputation as 'the Harrow of the Board Schools'.[3] This in turn became an

[1] Loc. cit.

[2] Apart from Westminster, which established a public library in 1857, Hampstead was only a few years behind other parts of London in opening a public library, and was ahead of many:

1857	Westminster
1881	Richmond
1883	Ealing
1886	Fulham
1887	Hammersmith
1888	Battersea, Kensington, Lambeth
1889	Camberwell, Finsbury
1890	Bermondsey, Chiswick, West Ham
1891	Chelsea, Holborn
1892	Lewisham, Penge, Shoreditch
1893	Edmonton, **Hampstead**, Leyton, Southwark
1894	Enfield, Poplar, Walthamstow
1896	Tottenham
1897	Bexley
1899	Hornsey
1904	Islington
1906	St Pancras
1908	Hackney
1919	Bethnal Green
1923	Marylebone
1930	Paddington

Source: Harrod, *The Libraries of Greater London* (1951).

[3] So called because of the enviable regularity with which Fleet Road children carried off a large number of the School Board's scholarships to secondary schools: Baines (ed.), op. cit., pp. 324–5.

argument, more powerful than the earlier and rather flimsy pleas for spreading the fruits of knowledge in front of the illiterate, for providing adequate libraries: the educated sons and daughters of the stablemen and tram workers needed something to read. The Vestry moved in its accustomed way, setting up a body of special Commissioners for Public Libraries and Museums in 1892; this body made an immediate start on remedying neglect and discrimination by opening a branch library in Kilburn at 48 Priory Road. A second branch library was built in 1896, in Antrim Street, for the Belsize area; and preparations went ahead for a Central Library which should be worthy of a cultivated urban community. A site was purchased from Sir Spencer Maryon Wilson on the corner of Arkwright Road and Finchley Road which made the library truly central; and Sir Henry Harben, sensing the central role which a well-founded public library should play in the life of a borough-to-be, gave the entire cost of the building, £5,000.[1] By the time it opened in 1897 Hampstead had its first librarian, W. E. Doubleday; and the Vestry, re-absorbing its Library Commissioners, had forged ahead to produce the rudiments of a library policy that went beyond the mere provision of rooms and shelves. In the course of 1896 it not only purchased the 8,000 volumes of the library of Henry Morley, Professor of English at University College, London, to form the basis of a scholarly reference library within the Central Library, but it also bought from a Cambridge college a volume containing the manuscript of a survey of the Heath in 1680, thus launching a local archive section in the Central Library. It was an inspired stroke, attaching to a public institution that sense of the possession of a past and a history which gives life and identity to a community.

In its final decade or so, therefore, the Vestry had become a busy, enterprising body. Its libraries, baths and electricity helped to improve the quality of the life of its citizens where the Vestry Hall of an earlier generation had only the limited ambition of helping its inhabitants to keep alive, through its sewers, and to be inoffensive in death, in its cemetery. The new blood of the newer residential districts had done its work in sweeping away the complacency which had set in under Town domination, and had done it in time to earn high marks from Booth. 'Hampstead Vestry has long enjoyed a reputation for good business-like management', he reported, 'and the change in form, to that of a Borough council, is unlikely to make any difference in this respect.

[1] Hampstead Vestry, *Annual Report* (1893), p. 13; *Annual Report* (1894), pp. 132–3; *Annual Report* (1896), pp. 87–9.
[2] T. J. Barratt, *The Annals of Hampstead*, iii (1912), 23; ii, 195.

FIGURE 6 The Central Library, Arkwright Road, architect Arnold S. Tayler, 1897

Men of High character are willing to serve, party politics are little regarded, and the difficulties to be encountered are moderate and manageable compared to those met with in Islington, St Pancras, or Marylebone.'[1] The more ambitious course in public administration came at the same time as Hampstead's intellectual and artistic life was stirring with vitality. The Hampstead Debating Society flourished from the 1880s, a mock parliament which took itself most seriously with its prime minister and its cabinet reshuffles; a Dramatic Society was founded and enjoyed great success; the Heath, which had long excited the attentions of a succession of committees, in 1897 attracted the services of a permanent Heath Protection Society; in the same year the interest and activities of the local antiquaries became great enough to support the formation of the Hampstead Antiquarian and Historical Society with Sir Walter Besant as its first president, and the work for Barratt's great *Annals* was well under way; and with the artists and architects drawn to Fitzjohn's Avenue something of an artists' colony, albeit of the wealthy and fashionable rather than the experimental and garret type, began to appear.[2] Hampstead might remain in estate agents' eyes 'a watering place in all respects but one, the exception being that there is no sea there'; and indeed there was still the resort atmosphere of donkey rides, bath chairs and summer lodgings taken for the season by well-to-do families.[3] There was more to it than that, however. All this show of activity meant that the long interval since the close of the eighteenth century, during which Hampstead had been steadily outgrowing a reputation for intellectual and artistic distinction as the solid family men of the City moved in, was coming to an end in a *fin de siècle* revival of a vigorous intellectual and cultural life. It was, as yet, highly respectable, conventional and well-heeled. The touch of excitement which made Hampstead adventurous, progressive, daring, outrageous, exotic, unconventional, or just plain disreputable came later. But at least an identity was being fostered and asserted against the menace of suburban anonymity.

The upsurge of activity which placed local government right in front of the eyes of Hampstead's citizens came in the nick of time to foster the growth of civic loyalties to replace the rapidly weakening earlier social ties. By the turn of the century the old resident gentry had decamped both from the town and West End, leaving no grand houses to give a

[1] Booth, *Religious Influences*, I, 212.
[2] *Hampstead and Highgate Express*, 8 January and 22 January 1887; Baines and Scarsbrook, *Local Guide and Almanac*, 1896 and 1900; Barratt, op. cit., II, 297.
[3] *Estates Gazette*, LXXII, 14 November 1908.

lead or form the centre of parish life. The sharp decline in the hold of religion had even more far-reaching implications for the character of urban life. The *Daily News* religious census of 1902–3 makes it clear that church attendance had fallen dramatically since the middle of the century. The observers counted 20,940 attendances at the various churches and chapels in Hampstead in the course of the chosen Sunday, which was about one in four of the total population. It was estimated, for London as a whole, that the 'twicers' who attended two services in the day formed 39 per cent of the total churchgoing group, reducing the Hampstead turn-out to an estimated 15,064 worshippers or 18 per cent of the population.[1] In the very much smaller population of 1851 church attendances, had, by the same reckoning, gathered in nearly three people out of every four, and the worshippers had formed half the total population. The decline in the churchgoing proportion of the population may well have set in as soon as population began to increase rapidly after 1851; but an absolute fall in the numbers of churchgoers seems to date only from the late 1880s. The *British Weekly* conducted a somewhat hurried religious census in 1886, using different methods from the later *Daily News* operation; but some individual Hampstead churches experienced steep declines in their congregations between the two counts. Christ Church blossomed with 2,325 attendances in 1886 but sank to only 909 in 1902–3; St Stephen's fell from 1,372 to 543, and Trinity, Finchley Road, form 2,050 to 951; by contrast the Lyndhurst Road Congregational Church remained flourishing, with 2,022 attendances in 1886 and 1,782 in 1902–3.[2] All over London the Church of England lost ground between 1886 and 1902–3, though the overall decline in attendances of 25 per cent was much more moderate than the 60 per cent decline apparently suffered by these three particular congregations; this collapse, however, was perhaps not unrepresentative of the wealthier districts, where the inroads of the new weekend habit were thought to have halved Anglican congregations since 1886.[3] No doubt it was correct to assume that Nonconformists did not surrender to such frivolity. Certainly chapel had virtually held its ground since 1886 while church had slumped. The result was that whereas in 1851 the Church of England attracted well over 80 per cent of Hampstead's churchgoers, by 1902–3 it retained barely 50 per cent; indeed while the total population had increased by 70,000 the Anglican

---

[1] R. Mudie-Smith (ed.), *The Religious Life of London* (1904), pp. 15, 131–4, 165–7.
[2] Ibid., pp. 283, 292.
[3] Ibid., pp. 281–3.

congregation had apparently grown by only some 2,300 members although the Dissenters and Catholics had multiplied wonderfully from well under one to well over six thousand.[1]

Booth had commented on the growing religious indifference of the middling and lower-middle-class clerk-land of West Hampstead with its raw new streets and its lack of defined neighbourhoods, its want of settled connections and general absence of substantial family life.[2] The *Daily News* figures, however, suggest very strongly that this growing indifference was by no means confined to the districts of most recent and most rapid development, but on the contrary affected the older, more respectable, more wealthy, and more fashionable parts of Hampstead at least as deeply. The relative and absolute decline in churchgoing in general cannot have failed to weaken very considerably the power of either church or chapel to act as the focus and mainspring of social organisation. The much more precipitate decline of the Anglicans, in comparison with Dissenters and Catholics, bit expecially deeply into the social fabric which had been established in the middle decades of the nineteenth century. The Church of England was obviously closely associated with established authority, so that its weakening created a need, among those who cared for seemliness, orderliness, and conformity, for a compensating strengthening of some substitute authority. More than this, the key position of the Church of England and its sense of duty to the general public had given it a geography of district churches with parochial responsibilities which meant that it, rather than any chapel, was the only possible centre for local residential communities. The weakening of the Church, therefore, signified the weakening of loyalties and attachments to the concept of a community at this intimate district level. All this did not necessarily reflect a widespread collapse of faith, growth of scepticism, and weakening of personal or public morality: if the weekend habit had really taken hold of wealthy Hampstead, then the richer quarters may simply have been exporting their religion to the countryside. But it did mean that the convention of regular attendance at the urban parish church had lost most of its force; and with the passing of this route to respectability and acceptance into a community there vanished also the chief prop of the early-suburban social system.

Nothing ever arose to replace this system satisfactorily, except possibly in 1940–1 when air raids brought forth an intense neighbourliness

[1] Calculated from the 1851 and 1902–3 figures on the assumption that 'twicers' formed 39 per cent of individual attenders.
[2] Booth, *Religious Influences*, I, 207–8.

street by street and square by square; although it is true that certain select groups, artists or left-wing intellectuals, were highly successful in forming vital, close-knit, élitist communities within the formal structure of Hampstead as a borough to which residents paid their rates. Nevertheless the decline of the churches did not reduce Hampstead to a mere collection of atomised individuals entirely lacking in cohesion. The municipal sense, already fostered in practice by many of the Vestry's activities in the 1890s, was actively stimulated when Hampstead became one of the new metropolitan boroughs in November 1900. Sir Henry Harben, the last acting chairman of the Vestry and first mayor of the new Borough, deliberately emphasised the sanitary role of the Vestry when summarising its achievements: 'Do you need any more proof of what the Vestry has done?' he asked, when pointing out that the death rate in Hampstead had fallen from 16·8 to 11·4 per thousand between 1851 and 1900.[1] The new Borough, it was implied, was going to set out to be a less remote, more popular, institution, released by past achievements from any need to concentrate too narrowly on the basic questions of public health. The new range of municipal services, admittedly, had in almost every case been pioneered by the Vestry, and the Borough was simply lucky enough to inherit a number of flourishing new ventures. But the new image of the Borough, and its widened electorate, undoubtedly attracted much wider interest than the Vestry had done; in the early years all the councillors faced contested elections and polls of 50 and 60 per cent of the electors were frequent, whereas it had been common for Vestrymen to be returned without a contest or for their elections at most to excite a very low poll.[2] In the few short years before 1914, while Hampstead had a largely stable population whose headlong growth had eased off and which by and large did not move frequently, and hence became attached to the locality, municipal loyalties and pride could grow, and the Borough could succeed in providing some of those social ties and shared purposes that go to make a community.

If the Borough did succeed in imparting some sense of coherence and of belonging to the varied districts and social elements of Hampstead, it

---

[1] *Hampstead and Highgate Express*, 27 October 1900, reporting the last meeting of the Vestry.

[2] Compare the last Vestry, in which 20 out of the 72 Vestrymen were returned unopposed, with the first Council, in which all 42 councillors had won contests: Baines and Scarsbrook, *Local Guide and Almanac*, 1900 and 1901. It must be conceded that popular interest in the Council elections was not sustained; by 1914 all 12 councillors for Adelaide and Central Wards were returned unopposed: ibid., 1914.

was more through a broadening feeling of participation in local government than because of any startling initiatives in municipal activity. Of these there were none. The library was well supported and energetic management by Doubleday backed up by reasonable funds made it, and its branches, into one of the leading public libraries in London. By 1911, with 61,000 books in its catalogue, the Hampstead library was way ahead of neighbouring St Pancras which had been a late starter and could barely muster 10,000 volumes for a population nearly three times as large. On a population basis Hampstead was way out in front with its public library. It had one book for every 1·4 inhabitants, the same ratio as in wealthier and longer-established Westminster, as against one to 2·4 and one to 4·1 inhabitants in Kensington and Islington; and the borrowing rate, the librarians' favourite gauge of success, showed that in Hampstead 4·5 books per inhabitant had been issued in the year, compared with figures of 3·3, 1·3 and 3·2 for Westminster, Kensington and Islington.[1] The figures revealed a scale of library provision and a rate of municipal reading which reflected credit on Hampstead's reputation for intelligence as well as on its wealth. In 1914 the cost of the library was still only a modest £4,373 out of a total Borough expenditure (excluding its contribution to the LCC and other metropolitan bodies) of £105,000, and was no greater than the expenditure on washhouses and baths. By 1939, however, the library was costing nearly £16,000 a year out of a total Borough budget of £224,000, and had grown to double the baths; while by 1963 the Borough's expenditure had tripled to £791,000, the library had grown even more, to £99,000, and absorbed more than three times as much as the baths.[2] The public library was indeed the Borough's fastest growing service, faster even than education. The administration of the public schools was always outside local hands, being run by the London School Board until 1902 and thereafter by the LCC; the Borough's contribution rose from £105,000 in 1914 to £1,234,224 gross and a notional £600,000 net in 1963.[3] In its closing days the Borough gave fitting recognition to the central importance of the public library in Hampstead's life by rehousing the central library in its present building, of striking architectural ingenuity, at

[1] Calculated from Accounts and Papers, *Public Libraries Act, Return of all places in which the Act has been adopted*, Parl. Papers, 1912/13, LXVIII.

[2] HBC *Abstract of Accounts*, 1914, 1939 and 1963. Years given in the text are those ending 31 March.

[3] Loc. cit. The expenditure on education in 1939 was £197,000. The difference between the gross and assumed net expenditure in 1963 is accounted for by the receipt of £737,000 in general grants from the Exchequer, most of which were to support education.

Swiss Cottage; true to the long association of municipal books and municipal baths, a new swimming bath went up alongside.

Municipal electricity, as well as municipal reading, was being successfully developed in the years before 1914. And the Borough sustained the tradition of the Vestry's support of open spaces by contributing £5,000 in 1908 towards the purchase of part of Wyldes Farm, over into Hendon parish, which was preserved as the northern extension of the Heath at the time when the rest of this Eton College property was made over to the curious experiment of Hampstead Garden Suburb. The Borough even went one better, by laying out £5,500 in 1912 to acquire Kilburn Grange and turn it into a public park for the Kilburn district. All these were well-established activities. The one new field entered by the Borough was that of housing, Hampstead becoming one of the very few London boroughs which had made a start before 1914 in providing the municipal housing which they were empowered to do under the Act of 1900 which set them up.[1] The chosen site was in Lower Cross Road (since renamed Garnett Road), in the seedy and deteriorated part of the St John's Park estate. Here, on a site purchased for £1,500, three blocks of tenements or working-class flats were erected in 1905–6 at a cost of £11,286. The forty-two tenements of these Park Dwellings were rapidly occupied, at rents of 5s. to 9s. a week, under a resident caretaker armed with a comprehensive rule book which among other things enjoined the tenants that 'all refuse vegetable matter such as potato and turnip peelings, cabbage leaves, pea shells, etc., shall be burnt in ordinary grates after slightly drying behind the fire, small quantities being placed on the fire at a time'.[2] Those who moved in were presumably content to accept such a strict regime, thankful to be housed in moderate comfort; at such rents they were likely to have come from the ranks of the respectable workers in steady jobs, not from the poorest sections. Park Dwellings were well-regarded at the time as proof of the Borough's public philanthropy and social conscience. They were, it is true, no more than a modest contribution to problems of poor housing, overcrowding and poverty; but then Hampstead of the 1900s tended to think that its own social problems were on a modest scale in any case. In comparison with any other London borough it was right

---

[1] By extending to the new metropolitan boroughs the powers of local authorities under the 1890 Housing Act, powers which the London vestries had not enjoyed. Before 1914 eleven boroughs had used these powers, Hampstead being far outpaced in council housing by Battersea, Chelsea and Westminster.

[2] HBC *Annual Report*, 1905–6, pp. 92–6; ibid., 1906–7, pp. 41–2. The Park Dwellings were aided out of the rates to the tune of £50–£150 a year.

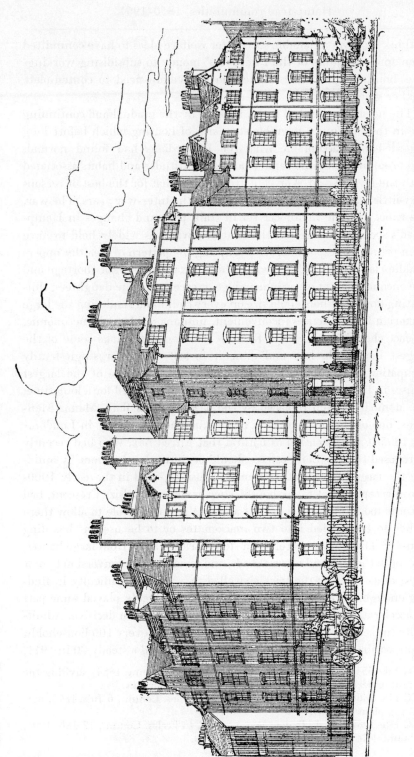

FIGURE 7 Hampstead's first council flats: Park Dwellings, Lower Cross Road (now Garnett Road), 1905

to think so; it was a notable success for welfare ideas to have committed even small amounts of the ratepayers' money to subsidising working-class housing, and there seemed no immediate need to contemplate further schemes.

The need was there all right, fostered by the gradual and continuing rise in the minimum tolerable standards of housing which before long regarded as unacceptable what the Edwardians had found normal, and brought out by the rapid changes in attitudes and habits associated with the First World War. The trouble was that for the best of reasons very little was done about the problem in the inter-war years. The war, the tube, and the motor car set in train profound changes in Hampstead's social structure. At the time the war was widely held to have been primarily responsible for disrupting the pattern of wealthy upper-middle-class family life, through high taxation, servant shortage and the encouragement of early marriage or careers for the daughters, thus cutting down the household size on every count and rendering the large Victorian family houses inconvenient, unmanageable and uneconomic. In fact changing tastes and fashions had begun to make some of the largest houses obsolete and difficult to sell or let for single-family occupation long before the war. As early as 1884 one of the largest houses in Belsize Park Gardens, after being unoccupied for a long time, was demolished and replaced by the large block of flats, Manor Mansions, one of the first blocks of residential flats to be built in London.[1] By 1893 it was regarded as natural that Alfred Bax, who had recently purchased the Ivy Bank estate, should begin its development by building the large luxury flats of Ornan Mansions;[2] and in the early 1900s it was accepted that many houses, such as those in Belsize Crescent, had become too large for the district and that it was sensible to allow them either to be divided into two maisonettes or to be used as boarding houses.[3] There was, therefore, a steady trickle away from large houses, except in the best and newest roads, and towards their conversion to new uses; after the war the trickle swelled to a torrent. Difficulty in finding enough servants to run such houses undoubtedly played some part in accelerating this trend, though it cannot have been decisive. Admittedly the servant ratio, the number of servants to every 100 households, slumped sharply from its peak of 81·4 in 1901 and a steady 80 in 1911,

---

[1] CC File 33405, Cluttons to Sir George Pringle, 9 June 1884, advising the grant of permission to demolish 48 Belsize Park Gardens.
[2] CC File 38689, Rye & Eyre, solicitors, to Eccles. Comm., 6 July 1893, outlining plans for flats.
[3] CC File 32878, S. A. Bailey, house-owner, to Eccles. Comm., 17 July 1903, obtaining leave to convert into maisonettes.

to 55 in 1921 and 47 in 1931. But this was not due to anything like a halving in the number of domestics, for there were still well over 11,000 of them in 1931 against the 14,000 of 1911, and the total population of the borough had grown very little in the interval. The effect was caused, rather, by the rapid growth in the number of separate households, which grew by 27 per cent while total population put on only 4 per cent.[1] This proliferation of households was caused by a number of factors, chief among which were the strong trend towards smaller families in the middle classes, and the equally strong urge to set up in the independence of a separate home as young as possible. Both these led to intensified demand for smaller houses or flats, a demand in which any absolute shortage of servants played a rather minor part.

It is probable that a high proportion of these smaller families and households were newcomers to Hampstead. Little is known about the normal length of residence of suburbans; but although Victorian middle-class families, who frequently rented their houses, often moved on to new districts when their five- or seven-year agreements ended, it seems likely that the rate of turnover speeded up considerably after 1918. The key to the process was the increased range and mobility of the groups which had previously supplied the more permanent residents. The wealthy and the fairly wealthy followed the old Hampstead gentry out into the country, at a half-century interval, placed in command of the new outer suburbs and the stockbroker belt by the motor car, the extended underground lines, and the improved commuter services of the main-line railways. The motor car had begun to make its presence felt in Hampstead before 1914, much of Princess Mews and Lancaster Stables being converted into garages and motor repair shops in 1911-13. In 1906 the horse trams had gone when the line to South End was electrified; after 1918 the horses disappeared rapidly from Hampstead's streets and stables, leaving much accommodation, some of it in large blocks like the Fleet Road depot, to be adapted to new uses. By the mid-1920s Bax's heirs, in completing the development of the Perceval Avenue–Belsize Lane–Haverstock Hill corner over the site of the Ivy Bank house, in one of the last pieces of fresh building in central Hampstead, found that it was very difficult to sell new houses unless garages were provided.[2] Cars inside the borough and cars taking

---

[1] *1911 Census*, Parl. Papers, 1913, LXXIX, Table 13; *1921 Census*, County of London, Table 16; *1931 Census*, County of London, Industry Tables. And see above, pp. 50–1.

[2] CC File 32878, Cluttons to Eccles. Comm., 10 July 1911, 26 April 1913 reporting on application to convert to garages; CC File 38689, Cluttons to

people outside it for ever were one of the main forces of change in inter-war Hampstead, even if it was not until much later, from the late 1950s, that they produced the modern problems of cars for everybody.

The broad effect of social change was for the wealthy, the smart, the fashionable and the intellectual to tend to retreat up the hill, to the newer quarters of large detached houses in spacious gardens of the Redington Road district, and to the charms of the old eighteenth-century town. Behind them a tide of multi-occupation swept in across the low ground, of a much poorer class than had been known before or than the houses had been built to receive. Social deterioration perhaps hit the Eton College estate most severely, particularly up to and along the line of Adelaide Road, though it was also apparent further west in Belsize Road; the threat of decay was held at bay in Eton Avenue, and stoutly repulsed by the redevelopment of the Haverstock Hill frontages whose leases fell in, with expensive flats in Eton Rise and Eton Hall. In the heartland of Belsize there was great change, some crumbling of the stucco, and some pockets of squalor; but no catastrophe. Here the social class of the residents did not shift much, rather they became less prosperous, or younger, representatives of the commercial or professional classes who had lived there before 1914. All around, in Belsize Avenue, Belsize Park Gardens, Belsize Crescent, Lyndhurst Road, the tall houses were converted into maisonettes and flats, or turned into boarding houses 'for persons of a good class suitable to the character of the premises and their neighbourhood.'[1] The tenants and the lodgers were for the most part young married couples and those with small families, of the middle classes, retired or distressed gentlefolk of small means, or young single people who were just beginning the bed-sitter way of life. Many of these were by nature transients, and when the bed-sitter habit exploded after 1945 it is easy to see how Hampstead acquired a population so volatile that perhaps as many as one-third leave the district every year.

Social change and flux on this scale posed many problems to the

---

Eccles. Comm., 11 December 1928, reporting the completion of Bax's building development, commenced in 1893.

[1] CC File 38689, Cluttons to Eccles. Comm., 14 July 1924, advising that 63 Belsize Avenue should be allowed to become a boarding house. In 1918 Cluttons had thought that 'the time has not yet come when the houses in Belsize Avenue should be converted', but by 1919 had changed their minds and recommended dividing the houses into two as the best way of ensuring that they remained occupied.

Borough. The moral and psychological problem of maintaining its identity and using its administrative unity to sustain some sense of cohesion and community among the different districts was probably insoluble in the face not only of the increasing social diversity but also of the growing impermanence and rootlessness of its residents. At any rate there is little sign that it was solved. The physical problems were more tractable; with health and education largely the responsibility of others, these boiled down to housing. Hampstead had practically no unemployed: a total of 405 in 1929 or 1·6 per cent of it insured working population, easily the lowest rate in London.[1] Its housing conditions, also, were by no means poor when compared to the slums of the East End or the degree of deterioration in Islington. But by the 1920s quite a proportion of its houses were ageing, and as their original use as private family dwellings tailed off and they were divided up and converted, maintenance was almost inevitably neglected, adding areas of shabbiness and decay to the several older pockets of twilight housing. There was scope here for municipal enterprise. Between the wars, however, not very much was done. In 1920, inspired by the spirit of post-war reconstruction and encouraged by the attractive government subsidies offered by Addison's Housing Act of 1919, the Council acquired a site at South End Green and built the South End Close council flats, at a cost of £201,000. There matters rested until 1936, when the Westcroft Estate was started to provide some relief for congestion on the Kilburn side, being placed in Cricklewood just over the borough boundary; the careful layout of houses grouped in fours forming a hollow square round a playground and community centre cost £158,000. The two schemes were decently planned and well executed; but they were the only two schemes of the period and made little impression on the general situation. More impression, indeed, was made by the private redevelopment which produced such buildings as the Eton flats, the massive 1930s concrete of Lawn Road Flats, the several large brick blocks at Swiss Cottage around the Odeon, and the shop parades in Finchley Road, which are all of the same decade.[2] These were declarations of confidence in a secure and prosperous future; but the most experienced land agents on the scene, Cluttons, seemed to be hoping for little more than a gradual and perhaps not too painful slide in the status of the once rich and proud residential properties towards the respectable mediocrity of improvised flatlets and genteelly

[1] Sir Hubert Llewellyn Smith, *The New Survey of London Life and Labour* (1934), p. 357.
[2] HBC *Abstract of Accounts*, Housing Accounts, especially 1920, 1939, 1963.

Hampstead
Housing Bonds

DO YOUR BIT
and make
"Happy Hampstead"
HAPPIER

FIGURE 8 Raising money for the South End Close housing scheme, 1922

complaining tenants who never had quite enough money to run their houses properly.[1]

In 1945, surveying the debris of the Second World War, it seemed only too likely that the worst forebodings were well on the way to fulfilment, and that once again war would prove to have given a strong shove to previous trends. People and property in Hampstead had not suffered at all badly from air raids in comparison with the badly-hit areas, though bombs had made not a few gaps near Swiss Cottage and alongside the Euston main line; the vast bulk of the Borough, however, and all the precious Georgian houses and terraces, were unscarred. Indirectly, nonetheless, the war laid its hands on all districts alike, bombed and upstanding; after the event some argued that the devastated areas were the more fortunate since they at least had the chance of a new start, much as German industry was said to have profited from its utter destruction. Thus Hampstead had been denuded of people, its population dropping from 90,000 in 1939 to 58,000 in 1942, and then beginning a slow recovery.[2] Houses stood empty and neglected, prey to decay and damage; and all those which remained occupied suffered the common and unavoidable neglect of repairs and maintenance. Seediness and dilapidation were in the air, and it seemed that wealth, respectability, colour and life would complete their retreat to the inner nucleus of the old Town and the social and intellectual security of the hill, leaving all else to the grey anonymity of the shifting population of bed-sitters, furnished flats and apartments in which no settled family life flourished. With the future promising at best rehabilitation to an uncertain but lower social level, Cluttons in 1951 persuaded the Church Commissioners to embark on the unprecedented policy of selling off the freeholds of selected parts of the Dean and Chapter's Belsize estate. The general object was to clear out of areas which were thought certain to go downhill in value and status, and to clear out before the leases fell in—many of them due in the early 1960s—and landed the ground landlords with unwelcome problems of dealing with decayed properties. Thus in the early 1950s the Church Commissioners were rapidly selling

---

[1] There was a considerable drop in property values; houses in Belsize Avenue which had changed hands at £2,000–£2,400 in the 1880s fetched £950–£1,100 in the 1920s and 1930s, while in Belsize Crescent rateable values fell from £145 in the 1890s to £52 in the 1930s. Cluttons generally advised, unenthusiastically, that licences to convert into flats or to run as boarding houses should be granted freely as the only alternative was to see houses standing empty, thus dragging whole streets further down: CC File 32878 and 38689, assignments of leases.

[2] HBC *Abstract of Accounts*, 1957, p. 104.

off freeholds, and for example by 1953 had disposed of all their property in Belsize Crescent to obscure property companies, and were congratulating themselves on being well-rid of a wasting asset.[1]

Instead of the expected continued slide from favour, somewhere around the mid-1950s the tide of fashion turned, and the grace of money and status flowed down the hill until by the 1960s most of Hampstead of the old great estates—Maryon Wilson, Dean and Chapter, Eton and Eyre—had been regained by its original nineteenth century affluence and desirability; west of the Finchley Road the reconquest was less secure, and in most of West Hampstead it had not even begun. Front doors were painted bright colours, stucco ceased to peel, and by night cars lined the streets of Belsize and Swiss Cottage. It was all part of the widespread rediscovery of the inner suburbs by the young executives and the professional classes, the Hampstead counterpart of the dramatic rehabilitation and soaring property values of Islington. The bed-sitter girls were certainly not routed in this social operation, indeed they probably continued to increase in numbers. But their speed of advance was checked, as also was the rate of conversion of Victorian family houses into apartments, by the strong reflux of complete families which were substantial socially if not in numbers of children. The solid evidence of this transformation was the fall in the number of unmarried girls from 31,000 in 1931 to 27,000 in 1961 even though total population had grown from 88,000 to 98,000; the old imbalance of the sexes in a middle-class servant-keeping suburb was slowly narrowing, the men having increased their share of Hampstead's population from 39 to 44 per cent in this period; while the number of independent households had rocketed from 23,000 to over 40,000. The family had made a strong comeback over the single lodger; and if not many families wanted, or could afford, to occupy the whole of a tall, four-storey, nineteenth-century house, plenty could tackle half a house, expensively converted.[2]

The rebirth of Hampstead was strongly assisted by the Borough Council, which was energetic in tidying up some of the poorest and most decayed areas that did not appeal to private developers, and in providing housing for the lower-paid for whom the private market

[1] CC File, 32878, general instructions to sell the freeholds of a list of selected properties 'for sale if opportunity offers', 8090 of 12 December 1951. Sales of Belsize Lane and Belsize Crescent were recorded 1951–4. The Church Commissioners at the same time decided to retain other areas, for later redevelopment: for example, the Englands Lane district.

[2] *Censuses of 1931, 1951 and 1961*, County of London, Tables of Ages and Marital Condition.

catered only inadequately. As people began to stream back into Hampstead towards the end of the war the Council was confronted by a growing list of applicants for housing and started to lay the plans for what became, in the post-war years, a mammoth enterprise completely eclipsing anything that had been done before. Work had started in 1939 on a block of 22 flats in Garnett Road, next to the original Park Dwellings, and had then been suspended; it was restarted in February 1946, in July a pre-war scheme for 24 flats at New End was dusted off and work begun, while 80 prefabricated houses were added to the pre-war Westcroft Estate. During 1944 the Council had started planning for larger projects, in Parkhill Road and in Well Walk, and these were both started by 1948, while preliminary moves had been made to provide a further 444 flats in schemes for King Henry's Road, Kilburn Priory, Broadhurst Gardens and West End Lane.[1] All this had been achieved while the private sector still took a generally gloomy view of Hampstead's prospects as a property investment, and may be reckoned as a sizeable contribution by municipal enterprise to swinging Hampstead towards prosperity through improving its amenities and appearance. In the 1950s the Borough embarked on many more, and much larger, schemes, some of them very large and ambitious indeed. Such were the great Harben Road redevelopment started in 1953, which by the end had cost little short of a million; and the huge complex of the Abbey estate, involving the complete obliteration of several roads off Abbey Road and the construction of great stilted tower blocks, which was only partly built when Camden Borough took over. Much criticised in some quarters for rehousing fewer people than were displaced to make way for them, such schemes were most considerable achievements in planning, in architecture, and in the high standards of accommodation provided. There were many more besides, on a slightly smaller scale, in Fleet Road, Rondu Road, Agamemnon Road, and Upper Park Road, to name only a few. Up to 1939 the Borough had laid out £370,000 in all on housing projects; by the time it ceased to exist £5,400,000 more had been spent.[2] It was little wonder that before 1939 there was no call for any separate organisation to administer the Council's house property, the engineer's and the treasurer's offices being well able to cope with all business; only from 1946 did the work become so great, and the new construction so large, that separate departments had to be created for a Housing Architect and a Housing

[1] HBC *Annual Report for 1947/48*, including a summary for 1939–47, pp. 61–3.
[2] HBC *Abstract of Accounts*, 1963, pp. 52–3.

Manager.[1] These two officers presided over perhaps the most exciting and most rewarding of the Borough's services.

As the pace of development increased from the middle of the 1950s it became clear that the tide of property values and social regeneration was flowing strongly in the Borough's favour. It may not have seemed that way to officials at the time, faced with mounting acquisition costs for sites for redevelopment. But in the long run the fact that private enterprise was joining in the work of rebuilding could not fail to contribute to the task of improving the amenities, attractions and value of the entire Borough. On the Eton College estate, indeed, where many leases were falling in, the redevelopment on either side of Adelaide Road, and facing Primrose Hill, was largely the work of private developers. Their tower blocks were not readily distinguishable from those of the Council, save that the one might well house hotels and the other council flats. With them the long cycle of redevelopment, from farmland to suburban country mansions to housing estates for prosperous Victorian families to apartments and rooms for clerks and secretaries, reached its current end. The last mayor of Hampstead, Councillor Oatway, accepted in a moment of rashness a Christmas-time fun motion from the opposition in the Council Chamber, that Borough funds should be spent on the writing of a history. The more lasting memorial to the Borough, however, lies in the bricks and the concrete which have been left behind, in patterns set by lines which run deep in the history of its landowners. The men, and the buildings, make Hampstead. The Borough's buildings will outlast many generations; for the steel and concrete of the 1950s will be harder to demolish than the Victorian bricks, in any new phase of redevelopment which may lie in the future.

[1] HBC *Annual Report for 1947/48*, p. 62.

Appendix

CENSUS HAMPSTEAD

A selection of demographic and occupational data from the decennial censuses relating to the Hampstead registration district.

Table A1   Total population, families, and houses, 1801–1961

Census	Total population	Males	Females	Households/ families	Inhabited houses
1801	4,343	1,799	2,544	953	691
1811	5,483	2,306	3,177	1,154	842
1821	7,263	3,104	4,159	1,455	1,047
1831	8,588	3,669	4,919	1,679	1,180
1841	10,093	4,323	5,770	n.a.	1,411
1851	11,986	4,960	7,026	n.a.	1,719
1861	19,106	7,332	11,774	n.a.	2,653
1871	32,281	12,466	19,815	n.a.	4,348
1881	45,452	17,569	27,883	n.a.	5,873
1891	68,416	26,777	41,639	13,168[a]	9,517
1901	82,329	31,828	50,501	16,998	11,359
1911	85,495	32,807	52,688	18,625	n.a.
1921	86,153	33,253	52,900	21,520	n.a.
1931	88,947	34,926	54,021	23,709	n.a.
1951	95,131	39,812	55,319	35,970	22,116[b]
1961	98,844	43,434	55,410	40,370	30,545[b]

[a] Separate tenements.
[b] Structurally separate dwellings.

Table A2 Population of new parishes or ecclesiastical districts, 1861–1901

Parish	1861		1871		1881		1891		1901	
	H	P	H	P	H	P	H	P	H	P
All Souls, St John's Wood, part (1865)	—	—	463	3,175	490	3,136	639	3,801	580	3,285
Christ Church (1852)	378	2,557	448	3,126	463	4,001	553	4,226	512	3,656
Emmanuel (1885)	—	—	—	—	—	—	1,143	7,431	1,374	9,923
Holy Trinity (1872)	—	—	—	—	419	3,220	594	4,016	661	4,419
St Augustine, Kilburn, part (1870)	—	—	302	2,399	307	2,521	698	5,341	679	5,248
St Cuthbert (1888)	—	—	—	—	—	—	549	4,479	804	6,055
St James (1888)	—	—	—	—	—	—	680	6,323	775	7,008
St John	1,558	11,271	766	5,953	703	5,592	915	6,244	988	7,701
St Mary (1863)	—	—	616	4,299	1,012	8,178	1,080	7,371	1,187	7,897
St Mary the Virgin, Primrose Hill (1885)	—	—	—	—	—	—	528	2,327	342	2,298
St Paul (1860)	310	2,333	333	2,608	393	2,852	513	3,527	556	3,661
St Peter (1861)	—	—	357	2,767	461	3,699	564	4,095	601	4,195
St Saviour (1856)	407	2,945	709	5,663	1,003	8,071	776	5,970	808	5,756
St Stephen (1880)	—	—	354	2,311	622	4,182	920	6,403	1,294	9,766
St Luke (1896)	—	—	—	—	—	—	—	—	395	2,613
St Paul, Kilburn, part (1897)	—	—	—	—	—	—	—	—	249	1,982

The Registrar remarked that as the boundaries of the new parishes were generally not well known, the accuracy of the figures could not be vouched for.

Dates of formation of new parishes are given in brackets.

H = Houses. P = Total population.

Table A3   Population of the wards, 1901–61

Ward	1901	1921	1931	1951	1961
Town (693)	11,895	12,852	12,481	12,832	12,656
Belsize (270)	12,915	13,562	14,334	15,894	15,873
Adelaide (318)	10,395	10,393	11,137	14,193	14,578
Central (314)	9,099	9,502	10,580	13,606	14,508
West End (248)	12,172	13,558	14,167	13,971	13,894
Kilburn (187)	14,777	15,669	15,124	12,929	12,993
Priory (235)	10,689	10,617	11,124	11,708	14,342

Seven wards were formed in 1901, replacing the previous four. The acreage of each ward is given in brackets.

The Ward boundaries are on O.S. 2½-inch map, Special Administrative Area Series, Greater London (1957 ed. overprinted 1965). The wards can be roughly identified with the following estates and districts discussed in the text:

Town: The old town from Downshire Hill northwards, plus the Redington Road–Telegraph Hill district.

Belsize: Belsize Avenue, Hillfield, Rosslyn Park, St John's Park, Fleet Road, and South Hill Park.

Adelaide: The Eton College estate, plus southern fringes of the Belsize estate.

Central: Fitzjohn's Avenue, Finchley Road, and the northern part of Maryon Wilson's Kilburn estate.

West End: West Hampstead north of the Midland Railway.

Kilburn: West Hampstead and Kilburn south of the Midland Railway.

Priory: The southern part of the Maryon Wilson Kilburn estate, the Bagot (Upton) estate, and the Hampstead section of the Eyre estate.

Table A4 *Selected occupations: male*

	1851	1861	1901	1911	1921	1931
Total occupied males	2,741[a]	3,998[a]	20,775[b]	22,308[b]	25,034[c]	25,296[d]
1. Civil servants	53	103	459	571	669	875
Local government, including police	51	53	316	486	459	1,027[e]
Armed services	32	36	104	99	165	153
2. Clergy	36	45	168	155	64[f]	137
Barristers	54	46	447[g]	476[g]	98	450[g]
Solicitors	55	92			267	
Doctors, surgeons, dentists, hospital service	34	42	203	230	330	516
Authors, editors	6	11	166[h]	263[h]	211	131
Artists, sculptors	15	30	626[j]	770[j]	174	191
Architects	13	22			88	92
Musicians	6	9			133	71
Actors	2	3			96	273
Teachers	29	35	216	249	313	280[k]
Civil engineers, surveyors	4	25	214	220	159	138
Law clerks	14	51	225	170	457	[m]
3. Domestic servants	116	118	264	285	338	951[n]
Outdoor servants, grooms, gardeners	60	162	637	665		
4. Merchants	48	132	1,314	1,515		1,206
Bankers, bank clerks, dealers in money	6	90	650	898		
Commercial clerks	38	101	2,011	1,790	2,489	
All commerce and finance					4,838	5,674[o]

	1	2	3	4	5	6
5. Railway staff	9	28	504	513	358	598
Livery stable-keepers, cab owners, garage owners	16	14		162		381
Coachmen, postboys	57	102	532	407	202	
Carriers, carters	27	63	411		78	144
Omnibus, tram drivers, conductors	24			123	690	302
Motor car drivers				100	52	
Grooms, horse-keepers	38	56	294	62		
Blacksmiths	19	27	74			
Vehicle makers, repairers			143	194	221	540
Vehicle dealers			136	185		164
6. Farmers	8	13				
Farm workers	78	56				
Gardeners (not domestic)	163	147	325	323		208
7. Builders	14	51	507	176	108	
Carpenters, joiners	101	129	328	301	294	
Bricklayers	70	114		192	108	
Masons, paviors	25	17		25		
Painters, plumbers, glaziers	58	99	659	720	672	
All building workers						1,794
8. Tailors, clothing trades	43	50	294	287	245	761
Shoemakers	85	95	168	145	116	
Cabinet makers, upholsterers	11	20	245	353	303	279
Electrical apparatus makers			225	280	460	525

Table A4—continued

	1851	1861	1901	1911	1921	1931
9. Cowkeepers, milk-sellers	19	37		288		232
Butchers	39	52		310		241
Poulterers, fishmongers	15	20				111
Greengrocers	20	19				158
Bakers	56	53		86	79	133
Brewers	13	22				47
Grocers	28	45		312		380
Wine and spirit merchants	11	28	110	72		95
Drapers	15	33	464	421		362
Booksellers, newsagents	10	18		226		
Tobacconists	1	5	56	60		55
Chemists, druggists	8	13	129	127		132
10. General labourers	260	250	427		423	
11. Gentlemen, independent	14	40	491	346		
Annuitants, retired from business	21	43	602	876	822	

Occupation tables showing the Hampstead District are available only in the censuses of 1851, 1861, 1901, 1911, 1921 and 1931. Definitions of individual occupations frequently altered between censuses; and the above table is an arbitrary selection of the larger, the more important, or the faster-growing occupations.

All gaps mean that a figure is not available or not applicable, for example because separate recording of a category was discontinued.

a All males over 20.
b All occupied males over 10.
c All occupied males over 12.
d All occupied males over 14.
e Including those employed in education.
f C. of E. clergy only.
g Barristers and solicitors.
h Those with literary and scientific pursuits.
j Those in art, music and drama.
k Excluding teachers employed by local government (see note e).
m Included, for 1931 only, with barristers and solicitors.
n Both indoor and outdoor domestic servants.
o Includes, for 1931 only, commercial clerks.

Table A5   *Selected occupations: female*

	1851	1861	1901	1911	1921	1931
Total occupied females	4,369[a]	7,308[a]	19,974[b]	22,856[b]	21,803[c]	23,224[d]
1. Local government					48	806[e]
2. Doctors, surgeons, dentists	52	29	5	9	43	
Nurses (not domestic)	51	86	497	1,104	830	1,180[f]
Governesses	58	114				
Teachers			848	849	1,004	704[g]
Art, music and drama	7	18	393	538	253[h]	
Literary and scientific			63	141	80	
Painters						147
Literary pursuits						91
Musicians						112
Actresses					135	200
3. Domestic servants, general	757	1,035	13,579	13,734	10,926	10,348
— housekeepers	82	50				
— cooks	230	662				
— housemaids	181	502				
— nurses	108	310				
	(1,358)[j]	(2,559)[k]				
Charwomen	62	71	240	275	295	m
4. Lodging and boarding house keepers	24	38	187	567	519	1,218
Barmaids, waitresses	23	12	160	654	237	412

Table A5—continued

	1851	1861	1901	1911	1921	1931
5. Milliners, dressmakers, seamstresses	176	213	1,388	1,449	1,176	1,180
Washerwomen, laundresses	376	407	311	176	129	120
Shop assistants					1,143	1,986[n]
6. Commercial clerks, typists			487	743	2,478	1,651[o]
7. Gentlewomen, independent	9	61	2,263	2,249		
Annuitants, retired	211	313	174	164	213	

All gaps mean that a figure is not available or not applicable, for example because separate recording of a category was discontinued.

[a] All females over 20.
[b] All occupied females over 10.
[c] All occupied females over 12.
[d] All occupied females over 14.
[e] Including those employed in education.
[f] All those engaged in medical work, including doctors.
[g] Excluding teachers employed by local government (see note e).
[h] Excluding actresses.
[j] Total of indoor domestic servants in 1851.
[k] Total of indoor domestic servants in 1861.
[m] Included under 'domestic servants, general'.
[n] Those employed in 'Commerce and Finance' minus the group employed in banking, insurance, estate agents, and other financial concerns.
[o] Those employed in banking and financial concerns (see note n) plus those employed by central government.

Index of subjects

231; solicitor, William Tooke, 216
Eyre estate, 64, 66, 76, 82, 215, 247–53; lack of records, 82

Ground rents, 88–90, 106–7, 223, 224, 231, 233, 238–9, 251, 257, 264, 273, 286, 288, 290, 293, 309, 320, 321–2, 347, 349n, 353, 360; peppercorn, 249–50, 282, 361–2; and house types, 365–70

Hampstead Borough Council, 422; council housing, 424–6, 429, 432–4; electricity supply, 414; Kilburn Grange, 424; North Heath Extension, 337, 424; and redevelopment, 253

Hampstead Heath: acquired by MBW 197, 202; artists and, 152–3; Bills to 'enclose', 138, 143, 149, 159; buildings on, 13–14, 15–17; donkeys on, 139, 197; the East Heath, 155; enclosures from, 138–9, 140, 177, 180; failure of Heath party, 183; fair on, 152, 327; final grants from, 202; ice cream on, 175n; laundry grounds on, 175, 251; masses and, 152, 169, 326; road and railway materials from, 114–15, 151, 193; value of, 194, 196; the West Heath, 128, 197

Hampstead Heath, the greater, 162, 164–5, 179, 185; abandoned, 198–9; revived, 324–9; achieved, 333; and propertied classes, 327–8; as ventilator of slums, 326; Heath Extension Committee, 329; Golders Hill Extension, 336–7; North Heath Extension, 336–7

Hampstead societies and associations, torpor of, 411; Antiquarian Society, 419; Committee to oppose Trams, 364; Debating Society, 419; Dramatic Society, 419; Heath Protection Society, 189, 419; Kyrle Society, 189, 325, 333

Hampstead town (village); origins, 18–20, 26; health resort, 20–2, 306; green belt, 124, ending of, 301; seclusion defended by Maryon Wilson, 115–24; unspoilt, 296–9, 301–2; insanitary, 400; slum clearance, 410–11

Hampstead Vestry: unreformed open, 390–3, and Metropolitan Police, 391; reformed, 396, first election, 184; composition of, 396–9; builders' group, 399; gentry control, 396; professional control, 399, 412; shopkeeper group, 396–7, 398n; lobbies Commons, 174n; and Heath, 184–5, 186, 187; opposes railway, 303; opposes trams, 364; Fitzjohn's Avenue, 312–15; Town Improvements, 316–17, 410–11; Heath Extension, 331–2; Golders Hill Extension, 337; and footpaths, 315, 356, 390; as road maker, 314; Burial Board, 407; Commissioners of Baths, 412; Library Commissioners, 417; high reputation, 417–19; *see also* Municipal activities, Vestry Offices, Vestry and Borough Officers

Hearth tax, 19–20

High Street traders: oppose gentry, 316; oppose trams, 364; support for Maryon Wilson, 160–1; and Vestry Hall, 408

Hospitals: Hampstead General, 161, 346; Kilburn Dispensary, 402; North-Western Fever, 270; Royal Free, 161, 270; Smallpox, 269, 294, 325, 355, 358–9

House prices and values: costs, 258, 369; prices, 87–8, 258, 266, 277, 293, 345, 354, 366–7, 431n; rents, 107, 126, 245, 287, 293

House types and styles: boarding houses, 345, 426; country mansions, 92–8; fourth rate, 71, 256; gothic, 66, 288, 290; Hollywood baronial, 338; Italianate, 234, 258; late classical, 234, 276; lodging houses, 268; maisonettes, 426; relation to ground rents, 365–70; semi-detached, 65–6, 87, 257; smart suburban, 347; with own stabling, 86, 100, 239, 248, 259, 292, 321; without stabling, 25, 248, 258; stuccoland, 288; terrace, 248–9, 252, 320; town houses, 25, 65; Victorian family, 241, 290; villas, 66, 87, 99; wealthy middle-class, 277, 290; workers' cottages, 85–6, 360

Index of people and places